ME

THE CONTRIBUTORS

Jennifer Merin wrote the chapters *Travel in Mexico 1991, Orienting Yourself, Setting Priorities,* and *Touring Ideas,* along with *Mexico City, Veracruz and the Gulf Coast, Acapulco and the Pacific Coast Resorts, Central Highlands,* and *The Yucatán Peninsula,* as well as the *Travel Arrangements* and *Cultural Timeline* sections. Ms. Merin is a well-known journalist whose nationally syndicated column on shopping around the world appears in the *Los Angeles Times, Chicago Tribune, New York Newsday, Miami Herald,* and other leading American newspapers. She has contributed numerous articles to major newspapers around the United States, including *U.S.A. Today,* the *Christian Science Monitor, Village Voice, Atlanta Journal & Constitution, Houston Chronicle, Denver Post,* and *Baltimore Sun,* among others. Ms. Merin authored *The Serious Shopper's Guide to Paris* and *The Serious Shopper's Guide to Los Angeles* (recently published by Prentice-Hall Press), and *The International Directory of Festivals of Theater, Dance, and Folklore* (Greenwood Press). She has contributed to leading American magazines including *Ms., Us, Diversion,* and others, and has been widely published in Canadian and European periodicals. Ms. Merin is also a correspondent covering news, entertainment, and travel for the NBC Radio Networks/Mutual Broadcasting System, and she has been a producer and/or writer for ABC News, Fox TV News, WNET-TV, WOR Radio in New York, and Swedish National Broadcasting.

A former Managing Editor of Hearst's *Colonial Homes* Magazine whose freelance articles have appeared frequently in *Travel and Leisure,* **Erica Kleine,** contributor of the *Oaxaca* and *Chiapas* chapters, has also written about travel and the decorative arts for publications which include *Travel/Holiday; Signature; Modern Bride; Home Decorating;* the *New York Daily News;* and *Antique Monthly.* She can sing the words to hundreds of *ranchera* songs, collects Mexican handicrafts, and maintains a profound love for the land and people of "Mexico, Lindo y Querido."

Eleanor S. Morris, who wrote the *Northern Mexico* and *Baja California, North and South* chapters, is a freelance travel writer and photographer living in Austin, Texas. Introduced to Mexico in her teens, she returns to that delightful country several times each year. She is a member of the Society of American Travel Writers, has published widely in national newspapers and magazines, and is the author of *Guide to Recommended Country Inns of Arizona, New Mexico, and Texas*.

The "Language" section was compiled by Marilee Crocker, a freelance travel writer living in Cape Cod.

We would like to thank Barbara J. Farmer and Matthew Karwowski for their tireless research efforts. We would also like to extend our deepest appreciation to the Mexican Consulate in New York City; Rolando Garcia, the Mexican Government Tourist Office, in Houston; Rafael Cruz Lozano, the Secretary of Tourism, the State of Oaxaca; M.P. Leal; and Javier Rivas and Eduardo Amezcua, also of the Mexican Government Tourist Office.

The New York editor for this book is Gail Chasan. Assistant editor is Debra Bernardi. Maps are by Swanston Graphics and R.V. Reise und Verkehrsverlag. Project management by Madigan Editorial Services.

BANTAM'S
MEXICO
1991

BANTAM

NEW YORK • TORONTO • LONDON • SYDNEY • AUCKLAND

MEXICO 1991
A Bantam Book / October 1990

Grateful acknowledgement is made to the following for reprint permission:
From Pleasure of Ruins, *by Rose Macaulay, copyright c. 1953. Reprinted by permission of Thames & Hudson, Ltd. From* The People's Guide to Mexico, *by Carl Franz, 7th Ed. copyright c. 1988 by John Muir Publications. Reprinted by permission. From* The Art of Mexican Cooking, *by Diana Kennedy, copyright c. 1989. Reprinted by permission of Bantam Doubleday Dell. From* Incidents of Travel in the Yucatan, *by John Stephens, copyright c. 1841 by Harper & Brothers. Reprinted by permission. From* Nothing to Declare, *by Mary Morris, copyright c. 1988 by Mary Morris. Reprinted by permission of Houghton Mifflin Company. From* So Far From God *by Patrick Marnham, copyright c. Patrick Marnham, 1985. All rights reserved. Reprinted by permission of Viking Penguin, a division of Penguin Books USA, Inc. and Jonathan Cape Great Britain. From* Another Mexico *by Graham Greene. Copyright 1939, renewed c. 1967 by Graham Greene. All rights reserved. Reprinted by permission of Viking Penguin, a division of Penguin Books USA, Inc. and Laurence Pollinger, Great Britain. From* The Pearl *by John Steinbeck. Copyright c. 1945 by John Steinbeck. Copyright renewed c. 1973 by Elaine Steinbeck IV and Thom Steinbeck. All rights reserved. Reprinted by permission of Viking Penguin, a division of Penguin Books USA, Inc. First published in 1948. Reprinted by kind permission of William Heinemann Ltd., Publishers, London. From* One Man's Mexico *by John Lincoln, copyright c. 1967 by John Lincoln. Reprinted by permission of The Bodley Head Ltd. London.*

ISBN 0-553-34941-4

Published simultaneously in the United States and Canada

Bantam Books are published by Bantam Books, a division of Bantam Double-day Dell Publishing Group, Inc. Its trademark, consisting of the words "Bantam Books" and the portrayal of a rooster, is Registered in U.S. Patent and Trademark Office and in other countries, Marca Registrada, Bantam Books, 666 Fifth Avenue, New York, New York 10103

CONTENTS

FOREWORD

How can you be sure that you choose the best guidebook for your needs? Fifty years ago the number of guidebooks available for any one destination could be counted on one or two fingers. Many destinations had no guidebook at all. So choice was usually nonexistant: if a guidebook existed, you bought it.

Today, the decision is not so simple. Some destinations have more than one hundred different guidebooks written about them. They cater to all tastes and all needs. Quality runs from excellent to poor. How, then, do you choose? The question is best answered by asking another question: How can a guidebook help you? At the very least it should 1. Help you plan your trip, and 2. Help you make choices during that trip. Surprisingly, many guidebooks fail at one or both of these minimal requirements.

Not surprisingly, however, Bantam does both of these jobs extremely well. And we do a lot more, too. We know that today's traveler is much more sophisticated than the traveler of fifty years ago. Today's traveler wants specifics—such as exact prices at each hotel and restaurant; merely saying that a place is in the moderate range, as many guidebooks do, is not enough. Today's traveler wants up-to-date information. Bantam Travel Guides are updated annually. Today's traveler wants honesty. Bantam's writers tell you what to avoid as well as what's worth seeing and doing. And as our cover quotes will corroborate, our attempts have been successful—in the short time Bantam Travel Guides have been available, we've received hundreds of rave reviews from critics and travelers alike.

Here are just a few reasons for you to choose Bantam:

- Bantam Travel Guides are updated annually.
- The guides include a full-color travel atlas plus numerous black-and-white maps throughout the text.
- The Priorities section of each guide lets you see at a glance what is most important to see and do—both in a city and in a region.
- Bantam Guides are organized geographically rather than alphabetically. Descriptions of what's available in a contiguous geographical area make it easier to get the most out of a city neighborhood or country region. For those who

still need to locate a place alphabetically, we provide a detailed index.

- Restaurants are reviewed in depth, giving examples of typical menu items, prices, and hours open. Restaurants are keyed into major-city maps so that you can locate these places on the map easily.
- Hotels are also reviewed in depth, providing descriptions of the amenities and decor, as well as actual room prices. Hotels are also keyed into major-city maps.
- Finally, we think you'll enjoy reading our guidebooks. We've tried hard to find not only informed writers, but good writers. The writing is literate and lively. It's honest. Most of all, it's a good read.

No matter how good a guidebook is, it cannot cover everything. It can't include every good restaurant, and it can't do justice to everyone's favorite place. Bear in mind, too, that prices can change at any time, and today's well-managed restaurant or hotel can change owners or managers tomorrow. Today's great food or service can be tomorrow's disappointment. We've recommended places as they are now and as we expect them to be in the future, but there are no guarantees. We've taken pains to insure the accuracy of all the information in this guide. Still, despite the best efforts of everyone involved, an error may occur from time to time. As guidebook publishers we take pride in our work, but we cannot take responsibility for errors that might occur. If a place described in this guide fails to justify its description, please write to us, and we'll investigate and revise our entry where indicated. Our address is Bantam Travel Guides, 666 Fifth Avenue, New York, NY 10103.

Richard T. Scott
Publisher
Bantam Travel Books

1

TRAVELING IN MEXICO, 1991

You're about to embark on a travel adventure through an exotic and festive land, with an extraordinary range of intriguing things to do and see, a remarkably beautiful and varied landscape, and a sophisticated and captivating cultural life. Mexico offers a wealth of sights and experiences that will keep you fascinated through a lifetime of vacations.

Many U.S. residents visiting Mexico for the first time are astonished to find the Amigo Country so near and yet so foreign. Mexico and the United States share a long, peaceful border and some mutual interests, but that's about all the two nations have in common. In its customs and ambience, its Spanish heritage and language, its lifestyle and outlook, Mexico has a decidedly Latin American accent. But Mexico's proximity to the United States offers the latter country's vacationing citizens the chance to vastly extend their cultural horizons by experiencing a markedly different culture without journeying to the ends of the earth.

Yes, Mexico is entertaining and uniquely exciting; and it is true, not all travelers adjust easily to unfamiliar customs and environments. But the key to enjoying a Mexican visit is flexibility. As a musician once commented, traveling in Mexico is like playing jazz—a constant improvisation. Get set to swing, and you'll have a swell time. Insist on following your original score, and you may well experience some disharmony.

Mexico, it seems, excels in friendliness and fails in efficiency. Expect service with a smile, but don't count on getting things done fast, or, occasionally, even at all. Yet despite the country's inefficiency, Mexico's tourist industry develops so quickly that it's difficult to keep up with the changes. From year to year, new hotels, new tours, new services are put into place. Does that seem like a contradiction? It is a contradiction, and it's typical of Mexico.

1

We wandered the hills on a dusty plateau and suddenly, in the middle of that desert devoid of any houses or buildings, we came upon an Olympic-size swimming pool filled with sparkling turquoise water. At first no one said a word. We assumed it was a mirage. But then we reached it. I bent over, touched the water, and established that it was real. Alejandro did not like to swim and Roger didn't have a suit, but Catherine and I stripped down to our bathing suits, dove in, and began swimming laps.

There is an anecdote about Mexico which perhaps I should tell here. André Breton, founder of the surrealist school in France and writer of *Les Manifestes du Surrealisme,* was invited to Mexico in the 1930s to teach Mexicans about surrealism. He wanted a table so he hired a carpenter and asked him to build it. Breton drew an architectural drawing of a table, diamond-shaped, foreshortened front legs, long back legs; and the carpenter took the drawing and made a table just like the one in the drawing— diamond-shaped, with short front legs and long back legs. When Breton saw the table, he said, "I have nothing to teach these people about surrealism." And he returned to France.

The reality of Mexico is really a dual reality. On the one hand there is the original indigenous culture—mystical, magical, communal, given to sacrifice and the worship of pagan gods. And then there is the reality of the conqueror—logical, precise, efficient. These two cultures exist literally one on top of the other. They account for what seems the utterly contradictory character of the Mexican. As Octavio Paz has described them, Mexicans are eternal adolescents, unable to find their true identity and hence unable to grow up into the adulthood that identity brings.

Whoever built that beautiful swimming pool in the middle of a desert with no houses in sight I'm sure did it for what he thought was a very pragmatic reason, but it eluded us at the time. That swimming pool, perfect and clean, was for me what that table was for Breton. A glimpse into the Mexican character that defies the logic of the Western mind.

—Mary Morris
Nothing to Declare, 1988

The hot new beach development of the nineties—in the state of Oaxaca—is Huatulco, and it features posh resorts along a series of bays, each with a distinct personality and package of activities and attractions. Other seaside resorts are scrambling to keep up their allure. Acapulco and Ixtapa are developing new properties. Cancún, Cozumel, and Isla Mujeres turned Hurricane Gilbert to their advantage as best they could: Resorts in the Yucatán have for the most part bounced back unbelievably from Gilbert's damage, and, where necessary, beaches are being rebuilt.

Mexico City, Guadalajara, and other urban areas continue their rapid growth. As their populations swell, so do their problems—overcrowding, unemployment, traffic congestion, and pollution. But the cities are also vital, sophisticated, and exciting centers of culture and commerce that offer visitors a substantial roster of brilliant attractions.

It's no secret that Mexico is having tough times. On the economic front, the constant devaluation of the peso and the rise of budget-busting inflation make it difficult for the majority of Mexicans to support their families. Mexicans generally assume that you, the foreigner, are rich. Now more than ever, the poor have their hands out for handouts, and all sorts of people expect tips for services you haven't requested and don't want. You may be sympathetic to their plight, but it's not pleasant to be made to feel like Scrooge because you're not as rich as Croesus. In addition, an increase in incidents of theft makes it necessary to safeguard your belongings.

While peso devaluation makes Mexico more affordable for foreign visitors with hard currency, persistent inflation somewhat offsets advantages. Don't expect Mexico to be dirt cheap. Hotel, restaurant, and tour prices have a way of sneaking upward, even though they're under strict regulation by the ministry of tourism.

Mexico has also had some political difficulties. The most recent national election, held in 1988 to choose a new president for a six-year term of office, was hotly contested. Nevertheless, the PRI's (Partido Revolucionario Institucionalisado) big candidate, Carlos Salinas de Gortari, assumed the presidency with a firm grip on the reins of power and the government seems quite stable. However, the supporters of the opposition have held frequent demonstrations throughout Mexico, and there have been several strikes and murders of union leaders. You would have to be either mighty unlucky or looking for trouble for these things to interfere with the success of your vacation, but you should know about them.

The new administration's revisions in monetary and fiscal policy; price controls; government-support of resort, road, and railway development; and other areas of operation *will* effect tourism. Salinas de Gortari has appointed Pedro Joaquin Coldwell as secretary of tourism, the head of the ministry that oversees front-line information booths and other direct tourist services, as well as behind-the-scenes regulatory activities and development schemes. And because Mexico relies heavily upon tourism for much-needed foreign revenue, it is safe to assume that the administration and ministry will try to establish conditions to make Mexico an even more popular tourist destination than it has been in past years. In fact, in his most recent State of the Nation Address, Salinas de Gortari emphasized his goal to improve the infrastructure of Mexico's tourist destinations and to assure visitors to Mexico of high standards of both safety and cleanliness.

The advice of a particularly knowledgeable, experienced, and reliable travel agent will prove invaluable to you in book-

Every Mexican is aware, subconsciously or otherwise, that he is not one person but two: the aggressive Spaniard and the proud but passive Indian; the eternal conqueror and the eternal victim. The facade covers the split. For a Mexican to feel secure against the weakness of his own duality he must protect it against the probing of friend and enemy alike.

That each Mexican is a fortress armed against other Mexicans as well as against foreigners is not easily understood. Faced with defences which are too threatening to be ignored or an inscrutableness too contrived to be discounted as reserve . . . the foreigner may feel himself rejected. He can make friends with Mexicans and enjoy their inexhaustible kindness and hospitality, but he can never get to know them. The guns may be lowered but the barricades are never down. If a chink does appear it usually reveals something so strange that he is left dazed with incomprehension. In a second it will be closed again. The facade will be as intact, mysterious and unreal as before.

—John Lincoln
One Man's Mexico, 1967

ing your Mexican vacation. And while it is undoubtedly more fun and often less expensive to explore this fascinating and friendly Mexico on your own, first-time visitors, those who tend to be a bit timid about travel, or anyone planning to venture off the beaten track may want to join a guided tour for at least part of the trip, just to avoid any hassles that might disrupt or undermine your budding relationship with a wonderful country—one that deserves to be one of your vacation mainstays.

2

ORIENTING YOURSELF

Mexico, the southernmost country on the North American continent, occupies 760,000 square miles of superbly varied land, covering deserts and jungle and including extensive coastlines and soaring mountain ranges.

As you look at the map, Mexico's shape resembles a cornucopia, the mouth of which borders the United States to the north and the tail of which curves to the east and forms the Yucatán Peninsula. To the south of the Yucatán Peninsula, part of which belongs to the nations of Guatemala and Belize, is Central America. To the west of Mexico's main landmass is Baja California, a long, narrow, hooklike peninsula that extends south from the U.S. border at California. The Gulf of California (to Mexicans, the Sea of Cortés), known for fine fishing, separates Baja California from Mexico's Pacific Coast, which stretches for about 4,560 miles and has terrific beaches. Mexico's East Coast, a jungle-like stretch of 1,743 miles along the inside curve of the cornucopia, is on the Gulf of Mexico. The Yucatán Peninsula, a flat, plateau-like landmass, is surrounded by the Gulf of Mexico and the Caribbean.

Mexico's Gulf Coast and the northern section of the Pacific Coast are bordered by low-lying plains, but further inland, the landscape is dominated by the Sierra Madre. Western, eastern, and southern branches of this mighty mountain chain, running more or less parallel to the coasts, create the northern and southern highland plateaus, where Mexico City and many colonial mining and agricultural towns are located.

For administrative purposes, Mexico is divided into 31 states and the Federal District (Distrito Federal) of Mexico City and surroundings. As with the United States—or any other federal system of government, for that matter—the individual Mexican states have distinct personalities and profiles, and there are regional rivalries between them. They root for their own sports teams, support their own celebrities, take pride in their unique culture, landscape, and cities. And the more you know of Mexico, the more intrigued you become with these regional differences. But ask any Mexican to name the 31 Mexican states, and you'll be lucky if you get a list of 25 with only one or two repeats. In case a Mexican asks you to name the states, and you want to show off, here, in alphabetical order, is the entire roster: Aguascalientes, Baja California, Baja California Sur, Campeche, Chiapas, Chihuahua, Coahuila, Colima, Durango, Guanajuato, Guerrero, Hidalgo, Jalisco, Mexico (state), Michoacán, Morelos, Nayarit, Nuevo León, Oaxaca, Puebla, Querétaro, Quintana Roo, San Luis Potosí, Sinaloa, Sonora, Tabasco, Tamaulipas, Tlaxcala, Veracruz, Yucatán, Zacatecas.

As a traveler, you probably won't visit all these states—and certainly not in alphabetical order. The following is a summary of what Mexico has to offer, region by region.

Mexico City, one of the world's most populous cities and the seat of the Mexican government, is an exciting and vital urban atmosphere enhanced by fabulous colonial and supermodern architecture, historical sights, museums and cultural events, and great shopping. In addition, fascinating Teotihuacán and archaeological ruins, and charming Taxco, among other colonial cities, are within day-trip distance.

Along Mexico's **Gulf Coast,** Veracruz and Villahermosa are particularly interesting modern business centers, with fascinating historical sites, wonderful anthropological museums, colorful local customs, and exquisite cuisine.

The **Pacific Coast** features Acapulco and Puerto Vallarta as the leading beach resorts, famous for their perpetual sunshine, terrific water sports, and swinging nightlife.

Northern Mexico, bordering on the United States, has a variety of attractions including Durango, the familiar backdrop to many Hollywood westerns; Monterrey, the dynamic and modern city that dominates Mexico's industrial development; and the Copper Canyon, the most spectacular gorge in the Sierras.

The **Central Highlands,** with its beautiful landscape sculpted of mountains, valleys, and plateaus, is the heart of Mexico's colonial trail, with interesting stops to be made at Guadalajara, Guanajuato, San Miguel de Allende, Querétaro, and Morelia, among other colonial cities.

Baja California and the **Northern Pacific Coast** are tops for fishing expeditions, as well as sun and surf vacations all the way from Cabo San Lucas to Mazatlán. And watch out for Loreto, Baja California Sur's peaceful little missionary town, slated for development into a major tourist resort within the next few years.

The **Yucatán Peninsula** offers a terrific combination of urban and resort environments, including Mérida and Campeche, Cancún and Cozumel. It also features the biggest concentration of fascinating archaeological zones, including Chichén Itzá, Uxmal, and Tulúm.

Peaceful **Oaxaca** and beautiful **Chiapas** are the contemporary strongholds of Mexico's ethnic cultures, with various Indian tribes living according to their ancient traditions within colonial cities such as Oaxaca and San Cristóbal de las Casas, or in their own rather isolated villages. And Oaxaca harbors Huatulco, slated as *the* hot Mexican resort area of the coming decade.

3

SETTING PRIORITIES

Mexico, due to its size and diversity, offers a myriad of vacation possibilities. Rather than assume that you are starting with a blank slate and relying on us to define where in the entire country you should go—an unlikely scenario at best—we are instead surmising that there are at least general areas of Mexico that you have chosen, or have been chosen for you, to visit, and we'll help you set your priorities within those parameters.

Mexico City is a must. The fabulous array of monumental colonial buildings and churches set amid magnificent modern skyscrapers, the fascinating historical sights, peaceful parks, and plazas, the museums and roster of cultural events surprise first-time visitors with their richness and variety. Those who are not deterred by this city's well-deserved reputation for crowds, clutter, and congestion will be captivated by the exciting pulse of Mexico's mega-capital. Don't miss the historic **Zócalo** with its government buildings, charming **San Angel** with its colonial mansions and fabulous Bazar Sábado, the **Zona Rosa** with its elegant shops and popular restaurants, and peaceful **Chapultepec Park,** where a day of satisfying sightseeing could easily be achieved, even if you never stray from the fascinating **National Museum of Anthropology,** with one of the world's most extraordinary collections of important archaeological artifacts. The great **Teotihuacán,** on the outskirts of Mexico City, is one of the most vital and fascinating archaeological zones in the Americas. Covering an area of about eight square miles, "The Place Where Man Becomes a God" has monumental pyramids and temples, with some dating from 200 B.C. And south of Mexico City, charming **Taxco,** a colonial mining town nestled in the Sierra Madre, boasts extraordinary silversmiths and shops set amid picturesque old mansions, gilded churches, and narrow cobblestone streets lined with lovely bougainvillea.

Farther south, on the Pacific Coast, is **Acapulco,** famous beach bastion of the jet set and glitterati. Get the best dazzling scenic overview of the Strip's sports and nightlife from the restful retreat provided by a **Hotel las Brisas** bungalow, perched on the palisades above the beautiful blue bay.

Puerto Vallarta, northwest of Acapulco on the Pacific Coast, has an appealing mixture of the unrushed *ambiente* of a Mexican fishing village and the attractions of a modern vacation haven. P.V.'s discos and bistros swing by night, but by day the town is sleepy, provincial, and wholly Mexican. You'll find great shopping throughout the town, and **Mismaloya Beach,** where *Night of the Iguana* was filmed, is a jungle paradise.

Inland from Puerto Vallarta, **Guadalajara,** favorite of U.S. vacationers and retirees, is known for mariachis, *charros* (cowboys), and the Mexican hat dance. Mexico's second-largest city has charming plazas, fabulous colonial buildings, and a rich cultural life. Don't miss José Clemente Orozco's awe-inspiring murals at the **Government Palace** and the **Hospicio Cabañas** (formerly an orphanage, now a cultural institute), or the magnificent **Teatro Degollado.** Shopping is superb at the **Mercado Libertad** and in **Tlaquepaque,** a charming suburb with terrific crafts and clothing boutiques.

East of Guadalajara and high in the Sierra Madre, **Guanajuato** is an enchanting and beautiful old mining town, rich with colonial churches, magnificent mansions, pleasant plazas, ancient arches, subterranean streets, and mysterious mummies. Guanajuato, important in the Mexican War of Independence, has fascinating historical sights and museums. If you're able to get reservations to visit during the annual **Cervantes Festival,** you'll enjoy first-rate concerts, dance, and theatrical performances presented in the exquisitely baroque **Teatro Juárez,** in Guanajuato's charming squares, and other intriguing venues. Scenic drives hugging the mountains around town provide thrilling, panoramic views of glorious Guanajuato.

San Miguel de Allende, east of Guanajuato, is another colonial city, so charming that it has—in its entirety!—been declared a national monument. This town, with its postcard-pretty square, ancient churches, monuments, and colonial mansions, is quintessentially quaint. San Miguel, yet another city enormously popular with U.S. travelers and retirees, has first-rate shopping and several outstanding cultural institutes offering courses in Spanish and the arts.

In the southern part of Mexico, the state of **Oaxaca** offers the city of Oaxaca, which has preserved and made an art of Mexico's traditional way of life. This unhurried, somewhat dusty town has miraculously avoided the congestion and cacophony of automation, perhaps because the largely Indian population tends to occupy itself with the more individualized arts of weaving, embroidering, and making pots rather than with more industrialized pursuits. And the products of this labor are sold in a superbly colorful *mercado.* Outside town, the ancient ceremonial center of **Monte Alban** is one of Mexico's most magical and moving ruins. As you enter, you pass a monumental cactus plant with thick and sturdy arms stretching toward the heavens. Next to it is a gigantic tree with gnarled branches and a crown of leaves rustling with the breeze. Having withstood the centuries, these ancient neighbors and best friends seem to symbolize the unique entwining of Mexico's Indian and European roots. And don't forget that Oaxaca also harbors **Huatulco,** Mexico's new up-and-coming resort development.

East of Oaxaca, **San Cristóbal de las Casas,** a sweet little provincial city with charming colonial buildings, is an excellent base for visiting **San Juan Chamula,** with its fascinating church where healing ceremonies are performed with Coca-Cola, as well as **Zinacantán** and **Tenejapa,** among other distinctive Indian communities, each with its own costumes, rituals, and language, which give the beautiful, densely forested mountain state of **Chiapas** its unique character and culture. The winding mountain roads between San Cristóbal and the Indian villages are often shrouded with clouds. As you turn on a curve, rays of sunlight explode through fog and spotlight three or four Indians, wearing pink Mexican ponchos and straw hats with multicolored streamers, weaving their way across a lush green field in a valley hundreds of feet below the roadway. This vision remains in your mind's eye without the aid of a snapshot.

Also in Chiapas, **Palenque** is one of Mexico's classical Mayan archaeological wonders. Built by the Maya on an unusually hilly site, Palenque has a unique style of architecture and is surrounded by dense rain forest.

The heaviest concentration of great Mayan ruins, however, is in the **Yucatán Peninsula,** in the states of **Yucatán** and **Quintana Roo.** There are three musts: **Chichén Itzá,** one of the largest Mexican archaeological zones, was for seven hundred years the chief Mayan ceremonial and sacred center, with impressive temples, palaces, ball courts, a *mercado,* and sacrificial well. **Uxmal,** with its rounded pyramids, is built in the distinctive Puuc style, probably the purest form of Mayan architecture, and has many impressive manmade cisterns for water storage in an otherwise dry landscape. **Tulúm,** surrounded by a stone wall built for defense, is perched on a cliff overlooking the blue-green Caribbean, and has astonishingly well-preserved frescoes depicting late Mayan life and religious beliefs.

The city of **Mérida,** with its neat gridlike streets lined with fabulous colonial palaces, mansions that once belonged to the area's millionaire henequen plantation owners, and brilliant restaurants serving famous Yucatecan cuisine, is a great base for visiting Chichén Itzá and Uxmal. Nearby, **Yaxcopoil,** a former henequen plantation with a beautifully preserved hacienda, factory, and administrative buildings, offers a fascinating glimpse into the Yucatán's past lifestyle.

The ultramodern beach resort at **Cancún,** a haven for hedonists and honeymooners, is an excellent base for touring to Tulúm and the more casual resorts at **Cozumel** and **Isla Mujeres.**

Obviously, Mexico has enough must-sees to satisfy a traveler through many more than one visit. In fact, you could easily spend a lifetime of vacations in this fascinating country and still not see all that warrants seeing.

HOLIDAYS AND SEASONAL EVENTS

Christmas, New Year's, and Easter are times when most Mexicans vacation. Therefore, a lot of offices, shops, and services will have limited hours and personnel during these holidays. In general, when planning your visit you should note the following national holidays: January 1 **(New Year's)** through January 6 **(Three Kings Day);** February 5 **(Constitution Day);** March 21 **(Benito Juárez's Birthday); Holy Week** and **Easter;** May 1 **(Labor Day);** May 5 **(Battle of Puebla);** September 1 **(President's annual address to the nation);** September 16 **(Independence Day);** October 12 **(Columbus Day and the Day of "La Raza," the Day of the Mexican Race);** November 20 **(Anniversary of the Revolution);** December 12 **(Day of the Virgin of Guadalupe);** and December 25 **(Christmas).**

In addition, each town in Mexico has its fiesta day, usually celebrating its patron saint, when businesses shut down and there are processions and ceremonies. Some of these events are very famous, and the town fills up with tourists. If you intend to attend one of the more famous of these fiestas, such as the **Day of the Dead** in Pátzcuaro (Dec. 1 and 2), and you plan to stay overnight, be sure to book your rooms far in advance. Again, arrive early in the day, with your written room confirmation in your hand.

4

TOURING IDEAS

Mexico offers abundant opportunities for travelers to pursue special interests. Packaged sightseeing tours organized by experts on travel to Mexico hit the highlights, and are first-rate introductions to the various areas of this vast and fascinating land, but are rarely capable of adjusting to individual tastes and curiosities. Although packaged tours often offer excellent value by making inexpensive group rates available to individuals, you can find yourself locked into an itinerary that is less than ideal for your interests. You might consider asking your travel agent to help you create an individualized tour, tailored to suit your favorite pastimes.

Shoppers for folk art and fine handicrafts, for example, can set up an exciting buying trip beginning with scheduled visits to **Mexico City**'s posh shops and **Insurgentes Market** in the **Zona Rosa** and **Bazar Sábado** in **San Angel,** as well as **Guadalajara's Mercado Libertad** and **Tlaquepaque,** for starters. More sophisticated collectors will want to tour towns and villages where potters, weavers, leather and metal workers, and carvers create wonderful objets d'art. Particularly interesting are **Morelia** and the city of **Oaxaca** and their surrounding areas, as well as **Chiapas.** Agendas should be arranged specifically around market days in little towns, when local artisans set up their stalls to sell their wares.

Another engaging pastime is **study.** The appealing and easily accessible alternatives include courses in Spanish and the arts—painting, sculpture, printmaking, ceramics, jewelry making, music, instrument making, ballet, and folk and modern dance. Excellent and reasonably priced cultural institutes in **Mexico City, Guadalajara, San Miguel de Allende,** and **Cuernavaca,** among other cities, offer light or intensive study programs for foreign and Mexican students. Further information on language schools is available for U.S. residents from the National Registration Center for Study Abroad; tel.

> If travel in Mexico involves hazards, what are the compensations which make it worth while or even enjoyable?
>
> There are obvious answers to this question: the beauty of the landscape, the picturesque appearance and intriguing character of its inhabitants, the exotic birds, animals and flowers, the ruins of the ancient civilizations, the crumbling churches and monasteries of New Spain, the new-world architecture of modern Mexico, the markets and festivals of the countryside, the jaguar-, crocodile- and turkey-hunting, the playground pleasures of Acapulco, its sun, sex, high divers and deep sea fishing. With such a wide range to choose from no visitor should be left unsatisfied, providing, to take an example, he is prepared to enjoy the hunt although the jaguar fails to show up. Even when he realizes that there is little hope of finding his chosen quarry he may still return to Mexico year after year just for the excitement of the quest. For there are pleasures related to the very hazards of a journey which can make Mexican travel for some people, especially if they stay in the country long enough, an obsession.
>
> —John Lincoln
> *One Man's Mexico,* 1967

414-278-0631 or 800-558-9988. Several of the best institutes are listed in the destination chapters that follow.

During the summer season, the Universidad Nacional Autónomia de México (UNAM) in Mexico City offers intensive courses of study for foreign students in anthropology, language, literature, sociology, international affairs, economics, and a wide variety of other subjects. For a list of courses, schedules, fees, and requirements, write to Curso de Verano, UNAM, Ciudad Universidad, Mexico City, D.F., Mexico.

If you are a student of **anthropology** or **archaeology,** you will find study in Mexico particularly rewarding, especially if you can arrange to work in the field. To do this, you don't need a degree as much as you need perseverance. Contact the anthropology department at your local university to find out whether any local teams are currently participating in digs on which you might assist, or inquire as to which institutes in Mexico might be accepting participants. You should know that working on a dig is often more grueling than glamorous, but there is tremendous satisfaction in sifting through the sands of time to seek the shards of the past. If you prefer, however, simply to see the sites, the **National Museum of Anthropology,** in **Mexico City; Teotihuacán; Palenque** in **Chiapas; Chichén Itzá, Uxmal,** and **Tulúm** on the Yucatán Peninsula are musts. Ethnologists should visit the various Indian communities in **Chiapas, Oaxaca,** and **Morelia.**

Of course, Mexico gives **history buffs** plenty to explore. From the time of the Conquest through the turn of the century, Mexican history reads like a best-selling novel with larger-than-life heroes and villains, high intrigue and adventure, thrilling romance. Some subplots are so dramatic you think a clever author must surely have invented them. But the evidence of events surrounds you, especially as you travel Mexico's Independence Trail. This remarkable route really winds through all of the country, along the coasts and across the Yucatán Peninsula, but it is most clearly defined and effectively packaged in **Guanajuato, San Miguel de Allende, Querétaro,** and other Central Highlands cities where Allende, Morelos, Hidalgo, and the heroes of the Mexican War for Independence lived, fought, and died. Following this route will entertain and yield valuable insight into Mexico's character.

If your special interests are **sports-** or **fitness-oriented,** Mexico promises challenges and rewards. **Golf** and **tennis** enthusiasts have great courses and courts at Mexico's major resorts, some of which feature workshops and clinics for those who wish to improve their skills. **Beach resorts** along Mexico's Pacific, Caribbean, and Gulf coasts provide an abundance of exciting seaside sports—swimming, surfing, snorkeling, scuba diving, sand-castle construction and more. Instruction and equipment rentals are readily available. **Cabo San Lucas, Mazatlán,** and other port towns are havens for **fishing enthusiasts.** Inland, the mighty **Sierra Madre** ranges challenge **mountaineers** and **hikers; highland roads** are tough training routes for serious **joggers** or **bicyclists;** and those who are keen on climbing stairs for aerobic exercise can work up a sweat and elevate their heart rates at the **pyramids.** Mexico also has several full-service **spas,** such as the **Hotel Ixtapan,** in Ixtapan de la Sal, outside Mexico City, and **Rancho la Puerta** in Tecate, Baja California, with weight-reduction programs, as well as a wide variety of mineral baths and hot springs for health enthusiasts.

5

MEXICO CITY

¡Bienvenido a la Ciudad de México! Mexico's capital is the world's largest city: In 1987, the population exceeded 18 million people. Mexico City covers an area of about 25 miles from north to south and 15 miles from east to west. The city borders are supposed to correspond to those of the Distrito Federal (DF), the area defined to establish the capital as a separate administrative entity. But Mexico City has expanded beyond those borders as wealthy residents have relocated to the outskirts of town to escape the crowds, and as thousands of campesinos flock to the city in search of work.

Mexico City, or simply México, as it is called by residents, makes an immediate impression on visitors. Some find the city's broad boulevards, parks, monuments, splendid colonial buildings, sophisticated modern architecture, and scattered remains of pre-Hispanic structures remarkably beautiful and fascinating. Others are upset by the signs of poverty, particularly the women and children begging for money; are frustrated by constant traffic congestion (which at press time has resulted in a policy restricting cars from being driven in the city on certain days of the week, a policy which does not affect tour buses or rental cars); and say the severe pollution and high altitude (about 7,200 feet) are health hazards, making breathing difficult. There is validity in both these perceptions: As the world's largest city, México combines the advantages and drawbacks of any big city, albeit in gigantic proportions.

There has been a city in this place since 1345, when the Aztecs (or Mexica, as they called themselves) settled here. They chose this site, on the shores of Lake Texcoco in the middle of the high mountain-ringed central valley known then as Anahuac (later, the Valley of Mexico) because their ancient teachings instructed them to build their city on the spot where they encountered an eagle perched atop a cactus plant and devouring a serpent. This was where they built Tenochtitlán (in Nahuatl, an Aztec dialect, "the place of the cactus fruit"),

15

their religious, economic, and political capital. To this day, the Mexican flag depicts an eagle, a cactus, and a serpent.

Tenochtitlán was a mighty city, a true triumph of engineering ingenuity and technical skill, and center of an empire with influence throughout most of what is now modern Mexico and Central America. The city of Tenochtitlán was built on an island in the middle of Lake Texcoco and the surrounding swamplands. Aztec engineers constructed three causeways from the mainland to the island and numerous canals that crisscrossed the island. Crops were farmed on floating sod platforms rooted to the lake bed. Dozens of pyramids, temples, palaces, marketplaces, and dwellings were built of stone and covered with painted stucco. In its heyday, the city had some three hundred thousand inhabitants, more than most European cities at that time.

No wonder Cortés and his men were awestruck when they first saw Tenochtitlán on November 8, 1519! The Aztecs welcomed the Spanish with honor and gifts. But Cortés and company, greedy conquerors that they were, besieged Tenochtitlán, took the city on August 13, 1521, and razed the Aztec pyramids, palaces, and temples. In 1522 they began to build their own city, Mexico City, on the ruins.

You can discern the fascinating history of Mexico in the city's architecture. Many of the early colonial buildings still stand, and major pre-Hispanic structures that lie beneath modern Mexico City are gradually being excavated. Other constructions tell the story of the brief empire of Maximilian and Carlota, of the struggle for independence, of the insurrections and influential presidencies. You can turn another page of Mexico's history on almost any corner.

In the meantime the capital strikes the observer as a place of spectacular contrasts. Here, in and around the Alameda, they are obvious enough: the glittering steel and glass of the new hotels beside the decaying stonework of the colonial churches; trees heavy with summer foliage jostling stark branches stripped as for winter; in the open the flat scorching gold of the sunlight, and in the shade the sharp alpine nip; the roar and surge of the traffic surrounding the relaxed indolence of the park; sleek American automobiles wing to wing with shambling tin buses; on the pavement the elegant business man strolling to his club, and on the grass the pregnant mother surrounded by her ragged children.

—John Lincoln
One Man's Mexico, 1967

PRIORITIES

Mexico City has so many genuinely impressive historical sites, museums, entertainment centers, and places of religious significance that it would take months, perhaps years, to see them all. If you're a first-time visitor to Mexico City, you need to get an overview of this vast and complex urban center. Begin your sightseeing with a general city tour (see **Connections and Touring,** below) to get your bearings—and a general idea of Mexico City's sophistication and richness. The following list of priorities will help you to determine your choice of important things to see. Notice that most of the sights are clustered in several specific areas, including Centro (Zócalo, Alameda, and other downtown locations); Zona Rosa; Polanco; Chapultepec; and the north and south of the city. Each attraction is keyed to the area of the city in which it is located. Also, sights are keyed to the color map of the city at the back of the book, referring to the page number of the map as well as the appropriate coordinates. *Mexico City by Neighborhood* (below) puts these priority sights into their geographical context and helps you organize your own sightseeing by area.

Alameda Park
DOWNTOWN, P. 15, 3E

Downtown, corner of Avenida Juárez and Dr. Mora, near the Zócalo

Metro: Hidalgo or Bellas Artes

A popular Sunday stroll through this beautiful park, with its fountains and filagree benches, is a must for resident and visitor alike. The park's rich history dates back to the Ancient Aztecs—but its modern-day offerings include free open-air concerts and a wide variety of vendors hawking merchandise.

In the Area: the Rivera Pavilion, featuring the monumental mural of Alameda Park, done by Diego Rivera, famous Mexican artist.

Basilica of the Virgin of Guadalupe
DOWNTOWN, P. 13, 2D

Plaza Hidalgo 1
Tel. 577-9396

Metro: La Basílica

This shrine, visited by hundreds of thousands of pilgrims each year, is considered by Catholics to be the most sacred spot in all of Mexico. In 1976, a new shrine was built here to allow for the huge numbers of worshipers, who can get a close-up view of the image via a moving walkway that passes directly below it.

In the Area: the tile-domed 18th-century La Capilla del Pocito (the Chapel of the Little Well).

Bazar Sábado   SAN ANGEL, P. 12, 4C
Plaza San Jacinto
Metro: Miguel Angel de Quevedo

Mexico City's most famous handicraft market is located in a wonderful old colonial mansion once occupied by the wealthy family of the counts of Oploca. You'll find a large open-air restaurant, along with many shops offering hand-made clothing and handicrafts here. The ambience is pleasant and chic; merchandise is above average in quality and even higher in price. Open Saturday only (as you could have guessed from the name) from 10 A.M. to 7 P.M.

Carrillo Gil Museum   SAN ANGEL, P. 12, 5C
Avenida Revolución 1608
Tel. 548-7467
Metro: Miguel Angel de Quevedo

Works by Rivera, Orozco, Siqueiros, Zuniga, and other great Mexican artists are the key to the collection here, but contemporary foreign artists are also represented. Open Tuesday through Sunday from 11 A.M. to 3 P.M. and from 4 to 7 P.M. Admission about $1.

Casa Colorada   COYOACÁN, P. 12, 5C
Calle de Higuera 57
Metro: Coyoacán

Hernán Cortés's wife disappeared mysteriously from this house shortly after the couple arrived in Mexico from Spain. The disappearance grew into a scandal when Cortés moved his Indian mistress—La Malinche—into the house.

Casa de Hernán Cortés   COYOACÁN, P. 12, 5C
Calle Aquayo, near Plaza Hidalgo
Metro: Coyoacán

This baroque building that housed Cortés in the 17th century now houses Mexican government offices. This site is reportedly where Cortés tortured Cuauhtemoc to get him to reveal the secret hiding places for the Aztecs' treasures.

Chapultepec Castle   CHAPULTEPEC, P. 14, 4A
Chapultepec Park 2da. Sección del Bosque de Chapultepec
Tel. 515-6304
Metro: Chapultepec

This magnificent 18th-century castle, in the corner of Chapultepec Park on Grasshopper Hill, overlooking Paseo de la Reforma and downtown México, houses the National Museum of History, with exhibits dating from the Conquest to the 1810 Revolution. Several important murals by Orozco, Siqueiros, and O'Gorman are located here.
In the Area: the Monument de los Niños Héroes.

Chapultepec Park   CHAPULTEPEC, P. 14, 4A
Metro: Chapultepec or Auditorio

Chapultepec Park is a welcome expanse of open space and greenery in one of the world's most crowded cities! The huge park (about two and a half square miles) has shady forests, beautiful gardens, a lake with rowboats, and much-used outdoor playing fields, as well as several of Mexico City's cultural treasures. The National Museum of Anthropology, Museum of Modern Art, Tamayo Museum, Chapultepec Castle (now housing the National Museum of History), Monument de los Niños Héroes, National Auditorium, and the Zoo are located here, as are a full-fledged amusement park (roller coaster and all!), Natural History and Technology museums, and relatively secluded jogging trails and picnic places.

Chapultepec Park is centrally located, near the Zona Rosa and the posh residential sections of Polanco and Lomas de Chapultepec, and easy to get to. Take a taxi, a collective cab, or bus along Paseo de la Reforma, which runs directly through the park, or take the Metro.

Convento del Carmen
SAN ANGEL, P. 12, 4C

Avenida Revolución 4

Metro: Miguel Angel de Quevedo

Formerly a Carmelite convent, this beautiful 17th-century building houses an eclectic collection of colonial art and artifacts. Open daily from 10 A.M. to 5 P.M. A small admission fee is charged.

Coyoacán
P. 12, 4C, 5C, 5D

Metro: Coyoacán

Coyoacán, an old and exclusive residential area in the south of Mexico City, has narrow cobblestone streets lined with colonial buildings noted for their fascinating architectural details, including fabulously carved wooden doors and walls built to accommodate branches of ancient trees. This is where many of the conquistadores, including Cortés, lived after the conquest of Mexico City. Today Coyoacán is the preferred address of leading Mexican artists and intellectuals.

Desierto de los Leónes (Desert of Lions)

Off the Toluca Highway (MEX15)

President Venustiano Carranza created this four-million-plus-acre national park by decree. It has many interesting attractions, including a former Carmelite convent built in the 17th century. This beautiful building has quiet cloisters and mysterious passageways. But whether you go to Desierto de los Leónes for the sights or for a picnic surrounded by cool pine forests, this is a great place to escape from Mexico City's congested traffic and pollution. Note that this park is difficult to get to if you don't have a car. The best alternative is to take a taxi and, for a flat fee, arrange to have it wait for you.

Diego Rivera Museum (The Anahuacalli)   P. 12, 5C
Calle del Museo 150, San Pablo Tepetlapa, a suburb to the south
Tel. 677-2984
Metro: Coyoacán, plus taxi

Designed by Diego Rivera, this building is an example of unusual modern architecture—a pyramid built out of *pedregal,* or lava. Dramatic lighting effects, including sunbeams filtered through translucent onyx, accent the exhibitions. The first floor has mostly Aztec artifacts. Upstairs floors exhibit artifacts from Nayarit, Colima, Jalisco, Oaxaca, and the Gulf Coast. The museum is out of the way, but very worth a visit. The best way to go is to take a taxi from Coyoacán or San Angel. Open Tuesday through Sunday from 10 A.M. to 6 P.M. Closed Mondays. Admission free.

Frida Kahlo House and Museum   COYOACÁN, P. 12, 4C

Calle Londres 127 and Allende
Tel. 554-5999
Metro: Coyoacán

The wonderful bright blue house that was occupied by painter Frida Kahlo and her husband, the famous muralist Diego Rivera, is filled with memorabilia and artwork by the couple. Of special interest is Frida's studio; a disability forced her to paint self-portraits while lying down, facing a mirror suspended over her bed. A must. Open Tuesday through Sunday, 10 A.M. to 6 P.M. Small admission fee.
In the Area: the Leon Trotsky House.

Hotel de México   P. 12, 3C
Toward the south of the city, at Insurgentes Sur and Filadelfia
Metro: San Pedro de los Pinos

The Hotel de México was once intended to be the largest hotel in Mexico City; work on it was abandoned when the developer ran out of funds. Now the building is just a shell, towering over this quiet residential neighborhood of Mexico City. But there is a revolving restaurant at the top of the hotel, open from 1 to 10 P.M. daily; AE, MC, and V are accepted.

Leon Trotsky House and Museum   COYOACÁN, P. 12, 4C
Viena 45
Tel. 554-4482
Metro: Coyoacán

The high stone walls and brick watchtowers of this house reflect the security-consciousness of its famous former resident, philosopher/revolutionary Leon Trotsky, who lived here from 1937 until his death in 1940. The house is filled with Trotsky's personal effects—papers, books, newspaper clippings. Trotsky's tomb, designed by Mexican artist Juan

O'Gorman, is in the garden. Open Tuesday through Friday from 11 A.M. to 4 P.M. A small admission fee is charged.
In the Area: the Frida Kahlo Museum.

Metropolitan Cathedral
DOWNTOWN, P. 15, 3F

North side of the Zócalo, between calles Monte de Piedad, Guatemala, and República de Argentina
Metro: Zócalo

Mexico City's enormous and almost overpowering cathedral, begun in 1573 and finished in 1667, is a fascinating combination of Renaissance, baroque, and neoclassical architectural styles. Outside, soaring towers and decorative carved stone detail dominate the building. The cathedral's interior houses the remains of many Mexican archbishops as well as the crypt of Augustín Iturbide, who was—albeit briefly—emperor of Mexico. Next to the cathedral, and connected to it, is el Sagrario, the parish church. And on the east side of the cathedral, you'll find major archaeological excavation at the site of Templo Mayor.

Ministry of Public Education
DOWNTOWN, P. 15, 3F

República de Argentina 28, near the Zócalo
Metro: Zócalo

The walls of the courtyards of this government building are covered with a series of more than one hundred murals, painted by Diego Rivera and other Mexican artists, and commissioned by José Vasconcelos, the post-revolutionary minister of public education and a great patron of the arts. Open Monday through Friday from 8 A.M. to 7 P.M. Admission free.

Monument to Mexican Independence
ZONA ROSA, P. 14, 4C

Paseo de la Reforma at the intersection of Florencia

Otherwise known as the Angel, the statue of the goddess of liberty, balanced atop a tall column, memorializes several of Mexico's revolutionary heroes interred here.
In the Area: the American Embassy; Hotel María Isabel Sheraton.

Monument de los Niños Héroes
CHAPULTEPEC, P. 14, 4B

Chapultepec Park, near Chapultepec Castle
Metro: Chapultepec

During the U.S. invasion in 1847, young Mexican cadets died trying to defend the Chapultepec Castle, then being used as Mexico's military academy. Throughout Mexico, these "Niños Héroes" are commemorated with monuments and streets named in their honor, but their tomb—and their official national monument—is here.

Museum of the City of Mexico
DOWNTOWN, P. 15, 3F

Calle Pino Suárez number 30, south of the Zócalo, just before the corner of Calle El Salvador

Tel. 542-0487

Metro: Zócalo or Pino Suárez

This museum features a wide array of exhibits on Mexican culture and history, along with fascinating maps and documents from the earliest Spanish incursions, as well as a huge model of Tenochtitlán, the capital city of the Aztecs, and exhibits depicting the present and future of Mexico City in photos and sketches. Open Tuesday through Sunday from 9:30 A.M. to 7:30 P.M. Admission is free, and there are regularly scheduled lectures Thursday evenings at 7.

Museum of Modern Art   CHAPULTEPEC, P. 14, 4A

Paseo de la Reforma, across the street from the National Museum of Anthropology

Tel. 553-6211

Metro: Chapultepec or Auditorio

The museum's great collections of contemporary art, including works by Mexican artists Rivera, Kahlo, O'Gorman, Tamayo, Siqueiros, and others, as well as Magritte, Delvaux, and other international modern masters, plus major traveling exhibitions of works by established artists and avant-gardists, are shown in two spacious, modern buildings that flank a small garden filled with contemporary sculpture. The museum is open Tuesday through Sunday from 10 A.M. to 6 P.M. There is a small admission fee. Enter the museum from Paseo de la Reforma or through a second gate located behind the Monument de los Niños Héroes.

National Auditorium   CHAPULTEPEC, P. 14, 4A

Paseo de la Reforma, in Chapultepec Park

Metro: Auditorio

This is Mexico City's primary exhibit hall and performing arts venue. Consult your concierge or the local newspapers for current schedules.

National Museum of Anthropology   CHAPULTEPEC, P. 14, 4A

Paseo de la Reforma, Chapultepec Park

Tel. 553-6266

Metro: Chapultepec or Auditorio

Mexico City's extraordinary National Museum of Anthropology houses the world's foremost collection of pre-Columbian artifacts. The museum offers archaeological artifacts from Mexico's important Indian cultures, along with exhibitions depicting the way Mexico's native populations live today. The National Museum of Anthropology is open Tuesday through Saturday from 9 A.M. to 7 P.M., Sunday from 10 A.M. to 6 P.M. There is a small admission fee, which is reduced on Sunday.

National Museum of History
(See **Chapultepec Castle,** above)

National Palace
DOWNTOWN, P. 15, 3F

On the east side of the Zócalo
Metro: Zócalo

The National Palace, now containing the office of the president along with several government departments, is on the site once occupied by Moctezuma's Palace. Over the central entrance to the National Palace hangs the original Mexican Liberty Bell, the one that was sounded by Miguel Hidalgo on September 16, 1810, to signal Mexican independence. A grand stairway leads to the balcony, where you'll find the magnificent murals of Diego Rivera.

The National Palace is open daily from 7 A.M. to 7 P.M. and Saturday and Sunday until 3 P.M. A small fee is charged for admission to Benito Juárez Museum only.

National Pawnshop
DOWNTOWN, P. 15, 3F

Monte de Piedad 7 and 5 de Mayo, near the Zócalo
Metro: Zócalo

Mexico's National Pawnshop is filled with all sorts of treasures, as well as a lot of junk. On a good day, you can make out like a bandit! Aside from that, the building is on the site of the Aztec palace where Moctezuma welcomed Cortés and company—and where they later killed him.

Olympic Stadium
At University City
Metro: Universidad

The former University Stadium was completely redesigned and rebuilt for the 1968 Olympics by architect Pedro Ramirez Vasquez. The new stadium, shaped like a pre-Hispanic pyramid, holds more than 72,000 spectators.

Palacio de las Bellas Artes
DOWNTOWN, P. 15, 3E

Avenida Juárez and Lázaro Cárdenas, downtown, near the Zócalo
Tel. 526-7805
Metro: Bellas Artes

A palatial building, constructed of gleaming white marble, the Palace of the Fine Arts, in the east end of Alameda Park, is home to the Ballet Folklórico and Mexico's National Symphony, and it also houses art galleries featuring temporary and permanent collections.

Pinacoteca Virreinal de San Diego
DOWNTOWN, P. 15, 3E

Dr. Mora 7, near Alameda
Tel. 510-2793
Metro: Zócalo

This beautiful 17th-century building, the former Monastery of San Diego, now houses a lovely art museum with an im-

pressive collection of 16th- and 17th-century colonial paintings, mostly with religious themes. The museum is open
Tuesday through Sunday from 10 A.M. to 5 P.M. Admission
is free.

On a more somber note: a plaque indicates the spot where
those found guilty of heresy were burned in the Inquisition.

Plaza Garibaldi
DOWNTOWN, P. 15, 2F

Avenidas Lázaro Cárdenas and República de Honduras, near
the Zócalo and Alameda
Metro: Zócalo or Bellas Artes

This square, Mexico City's mariachi headquarters, is always filled with the bands of musicians waiting to be hired.
Action around the square is usually most intense at around
nine at night, especially on Sundays. Often it seems to have
more to do with the hustle of getting hired than with the actual
playing of music. You can order a performance on the spot
for about $5 per song, or you can arrange to be serenaded
at your hotel for a slightly higher rate.
In the Area: bars and bistros such as Tenampa, Tlaquepaque, and Pulqueria la Hermana Hortensia.

Plaza of the Three Cultures
Several miles north of Alameda Park, in Tlatelolco
Metro: Tlatelolco

The three predominant aspects of Mexican culture are represented in this square, with its Aztec ruins, a colonial church,
and modern buildings.
In the Area: the Ministry of Foreign Affairs.

Pyramid of Cuicuilco
Near the Periférico (Freeway) in the south of the city

This, thought to be the oldest manmade structure in North
America, was only recently discovered. The circular shape of
the pyramid has raised a great deal of speculation about its
origins.

Reino Aventura
Carretera Picacho Ajusto sin/nombre
Tel. 652-2231

An amusement park with thrill rides and six different theme
sections, with good food and special rides in each section.
Open daily except Tuesday. An afternoon of rides costs about
$8 and up.

Sanborn's House of Tiles
DOWNTOWN, P. 15, 3E

Madero 4, near the Zócalo
Tel. 521-6058
Metro: Zócalo

If you want to get a good look at beautiful blue and white
Puebla tiles, here's your chance! This four centuries-old colonial mansion is completely covered with them, although they

were not the innovation of the counts of Orizaba, the original inhabitants, but were rather added by a later resident. Inside is an enormous glass-covered courtyard surrounded by columns supporting balconies lined with tiles and decorated with carved stone details. The House of Tiles is now occupied by Sanborn's Restaurant and is a perfect place to rest and snack. Open daily 24 hours.

San Carlos Museum
DOWNTOWN, P. 15, 2D

Puente de Alvarado 50
Tel. 535-4848
Metro: Zócalo

This lovely museum, set in a splendid colonial mansion, exhibits a collection of works by Mexican painters and various European masters, including Fragonard, Tintoretto, Sir Joshua Reynolds, Lucas Cranach the Elder, Rubens, and Rembrandt, among others. The museum is associated with the San Carlos Academy, Mexico's finest art school, which counts Diego Rivera among its graduates. The museum is open Monday, and Wednesday through Sunday from 10 A.M. to 3 P.M. and 4 to 7 P.M. A minimal admission fee is charged.

Siqueiros Polyforum
SOUTH OF THE CITY, P. 12, 3C

Insurgentes Sur and Filadelfia
Tel. 536-4524
Metro: San Pedro de los Pinos

Famous muralist David Siqueiros's monumental *March of Humanity on Earth* and *Toward the Cosmos* are on display inside this unique, multifaceted art center. But you don't really have to go inside to experience the impact of Siqueiros's work: the building's exterior is covered by another 27,000-square-foot Siqueiros mural. The Polyforum, a monument to this master artist, is open daily from 10 A.M. to 2:30 P.M. and 3:30 to 9 P.M. Siqueiros Polyforum is located directly in front of the **Hotel de México** (see above).

Tamayo Museum
CHAPULTEPEC, P. 14, 4A

Paseo de la Reforma, Chapultepec Park
Metro: Auditorio

Containing a substantial collection of works by the renowned Mexican painter Rufino Tamayo, as well as his personal collection of works by his contemporaries, the museum, located in a pleasant parklike area, was built by architect Pedro Ramirez Vasquez.
In the Area: the Museum of Anthropology.

Templo Mayor
DOWNTOWN, P. 15, 3F

On Seminario, east of the Metropolitan Cathedral, near the Zócalo
Metro: Zócalo

This major archaeological site, located to the east of the Metropolitan Cathedral in the heart of Mexico City's prime

Mexico City is a city with a secret, and to live here requires both imagination and will. It is like a person who seems incredibly disheveled but whose core, if you dig deep enough, is ordered, sure, and compelled by belief. What you see when you arrive in this smog-ridden, traffic-heavy city of eighteen million people—many of whom are unemployed peasants from the campos who haven't yet made it to the border—will make you crazy. But its secret is this: beneath its poverty, its filth, its damaged people, another reality exists. . . .

The past repeats itself. History builds layer upon layer. Mexico City is an archaeologist's dream and an urban planner's nightmare. If you try to dig a subway tunnel or excavate for a new building, you will come across the ruins of the Temple Major or of a monument to Quetzalcóatl. The Spaniards built their new city—their enormous colonial churches and houses of justice—directly on top of the Aztec temples and houses they destroyed.

What remains in Mexico today, four hundred years after its past was buried, is an incompatible mix of cultures—Spanish, French, United States, and indigenous Mesoamerican. The conquistadors, through genocide, cultural destruction, and miscegenation, managed to obliterate the great empires of North and South America: the Incas, the Mayas, the Aztecs, and the North American tribes. But in Mexico it is still all there—beneath the city the Spaniards built. The language, the culture, the artwork, the sense of time, the spiritual beliefs, the connections to earth and sky, remain beneath the structure of Western values and Christianity. It is all there.

—Mary Morris
Nothing to Declare, 1988

commercial real estate, was accidentally discovered in 1978. At present, continual excavation is under way. Walkways around the site allow the public to observe archaeologists' progress without hindering it, and many of the structures are clearly visible from the edges. The best vantage point is had from the south side of the excavation, on the corner of Calle República de Guatemala and Calle Verdad. Or you can actually tour through the dig, with English-speaking guides who explain the various buildings and their significance. The site is open Tuesday through Sunday from 9 A.M. to 5 P.M.; free tours begin when enough people have arrived and there is an available guide. There is also a small museum, open Tuesday through Sunday from 10 A.M. to 1 P.M., located on the northeast side of the dig, at the corner of Calle Correo Mayor and Calle Justo Sierra. A small admission fee is charged.

In the Area: Mexico City Historical Center.

La Torre Latinoamericana (The Latin American Tower)

DOWNTOWN, P. 15, 3E

Corner of Avenida Juárez and Lázaro Cárdenas, near Alameda Park

Metro: Bellas Artes

The tower's observation deck, on the 42nd floor, is *the* place for a spectacular bird's-eye view of downtown Mexico City. On a clear day, you can see as far as Chapultepec Park (at the other end of Paseo de la Reforma) and the mountains in the distance beyond. The deck is open daily from 10 A.M. to midnight. Buy tickets (about 50¢) and tokens for the deck's telescope at the booth near the elevator.

University City

Jardines del Pedregal, in the south of the city

Metro: Universidad

This is the seat of the Universidad Autónoma Nacional de México (UNAM), which claims to be the oldest university in the New World. The eight-hundred-acre campus, established about thirty years ago, contains many fascinating examples of contemporary Mexican architecture, including Sala Nezahualcoyotl, a 2,500-seat modern concert hall with fabulous acoustics and famous guest artists (including the Moscow Philharmonic, London Symphony, and Cleveland Orchestra, among others), and the University Library, with a ten-story monumental mosaic mural by artist Juan O'Gorman.

Xochimilco

Suburb, about thirty minutes by car to the south of Mexico City

In ancient times, Aztec farmers grew their crops here, on sod-filled barges; this area became known as the "floating gardens of Xochimilco." Today you can buy a ride for about $10 or $15 on one of the boats that sail through the complex system of canals. Food and entertainment are available. Open daily. Much fun and local color, especially on Sunday afternoons.

Zócalo

DOWNTOWN, P. 15, 3F

Metro: Zócalo

Mexico City's principal square, known officially as Plaza de la Constitución and unofficially as the *zócalo,* is the world's third largest city square (after Tiananmen Square in Beijing and Red Square in Moscow). Once a parklike space filled with trees, the Zócalo is now an open, shadeless area, surrounded by fabulous colonial buildings.

In the Area: National Palace; Metropolitan Cathedral.

Zona Rosa

P. 14, 4C

Bounded by Paseo de la Reforma, Niza, Liverpool, and Florencia

The Zona Rosa, or Pink Zone, is the embodiment of European influence and style in the heart of Mexico City. Even the area's streets are named after European cities—Génova, Hamburgo, Copenhague, Londres. Formerly primarily residential, the Zona Rosa is now known for fashionable shopping and a wide array of restaurants. Fortunately, some of the streets are closed to cars—so the daytime shoppers and nighttime revelers can relax their pace.

Zoo

CHAPULTEPEC, P. 14, 4A

Chapultepec Park, off Paseo de la Reforma
Tel. 277-7239
Metro: Chapultepec or Auditorio

Recent news of pandas born in captivity here has captured the world's imagination about the Mexico City Parque Zoologico. Less famous but equally entertaining residents include imported big cats, bears, deer, and local exotic creatures, including iguanas. A mini-railroad runs through the zoo, and rowboats can be rented at a nearby lake.

CONNECTIONS AND TOURING

Mexico City's sprawl means tourists must spread themselves a bit thin to see all its interesting corners. Fortunately, most sights that tourists wish to see, with some key exceptions, are clustered in distinct areas, and transportation between these is fairly easy.

Modern Mexico is divided into 16 large administrative units called *delegaciós,* or districts, with 240 smaller *colonias,* or neighborhoods. Streets within each *colonia* usually have similar names: names of rivers, for example, or cities, writers, or doctors. Be familiar with the term *colonia.* It is often used in addresses.

The Paseo de la Reforma is a key east-west route through the city, linking downtown areas, including the Zócalo and Alameda Park, with the Zona Rosa and, farther west, with Polanco and Chapultepec Park. The distance between the Zócalo and Chapultepec Park is about 2½ miles. Most of Mexico City's major attractions and best hotels are along this route. Around the Alameda Park, Paseo de la Reforma swings northward, and along this extension, you'll find the Basilica of the Virgin of Guadalupe and Plaza of the Three Cultures. Insurgentes Sur and the Periférico are two main north-south roads, leading to additional attractions in the south of the city, at San Angel, Coyoacán, and University City. These areas are fairly close to each other and are easily reached by taxi or Metro.

There are several reliable options for transportation around Mexico City. Rental cars are available, but driving yourself is not recommended for several reasons. The traffic is congested enough to turn even angels into monsters, and Mexican drivers seem to take their aggressions out on the road. In addition, the street layout is confusing, especially when one-way streets suddenly change directions. Finding a parking space is almost impossible, and if you do find one, you'll probably have to pay some kids or an older man in uniform to watch your car. You may also have to pay a "fine" for some imaginary infraction of the law, if you have the misfortune of being pulled over by one of Mexico City's finest. It's better to take a taxi. If, however, you insist upon driving yourself, National Car Rental's (tel. 5-784-2241, 5-571-8889 or, in the United States, 800-227-3876) Mexican operation is reliable and offers competitive prices and convenient office locations. If you're traveling from the United States, note that for some reason cars reserved in the United States rent for less than those reserved in Mexico.

If you opt for taxis, take comfort in the fact that these are plentiful. They come in several varieties that you should know about. Hotel taxis are most convenient, but they cost more—sometimes double the rate charged by taxis you hail on the street. Street taxis are yellow and white or orange and white—usually Volkswagen Beetles or Datsun sedans. These may be lined up at a *sitio,* or taxi stand (from which they may be ordered by telephone, except if you're being picked up at a hotel), or they may be cruising the streets. *Sitio* cabs cost more than cruising cabs and less than hotel cabs.

In Mexico, taxi fares are not determined by a ticking meter. You must negotiate the fare with the cabby before accepting the ride. Though their rates are set, hotel and *sitio* taxis charge higher fares than cruising cabs. If you decide to take a cruising cab, you'll have to bargain to get the going rate.

Let's say you want to go from Polanco to the Zona Rosa. You hail a taxi and ask, "How much?" The cabby says, "Ten thousand pesos." You look astonished and say, "That's very expensive." He'll say, "How much you wanna pay?" You offer five thousand. He'll try for eight thousand. You counter with six thousand—and probably wind up paying seven thousand.

Sometimes bargaining seems like too much trouble. You're too tired. Or haggling over three thousand pesos makes you feel cheap. So you avoid the whole issue by agreeing to pay the ten thousand pesos the cabby asked for in the first place. But then, as you ride, you stew about letting a cabby take you to the cleaners while transporting you to the Zona Rosa. And that stew turns into a burn when, the next day, another cruising cabby asks you for only four thousand pesos to make exactly the same trip.

Taxi fare is not always fair in Mexico.

Mexico City also has *peseros.* These are vans used as shared taxis that run along set routes. You'll pay about $.50 per ride for a great way to travel, especially along the popular route from Polanco and the Chapultepec area along Paseo de la Reforma to downtown and the Zócalo. You might have to change *peseros,* but even a double fare is easy on the budget.

Public buses along Paseo de la Reforma are inexpensive and reliable. Buses heading downtown along this route are marked "Zócalo"; those headed in the other direction are marked "Auditorio," "Lomas," and "Palmas." Another important bus route runs along Insurgentes, to the south of the city. Heavy traffic and frequent stops make bus travel time-consuming.

The Metro is a time-saving alternative. It is modern, clean, efficient, inexpensive, and has seven lines that will take you just about everywhere in the city. (See the color metro map at the back of the book.) The subway is always crowded, but there are special cars for women and children, and luggage or large items may not be carried aboard. Signs are in Spanish: *Salida* marks exits, and *Correspondencias* shows where you can transfer from one line to another. On weekdays, subways run from early morning (5 or 6 A.M.; 7 A.M. on Sun.) until 12:30 A.M. (1:30 A.M. on Sat.). Watch your wallet and other valuables when it's crowded. The pickpockets are pros!

If you have limited time or wish to cover specific sights that are some distance from one another, it's a good idea for you to take a day tour of the city. You can book a city tour covering the Zócalo and nearby sights; Chapultepec Park museums and nearby sights; San Angel and Coyoacán and nearby sights; or any combination thereof, or you can organize your own individualized itinerary to suit your particular needs. A dozen or more local tour companies would love to accommodate you, and your hotel desk should be able to match you up with a suitable tour or guide with no difficulty. In addition, **Mexico Travel Advisers (MTA),** one of the largest and most reliable of the tour companies, offers a broad range of reasonably priced tour services, including regularly scheduled city tours in air-conditioned buses or vans, or individual tours in vans or private cars. The latter naturally cost more, but MTA's rates are competitive. MTA's services are also recommended for day and overnight excursions from Mexico City (see **Excursions,** below). MTA's Mexico City office is at Génova 30, in the Zona Rosa; tel. 525-7520. Tours may be booked by telephone, and you can arrange to be picked up at your hotel. However, before you book any tour, make sure the itinerary is to your liking. Avoid tours that schedule lengthy stops at tourist shops (where the guide and driver get commissions), which cut into your time to see the sights.

🧳 HOTELS

Mexico City has dozens of hotels of all categories and descriptions. There are super-deluxe soaring towers of glass and steel, converted colonial mansions, and budget bedrooms: in other words, a space to suit everyone's taste and pocketbook. The best choices are close to the tourists sights—around the Zócalo, along Paseo de la Reforma, or near Chapultepec Park, in the neighborhoods described in **Priorities,** above. The staff of Mexico City hotels is for the most part very friendly, and workers will try to be accommodating and obliging. However, the pace at which people operate here is different from what you are probably accustomed to, and by North American standards in general, service would certainly be considered slow.

The same neighborhood and map keying system used in **Priorities** is also utilized here. All selections described below are air-conditioned unless otherwise noted. Here are some sound selections:

Calinda Geneva Quality Inn
ZONA ROSA, P. 14, 4C

Londres 130, 06600
Tel. 5-211-0071 or 800-228-5151
Doubles, from $60

This very popular hotel has a history: It was opened in 1907! Now, under the capable management of the Calinda Quality chain, the Geneva has been refurbished. The lobby is deep red and elegant, with evening mariachis or other entertainment. This is a popular meeting place, even for nonguests. The 350 rooms are freshly painted but vary in size and, consequently, in comfort (some suffer from Zona Rosa traffic noises, too; ask for rooms facing the interior courtyard). Color TV and direct-dial phones are in all rooms. The restaurant is good enough to compete with other Zona Rosa eateries for your dining pleasure. Credit cards: AE, CB, DC, MC, V.

Camino Real
CHAPULTEPEC, P. 14, 3A

Mariano Escobedo 700, 11590
Tel. 5-203-2121 or 800–228–3000
Doubles, from $110

The location, fabulous architecture, quality service, and a coterie of influential guests who call this hotel their Mexico City home, make this one of Mexico City's top choices for both business travelers and vacationers. The hotel is a self-contained complex with a distinctly Mexican look. Exterior walls are slightly sloped, following the model of ancient pyramids. Inside, spacious multilevel lobbies are decorated boldly with pinks, purples, and orange expanses of wall and feature fine murals, paintings, and sculptures, including works by Tamayo and Calder, as decorative accents. The seven hundred rooms are large and cheerfully decorated with brightly colored bedspreads, curtains, and colonial-style furniture. All have color TVs with English-language channels and servibars. The hotel has five heated swimming pools and rooftop illuminated tennis courts. Excellent shops offer everything from clothes to handicrafts, and several fine restaurants, including **Azulejos** and **Fouquet's de Paris** (see listings for both in *Restaurants,* below), are on the premises. Credit cards: AE, DC, MC, V.

Century
ZONA ROSA, P. 14, 4C

Liverpool 152 (at Amberes), 06600
Tel. 5-584-7111
Doubles, from $70

In the heart of the Zona Rosa, this modern hotel has 143 rooms on 19 floors. Though the rooms are small, they all have balconies; those on the top floors have spectacular views. Bathrooms have marble bathtubs. Color TV with English-language channels is offered. The hotel restaurant, **Regine's,** is pleasant. Swimming pool and sauna are both welcome retreats from Mexico City hustle and bustle. Credit cards: AE, DC, MC, V.

De Cortés
DOWNTOWN, P. 15, 3F

Avenida Hidalgo 85 (near Zócalo), 06300
Tel. 5-518-2181 or 800-528-1234
Doubles, from $50

This is the oldest hotel in Mexico City, and it still retains much of its colonial charm. Originally an inn for monks in transit through Mexico City, the two-story hotel was built in the 18th century. There are 27 rooms and several suites, all decorated with modern furniture and surrounding a traditional arcaded courtyard with fountain, shade trees, bougainvillea, and a pleasant open-air restaurant. Corner rooms overlooking the Alameda Park are best, although some may find city noises distracting. All in all, a very good find. Credit cards: AE, CB, DC, MC, V.

Emporio   DOWNTOWN/ZONA ROSA, P. 15, 3D
Paseo de la Reforma 124, 06600
Tel. 5-556-7766
Doubles, from $50
Ideally located between the Zona Rosa and the Zócalo, the newly refurbished Hotel Emporio is a real find. The lobby is all marble and sparkling chandeliers. Rooms are tastefully modern, with built-in furniture, and each has a terrific red Jacuzzi. The staff members seem to take a personal interest in the hotel and work hard to make a good impression on guests. Credit cards: AE, DC, MC, V.

Fiesta Americana Airport   SOUTH OF CITY
Fundidora Monterrey 89, Peñon de los Baños, 15520 (across from Aeropuerto Benito Juarez)
Tel. 5-762-0199 or 800-223-2332
Doubles, from $115
A deluxe and convenient hotel for business travelers on the fly in and out of Mexico City for meetings: the 272-room modern building is across the road from the domestic-arrivals building and can be reached by a covered walkway. Rooms are spacious, comfortable, modern, and clean. There's a TV monitor with flight schedules in the lobby, plus satellite TV from the United States in all rooms, along with restaurants, bar, nightclub, and just about everything else you'd need for a short and self-contained hotel stay. This place is often booked full—but the location is a drawback for nonbusiness travelers because it is so far from most of the Mexico City sights. Credit cards: AE, DC, MC, V.

Galería Plaza   ZONA ROSA, P. 14, 4C
Hamburgo 195, 06600
Tel. 5-211-0014 or 800-228-3000
Doubles, from $90
A large, convenient, modern, and well-run hotel in the heart of the Zona Rosa. The 430 rooms are pleasantly decorated in contemporary style and have English-language TV and servibars. Those rooms on upper floors have attractive city views. A spacious lobby has a refreshing fountain and pleasant greenery. Three restaurants and a popular disco are on the premises. Credit cards: AE, DC, MC, V.

El Gran Hotel
16 de Septiembre 82, 06000

DOWNTOWN, P. 15, 3F

Tel. 5-510-4040/49 or 800-654-2000

Doubles, $75

El Gran Hotel is representative of Mexico's grand dreams and designs. And like Mexico, it has survived and triumphed through troubled times.

The impressive building, wonderfully located, just a pulse beat away from Mexico's National and Municipal palaces, was constructed between 1895 and 1899 and inaugurated in the grand old style, with a celebrated event attended by President Porfirio Díaz. Initially, the structure housed a commercial center and office spaces. It had 23 stores (including Mexico's haute clothiers) and one hundred offices, and it boasted its own electrical generator and two panoramic elevators, plus running water, telephone and telegraph service, mail delivery, and other modern conveniences in every room. It astonished the public with its modernity. And its eclectic facade—with both fluted and smooth columns used to support a ledge with bronze and zinc statues, its sculptural representation of industry and commerce, and statues of two proud lions guarding the entrance—was acclaimed a work of art. No less so the interior, with two hundred Czechoslovakian crystal chandeliers, gilded iron lamps with ornate floral designs, a grand sweeping staircase, enormous gold cages filled with canaries, Greek columns, exquisite stained-glass roof and domes, and beautiful wrought-iron trellis work. The building was, indeed, a marvel.

Eventually the entire space was occupied by el Centro Mercantil, a commercial enterprise. In the late 1950s, this company attempted to tear the building down, and actually sold off various fixtures—including the sweeping staircase—before a new owner (Inversiónes y Valores de México, S.A.) stepped in to save the place from destruction. The building was converted to a hotel that had 120 rooms and twenty suites. Today, the rooms are comfortable enough—especially the roomier ones with windows facing the street—and pleasantly furnished, and the hotel has a considerate staff, two very decent restaurants and is still located just minutes away from the heart of Mexican political and economic activity. But the real thrill of staying at El Gran Hotel is walking into that Deco lobby and looking up at that stained-glass ceiling, staring at the rays of sunlight as they filter down, and the blues, greens, reds, and yellows that create undulating patterns in this historic and amazing place. Credit cards: AE, CB, DC, MC, V.

Holiday Inn Crowne Plaza
Paseo de la Reforma 80, 06600

DOWNTOWN, P. 15, 3D

Tel. 5-705-1515 or 800-HOLIDAY

Doubles, from $107

This luxury high-rise hotel, situated midway between the Zócalo and the Zona Rosa, is ideally located for both sightseers and shoppers. The pleasant lobby and lobby bar are always bustling. The first floor has meeting rooms that can be adjusted to suit your size requirements. The hotel is 25 stories tall, and rooms on higher floors have spectacular views of the city. Floors 22 and 23 offer Plaza Club service, with an elegant private lounge and concierge, complimentary breakfasts and cocktails, and other special amenities. But all the hotel's 630 rooms have been recently redecorated, with pleasant and cheerful pastel-colored furnishings. The hotel's popular restaurant, **la Hacienda,** offers a spectacular and reasonably priced Mexican buffet lunch every Thurs. An in-house booking agency has information about current performances, sports meets, and other events, and can get you tickets for just about anything in town. Pleasant and reliable service, especially on the Plaza Club floors. No swimming pool. Credit cards: AE, DC, MC, V.

Krystal Rosa   ZONA ROSA, P. 14, 4C
Liverpool 155, 06600
Tel. 5-211-0092 or 800-231-9860
Doubles, from $90

This 17-story centrally located hotel has 355 spacious, modern rooms, with English-language TV and servibars. The mirrored lobby, with chrome and velvet furniture, has an elegant and polished appeal, and you'll find a swimming pool and restaurants on the premises. Credit cards: AE, CB, DC, MC, V.

María Christina   ZONA ROSA, P. 14, 4C
31 Lerma 5, 06500
Tel. 5-546-9880
Doubles, from $45

This inexpensive hotel, located conveniently near the Zona Rosa, has 110 rooms—all recently refurbished. The ambience is definitely Mexican and slow-paced. Sometimes the staff is inattentive, but the rooms are pleasant and clean, and the price is right. The garden restaurant isn't always open for business, but the food is good when there is service. Credit cards: AE, DC, MC, V.

María Isabel Sheraton   ZONA ROSA, P. 14, 4C
Paseo de la Reforma 325, 06500
Tel. 5-207-3933 or 800-325-3535
Doubles, about $125

One of the most popular of Mexico City's modern high-rise luxury hotels, the María Isabel Sheraton is located next to the American Embassy and across the street from the fashionable Zona Rosa. The busy lobby is a favorite meeting place. The hotel's 850 rooms have recently been refurnished with pleasant pastel decor. There's a heated pool, and tennis courts on the roof, and a guests-only health club with weight-training equipment and sauna. Two fine restaurants, three bars, a nightclub, and shopping arcade with Gucci and other fine boutiques complete the picture. Credit cards: AE, CB, DC, MC, V.

Nikko Hotel   CHAPULTEPEC, P. 14, 3A
Campos Elíseos 204 (corner of Arquimedes), 11560

Tel. 5-203-4020 or 800-645-5687
Doubles, from $100

The newest of Mexico City's deluxe hotels, this high-tech high-rise is a joint Japanese and Mexican venture and is very popular with traveling business executives and vacationers who require efficient service. Nikko is located in residential Polanco, away from the downtown rush but close enough to all the action: Chapultepec Park, the National Museum of Anthropology, and other museums are within walking distance; and the Zona Rosa is a short cab or bus ride away. The spacious atrium lobby of sparkling marble accommodates the reception desk, concierge, waiting area with comfortable sofas and easy chairs, shops, a gallery, and lobby bar. Seven hundred fifty rooms and suites have pleasant gray-and-pink decor, with English-language TV, servibars, and key cards. Several units are specially equipped for disabled guests, and there are two Japanese tatami suites. The hotel's top four floors are "Nikko Floors," with special amenities including private lounges, concierge services, complimentary breakfasts and cocktails, as well as secretarial services for traveling executives. The hotel's Japanese restaurants are highly recommended, as is **les Celebrities** (see **Restaurants,** below), with exceptionally fine French cuisine. **El Jardín** (see **Restaurants,** below) serves excellent breakfast and lunch buffets, and à la carte dinners. A heated pool, tennis courts, and a health club with separate facilities for men and women are also on the premises. The Nikko is one of the most expensive hotels in Mexico City, and it is considered one of the best. Credit cards: AE, CB, DC, MC, V.

Polanco Hotel
CHAPULTEPEC, P. 12, 3B

Edgar Allan Poe 8, 15060
Tel. 5-520-6040/1/2 or 5-520-2085
Doubles, about $50

This modest little hotel, nestled in a quiet park-like corner of residential Polanco, offers a restful and reasonably priced retreat from the hustle and bustle of Mexico City. The modern five-story elevator building, with its unpretentious lobby, 72 small but comfortable and recently redecorated rooms, and six junior suites is less than a block from Paseo de la Reforma, and within easy access of the Museum of Anthropology, the Zona Rosa, and the Zócalo. All rooms have phones, color TVs broadcasting English-language channels, private baths, and central heating; some rooms provide pleasant views of the park. The restaurant **La Bottiglia,** with Spanish cuisine, is accessible from the lobby. Credit cards: AE, MC, V.

Stouffer's Presidente
CHAPULTEPEC, P. 14, 3A

Campos Elíseos 218, 11560
Tel. 5-250-7700 or 800-472-2427
Doubles, about $120

This modern monolithic high-rise towers over Polanco's palatial residences and affords stunning views of nearby Chapultepec Park from its upper-story windows. There are 726 rooms and 26 suites, all with modern and soothingly simple decor. The spacious lobby, with its comfortable leather couches and high ceilings, is a popular place for friends to gather before dining at one of the hotel's pleasant restaurants. El Presidente is well situated for tourists who don't want to be in the middle of downtown. It's possible to walk from here to Chapultepec Park or to the Museum of Anthropology or the Contemporary Art and Tamayo museums, and the Zona Rosa and downtown are a short ride down Paseo de la Reforma by taxi, bus, or Metro. Aeromexico and Mexicana have reservations desks off the lobby. Service is capable and pleasant. Credit cards: AE, DC, MC, V.

Suites Amberes   ZONA ROSA, P. 14, 4C
Amberes 64, 06600
Tel. 5-533-1306
Doubles, from $60
   This residential hotel, comfortable, convenient, and reasonably priced (especially for those who wish to do their own cooking), allows you to set up a home away from home in the middle of the Zona Rosa. You can entertain all you wish—or set up a temporary office. The 28 suites have colonial-style furniture, and the hotel staff offers good service. Credit cards: AE, MC, V.

MEXICO CITY BY NEIGHBORHOOD

Mexico City is divided into neighborhoods, called *colonias,* that have distinct personalities and are almost small cities in their own right. Many of the *colonias* are charming, but their borders do not necessarily indicate areas that are of particular interest to travelers. The following descriptions of neighborhoods are based on groupings of tourist sights and attractions and are intended to make it easy for visitors to Mexico City to see as much as possible in relatively little time.

El Centro

El Centro, the downtown area, is dominated by Mexico City's principal square, known officially as Plaza de la Constitución and unofficially as the Zócalo. For centuries, it has been the heartbeat of this land. In pre-Hispanic times, this was the seat of the Aztec city of Tenochtitlán, and it was filled with impressive palaces, pyramids, and temples. The Spanish conquerors replaced these structures with their own cathedral and government palaces, the most important buildings in colonial New Spain.

   The Zócalo is still the city's core. Until recently it was a parklike tree-filled space. Now, for security reasons, it is a paved area. But it is still surrounded by fabulous colonial buildings filled with activities essential to the life of Mexico.

   Every colonial town in Mexico has its *zócalo,* laid out according to the established model, with church, government, palace, and military offices surrounding the square—and a gazebo/bandstand in the center. Although the Mexico City Zócalo is missing its bandstand, it is by far the grandest *zócalo* in the land.

The **National Palace,** constructed in 1692 and 1693 on the site once occupied by Moctezuma's palace, has long been the seat of the Mexican government. It was occupied by the Spanish viceroys during colonial times, and subsequently by the emperors Iturbide and Maximilian, and many Mexican presidents. Today it houses the office of the president and several government departments.

Over the central entrance to the National Palace hangs the original Mexican Liberty Bell, the one that was sounded by Miguel Hidalgo on September 16, 1810, to signal Mexican independence. Each year on September 16, the current president of Mexico ceremoniously rings the bell, here, at the National Palace.

Inside the building are several large courts. Mexico's first bullfight was held here, in celebration of Cortés's return from Honduras.

Diego Rivera's murals can be found on the balcony. Painted over a 25-year period, the murals depict the history of Mexico from before the Conquest to modern times. Mexico's pantheon of heroes appears, surrounded by a cast of thousands of Indians, peasants, and workers. Guides and books are available to give detailed explanations of the murals.

The **Benito Juárez Museum** (tel. 522-5646) is also located in the National Palace. To get to it, use the left-most entrance to the palace, cross the courtyard to Benito Juárez's statue, and go up the flight of stairs. Juárez lived in these rooms, and he died here is 1872. All around are personal effects—papers, a dressing gown, and even a chamber pot.

The National Palace is open daily from 7 A.M. to 7 P.M. The Juárez Museum is open Monday through Friday from 10 A.M. to 7 P.M., and Saturday and Sunday until 3 P.M.

The **Metropolitan Cathedral,** Mexico City's mammoth cathedral, begun in 1573 and finished in 1667, is a fascinating combination of three architectural styles—Renaissance, baroque, and neoclassical. Outside, soaring towers and decorative carved stone detail dominate the building. The cathedral's interior is shaped like a cross, with a central nave and side aisles containing 16 small chapels, most notably the Capilla de San Isidro Labrador (second on the right), which contains the famous Black Christ, and Capilla de San José (third on the left), with a famous statue of Christ known as the *Lord of Cacao.* The tomb of Augustín Iturbide, the revolutionary leader who briefly became Mexico's emperor, was placed in the cathedral in 1838, and the remains of Mexico's archbishops are in the Crypt of the Archbishops located in the west transept.

Notice that the stone holy water founts ring like bells when they are struck lightly with a coin or other metal object. And

notice also that the cathedral, like many other colonial structures in Mexico City, is sinking: It was built on a filled-in lake
that is not solid enough to carry the weight of its heavy stone
towers and ornaments. Recently, however, the foundation has
been stabilized—a miracle of modern engineering.

Next to the cathedral, and connected to it, is **El Sagrario,**
the parish church. It is an architectural gem, built in the mid-
1700s in the marvelous baroque churrigueresque style.

On the east side of the cathedral, past a cluster of carpen-
ters, plumbers, and other tradesmen who try to drum up business with pictures of their prior accomplishments, you'll find
a major archaeological excavation on the site of **Templo
Mayor** (see below), the principal religious structure of the
Aztecs in Tenochtitlán.

East of the cathedral is **Templo Mayor,** a major archaeological site in the heart of Mexico City's prime commercial
real estate, accidentally discovered in 1978 when power company workers digging on the job unearthed a huge (ten feet
in diameter), round-shaped stone votive sculpture of the
Aztec moon goddess Coyolxuahqui. Further digging by the
experts revealed that this site had been the location of Tenochtitlán's religious and ceremonial center, with major temples to Huitzilopochtli, the Aztec patron deity and war god,
and Tlaloc, the god of rain. The structures had been razed
by the Spanish conquistadores, lead by Cortés: Spanish missionaries then constructed a church on the rubble. That
church was demolished in 1573, and the **Metropolitan Cathedral** (see above) was built in its place. At present, continual excavation is under way to the east of the Metropolitan
Cathedral. You can walk around the site and observe the archaeologists' progress; many of the structures are clearly visible from the perimeter. The best overview is had from the
south side of the excavation, on the corner of Calles República
de Guatemala and Verdad. Tours through the dig, with English-speaking guides who explain the various buildings and
their significance, are also available. The site is open Tuesday
through Sunday, from 9 A.M. to 5 P.M.: tours begin when
enough people have arrived and there is an available guide.
There is also a small museum, open Tuesday through Sunday
from 10 A.M. to 1 P.M., located on the northeast side of the
dig, at the corner of Calle Correo Mayor and Calle Justo Sierra.

The area surrounding the Templo Mayor dig was declared
an **Historic Zone** in 1980, and many of the historic colonial
buildings are being restored. One of these, the 18th-century
home of Don Manuel de Heras y Soto, one of the signers of
Mexico's National Act of Independence, has been converted
to the **Mexico City Historical Center.** This beautifully restored mansion is located at the corner of República de Chile
and Donceles.

Another colonial building serves as the **Museum of the City of Mexico.** This museum, dedicated to the history and culture of the Valley of Mexico, from the first arrival of man in about 8000 B.C. to the present, has been located since 1964 in a marvelous mansion built in 1528 as the Mexico City seat of the house of the counts of Santiago de Calimaya. The museum has fascinating maps and documents from the earliest Spanish incursions, as well as a huge model of Tenochtitlán. Also cataloged in fine paintings, documents, costumes, artifacts, and photographs is the history of Mexico City, of its founding fathers, fashion, mode of transportation, and other aspects of city life. The present and future of Mexico City is shown in photos and sketches. The museum, which has free admission, is open Tuesday through Sunday from 9:30 A.M. to 7:30 P.M. Lectures are regularly held on Thursday evenings at seven.

North of the Templo Mayor, on Argentina, is the **Ministry of Education.** The walls here are covered with a series of more than one hundred murals by Diego Rivera, painted between 1923 and 1928, as well as works by other Mexican artists. All were commissioned by José Vasconcelos, the post-revolutionary minister of public education and a great patron of the arts. These Rivera murals seem to be less didactic and political than usual, and more a pure celebration of Mexican culture. Open Monday through Friday from 8 A.M. to 7 P.M. No admission fee.

Nearby, stop in at the **National Pawnshop,** where you'll find all sorts of treasures—jewelry, crystal chandeliers, bentwood furniture, china dinner sets, old books and records, TV sets, and bicycles, along with the usual amount of junk. But you never know what you might find here! And the pawn shop is located on the site of the Aztec palace where Moctezuma welcomed Cortés and company, and where they later killed him.

As you walk west from the Zócalo on Madero, you'll reach the easily recognizable **Sanborn's House of Tiles.** The exterior of this wonderful colonial mansion, built at the end of the 16th century for the counts of the Valley of Orizaba, is completely covered with beautiful blue-and-white Puebla tiles, which were added by a later resident. Inside is an enormous glass-covered courtyard surrounded by columns supporting tile-lined balconies and decorated with carved stone details. The House of Tiles, now occupied by Sanborn's, is a great place to relax and grab a bite.

As you cross Lázaro Cárdenas, Madero turns into Avenida Juárez, and here, almost directly in front of Sanborn's House of Tiles, is the **Palacio de las Bellas Artes.** This gleaming white marble building dominates the east end of **Alameda Park.** The Revolution interrupted the Palacio's construction (begun in 1900) for 24 years. But since the Palacio de las Bellas Artes opened in 1934, it has been Mexico City's premiere showcase for the arts. The outside is ornate and Italianate, but the inside has an Art Deco design, with sweeping staircases leading to theaters and galleries on upper floors.

Bellas Artes is home to the Ballet Folklórico and Mexico's National Symphony. Both perform in the main theater, a beautiful house with a remarkable Art Nouveau curtain created by Louis Comfort Tiffany's New York studio out of thousands of pieces of shimmering colored glass. This fabulous curtain, modeled after a mural of the Valley of Mexico by Dr. Atl (the Mexican painter Gerardo Murillo), has also been raised on performances by a long roster of the world's leading musical and dance ensembles during their Mexico City engagements. For current performance schedules, consult your hotel concierge or the local newspapers.

In addition, Bellas Artes has art galleries displaying several murals painted by the Mexican masters—Rivera, Orozco, Siqueiros, and Tamayo. Most famous is the Diego Rivera mural *Man at the Crossing of the Ways,* on the western wall of the third floor. This work was originally commissioned for and painted in Rockefeller Center in New York in 1933. But the Rockefellers rejected the painting, then known as *Man in Control of His Universe,* because of its obviously socialist orientation, and painted over it. Rivera reconstructed the mural in Bellas Artes.

Other galleries exhibit permanent collections of paintings by other Mexican artists, plus top traveling exhibitions from all over the world.

Like many of the other heavy stone buildings around the Zócalo, Bellas Artes is actually sinking into the soft bed of Lake Texcoco. In fact, its base has "settled" about 12 feet since construction was begun in 1900.

Nearby, the **Pinacoteca Virreinal de San Diego** at Dr. Mora 7, formerly the Monastery of San Diego, is a lovely 17th-century building that now houses a delightful art museum with an impressive collection of 16th- and 17th-century colonial paintings, mostly with religious themes. The museum is open Tuesday through Sunday from 10 A.M. to 5 P.M. Admission is free.

It was outside this building that those found to be heretics were burned during the Inquisition. There is a plaque to mark the spot.

Stop at the **San Carlos Museum** at Alvarado and Azripe for a collection of works that includes Mexican painters and various European masters, such as Fragonard, Tintoretto, Sir Joshua Reynolds, Lucas Cranach the Elder, Rubens, and Rembrandt, among others. The museum is associated with Mexico's finest art school, the San Carlos Academy, alma mater of Diego Rivera and many of the country's other great painters. The museum is open Monday, and Wednesday through

Sunday from 10 A.M. to 3 P.M. and 4 to 7 P.M. Closed Tuesday. A small admission fee is charged.

Alameda Park is filled with French statuary, fountains, filigree benches, strollers—and history. In ancient times, this was an Aztec marketplace. Alameda, turned into a public park in 1592 by order of the Spanish viceroy Luis de Velasco, has been a popular place for promenades ever since, especially on Sunday afternoons, when there are free open-air concerts and vendors selling a wide variety of merchandise. Around Christmastime, on the Day of the Three Kings, the perimeter of the park, especially along Avenida Juárez, is lined with Santa Clauses ready to pose with passersby for photos taken in front of inventive cutouts of festive present-filled rooms, Arctic houses, chimneys, and other scenes. This is a much-loved Mexico City tradition, and a must if you're in town for Christmas.

Diego Rivera, Mexico's most famous artist, used the Alameda Park as the subject for one of his most important murals, *A Sunday Dream in Alameda Park,* painted in 1947. Formerly located in the Hotel del Prado (destroyed in the 1985 earthquake), the mural now has its own showplace, the **Rivera Pavilion,** at Balderas and Colon, near Alameda Park. The mural is monumental in size (50 feet long by 13 feet high), and depicts an imaginary promenade of men and women who most influenced Mexico's political and cultural history, surrounded by symbols of Mexican culture. Rivera painted himself into the picture, as a little boy holding hands with a fashionably dressed skeleton. Behind him is a portrait of his wife, painter Frida Kahlo. There are mural "maps" that identify the various characters and explain the whole story of the mural.

On Avenida Juárez, across from Alameda Park, you'll find the wonderful **FONART** and **Museo Nacional de Artes y Industrias Populares** handicrafts shops (see **Shopping,** below).

Sunday strollers might move from the Alameda to **Plaza Garibaldi,** Mexico City's mariachi headquarters! This square is always filled with the bands of musicians waiting to be hired to play parties, celebrate anniversaries, or create impromptu fiestas for no reason at all. They wear characteristic costumes: tight trousers with silver spangles and bolero jackets with silver studs, big black floppy bow ties, and broad-brimmed sombreros. The tradition dates back to the French occupation, and the name *mariachi* is said to be a Mexican mispronunciation of the French word for marriage—since these musicians often sang and played at French weddings.

Look for the action around the square to intensify at around 9 P.M., especially on Sundays. Sometimes a group just bursts into song to impress potential patrons. An on-the-spot performance will run about $5 to $8 per song—or you can arrange to be serenaded at your hotel for a slightly higher rate.

Garibaldi Square is ringed with bars and bistros; the most popular are **Tenampa, Tlaquepaque,** and **Pulqueria la Hermana Hortensia.** All are filled with local color and are good places to stop for a brew and, perhaps, a tune from some mariachis who happen to stroll in for some refreshment.

Near Plaza Garibaldi, **Lagunilla** market (see **Shopping,** below), on Ecuador between Allende and Chile, is great for browsing, especially on Sunday when additional vendors crowd the surrounding streets.

Farther north, along Paseo de la Reforma past Avenida Juárez, is the **Plaza of the Three Cultures,** representing the three predominant aspects of Mexican culture—there are Aztec ruins, a colonial church, and modern buildings. The ruins are from Tlatelolco, an important Aztec center: This is where Cuauhtemoc and his armies withstood the forces of Cortés, and where, after three long months of siege, the Aztec emperor finally took his own life and cleared the way for Spanish domination of Mexico. The colonial church, the Church of Santiago Tlatelolco, was constructed in 1609 of the same volcanic stone as the Aztec pyramids. The colonial building next to the church, long ago used to educate the children of Aztec nobles, is where Father Bernardino de Sahagun wrote *Historia de Las Cosas de Nueva Espana,* an important source book about life in 16th-century Mexico. The remainder of the buildings surrounding the square are modern residential highrises and government offices, including the Ministry of Foreign Affairs.

Nearby, the **Basilica of the Virgin of Guadalupe** is considered by Catholics to be the most sacred spot in all of Mexico, and each year hundreds of thousands of pilgrims visit the shrine, many of them approaching on their hands and knees, especially on December 12, the anniversary of the Virgin's miraculous appearance. The story of that appearance is as follows: In 1531, Juan Diego, an Indian who had converted to Catholicism, was walking across this hill when the Virgin appeared before him. She asked Juan to have a church in her name built on this site, which before the Conquest had been the location of an Aztec temple dedicated to the earth goddess Tonantzin. Juan asked help of Mexico's bishop, who did not believe that the Virgin had appeared to the Indian. On December 12, the Virgin appeared again, and this time instructed Juan to pick some roses growing on the top of the hill, a rocky place where normally only cactus grew, and to take the roses to the bishop as a sign. Juan picked the roses, as instructed, wrapped them in his cape, and went to see the Bishop. When he unfolded his cape, he found an emblazoned image of the Virgin where the roses had been. The bishop was convinced and ordered that the church be built, and that the cape, framed in gold, be prominently displayed on the altar.

From that time to the present, the Virgin of Guadalupe has played a significant role in the development of Mexico, especially during the struggle for independence, when both Father Hidalgo and later leaders of the movement carried the image of the Virgin into battle.

In 1976 a new shrine was built to house the original cape and the image. It was designed by Pedro Ramirez Vasquez, the architect who designed the National Museum of Anthropology and the Olympic Stadium. Huge, modernistic, and sweeping in design, the structure is intended to easily accommodate the masses who come to worship here. The image, still framed in gold, is rather remote, placed behind the altar. But everyone can get a closer look by riding on a moving walkway that passes directly beneath the image.

Nearby, the lovely tile-domed 18th-century **la Capilla del Pocito** (the Chapel of the Little Well) has a well that supposedly opened under the feet of the Virgin as she addressed Juan Diego. The well is said to have healing properties.

Zona Rosa

This fashionable enclave of European influence and style in the heart of Mexico City is known as the Zona Rosa, or Pink Zone. The area's streets—Génova, Hamburgo, Copenhague, and Londres, for example—are named after European cities. The Zona Rosa used to be primarily residential, but it has evolved over the years into one of Mexico City's main entertainment centers. Most of the old mansions and lesser buildings now house exclusive shops and popular restaurants, offering all types of cuisine. Some of the streets are closed to cars, so strollers can amble along at leisure, without minding Mexico's ever-aggressive traffic. The Zona Rosa is usually crowded—with shoppers during the day and with pleasure seekers out on the town until the wee hours of the night.

On Londres, the **Insurgentes Market** (see **Shopping,** below) is a good place to buy typical Mexican handicrafts everyday of the week, and **Centro de Antiguedades** (see **Shopping,** below) is a wonderful source of antiques—on Saturday only, however.

A Zona Rosa landmark is the **Monument to Mexican Independence,** otherwise known as "the Angel." This statue of the goddess of liberty, balanced atop a tall column, pays tribute to several of Mexico's revolutionary heroes who are buried here. The monument is right in front of the American Embassy and Hotel María Isabel.

For those who wish to study Spanish in Mexico City, excellent intensive courses are offered at **Instituto Mex-**

icano/Norteamericano de Relaciónes Culturales (Hamburgo 115; tel. 5-525-3357). The reasonably priced courses last for one to four weeks, and the institute will help you to arrange accommodations, possibly with a Mexican family. Even if you don't intend to study there, it's fun to drop in at the institute to chat with Mexican students who are studying English and wish to practice, or visit the institute's interesting Mexican-American exhibitions.

Chapultepec Park and Polanco

Lovely **Chapultepec Park** is Mexico City's major recreation area, and one of the few places in the city where you get a feeling of expansive greenery and open space. The huge park (about two and a half square miles) has shady forests, beautiful gardens, a lake with rowboats, and much-used outdoor playing fields, as well as several of Mexico City's cultural treasures.

Magnificent **Chapultepec Castle,** built during the 18th century, is in the corner of Chapultepec Park, on a high hill, known as Grasshopper Hill, overlooking Paseo de la Reforma and downtown Mexico. In pre-Hispanic times, this is where the Aztecs built the temple to the rain god Tlaloc. During the 18th century, the Spanish viceroys used the castle as their residence. It later became a military school. It was here that the young Mexican cadets defended to the death their quarters during the U.S. invasion of 1847, and their heroism is memorialized in the nearby **Monument de los Niños Héroes.** These "Boy Heroes" are memorialized with monuments and streets named in their honor. This simple and impressive collection of marble columns serves as their tomb; it is also their official national monument.

Emperor Maximilian and his wife Carlota lived in Chapultepec Castle during their troubled reign, adding the Alcazar imperial living quarters as well as the castle's fabulous gardens. It is said that Carlota took great pleasure in standing on her balcony to watch Maximilian as he rode off in his royal carriage down Paseo de la Reforma toward the Zócalo.

With the demise of the French Empire, Chapultepec Castle fell out of fashion. In fact, it was all but abandoned until the late 19th century, when the Mexican presidents began to use it as their official residence. President Porfirio Díaz, famous for his love of luxury and things French, was particularly fond of the castle, and spent a good deal of his 35-year term of office in it.

In 1944, President Lázaro Cárdenas turned the castle into the **National Museum of History,** which exhibits documents, artifacts, and artwork having to do with Mexican history from the time of the Conquest of the 1810 Revolution.

There are several important murals by Orozco, Siqueiros, and O'Gorman here.

The **Museum of Modern Art** nearby offers a vast contemporary art collection. Works by Mexican artists Rivera, Kahlo, O'Gorman, Tamayo, Siqueiros, and others, as well as Magritte, Delvaux, and other international modern masters, plus major traveling exhibitions of works by established artists and avant-gardists, can be found here. All are shown in two spacious modern buildings that surround a small garden filled with contemporary sculpture. The museum is open Tuesday through Sunday from 10 A.M. to 6 P.M. There is a small admission fee. Enter the museum from Paseo de la Reforma or through a second gate located behind the Monument de los Niños Héroes.

Farther down the Paseo de la Reforma is the **Zoo,** where recent news of pandas born in captivity has captured the world's imagination. But the zoo features some less famous but equally entertaining residents, including imported big cats, bears, deer, local exotic creatures, and iguanas. A mini-railroad runs through the zoo; rowboats can be rented at a nearby lake.

Beyond the zoo, on the same side of the Paseo de la Reforma, you'll find the **National Auditorium,** a modern covered stadium and exhibition hall used for a wide variety of interesting performances, concerts, conventions, expos, exhibitions, and other events that require a lot of space and great seating capacity. Consult your concierge or the local newspapers for current schedules.

Across the Paseo de la Reforma is Mexico City's extraordinary **National Museum of Anthropology,** featuring the world's foremost collection of pre-Columbian artifacts in a unique environment designed by architect Pedro Ramirez Vasquez. The museum has 23 rooms, of which 12 on the ground floor are used to display archaeological artifacts from Mexico's important Indian cultures; the 11 on the second floor contain ethnographic exhibitions depicting modern life among Mexico's indigenous populations. Ground-floor salons surround a large central patio covered by a huge umbrella-like concrete-and-steel structure that offers protection against the sun or rain and also functions as a cooling and decorative fountain.

The museum's floor plan is easy to follow. Galleries, called *salas,* are arranged by archaeological period, region, and culture. You have the option of seeing the entire museum by moving from gallery to gallery in proper order or, by cutting across the central patio, skipping around to exhibits that most interest you. The museum is really too big and too complete to see fully in one day, so strategic viewing is probably advisable. Here's a list of highlights: The Orientation room has audiovisual presentations on pre-Hispanic cultures. The

Introduction to Anthropology has exhibits about anthropology, Mesoamerican cultures, and the origins of Mexico's indigenous populations. The Pre-Classic gallery exhibits Central Highlands artifacts dating from two thousand years ago, including Olmec-influenced pieces from Tlatilco, as well as models of the Aztec ceremonial center at Teotihuacán. The Teotihuacán gallery has reproductions of the Temple of Quetzalcoatl and fine examples of pottery and ceramics. The Toltec room has artifacts from Tula, including the reclining figure of the god Chacmool, and a 14-foot-high column representing a warrior. The Mexica gallery features the art of Aztecs, including the 24-ton Sun Stone, a calendar illustrating the Aztec cosmos, with remarkable statues of Coyolxuahqui, the moon goddess, and Coatlicue, the earth goddess. A replica of Moctezuma's headdress of quetzal feathers and a model of Templo Mayor are also featured. The Oaxaca room has objects from the Zapotec and Mixtec cultures at Monte Alban and Mitla, including urns and jaguar statues and replicas of tombs found at Monte Alban. The Gulf of Mexico gallery has an Olmec colossal stone head and exquisite small jade sculptures typical of Olmec art, including a remarkable set of 16 figurines—all in jade except for the one carved of basalt (thought to represent a sacrificial victim). The Maya room has artifacts from the classic period of Mayan art, including carved limestone stelae from Yaxchilan showing Mayan rulers and recording historic events. There are also ceramic figurines and pre-Hispanic clothes. An outdoor garden has a small temple with reproductions of battle murals from Bonampak. The rooms for North and West Mexico show clay figurines from Colima, Jalisco, and Nayarit, including the famous Colima dogs and warriors. Ethnography rooms on the second floor have extraordinary collections of regional handicrafts, interestingly exhibited in settings that show how Mexico's indigenous populations—including the Huichols, Tarascans, Coras, Otomis, Nahuas, Seris, Tarahumaras, Yaquis, and other groups—live today.

The National Museum of Anthropology is open Tuesday through Saturday, from 9 A.M. to 7 P.M., Sunday from 10 A.M. to 6 P.M. There is a small admission fee, which is reduced on Sunday.

Next door is the **Tamayo Museum,** housing a substantial collection of works by the renowned Mexican painter Rufino Tamayo, as well as his personal collection of works by his contemporaries. The museum, another structure built by architect Pedro Ramirez Vasquez (who also designed the Museum of Anthropology), is in a pleasant park-like area.

A recently opened area known as **New Chapultepec Park,** or the Third Section, has a full-fledged amusement park (roller coaster and all!), plus museums of natural history and technology, as well as relatively secluded jogging trails and picnic places.

The Chapultepec Park area is centrally located, near the Zona Rosa and the posh residential sections of Polanco and Lomas de Chapultepec, and easy to get to. Take a taxi, a collective cab, or bus along Paseo de la Reforma, which runs directly through the park, or take the Metro to the Chapultepec or Auditorio stations.

Chapultepec Park is bordered by **Polanco,** an area of quiet tree-lined streets with a wealth of handsome homes. Many of the mansions along **Avenida Presidente Mazarik** have been converted to exclusive shops and boutiques offering all sorts of finery, making Polanco a prime destination for shoppers (see **Shopping,** below). For exceptional handicrafts, stop in at **La Casa de las Artesanias de Michoacán,** on Campos Elíseos, across the street from the Nikko and Presidente Chapultepec hotels.

Continuing along Paseo de la Reforma, past Polanco, you come to **Lomas de Chapultepec,** a hilly residential district with fabulous mansions of traditional and very innovative design. This is a great place to get a peek at the lifestyles of Mexico's rich and famous.

The South: San Angel, Coyoacan, Pedregal, University City

The southern section of Mexico City is in reality a huge area, comprising several sightseeing zones and distinct neighborhoods. For convenience's sake they are grouped together here, because they are all in the same general direction and might best be visited in one or several grand sweeps.

Avenida Insurgentes Sur is one of the main arteries from the Zona Rosa to the southern part of the city. Along this boulevard, at the corner of Filadelfia, about midway between the Zona Rosa and San Angel, you'll find the **Siqueiros Polyforum.** The Polyforum is a tribute to renowned muralist David Siqueiros, whose murals, the *March of Humanity on Earth* and *Toward the Cosmos,* two extraordinarily complex and somber sculptural murals, are on display inside this unique, multifaceted art center. But you really don't have to go inside to experience the impact of Siqueiros's work: The building's exterior is covered by another 27,000-square-foot Siqueiros mural. The Polyforum is open daily from 10 A.M. to 2:30 P.M. and 3:30 to 9 P.M. Siqueiros Polyforum is located directly in front of the **Hotel de México,** once intended to be the largest hotel in Mexico City. Work on the Hotel de México was abandoned when the developer ran out of funds.

Now the building is just a shell, towering over this quiet residential neighborhood of Mexico City. It's actually quite eerie, despite its revolving rooftop restaurant, known more for the view than for the food. The restaurant is open from 1 P.M. to 10:30 P.M. daily. Recently plans have been announced to convert the Hotel de México into a world trade center, but the schedule for that is still sketchy.

Continue along Insurgentes Sur to get to **San Angel,** a charming and pricey residential area, with several must-see attractions. It's best to visit San Angel on a Saturday, when the famous **Bazar Sábado** at Plaza San Jacinto, is in full swing. The bazaar, located in a wonderful colonial mansion once occupied by the wealthy family of the counts of Oploca, is Mexico City's most famous handicrafts market. In 1847 it reportedly housed invading American troops, and in 1863 was used to headquarter French invaders. Today the spacious courtyard is used for an open-air restaurant, and the rooms surrounding it have dozens of small stall shops and boutiques with a wide array of handmade clothes and objets d'art. A second floor and balcony have more shops, and additional merchants set up stalls outside the building and in a small nearby park. The goods here, though somewhat high priced, are also high quality, and the ambience is pleasant and chic.

Additional crafts are sold at **FONART** (see **Shopping,** below) and shops around **Sanborn's San Angel** (see **Restaurants,** below), as well.

San Angel has two outstanding museums: The **Carrillo Gil Museum,** at Avenida Revolución 1608, shows works by Rivera, Orozco, Siqueiros, Zuniga, and other great Mexican artists. Contemporary foreign artists are also represented. This museum has terrific temporary exhibitions, often exploring new directions in the Mexican and international art scene. The museum's modern architecture and spacious galleries reflect its contents. Open Tuesday through Sunday from 11 A.M. to 3 P.M. and from 4 to 7 P.M. An admission fee of about $1 is charged.

The **Convento del Carmen,** at Avenida Revolución 4, formerly a Carmelite convent, is a beautiful 17th-century building used to house an eclectic collection of colonial art and artifacts: religious paintings, furniture, tiles, murals, and the mummified remains of several priests and nuns. The structure of the building is somewhat eclectic, too, what with its mysterious maze of darkened hallways, interlocking rooms, and chapels, and lovely garden-like patios filled with sunlight and flowers. Open daily from 10 A.M. to 5 P.M. A small admission fee is charged.

Stop at the **San Angel Inn** (see **Restaurants,** below), an 18th-century hacienda, for a lavish luncheon or elegant dinner.

Coyoacán is a short taxi ride from San Angel. This old and exclusive residential area in the south of Mexico City offers narrow cobblestone streets lined with wonderful colonial buildings noted for their fascinating architectural details, including fabulously carved wooden doors and walls built to accommodate branches of ancient trees. Many conquistadores, including Cortés, lived here following the conquest of Mexico City. Today this is the preferred address of leading Mexican artists and intellectuals. Two lovely squares, **Plaza Hidalgo** and **Jardín Centenario,** are set with pretty filigree benches and are great places for Sunday sunning or strolling. The very pretty **Church of San Juan Bautista,** built in 1583, is a favorite for weddings.

Near Plaza Hidalgo, on Calle Aquayo, the baroque **Casa de Hernán Cortés** was occupied in the 17th century by the conquistador. It now houses Mexican government offices. The *casa* is reputed to be where Cortés tortured Cuauhtemoc to get him to reveal the secret hiding places for Aztec treasures. Nearby **Casa Colorada,** at Calle de Higuera 57, is the house from which Cortés's wife disappeared mysteriously, to be quickly replaced by his mistress, La Malinche.

Visit the **Frida Kahlo House and Museum,** at Londres and Allende, to get an inside glimpse at the lives of this famous artist and her equally famous husband, muralist Diego Rivera. Memorabilia and artwork by the famous couple fill the bright blue house. Visitors can view studios, bedrooms, kitchen, and gardens, for a fascinating look into Mexican cultural and social history. Especially intriguing is Frida's studio; a disabled artist, she painted many of her best-known self-portraits while lying down and looking into a mirror suspended over her bed. The collection of retablos hung in one stairway is magnificent, as are the delicate illustrations on the kitchen walls. Open Tuesday through Sunday, 10 A.M. to 6 P.M. A small admission fee is charged.

Nearby, the **Leon Trotsky House and Museum,** at Viena 45, is where the Russian philosopher and revolutionary lived and wrote from 1937 until his death in 1940. Following Lenin's death, Stalin's and Trotsky's ideologies clashed violently, and Stalin exiled Trotsky from Russia. Trotsky was obviously security-conscious; the house has high stone walls and brick watchtowers, and the entrance to Trotsky's bedroom is a steel door. Most of these measures were installed after a failed attempt on Trotsky's life. They did not, however, foil a second attempt: An agent of Stalin's, posing as Trotsky's friend, gained access to the house and killed him. The house is filled with Trotsky's personal effects—papers, books, newspaper clippings. Trotsky's tomb, designed by Mexican artist Juan O'Gorman, is in the garden. Open Tuesday through Friday, 11 A.M. to 4 P.M.

You have to take a taxi, preferably from Coyoacán or San Angel, to get to the **Diego Rivera Museum,** in San Pablo Tepetlapan, a suburb farther to the south. This splendid museum was designed by Diego Rivera to house his personal collection of pre-Columbian artifacts that he was rededicating to the Mexican people. The building, a pyramid built out of pedregal, or lava, is an example of unusual modern architecture. Dramatic lighting effects, including sunbeams filtered through translucent onyx, accent the exhibitions. The first floor has mostly Aztec artifacts. Upstairs floors exhibit artifacts from Nayarit, Colima, and Jalisco, as well as Oaxaca and the Gulf Coast. The museum is certainly off the beaten path but worth a visit. Open Tuesday through Sunday, from 10 A.M. to 6 P.M. Closed Monday. Admission is free.

Near Coyoacán, and as far south as University City, the posh residential area known as the **Pedregal** has some extraordinary homes built on lava beds. This is a great place to ogle great avant-garde architecture.

Further south, and easily accessible from downtown by Metro, **University City** is the eight-hundred-acre campus of the Universidad Autónoma Nacional de México (UNAM), with fine contemporary Mexican architecture, including **Sala Nezahualcoyotl,** a twenty-five-hundred-seat concert hall, and the **Olympic Stadium,** the former University Stadium, completely redesigned and rebuilt for the 1968 Olympics by architect Pedro Ramirez Vasquez. The new stadium is shaped like a pre-Hispanic pyramid and holds more than seventy-two thousand spectators. A three-dimensional multicolored mosaic sculpture of a design by muralist Diego Rivera dominates the stadium's main entrance.

If you return to the center of town via the Periférico, be on the lookout for an ancient pyramid, the **Pyramid of Cuicuilco,** considered to be the oldest manmade structure in North America. This pyramid was built, according to current estimates, around 3000 B.C. It was covered by lava from a nearby volcano, experts estimate, about A.D. 300 and was only recently discovered. The pyramid's unusual circular shape has caused great curiosity and much speculation about its origins. Cuicuilco is the Nahuatl (Aztec) word for "place to sing and dance."

Also along the Periférico, **Reino Aventura** is an amusement park with thrilling rides and six different theme sections, including Mexican, Western, Swiss, Polynesian, and French villages, and a Children's world. Good food and special rides in each section. Open daily except Tuesday. An afternoon of rides costs about $8 and up.

Nearby is **Centro Comercial Perisur,** Mexico City's showcase shopping center.

Two additional attractions in the south of the city should probably be approached as day trips. Best reached by car, the

Desierto de los Leónes, off the Toluca Highway, is a huge recreation area, with many interesting attractions, including a beautiful 17th-century former Carmelite convent, with quiet cloisters and mysterious passageways. And Desierto de los Leónes is a wonderful place to escape from the crowded city for a picnic surrounded by cool pine forests. If you don't have a car, the best alternative is to take a taxi and, for a flat fee, arrange to have it wait for you.

Xochimilco, in a southern suburb, about thirty minutes by car from downtown Mexico City, is the last trace of the extensive waterways that criss-crossed ancient Tenochtitlán. In ancient times, Aztec farmers used sod-filled barges to grow their crops, and this area became known as the "floating gardens of Xochimilco." Gondola-like craft propelled by tenders with long poles ply the water these days. The boats, festooned with colorful flowers and streamers and given women's names, are large enough to carry a dozen or so passengers, and are often used by families celebrating birthdays or anniversaries. Smaller boats carrying mariachis or food vendors ride alongside, selling songs or snacks. Open daily. Much fun and local color, especially on Sunday afternoons. Though rates vary, depending largely upon your bargaining skills, count on spending between $5 to $10 per hour.

☕ RESTAURANTS

Mexico City is a gourmet's delight. Fabulous restaurants offer all types of cuisine, including the rich array of regional Mexican dishes and savory samplings the world over. If you are concerned about digestive disorders, drink only bottled water (*agua mineral* or "Tehuacan") and stick to better-known restaurants. Those listed below are generally clean and trustworthy. As they say in Mexico, "!*Buen provecho*!" (bon apetit!)

Prices in Mexico City restaurants will generally strike most visitors as remarkably reasonable, and a full-course meal in a first-rate Mexico City restaurant will generally cost considerably less than would a similar meal in a top-notch restaurant in most other major cities. And it is important to note that mealtimes in most family-, as well as business-oriented establishments, are considered social gatherings, and as such can take hours: go with time to spare.

A word about meal times: lunch is usually the biggest meal of the day, and it is eaten in the afternoon, between 2 and 4 P.M. Dinner may be a full meal or a light snack and is usually served at about 9 or 10 P.M. Recently, early-morning business breakfasts, beginning no later than around eight, have become popular, especially in hotel dining rooms. No matter when you're dining out, reservations are always a good idea, except when otherwise noted, especially if you're planning to dine during the busy hours.

Each restaurant is keyed to the area of the city in which it is located, and keyed to the color map of the city at the back of the book, referring to the page number of the map as well as appropriate coordinates.

Anderson's

ZONA ROSA, P. 14, 4C

Paseo de la Reforma 400
Tel. 525-1006

Anderson's is certainly the place for hearty fare and fun. The restaurant is first in the Carlos Anderson chain, famous for its fun-house ambience and waiters who love to fool around. The decor, eclectic to say the least, features wooden carousel horses, photos of fifties movie stars, balloons, antique odds and ends, and a collection of cowboy and hard hats. Loud rock music always rings through the air, and the place is usually crowded. The cutesiness extends to the menu, which features catchy captions: under "moo," you'll find steaks and hamburgers; the famous barbecued ribs (a specialty) are listed under "oink"; and soups are headlined "slurp." Anderson's draws a young, hip, and monied crowd. Reasonable wine list, and mixed drinks—but they tend to be expensive. A meal for two, including a moderate wine, costs about $50. Mon.–Sat., 1 P.M.–midnight, Sun. 1–5:30 P.M. Reservations suggested. Credit cards: AE, MC, DC, V.

Azulejos

POLANCO-CHAPULTEPEC, P. 14, 3A

Hotel Camino Real, Mariano Escobedo 700
Tel. 203-2121

The appealing and comprehensive menu of the Hotel Camino Real's pleasant all-day dining room features a wide variety of breakfast, lunch, and dinner selections. Well-prepared Mexican favorites range from *huevos rancheros* to *enchiladas suizas,* and the international fare includes ample hamburgers and sandwiches, as well as steaks and seafood. The Sun.-brunch buffet, served 1–4 P.M., can make Sun. a one-meal day: choose from fresh seafood salads, ceviche, oysters, shrimps, eggs prepared as you like them with or without ham or sausage, exotic fruits, roast beef, turkey, breads, sweet rolls, and tantalizing desserts. The room is spacious and airy, and the walls accented with tiles make for a cheerful decor. Beer and wine served. Meals average about $20 and up per person. No reservations required. Credit cards: AE, DC, MC, V.

Bellinghausen

ZONA ROSA, P. 14, 4C

Londres 95
Tel. 511-1056

A favorite for business lunches and leisurely evening meals, Bellinghausen offers primarily German cuisine in a comfortable, unpretentious, somewhat old-fashioned and familial ambience. The walls exhibit paintings and prints of horse and hunt scenes; polished old-wood paneling adds to the traditional air. In mild weather, the tables in the tree-shaded courtyard are particularly attractive. Waiters are friendly and efficient but never rush you, even if people are waiting in line, as they sometimes are, for your table. The menu features schnitzels, wursts, and osso buco, as well as a good selection of fish dishes. Chefs and quality are both reliable. A good selection of beers, wines, and mixed drinks is available. Mon.–Sat., 1–11 P.M. The average cost of a meal for two, including wine, is about $45. No reservations. Credit cards: AE, DC, MC, V.

Café de Paris   POLANCO-CHAPULTEPEC, P. 14, 3A
Campos Elíseos 164
Tel. 531-6646

Founded by chef Jacques Bergerault in 1968, Café de Paris has a well-established reputation as one of Mexico City's finest French restaurants. Located in residential Polanco, within walking distance of the Nikko Hotel and the Hotel Presidente Chapultepec, the restaurant occupies a former mansion, the exterior of which is now painted a cheerful pink. The interior, with several dining rooms, offers French Provincial decor—subdued pink walls covered with French Impressionist prints and light-pine furnishings. Service is unimpeachable. The menu suggests several specialties, including coq au vin and *confit du canard au poivre vert* (confit of duck with green peppercorns). Onion soup and *huîtres Bienville* are listed among the appetizers, and desserts include crêpes suzettes for two. The menu also offers some Mexican dishes, including ceviche. There is a limited selection of French wines, ranging in price from about $45–$90 per bottle. Without wine, dinner for two costs about $50. Reservations a must. Open daily. Lunch, 1:30–7 P.M.; dinner, 8 P.M.–1 A.M. Credit cards: AE, MC, V.

Café de Tacuba   DOWNTOWN, P. 15, 3F
Tacuba 28, near the Zócalo
Tel. 512-8482

Truly a Mexico City tradition, Café de Tacuba serves superbly prepared Mexican meals and munchies in a delightfully old-fashioned ambience. The restaurant's decor—its high ceilings, tiled walls, dark wooden trim and arches, chandeliers, and profusion of plants in colored or terra-cotta pots—makes you feel as though you've been transported into a peaceful moment in Mexico's colorful colonial past. In fact, Café de Tacuba has been around for quite a number of years—since 1912. A must on the menu is café con leche prepared the old-fashioned way. This can be accompanied by a variety of fabulous sweet rolls and pastries, all baked on the premises. More substantial items include enchiladas, quesadillas, and tacos, prepared as you prefer them. A favorite late-night hangout for artists, intellectuals, and anyone who happens to be downtown or feels like going downtown for a snack. Open daily, 8 A.M.–midnight. Credit cards: AE, DC, MC, V.

Las Cazuelas   DOWNTOWN, P. 15, 3F
Colombia 69, near the Zócalo
Tel. 522-0689

This festive, family-style restaurant is a favorite with the Mexican people. The ambience is that of an ongoing fiesta—crowded, noisy, fun-filled, colorful. Located in a working-class neighborhood within walking distance from the Zócalo, Las Cazuelas utilizes Mexican handicrafts, especially decorative tiles in a cacophony of colors and hand-painted chairs with cheerful designs, in its decor. The walls are covered with murals of Mexican daily life and legend. Mariachis liven things up with love songs and other Mexican favorites. The menu features everything Mexican—*carnitas* (meat pies), mole *poblano, cerdo* (pork) or *pollo* (chicken) with pumpkinseed sauce, enchiladas, tacos, *chiles rellenos, cecina* (specially seasoned dried beef), and more. All are freshly prepared in an open, aromatic kitchen. Beer is served. Open daily for lunch and dinner—the liveliest time to dine here is on Sun. afternoon, but if you're not here by 2 P.M., you'll probably face a long wait for a table. Evenings are quite quiet. A meal for two, with beer, costs about $30. No reservations. No credit cards.

Les Celebrities   POLANCO-CHAPULTEPEC, P. 15, 4A

Nikko Hotel
Campos Elíseos 204 (corner of Arquímedes)
Tel. 203-4800

This gourmet restaurant in the Hotel Nikko offers both cuisine and environment worth celebrating. The multilevel interior is arranged to allow patrons maximum privacy, whether they are there for an intimate tête-à-tête or a high-powered business dinner. The elegant atmosphere is all pastels and candlelight, banquettes and armchairs comfortably padded in lavenders and pinks, silver table settings, gleaming brass railings, gossamer window curtains, fresh flowers, unobtrusive piano music, and attentive waiters. The cuisine, supervised by chef Philippe Braun, is perfectly French, without the slightest hint of Mexican influence. For starters, salmon tartar with crisp toast, smoked oyster salad with ginger sauce, or *beignets d'escargots à la crème de persil* (breaded snails with creamed parsley sauce) are exquisite. Fabulous fish entrées include sea bass with oyster sauce, red snapper with curry sauce, and poached salmon with chive sauce. For meat eaters, the lamb with rosemary sauce is tender perfection. The brilliant wine list has exorbitantly priced imports—and several moderately priced domestic vintages. The restaurant also offers special dress-up banquets based on themes that intrigue the management: For the *Cena Concierto Traviata* (Traviata Concert Dinner), the restaurant became a private opera house, and waiters in period attire attended similarly dressed patrons as they dined and enjoyed a performance of *La Traviata*. Les Celebrities is open for dinner only, 7–11:30 P.M. The average cost of dinner for two, including a moderately priced wine, is about $100. A prix fixe menu is available for about $40 per person. Reservations suggested. Credit cards: AE, DC, MC, V.

Chalet Suizo   ZONA ROSA, P. 14, 3B

Niza 37
Tel. 511-7529

Pseudo-chalet decor serves as a fun, if a bit overdone, backdrop to typical Swiss cuisine. The menu, which includes favorite fondues, schnitzels, and other Swiss dishes offers a nice change from Mexican cuisine and ambience. Beer and wine are served. Open daily, lunch and dinner, noon–midnight. Dinner for two, with wine, averages about $30. No reservations necessary. Credit cards: AE, DC, MC, V.

Champs-Elysées

ZONA ROSA, P. 14, 4C

Amberes 1, corner of Paseo de la Reforma
Tel. 514-0450

This charming French restaurant is favored for its fine food and convenient location. It occupies the second floor of a modern two-story building along the Paseo de la Reforma, in the heart of the Zona Rosa, and window tables in the front dining rooms provide pleasant views of that tree-lined boulevard. The decor is light and airy, and the menu is primarily French, with a slightly Mexican flavor. The bouillabaisse is particularly popular, as are the clam soup, super-fresh ceviche, and excellent house pâtés. The extensive wine list offers both Mexican and imported vintages; the imported wines, however, are very expensive. Lunch or dinner for two, with moderately priced wine, costs about $50. Mon.–Fri., 1–11 P.M.; closed Sat. and Sun. Reservations recommended. Credit cards: AE, MC, V.

Del Lago

CHAPULTEPEC, P. 15, 3B

New Chapultepec Park
Tel. 515-9585

This restaurant, on the lake in the middle of Chapultepec Park, features unusual ultramodern architecture. The beautiful glass facade that fronts the lake offers spectacular views, especially after dark, when a dramatically lit, undulating fountain sprays shimmering streaks into the night. After 8:30 P.M., live-band dance music resounds through the spacious, high-ceilinged, plant-filled interior, encouraging diners to dance between courses. The menu features Chateaubriand, roast duck, stuffed shrimp, and other international delicacies. Beer, wine, and mixed drinks are offered. Dress up: This crowd is elegant. A meal for two, with wine included, averages about $60. Open daily for lunch and dinner, 1:30 P.M.–12:30 A.M.; closed Sun. Reservations suggested, especially for dinner, when there is an entertainment charge. Credit cards: AE, DC, MC, V.

Delmonico's

ZONA ROSA, P. 14, 4C

Londres 87
Tel. 514-7003

Chateaubriand, rib-eye steaks, and roast beef (served with Yorkshire pudding) are top selections at this pleasant restaurant, which seems to be a favorite with American travelers. In addition to the beef (which is reportedly flown in from Chicago and Denver), the menu offers veal, chicken, and seafood prepared with international style. The decor is posh without being heavy—except for a gravity-defying wrought-iron chandelier. In contrast to the brightly lit dining rooms, the bar is dark and wood-paneled—a good place for an intimate drink. Adequate but expensive wine list. Daily, 7:30–11 A.M. and 12:30 P.M.–midnight. Weekday executive breakfasts and the elaborate weekend brunches are gustatory events. Dinner for two, with wine, costs approximately $60. Reservations recommended. Credit cards: AE, MC, V.

Denny's
THROUGHOUT CITY

Bulevar M. Avila Camacho 3228 and other locations
Tel. 562-9085

A chain of restaurants that specializes in hamburgers, sand-wiches, and light meals, Denny's is clean, reliable, and has branches throughout downtown, in the Zona Rosa, and just about every place else a traveler is likely to wander in Mexico City (and in popular Mexican resort areas as well). If you tire of tacos and refried beans, stop by Denny's for some good old American fast food. Most branches are open daily, 7:30 A.M.–midnight. The average cost of a meal for two is about $15. No reservations. Credit cards: AE, DC, MC, V.

Estoril
ZONA ROSA, P. 14, 4C

Génova 75
Tel. 511-3421

The menu features an appealing combination of Mexican and international cooking styles, with traditional Mexican ingredients used in inventive ways: *huitlacoche,* the tasty and exotic Mexican fungus that grows on corn, is used in season to fill otherwise mundane crêpes; various inventive preparations of *róbalo* (sea bass) are also specialties; and fish fillets and fresh artichokes are accompanied by a superb Hollandaise sauce. The restaurant is as elegant as it is inventive, and it attracts an attractive and fashionable crowd that enjoys the intimate ambience of Estoril's several small semiprivate dining rooms, decorated with fine Mexican contemporary art. Nice wine list. Daily, 1–10:30 P.M. The average cost of dinner for two, with wine, is about $50. Reservations suggested. Credit cards: AE, MC, V.

Focolare
ZONA ROSA, P. 14, 4C

Hamburgo 87
Tel. 525-1487

Long a favorite with the Mexican upper crust and local celebrities, Focolare offers its loyal patrons more than snob appeal: dishes representing various Mexican regional cuisines, all prepared with finesse. Each day of the week, a different Oaxacan mole sauce is offered, and there are numerous Yucatecan samplings as well. The restaurant takes full advantage of its setting—a former town house—to establish an atmosphere of easy elegance. Good, but fairly expensive, wine list. Daily, 8 A.M.–midnight. The average cost of dinner for two, with wine, is about $45. Reservations suggested. Credit cards: AE, MC, V.

Fonda del Recuerdo
COLONIA ANZURES, P. 12, 3A

Bahía de las Palmas 39
Tel. 545-1652

Music is as much a feature of this lively restaurant as is the menu. The music is supplied by one or more bands (sometimes playing at the same time) from the state of Veracruz. The menu is pure Mexican and lists tacos of every variety, tamales, enchiladas, *chiles rellenos,* and *pozole* (a thick corn soup made with bits of chicken, lettuce, radishes, and chiles), among other tempting items. The house specialties are *huachinango relleno de mariscos* (red snapper stuffed with seafood) and *sábana a la tampiqueña* (a beef filet that's been beaten until it's paper-

. . .[Mexican] popular, traditional foods are so regionally diverse, and so varied within those regions themselves, that they defy a cohesive, all-embracing definition. A certain homogeneity has indeed come about through improved transportation and other communications. But the basic differences remain, perhaps more because of the inability to reproduce the same *chiles* and herbs unique to one area in another (owing to climatic and topographical conditions) rather than from the strong dictates of local cultures. They vary in levels of sophistication from those that are wild and gathered at random—often eaten raw—to dishes that call for a number of nonindigenous ingredients requiring more intricate methods of preparation. But while peasants and urban gourmets alike can lick their lips over a snack of grilled grasshoppers or a *taco* of *colorín* (coral tree) flowers with a sauce of grilled *tunas* (prickly pears), the peasants would go hungry rather than eat, say, a *crêpe* of *sautéed* sweetbreads in a *pulque*/cream/*pasilla* sauce, or a chicken breast stuffed with *cuitlacoche* in a cream of squash flower sauce à la nouvelle. Nor would a Sonorense or Campechana necessarily delight in a *chichilo negro* from the Oaxacan coast, redolent of charred *chiles* and avocado leaves.

—Diana Kennedy
The Art of Mexican Cooking, 1989

thin, then lightly cooked and served with strips of chile). Fonda del Recuerdo is a great place to sample Mexico—both the cuisine and ambience. Beer and wine served, but the wine list is not extensive. Daily, 8 A.M.–midnight. The average cost of a meal for two, with wine, is about $40. Reservations suggested. Credit cards: AE, DC, MC, V.

Fonda del Refugio
ZONA ROSA, P. 14, 4C
Liverpool 166
Tel. 528-5823

A festive colonial ambience embraces you as you enter the first-floor dining room, decorated with wonderful Mexican handicrafts—copperware, textiles, items made of clay and straw. This definitely establishes a mood for fine Mexican cooking, and the menu of Fonda del Refugio obliges in every respect. For traditional favorites, try the mole *poblano* or *chiles rellenos.* More inventive selections are served as daily specials, including Wed.'s delicious chicken with mole *verde de pepita* (a green sauce made with chiles and pumpkin seeds). Mon.–Sat., 1 P.M.–1 A.M.; closed Sun. Beer and wine served, along with fabulous *aguas frescas* (refreshing nonalcoholic drinks made of fresh fruits, flowers, seeds, and sugar). A meal for two, including beer or wine, costs about $50. Reservations not required. Credit cards: AE, DC, MC, V.

Fouquet's de Paris
POLANCO-CHAPULTEPEC, P. 14, 3A
Hotel Camino Real, Mariano Escobedo 700
Tel. 203-2121

A little corner of Paris imported to Mexico City, Fouquet's de Paris is a clone of the famous and sophisticated Parisian dining spot and serves the same fine fare. The setting is chic, and service attentive; soft piano music accompanies evening meals—otherwise the restaurant has an appealing hush about it. The cuisine is classic. Pâtés are excellent, and the sensational desserts deserve their own menu. The wine list features French imports at astronomical prices. Mon.–Fri., 2–4:30 P.M. and 8–11:15 P.M.; Sat. 8–11:15 P.M. only. Closed Sun. The average cost of a meal for two, including wine, is about $90. Reservations suggested. Credit cards: AE, DC, MC, V.

Las Fuentes
ZONA ROSA, P. 14, 4C

Panucho 127, corner of Tiber
Tel. 525-0629

Lentils, beans, rice, big plates of freshly steamed or lightly sautéed vegetables, tacos and enchiladas stuffed with carrots and potatoes, and most other vegetarian staples are offered at Las Fuentes, and they're served in sizable portions. This is the place to avoid heavily salted and sauced foods and still enjoy a satisfying meal—for a very reasonable price. Choose honey or banana cake for dessert. The decor is pleasantly modern, and the atmosphere is cheerful. Open Mon.–Sat., 8:30 A.M.–11:30 P.M., to 10:30 P.M. on Sun. The average cost of a meal for two is about $20. No reservations. Credit cards: AE, MC, V.

La Góndola
ZONA ROSA, P. 14, 4C

Génova 21
Tel. 511-6908

Popular with Mexicans and travelers alike, La Góndola serves satisfying pastas and a superb lasagna. The house specialty is spaghetti Vivaldi, done up with a bouquet of fresh vegetables. In addition, there are veal, chicken, and seafood entrées, and several appealing Mexican dishes, including a tasty Xochitl soup (pieces of chicken, avocado, rice, raw onion, and chile sauce, in a rich chicken stock). La Góndola's decor is a bit hokey—red tablecloths, coats of arms, and that sort of thing. Italian wines on the list are much more expensive than the domestic vintages. Open daily, 1 P.M.–1 A.M. The average cost of a dinner for two, with wine, is about $35. Reservations suggested. Credit cards: AE, MC, V.

La Hacienda de los Morales
COLONIA MORALES,
P. 12, 3B

Avenida Vasquez de Mella 525, off Avenida Ejército Nacional
Tel. 540-3225.

One of Mexico City's most elegant and refined dining spots, La Hacienda de los Morales actually occupies a 16th-century hacienda, with beautiful courtyards and gardens. Several dining rooms—all spacious with wood-beamed high ceilings—are decorated with beautiful Mexican colonial-style furniture and ensure diners privacy and quiet. Windows offer views of garden pools, complete with swimming swans. A trio of guitars and a piano provide soothing background music. The fine menu offers a wide selection of meat and seafood entrées; specialties include chicken with mole, and duck in pumpkinseed sauce. Attention is paid to detail: You are, for example, offered a choice of Parma or Serrano ham with your melon—depending upon whether you prefer the Italian or Spanish style of curing. Desserts are delightful: Try the pastries or homemade sorbets for a special treat. Daily, 1 P.M.–1 A.M. High-priced wine list offers Mexican and imported selections. Dinner for two, without wine, starts at about $75. Reservations required. Credit cards: AE, DC, MC, V.

El Jardín
CHAPULTEPEC, P. 14, 3A

Nikko Hotel, Paseo de la Reforma, corner of Arquimedes
Tel. 203-4020

This airy eatery, on a balcony overlooking the atrium lobby of the fancy Nikko Hotel, is open for daylong dining. A fabulous breakfast buffet with everything from scrambled eggs and sausages to pork rinds and refried beans, accompanied by a marvelous medley of fresh fruits, juices, and sweet rolls, is a popular draw for early-morning business meetings. There is also an appealing lunchtime buffet, and the evening menu, featuring steaks, chops, and seafood prepared in both Mexican and international styles, is offered à la carte. Waiters are accommodating and efficient. There is one unpleasant note: music generated by mariachis or other bands playing in the evening in the hotel lobby bar echoes off the atrium walls and is loud enough to deter dinner conversation. Per person, the breakfast buffet costs about $10; an à la carte meal, including beer or soda, starts at about $15 and up. Open daily, 6:30 A.M.–2 A.M. No reservations. Credit cards: AE, MC, V.

La Lanterna
ZONA ROSA, P. 14, 4B

Paseo de la Reforma 458 (Colonia Cuauhtemoc)
Tel. 528-5269

The friendly Petterino family has run La Lanterna for more than twenty years, and has during that time established a well-deserved reputation for good food and excellent service. This is a family-style restaurant, unpretentiously decorated with rustic wood-paneled walls and red-checked cloth-covered tables in street-level and second-floor dining rooms. Pastas, made on the premises, are prepared with a pleasing variety of sauces: the Bolognese sauce is considered a specialty. Besides pasta, the *osso buco alla milanese* and *saltimbocca alla romano* are excellent choices, as are the beef and rabbit dishes. Salads are always fresh and prettily presented, and desserts range from Italian specialties such as zabaglione to apple pie topped with ice cream. The wine list includes some lovely Italian imports, offered at high prices, as well as their more moderately priced Mexican counterparts. House wines, red and white, are usually reliable. Open Mon.–Sat., 1 P.M.–1 A.M. The place is usually crowded at lunchtime and late at night. The average cost of a meal for two, including some house wine, is about $35. No reservations. Credit cards: AE, MC, V.

Loredo
ZONA ROSA, P. 14, 4C

Hamburgo 29
Tel. 566-3433

The sophisticated Mexican cooking here is arguably the best in town. Owner José Loredo created the ever-so-popular *carne asada a la tampiqueña,* a dish featuring a grilled steak surrounded by baked cheese, enchiladas, and chiles. Fresh fish is beautifully prepared in a variety of Mexican recipes. The Mixteca soup, thick with fresh vegetables, is superb. Open weekdays and Sat. for lunch and dinner, for lunch only on Sun. Beer and wine served. A meal for two, with moderately priced wine, costs approximately $40. Reservations suggested but not required. Credit cards: AE, MC, V. Additional **Loredo** restaurants are located at Homero and Suderman (Polanco; tel. 531-2217); Avenida Universidad 1122 (Coyoacán; tel. 604-8301); Avenida Revolución 1511 (San Angel; tel. 548-6717). **Mesón del Caballo Bayo** (see below) also belongs to this chain.

Lory's   ZONA ROSA, P. 14, 4C
Génova 73, in the Zona Rosa
Tel. 514-6594

The menu is simple and straightforward: roast beef, Yorkshire pudding, baked potatoes, and fresh tossed salads. The ambience is Scottish, with clan tartans adorning the walls and covering the tables. Hearty and pleasant in every respect. Open for lunch and dinner. A meal for two costs about $30. Reservations not required. Credit cards: AE, MC, V.

Las Mercedes   POLANCO-CHAPULTEPEC, P. 14, 3B
Leibnitz 67, corner of Darwin
Tel. 525-2099

Billed as a *"restaurante de época,"* Las Mercedes offers traditional Mexican regional fare, much of it prepared according to recipes that have been handed down through the generations. Favorites are *huachinango a la veracruzana* (red snapper), chicken mole from Puebla, and *carne a la tampiqueña.* The soups, especially the tortilla soup, a rich *sopa de fideo* (vermicelli soup), and a perfumy Yucatecan lime soup, are notable. The restaurant's exterior has a modernistic angular facade; the inside is more traditional, with rustic pine furniture and cane chairs set attractively against terra-cotta–colored walls. A curved staircase leading to second-floor dining rooms adds a measure of drama here. The restaurant is particularly popular with well-heeled Mexicans for weekday breakfasts and Sun. brunches. At other times, it is usually fairly quiet and requires no reservations. Open Mon.–Sat., 8 A.M.–midnight; Sun., 9 A.M.–11 P.M. Wine available from a limited list. A meal for two, without wine, averages about $30. Credit cards: AE, MC, V.

Mesón del Caballo Bayo   CHAPULTEPEC, P. 15, 3B
Avenida del Conscripto 360, near Hipodromo Racetrack
Tel. 589-3000

Take a step into Mexico's wild west at Mesón del Caballo Bayo (Bay Horse), located near the Hipodromo Racetrack and decorated with saddles and *charro* (cowboy) costumes and equipment. The restaurant occupies a spacious old mansion in one of Mexico City's prime residential areas, and the atmosphere is festive, with mariachi musicians strolling to serenade different tables with special requests. The food is typically Mexican, with meat dishes the specialty; the menu is similar to that offered by the **Loredo** restaurant chain (see above), which owns

Carne Asada a la Tampiqueña
(Tampico Grilled Meat)

Serves 6

Two of the most popular meat dishes in Mexico are undoubtedly *carne asada a la Tampiqueña* and *la sabana,* both of which were invented by the founder of the Loredo chain of restaurants, José Inez Loredo. Born in Tampico, he came to Mexico City in 1941 to found the Tampico Club, which was first famous for its seafood and then for these two meat dishes, using the best produce from his native region.

The recipe for *carne asada* has been interpreted in many different ways by other restaurateurs and no doubt has undergone modifications in the Loredo restaurants themselves, but here is the recipe as it is today.

A thin strip of butterflied fillet of beef is quickly seared and served with two *enchiladas verdes,* strips of *chiles poblanos,* a square of grilled *panela* cheese, with a small bowl of *frijoles charros* on the side and a *salsa mexicana* passed separately. It is perfect for the restaurant kitchen that has many of those already prepared ingredients and the happiest example that I know of a "combination plate"—usually anathema to me.

For this recipe a thick slice of fillet steak about 3 inches is butterflied out to a strip about ¼ inch thick.

1 6-ounce slice *filet mignon,* cleaned of any gristle or connective tissue
salt and freshly ground pepper to taste
squeeze of fresh lime juice (optional)

With the cut side of the meat toward you and holding it firmly on top, make a horizontal cut through the center of the meat to within ¼ inch of the other side. Open meat out and cut on both sides, turning the meat (unless you are ambidextrous), and make a second cut to butterfly it on both sides. Turn meat over and cut again. Continue turning and cutting until you have an even strip of steak that is about ¼ inch thick.

Season the meat lightly on both sides, and if you're not going to cook it immediately, roll it up and set aside in a cool place.

When ready to cook, heat a very lightly greased griddle over very high heat. Lightly sprinkle water on the griddle; it should sizzle and jump fiercely when the griddle's ready. Squeeze a little lime juice on both sides of the meat and quickly sear and brown the meat on each side. It only will take about 2 minutes on each side for medium-rare.

—Diana Kennedy
The Art of Mexican Cooking, 1989

Mesón del Caballo Bayo. Daily, 8 A.M.–midnight. Adequate wine list. A meal for two, with wine, costs an average of $45. Reservations suggested. Credit cards: AE, DC, MC, V.

Mesón del Cid
DOWNTOWN, P. 15, 3F

Humboldt 61, near the Zócalo and Alameda Park
Tel. 521-1940

Superb gazpacho and paella top the menu of this traditional Spanish tavern, offering authentic Andalusian dishes. The ambience is Spanish too: Listen to lively guitar music; before your meal, sit in the restaurant's patio bar, located in an attractive courtyard, and sip a light Spanish wine; nibble on Spanish *chistorra* sausage or *jamón serrano* (highland ham). On Sat. nights, the restaurant presents a rib-splitting medieval feast, complete with suckling pig and all the trimmings. Open daily for lunch and dinner; closed Sun. The average cost of a meal for two, with wine, is about $45. Reservations suggested. Credit cards: AE, MC, V.

Mesón del Perro Andaluz
ZONA ROSA, P. 14, 4C

Copenhague 26
Tel. 533-5306

A popular midday and evening bistro, Mesón del Perro Andaluz has umbrella-covered outdoor tables on the pedestrians-only Calle Copenhague, in the heart of the Zona Rosa. You can alight for a quick and delicious snack of Mexican *antojitos* (appetizer-type snacks)—quesadillas, tacos, and the like—or linger over a leisurely cup of coffee or beer while you read the newspaper or study the continual stream of strollers-by. More substantial dishes include giant shrimps in garlic sauce, trout with anchovy sauce, and fried squid. In case all the outdoor tables are taken, there is also indoor service on the first and second floors. The food is good and reasonably priced. An average meal costs about $12–$15 per person, including beer or wine (but the selection is limited). Daily, 1 P.M.–1 A.M. No reservations. Credit cards: AE, DC, MC, V.

Les Moustaches
ZONA ROSA, P. 14, 3C

Río Sena 88 (Colonia Cuauhtemoc)
Tel. 533-3390

The setting: a marvelously restored old mansion with a beautiful covered patio area done in creamy beiges and whites; exquisitely groomed greenery; small intimate dining alcoves; and a sweeping staircase to second-floor dining rooms. Complete the scene with soft, romantic piano music. The menu: haute international, featuring a fine selection of the standard cuts of meats, fish, and fowl, all prepared with delectable sauces, as well as inventive items, such as cream of smoked-salmon soup. The ambience: refined and formal (jackets and ties for men, and the equally formal dress counterpart for women required at all times). In addition to the above, Les Moustaches' location near both the American and British embassies makes it particularly popular with the international crowd either living in or visiting Mexico. The wine list includes domestic labels and high-priced imported vintages. Open Mon.–Fri., 1 P.M.–1 A.M.; closed Sat. and Sun. A meal for two, including wine, averages about $50. Reservations suggested. Credit cards: AE, MC, V.

Restaurantes Lincoln

Amberes 64
Tel. 533-4296 or 511-0308
also Revillagigedo 24, near the Zócalo and Alameda Park
Tel. 510-1468 or 510-1102

Especially popular with businessmen enjoying lengthy lunches, this downtown restaurant, established in 1943, is particularly well known for its fresh and flavorful seafood dishes. *Huachinango* (red snapper) *a la veracruzana* (sauce made with tomatoes, olives, capers, onions, chile, and butter), *jaibes en chipachole* (a spicy, thick soup with crabs in a tomato base), and *camarones gigantes al mojo de ajo* (giant shrimp in garlic sauce) are specialties, but the menu has some meat dishes as well. The decor features leather-lined booths and wood-paneled walls; tuxedo-clad waiters are always at the ready. Open daily for breakfast, lunch, and dinner. Good Mexican beer and soft drinks. No reservations. No credit cards.

San Angel Inn

Palmas 50 at Altavista
Tel. 548-6746

The San Angel Inn, one of Mexico's most celebrated restaurants, is often used by affluent Mexicans to celebrate special occasions—weddings, birthdays, anniversaries, graduations. Located in a magnificent 18th-century hacienda and former convent, the restaurant has a series of beautiful dining rooms—decorated with antique mahogany chairs and tables covered with crisp white cloths and set with magnificent blue-and-white Talavera service—overlooking perfectly manicured gardens, with fragrant flowers and cooling fountains. The lengthy menu and superb food preparation are as exquisite as the surroundings. *Filete* (steak) and *huachinango* (red snapper) are presented in a number of appealing ways, all delicious, and the restaurant's duck in blackberry sauce is a very popular choice. The dessert trolley is laden with riches, ranging from cakes with cream to crème caramel or fresh fruit. The wine list is extensive and expensive. Daily, 1 P.M.–1 A.M. A meal for two, with wine, averages about $80. Reservations required, especially on weekends. Credit cards: AE, DC, MC, V.

Sanborn's House of Tiles

Madero 4, near the Zócalo
Tel. 521-6058

This historic and beautiful tile-covered 16th-century colonial mansion, in the heart of downtown Mexico City, is the crowning glory of the Sanborn group, a reliable and reasonably priced chain of combination restaurants/gift boutiques/drug stores/newspaper stands/bookshops. Shop and eat, or eat and shop, as you will. The food is served fast and is quite tasty, especially the *enchiladas suizas* and the American-style hamburgers. *Huevos rancheros* and other Mexican-style egg dishes are good anytime day or night. The decor matches the mood of the exterior, with sturdy wooden tables, potted plants, and waitresses clad in colorful Indian skirts and headdresses. Be sure to take a peek at the Orozco mural at the top of the stairway to the second floor, where you'll also find the refreshingly clean rest rooms. Open daily 24 hours (shopping sections close at around midnight). Beer, wine, and mixed drinks are served. The average cost of a meal for two is about $25. No reservations. Credit cards: AE, MC, V.

Sanborn's Reforma
ZONA ROSA, P. 14, 4C

Paseo de la Reforma 333
Tel. 533-1843

This modern branch of the Sanborn's chain (see **Sanborn's House of Tiles,** above) is conveniently located near the Zona Rosa hotels and shopping areas, and near the American and British embassies. Credit cards: AE, MC, V.

Sanborn's San Angel
SAN ANGEL, P. 12, 4C

Insurgentes Sur 2105
Tel. 550-1033

This, a particularly charming branch of the Sanborn's chain (see **Sanborn's House of Tiles,** above) is a popular after-work or Sat. meeting place. It is surrounded by an unusually large number of shops selling Mexican handicrafts and is located conveniently near the famous Bazar Sábado. Credit cards: AE, MC, V.

Suntory
CHAPULTEPEC-LOMAS, P. 12, 3A

Montes Urales 535, off Las Palmas
Tel. 536-9432

While dining on Japanese steak and sukiyaki, you're treated to a spectacle of flashing knives and scrambling spatulas. The food is tasty and reliable, and the show is always exciting and good fun. This is a good place to go with a crowd, because the more food ordered, the more show there is. Suntory's Mexican outposts are decorated very much like all the other restaurants belonging to this well-known international chain: peaceful rock gardens, rice-paper screens, tatami mats, dim lighting, and highly polished teak tables with grills set in the middle, plus traditional sushi bars. But here, the kimono-clad waitresses are mostly Mexicans! Beer and saki are served. Open Mon.–Sat., 1–5:30 P.M. and 7:30–11 P.M.; Sun., 1–5:50 P.M. A meal for two, with beer or saki, averages about $60. Reservations are suggested. Credit cards: AE, DC, MC, V. Another Mexico City branch of **Suntory** is located at Torres Adalid 14 (near Insurgentes Sur in Colonia del Valle); tel. 536-9432 for reservations at both Mexico City locations. **Suntory** also has a restaurant in Acapulco.

Tokyo
ZONA ROSA, P. 14, 4C

Hamburgo 134
Tel. 525-3775

This unpretentious second-floor restaurant, with its straight-back chairs and laminated square tables, is frequented by Japanese and savvy Mexicans who go in for great food rather than a lot of show. The sashimi is as fresh as can be, and other favorites, including *shabu-shabu* and tempura, are delicately flavored and cooked to perfection. Appetizers include all the standard Japanese offerings, and Japanese beers, hot or cold saki, and plum wine are served. The restaurant has several rooms: Tables with a view of the street are the most fun. Open Mon.–Sat., lunch and dinner, 12:30 P.M.–midnight; Sun., 2–10 P.M. Dinner for two, including saki or beer, costs around $40. No reservations. Credit cards: AE, MC, V.

Tortas la Perla

ZONA ROSA, P. 14, 3C

Río Rhin 51, between Lerma and Panuco
No tel.

Tortas are the Mexican equivalent of hero sandwiches, and la Perla is sort of the local Blimpie. Hardly elegant or sophisticated—but great for a satisfying light meal on the run. La Perla is actually tiny—a counter without stools, tables, or chairs—so your choices are either take-out or eat-on-your-feet. However, don't be scared off: The place is clean and the quality reliable. Sandwich fixings include ham, cheese, chicken, or roasted pork with tomatoes, avocado, sour cream, refried beans, onions, and chiles. Fabulously flavorful and very reasonably priced at about $5 or less per *torta.* Sorry, no reservations—and you'll have to stop elsewhere for wine. Open Mon.–Sat., mainly for lunch; closed by 8 P.M. and all day Sun. No credit cards.

VIPS

THROUGHOUT CITY

Avenida Juárez 64B and other locations
Tel. 521-0516

A reliable chain of fast-food restaurants that serve American favorites: hamburgers, french fries, milk shakes, fried chicken. Some typical Mexican dishes, including the standard enchiladas, tacos, and soups, are also on the menu. The decor is pure plastic, but VIPS is open 24 hours a day and has many loyal patrons. The average cost of a meal for two is about $18. No reservations. Credit cards: AE, MC, V.

SHOPPING

ZONA ROSA

The Zona Rosa has, overall, Mexico's best collection of shops, offering a wide variety of contemporary and ethnic clothing, jewelry, handicrafts, leather goods, and shoes. Attractive boutiques and charming *tiendas* line the neighborhood's crowded streets. Some of the streets are pedestrian-only—great for browsers who drift from one sidewalk to another without minding Mexico's hectic traffic. There's enough attractive and affordable merchandise in the Zona Rosa to stuff many a suitcase, as well as some stunning suitcases just waiting to be stuffed.

Most better Mexico City shops take major credit cards, while *mercados* and stalls seldom do.

Before you hit the shops, visit the **Insurgentes Market** (see **Markets,** below), at Londres 154, where you'll find rows of stalls bursting with colorful clothing and handicrafts from all regions of Mexico. The *mercado* generally has a greater variety of merchandise and better prices (if you know how to bargain) than nearby shops that sell similar wares and cater especially to tourists. Seeing what's available at the market gives you a valuable point of comparison, but always check for quality and authenticity. Market vendors have been known to sell alpaca (so-called "Mexican silver" and in fact nickel silver) for silver and onyx for jade, and the weave on their hammocks may be flawed. Always check carefully before buying. While vendors usually do not accept credit cards, most often they will accept U.S. dollars and traveler's checks.

You can be more confident about the quality of merchandise in the better shops, but always get a sales receipt that describes the article and records the price. Here are some favorite Zona Rosa shops:

ACA Joe, at Amberes 19, has great casual and sports clothes. The company has outlets in the United States, but prices in Mexico are often fifty percent less. Displays include stacks of colorful cotton mix-and-match resortwear, cotton sweat clothes, T-shirts, and baseball jackets with team logos.

Antil, at Florencia 22, has an extensive range of sumptuously soft and fabulously fashionable expensive leather clothes designed by Rosario Maroto de Lavin. There are also roomy handbags and sensational luggage, plus handsome desk accessories in a wide range of colors and styles. Antil's own factory makes most of the merchandise, the men's shoes being the main exception. Prices are high, but so is quality—and these are long-lasting purchases.

Aries, with branches at both Amberes 24 and Florencia 14, is one of Mexico's finest leather chain stores, with branches as far away as Beverly Hills and Paris. Aries specializes in everything beautiful in leather clothing—coats, jackets, skirts, and slacks—and accessories. There are handbags, belts, briefcases, wallets, golf bags, large black leather carryalls, handsome briefcases of black leather with red piping trim and handles or shoulder straps, stunning clutch bags, and beautifully constructed backgammon sets. All are beautifully designed and well crafted. Prices are high, but much less so here than in the United States or France. The Florencia shop is larger, but sales personnel in the Amberes store are much friendlier and more helpful.

Arte En Plata, at Amberes 24, displays its fabulous silver jewelry, much of it richly inlaid with malachite, onyx, obsidian, and turquoise, in gleaming glass and oak cases. Most distinctive are the bracelets and necklaces in which a silver band with two hands embraces the wrist or neck; sometimes the hands clasp a glittering gem. Other designs utilize tiny silver animals and flowers or geometric shapes in unusual, almost mystical settings. The sales staff is particularly pleasant and attentive.

Artesca, at Florencia 13, is a government-sponsored shop selling handicrafts from the state of Guerrero. Look here for delightful wooden masks of animals' heads or demi-demons (some more amusing than scary), in a variety of sizes—always colorful. Also special is the lacquerwork from Olinala, a remote and tiny town hidden in the Guerrero mountains, where lacquerwork has been a way of life for some three hundred years. Artesca sells Olinala dining-room tables, headboards, and screens, all done with painstaking care and completely exquisite. These are expensive and worth every penny.

Art-Jonilla, at Génova 39B, sells spectacular one-of-a-kind ceramics that owner Manuel Arjonilla has collected from master craftsmen and state-competition prizewinners throughout Mexico's 31 states. The selection includes everything from vases to full dinner sets. Best represented are Michoacán's beautiful earth-colored pottery decorated with flowers and animals, and Guanajuato's lovely floral and geometric designs in cheerful blue, green, yellow, and orange on a white background. The shop also sells some unusual papier-mâché sculptures.

La Boutique, at Génova 59F, is the place to buy *ropa típica,* or typical clothes, but the colorful embroidered dresses, caftans, and blouses sold in this store are all highly unusual. Most are one of a kind, created by women who have moved to Mexico City from all over the country, bringing with them their sewing skills and a great need for cash. Their one-of-a-kind garments, frequently trimmed with lace and usually hand-dyed, are feminine and fun to wear, and definitely a cut above the *ropa típica* found in the *mercados* and more touristic *tiendas.*

Bye Mexico, at Londres 106, has more than two hundred T-shirt designs with colorful Mexican themes, including palm trees and parrots. They're terrific souvenirs. So are the sturdy beach bags in bold colors and designs, and the easy-to-wear sports clothes in natural cottons and colors. Moderately priced, unless you buy out the store.

Los Castillos is a famous Taxco silver shop, and this Mexico City branch, in a converted mansion at Amberes 41, is a shining sea of tempting sterling, silver plate, and alpaca objects. Jewelry includes earrings, bracelets, and necklaces, and designs range from traditional Aztec to ultramodern. Many of the pieces are set with lapis lazuli, onyx, turquoise, and other semiprecious stones. There are inexpensive alpaca pillboxes encrusted with abalone shell, and pricey sterling silver platters with finely engraved designs. Los Castillos specializes in three-tone decorative items, such as mirror frames and cream and sugar sets, designed with combination of silver, copper, and brass.

Colección de Felguras, at Hamburgo 130A, is a postage-stamp-sized shop filled with amazingly detailed miniatures of everything from cups and saucers to animals, cacti, and people—even mariachis. Encased in little glass boxes are entire offices, barnyards, pool halls, and bakeries. These are funny little things to bring home—and there's no problem fitting them into your bulging suitcase.

Flamma, at Hamburgo 177, will light up your life with candles galore. There are traditional tapers in all colors, lengths, and widths, plus a complete zoo of inventive sculptural animals, as well as flowers, fruits, figurines, and ice-cream sundaes. Some are sweetly scented, many are too unusual or amusing ever to be lit, and all are reasonably priced.

FONART, at Londres 36, has a wonderful selection of handicrafts from all regions of Mexico (see **Handicrafts,** FONART, below).

Furor Products, Hamburgo 118 and 122, is the hot shop for Mexico City's young trendies, and with good reason. The shop's pleated trousers and oversized shirts are big and baggy enough to cover up the pudgies or fill out the skinnies. Pants and shirts are mostly in primary colors, and they are made in attractive, textured cottons or linen. Men and women, short and tall, flock to these shops for the garb of the moment.

Gaitan, at Copenhague 32, has tooled leather bags, belts, briefcases, eyeglass cases, card cases, key cases, coin purses, agendas, wallets, tennis racquet covers, and golf-club bags. And more. An interesting array, and very good value.

Galería de Arte Misrachi, at Génova 20, one of Mexico's finest art galleries, exhibits the works of outstanding Mexican contemporary artists, including such masters as Siqueiros and Zuniga, along with lesser-known but very collectible painters, such as Rafael Caudur, whose works are intriguing explorations of traditional Mexican themes and elements. The gallery has ten individual shows annually, as well as ongoing collective shows. About one-quarter of the gallery's sales are exported, but works for sale by Diego Rivera or Juan O'Gorman are for your viewing only—these are considered national treasures and may not be taken out of Mexico. If you're planning to relocate, however, shop to your heart's content.

Galería Pecanins, at Durango 186 (actually several blocks north of the Zona Rosa), has interesting and affordable contemporary Mexican paintings, prints, and sculptures. This is a great place to learn about who and what is up and coming in the Mexican art world. Exhibits change frequently, and the ambience is both sophisticated and genteel.

Galería Sergio Bustamente, at Amberes 14, shows the famous ceramicist's intriguing sculptures, many of which are somewhat surreal in style. There are, for example, all sorts of wildly exotic creatures, some of which are born completely of the artist's imagination, emerging from large eggs, and richly detailed miniature houses have iguanas or rabbits peeking out of every window. Bustamente, who has galleries in the United States, has been widely copied. In fact, he now employs an atelier of assistants, but all pieces sold in his galleries are signed by him. Bustamente's headquarters are in Guadalajara, at his Tlaquepaque gallery.

Girasol, at Génova 19, features Mexican designer Gonzalo Bauer's clothes, including lovely heavyweight, brightly colored cotton dresses, shirts, and skirts richly embellished with ribbons, appliqué and embroidery, to be worn with broad silk sashes with fringed ends; beautiful patchwork and embroidered jackets of velvet and silk; and embroidered velvet pouches. Girasol also has lovely leather and suede handbags with patchwork lions and other animals.

Gucci, at Hamburgo 136 and at the María Isabel Sheraton Hotel, has the Italian designer items, monogram and all, at prices that seem too good to be true. That's probably because this shop's goods are Mexican-made. But you will find the key chains, handbags, shoes, desk sets, wallets, and luggage that are ever-popular purchases with both Mexicans and tourists.

Guess?, Amberes 17, has casual clothes bearing the familiar *Guess?* logo, including denim jackets with leather trim, cotton trousers, and chic jeans for adults and children, at terrific prices. The sales staff assures customers that these are the original *Guess?* products, not copies; labels, however, read *"Hecho en México."* Who to believe? Your guess is as good as mine.

The owner of **Muller's,** at Florencia 52, Gary Muller, is known as Mr. Onyx, and this shop offers you beautiful boxes, chess sets, goblets, sculpted animals, bowls, and other items made of the stone the Aztecs once thought was too sacred to be used by humans. Also sold are larger items, including dining-room and coffee tables, plain or engraved. In fact, Muller's will create large pieces to your specifications and ship them to your home. Reliable quality and reasonable prices.

Don't miss **Tane,** at Amberes 70, one of Mexico's finest silver shops, where you're greeted with a red carnation and a bag of bonbons wrapped in silver foil. There are dazzling silver and gold bracelets, neck chains, and other baubles, all designed by Pedro Tane, plus baroque and modern-style silver picture frames, two-spouted ewers, solid silver candlesticks and woven silver baskets.

Telas Escalera, at Génova 65B, is where Spanish designer Luis Martin Escalera, who has lived in Mexico for years, sells his beautiful silk-screened cotton, either by the bolt or stitched into attractive puff-sleeved blouses and flowing skirts or pillows and other home accessories. The colorful fabrics are patterned after traditional Mexican elements—pyramid figures, flowers, and birds—and look almost like Oriental batik. Escalera's other stores (Neus, at Génova 65F, and Palenque, at Londres 119) are nearby and are similarly stocked.

POLANCO

Polanco's **Avenida Presidente Mazarik,** a tree-lined boulevard that cuts through the quiet residential district, is one of Mexico City's most fashionable shopping streets. Fabulously elegant old residences now house exclusive boutiques, filled with finery. These offer high-quality clothing, gift items, and household goods. Unfortunately, some lovely old architecture has been replaced by glass-front shops, but many buildings still have impressive classic exteriors, while interiors are modern, with dramatic lighting to enhance merchandise displays. The shops are concentrated within a dozen or so blocks, beginning near **Avenida Mariano Escobedo** and stretching toward **Pasaje Polanco,** a grouping of handsome shops and eateries around a charming courtyard. Some of the boutiques are outlets of the Zona Rosa's top shops, but the Polanco branches are usually less crowded and more accommodating. Visit the following for a rewarding afternoon's shopping stroll:

ACA Joe's (see **Zona Rosa,** above) sizeable Mazarik store, at number 310 to 318, has three distinct sections offering the full line of designer sportswear, plus a discount outlet where shirts, slacks, jackets, and sweat clothes are practically given away.

Ruben Torres, at number 318 bis, is another casual clothes label popular in Mexico but still relatively unknown in the United States. The clothing is similar to that of ACA Joe, but colors are softer and patterns less bold. Prices for mix and match shorts, slacks, and shirts are about equal to those at ACA Joe.

Girasol (see **Zona Rosa,** above), at number 318 bis, upstairs from Ruben Torres, has a wonderful selection of heavy cotton dresses in bright colors, plus shirts and skirts with colorful appliqué and embroidery. This boutique also has some terrific sweaters, many with leather appliqués.

Guess? (see **Zona Rosa,** above), at number 326, is located in a wonderful old house that adds a note of class to these trendy casual clothes. Browse through the various salons, selecting chic jeans and jackets for the whole family.

Express, at number 332 bis, is another casual clothes shop. The interior is designed like a pastel boiler room—pink and baby blue pipes everywhere. The clothes are trendy: Mix-and-match golf shorts-and-shirt sets are in bold floral patterns; safari tops and shorts are in fashionable khakis and olive drab. There are figure-fitting stone-washed denim dresses with zippers up the front and matching coats or jackets. Men's jeans, jackets, and shirts look Hawaiian rather than Mexican.

On the corner of Mazarik and Alejandro Dumas is the first of three fine leather shops. **Regina Romero's** boutique sells stylishly attractive leather clothes, shoes, belts, and handbags. Look for white strapless leather gaucho dresses with fringed jackets, and aqua leather skirt and cape ensembles with studs and fringe, plus large leather handbags and belts. Hardly inexpensive—but you'll pay much less here than you would in the United States.

Nearby is **Aries** (at Palmas 50; see **Zona Rosa,** above) with exceptional leather goods. This branch is small but well stocked with beautiful bags, belts, briefcases, and the other accessories for which the chain is famous. Look for clothing in the Zona Rosa shops.

Inside Pasaje Polanco (number 360), **Keko** sells lovely women's clothes, including stylish dresses, tiered skirts and matching tops, cotton jumpsuits, and denim mini-skirts with matching vests.

Tapanco Artesanias, in the Pasaje, sells Mexican handicrafts, including lovely jewel boxes with etched lacquer exteriors, glassware, handcrafted and painted vases by J. Benabe and other well-known artisans, and complete sets of colorful Talavera tableware. This is not the least expensive place to shop for these items, but the selection is good.

Nearby, also in the Pasaje (though there is an entrance on Avenida Presidente Mazarik), **Michel Domit,** an excellent shoe store, has great Topsiders in all colors for children and adults, plus fine men's leather boots and tasseled loafers. The shop also has handsome men's accessories, including leather jackets, belts, portfolios, and silk ties and shirts.

Before leaving the Pasaje, stop in at *Snob*. This fashionable tea shop has fabulous cakes and pastries and serves a super-rich cappuccino. Tables in the courtyard are prime for people watching.

Tane (see **Zona Rosa,** above), at the corner of Avenida Presidente Mazarik and Edgar Allan Poe (several blocks beyond the Pasaje), is all elegance in silver. You'll be dazzled by the collection of baubles and beautiful home accessories of gleaming silver and gold, and by the genteel reception you're given by attentive salespeople who meet you at the door (which is heavily guarded!) with a red rose and a small sack of sweets wrapped in silver foil. Don't miss this.

Before you leave Polanco, take a detour off Mazarik (better yet, take a taxi!) to **La Casa de las Artesanias de Michoacán** (see **Handicrafts,** below), on the corner of Campos Elíseos and Temistocles (across the street from the Nikko and Presidente Chapultepec hotels), for an awesome selection of ceramics, copper, woodwork, weavings, and textiles from Michoacán State.

DEPARTMENT STORES

Mexico's two major department stores, **Liverpool** and **Palacio de Hierro** (Iron Palace), are good places to buy quality goods and to get a glimpse into the kinds of objects you might

A word about hours: Most Polanco and Zona Rosa shops open at 10 A.M. (though that often becomes 10:30 or 11 A.M.) and close at about 8 P.M. (though that sometimes becomes 7 P.M.). Most shops stay open during lunch hour (generally 3 to 5 P.M.), but don't be surprised to see a small handwritten sign saying *"Regreso in diez minutos"* ("Back in ten minutes"—or more like thirty minutes) taped to a locked shop door. Mexican shopkeepers, like most Mexicans, simply don't live strictly by the clock. So shop when you have plenty of time to roam around and return to a closed shop for another try.

find in most Mexican upper-middle-class homes—the clothes, cosmetics, linens, furniture, dishes, cooking utensils, small appliances, games, and toys that are so much a part of daily life. Not surprisingly, the goods sold here are similar to those found in department stores everywhere, including the internationally known labels and brands that register prestige wherever they are sold. Liverpool and Palacio de Hierro compete neck and neck; and both call for generous outlays at cash registers.

Liverpool and Palacio de Hierro each have several branch stores in upper-class neighborhoods and shopping centers, but both have their flagship stores downtown, near the Zócalo, at the corner of Venustiano Carranza and 20 de Noviembre, across the street from each other. Liverpool, established in 1847, is the elder of the two, but the store was given a streamlined Art Deco facade in the 1930s. Palacio de Hierro, open here since the 1870s, is decidedly Art Nouveau, with a great display of blue-and-white tiles listing the types of goods for sale inside. Curiously, both stores were founded by Frenchmen.

The atmosphere in Liverpool's downtown store actually seems a bit close and cluttered. Other Liverpool branches at Centro Comercial Perisur, in Polanco on Horacio, and at Coyoacán on Insurgentes Sur are much more spacious, well planned, and accommodating.

A visit to the downtown Palacio de Hierro is, however, a must. The store is modeled after the great French *magasins,* Galleries Lafayette and Au Printemps, and has its departments on balconies surrounding a central atrium, covered with a splendid Art Nouveau stained-glass dome. The pretty wrought-iron grillwork around the balconies is painted pale lavender. Additional Palacio de Hierro stores are located in Colonia Roma on Durango (near the Zona Rosa) and at Perisur.

Mexico City also has branches of **Sears** (call it reliable or predictable, depending upon your point of view) and **Paris Londres,** a less stylish and expansive department-store chain than either Liverpool or Palacio de Hierro. Both accept major credit cards.

Department stores are generally open Monday, Tuesday, Thursday and Friday from 10 A.M. to 7 P.M., and from 10 A.M. to 8 P.M. on Wednesday and Saturday. Department stores have their own credit cards, but will accept most major credit cards as well.

HANDICRAFTS

The variety and inventiveness of Mexican handicrafts are awe-inspiring. Twigs are turned into fabulous animal sculptures, rags become adorable dolls, and straw is woven into phenomenal baskets and toys. Highly skilled craftspeople turn out exquisite lacquerware, glassware, and ceramics. It would seem that Mexico in general is artistically inclined, and it is difficult to resist falling in love with this aspect of Mexican culture.

Every region of Mexico has its own special handicrafts, and such information is given in chapters that follow. But if you're not traveling through the country, you can still see and buy products from most of the Mexican states at excellent government-sponsored and privately owned crafts shops in Mexico City. Some shops specialize in a type of craft or crafts from one state; others have a little bit of everything.

FONART (Fondo Nacional para el Fomento de las Artesanias) is a large government-operated chain of craft stores, with Mexico City locations at Avenida Juárez 89 (across from Alameda Park, downtown); Londres 36 (Zona Rosa); Avenida de la Paz 37 (San Angel, near the Bazar Sábado); and Patriotismo 691 (Colonia Mixcoac). The largest of these is the Juárez shop, but all are well stocked with pottery from Puebla, Michoacán, Jalisco, and Guanajuato, as well as woven and embroidered clothing, bags, blankets, and rugs; silver and filigree jewelry; statues made of wood, clay, and papier-mâché; paintings on bark; drawings etched into glass and created with yarn pasted on wood; plus lacquerware chests, headboards, boxes, and trays of all sizes; and more. Of course, stock varies almost daily, but there is always something beautiful and fascinating to capture your fancy. If you buy something large, you should arrange to ship it yourself; FONART is notoriously late on delivery of sent items.

Artesca, at Florencia 13 (see **Zona Rosa,** above).

La Casa de las Artesanias de Michoacán, at Campos Elíseos and Temistocles (in Polanco, across the street from the Nikko and Presidente Chapultepec hotels) is a government-sponsored boutique with an extraordinary display of the absolutely exquisite ceramics, copper, woodwork, weavings, and textiles from Michoacán state, known for producing the finest crafts in all of Mexico. Ceramics are really the specialty here. The hand-painted dinner sets, serving vessels, and vases in floral and geometric patterns with color combinations ranging from classic blue and white to the fabulous flair of green and yellow on a black background, would make an event of any meal. Señora Guadalupe Prieto de Zulbaran, who runs the store, is very helpful—and generous with her extensive knowledge of crafts from Michoacán. The goods are not inexpensive, but they are priceless!

Mexico City's **Markets** (see below) usually have an ample selection of crafts. Merchandise here is generally of lower quality, and you usually won't find any collectible folk art, but you can bargain for lower prices on standard items such as serapes, rugs, leather goods, woolen sweaters, woven bags, and some embroidered clothing.

Museo Nacional de Artes y Industrias Populares, at Avenida Juárez 44 (near the Juárez FONART shop), is a first-floor shop with a wide variety of carefully selected crafts of all types from all the Mexican states, and a second-floor museum with antique masks, musical instruments, weavings, and lacquerware.

Sanborn's, at various locations, is a restaurant/gift boutique/drug store/newspaper stand/bookshop chain, with a nice selection of woolen blankets, brass, glass, ceramics, and other handicrafts.

Victor's, at Madero 8 and 10 in Room 305 (near the Alameda Park), is celebrated for its selectivity in gathering crafts, many of them antiques, from all over Mexico—thanks to the persistence and dedication of owner Victor Fosado. The place is like a museum. In fact, part of Victor Fosado's personal collection (gathered during more than sixty years of combing the country for treasures) has been donated to the National Museum of Anthropology, where it is currently on display. Items for sale include old lacquerware chests and gourds, musical instruments and ceramics, antique weavings and embroidered clothes, beadwork bags and bowls, regional masks, and traditional Indian jewelry made in a family-owned workshop. The shop's hours are irregular; it's best to call 512-1263 to see if they are open.

MARKETS

Visiting a Mexican market is a must. Almost every neighborhood in Mexico City (and every town in the country, for that matter) has either a permanent *mercado* with well-established food, clothing, gadget, and artisan shops, or weekly *tianguis,* where vendors set up in temporary stalls to sell fresh fruits, spices, sweets, and a wide variety of handicrafts. The quality of merchandise and ambience vary greatly, but the experience is always fascinating. Unless you restrict your browsing to the best (read cleanest and most expensive) markets, be prepared for some strange smells, sights, and sounds. For example, you might encounter a side of beef that's been hanging

San Angel's Bazar Sábado: The Ultimate Mexican Crafts Market

Bazar Sábado (see **Priorities,** above) is a browser's dream come true. It's the ultimate crafts market, set in a marvelous old mansion, originally the family seat of the wealthy and influential counts of Oploca. Inside this sprawling colonial structure, located at Plaza San Jacinto 11, in the heart of the exclusive San Angel residential area, are dozens of stalls and small shops, set up throughout the first floor and on a second-floor balcony. The umbrella-covered central patio has a restaurant that serves typical Mexican dishes. Outside the walls surrounding the mansion, other vendors set up their stands, and, across the street, artists turn a small park into an outdoor gallery. There's usually a hurdy-gurdy man playing on the corner.

Inside the Bazar Sábado, you'll find the best-quality typical handicrafts, including embroidered clothing, boxes of brass and glass, ceramics from Puebla and Jalisco, hand-blown glass goblets, papier-mâché and ceramic figurines of devils and peasants, carved wood masks, hand-woven blankets and rugs, hand-knit sweaters, lacquered Olinala chests and trays, and more. But the Bazar Sábado also exclusively features the work of some highly individualized artists. In one stall, there's a display of large and intriguing futuristic automobiles, airplanes, submarines, and bicycles made out of discarded bolts, spatulas, saw blades, and screwdrivers, and scraps of metal. Nearby, another booth offers exceptional crystals set delicately in silver and gold settings to be worn as rings or pendants, or carefully mounted on wooden base blocks to be displayed on mantels or night tables. You'll also find Girasol, the Mexican fashion label, sold in a boutique filled with long and short white cotton dresses decorated with colorful embroidery and ribbon trim, colorful pantsuits and hand-knit sweaters. Another boutique has handmade Christmas-tree ornaments that are out of this world.

You'll notice that prices are higher at Bazar Sábado than they are at other crafts markets, but in general the quality is better. For some of the more standard items—the brass and glass boxes and hand-woven rugs, for example—you'll do better to buy at the Insurgentes, La Ciudadela, or San Juan markets (see **Markets,** below). But Bazar Sábado's ambience and unique products cannot be beat. Don't miss this Saturday-only shopping special. The hours are from 10 A.M. to 7 P.M. Some of the vendors take credit cards; most do not.

in the open air for some time and has attracted a swarm of buzzing flies. So, steer clear of meat sellers and head for hats or handicrafts. But even the smaller and less-affluent markets can provide unexpected triumphs for serious shoppers, although larger markets, accustomed to dealing with tourists, are the safer bets. Most vendors in markets do not accept credit cards, but they usually do accept U.S. dollars and traveler's checks.

Insurgentes Market, in the Zona Rosa at Londres 154, presents a mazelike little alley with about two hundred stalls filled to overflowing with wonderful embroidered clothing, heavy woolen hand-knit sweaters, baskets, blankets, glassware, ceramics, wood, leather, silver and gems (including some psuedo-silver and gems, so watch out!), copper and brass and papier-mâché items that are functional or fanciful, blankets, rugs, and *rebozos* (shawls). Price-wise, merchandise is reasonable, especially if you know how to bargain. Think of this as a sporting event: sparring with charm to save dollars. Quality-wise, the *mercado* has a mixture of good and bad. Be on your guard against onyx that is sold as jade, or red and blue dyes that will mix to make purple during a garment's first washing.

Best-bet stalls include Bertha de Ponce's silver shop at number 145 (heavy silver and lapis necklaces, wide-band silver bracelets, and terrific eye-catching earrings of monumental proportion), Juanita Garcia's lacquerwork shop at number 154 (black lacquer boxes with gold-leaf decorations, brooches, and pendants—all from the state of Michoacán), and Artesanias Patricia at number 174 (specializing in all sorts of textiles and embroidered wearables from the states of Oaxaca, Jalisco, and Chiapas).

Some stalls here accept credit cards, but you'll usually get a better price if you offer cash. Open daily from 10 A.M. to 7 P.M. And some vendors close for lunch, or on Sunday afternoon.

Centro de Antiquedades is a Saturday-only (usually 10 A.M. to 6 P.M.) antiques fair, in the Zona Rosa at Londres 161, in the Plaza del Angel, a series of little alleys and a picturesque courtyard. An amazing variety of material is sold here, some of it quite magnificent. Antique armoires, for example, made of richly carved wood, are too large (or too grand) to fit anywhere other than a hacienda similar to the one in which it undoubtedly originated. The huge crystal chandeliers deserve modern-day palaces. Smaller items include ancient tomes, vintage sheet music, coins, lamp fixtures, jewelry, china, photos, and, best of all, *retablos* (religious paintings done with oil on tin). Bargaining is an essential part of the action, and be prepared to pay cash.

Lagunilla, downtown, eight blocks north of Madero, on Ecuador between Allende and Chile (near Plaza Garibaldi), is a multibuilding market with stalls selling food, clothing, household items, handicrafts, and leather goods—all fairly unexceptional in quality. However, every Sunday, the surrounding area becomes a giant flea market, with hundred of vendors selling antiques and secondhand paraphernalia that they got hold of only God knows where—and nobody else is asking.

The range of objects includes crystal and china, old photos and watches, jewelry, paintings, vintage clothes, and antique electrical devices for every imaginable application. The Sunday market is very popular with Mexicans and tourists, who come in search of the rare masterpiece that's been obscured by dust—or the bustling ambience. Bargain hard, pay in cash, and watch out for hustlers and your wallet.

La Ciudadela Arts and Crafts Market, downtown at the corner of Balderas and Ayuntamiento, is a big pink Mexican building with 256 stalls selling some really wonderful pieces of folk art, mixed in with the standard variety of handicrafts and a whole lot of junk. In the folk art category, best of all are the painted wood masks from the state of Guerrero, most typically of tigers, pirates, and demons with horns, and simple Nativity scenes made of wood, ceramics, or papiermâché. There are also colorful lacquerware chests, tables, and trays with great character, and copper and earthenware pots. Jewelry isn't all that reliable or attractive here, but there are nice textiles, including woolen *rebozos* and ponchos, and a selection of fine embroidered dresses, including the pretty floral patterns that hail from Oaxaca. Even if you don't intend to buy anything (and that would be foolish), visit La Ciudadela to see *artesanías* (craftspeople) at work. There are seventy ateliers in the *mercado,* producing everything from weavings to woodwork. Prices here depend on your persistent bargaining. Be prepared to haggle down to the last peso and to pay cash (either pesos or dollars). Open daily from 11 A.M. to 7 P.M. Some stalls close for lunch or on Sunday afternoon.

San Juan Market, at Ayuntamiento and Arranda, several blocks away from La Ciudadela, is usually quieter, less crowded, and somewhat less exciting than the other market, but offers a similar array of goods.

Sullivan Park Art Market, held Sundays only (from 10 A.M. to 4 P.M.) at Sullivan Park in Colonia San Rafael, just off Insurgentes Centro, is an outdoor gallery of modern Mexican art. It's very informal. The artists set up their canvases and sculptures on the park's lawns, and sketch or read or snack on fresh fruit and cheese from the neighboring produce market, while browsers stroll by. The artists aren't pushy, but they're always ready to chat with prospective patrons. The work varies widely in style and media. There are watercolors of typical Mexican town scenes or landscapes, oil or pastel portraits of Indians or beautiful nudes, and bold geometric abstractions in acrylic. Sculptures include depictions of beggar women in bronze and ceramic busts of Mayan or Aztec chieftains. Some are sophisticated, others rather amateurish. But the event is certainly pleasant enough, what with the outdoors, some good art, and interesting conversation—and you don't have to buy anything, unless it's perfect for that big blank space over the mantelpiece. Stop by the produce market, too, for some tasty nibbles of cheese from Chihuahua or Oaxaca and exotic fruits.

ENTERTAINMENT

Mexico City has a fabulously rich cultural life, with frequent performances by national and international artists of note, and an active and adventurous contingent of avant-garde performers. The best way to find out what's on when you're in town is to check in the Friday edition of the *News,* Mexico's English-language daily newspaper. Here you'll find a complete listing of interesting cultural events and popular performances. Here's a list of some items to look for especially:

Ballet Folklórico de México
The Ballet Folklórico de México takes you on a cultural tour of this country through music and dance. The performance is an entertaining, colorful, and high-energy revue of Mexico's regional dances, presented with fabulous costumes and choreography. Shows are presented at the Palacio de las Bellas Artes (tel. 585-4888, ext. 29) on Sunday at 9:30 A.M. and 9 P.M. and Wednesday at 9 P.M., with additional performances scheduled to meet the great demand for tickets. Consult your hotel concierge or local newspaper for current schedules.

Tickets ($5 and up) can be bought at the Bellas Artes box office (open from 10:30 A.M. to 1 P.M. and 4 to 7 P.M.), but tickets for a given performance do not go on sale until three days before that performance. Tickets may also be ordered through travel agencies, but these may cost twice as much as the face value.

A less famous group, the **Ballet Folklórico Nacional Aztlan** presents similar performances at the beautiful belle époque Teatro de la Ciudad (Donceles 36, between Allende and Xicotencatl, just about a block away from Bellas Artes; tel. 521-2355 or 510-2942). Shows are scheduled on Sun. at 9:30 A.M. and 9 P.M., and on Thurs. at 8:30 P.M. Tickets are both less expensive and easier to get than are those for the Ballet Folklórico de México.

Palacio de las Bellas Artes
Mexico City's beautiful Palace of the Arts, located near the Zócalo and Alameda Park, presents not only the famous Ballet Folklórico de México and Mexico's National Symphony Orchestra but also other leading dance and musical ensembles from around the world. Tickets can be bought at the box office. Check with your hotel concierge or local newspaper for current schedules.

National Auditorium

The National Auditorium, located in Chapultepec Park (across the street from the Nikko and Presidente Chapultepec hotels), presents performances by pop stars, visiting symphonies, dance and theater ensembles, and the like. Tickets can be bought at the box office, and again, check with your hotel concierge or local newspaper for current schedules.

University Concerts

In the south of the city, the **University Cultural Center** (Insurgentes Sur 3000) presents excellent music, dance, and theatrical performances by both well-established and up-and-coming ensembles, in the Nezahualcoyotl and Miguel Covarrubias concert halls. For current schedules, consult your hotel concierge or local newspaper.

Teatro Blanquito

This showplace (at Lázaro Cárdenas and Mina) presents a lively vaudeville revue headlined by some of Mexico's top pop singers and acts and is enormously popular with Mexican audiences. The place is fun and full of local color—a real change from the tame, highbrow scene. The curtain usually goes up at 7:30, but it isn't necessary to get there right at the beginning. The best acts are usually on a little later. Tickets are sold at the box office on the day of the performance. Consult your concierge or one of the Spanish-language newspapers for current schedules.

Plaza Garibaldi

Mexico City's mariachi headquarters, at Lázaro Cárdenas and Honduras, is always filled with bands of musicians wearing tight trousers, bolero jackets, and broad-brimmed sombreros. The place is liveliest at around nine at night, especially on Sundays. Sometimes groups burst into song, but mostly they're just waiting to be hired to play. You can order a performance on the spot for about $6 per song, or hang around at Tlaquepaque, Pulqueria la Hermana Hortensia, or other bars and bistros that ring Garibaldi Square.

Fonda Del Recuerdo

This restaurant (at Bahía de las Palmas 39A; tel. 545-7260) features musical entertainment from the state of Veracruz. The bands, playing guitars and harps and dressed all in white, are paid by the song. You can call them over for your own serenade, or simply enjoy the music they play for other tables. The ambience is quite festive, and the food is good.

NIGHTCLUBS, BARS AND COCKTAIL LOUNGES

Some of the most popular night spots in town are the hotel bars. **Hotel Presidente Chapultepec's** cocktail lounge is usually full of chic Mexicans on dates, and the atmosphere, enhanced by a lively band, is friendly and upbeat. Next door, the **Hotel Nikko's** lobby bar is frequented by an international set of businesspeople. The bar is beautifully set at the base of an airy atrium. Mariachis or pop singers add a festive note, but the sound level is sometimes deafening. For a more intimate setting, try the lounge at **Les Celebrities,** the Nikko's gourmet restaurant. The background noise in this gentle candlelit environment is soothing piano music. The mood at the Hotel María Isabel Sheraton's popular **Jorongo Bar** is festive, and you'll find mariachis serenading a crowd of international vacationers and businesspeople out for a night on the town.

Away from the hotel scene, **La Muralta Bar,** atop the Torre Latinoamericana, at Juárez and Lázaro Cárdenas, provides a romantic setting and spectacular views of Mexico City by night. **Bar L'Opera** (5 de Mayo 15, corner of Mata) is a wonderful old wood-paneled bar that used to be for men only. Now women, too, may enjoy the clubby atmosphere while they sip a brew or throw back a tequila. L'Opera is open daily, but closes at 9 P.M. on Saturday night. **Le Rendezvous** (Madero 29, near the Zócalo; tel. 518-3955) is a rocking night spot with a nightly roster of jazz and pop bands. The action begins at about eight and continues until around midnight. Very popular with the younger set. **Gitanerias** (Oaxaca 15; tel. 511-5283) is a good nightclub for drinks and Flamenco dancing. Also Spanish in theme, **Mesón del Perro Andaluz** (Copenhague 26, in the Zona Rosa; tel. 533-5306; see **Restaurants,** above) is a popular sidewalk café where you can nurse a drink for hours and watch the world stroll by.

DISCOS

Mexico has many popular discos, but currently topping the "in" list are the Hotel Camino Real's **Cero,** with live and taped music and a great light show; the Hotel Plaza Galeria's totally modern **Le Chic,** with its popular backgammon room; and **Senorial** (Hamburgo 188, across the street from the Galeria Plaza), with its tunnel-like entrance and cavernous interior. Security is tight at Mexico's discos. At some of them, you'll be frisked as you enter. So, be prepared—leave anything questionable at the hotel!

SPORTS

Baseball

Mexico's baseball season runs from April through August. Two popular Mexico City teams, the Red Devils and the Tigers, compete at Parque de Seguro Social, located at Avenida Cuauhtemoc and Obrero Mundial, near the Medical Center. Check newspapers or your hotel concierge for weeknight and Sunday afternoon schedules.

Boating

From 8 A.M. to 4 P.M., you can rent boats and row around the lake in Chapultepec Park. The three rental stations, located at different points around the lake, are open from 8 A.M. to 4 P.M. daily except Monday.

Boxing and Wrestling

Matches are scheduled on Saturday nights at the Arena de México, located at Dr. Lucio and Dr. Lavista, and at Arena Coliseos, located at Peru 77, near Garibaldi Square. It's obvious that the cheering, jeering spectators love a good fight—sometimes enough to get into one themselves. The action starts at 9 P.M. Tickets are available at the gate. Check newspapers or your hotel concierge for current schedules.

Bullfights

Mexico City's Plaza México, located on Insurgentes Sur between Holbein and San Antonio in the south of the city, is the largest bullring in the world. On Sundays at 4:30 P.M., most of the fifty-thousand-plus seats are filled with spectators. The most important season for the *corrida* runs between December and March. Bullfights during other months tend to be with less famous matadors and less powerful bulls. You can purchase tickets for Plaza México at the gate or at Boletronico ticket booths, as well as through most hotels and tour agencies. Try to get seats in the shade. On Sundays, special buses marked "Plaza México" run along Insurgentes Sur and go directly to the bullring; in addition, buses marked "C.U." (Ciudad Universidad) pass Plaza México in their regular route.

Charreadas

These traditional Mexican rodeos are action-filled and full of local atmosphere. You'll see plenty of roping and riding, plus colorful costumes and lots of hoopla. There are two Mexico City venues: Rancho de la Villa, at the northernmost end of Avenida Insurgentes, and El Rancho de San Angel del Pedregal, in the south of the city. In the northern suburbs of Mexico City, you'll find *charreadas* at Rancho de Tlanepantla (near the *zócalo* in the town of Tlanepantla). Held on Sundays only, the actual action begins at noon and runs until 2 P.M., but the arenas are open from 9 A.M. Get there early, so you can see horses and soak up atmosphere. Tickets are sold at the gate.

Golf

Mexico City has two excellent golf courses: Deportivo Linda Vista and Club Banquero. Both are in the south of the city, and, unfortunately for foreign visitors, both belong to private clubs and are for the use of members only. The best way to gain entry is to get a member to sponsor you for the day. Of course, if you're completely new in town, that might be difficult. One alternative that is sometimes effective is to ask the pro at your club to contact the pro at a Mexico City club on your behalf. If that doesn't work, you're probably wise to leave your clubs at home. It's easier to gain access to the 18-hole course at Hacienda Cocoyoc, a resort near Cuernavaca and at least an hour's ride from Mexico City. Ask your hotel concierge to make arrangements.

Horseback Riding

There are several public stables in Mexico City's park areas, including Desierto de los Leónes and La Marquesa, located on the outskirts of the city, just off the highway to Toluca. The riding trails are pleasant, but horses aren't always available, and fees are very changeable. Your best bet for booking a ride is through your hotel concierge.

Horse Racing

During the season, from mid-October through the following mid-September (a total of 48 weeks), races are held daily (except Monday and Wednesday) at 2 P.M. at Mexico City's Hipodromo de las Americas. This beautiful track is located near Chapultepec Park, off Calzado Conscripto, in the north part of the city. Buses marked "Hipodromo" run along Reforma, and just before race time, there are special *peseros* heading directly to the race track. Drivers signal their destination by holding up their hands and "galloping" with their fingers as they drive along.

Jai Alai

Jai alai is a popular betting sport in Mexico, with gambling action almost as lively as the fast-moving ball game. It's fun to watch both at Frontón México, near the Plaza de la República, and the Monument to the Revolution. The game is Basque in origin, and somewhat resembles squash or handball. But in jai alai, the players use lightweight curved baskets, tied to their arms, to sling a small hard rubber ball at great velocity against the wall. It's fast and fascinating, especially during doubles matches. Bets are placed before the game begins. But there are bookies in the stands to watch the action, and as points are scored, they escalate the odds. At this point, they make bets by tossing around tennis balls with slits in which wagers have been secreted. It's boisterous and lots of fun. Games take place every evening, except Monday and Friday, at 6:30 P.M. Get tickets at Frontón México.

Jogging

Jogging is very popular in Mexico, and you see many runners sprinting up and down mountain roads around the city. There are also attractive and well-trafficked jogging paths in Chapultepec Park, but unless you're extremely fit, take it easy when running in Mexico. Doctors warn that Mexico City's pollution can be hazardous, and the high altitude does strange things to blood pressure and stamina. If you do jog, don't push it. You probably won't be able to do what you do at home.

Soccer

The Mexicans are almost fanatic about *fútbol,* and competitions are intense. Professional teams are tops, and the matches are fast-paced and exciting. See for yourself at Estadio Azteca, located near Calzado Tlalpan and Periférico Sur, in the south of the city. Games are held on Sundays and irregularly on weekdays, and it's best to check with your hotel concierge for current schedules. The arena has 105,000 seats, but try to reserve: Soccer is very popular, and seats are sold quickly.

Swimming

There are a number of public pools located throughout Mexico City, but these tend to be quite crowded. Other pools belong to private country clubs and are for use by members only. You'll have a tough time getting in, unless a friend or business acquaintance has a membership card. Best bet is to stick to your hotel pool. Many of the luxury hotels have pools reserved for use, without an additional fee, by guests. If you want to try a public pool, ask your hotel concierge for the nearest one.

Tennis

In general, public tennis courts are as crowded as public pools, and if you play on them, you have to bring your own net. Courts in country clubs are for the exclusive use of members. Many of the luxury hotels have one or several courts for guests' play, at no additional cost. Reserve as soon as you arrive in order to ensure yourself court time.

CITY LISTINGS

The following is a listing of the sights and shops discussed in this chapter, with addresses, phone numbers, and hours for easy reference. Keys refer to the page number of the color map insert and map coordinates at which the sight/establishment is located.

Churches

Basilica of the Virgin of Guadalupe   P. 13, 2D
Plaza Hidalgo; 577-9396

La Capilla del Pocito   P. 13, 2D
Bulevar B. Domínguez and L. Valle

Church of San Juan Bautista   P. 12, 5C
Avenida Hidalgo and Caballo Calco

Metropolitan Cathedral   P. 15, 3F
North side of the Zócalo, between calles Monte de Piedad, Guatemala, and
República de Argentina

El Sagrario   P. 15, 3F
Connected to the Metropolitan Cathedral

Museums and Galleries

Benito Juárez Museum   P. 15, 3F
In the National Palace, at Calle La Moneda, on the east side of the Zócalo;
522-5646; Mon.–Fri., 10 A.M.–7 P.M., Sat. and Sun., 10 A.M.–3 P.M.

Carillo Gil Museum   P. 12, 5C
Avenida Revolución 1608; 548-7467; Tues.–Sun. 11 A.M.–3 P.M., 4–7 P.M.

Convento del Carmen   P. 12, 4C
Avenida Revolución 4; daily 10 A.M.–5 P.M.

Diego Rivera Museum   P. 12, 5C
Calles del Museo 150; 677-2984; Tues.–Sun. 10 A.M.–6 P.M.

Frida Kahlo House and Museum   P. 12, 4C
Calle Londres 127 and Allende; 554-5999; Tues.–Sun. 10 A.M.–6 P.M.

Leon Trotsky House and Museum   P. 12, 4C
Viena 45; 554-4482; Tues.–Fri. 11 A.M.–4 P.M.

Ministry of Education   P. 15, 3F
República de Argentina 28; Mon.–Fri. 8 A.M.–7 P.M.

Museum of the City of Mexico   P. 15, 3F
Calle Pino Súarez, no. 30; 542-0487; Tues.–Sun. 9:30 A.M.–7:30 P.M.

Museum of Modern Art   P. 14, 4A
Paseo de la Reforma; 553-6211; Tues.–Sun. 10 A.M.–6 P.M.

National Museum of Anthropology   P. 14, 4A
Paseo de la Reforma; 553-6266; Tues.–Sat. 9 A.M.–7 P.M., Sun. 10 A.M.–6
P.M.

National Museum of History   P. 14, 4A
2da. Sección del Basque de Chapultepec; 555-6304; Tues.–Sun. 10 A.M.–5
P.M.

National Pawnshop   P. 15, 3F
Monte de Piedad 7 and 5 de Mayo

Palacio de las Bellas Artes   P. 15, 3E
Avenida Juárez and Lázaro Cárdenas; 526-7805

Pinacoteca Virreinal de San Diego   P. 15, 3E
Dr. Mora 7; 510-2793; Tues.–Sun. 9 A.M.–5 P.M.

San Carlos Museum   P. 15, 2D
Puente de Alvarado 50; 535-4848; Wed.–Mon. 10 A.M.–3 P.M., 4–7 P.M.

Siqueiros Polyforum   P. 12, 3C
Avenidas Insurgentes Sur and Filadelfia; 536-4254; daily 10 A.M.–2:30 P.M.,
3:30–9 P.M.

Tamayo Museum   P. 14, 4A
Paseo de la Reforma; Tues.–Sun. 10 A.M.–6 P.M.

Historic Sites
Casa Colorada   P. 12, 5C
Calle de Higuera 57

Casa de Hernán Cortés   P. 12, 5C

Chapultepec Castle   P. 14, 4A
Chapultepec Park

Monument de los Niños Héroes   P. 14, 4B
Chapultepec Park, near Chapultepec Castle

Monument to Mexican Independence   P. 14, 4C
Paseo de la Reforma at the intersection of Florencia

National Palace   P. 15, 3F
Calle La Moneda, on the east side of the Zócalo; 522-5646;
daily, 7 A.M.–7 P.M.

Pyramid of Cuicuilco
Near the Periférico (freeway), in the south of the city

Sanborn's House of Tiles   P. 15, 3F
Madero 4; 521-6058

Templo Mayor   P. 15, 3F
On Seminario, east of the Metropolitan Cathedral, near
the Zócalo; Tues.–Sun. 9 A.M.–5 P.M.

La Torre Latinoamerica   P. 15, 3E
Corner Avenida Juárez and Lázaro Cárdenas; daily
10 A.M.–midnight

Universidad Autónoma Nacional de México
C.D. Universitaria; 550-5215

Parks and Gardens
Alameda Park   P. 15, 3E
Corner Avenida Juárez and Dr. Mora

Chapultepec Park   P. 14, 4A
Bounded by Paseo de la Reforma and Avenida Constituventes

Desierto de los Leónes
Toluca Hwy. (MEX15)

Jardín Centenario   P. 12, 5C
Along with Plaza Hidalgo, bounded by calles Hidalgo,
Aquayo, and Caballo Colco

Plaza Hidalgo   P. 12, 5C

Plaza Garibaldi   P. 15, 2F
Avenida Lázaro Cárdenas and Avenida República de Honduras

Reino Aventura
Carretera Picacho Ajuso sin/nombre; 652-2231

Zoo (Parque Zoológico)   P. 14, 4A
Chapultepec Park, off Paseo de la Reforma; 277-7239

Shops
ACA Joe
Amberes 19;   P. 14, 4C
Avenida Presidente Mazarik, Nos. 310–318   P. 12, 3B

Antil   P. 14, 4C
  Florencia 22

Aries
  Amberes 24;   P. 14, 4C
  Florencia 14; Palmas 50   P. 12, 3B

Arte En Plata   P. 14, 4C
  Amberes 24

Artesca   P. 14, 4C
  Florencia 13

Art-Jonilla   P. 14, 4C
  Génova 39B

La Boutique   P. 14, 4C
  Génova 59F

Bye Mexico   P. 14, 4C
  Londres 106

La Casa de las Artesanias de Michoacán   P. 12, 3B
  Campos Elíseos and Temistocles

Los Castillos   P. 14, 4C
  Amberes 41

Centro Comercial Perisur   P. 12, 4C
  Periférico Sur 690

Centro de Antiquedades   P. 14, 4C
  Londres 161; Sat. 10 A.M.–6 P.M.

La Ciudadela Arts and Crafts Market   P. 15, 3E
  Balderas and Ayuntamiento; daily 11 A.M.–7 P.M.

Colleción de Felguras   P. 14, 4C
  Hamburgo 130A

Express   P. 12, 3B
  Avenida Presidente Mazarik No. 332 bis

Flamma   P. 14, 4C
  Hamburgo 177

FONART
  Avenida Juárez 89;   P. 15, 3E
  Londres 36;   P. 14, 4C
  Avenida de la Paz 37;
  Patriotismo 691

Furor Products   P. 12, 4C
  Hamburgo 118; Hamburgo 122

Gaitan   P. 14, 4C
  Copenhague 32   P. 14, 4C

Galería de Arte Misrachi   P. 14, 4C
  Génova 20

Galería Pecanins   P. 15, 4D
  Durango 186

Galería Sergio Bustamente   P. 14, 4C
  Amberes 14

Girasol
  Génova 19;   P. 14, 4C
  Avenida Presidente Mazarik No. 318 bis   P. 12, 3B

Gucci
Hamburgo 136;   P. 14, 4C
Paseo de la Reforma 325 (at the María Isabel Sheraton)   P. 14, 4C

Guess?
Amberes 17;   P. 14, 4C
Avenida Presidente Mazarik No. 326 bis   P. 12, 3B

Insurgentes Market   P. 14, 4C
Londres 154; daily 10 A.M.–7 P.M.

Keko   P. 12, 3B
Pasaje Polanco

Lagunilla   P. 15, 2F
Ecuador between Allende and Chile

Liverpool
Venustiano Carranza and 20 de Noviembre   P. 15, 3F
Centro Comercial Perisur;   P. 12, 4C
Horacio; Insurgentes Sur   P. 12, 3B

Michel Domit   P. 12, 3B
Pasaje Polanco

Muller's   P. 14, 4C
Florencia 52

Museo Nacional de Artes y Industrias Populares   P. 15, 3E
Avenida Juárez 44

Palacio de Hierro   P. 15, 3F
Venustiano Carranza and 20 de Noviembre

Paris Londres   P. 12, 4C
Avenida Insurgentes Sur 1235; 563-1211

Plaza Polanco   P. 12, 3B
Jaime Balmes 11

Plaza Satelite
CECO Plaza Satelite; 572-3640

Plaza Universidad
Avenida Universidad 1000

Regina Romero's   P. 12, 3B
Corner of Avenida Presidente Mazarik and Alejandro Dumas

Ruben Torres   P. 12, 3B
Avenida Presidente Mazarik No. 318 bis

San Angel's Bazar Sábado   P. 12, 4C
Plaza San Jacinto 11

San Juan Market   P. 15, 3E
Ayuntamiento and Arranda

Sanborn's   P. 15, 3F
Madero 4; 521-6058

Sears   P. 14, 3C
Montevideo 363; 586-4600

Sullivan Park Art Market   P. 12, 3B
Colonia San Rafael; Sun. 10 A.M.–4 P.M.

Tane
Avenida Presidente Mazarik and Edgar Allan Poe;   P. 14, 4C
Amberes 70   P. 14, 4C

EXCURSIONS

There is more than enough to keep anyone occupied in Mexico City for an indefinite amount of time, but at a certain point you might want to get away from the bustle of the city and see something else of this vast and varied country. A number of day or overnight excursions are available and are certainly of interest. Consider the following:

Teotihuacán

Teotihuacán, about thirty miles northeast of Mexico City, is one of the biggest and most important archaeological zones in the Americas. In fact, it's so important that volumes have been written about it, and almost everyone who visits Mexico City makes the hour-long trip by car, public bus, or guided tour to see its great pyramids.

The name Teotihuacán, meaning "Place Where Man Becomes a God" in the Aztec dialect of Nahuatl, was assigned to this place by the Aztecs. They did not build it, however. This city had been abandoned and was in ruins by the time the Aztecs took power in this region. The Aztecs thought this was a center with mythical importance belonging to a civilization of legendary proportions—thus the name.

Teotihuacán's original name is not known, nor is much known about the civilization that built and inhabited this place that was, in its day, the most influential religious, economic, and cultural center in Mesoamerica. At the height of its development Teotihuacán had two hundred thousand inhabitants and extensive intercultural and commercial dealings with civilizations as far away as Guatemala and Honduras.

The site of the ancient religious, economic, and cultural center of Teotihuacán covers about eight square miles. Excavations began here in 1864, and despite extensive digs in the area in the 1880s, 1920s, and from 1962 to the present, much of the city is still covered with dirt and grass or is in a state of ruin. The ruins of the major ceremonial temples, palaces, and pyramids are in a core section that's about two square miles in size. You'll do a lot of walking, so wear comfortable shoes and bring along sunscreen.

For convenience, a road, *carretera de circunvalación,* has been built around the site. There are several parking lots located near important structures. Most visitors enter at the southern end of the site, near a small **museum,** with exhibitions, maps, and models dealing with the site and its history. Directly across from the museum is the **Citadel,** a huge complex with a dozen buildings on three sides of a plaza area, and a pyramid on the fourth side. In this complex is the twice-built **Temple of Quetzalcoatl,** with 336 sculpted figures of feathered serpents and masks (assumed to be of Tlaloc, the rain god). It is assumed that the Citadel was used to house priests and dignitaries.

In front of the Citadel is the two-mile-long Miccaotli, or main street, known as the **Street of the Dead.** As you walk north along the Street of the Dead, you pass dozens of two-story buildings that were probably once topped by ceremonial temples. Some of the buildings have frescoes. On the right is a structure known as the **Priest's House,** and beyond it is the path to the **Pyramid of the Sun,** the second-largest pyramid in the Americas (after Cholula; see below), covering 720 by 740 square feet at its base and measuring 207 feet in height, with a volume of thirty-five million cubic feet. It is situated so that on the day of the summer solstice, the sun sets directly opposite its main facade. Anyone with enough stamina can climb the pyramid: A very steep stairway with several plateaus leads to the top. It's a big challenge, especially at this altitude (7,484 feet). Take your time. It's worth the effort—the view is spectacular.

Across from the Pyramid of the Sun are four small temples. To the right, as you continue north on the Street of the Dead, there is a wall with an impressive fresco of a jaguar that measures more than six feet in length. At the end of the Street of the Dead is the **Pyramid of the Moon,** covering a base of 460 feet by 490 feet, and measuring 152 feet in height. It too can be climbed to the top. Surrounding the Pyramid of the Moon is a plaza containing the **Jaguar Palace,** with wall paintings; a substructure known as the **Temple of Feathered Shells,** with bas-relief carvings of plumed conch shells; and the **Palace of the Quetzalpapalotl.** Also known as the Palace of the Quetzal Butterfly, this completely restored residence gives a good idea of what an important person's life in Teotihuacán must have been like. The rooms are filled with murals and carved columns. There's a drainage system, and interior courtyards provide for ventilation.

One can only imagine what this city was like during its heyday. All the buildings were then covered with stucco and painted with religious and ceremonial symbols. In addition to the large population, thousands of pilgrims and traders came here to worship and conduct business. Today you won't see any of that grandeur. The only people at the site are other curious tourists. But give yourself time to wander off and explore and to wonder about the extraordinary achievement known as Teotihuacán. For dramatic assistance in your wondering, there's a nightly (except during the rainy season, from July to September) sound-and-light show narrated in English at the pyramids at 7 and at 8:15 in Spanish.

CONNECTIONS AND TOURING

Frequently scheduled public buses for Pirámides-Teotihuacán leave Terminal Central del Norte (near the Terminal Autobuses del Norte Metro station). Return buses destined for México-Metro leave the ruins from near the museum. Special buses leave for the sound-and-light show. Check with your hotel concierge or local travel agent for special bus schedules and points of departure.

Most local tour companies offer guided day trips to Teotihuacán; some include stops at local craft shops, the 16th-century **Acolman Monastery** (about 8 miles from Teotihuacán), or the sound-and-light show. One of the best of these services is MTA (5-525-7520). You can also hire hotel-based taxis for the day trip to Teotihuacán. The drive by private car is fairly easy if you don't hit traffic. Take Insurgentes Norte to MEX85, a toll road, and follow the signs to Pirámides and MEX132. Take the toll roads to avoid traffic jams.

🧳 HOTELS

If you want to overnight in Teotihuacán the best place is **Club Med's Villa Arqueológica,** where a room for two with two twin beds and private shower costs $50 per night, double, excluding meals. Reserve at 800-CLUB-MED or 595-6-02-44, or take your chances on the spot. If you don't have a prepaid reservation, you'll have to pay cash, in pesos.

☕ RESTAURANTS

There are food stalls and several restaurants near the ruins, but you may prefer to bring a picnic lunch from your hotel. Or try **La Gruta Restaurant,** located a ways behind the Pyramid of the Sun. The food is Mexican and good, and the place is unusual. Some call it imaginative; others say it's touristy. What it is, is a cave. The average cost of a meal for two is about $30. Credit cards: AE, MC, V.

Cuernavaca

Perpetual springlike weather and temperatures that hover around 75 degrees Fahrenheit have made Cuernavaca a favorite Mexico City weekend retreat and one of the Mexican headquarters for the international retirement community. The city, capital of the state of Morelos, is about forty miles south of Mexico City on MEX95 (the road that continues on past Taxco to Acapulco).

From pre-Hispanic times to the present, this garden-like spot, sometimes referred to as the "City of Eternal Spring" or the "Garden City," has been a favorite vacation place. The Aztecs set up hunting preserves and used to winter in this place that they called Cuauhnahuac (the Nahuatl word meaning "beside the forest"). Apparently, the conquistadores heard that word as *Cuerna-de-vaca* (Spanish for "cow's horn"), which they shortened to Cuernavaca.

Cortés was given Cuernavaca as a fief by Charles V of Spain. In 1532, the conqueror built a mighty palace-fortress on the rubble of the once-mighty Aztec settlement and lived here for about six years toward the end of his stay in Mexico. During the 18th century, José de la Borda, the fabulously wealthy Taxco silver-mine magnate, built a splendid mansion in Cuernavaca, later used as a vacation getaway by Emperor Maximilian and Carlota during their short and troubled reign.

Today Cuernavaca is an industrial and commercial center. With a population of about four hundred thousand, it offers the advantages of city life in a rather relaxed atmosphere. Upper-class Mexican weekenders are joined in their enjoyment of Cuernavaca by international jet setters and well-to-do retirees. They inhabit palatial mansions discreetly tucked away behind high stucco walls. What day-trippers see of their lives is the ever-blooming bouquet of pink bougainvillea and violet jacaranda, perhaps peeking over the tops of the stucco walls—and that's about all.

PRIORITIES

But day-trippers can visit a wealth of worthy sights. Begin at the *zócalo,* really two adjacent plazas. Stroll around **Jardín Juárez,** take a seat on a filigree bench, and gaze at the bandstand designed by Louis Eiffel (of Eiffel Tower fame). There are public concerts presented here on Thursday and Sunday evenings. The **Jardín de los Heroes** (also known as the Plaza de Armas), the official *zócalo,* is where you'll find **Cortés's Palace.**

From the outside, the palace looks like a forbidding fortress, and you expect the interior to be dark and dingy. Surprise! Inside there are sweeping stairways and huge open rooms with high arches. Perhaps the airy quality is the product of reconstruction—the palace now houses the **Museum of Cuauhnahuac,** with a simply marvelous collection of colonial furniture, clothing, cooking utensils, carriages, arms, paintings, and personal accessories that give you a very good idea of what life in old Mexico must have been like. In addition, there is a fascinating display of photographs and documents having to do with the life and times of Emiliano Zapata, the revolutionary leader whose near-legendary exploits began with his birth in the environs of Cuernavaca. On the balcony, which provides a super panoramic view of Cuernavaca, is a famous Diego Rivera mural that depicts Mexican history from pre-Hispanic times to the Revolution of 1910. The mural was commissioned by Dwight Morrow, U.S. Ambassador to Mexico during the 1920s. The museum is open Tuesday through Sunday from 9:30 A.M. to 6 P.M. There is a small admission charge.

The **Cathedral de la Asunción,** built in the 1530s shortly after the conquest of Tenochtitlán, looks like a fortress. Located at the corner of Hidalgo and Morelos (three blocks away from Jardín de los Heroes, one of the only Mexican cathedrals not built in the *zócalo!*), it is stark and severe in style and definitely gives the impression that life in this land of eternal spring was not always a bed of roses. The cathedral has interesting frescoes depicting the sad story of some missionaries whose ship ran aground in Nagasaki and who were subsequently crucified.

The **Palacio Municipal,** nearby at Morelos and Callejon Borda, has murals depicting local history and showing how the Indians lived and worked from ancient to modern times. Most interesting are the scenes of Maximilian and his lover, la India Bonita (Margarita Leguisamo Sedano), and his court. There are also oil paintings of other local historical personalities. The building is open Monday through Friday from 9 A.M. to 2 P.M. and 4 to 6 P.M.

Jardín Borda, on Morelos and Hidalgo, was once the private park next to the mansion built by José de la Borda in the late 1700s, and later used by Emperor Maximilian. The park was neglected for years, but the garden is currently being reconstructed and is worth a look-see.

Actually, you can get more than an over-the-wall glimpse of Cuernavaca's fabulous private residences by taking a homes and gardens tour. These are irregularly scheduled, but usually occur on Thursdays. Ask your concierge or Mexico City travel agent about schedules, reservations, and fees.

A day trip to Cuernavaca will give you time to cover the basics, but there is plenty to do in town to hold your interest for longer periods of time. For one thing, Cuernavaca has excellent Spanish-language schools, offering intensive courses for those who wish to learn to *habla con los Mexicanos,* like a native. For a listing of recommended schools, contact the Mexican Government Tourism Office nearest you (see **Travel Arrangements,** below), or call the Mexican Student Program Coordination hotline at 800-558-9988.

CONNECTIONS

If you're driving, take Periférico Sur to MEX95, the toll *(cuota)* road that goes south, all the way to Acapulco. Get off at the Cuernavaca exit and follow the signs to the *zócalo.* The trip should take about an hour and a half, except on weekends when the traffic from Mexico City is often bumper to bumper. It's best to visit Cuernavaca Tues. through Thurs.

That's true even if you're leaving the driving to the bus operators. Along with its colonial charm, cobblestone streets, and beautiful old mansions, Cuernavaca has traffic jams, pollution, and the other urban maladies—especially on weekends.

The several bus lines that run between Mexico City and Cuernavaca, and on to Taxco and Acapulco beyond, use the Centro de Autobuses del Sur (next to the Tasquena Metro stop). First-class Estrella de Oro buses allow you to select your seat by computer, advisable if you're riding to Taxco or Acapulco, but unnecessary if you're making the short hop to Cuernavaca. Autobuses Pullman de Morelos isn't as high tech but has more frequent service to Cuernavaca, with buses leaving about every 15 minutes. The Pullman de Morelos downtown Cuernavaca terminal, El Centro (there's another terminal at La Selva, on the edge of town—you don't want it!), is at Abasolo and Netzahualcoyotl, within walking distance of the *zócalo*. The ride takes about an hour and costs several dollars.

Mexico City tour operators, including the reliable Mexico Travel Associates (MTA), have day or overnight tours, some with stops in Taxco and/or Acapulco. For current tour schedules, rates, and reservations contact MTA's Mexico City offices at Génova 30, in the Zona Rosa; tel. 5-525-7520. MTA tours may also be booked through most U.S. travel agents.

📖 HOTELS

Should you decide to stay in Cuernavaca for a few days, the town has several excellent hotels to accommodate you, including the following:

Cuernavaca Racquet Club

Francisco Villa 100, 62120
Tel. 73-13-61-22 or 800-228-5151

Run by the Calinda Quality chain, the Cuernavaca Racquet Club is a luxurious retreat with 36 charming villas and garden suites, all with their own living rooms, some with fireplaces. About three miles from the *zócalo,* the property is the former mansion of a Swedish millionaire and has a heated pool, sauna (men only), and nine tennis courts (tennis whites only), plus a clubhouse, restaurant, and disco. A double room for two persons costs about $90 and up per night. Credit cards: AE, DC.

Las Mañanitas

Linares 107, 62000
Tel. 73-12-46-46

This elegant, self-contained compound, behind a pretty pink wall, has 23 rooms and suites arranged around an interior courtyard and garden (with African storks, macaws, and pink flamingos!). It is the best, best-known, and most exclusive hotel in town. Within the compound, **Las Mañanitas Restaurant,** considered to be one of the best in all Mexico, has a living-room-like bar, elegant formal terrace, and umbrella-shaded garden tables. Lunch and dinner are served. The menu features sophisticated Mexican specialties and international standards—all prepared to perfection—and the wine list is superb. Rooms and restaurant are often fully booked, so reserve your place well in advance. Double rooms cost from $75 and up per night. The cost of a meal for two, including wine, averages about $80. No credit cards.

Hotel Palacio

Morrow 204 (near Matamoros), 62000
Tel. 73-12-05-53

The Palacio is another downtown Cuernavaca town house, vintage 19th century, converted into a small hotel. There are 16 comfortable rooms and a glass-covered courtyard that serves as a restaurant. It's charming, and the service is good. So is the price: A double room for two costs about $25 per night. Credit cards: MC, V.

Posada de Xochiquetzal

Leyva 200 (near Abasolo), 62000
Tel. 73-12-02-20

This lovely old town house in the heart of Cuernavaca has 14 charming rooms, a handsome courtyard garden with a pool and fountain, and restaurant and bar. The restaurant is open for breakfast, lunch, and dinner. Entrées include steaks, osso buco, and spareribs; meals cost about $15 per person. The hotel's location, just two blocks from Cortés's Palace, is convenient. A double room for two costs about $40 per night. Credit cards: MC, V.

■ RESTAURANTS

Try **Las Mañanitas** and **Posada de Xochiquetzal** (see **Hotels,** above), which are in a class by themselves. Otherwise, Cuernavaca has some fun and fine eateries, including the following:

La India Bonita

Morrow 6B, near Matamoros
Tel. 73-12-12-66

Named after the Cuernavaca mistress of Emperor Maximilian, La India Bonita's lunch and dinner menu offers appealing grilled steaks and mole *poblano* (chicken with a chocolate-based sauce), as well as lighter meals. This is a good morning eatery, especially for the big breakfaster who may enjoy—but not be able to finish—the "Maximiliano," a plate piled high with enchiladas and other victuals. Reasonably priced; a meal for two costs about $20. Credit cards: AE, MC, V.

La Parroquía

Guerrero 102, near Jardín Juárez
Tel. 73-12-54-00

Enchiladas and hummus, tacos and shish kebab, french fries and quesadillas. This crazily mixed menu works rather well in its casual open-air setting. Beer and wine. Pleasant service. A meal for two, including beer or wine, costs about $15. No credit cards.

Restaurante los Arcos
Jardín de los Héroes 4, on the *zócalo*
Tel. 73-12-44-86

Within view of Cortés's Palace, this open-all-day restaurant serves snacks and full meals, including the *menú del día,* a set-price lunch for about $6. Good, wholesome food, including steaks, shrimp, and chicken prepared as you like them, as well as quickie quesadillas for those on the run. The outdoor tables are best. A meal for two averages about $15. Credit cards: AE, MC, V.

Viena Cafetería
Guerrero 104, near Jardín Juárez
No telephone

Indulge in a feast of sweets at Viena, which has the best pastry, ice cream, and cappuccino in Cuernavaca, plus sandwiches and salads for the serious eaters. A nice place, too, to watch the world walk by. You have a front-row seat, all for the price of a snack—which costs about $5 or $6 per person. Open all day. No credit cards.

Taxco

Nestled high in the Sierra Madre in the state of Guerrero, Taxco is a charming old colonial mining town, with narrow, winding cobblestone streets that lead past panoramic views to shady plazas surrounded by splendid colonial buildings. During much of the year, bougainvillea blossoms cascade off balconies and past terraced gardens, creating a profusion of purples and pinks against the town's orange tile roofs. The entire town has been declared a national monument, protected by law from alteration and overdevelopment.

Taxco is a shopper's paradise, especially if silver is what is wanted. They say that 19 out of twenty doors in town lead to *platerías.* Perhaps that's an exaggeration, but Taxco boasts well over one hundred silver shops offering a vast array of jewelry, personal and home accessories, and other objects carefully handcrafted from the precious metal (see **Shopping,** below).

PRIORITIES

The town's real treasure is **Santa Prisca Church,** constructed in 1759 in the ornate Mexican churrigueresque style, with carved stone exterior and an interior of magnificent carved wood altars of figurines, foliage, and reduplicated molding—all completely coated with twenty-karat gold! Santa Prisca, an amazing piece of work, dominates the *zócalo,* **Plaza Borda.** The church was funded by José de la Borda, who owned Taxco's richest mine (and for whom the *zócalo* is

Taxco's silver industry predates the Conquest. Indians mined in these mountains long before the Spanish arrived. Hernán Cortés, following the natives' lead, founded Taxco as a mining base in 1522. The local yield of silver was so high that Taxco, due largely to silver extracted from the mountains of Mexico, became one of the colonial crossroads of Spain's economy. Taxco was also an important stop on trade routes for transporting luxury goods from the Orient to Europe via the Pacific Coast port of Acapulco, over land through Taxco and Mexico City, and across the Atlantic from the Gulf Coast's port of Veracruz.

By the 18th century, mining had made Taxco a very wealthy colonial community, and the trade route had provided wealthy mine owners with access to the luxuries they could afford. In fact, wealthy miners poured money back into the town, building lavish mansions and public buildings that turned Taxco into a colonial gem.

As the area's silver mines declined, so did Taxco's population and commerce. The town was more or less ignored for many years, but its colonial charm, though somewhat run down, was preserved more or less intact.

In the 1930s, Taxco's silver industry began to shine again, mostly because of the brilliant activities of William Spratling, an American silversmith. Spratling moved to Taxco, set up a workshop, and trained local craftsmen in advanced techniques of working silver. The Spratling studio used traditional Indian designs to make jewelry and created exquisite silver platters and serving sets with rosewood handles. News of Spratling's work spread to collectors around the world, and Taxco's silver industry was again on the world's treasure map—where it has remained to date.

named). This was his way of saying thanks for his good fortune.

The **Spratling Museum,** located just behind Santa Prisca Church, has exhibits depicting the silver industry in Taxco and displays Spratling's personal collection of pre-Columbian and silver objects. Open Tuesday through Saturday from 10 A.M. to 5 P.M. Small admission fee.

Behind the *zócalo,* on Plaza de los Gallos, is **Casa Figueroa,** known in colonial times as the House of Tears because Count Cadena, the magistrate, forced debtors to build his home. Go straight to the second floor, completely restored with Puebla tiles. Open Monday through Saturday from 9 A.M. to 1 P.M. and 3 to 7 P.M. $1.50 admission fee.

Casa Humboldt, on Calle Juan Ruiz de Alarcon, was built as an inn to accommodate traders en route between Acapulco and Mexico City. A beautiful building with obvious Moorish influence, it now houses a fine government-sponsored handicrafts shop named after Baron Alexander von Humboldt, the

German naturalist, who stayed here while he visited Taxco in 1803.

CONNECTIONS

Taxco is about 104 miles south of Mexico City. If you're driving, take Periférico Sur to MEX95, the toll *(cuota)* road to Cuernavaca, Taxco, and Acapulco. After passing Cuernavaca, take the toll road marked "Iguala/Acapulco." The trip to Taxco should take about three hours, depending upon traffic conditions.

Many bus lines travel between Mexico City's Centro de Autobuses del Sur (Calzada Tlalpan 2205; tel. 549-8520; Metro stop: Tasquena) and Taxco. The first-class Estrella de Oro is probably the best of these, and it has five buses daily to Taxco. The trip takes about three and a half hours. The bus will pick you up in Cuernavaca, if there are empty seats. From Estrella de Oro's Taxco terminal (Avenida JFK and Calle Pilita), you can get to the *zócalo* by taxi or collective vans that follow a set route from Avenida JFK via the aqueduct, Benito Juárez, the *zócalo,* Cuauhtemoc, San Juan Plaza, Hidalgo, San Miguel, and back to JFK. Stops along the route are called *paradas.*

State tourism offices with maps and other information are located at both ends of Avenida JFK (as you enter Taxco), and in Plazuela Bernal. Offices are open Mon. through Fri. from 9 A.M. to 2 P.M. and 5 to 7:30 P.M.

Many Mexico City travel companies offer guided tours of Taxco; some include stops in Cuernavaca and/or Acapulco (about 170 miles south of Taxco). One of the best and most reliable tour operators is Mexico Travel Associates (MTA), with day or overnight tours, some with stops in Cuernavaca or traveling on to Acapulco. For current tour schedules, rates, and reservations contact MTA's Mexico City offices at Génova 30, in the Zona Rosa; tel. 5-525-7520. MTA tours may also be booked through most U.S. travel agents.

🧳 HOTELS

Hotel los Arcos
Juan Ruiz de Alarcon 2, 40200
Tel. 732-218-36

Conveniently located in the center of town, this small hotel was a monastery once upon a time. The decor of the 26 comfortable rooms is cheery, if a bit worn. Local traffic and the hotel's lively disco can be distracting if you're sensitive to noise. Double, from $35. No credit cards.

Hacienda del Chorrillo
Calle Los Arcos 1 and Avenida Florida
Tel. 732-234-09

This charming small hotel with 15 rooms and suites, some with wonderful stone fireplaces, shares the beautiful grounds of a 16th-century hacienda with the interesting Instituto de Artes Plastico. Good restaurant, pleasant bar, and pool for diversion. A bit out of town, but the combivans described above begin their regular route nearby. Doubles, from $45. Credit cards: AE, MC, V.

Hotel Hacienda del Solar

Calle del Solar (two miles south of town, off MEX95), 40200
Tel. 732-203-23

This accommodating rancho has charming villas with comfortable living rooms, fireplaces, and great views. Swimming pool, tennis court, putting green, access to a nearby nine-hole golf course and bar with entertainment make this a self-contained resort. It is a restful retreat, but you do need a car to get to Taxco for sightseeing, shopping, or eating out. Doubles, with breakfast and lunch or dinner for both people, from $100 (meal plan usually required). Credit cards: MC, V.

Posada de la Misión

Avenida JFK 32, 40230
Tel. 732-200-63

This self-contained small resort has 150 comfortable rooms, swimming pool, whirlpool, tennis court, and an excellent restaurant. The hotel is located near the edge of town, on busy Avenida JFK. Be sure to request a room away from the road—for quiet, freedom from fumes, and a better view of the hotel's gardens and of Taxco. Double, from $50, including breakfast for two people. Credit cards: AE, MC, V.

Posada de los Castillos

Juan Ruiz de Alarcon 7, 40200
Tel. 732-213-96

This restored colonial mansion, with just 15 rooms, has the feel of a private home—quiet, peaceful, and accommodating. Room decor is unpretentious and comfortable; bathrooms have been completely modernized. Doubles, from $20. Credit cards: MC, V.

📖 RESTAURANTS

Celito Lindo

Plaza Borda 14, on the *zócalo*
Tel. 206-03

Clean, reliable, and usually crowded, this restaurant serves up Mexican standards, including good enchiladas, plus tender roast chicken and sandwiches. Open daily, 10 A.M.–10 P.M. (will stay open later if there are customers). A meal for two averages about $18. No credit cards.

La Pagaduria del Rey

Cerro de Bermeja
Tel. 234-67

Set in a lovely colonial building atop the hill that once yielded much silver for the Spanish crown, this restaurant offers fine dining on steaks, chops, seafood, and Mexican specialties—and the views are spectacular. Good wine list. Open 1–11 P.M. A meal for two, including wine, costs about $60. Credit cards: AE, MC, V.

Señor Costilla's

Plaza Borda 1, Second Floor, on the *zócalo*
Tel. 232-15

This is the Taxco edition of the Carlos Anderson chain of restaurants, with a circus-like ambience and fun-house decor. Ribs are the specialty, but the menu also offers fine fish and chicken entrées, plus excellent soups and Mexican specialties. Try to get a table on the balcony, overlooking the *zócalo* and away from the ever-present throb of rock music. Open 1–10 P.M. Average cost of a meal for two, including drinks, is about $40. Credit cards: AE, MC, V.

La Ventana de Taxco

Calle del Solar, two miles south of town, off MEX95
Tel. 205-87

A romantic, elegant hideaway with terrific panoramic views of beautiful Taxco. The menu is international with a charming Northern Italian accent. Fine wine list, with imported vintages on the pricey side. Open 1–11 P.M. The average cost of a meal for two, with wine, is about $70. No credit cards.

SHOPPING

Taxco's profusion of silver shops is confusing, especially because prices and quality vary on designs that look similar. The problem of choice is amplified by the fact that guides deliver tourists to shops that give them generous commissions, with commission costs generally passed along to the buyers.

Beware excessive bargains. Most shops are honest, but always make sure the items you've select have "sterling" or ".925" clearly stamped on them. Check workmanship to see that fastenings and hinges are well made and that there are no rough spots that might snag clothes. Prices in Taxco are not necessarily lower than they are in other Mexican cities where Taxco silver is sold, but there is greater variety.

Los Castillos (Plazuela de Bernal 10) invites shoppers into its workshops to see how the beautiful things that are sold in the shop are made. The shop is a shining sea of sterling, silverplate, and alpaca (nickel silver) objects. Los Castillos makes three-tone decorative items, such as mirror frames and cream and sugar sets, designed with a combination of silver, copper, and brass, and specializes in silver plaques and platters with cut out designs that have been filled in with colorful birds' feathers, and then coated with clear resins to prevent deterioration. Credit cards: AE, MC, V.

Several excellent silver shops are on the *zócalo:* **Pineda's** has fine jewelry and silver table service. The square-shaped, solid silver candlesticks are gorgeous. So is a domino set made of rosewood with silver dots. **El Mineral Joyeros** is designed to look like a mine, with jewelry displayed on huge hunks of rock crystals. The shop specializes in attractive work inlaid with turquoise, onyx, chrysoprase, lapis lazuli, and other semiprecious stones set into modern designs. Credit cards: AE, MC, V. **Sociedad Cooperativo Artesanal José de la Borda** (long name, tiny shop) has very unusual pieces. A remarkable purse-sized six-photo picture frame folds up into a ball! Credit cards: AE, MC, V. And **La Jaula** is a very good place to get belt buckles. Credit cards: AE, MC, V.

Ixtapan de la Sal

Ixtapan de la Sal is a small town that abounds in mineral hot springs and boasts Mexico's most famous health resort. In a landscaped setting of terraced gardens with statuary, pools, playgrounds, and jogging trails, the lavish 250-room **Hotel Ixtapan,** at Boulevard las Jacarandas and Diana Circle, offers guests regimented week-long weight-reduction programs combining low-calorie diet, rigorous physical exercise, massage, and beauty treatments. Guests may sign up for the complete package or participate on a treatment-by-treatment basis. Or they may stay overnight at the hotel and enjoy a good soak in the hot springs, have a facial, play tennis, and enjoy non-low-calorie meals from the dining room's regular menu. Organized evening entertainment includes film showings, concerts, and theatrical and nightclub performances. Rates for the Hotel Ixtapan are about $120 per person per night, including three meals. Credit cards: AE, MC, V.

The Hotel Ixtapan offers bus or limo transportation from its Mexico City offices at Paseo de la Reforma 132 (tel. 535-2553). Ixtapan de la Sal is about eighty miles southwest of Mexico City, on MEX55, the road that runs between Toluca and Taxco. If you're driving yourself, the easiest route from Mexico City is via the Toluca road, MEX15, to the MEX55 turnoff at La Marquesa, just before you reach Toluca. The drive takes about two hours.

Puebla and Cholula

Puebla **(see map, Page 505),** about eighty miles east of Mexico City, is capital of the state of Puebla. The city is the fourth largest in Mexico and an industrial center. About seven miles away is the provincial town of Cholula. In pre-Hispanic Mexico, Cholula was a major religious and economic center, with its greatest influence between the fall of Teotihuacán (about A.D. 750) and the rise of Tula (about 950). Legend has it that the god-king Quetzalcoatl stayed in Cholula after he left Tula and before he moved on to the Yucatán. Cholula is the site of the world's largest pyramid, now in ruins.

Puebla and Cholula are situated on a fertile high plain, ringed by mountains. The famous Popocatépetl, Iztaccihuatl, and La Malinche volcanoes are within view. Puebla was founded in 1531 (with the name "Ciudad de Los Angeles") by Franciscan missionaries. In 1539, it became a bishopric, and its name was changed to Puebla de los Angeles. Until the religious orders were expelled from Mexico, Puebla was an important church center, with more than one hundred churches. Many of these functioned secretly during Mexico's severe religious reform, and many are still active today.

Both Puebla and Cholula were important stops on the busy overland trade route from Acapulco, through Taxco, Mexico City, and east to Veracruz. However, Puebla eclipsed Cholula in influence, perhaps because of the plague that swept Cholula, or because Puebla was a more thoroughly Spanish town.

PUEBLA

Because of its strategic location, Puebla was often the scene of crucial battles, including the famous May 5, 1862, battle against the French, in which two thousand Mexicans defeated six thousand French troops. Streets throughout Mexico named 5 de Mayo commemorate this battle, as does a national holiday that is rigorously observed in Puebla.

For hundreds of years, Puebla has been known for ceramics, especially Talavera-style dishes and jars, and tiles, hand-painted in traditional blue, yellow, and white designs. Many of the town's colonial mansions are covered with colorful tiles—thus, the town's nickname, "City of Tiles."

Today Puebla's colonial charm is overshadowed by severe air pollution and traffic problems. A day's visit is very worthwhile, but you're probably better off moving on quickly, perhaps to look at Cholula, after you've seen Puebla's colonial treasures and other highlights.

PRIORITIES

Begin at the *zócalo,* with the 17th-century **cathedral,** the second largest in Mexico (after the Metropolitan Cathedral in Mexico City), known for its marvelous religious paintings. Nearby, at Calle 16 de Septiembre and Avenida 5 Oriente, is the **Palafox Library,** in the former Archbishop's Palace. The library, the oldest and one of the finest in the Americas, was assembled by Bishop Juan de Palafox y Mendoza in 1646 and contains more than 46,000 books, maps, and documents from 17th-century Mexico. Open Tuesday through Sunday from 10 A.M. to 5 P.M. Small admission fee. North of the *zócalo,* on Calle 5 de Mayo near Avenida 4 Poniente, is the Church of Santo Domingo, with the magnificent gilded interior of the 17th-century chapel, the **Capilla del Rosario.** Open daily from 7 A.M. to 1 P.M. and 3 to 7:30 P.M. The 17th-century **Convent of Santa Monica** (Calle 3 Norte and Avenida 18 Poniente) functioned secretly for about eighty years following

Mexico's Reform Laws of 1857, which made convents and monasteries illegal and gave the government the right to confiscate church properties. Somehow this convent escaped detection until 1934. Somehow? Perhaps it's because you enter the place through a cupboard in what looks like an ordinary residence. The convent is now a museum displaying documents as well as personal and religious articles found in three secret convents. Open Tuesday through Sunday from 10 A.M. to 5 P.M. Small admission fee. The former **Convent of Santa Rosa** (Calle 5 de Mayo and Avenida 14 Poniente) has a beautiful tiled kitchen where, it is said, the Dominican nuns invented the famous Puebla mole and other regional recipes. The convent now houses the **Museo de Artesanias,** with fabulous state of Puebla crafts exhibitions and a government-sponsored shop offering terrific tiles and ceramics.

Additional sources of Puebla tiles and ceramics are the local **azulejerías** (tile merchants), including **Casa Rugerio** (Avenida 18 Poniente 111) and **La Trinidad** (Avenida 20 Poniente 305). Another place to shop for crafts is **Mercado Parian** (Calle 6 Norte between avenidas 2 and 4 Poniente), a charming colonial arcade where you'll find thousands of onyx bowls, platters, boxes, tabletops, chess sets and trinkets, as well as other local craft items. Nearby, the Barrio del Artistas (Calle 8 Norte) has interesting paintings and sculptures by local artists.

Two marvelous old mansions have been converted to intriguing museums. The **Casa de Alfenique Museum** (Calle 6 Norte and Avenida 4 Oriente) is an 18th-century building with a gingerbread facade in the most elaborate Puebla architectural tile tradition. Inside, the museum displays period furniture, documents, and 19th-century historical photographs. Open Tuesday through Sunday from 10 A.M. to 5 P.M. Small admission fee. The **Bello Museum** is housed in a 19th-century private residence, the owner of which, Señor Bello, put together a great collection of 17th-, 18th-, and 19th-century fine and decorative art and antique furniture. Visitors to the museum must be accompanied by guides, most of whom speak Spanish only. Open from Tuesday through Sunday from 10 A.M. to 5 P.M. Small admission fee.

CONNECTIONS

There is frequent, first-class bus service between Mexico City and Puebla. The ADO (Autobuses de Oriente) line's buses leave from Terminal Oriente (near San Lazaro Metro stop), and the trip usually takes about two hours. Puebla is also easily accessible by car via two alternative routes. But traffic on these roads is so congested that you're much better off leaving the driving to the bus driver while you read a good book.

Perpetual traffic jams mean that walking is the best means of transportation around Puebla. The town is easy to walk, once you've got the somewhat confusing system of street names and numbers straight. Streets running east and west are *avenidas;* those running north and south are *calles.* The city is divided into quadrants by Avenida Reforma (which separates north and south, with even-numbered streets to the north and odd-numbered streets to the south) and Calle 16 de Septiembre adjoined to Calle 5 de Mayo (which separates east and west, with even-numbered streets to the east and odd-numbered streets to the west).

🧳 HOTELS

While Puebla is not exactly the resort center of Mexico, there are a couple of first-class establishments worth recommending. **El Mesón del Angel,** Hermanos Serdan number 807, 72000, tel. 22-48-21-00 and **Misión de Puebla,** 5 Pte. 2522 72160, tel. 22-48-96-00 both have decent rooms, restaurants and/or dining rooms on the premises, and sports facilities.

☕ RESTAURANTS

Another thing you must do in Puebla is eat. The regional cuisine is extraordinary. Most famous is mole *poblano,* the preparation of chicken, turkey, and enchiladas in a rich, thick, spicy dark brown sauce made from a blend of chocolate, chiles, nuts, seeds, spices, and herbs. Recipes vary—and are usually kept secret. The mole at **Fonda de Santa Clara** (across from the Bello Museum, at Avenida 3 Poniente 307; tel. 22-42-50-03) is fabulous. But don't hesitate to try some of the other Puebla delicacies, including *chiles en nogada* (chiles in walnut sauce), or the shredded pork with tomatoes, cheese, and avocado known as *tinga poblano.* Open noon–11 P.M. every day but Mon. The average price for a meal for two is about $20. Credit cards: AE, MC, V.

Restaurante del Parian (Calle 6 Norte and Avenida 2 Oriente; tel. 22-46-47-98) is another favorite for mole, and for ambience. The place is full of earthenware pots, old tiles, and carved wood moldings. The menu offers more than mole: other regional specialties include *pipián* (pumpkinseed) sauces and *adobos* (chile blend) sauces. Very tasty—sometimes very spicy. Open for lunch and dinner. The average price for a meal for two is about $20. No credit cards.

El Cortijo (Calle 16 de Septiembre near Avenida 7 Poniente; tel. 22-42-05-03) has mole on the menu, but specializes in Spanish cuisine and seafood. The restaurant, set in a colonial courtyard, is a charming escape from Puebla traffic. Open 1–6 P.M. The average price of a meal for two, with wine, is about $30. Credit cards: AE, MC, V.

If you want to stick to the tried and true, there's a modern **Sanborn's** (Avenida 2 Oriente 6; tel. 22-42-94-36), with reliable enchiladas and sandwiches. Open 7 A.M.–11 P.M. The average cost of a meal for two is about $20. Credit cards: AE, MC, V.

CHOLULA

To get to Cholula, take the public bus marked "Cholula" on the corner of Calle 7 Norte and Avenida 8 Poniente. The trip from Puebla takes about half an hour.

The great **pyramid** is still being explored and excavated. Most of it is covered by grass, and it looks like one of the surrounding hills. Its size is astonishing; the base covers 45 acres, its summit is 198 feet high, and it has a volume of about three million square meters. Climb to the top of the pyramid to see the **Iglesia de la Virgen de los Remedios** and get a spectacular overview of the entire valley below. You can enter the pyramid through a maze of tunnels and see several fascinating murals. Outside, on the south side of the pyramid, there are murals and carvings. There are local guides who will take you around the area. Some of their explanations are elaborations, but they'll help you to see the pyramid's important aspects.

Cholula itself is kind of dusty—not much to write home about, except for the churches. They say there's a church for every day of the year in this little town. Especially lovely are **Santa María Tonanzintla** and **San Francisco Acatepic.** On the outskirts of Cholula, these churches are easily reached by bus, and are exquisite gems of the colonial churrigueresque style of architecture.

▥ HOTELS

If you want to stay overnight in Cholula, the best place is **Club Med's Villa Arqueológica,** on the south side of the pyramid. A room for two with two twin beds and private shower costs about $50 per night, with breakfasts for an additional $4 and lunch or dinner for an additional $9. No credit cards accepted, and you must pay in pesos (unless you've prepaid in the United States in dollars). It's best to make reservations, and you can do so by calling 800-CLUB-MED or, in Cholula, 22-47-19-66.

6

VERACRUZ AND THE GULF COAST

Mexico's Gulf Coast stretches from the tip of Texas in the north to the Yucatán Peninsula in the south, and is bordered by four Mexican states: Tamaulipas, Veracruz, Tabasco, and Campeche (from north to south). Of these, Veracruz, Tabasco, and Campeche are of interest to tourists. (Campeche is covered in Chapter 11, **The Yucatán Peninsula.**)

The state of **Veracruz,** a long and relatively narrow strip of land that hugs the coast, is a wealthy and populous region with a varied landscape and diversified economy. Along the coast, Veracruz has long beaches backed by plantations cut out of jungle-like countryside. The climate is hot and humid (except during the occasional *nortes,* chilling winds that blow in from the sea). Inland, especially in the northern part of the state, the Sierra Madre Occidental creates plateaus where the weather is mild and mostly balmy. Farther inland, Orizaba Peak (18,700 feet) is the highest mountain in Mexico. Oil production, shipping, agriculture, and industry have made Veracruz the fourth-richest state in Mexico after the states of Mexico, Jalisco, and Nuevo León. The state's major cities are the **Port of Veracruz (see map, Page 507),** Mexico's principal port, and **Jalapa,** the state capital, which is inland. Other places of interest include **Papantla,** the center of Mexico's vanilla industry and home of the famous *voladores,* or pole dancers; **El Tajín,** a significant archaeologic site attributed to the Totonacs; and **Orizaba,** the city where most of Mexico's beer is brewed.

The state of **Tabasco,** south of and smaller than Veracruz, is mostly flatland covered by swamp, rain forests, and plantations for bananas, coconuts, coffee, cacao, and sugarcane. The state's capital, **Villahermosa,** is a boom town and center for

Mexico's oil industry. Of primary interest to travelers is the outdoor archaeological museum, La Venta.

The Gulf Coast area, and especially the Port of Veracruz, played a significant role in Mexican colonial and modern history, but even before the Spanish arrived, this region was an important center of civilization. In fact, many archaeologists believe this was the cradle of civilization in Mesoamerica. It was in the jungles and rain forests of the southern Gulf Coast, between Veracruz and Tabasco, amid an abundance of wildlife and profusion of year-round crops, that the Olmec culture began as early as 1200 B.C. and flourished until about 400 B.C. The Olmecs (the name means "people from the land of rubber" in Nahuatl, an Aztec dialect) built great cities and ceremonial centers, notably at San Lorenzo, La Venta, and Tres Zapotes. Their trade routes extended throughout Mesoamerica, and they had a glyphic script and numeric system that influenced development of subsequent Indian civilizations throughout Mesoamerica. Olmec theology included deities, such as the feathered serpent god Quetzalcoatl and the rain god Tlaloc, who were significant in later cultures. In fact, centuries later, after the power center in Mesoamerica had shifted from the Gulf Coast to Mexico's Central Highlands, the Aztec emperor Moctezuma thought Hernán Cortés might be the god-king Queztalcoatl returning, as prophesied by legend, from across the sea, and so he received the conqueror in friendship.

Port of Veracruz

It was near Veracruz, close to the heart of the ancient Olmec domain, that Cortés the conqueror landed in Mexico and established his first settlement. It was to this place, the birthplace of the ancient Mesoamerican civilizations, that Moctezuma sent his envoys to welcome Cortés and escort him to Tenochtitlán. And shortly thereafter, Cortés did, in very little time, what had taken centuries and the rise and fall of several civilizations for the Indians to do. The conqueror shifted his power base from Veracruz to Mexico City, which he founded as his capital on the rubble of the great Aztec capital that he had defeated and razed.

However, throughout the colonial period, Veracruz continued to be Mexico's principal port, the last stop on the overland trade route from Acapulco via Taxco, Mexico City, and Puebla, for silver and gold mined in the highlands and luxury goods being imported from the Orient. Veracruz was frequently attacked and ransacked by pirates, despite the protective presence of the mighty fortress of San Juan de Ulua, which had behind its impenetrable walls a customs house, warehouses, barracks, and a death-dealing dungeon for captured pirates, rebels, and, later, political dissenters. Perhaps it was because of the pirate threat, or because of the presence of malaria and other tropical diseases, that the population of Veracruz was never very large until modern times. But the Spanish presence in Veracruz was strong throughout colonial times. Veracruz is where the Spanish first entered Mexico, and it is where Spanish troops lowered their last flag before leaving Mexico after the country won independence.

The strategically located Port of Veracruz has been the principal depot for foreign goods entering Mexico, and customs duties on these goods have been a main source of revenue for the Mexican government. Consequently, foreign governments attempting to enforce payment of Mexico's debts have occupied Veracruz several times since Mexico won independence from Spain. In 1838 French troops took Veracruz to ensure payment of compensation to France. In 1847 U.S. troops took Veracruz during the war between the United States and Mexico. In 1864 Maximilian landed in Veracruz en route to Mexico City to become emperor, and, three years later, French troops left Mexico from Veracruz after the fall of the imperial government. In 1914 U.S. troops again occupied Veracruz.

Today Veracruz is a large and thriving port city, known for its very friendly population and exceptional cuisine. People come to Veracruz mostly to do business and to eat— especially if some of Mexico's best seafood prepared *a la veracruzana*—with rich and spicy tomato-based sauces—is in the offing. Veracruz also has a great café life, fascinating historical sights, pretty residential areas, fun shopping, marimba music, and typical dances, beaches, and some wonderful day trips too. This city welcomes visitors but isn't preoccupied by them. There's service with a smile, but people don't seem to trip over one another to get to your tip.

In Veracruz, daily life centers around the **zócalo** (here, Plaza de Armas), as it is in most Mexican cities. However, only the pretty *zócalo* in Veracruz has **Café la Parroquia** (see **Restaurants,** below).

Café la Parroquia is directly across the street from **La Parroquia** (the parish church), dedicated in 1743 and now named Catedral de Nuestra Señora de la Asunción. Nearby is the **Municipal Palace,** an attractive Moorish-style building that houses local government. The *zócalo* also has a kiosk where you can hear local marimba bands from 1 to 2 P.M. daily except Thursday and Sunday, when they play from 7 to 10 P.M. Surrounding the *zócalo* are **Los Portales,** a long covered arcade with a dozen or so popular bars and cafés that spill over into one another's domain. The Veracruzanos who hang out here call this place the world's longest bar, and they cruise from

one end to the other, stopping to visit friends at various tables
en route. A beer costs less than 50¢. Snacks and light meals
are also served.

Near the *zócalo* is the **Malecón** (the city's principal quay),
which provides a marvelous vantage point for viewing the active harbor. The modern high-rise overlooking the water is
the **Bank of Mexico** building, also called El Faro Nuevo
(New Lighthouse), which is one of several functioning light-
houses in Veracruz. Midway between the Malecón and the
Hotel Emporio is the **Venustiano Carranza Lighthouse,**
part of Naval Headquarters. Here you'll find the **Museo His-
tórico de la Revolución Venustiano Carranza,** with a
display of photographs and documents about Carranza's life
and times. The setting of the museum is perhaps as interesting as its contents. You actually go into Naval Headquarters,
past armed sailors, and must show some ID and sign a regis-
try. The museum is open Tuesday through Friday from 9 A.M.
to 1 P.M. and 4 to 6 P.M.; on Saturdays from 9 A.M. to 1 P.M.;
and on Sundays and holidays from 9 A.M. to noon. Admission
is free.

Across the water from the Malecón you can see thick stone
walls surrounding the island **Fortress of San Juan Ulua,**
one of the most interesting sights in Veracruz. It has an important and frightening history. To get to the fortress, drive
across a causeway and bridge from the northern end of the
Malecón. When you reach the island, continue past the docks.
Or you can take a bus from the corner of Lerdo and Landero
y Coss. The fortress is open Tuesday through Sunday from
9 A.M. to 5 P.M.

Construction of the fortress was begun in 1528 on a coral-
reef island. It is estimated that five hundred thousand slaves
of Indian and African descent died as they were used to level
the reef and cut the coral into huge blocks for building the
fortress. Today, you can see fossilized marine life in the original walls and the stone walkways. Initially the walls were covered with stucco made from sand, coral, and crushed turtle
eggs. The fortress was built to defend the Port of Veracruz
from pirates, and it wasn't always up to the task. In fact,
Chucho El Rato (a nickname for the infamous pirate Jesus Arriaga) sacked Veracruz three times. But within the fortress's
protective walls a number of warehouses were constructed
to keep safe large deposits of gold, silver, and other treasures
awaiting export to Spain. The arched warehouses were also
constructed of the coral stone, which is porous and conducts
moisture in such a way that today, after years of disuse, the
ceilings of the warehouses are covered with stalactites.

The same porous stone was also used to build a terrifying
dungeon. It is actually on another island, where the Spanish
had their arsenal; you cross to it on a bridge called the Last
Breath, so named because only very rarely did prisoners

make it back over that bridge alive. Prisoners in those days were kept in the dark, many were chained tightly to the wall, and the porous stone would allow water to drip regularly on their heads. In addition, during periods of high tide, the dungeon would fill with water and some prisoners would drown. Since the dungeon was first used by the Holy Inquisition in 1755, many important Mexicans have been locked up in it. Among the most famous—and among those who made it out alive—were Santana and Benito Juárez (the latter was incarcerated here for 11 days in 1853). And Porfirio Díaz imprisoned dissenting journalists and labor leaders in the dungeon. When, however, U.S. invading forces took Veracruz in 1914 and set free the prisoners of San Juan Ulua, the prisoners attacked the Americans in defense of the fortress. Following that, the Mexican government freed all the prisoners in San Juan Ulua and declared that the fortress could not be used again as a prison for one hundred years—until 2015. What happens then remains to be seen.

The fortress has a customs house and a residence that was occupied by governors of the island and by various Mexican leaders, including Benito Juárez, Porfirio Díaz, and Venustiano Carranza.

From the fortress's high lookout points you have a splendid view of Veracruz, especially of the docks that Porfirio Díaz ordered built in 1902 by the Pierson Company, an American firm. You can also see nearby **Isla de Sacrificios,** where the Spanish conquerors supposedly witnessed human sacrifices. Today, there is a popular beach on the island. You can get there by boats that leave from in front of the Hotel Emporio.

Back in Veracruz, on the corner of 16 de Septiembre and Rayón, the **Baluarte,** or **Fort of Santiago,** built in 1636, is all that remains of a fortified wall that encircled the city. Inside is a small museum with a limited collection of antique arms and other relics from early colonial days. The museum is open Tuesday through Sunday from 10 A.M. to 1 P.M. and 4 to 7 P.M.

The 16th-century **Church of Santo Cristo del Buen Viaje,** a simple and beautiful white building on the Plaza Gutierrez Zamora, is said to be the oldest church in Mexico.

The **Museo de Arte e Historia Veracruzana** (the city museum), at Zaragoza 397, exhibits artifacts from the important pre-Hispanic cultures in the state of Veracruz, including the Olmec (southern part of the state), Totonac (central part of the state), and Huasteca (northern part of the state). Other exhibitions include regional costumes and crafts. The museum occupies a lovely building, constructed during the 1860s as an orphanage, surrounded by a pretty courtyard and gardens. The museum is open Tuesday through Sunday from 10 A.M. to 6 P.M. Admission is free.

The biggest market in town is the **Mercado de Hidalgo** at Cortés and Hidalgo, where hundreds of stalls sell fresh fruit and vegetables, meats and other foodstuffs, clothing and household goods, and some handicrafts, including Panama hats and all sorts of items made out of sea shells. Veracruz's biggest shopping street is **Avenida Independencia,** with the choicest boutiques and best gift shops in town.

In addition to the sandy strip on Isla de Sacrificios, Veracruz has several popular beaches. In town, Avenida Avila Camacho (the southern extension of the Malecón) is fronted by a long beach called **Villa del Mar.** This strip is especially busy in the morning and evening when joggers crisscross the light brown sand, and in the afternoon when ball players kick around a soccer ball. Swimmers find the water pleasantly calm, although it is shallow in some places. Farther south, about six miles from the center of town, is **Mocambo,** considered to be the prettiest beach in the area. You'll find amenities, including beach chairs for rent, food and drink vendors, and musicians, plus the pretty Mocambo Beach Hotel (see **Hotels,** below).

CONNECTIONS

Mexicana Airlines has several flights daily from Mexico City to Veracruz. Aerotur, a regional airline, operates small planes between Veracruz and Villahermosa and between Veracruz and Mérida. The airport is about 5 miles from town. Transportación Terrestre operates taxis and combis to all areas of Veracruz. For about $7, the combis will take you to your hotel. Combis are also available to take you back to the airport. Have your hotel concierge call at least 24 hours before your scheduled departure to arrange for you to be picked up to go back to the airport.

First-class train service between Mexico City and Veracruz is excellent; Mexico's national train system, the Ferrocariles Nacionales de México, offers the Servicio Estrella de Pasajeros. The overnight train leaves Mexico City at 9:15 P.M. and arrives in Veracruz the following morning at 7 A.M., with stops in Orizaba (4:05 A.M.), Fortín de las Flores (4:35 A.M.), and Córdoba (4:55 A.M.). Single and double sleeperettes are available. The train has a pleasant dining car, and both dinner and breakfast are included in the price of the train ticket. One-way tickets from Mexico City to Veracruz cost from about $9 (regular first class) to $25 (double sleeperette). Return trains leave Veracruz at 9:30 P.M. and arrive in Mexico City the following morning at 7:40 A.M., after stopping at Córdoba (11:45 P.M.), Fortín de las Flores (midnight), and Orizaba (12:35 A.M.). Reserved seating only. If you're interested, call 5-547-5819 or 5-547-3190 from Mexico City, 29-32-25-69 from Veracruz.

Buses connect Veracruz to most other cities in Mexico. There are several buses daily to and from Mexico City, three to and from Mérida, and one night bus to and from Oaxaca. You can also get to Veracruz from Northern Mexico—and back again—

by bus. The ADO line operates most of the first-class buses in the area, and the fares are quite inexpensive.

Roads between Mexico City and Veracruz are quite good, and driving yourself allows you to vary your route to cover sights of particular interest. The most direct route takes at least six or seven hours, depending upon the amount of traffic you encounter leaving or entering Mexico City and around Puebla. From Mexico City, take Frey Servando Meir to Zaragoza to MEX190 to Puebla. At Puebla, you can take MEX150 (take the toll, or *cuota,* road) via Fortín de Las Flores and the Orizaba Pass (this is a heavy truck route, and traffic is frequently backed up for miles) to MEX180, and on to Veracruz. The alternate route is to take MEX190 from Puebla via Jalapa to MEX140 to Veracruz.

Having a car in Veracruz is great for getting around and especially for getting out of town on day trips (see **Excursions,** below). Traffic is not unduly congested, and it isn't impossible to find a parking place. If you're planning to rent a car upon arriving in Veracruz by plane or train, National (tel. 29-31-17-56), among other rental companies, has offices conveniently located at the airport and in town. Remember that you save money on rates and get free mileage if you book in advance in the United States.

But you really don't need a car to get around Veracruz. There are plenty of taxis, and public transportation is reliable. Regular bus routes take you to and from the *zócalo,* the beaches, the Fortress of San Juan Ulua, and other places of interest.

🧳 HOTELS

Most of the hotels in Veracruz are small and independent. Many have long-term patrons who stay for months while they're working or otherwise doing business in Veracruz. In general, you'll find a high standard of service in the following:

Hotel Baluarte
Canal 265 (at 16 de Septiembre), 91700
Tel. 29-36-08-44
Doubles, from $35

This five-story hotel is modern, clean, inexpensive, and well located—near the Fort of Santiago and a ten-minute walk from the *zócalo.* The hotel's 73 rooms are comfortable and air-conditioned. The on-premises restaurant serves only breakfasts and light meals. No credit cards.

Hotel Colonial
Miguel Lerdo 117, 91700
Tel. 29-32-01-97
Doubles, from $45

The Colonial is ideally located on the *zócalo.* The hotel's style is, needless to say, colonial, but the 180 rooms have been modernized. Most have air-conditioning, but some are still cooled with ceiling fans. The heated indoor pool is especially useful during the chilling *nortes,* and the sidewalk café/bar is popular. Credit cards: CB, MC, V.

Hotel Emporio
Paseo de Malecón, 91700
Tel. 29-32-75-20 or 29-32-00-20
Doubles, from $65

This recently remodeled hotel is right on the Malecón, and some of the 207 spacious rooms have nice views plus color TV with cable channels. The Emporio's elaborate terraced recreation area, with several outdoor pools and a heated indoor pool, makes you forget you're in the heart of a big city. In addition, the lobby bar is **Tilingo Charlie's,** part of the Carlos Anderson group and a very popular hangout for the young and affluent of Veracruz. Credit cards: AE, MC, V.

Hotel Hostal de Cortés
Bulevar Avila Camacho (corner of Las Casas), 91910
Tel. 29-32-00-66
Doubles, from $70

This pleasant six-story hotel faces the sea, and many of the 103 rooms have small balconies and views of the ocean and a beach (across from the hotel) that's popular with joggers. The spacious lobby has comfortable sofas and lots of potted palms. The rooms are small but comfortable: All have color TV with cable channels, as well as servibars. The pleasant and reliable staff is very helpful with traveler's tips and directions to various sights in Veracruz. A restaurant, coffee bar, and very pleasant pool and patio area are also on the premises. Credit cards: AE, CB, DC.

Hotel Mocambo
Apdo. Postal 263, Boca del Río, 94260
Tel. 29-37-17-10
Doubles, from $65

This old-fashioned and pleasant ninety-room resort hotel is on Mocambo Beach just outside of town. It's away from the sights and sounds of Veracruz, but there is public transportation to get you into the *zócalo* or to the Malecón. The building is surrounded by gardens, and a terraced walkway leads down to the beach. All rooms are air-conditioned; many have been recently refurbished, but some are a bit run-down. The Mocambo also offers a restaurant and bar, pool, and tennis court. Credit cards: AE, CB, DC.

Hotel Playa Paraiso
Km. 3.5, Bulevar Veracruz Mocambo, Boca del Río, 94290
Tel. 29-37-83-99
Doubles, from $85

Located on the beach south of Veracruz, this modern *casita*-style resort hotel has 56 one- or two-bedroom suites, and is a good place for family vacations. The grounds have a pool and tennis court, plus a restaurant and bar. Credit cards: AE, DC, V.

Hotel Prendes
Independencia and Lerdo, 97000
Tel. 29-31-03-66

Doubles, from $50

In the heart of Veracruz, on the *zócalo*, the Prendes is a small hotel with a tiled lobby and 34 recently refurbished colonial-style rooms with louvered French doors and small balconies. The hotel's restaurant is very popular, and its location can't be beat. Outside rooms can be a bit noisy, though. Credit cards: AE, V.

🍵 RESTAURANTS

Veracruz, one of Mexico's gourmet capitals, has its very own style of cuisine, and you can sample it in dozens of fine eateries (in fact, in just about every restaurant, fancy or family-style) in the city. Seafood and fish predominate, but menus offer meat and chicken dishes too. *A la veracruzana,* the term frequently applied to the Veracruz style of preparing food, most often refers to a thick and spicy tomato-based sauce with onions, capers, olives, garlic, and dozens of herbs and spices. Veracruz-style cooking frequently stuffs, broils, and steams fish. Additional favorites are shrimp soup and *chipachole* crabs, made with a fiery tomato-based sauce. In Veracruz, precious family or restaurant recipes are kept secret and handed down from generation to generation. These restaurants allow you to savor the special flavor of Veracruz:

Café de la Parroquia
Independencia 106–107, off the *zócalo*
No telephone

This is where local politicians and businesspeople have their power breakfasts and power lunches. The outdoor tables are usually full, and you're considered lucky if you can even find a seat in the white-tiled interior. This coffeehouse serves its own blend of strong freshly brewed java with a pitcher of steamed milk on the side: You mix the two to your taste. It's delicious, and so is the cappuccino. Light meals and snacks are also served. Open daily 7 A.M.–midnight. Coffee costs about $.50; snacks are about $2 and up. No reservations. No credit cards.

El Chato Moyo
Landero y Coss 142, near Insurgentes Veracruzanos
Tel. 29-22-50-78

This restaurant, with fine food and pleasant ambience, allows you to sit on the outside dining terrace and watch the world parade by as you dine on fresh fish or seafood, prepared *a la veracruzana* or simply grilled. The seafood cocktails—shrimp, octopus, and oyster—are exceptionally fresh and delicious. Open 11 A.M.–7 P.M. Fish dishes are priced by weight, and the average cost of a meal for two is about $20. No reservations. No credit cards.

Garlic's
Bulevar Avila Camacho (no number)
Tel. 29-35-10-34

Garlic's ocean-view location on Avila Camacho, toward Mocambo, is a real asset. This spot is easy to get to—yet away from the bustle of downtown. Even more appealing, Garlic's has great seafood. Red snapper and shrimp top the menu—and they can be prepared in dozens of ways. Another specialty is paella, here a satisfying and rich mixture of shrimp, crab, oysters, snails, fish, and chicken. The wine list has domestic and imported labels. Open 1 P.M.–1 A.M. The average cost of a meal for two, including wine, is about $30. Reservations suggested. Credit cards: AE, DC, MC, V.

Lorencillo's

Paseo del Malecón and Bulevar Avila Camacho
Tel. 29-32-53-55

Lorencillo's is one of the more elegant restaurants in Veracruz, a place to celebrate special occasions. A pretty ocean view is a backdrop to the fine service and excellent food. The menu offers a nice variety of steaks, chops, chicken, and seafood and fish dishes. The wine list has both domestic and imported labels and is on the pricey side. Open 1–11 P.M. The average cost of a meal for two, including wine, is about $45. Reservations suggested. Credit cards: AE, MC, V.

La Paella

Zamora 138
Tel. 29-32-03-22

The facade of this restaurant is completely colonial in style, and the menu is almost purely Spanish. Specialties include delicious paella *valenciana,* sea bass prepared the Basque way, and *caldo gallego,* a lovely fish soup. For lunch, the daily special five-course meal costs about $9–$10 and includes a glass of domestic wine. No reservations. No credit cards.

Paraiso del Mar

Gomez Farias 37
No telephone

This is a simply decorated, moderately priced, and reliable seafood restaurant with typical Veracruz-style cooking. It's conveniently located near the Malecón and is a real favorite with Veracruzanos in the know. Open 11 A.M.–11 P.M. The average cost of a meal for two is about $20. No reservations. Credit cards: AE, MC, V.

El Pescador

Zaragoza 335
Tel. 29-32-52-52

El Pescador is bound to delight seagoers—and seafood lovers. The restaurant is decorated with all sorts of ocean paraphernalia and knickknacks—full-rigged sailing ships in miniature, shark's jaws, turtle shells, anchors, and more. The menu has everything from shrimp cocktail to turtle stew, and a very extensive selection of fish dishes. Open daily 10 A.M.–7 P.M. The average cost of a meal for two is about $25. No reservations. Credit cards: AE, MC, V.

Tilingo Charlie's

Hotel Emporio
Paseo de Malecón
Tel. 29-32-75-20 or 29-32-00-20

This, the Veracruz edition of the ever-popular Carlos Anderson chain of fun and fashionable eateries, with kibitzing waiters, rock music, and amusing decor, is where the young and chic of Veracruz amuse themselves. The menu features barbecued ribs, hamburgers, and various seafood dishes, as well as good salads and soups. A bar and nice wine list complete the picture. Open 1 P.M.–midnight. The average cost of a meal for two, including wine, is about $45. Reservations suggested. Credit cards: MC, V.

EXCURSIONS

While the Port of Veracruz has some interesting historical sights, terrific restaurants, and a generally pleasant ambience for ambling about, your visit will be very much enhanced by a day trip to one or several nearby sites of charm and interest, including quaint fishing villages, sleepy little pueblos, ancient ruins, and the colonial capital of the state. The following are sure to intrigue and to please:

BOCA DEL RÍO AND TLACOTALPAN

On the eastern outskirts of Veracruz, **Boca del Río** is located on the banks of the Jamapa River as it flows into the gulf. The town has been growing so rapidly that it was recently given city status. But it still has the look and feel of a little town, and a charming one at that. Veracruzanos make regular journeys to Boca del Río to eat, and with good reason. There are charming restaurants that serve very fresh and finely prepared seafood, and prices in Boca del Río are about one-third of what they are in Veracruz. This is the place to stop for lunch en route to or from Tlacotalpan.

The best of all Boca del Río's eateries is **Boulevard,** with a lovely terrace dining area overlooking the river. Boulevard is the three Bs—*bueno* (good); *barato* (inexpensive); and *bonito* (pretty). Specialties include *caldo de pescado* (fish soup); *pulpos a la veracruzana* (octopus in a spicy tomato-based sauce); and *jaibas rellenos* (stuffed crabs). The seafood is superb, but you can order steaks and chicken dishes, too. Try some *Torito,* a locally blended peanut crème liquor. Open daily from 11 A.M.–7 P.M. No reservations. No credit cards. The average cost of a meal for two is about $20. Two other popular Boca del Río seafood restaurants are **Restaurante Pardinos** and **Las Brisas del Mar.** Menus and prices are similar to those at Boulevard, and both restaurants have charm, but neither has that delightful outdoor terrace overlooking the water.

On the way to Tlacotalpan, you pass **Alvarado,** a town that's famous for catching and preparing shrimp. Stop for a sample, or just enjoy watching the parade of shrimp boats sailing in and out of this marvelous little harbor.

Tlacotalpan, a delightful old-fashioned town on the banks of the Papaloapan (meaning Butterflies) River, is about fifty miles southeast of Veracruz in an area of rolling plains with pineapple and sugarcane plantations. This is gentle, slow-paced bayou country—and it is gorgeous! The town itself looks like a movie set of old Mexico. It was built during colonial days by wealthy Veracruzanos seeking refuge from pirate attacks on the port or escape from unhealthy, steamy seaside weather.

There are two interesting and contrasting churches of colonial vintage here. The **Santuario de la Virgin de la Candélaria** is an exceptionally beautiful, and quite cheerful, church. The entire interior is covered with baroque and Moorish patterns, painted in pink, blue, and gold. The **Parroquia** is more austere, with white walls and an impressive wooden altar. The **San José Pharmacy,** at Carranza 4, is one hundred years old and has, thank goodness, avoided modernization. The old wooden cases are lined with antique glass bottles and vials, some with their original contents. This drugstore has been run by the same family for four generations. Buy a pack of gum or some aspirin just to do some business here. You'll enjoy the experience.

Parque Zaragoza has an English garden with a 19th-century gazebo and lots of filigree benches to sit down on. The nearby **Museo Salvador Ferrando,** at Parque Zaragoza's Capilla de Candelaria, has a remarkable collection of antiquities assembled in a colonial chapel built in 1779. Salvador Ferrando (1830–1906) was a noted portrait painter, and the canvases displayed here depict his family, Benito Juárez, and Porfirio Díaz. The building is decorated with 19th-century furniture, and from it you get a good idea of what life might have been like in this sleepy little town way back when. You will find a bedroom with a huge armoire, a wooden baby cradle, and a four-poster bed with a lace canopy above and a bedpan below. Another room has antique machinery; there are also antique violins and guitars, artifacts found in nearby archaeological zones, tiled bathtubs, old photos, and more. The museum caretaker is a delightful and knowledgeable gentleman whose anecdotes are sure to entertain. Tlacotalpan was the birthplace of Augustin Lara, and the **Bar/Museum Augustin Lara** celebrates this famous poet and local hero with photos, thematic graffiti, paintings—and good, cold beer.

Walk down to the riverfront, along Avenida Carranza, and at number 11 you'll find **Posada Dona Lala** (tel. 29-34-25-80), the best restaurant and hotel in town. Dona Lala offers fresh fish and seafood, prepared to your taste. An average meal for two, with wine, is about $25. The hotel rooms are charming and varied: Some are suites; some have three beds; and number 113 has the best view overlooking the river. An air-conditioned room with a servibar, TV, and two beds costs $30 per night. Credit cards: AE, MC, V. A few doors down Avenida Carranza is **Restaurante la Flecha,** another good family-style seafood restaurant, and across the road, on the banks of the river, you'll find a dozen or so small shack-housed restaurants selling fresh fish and seafood.

By the way, don't expect the citizens of Tlacotalpan to direct you to an address in their town. They'll show you where restaurants, museums, and churches are located, but most often they don't know the street number or even the street name. It's all part of the innocent small-town charm here. Tlacotalpan is very small and very naive.

PAPANTLA AND EL TAJÍN

In the heart of Mexico's vanilla country, about 150 miles from Veracruz, the provincial town of **Papantla** is best known as the home of the daring and death-defying **voladores,** or pole dancers, who perform an ancient Totonac Indian ritual. A team of five male dancers climbs to the top of a high pole. Four of the dancers, representing the four directions of the universe, tie ropes to their ankles and dive downward, arcing around the pole, supposedly 13 times, and eventually landing on the ground on their feet. The fifth dancer, usually the leader of the team and representing the fifth direction of the universe (the center), balances on top of the pole while he stamps his feet on a small drum and plays a flute. Nobody knows the original significance or meaning of this ritual, but it is one of the few ancient rites that were not forbidden by the conquerors. It is assumed that the Spanish thought the dance was merely sport rather than religion, and so allowed the practice to continue. Actually *voladores* are hired to perform the ritual as a tourist entertainment in Acapulco and other resorts, but this is where the custom originated and this is where it continues in its purest form. The *voladores* used to perform only on Corpus Christi Day (sometime in May or June), but the ceremony is currently enacted in Papantla every Sunday evening at 8 P.M. in the churchyard, and often at the entrance to the nearby ruins of El Tajín, again on Sunday, at 11 A.M. and 3 P.M.

Other than the *voladores,* vanilla extract and beans shaped into crucifixes or scorpions by local craftspeople, and some dusty colonial architecture, Papantla has little to offer tourists. But it is an excellent base for a visit to the archaeological zone at **El Tajín,** located about ten miles from town.

For many years, archaeologists attributed the construction of El Tajín to the Totonacs who lived around the ceremonial center when the Spanish arrived on the Gulf Coast. However, recent finds indicate that the ruins had probably been built by the Olmecs or Maya, with significant influences from other ancient civilizations during the fourth or fifth century, and abandoned during the 12th century, after which the Totonacs moved into the area. By the time the Spanish arrived, the Totonacs were under the influence of and had to pay tribute to the Aztecs. The Totonacs allied themselves with Cortés in his battle for Tenochtitlán.

El Tajín was ignored after the Conquest. More than 250 years had elapsed before the first Spaniard (Diego Ruíz) visited the site in 1785. In 1811 Alexander von Humboldt visited and made valuable notes about El Tajín, but excavations weren't begun until 1934. To date only about one-tenth of the site's thirty acres has been uncovered.

Most famous and important at El Tajín is the **Pyramid of the Niches,** built between the sixth and seventh centuries. This unusual structure has 365 (one for each day of the year) shallow square niches evenly spaced around all seven levels (including the temple on the top) of the pyramid. The niches are framed by protruding stone slabs. Originally, the pyramid was covered with stucco, and it is thought that these niches were painted brilliant colors to create a dramatic effect of light and shadow. In the front of the pyramid is an extremely steep staircase that's about 33 feet wide and has five groups of three smaller niches built into it at regular intervals. The staircase is bordered by a balustrade carved with irregular mosaic patterns.

The fascinating **Building of the Columns,** in the Plaza of El Tajín Chico, also has niches and staircases, both of which were apparently purely decorative. There is evidence that ladders were used to get to the upper levels of the building. There was a gallery that ran along the front of the building, but only sections of the supporting columns are left. These are covered with bas-reliefs showing scenes of war and religious ceremonies, including human sacrifice.

More bas-reliefs with sacrificial themes are found in the **North** and **South Ball Courts.** Archaeologists believe that El Tajín was a center for the ball-game ritual, which apparently originated along the Gulf Coast and spread to other civilizations throughout Mesoamerica.

There is a small museum at El Tajín with parts of columns from the Building of the Columns and sculptures retrieved from the Pyramid of the Niches. The artifacts aren't beautifully displayed, but they are fascinating.

The trip to Papantla from Veracruz takes about three and a half hours, and you can either drive or take the bus. The route follows coastal road MEX180, going northwest toward Poza Rica. Just past the Tecolutla Bridge MEX180 veers inland and uphill to Papantla. If you drive, keep a constant lookout for unmarked *topes* (speed bumps), especially as you enter and leave the many small towns along the road.

You can also get to Papantla from Poza Rica, a nearby oil town. Aeromexico used to fly between Mexico City and Poza Rica, but the route was dropped after the airline's reorganization. It may be reinstated in the future. Call 800-237-6639 in the United States for information. Poza Rica is about 12 miles from Papantla. Both bus and taxi service are available for the trip.

To get from Papantla to El Tajín, follow the road to Poza Rica for about three miles and turn right onto the road that leads to the entrance to the ruins. Taking the bus is a chore, because you have to take two second-class buses (the first to Chote, and the second to Poza Rica), ask to be dropped off by the El Tajín access road, and then walk a little more than half a mile up the access road to the entrance to the ruins. See if you can cut a deal with a local cabby for a flat day rate. But this is one excursion where having a car is almost essential.

 As you may have gathered from the type of bus service available, this area is not much trafficked by tourists. Accommodations, too, reflect that fact. However, you'll probably want to (or have to) overnight in Papantla. There are several small and unassuming hotels. The best of these is **Hotel Tajín,** at José Nuñez 104, near the Papantla *zócalo.* There are sixty pleasantly furnished rooms, some with air-conditioning, and a restaurant and bar. Call 784-2-01-21 for reservations. Credit cards: AE, MC, V. Doubles, from $23.

JALAPA AND ZEMPOALA

The charming colonial city of Jalapa (sometimes spelled Xalapa) is the capital of the state of Veracruz, located about 75 miles northwest and inland of the Port of Veracruz. When the Spanish arrived on the Gulf Coast, Jalapa was a thriving Indian community under the influence of the Aztecs. After the fall of Tenochtitlán, many Spaniards chose to settle in Jalapa and enjoy its gentle climate rather than live in the steamy and unhealthy climate around the Port of Veracruz. Jalapa was an important stop on the overland trade route from Acapulco via Taxco, Mexico City, and Puebla, en route to Veracruz, and it became a base for the distribution of goods brought from Spain on returning "silver ships." Jalapa's annual fair attracted merchants and traders from all parts of New Spain.

Much of the town's colonial atmosphere—the charm of winding narrow cobblestone streets bordered by beautiful parks and gardens or lined with lovely old public buildings and mansions—has survived to present times. The public buildings around **Parque Juárez,** the *zócalo,* are attractive—but not that old. There is the huge **Catedral Metropolitana de Jalapa,** built in 1773, and the **Palacio de Gobierno,** with some interesting murals by José Chavez Morado.

Within its colonial framework, Jalapa is a modern government center with a very sophisticated cultural life. It has an excellent university that offers summer courses to foreigners, and a critically acclaimed symphony orchestra. Jalapa has an important **Museum of Anthropology,** with a fine collection of terra-cotta and jade sculptures and figurines from all periods of the Olmec civilization and from the Totonac culture at the time of the Conquest. The newly remodeled museum is located on Avenida Xalapa, on the northwest outskirts of town. Open Tuesday through Sunday from 10 A.M. to 6 P.M. There is an admission fee.

🧳 Should you decide to overnight, Jalapa has several nice hotels. Among these, the **Hotel María Victoria** (Calle Zaragoza 6, 91000, tel. 281-7-56-00; AE, MC, V; doubles, from $30), a pleasant old hotel located behind the Palacio de Gobierno, and the newer **Hotel Xalapa** (Victoria and Bustamante, 91000, tel. 281-8-25-52; AE, MC, V; doubles, from $40) offer satisfactory accommodations.

☕ These and other hotels have reasonably priced restaurants, or you might try **La Casona del Beaterio** (Calle Zaragoza 20, 91000, tel. 281-8-21-19). This wonderful cafeteria-style restaurant occupies an old house of several rooms around a central courtyard with working fountain. The old photos used for decoration are fascinating; the menu is varied; and the food is good. You can get meat or fish dishes for under $8, chicken dishes for slightly more. Open daily from 8 A.M.–10 P.M. Credit cards: MC, V.

　　Restaurante el Diamante (Calle Antonia María de Rivera 16; tel. 281-7-13-26) is a charming place decorated with earthenware. The menu offers meat, fish, and chicken dishes, prepared with spicy Mexican sauces or grilled. Open daily from 11 A.M.–10 P.M. Credit cards: MC, V. The average price of a meal for two is about $18.

　　Jalapa's **Café la Parroquia** (Zaragoza 18) has different owners than the Veracruz café of the same name, but both serve terrific coffee. They also offer Mexican meals for under $5. No credit cards accepted. Open daily from 7:30 A.M.–10:30 P.M.

To get to Jalapa from Veracruz, you can take the first-class ADO bus or drive northwest on MEX140. At most, the trip takes about two hours.

En route, you might want to stop off at **Zempoala** (sometimes spelled Cempoala), off MEX140, about 25 miles northwest of Veracruz. Zempoala was the last Totonac capital. This is where Cortés met Chicomacatl (nicknamed *Chacque Gordo,* or fat chief), the Totonac king who became the conqueror's first ally against the Aztecs.

　　The central plaza has been restored to resemble Zempoala as the Spanish found it when they arrived on the Gulf Coast, but it is believed that there was a settlement at this site from about A.D. 1000. Not all of the structures have been excavated, but you can walk around the **Temple of the Chimneys,** where Cortés and his men camped when they arrived in town. This six-story structure is named for the series of broken columns found in front of the grand stairway leading to its platform. Most interesting is the **Temple of the Little Heads,** so named for the small terra-cotta skulls that once filled 365 niches in the walls of this temple. There is a small museum with artifacts found at the site.

You can also get to Zempoala from Veracruz by second-class Las Fuega buses. These are locals, so the trip takes about an hour and a half. But the lush and beautiful country-side makes the time, if not the bus, go faster. Zempoala is open daily from 8 A.M. to 6 P.M. There is an admission fee.

Villahermosa

Villahermosa (Spanish for "beautiful city"), capital of the oil-rich state of Tabasco, until quite recently lived up to its name. Founded in 1596 as Villa Felipe II, and renamed Villahermosa in 1598, the town remained quiet and colonial through the years. But black gold has changed all that. Villahermosa is Boom Town, Mexico. The city has grown very rapidly—some say too rapidly. Modern buildings now eclipse the town's 17th-century cathedral. And there are more new roads, more people, more traffic, and less charm. Nevertheless, Villahermosa's new wealth has provided the means to invest in local culture, and that has resulted in the establishment of two of Mexico's best archaeology museums. People come to town for either one or for all of three reasons: to work in the oil industry; to see Villahermosa's fabulous museums; and/or to use the town as a point of departure for touring the cities and ruins in the state of Chiapas (see Chapter 13).

Most famous and dramatic of Villahermosa's museums is **Parque Museo la Venta,** an open-air museum on the south-western shore of Laguna de los Ilusiónes (Lake of Illusions), in the suburbs of Villahermosa on MEX180. A parklike setting has been created for major archaeological finds from the rather inaccessible Olmec ruins at La Venta, San Lorenzo, and Tres Marías. Parque Museo la Venta is unique because it gives you the feeling that you're at the actual site (complete with crocodiles), without having experienced the inconvenience of a long trek into Veracruz and Tabasco swampland. The artifacts are quite impressive, especially the colossal heads that the Olmecs carved from basalt. The heads measure up to ten feet tall, and weigh up to twenty tons. Archaeologists haven't a clue as to how the Olmecs succeeded in bringing the huge basalt boulders to their ceremonial centers from sources that were at least seventy miles away. Although other artifacts indicate that wheels were used on small-scale toys, apparently the Olmecs knew nothing of the practical applications of the principle of the wheel. Nor do archaeologists understand how the Olmecs were able to so skillfully carve the stone without the benefit of metal tools: They worked exclusively with obsidian blades. Typically, the heads have helmets. Some are thought to be portraits of rulers; others, with their full, fleshy-looking mouths, suggest jaguar-like snarls. These jaguar-type faces, seen on other sculptures as well, have given the Olmecs their modern nickname, the "Jaguar People." In addition to the heads, Parque Museo la Venta exhibits large Olmec altars and stelae, as well as finely carved smaller figurines, toys, and other fascinating evidence of the belief system and way of life in Mesoamerica's earliest known civilization. Parque Museo la Venta is open daily from 8 A.M. to 5 P.M. There is a small admission fee. Guides are available, but many of them speak Spanish only. By the way, next to Parque Museo la Venta is the **Tabasco 2000 Exposition Park,** a complex of modern buildings including a planetarium, conference center, shopping malls, and city hall.

Villahermosa's other great museum is the **Carlos Pellicer Camara Regional Museum of Anthropology,** one section of the Centro de Investigaciónes de las Culturas Olmeca y Maya, otherwise known as CICOM, a cultural complex that opened in 1980 on the banks of the Grijalva River. The Museum of Anthropology is named after a famous Mexican poet and benefactor who was influential in the founding and design of Parque Museo la Venta. The museum's three stories are filled with fascinating exhibitions of artifacts and excellent reproductions of objects found in Olmec and Mayan sites in the state of Tabasco, and from other ancient civilizations in other parts of Mexico. The museum is open daily from 9 A.M. to 7 P.M. There is an admission fee.

CONNECTIONS

Mexicana and Aeromexico have daily service between Villahermosa and Mexico City, Mérida, Tuxtla Gutiérrez, Oaxaca, Mazatlán, Acapulco, Bahias de Huatulco, Ciudad Obregon, Guadalajara, Ixtapa/Zihuatanejo, La Paz, and Cancún. International flights can connect through Mexico City, Mérida, and Cancún. Aerotur, a regional airline, flies between Villahermosa and Veracruz. The airport is about 6 miles from town. Transportación Terrestre operates flat-fee taxis into Villahermosa; the ride costs about $9. National (931-9-19-31 or 931-2-03-93) and other car-rental companies have offices at the airport and downtown. Despite traffic congestion in the area, it's a good idea to have the use of a car in Villahermosa to get to Parque Museo la Venta and perhaps for touring to Chiapas. Remember that you save money on rates and can usually obtain free mileage if you book in advance in the United States.

To get to Villahermosa from Veracruz by car, take MEX180 for about 300 miles east through flatland swamps and jungles. The trip takes about eight hours and is usually traffic-free, except as you near Villahermosa, where road conditions tend to be worse, too, due to heavy truck traffic in the area. To drive to or from the Yucatán Peninsula to the east, and from the cities of Campeche or Mérida (about 400 miles), take MEX186. To drive south to Tuxtla Gutiérrez (about 120 miles) or San Cristóbal de las Casas, take MEX195.

First-class ADO buses serve all these routes with frequent departures.

🧳 HOTELS

If you plan to stay overnight in Villahermosa, book well in advance. Hotel space in this very busy business town is limited, and the good hotels are usually booked up.

Hotel Exelaris Hyatt

Avenida Juárez 106, 86050
Tel. 931-3-44-33 or 800-228-9000
Doubles, from $80 (weekend rates from $35)

This modern high rise, a 215-room Hyatt, is located conveniently near the Parque Museo la Venta and Tabasco 2000. Rooms are spacious and recently refurbished with pastel decor, cable TV, and servibars. The hotel's restaurant has a good international and Mexican menu, and the bar has live entertainment. The hotel also has a large pool and tennis court for guests' use. Credit cards: AE, DC, MC, V.

Holiday Inn

Paseo Tabasco 1407, 86030
Tel. 931-3-44-00 or 800-465-4329
Doubles, from $80

With an advantageous location in the Tabasco 2000 complex, the Holiday Inn is ideal for tourists who want to spend time at Parque Museo la Venta and shop in local malls. The hotel has 270 spacious modern rooms with cable TV and servibars. You'll also find a large and attractive tiled lobby, plus pleasant restaurant and bar and sizable swimming pool. Credit cards: AE, DC, MC, V.

Hotel Miraflores

Reforma 304, 86000
Tel. 931-2-00-22 or 931-2-00-54
Doubles, from $40

Sixty-eight modern and very plastic—but clean and inexpensive—rooms in a downtown hotel on a traffic-free street. Not much atmosphere . . . but the building has central air-conditioning, an elevator, a restaurant, and bar. Credit cards: AE.

Maya Tabasco Hotel

Bulevar Ruíz Cortines 907, 86000
Tel. 931-2-11-11
Doubles, from $60

A cheerful and lively Mexican ambience adds flavor to this business hotel with 140 pleasant and adequately sized rooms. The best rooms have views overlooking a garden. There's a large swimming pool, plus two restaurants and bars, and a disco. The hotel has a terrific Sun. buffet lunch (1–5 P.M.) with unusual local dishes. Credit cards: AE, DC, MC, V.

☕ RESTAURANTS

When it comes to food, Villahermosa comes in a distant second to Veracruz. Nevertheless, there are several reliable restaurants where you can get savory local seafood specialties and well-prepared steaks and chicken dishes.

Leo's

Paseo Tabasco 429
No telephone

This popular fast-food joint is always packed. The decor is somewhat garish, but the food is really good and inexpensive. The favorite way to order here is to get some beef or pork, plus salad fixings, and make your own tacos. You can also get a tasty hamburger and crisp French fries. Leo's is conveniently located between CICOM and Parque Museo la Venta. Open 12:30 P.M.–1 A.M. The average cost of a meal for two is about $18. No reservations. No credit cards.

Maya Tabasco

Bulevar Ruíz Cortines 907
Tel. 931-2-11-11

Try the Sun. buffet lunch here for a taste of regional cuisine, including turtle, local fish dishes, and *chanchamitos caseros* (a local type of tamale). Served Sun., 1–5 P.M. At other times, the restaurant offers a standard Mexican and international menu. The average cost of a meal for two is about $30. No reservations. Credit cards: AE, DC, MC, V.

Restaurante los Guayacanes

CICOM Complex
No telephone

Conveniently located near the Regional Museum of Anthropology, los Guayacanes offers a fine selection of spicy local seafood dishes, as well as tender steaks. The restaurant is clean and modern. Open Tues.–Sun., 11 A.M.–8 P.M. The average cost of a meal for two is about $25. No reservations. Credit cards: AE, DC, MC, V.

Restaurante los Pepes

Madero 610
Tel. 931-2-01-54

This popular, clean, and reliable outdoor café has an extensive menu with seafood, chicken, beef, and pork dishes, mostly prepared with a Mexican accent. Los Pepes is friendly and cheerful, with bright mats on the tables and cooling overhead fans. Open Mon.–Sat., 7 A.M.–11 P.M. The average cost of a meal for two is about $18. No reservations. No credit cards.

EXCURSIONS

The archaeological zone closest to Villahermosa is the Mayan ruins near the town of **Comalcalco,** about 37 miles north-west of Villahermosa. During the late-Classic period (approximately A.D. 600 to 900), Comalcalco, westernmost of the

Mayan centers, was a thriving community with an economy probably based on cacao beans, which are still cultivated in the area. It was perhaps a province of Palenque, to which it bears much similarity. Like Palenque, Comalcalco has a tomb, the **Tumba de los Nueve Señores de la Noche,** with carvings of what are thought to be the Nine Lords of the Underworld. However, Palenque and other Mayan ruins were built of stone, but the structures at Comalcalco were built of fired bricks because there was no limestone available. This is the only Mayan city to use bricks, and the bricks were treated in a very interesting fashion. Before they were covered with stucco and painted, the bricks were completely covered with inscriptions and elaborate paintings that could not be seen while the building was intact. But these bricks can be seen now, in the Comalcalco Museum. Also in the museum, and in special niches with thatched roofs located around the **Plaza Norte** and pyramid, are stucco sculptures, mostly in fragments. These, too, indicate a connection with Palenque. Because Comalcalco was built of brick and has been plundered several times, the site, discovered in 1880 and excavated by a team of archaeologists from Tulane University in 1925, is badly deteriorated. But a sense of vitality lingers from its ancient days.

To get to Comalcalco by car, take Bulevar Ruíz Cortines to Avenida Universidad, turn north, and follow the signs for Comalcalco. Drive cautiously, as there are an unusually large number of *topes* (speed bumps) on this road. About twenty miles down the road, you'll pass Cupilco Church, with a beautiful blue-and-yellow facade painted with flowers, angels, and a mural of the Virgin of Guadalupe. Beyond the town of Comalcalco (about one mile in the direction of Paraíso Beach) is the access road to the ruins. There are buses from Villahermosa to Comalcalco and Paraíso Beach (about ten miles beyond Comalcalco). If you take the bus, you can get off in Comalcalco and take a taxi to the ruins or continue on the bus toward Paraíso Beach and get off at the access road and walk from there. Comalcalco is open daily from 7:30 A.M. to 5 P.M. There is an admission fee. Bring sunscreen and insect repellent, and—if you're making a day of it—a picnic. There is a food stand at the site, but you'll be happier if you bring your own lunch.

Just as Villahermosa can be an excursion from Veracruz, so **Veracruz** can be an excursion from Villahermosa. Villahermosa is easier to get to from the outside world and has more daily flights, the great museums, and easier access to the wonderful cities and ruins in Chiapas. Veracruz is a more interesting town, with the port, the fort, all that history, better hotels, and superb food; it's also close to the rather sophisticated city of Jalapa and is convenient to El Tajín.

7

ACAPULCO AND THE PACIFIC COAST RESORTS

Mexico's scenic Pacific Coast features the dramatic, craggy landscape of steep cliffs and secluded beaches formed by the mighty Sierra Madre as it falls off into the sea. Beginning with Acapulco in the south and continuing farther north than Mazatlán, Mexico's thousand-mile stretch of Pacific Coast shoreline boasts dozens of beautiful bays with pure-white palm-studded sands and inviting bright-blue waters.

Some of these bays have been developed into fabulous resorts with first-class and high-tech hotels, fabulous restaurants, and exciting dance clubs and nightclubs that attract high-living sun worshipers from around the globe. Other bays harbor typical tropical fishing villages that have been pretty much untouched by time, and are all but devoid of modern conveniences. These villages are usually bypassed by the flocks of tourists but are treasured by nature lovers who seek seclusion and simplicity.

All along the Pacific Coast, whether in sizzling Acapulco or sleepy Zihuatanejo, the emphasis is on surf and sand. Don't expect to find high culture hanging out poolside or hiding between the sheets in a seaside hotel. You probably won't hear any symphonies or see any ballets during your entire vacation. This is decidedly the land of contemporary pop culture. Along Mexico's Pacific Coast, you'll do your *pas de deux* on the disco floor.

Five world-class resorts dominate Mexico's Pacific Coast. From south to north, they are Acapulco, Ixtapa-Zihuatanejo, Manzanillo, Puerto Vallarta, and Mazatlán. All offer the pleasures of superb beaches and a variety of water sports, but each has its very own personality and will appeal to vacationers with different interests, tastes, priorities. The hotels and attractions of these Pacific Coast resorts are covered in this chapter, with the exception of those belonging to Mazatlán, described in Chapter 8.

Of all the Pacific Coast resorts, Acapulco is the most famous. In fact, Acapulco is the Number One tourist destination in all of Mexico. Its reputation elicits jet-set expectations of constant activity and excitement, of high living among the rich and famous, of stars trying to hide away in the limelight, of nonstop sun and surf flowing into nonstop nightlife. How much of this reputation is fact and how much is fantasy probably depends somewhat from week to week, and varies on who's around. But travelers can *always* count on the fact that Acapulco has plenty of outdoor attractions and plenty of nightlife—enough to keep them so busy and to so exhaust them that they'll need a vacation from their vacation.

During any given week, however, Acapulco seems to be a haven for honeymooners. The hotels are filled with attractive, energetic, and glowing—perhaps from too much sun?—young couples. A lot of hotels have special honeymoon packages and special honeymoon events. If you're going to Acapulco on a honeymoon, consult your travel agent for details.

Farther up the coast, about 150 miles west of Acapulco, is the resort of Ixtapa-Zihuatanejo. These are sister cities with very different personalities that complement each other nicely. Ixtapa is a resort area, a sort of Acapulco Junior, with modern high-rise luxury hotels, restaurants, shopping plazas, and night spots built along a strip of pretty Pacific beachfront. Zihuatanejo, about six miles away, is a traditional, somewhat sleepy little fishing village and commercial center with unpretentious hotels, a port, *mercados,* and terrific family-style seafood restaurants. Combined, the two cities offer the best of Pacific Coast beach vacations—a blend of the glamour and excitement of life along the fast-paced strip, and of the down-to-earth, simple, traditional Mexican lifestyle.

About 240 miles west of Ixtapa-Zihuatanejo is Manzanillo, a port town and resort in the state of Colima. Manzanillo is famous as the background to the exotic and exclusive Las Hadas resort, brought to the world's attention in the motion picture *10.* Of the Pacific Coast resorts covered in this chapter, Manzanillo is perhaps the least developed, the least accommodating to tourists. There are a few good hotels and several popular time-share condominium developments, but Manzanillo doesn't offer the abundant selection of restaurants and night spots available in the other Pacific Coast resorts. Manzanillo is, however, an important port and is an extremely popular point of embarkation for deep-sea fishing.

Puerto Vallarta is about 160 miles northwest of Manzanillo, in the state of Jalisco (about 220 miles west of Guadalajara, the capital of the state of Jalisco). Like Manzanillo, Puerto

Vallarta was made famous by the movies. Life in this old port was never the same after the cast and crew of *Night of the Iguana* came to town, and some of them—including stars Elizabeth Taylor and Richard Burton—settled here. They were followed by many other celebrities, wealthy retirees, and thousands of travelers, all of whom adore the town's delightful, somewhat artsy ambience and hothouse climate.

Puerto Vallarta is a very swinging little town that attracts a lot of young, fun-loving vacationers with its pretty beaches, renowned hotels and restaurants, lively discos, and myriad shops. At the same time, however, Puerto Vallarta is a real town and as such has a genuine rhythm of its own, apart from its visitors. Perhaps that's why it is a favorite vacation spot; once people have discovered it, they return to it year after year, making Puerto Vallarta the third most-visited tourist destination in Mexico.

All of the Pacific Coast resorts are served by Mexican and international airlines, with direct flights or flights via Mexico City or Guadalajara available. Several flights are routed so that they stop at more than one Pacific Coast resort, but if, for example, you want to fly from Manzanillo to Puerto Vallarta or Ixtapa-Zihuatanejo, you may have to connect through Mexico City. Consult airline schedules for detailed information. It is possible to follow coast roads all the way from Acapulco to Puerto Vallarta, and on to Mazatlán. But this is not advisable. Although coastal roads have been recently improved, driving them can be very time consuming, especially if you wind up behind a slow-moving truck and cannot pass because of heavy oncoming traffic. On a more serious note, recently there have been reports of highway robberies of individual cars, and even in buses on their regularly scheduled routes. Of course, driving gives you the wonderful adventure of discovering those hidden beaches and ports as yet unknown to other tourists—but the thought of getting to know a *bandido* will perhaps dampen your spirit of adventure.

Acapulco

Alluring Acapulco, queen of Mexico's Pacific Coast resorts, is the glamorous beach bastion of jet setters and glitterati from around the world—and the country's most expensive city.

Acapulco is a quick-paced haven of sun and fun—and both are available in abundance. Daytime is for sunbathing, swimming, sightseeing, and shopping; nighttime's for dining and discohopping. This dawn-to-dusk-to-dawn activity makes Acapulco an ideal vacation place for the excitement seeker.

Much of the excitement in Acapulco takes place along the Costera Miguel Alemán, a broad boulevard that hugs the pretty crescent-shaped bay. The two-mile Strip, as it is commonly known, between Icacos Beach to the east and Papagayo Park to the west is where most of the luxury hotels, popular restaurants, night spots, and shops are located. Hotels are mostly clustered around the famous beaches—Icacos, Condesa, El Morro, Paraíso—which, as more and more hotels are built, are blending into one another. The most expensive hotels on the Strip are on the bay side of the Costera Miguel Alemán, and have beachfronts. But all beaches in Mexico are public— you can use any beachfront, even if you're not staying at the hotel that's on it. To the east of the Strip, Costera Miguel Alemán runs into the Carretera Escénica, a scenic drive that twists through the hills overlooking the bay, and past roads leading to the beaches at Puerto Marqués (where you'll find many private residences and condominiums) and Revolcadero (where the Acapulco Princess and Pierre Marqués hotels are located), all the way to the airport.

West of the Strip, the Costera Miguel Alemán goes through an underpass, past Papagayo Park, and past Hornitos and Hornos beaches (popular with the locals; there are no hotels here), and past the Malecón (waterfront, dock area), *zócalo*, and downtown shops, and around a small peninsula, where an offshoot leads to Caleta and Caletilla beaches. This is Old Acapulco, the original tourist area that made this town famous. La Roqueta Island, with a lovely beach and underwater Shrine of Our Lady of Guadalupe, is in front (ten minutes by boat) of Caleta Beach. La Quebrada, where daring young men dive from high cliffs, is on the west side of the peninsula.

People have probably been diving from those cliffs for hundreds of years, but the first record of Acapulco's existence came with the Aztec conquest of the area at the end of the 15th century, and the first European to see the bay was Gil Gonzales Avila in 1521. Acapulco was an important port during colonial times, first as a base for expeditions to the Orient and South America and, later, during the 16th century, as a key transit point on the trade route that brought silks, porcelain, and other luxuries from the Philippines and China, via Acapulco, and overland through Taxco and Mexico City to the Gulf Coast's Port of Veracruz, then by sea to Spain. Acapulco was attacked repeatedly by pirates—some of the best, or actually worst, in the business—during the 17th and 18th centuries. At the end of the 18th century, Acapulco's importance waned as new trade routes from the Orient brought goods to Spain through the Indian Ocean and around the Cape of Good Hope. After Mexico won its independence, the once important port was all but forgotten. Then, in 1927, a road was built from Mexico City to Acapulco, and, little by little, vacationers discovered this charming old port town and its marvelous bay. The real tourist boom began after World War II, during the presidency of Miguel Alemán Valdes, who poured funds into developing Acapulco's tourist infrastructure, including its main road, the Costera Miguel Alemán. Acapulco now has a superb tourist infrastructure and all the amenities to keep people coming to the resort. As Mexico's top tourist destination, Acapulco presents the face of modern Mexican culture to much of the world, and it's a major source of much-needed foreign income.

CONNECTIONS

There is frequent and reliable bus service between Mexico City and Acapulco (direct or via Cuernavaca or Taxco). First-class Estrella de Oro (tel. 5-549-8520) buses depart for Acapulco almost hourly from Terminal Central de Autobuses del Sur (near the Tasquena Metro station). You can reserve seats. The one-way fare is less than $10. The trip usually takes about seven hours, but on weekends, bumper-to-bumper traffic between Mexico City and Cuernavaca can make for frustrating delays. The route winds through some pretty mountain scenery. You can make the trip by car as well: Take MEX95 all the way, via Cuernavaca and Taxco, to Acapulco.

However, most international visitors arrive in Acapulco by air. The resort's busy airport handles dozens of international and national flights every day. From the United States, there are direct flights from Los Angeles, Atlanta, Chicago, New York, and Dallas/Fort Worth. Airlines with direct flights between U.S. cities and Acapulco include Continental, Mexicana, American, Delta, and Aeromexico. In addition, there are connecting flights, through Mexico City or through Guadalajara, from most cities in the United States, Canada, and Mexico. The Mexico City–to–Acapulco route has frequent air service too. For example, Mexicana Airlines has four daily nonstop flights (at 5:35 A.M., 10:40 A.M., 1:15 P.M. and 8:40 P.M.) between Mexico City and Acapulco, plus seven additional flights that operate from one to six days per week. Aeromexico also has several daily nonstop flights between Mexico City and Acapulco.

Acapulco's airport is located about 12 miles south of the Strip, or 14 miles south of the center of town. You have several options for getting to your hotel. You can take a *colectivo* (a group taxi) or a standard taxi. Both are operated by Transportación Terrestre (tel. 5-23-32). You pay a flat rate, per person, determined by the distance to your hotel. You can purchase a one-way or round-trip ticket for the service. If you plan to ride with Transportación Terrestre on your return to the airport, you must advise them of your departure time (by calling the number given above) at least 24 hours in advance. Fees for *colectivo* rides are under $12 per person. Taxis are obviously more expensive.

The airport also has car-rental agencies. If you plan to rent a car or jeep while you're in Acapulco, you might as well pick it up here and drive yourself to your hotel. Car-rental rates in Mexico are on the high side. You will, however, save money by reserving your car in the United States, if at all practical: For some reason, the major U.S. car-rental companies with agents in Mexico offer lower rental rates for cars used in Mexico if those cars are reserved in the United States rather than rented directly in Mexico. For example, National charges $210 for a weekly rental of a Volkswagen sedan, with unlimited free mileage, if you reserve the car at least seven days in advance in the United States. But if you rent the same car from National in Mexico, the charge will be about $485 per week, including 1,400 free kilometers. Both of these rates are subject to a 15 percent sales tax and do not include liability or personal insurance. If you're renting a jeep, however, you'll probably have to do it in Acapulco because most of the larger car-rental agencies don't deal in jeeps. Jeeps rent for about $50 per day, including insurance (and, in some cases, gas) and are a fun way of getting around Acapulco.

Is it a good idea to rent a vehicle for use in Acapulco? In general, yes. Acapulco's Strip is about 4 miles long. You'll want some form of wheels unless you're a world-class runner, and the need for a car becomes even more essential if you're staying in one of the more isolated hotels along the Carretera Escénica, or if you plan to hop back and forth between the Strip and Old Acapulco.

Driving in Acapulco is easy. The Ccstera Miguel Alemán is a wide, well-paved boulevard. Traffic can be heavy, but there are rarely jams. Most of the hotels, restaurants, and other attractions are along the Costera. If you're looking for an address off the main drag, you may have some difficulty because streets are not always well marked. Ask your hotel concierge for detailed directions, and always carry a map with you. If you're in one of the outlying hotels, you'll have to drive along the Carretera Escénica. In addition to being scenic, it's steep and, in some places, without guard rails. Be careful, especially after a night on the town. Many of the hotels have parking facilities, or you can park on the street without much difficulty.

Without a car, you'll have to rely on taxis or buses. Both are plentiful. Taxis stationed at hotels usually charge more than taxis hailed in the street. With cruising cabs, you'll probably have to bargain about the fare. Don't be embarrassed. This is an accepted, expected practice. Whenever you're taking a taxi, ask your concierge what's the going rate, and before you get into a cab always agree on a fee. Buses are much cheaper than taxis and run up and down the Costera, from Puerto Marqués to Caleta, at all times of the day and night. However, if you're staying at one of the outlying hotels, you're better off taking taxis. Acapulco also has horse-drawn buggies that ride up and down the Strip. For a real treat, and when you're not in a hurry, take one of these for an evening drive.

In Acapulco, beaches are the main attraction, and there are several to choose from. You can select one and spread your blanket, or you can cruise up and down the coast. From east to west, here are the choices: **Revolcadero,** off the airport road to the east of Acapulco Bay and facing the open sea, is a quiet, secluded beach, surrounded by jungle-like greenery. The Acapulco Princess and Pierre Marqués hotels are nearby. **Puerto Marqués,** off the Carretera Escénica and along an inlet east of Acapulco Bay, is surrounded by private mansions and luxury high-rise condominiums. This beach is a favorite with Mexican families. **La Concha,** off the Carretera Escénica, is the "private" beach club of Las Brisas Hotel. This beautiful beach is clean and quiet and provides a fabulous panoramic view of Acapulco Bay, with the Strip sparkling in the distance. It is a favorite with honeymooners. Bordered on both sides by rock formations, the beach has guards posted to keep trespassers (mostly vendors and locals) out. But all Mexican beaches are, by law, open to the public. And foreign tourists usually have no trouble gaining entry. **Guitarrón** and **Icacos** flank the Icacos Naval Base and are, to some extent, dominated by it. Icacos is, however, near some hotels (Exelaris Hyatt Regency, Copacabana, La Palapa, Posada del Sol, Elcano, and El Tropical, among others) and is popular with some swimmers. More popular is **Condesa** (near the Calinda Quality Acapulco, Condesa del Mar, El Presidente, and other hotels), which is usually quite crowded and where you can always find an active water-sports scene. **El Morro** (near the Acapulco Plaza, Acapulco Ritz, Maralisa, Exelaris Hyatt Continental, and other hotels) is similar to Condesa in the kinds of activities it offers, and it attracts a similar crowd. At both Condesa and El Morro, you'll find brigades of street vendors, as well as attentive waiters who are very willing to fetch you refreshments from the nearest hotel bar. **Paraíso** (near Paraíso Radisson Acapulco and other hotels) is the last beach on the Strip. It is somewhat quieter than Condesa and El Morro, but still has sports and beachfront bar service. **Hornitos** and **Hornos** are "public" beaches—that is, they have no hotels on them, and they're popular with the locals. When Hornitos and Hornos aren't crowded, they can be perfectly delightful. For one thing, there are fewer vendors to pester you. Farther west, on a small peninsula, are **Caleta** and **Caletilla.** These beaches are Acapulco's oldest tourist attractions, popular long before the Strip became a reality. They are surrounded by relatively inexpensive hotels and are frequented primarily by Mexican families on budget vacations. In front of Caleta and Caletilla is **La Roqueta Island,** with a peaceful beach that's popular with snorklers. Also on La Roqueta is the underwater Shrine of Our Lady of Guadalupe, a submerged bronze statue of the Virgin. On the west side of the peninsula is **Langosta,** a small cove and beach, and nearby are the high cliffs known as **La Quebrada,** where young men defy death by diving into the rocky sea. **Pie de la Cuesta Beach,** about eight miles from Acapulco on the coastal road MEX200, has rough currents that make swimming impossible but is a favorite spot for sunset watching.

Several words of caution concerning all of Acapulco's beaches: Currents in and around the bay can be strong and unpredictable, and there is often a mighty undertow. Every year, there are several deaths by drowning reported in Acapulco. Swimmers are warned to stay in the bay area, never to swim in the open sea, to pay strict attention to warning flags that indicate rough seas, and never to swim alone. In addition, Acapulco Bay is quite polluted, despite recent government clean-up efforts. Some people feel that it's a good idea to lounge on the beach but swim in the hotel pools. Use your own discretion.

Water-sport activities, including parasailing, scooter boating, waterskiing, snorkeling, scuba diving, and deep-sea fishing, can easily be arranged through your hotel concierge, a local travel agency, or on the beach. But use your head. If you're going on a fishing or diving expedition, hire the services of an authorized guide.

Après beach, the most popular activities in Acapulco are dining, dancing, and shopping. Popular restaurants, discos, and shops are described below under separate headings.

Boat cruises around Acapulco Bay are entertaining and give you an opportunity to see the Strip and Old Acapulco from another perspective. The *Fiesta* and *Bonanza* yachts have daily departures from the waterfront west of the *zócalo,* for daylight (at 11 A.M. and 4:30 P.M.; about $12); dinner (at 7:30 P.M.; about $25); and moonlight cruises with dancing (at 10:30 P.M.; about $25).

In Old Acapulco, it's fun to wander around the **zócalo** and browse in the *mercado* (see **Shopping,** below). **Fort San Diego,** high atop a hill overlooking the Costera east of the *zócalo,* was built in 1616 to protect Acapulco, then a busy port handling trade with the Philippines, from invading pirates. The original fort was destroyed in an earthquake in 1776. This structure was built to replace it. The fort is now a museum with exhibits about Acapulco's history. It is open Tuesday through Sunday from 10 A.M. to 6 P.M., and there is a small admission fee.

Also diverting are two amusement parks. **Papagayo Park** (off Costera Miguel Alemán, near the underpass to Old Acapulco) is a zoo, botanical gardens, and amusement park—fun for kids of all ages. **Cici** (on the bay side of the Costera, near Icacos Beach) has a huge swimming pool with a water slide, another pool with artificial waves, a dolphin show, and shark tank, all hidden away behind a bright blue wave-shaped stucco wall.

In a shady grove of trees along the Costera Miguel Alemán, near Cici, the **Acapulco Cultural Center,** run by the state of Guerrero, has a small archaeological museum with artifacts from the area and exhibitions of local handicrafts.

Centro Acapulco, a huge convention center toward the eastern end of the Strip, has impressive exhibition halls and meeting rooms. The place is worth a visit even if you're not in Acapulco on business. The complex also has restaurants, bars, a disco, and both legitimate and movie theaters. Check with your hotel concierge or call 748-4-70-50 for a schedule of current events.

💼 HOTELS

Choice of hotel is more important in Acapulco than it might be in some other vacation spots. Acapulco's accommodations vary greatly in price and ambience, and, more significantly, in location. You may not spend a lot of time in your room, but your hotel's location can really influence your vacation's tone. Do you want to be in the center of the action, or away in a more secluded setting? That's the key question to keep in mind as you consider the following. You'll note that several hotels require you take some of your daily meals there—especially during the popular winter season. This is referred to below as Modified American Plan. Rates vary significantly according to the season.

Deluxe

Acapulco Plaza
Costera Miguel Alemán 123 (on El Morro Beach), 39580
Tel. 748-5-90-50 or 800-HOLIDAY
Doubles, from $140

This well-maintained hotel always seems to be filled with activity. The lobby has an unusual feature: the Jaula Bar, suspended on ropes from the lobby's high domed ceiling and filled with loud music, screeching birds, and chattering guests. Surrounding this very busy and somewhat noisy core are one thousand modern rooms and suites—all relatively quiet. They are elegantly appointed with modern furniture, servibars, color cable TV, and other amenities. All rooms have at least partial sea views. The beachside leisure complex has a large patio, two pools and Jacuzzis, plus a health club with steam rooms and sauna, and tennis courts. The restaurants and bars are popular and usually packed. The shopping arcade has excellent boutiques and specialty shops. You could happily spend all your time in Acapulco at the Plaza, but the hotel's convenient location provides irresistibly easy access to the town's other attractions and entertainments. Credit cards: AE, DC, MC, V.

Acapulco Princess Hotel
Apdo. Postal 1351, Playa Revolcadero, 39370
Tel. 748-4-31-00 or 800-223-1818
Doubles, from $150 (Modified American Plan required in winter only, from $220)

The main building is a twenty-story pyramid—very dramatic— with an interior atrium of open hallways and balconies, with thick

foliage and abundant flowers. The top floor has pricey pent-
houses with fabulous wraparound balconies, sunken tubs, and
kitchens. Other rooms are spacious and nicely decorated but
not all have ocean views. Rooms do not have TV. Additional
rooms are located in two towers on either side of pyramid. The
hotel's public areas are outstanding: You are greeted by a tall
man-made waterfall at the hotel entrance; there are trees all
around the interior; and the wide-open lobby allows a constant
breeze to circulate through the building, from beach to golf
course. The 18-hole golf course ($48 greens fee and $28 for
use of cart) is beautifully cared for, and another course is available at the Pierre Marqués Hotel, just down the road, with a free
shuttle bus that runs every ten minutes. Grounds feature a huge
saltwater pool with water toboggan, plus four smaller-but-still-
large freshwater pools. Dramatic water effects include an in-pool
waterfall with swim-up bar behind it. Lots of conventions take
place at the Princess: It's really large enough so that conven-
tioneers can have some privacy, too. And it's a haven for honeymooners. One drawback: The Princess is just over 10 miles from
town, and the hotel does not provide shuttle service. Taxis back
and forth can be very costly. During the winter, room rates include a mandatory meal plan, but guests have a choice of restaurants—six in all. Several offer attractive buffets, and the
higher-priced gourmet restaurants with à la carte menus grant
a credit toward meals. Credit cards: AE, DC, MC, V.

Las Brisas

Apdo. Postal 281, Carretera Escénica 5255, 39868
Tel. 748-4-15-80 or 800-228-3000
**Doubles, from $220, Continental breakfast and gratuities in-
cluded**

In a category all its own, Las Brisas is a pink-and-white tropical
village covering the side of a mountain that overlooks all of Acapulco—city, beaches, and bay. Views are exquisite any time of
the day or night. Guests are shuttled up and down the mountain,
along twisting and seemingly treacherous little alleys with pink
stripes down the middle, via pink-and-white jeeps from the
breezy reception area to little *casitas,* with private or semiprivate
swimming pool. These private pools are intended for sitting or
splashing about; they're not really large enough for serious
swimming. Everywhere there are bright pink hibiscus flowers—
floating in the pools, decorating the rooms, on the turned-down
beds. The *casitas* have great views—all of them have balconies
overlooking the bay and the town. During the day, you get the
sea view; at night, the twinkling lights from town are glorious.
Every morning, a pot of hot coffee and a basket of sweet rolls
and fresh fruit are delivered to each *casita.* The **Belle Vista** and
El Méxicano restaurants offer fine food and views but are on
the pricey side. On Friday nights, Las Brisas puts on a terrific
Fiesta Méxicana, with buffet, Ballet Folklórico, mariachi music,
and other entertainment. No televisions in the rooms, but the
Tulipan Club, just about the only place in the whole hotel that
facilitates mingling among the guests, has music videos, satellite TV, game tables, and movie screenings. Las Brisas in general is better suited to honeymooners than singles, although

reserve your *casita* carefully—the degree of privacy you enjoy will depend upon its location. The *casitas* that overlook the pools afford more privacy than do those that overlook other *casitas.* So if you want seclusion, be sure to specify that when you make your reservation. The higher up the hill, the bigger the *casita,* the bigger the pool, the more privacy—and the higher the price. Jeeps with names like "Snoopy," "Brenda Vacarro," "Plácido Domingo," and "Sylvester Stallone" are available for rent for about $49–$70 per day, including insurance and gas. If you intend to go to town, it might be a good idea to rent one of these: They give a lovely sense of freedom. La Concha beach club, down the road by the water, is wonderful for activities. You can sunbathe on a private deck that surrounds two pools of enclosed ocean. There is a roped-off section of ocean for safe swimming, complete with floaters with the pretty pink hibiscus logo of Las Brisas. The hotel also offers jeep safaris through villages near Acapulco, as well as boat trips to the nearby island of Mandinga. Lots of beer, lunch, and donkey rides are part of the package. Book through the hotel concierge. Credit cards: AE, DC, MC, V.

Exelaris Hyatt Continental
Apdo. Postal 214, Costera Miguel Alemán (on El Morro Beach), 39580
Tel. 748-4-09-09 or 800-228-9000
Doubles, from $150

Like its sister hotel, the Exelaris Hyatt Regency (see below), the Exelaris Hyatt Continental is a modern efficient high-rise retreat with a well-tended expanse of beachfront. The spacious marble-lined lobby provides a cool and welcome retreat from the Acapulco sun and humidity. The 435 rooms have balconies and offer bay views. The pool area is splendid, jungle-like. You get to it by following a stone path that meanders through lush greenery, over little streams, and past shallow goldfish ponds with waterfalls. The pool is big and free-form, with lots of little nooks and a pleasant swim-up bar. The main drawback here is that the Continental is sometimes used for big fiestas, and the music and noise reverberate through hotel rooms on lower floors. Good on-premises restaurants offer pleasant service—especially **La Isla,** located on an island in the middle of the swimming pool. Regency Club floors provide extra amenities, including a private lounge with Continental breakfasts and cocktails. All guests may use the facilities at the Exelaris Hyatt Regency, and there's frequent shuttle service between the two hotels. Credit Cards: AE, CB, DC, MC, V.

Exelaris Hyatt Regency
Costera Miguel Alemán 1 (on Icacos Beach), 39869
Tel. 748-4-28-88 or 800-228-9000
Doubles, from $150

Recently refurbished and offering all the amenities of the Hyatt chain, this towering hotel is at the easternmost end of Costera Miguel Alemán, Acapulco's posh hotel strip. The lobby is a spacious, high-ceilinged, wood-paneled oval ringed by reception desk, seating areas, and shops. Restaurants and additional designer shops are beyond the lobby, toward the beach side of the hotel, where an open-air café and balcony leads to an expansive pool, sun deck, and beach area, with lots of *palapas* and palms to provide shade. In addition to swimming, sunning, and water-sports activities, the hotel has artisans on hand who demonstrate painting ceramic objects and show you how to do it—all free of charge. The recently remodeled rooms—690 of them—are outfitted in soothing shades of pale green and coral, with attractive art. All have balconies, color cable TV, and servibars. Rooms with sea views are more expensive, as are suites with spectacular wraparound views. The Regency floors numbered 20 and 21 provide Continental breakfast buffets and a cocktail hour, as well as special concierge service. **El Pescador,** the delightful seafood restaurant, serves fish dishes ranging from sashimi to shrimp tacos. The shopping arcade has Gucci, Michel Domit, Tane, Fiorucci, and other top boutiques. Credit cards: AE, DC, MC, V.

Hotel Pierre Marqués

Apdo. Postal 474, Playa Revolcadero, 39370
Tel. 748-4-20-00 or 800-223-1818
Doubles, from $100 (Modified American Plan required in winter only, from $220)

Located just to the north along Revolcadero Beach and sister to the Princess, the Pierre Marqués is much smaller, with only 334 rooms, and quieter than the Princess. It is like a modern hacienda, with great open spaces and rooms clustered into little buildings. Each building contains 12 suites, and there are also exclusive bungalows. The grounds offer fabulous swimming pools, and there is an 18-hole golf course. Rates are the same as the Princess in the winter high season; the meal plan is mandatory in winter and is included in the room rate. Credit cards: AE, DC, MC, V.

Villa Vera Racquet Club and Hotel

Loma del Mar 35, 39830
Tel. 748-4-03-33 or 800-333-8847
Doubles, from $160

An exclusive retreat from the bustle of the beach and Costera Miguel Alemán, this hilltop hideaway is frequented by celebrities and sophisticates. Public areas and activities are kept to a minimum in order to maximize privacy. There is, however, a pool surrounded by deck chairs, and a breezy open-air restaurant offers a spectacular view of the Costera and the sea beyond. Guests are housed in small *casitas* situated to provide as much seclusion as possible. Credit cards: AE, CB, DC, MC, V.

Expensive

Hotel Elcano

Apdo. Postal 430, Avenidas del Parque and Palmas (off the Costera, near Icacos Beach), 39300
Tel. 748-4-19-50 or 800-458-6888
Doubles, from $120

The 140 rooms in one of Acapulco's grand old dames have been recently redecorated and offer budget-minded travelers ample accommodation. Rooms have color cable TV and furnished balconies, large enough for comfortable sunbathing, and offering wonderful views. The pool area, surrounded by lush greenery, is particularly attractive. Credit cards: AE, DC, MC, V.

Paraíso Radisson Acapulco
Costera Miguel Alemán 163, 39670
Tel. 748-5-55-96 or 800-777-7800
Doubles, from $125

Located at the end of the Costera Miguel Alemán, just before the tunnel that leads to Old Acapulco, the Paraíso has a large return clientele. The hotel has been operated by several major chains, and is currently under the Radisson umbrella. The lobby is pleasant, with marble floors, dark wood walls, and breezy open areas. The hallways seem dingy because of the dark wood paneling and doors to the rooms, but beyond those dark doors, the rooms are cheery. Best, and somewhat more expensive, are the suites at the ends of the hallways: These have splendid two-sided views of Acapulco and the bay. The hotel's rooftop restaurant, **La Fragata,** is decorated like an old ship, has candlelight and lacy table coverings, and offers fine seafood and great views. The hotel puts on a fun Mexican fiesta every Thur. and Sat. night, with buffet, live entertainment, games, and prizes. Credit cards: AE, CB, DC, MC, V.

Hotel Presidente
Apdo. Postal 933, Costera Miguel Alemán (on Condesa Beach), 39580
Tel. 748-4-17-00
Doubles, from $110

Another favorite with Mexican tourists, this twin-towered hotel has four hundred rooms, all recently redecorated, many with spectacular views. The hotel has two pools, along with tennis courts and scheduled social activities for both adults and children. Several eateries, one of which is kosher, are located on the premises. Lobby bar with live entertainment, plus disco. Credit cards; AE, MC, V.

Moderate

Hotel Boca Chica
Apdo. Postal 1211, Costera Miguel Alemán (at Caletilla Beach), 39390
Tel. 748-3-66-01 or 800-34MEXICO
Doubles, from $110 (Modified American Plan required in winter only)

Hotel Boca Chica has 45 charming rooms, all with small balconies and panoramic views, on five stories, and multilevel grounds with restaurant, bar, pool, and patios. During the winter season, the Modified American Plan, including breakfasts and dinners at the hotel, is mandatory. But both food and service are good. The hotel occupies a terrific spot on the headland of Caletilla Beach, on the Costera, but away from the high-rise and high-cost Strip. Boca Chica overlooks La Roqueta Island and has easy accessibility for waterskiing and deep-sea fishing. Credit cards: AE, MC, V.

Calinda Quality Acapulco
1260 Costera Miguel Alemán (on Condesa Beach), 39300
Tel. 748-4-04-10 or 800-228-5151
Doubles, from $100

Formerly under the Holiday Inn banner, this big white beehive-like hotel has 358 rooms facing in all directions. The spacious rooms are all pleasantly decorated with modern furnishings and colorful accents. Obviously, the most popular choice is for rooms with sea views. The public areas, including lobby, bars, restaurants, pool, and patio are airy and accommodating. The beach area has shade-providing *palapa* huts, where drinks are served and beach towels are dispensed. Restaurants and bars are lively. The nightclub is a popular spot for dancing. Credit cards: AE, DC, MC, V.

Condesa del Mar
Costera Miguel Alemán 1220 (on Condesa Beach), 39360
Tel. 748-4-26-03
Doubles, from $85

This hotel's location, right in the middle of the Costera Miguel Alemán, is advantageous for those who intend to enjoy activities along the Strip. The hotel draws a young international crowd and many vacationing Mexican families. The greenery-filled open-air lobby features a waterfall and is a pleasant background to the hotel's very popular and crowded happy-hour festivities. All of the 470 rooms and thirty suites are pleasantly furnished with cheerful decor—beginning, perhaps, to show signs of age. All have splendid ocean views, however. Two pools adjoin an open patio—overlooking the sea—with umbrellas, snacks, and bar. Children's activities, including water volleyball, as well as games for adults, are available. The hotel has popular restaurants and bars, including **Techo del Mar** (Roof of the Sea) for elegant dinners, dancing, and great views of sunset and stars. Credit cards: AE, DC, MC, V.

Copacabana Hotel
Tabachines 2 (on Icacos Beach), 39690
Tel. 748-4-31-03, 800-327-9408
Doubles, from $100

A relatively new hotel, opened in 1984, the Copacabana is a 16-story curved white tower located on the busiest section of the Strip and about two blocks from the Acapulco Convention Center. The hotel has 430 rooms, all with small furnished balconies and slightly elliptical ocean views. The beach, a wide expanse of white sand dotted with umbrellas, is very popular, as is the pool area. There are restaurants and four action-packed bars. Credit cards: AE, DC, MC, V.

Hotel Maralisa
Enrique el Esclavo (near Costera Miguel Alemán, on El Morro Beach), 39580

Tel. 748-5-6667
Doubles, from $80

This seafront sister to the pricey hilltop Villa Vera Racquet Club and Hotel is a small, intimate retreat. The Maralisa is on the Strip but still has a quiet, almost secluded atmosphere. The hotel has one hundred rooms, all pleasantly furnished, and surrounding patios and swimming pools. The bar and restaurant overlook the beach. Guests may use the tennis courts at the Villa Vera. Credit cards: AE, MC, V.

Hotel la Palapa

Fragata Yucatán 210 (at Icacos Beach), 39850
Tel. 748-4-53-63 or 800-528-1234
Doubles, from $100

Conveniently located across the Costera from the Acapulco Convention Center, la Palapa is an informal and pleasant hotel with 340 junior suites, many with balconies overlooking the bay. Suites and public areas are pleasantly decorated with tropical wicker furniture. La Palapa offers free-form swimming pools and organized water sports on the beach. Lush patio area, restaurants, bars. Credit cards: AE, CB, DC, MC, V.

Budget

Hotel Belmar

Gran Vía Tropical and Avenida Combres
Tel. 748-2-15-25
Doubles, from $60

Known as a good buy, this charming hotel in Old Acapulco, away from the hustle and bustle of the Strip, on a hill a few blocks away from Caleta Beach, is quiet, clean, and comfortable. Rooms are simple and spacious, many with views overlooking the hotel's lovely gardens. A good restaurant and two small but adequate pools are on the premises. Credit cards: AE, MC, V.

Hotel Caleta

Cerro de San Martin (on Caleta Beach), 39350
Tel. 748-3-99-40 or 748-3-93-34
Doubles, from $65

The Hotel Caleta is an Acapulco tradition, the classic stopping place in Old Acapulco. This section of town, off the Strip, offers the atmosphere and charm typical of a Mexican port town. There are lots of small hotels here, all of them less expensive than the hotels along the Costera. Hotel Caleta, especially since its face-life several years ago, is the best of these, and offers excellent accommodations. It is clean and well cared for. The 250 rooms are on the small side, and comfortably—though not elegantly—furnished with wicker. Rooms with views overlooking the activity on Caleta Beach are premium. The hotel's terrace restaurant serves well-prepared fresh seafood and offers breezy appealing vistas of Old Acapulco. Credit cards: AE, MC, V.

Hotel Linda Vista

Apdo. Postal Caleta Beach
Tel. 748-2-27-83 or 748-2-54-14
Doubles, from $35

This modest hotel, located on a hillside, is popular with older vacationers, who enjoy its relative quiet, reasonable rates, and competent service. The simply furnished rooms have delightful views of the beach and the town. All rooms have ceiling fans; there are some air-conditioned rooms, and these are slightly more expensive. Specify your preference when you make your reservation. The pool is small, but the hotel's terrace, with a lovely restaurant, is a great place to sit and gaze at the sea. Credit cards: MC, V.

Hotel Majestic

Avenida de la Aguada (near Caleta Beach), 39830
Tel. 748-2-49-50
Doubles, from $30

Although Hotel Majestic is not located directly on a beach, free van service to and from Caleta Beach is provided for its guests—or you can enjoy the sun while sitting poolside. The 146 rooms of this hotel are spacious, and many have large balconies with sea views. Public areas are pleasantly furnished, and the restaurant serves good home-style meals at reasonable prices. Credit cards: AE, MC, V.

Hotel Versalles

Gran Vía Tropical (near Caleta Beach), 39390
Tel. 748-2-60-02
Doubles, from $48 (Modified American Plan)

This small hillside hotel offers fifty clean, cool rooms, many with small balconies and views overlooking Acapulco and the bay. There is a small pool for cooling off, and the hotel is within walking distance from Caleta Beach. Versalles is ideal to use as a base for seeing the rest of Acapulco. You can go out on the town—and then retreat to relative peace and quiet. No credit cards.

🍵 RESTAURANTS

Acapulco's eateries offer every type of cuisine, but the area's specialty is undoubtedly seafood—fresh, varied, and beautifully prepared. Most menus offer shrimp, lobster, and all sorts of fish cooked Mexican-style, marinated, or simply grilled. If you don't like fish, you'll find steaks and chicken readily available—in the midst of what is most often a maritime decor. Mexican buffets and plates offering a variety of typical Mexican tidbits (which can be viewed as the southern counterpart to the North American *tapas* craze) are also enormously popular.

Perhaps you're a little finicky about wandering into a questionable establishment, where food (or hygiene!) may take a backseat to atmosphere. If so, remember that you're usually safe at hotel restaurants, many of which offer both ambience and excellent food. Also reliable are **Sanborn's** (Costera Miguel Alemán, next door to Condesa del Mar Hotel), **VIPS** (Costera Miguel Alemán 1252), and **Denny's** (Costera Miguel Alemán 650 and 4085). All are open morning to night and serve breakfast, selected Mexican specialties, sandwiches, shakes, hamburgers, and french fries; the tab usually comes to about $5–$8 per person. All have convenient locations.

The restaurants described below have atmosphere—ranging from the fun-filled (if a bit touristy) to the sublime and refined. Food-wise, you should be both safe and satisfied with the following:

Antojitos Mayab
Costera Miguel Alemán, at Hornos Beach
No phone

This family-style Mexican restaurant is hidden away behind a lush growth of bushes and vines on the Costera at Hornos Beach, just beyond the underpass from the Strip. The decor is simple, but the food is spectacular. The specialty is Yucatán cuisine, with items such as *sopa de lima* (lime soup) and *pollo pibil* topping the menu. Most of the customers are Mexican, attracted here by the great food at good prices. Open 9 A.M.–10 P.M. The average cost of a meal for two is about $15. No reservations. No credit cards.

Barbarroja (Red Beard)
Costera Miguel Alemán, at Condesa Beach
Tel. 748-4-59-32

Located along the busiest section of the Strip, Barbarroja is a tourist restaurant with a pirate atmosphere and good seafood. The restaurant is an old ship, complete with masts and riggings. The best tables are by the railing (reservations a must for these; suggested otherwise), where you do get a sense of getting away from it all. Open daily for dinner only, 6:30 P.M.–12:30 A.M. The average cost of a meal for two, including wine, is about $42. Credit cards: AE, MC, V.

Barbas Negras (Blackbeard's)
Costera Miguel Alemán, at Condesa Beach
Tel. 748-4-25-49

The milieu here—that of a pirate ship—is very similar to **Barbarroja**'s (see above), as is the menu, which features fresh fish and seafood, as well as steaks. Open daily for dinner only, 6:30 P.M.–12:30 A.M. The average cost of a meal for two, including wine, is about $40. Reservations suggested. Credit cards: AE, MC, V.

Beto's
Costera Miguel Alemán, at Condesa Beach
Tel. 748-4-04-73

A beachfront bistro in the midst of the busiest section of the Costera Miguel Alemán, Beto's attracts a young, touristy, fun-loving crowd. You enter by following a tree-lined, curving stairway down to a large *palapa*-covered bar, with other deck areas also covered by *palapas*. During the day, there's meal service on the beach, where you'll find umbrella-covered tables. After dusk, service is only in the enclosed part of the restaurant. The menu emphasizes a large variety of fish and seafood entrées (with grilled or garlic shrimp the real specialty) but also offers steaks and chicken dishes. Mexican specialties include the standard enchiladas and quesadillas. Beto's is big on drinks and serves all the tropical coladas and margaritas, plus some exclusive and lethal recipes. Open daily for lunch and dinner, 1 P.M.–midnight. The average cost of a meal for two is about $40. No reservations. Credit cards: AE, MC, V.

Coyuca 22
Avenida Coyuca 22
Tel. 748-2-34-68

One of the most expensive and exclusive restaurants in Acapulco, Coyuca offers the ambience of a lovely garden in a private estate. The menu is limited to standard international preparations of steaks, chicken, and fish entrées, and the wine list is no more than adequate. But the view is spectacular: The restaurant is located on a hilltop in the Caleta section of Old Acapulco. It has a multilevel design and terraced gardens that allow you to gaze out over the bay on one side, and over the Pacific Ocean on the other. Open daily, Nov.–Apr., for dinner only, 7–11 P.M. The average cost of a meal for two, including wine, is about $100. Reservations are a must. Credit cards: AE, DC, MC, V.

El Embarcadero
Costera Miguel Alemán 25
Tel. 748-4-87-87

El Embarcadero is on the beach side of the Costera Miguel Alemán, in a jungle-like setting that has been decorated to look like an old ship. Moats and planks abound; crates serve as tables and chairs. In the midst of all this atmosphere, you can get some fresh and decently prepared fish and seafood, including red snapper, bass, lobster, and shrimp, plus steak and chicken entrées. But the real specialties are Polynesian—Rangoon chicken and Tahitian tempura included. This is a nice change from Mexican, and the South Seas trip is fun, to be sure. Open for lunch, 1–5 P.M.; for dinner, 6–11 P.M. Adequate wine list. The average cost of a meal for two, including wine, is about $60. Reservations suggested. Credit cards: AE, MC, V.

La Fragata
Hotel Paraíso Radisson
Costera Miguel Alemán (no number)
Tel. 748-5-55-96

On the top floor of the Paraíso Radisson Hotel, this restaurant is outfitted like an old ship, complete with dark wood fittings and rope riggings, which clash rather conspicuously with plush red carpets, white lace tablecloths, and candlelight. The view of Acapulco Bay is spectacular. The menu features Continental specialties and seafood. Lobster is a favorite, but thick steaks are available for landlubbers. A fine wine list, with both domestic and imported vintages, is offered. The average cost of a meal for two, including wine, is about $60. Reservations suggested, especially on weekends. Credit cards: AE, MC, V.

Huachinango Charlie's
Costera Miguel Alemán, at Andrea Doria

Tel. 748-4-04-93

This ever-popular Acapulco outpost of the famous Carlos Anderson chain of restaurants is always crowded with those who enjoy the fun-house ambience here. The decor features photos of fifties movie stars, balloons, antique odds and ends, cowboy and hard hats, and dozens of business cards that patrons have pinned to the walls. Loud rock music prevails over conversation. The menu offers hamburgers and steaks, barbecued ribs (a specialty), soups, and other well-prepared goodies. Huachinango Charlie's captures the spirit of Acapulco, and attracts the young, the hip, and the fun-loving. Wines here are reasonably priced, mixed drinks considerably less so. Open Mon.–Sat., 1 P.M.–midnight; Sun., 1–5:30 P.M. The average cost of a meal for two, including a moderately priced wine, is about $50. Reservations suggested. Credit cards: MC, V.

Madeiras
Carretera Escénica 39
Tel. 748-4-69-21

Certainly one of the most highly regarded restaurants in Acapulco, Madeiras is known for its fine food and ambience and spectacular views. Perched on a hill, on the beach side of the Carretera Escénica, the dining room overlooks all of Acapulco. The menu is international with a French accent and features terrific seafood. *Huachinango* (red snapper), either *relleno* (stuffed) or *al mojo de ajo* (with garlic), is superb. For an appetizer, the coquilles St. Jacques are a nice change from the typical Mexican ceviche. Indulge in one of the sinful desserts! Open Mon.–Sat., for dinner and cocktails only, with two seatings, at 7 and 10 P.M. Good wine list, with fine imports at fine prices. The average cost of a meal for two, including wine, is about $90. The place is usually packed; make reservations as far in advance as possible. Credit cards: AE, MC, V.

Mimi's Chili Saloon
Costera Miguel Alemán, at Condesa Beach
No phone

The exterior of this cheerful restaurant is painted a bright blue and covered with amusing posters with slogans about chile. Mimi's chile is, in fact, palate-pleasing, as are her hamburgers, French fries, onion rings, hot dogs, fried chicken, and other homespun favorites that will remind you of, well, home. Exotic large drinks, including mango or strawberry margaritas, are pleasantly lethal: two for the price of one during happy hour, 4–6 P.M. Open daily, 2–11 P.M. The average cost of a meal for two, including drinks, is about $20. No reservations. No credit cards.

Miramar
Carretera Escénica, at La Vista Shopping Center
Tel. 748-4-78-74

In a splendid setting, atop a hill and overlooking Acapulco Bay, the Miramar signals its exclusivity with quiet and refined Mexican decor, complete with hand-painted tiles and cooling fountains. The menu offers haute French cuisine including Chateaubriand and coq au vin. The wine list includes top imported and Mexican vintages. The service is excellent and very formal.

Open daily for dinner only, from 7 P.M. The average cost of a meal for two, including wine, is about $70. Reservations are a must. Credit cards: AE, MC, V.

Palenque

Carretera Escénica, across from La Vista Shopping Center
Tel. 748-4-59-98

Palenque is perched atop a hill, above the Carretera Escénica. The road up is steep and a bit scary, especially at night. Palenque offers dining in the round: The restaurant is a pink adobe circular space with tiered seating. Colorful crêpe chain decorations are strung across the ceiling, and leather-covered chairs and tables, the latter decked with cheerful red cloths, enhance the Mexican flavor of the place. In addition to the regular menu, featuring steaks and fish prepared Mexican-style or grilled, Palenque periodically presents Mexican fiestas with big buffets, folkloric dancing, mariachi music, and cockfighting. Open daily, Mon.–Wed., Fri., and Sat., 7–11 P.M.; on Sun., 2–11 P.M.; and on Thurs., 4–11 P.M. Reservations are not required, but call before making the trip; the hours, we are informed, are subject to change. Palenque's wine list features mostly domestic labels. The average cost of a meal for two, including wine, is about $50. Credit cards: AE, MC, V.

Suntory

Costera Miguel Alemán, near La Palapa Hotel, at Icacos Beach
Tel. 748-4-80-88

Suntory takes Acapulco's reputation for fresh fish and seafood a step further, as it offers sashimi and sushi. This Acapulco outpost is decorated very much like all the other Suntory restaurants: peaceful rock gardens, rice-paper screens, tatami mats, dim lighting, and highly polished teak tables with grills set in the middle, plus traditional-style sushi bars. The food is fresh and reliable. Beer and saki served. Open Mon.–Sat., 1–5:30 P.M. and 7:30–11 P.M.; Sun., 1–5:50 P.M. A meal for two, with beer or saki, averages about $65. Reservations are suggested. Credit cards: AE, MC, V.

SHOPPING

Shopping is Acapulco's most popular attraction—after sun, surf, and nightlife. The resort's hundreds of tempting shops offer just about anything anyone could possibly want. Browsing around town is quite delightful—the merchandise on display is glorious, and the shops are refreshingly air-conditioned!

Acapulco is Mexico's most expensive destination. That mark of distinction applies to the town's boutiques and gift shops as well as its hotels and restaurants. Attractive beach and casual wear, handicrafts, souvenirs, and gift items—in fact, all the items you'd be most likely to buy in Acapulco—are somewhat more expensive here than they would be elsewhere in Mexico. So if you're planning to visit other Mexican cities or beach resorts, consider the possibility of saving your shopping spree for other stops. You'll probably stretch your shopping dollars by doing so.

Actually, price tags tend to be higher during the peak season, from December through February. Even so, with the peso's built-in devaluation, you'll get good value for your dollars. And in comparison to prices in the United States Acapulco still offers good buys, especially on items that are *"Hecho en México."* Many shops sporting designer names actually sell *"Hecho en México"* copies of designer creations, some without designer permission. If you're a stickler for authenticity, ask before you buy.

Some of the best buys include casual cotton clothes, beach attire, souvenir T-shirts and towels, leather goods, baskets, silver (but make sure the item you're buying has the "sterling" or ".925" stamp), ceramics, embroidered clothing, onyx trinkets, hand-blown glass, and other handicrafts.

On the other hand, Acapulco is not a good place to buy high-tech things like hair dryers, electric razors, cassette players, portable TVs, or other personal small appliances. These are expensive in Mexico, and very often, they are not particularly well made. In fact, even the ordinary Duracell batteries that power these accessories are quite costly in Mexico. Bring all these things from home, or buy them in the duty-free shop at the airport when you're leaving for Mexico.

Don't think you can avoid shopping in Acapulco. Even if you're too busy or too tired to move yourself in the direction of the shops, the merchants will come to you. Street and beach vendors greet you at every corner of the Costera Miguel Alemán and approach you as you're lounging by the shore. Some of the street vendors look like walking hat racks; others seem to be burros overburdened with far too many blankets and baskets. Whether the vendors are old or young, they have a way of making you feel guilty if you don't buy something. They're very persistent, and they're hawking everything. "Hammocks?," says one. "Silver?," smiles another. "Nice T-shirt?," offers a third. All insist that their goods are "very, very good and very, very cheap. Especially for you. Today."

With street vendors, and in most outdoor or *mercado* stalls, the price you pay for something depends largely upon your bargaining skills. If you are quoted a price, offer half. Then work your way, peso by peso, to a decent price. You can haggle over pennies or be a brutal cheapskate, and it won't phase the vendors in the least. Remember, they're the pros, and you're not getting away with a thing. When it comes to buying silver in the street and stalls, be especially careful. Such venues offer attractive jewelry, but much of it is alpaca (nickel silver) rather than actual silver, and even a superb bargainer can't transform it into the real thing.

Acapulco street vendors, like street vendors anywhere, can be annoying. Often they stick to you like glue, especially if you've expressed any sort of initial interest, or sometimes if you've merely been polite. If you want to get rid of them, you may have to be obviously rude. One way is to offer them an insultingly low amount for their wares. Of course, you can avoid this unpleasantness by waving them off in the first place. A definite no with a shaking index finger is usually effective. Otherwise, you may wind up with some serapes and reproductions of artifacts (often billed as "the real thing") that you don't really want—and that probably aren't worth whatever you paid for them—just to get rid of a vendor who wouldn't take no for an answer.

In general, shops along the posh Costera Miguel Alemán and in the luxury hotels are more expensive than those in the old section of town, and the prices charged by vendors stationed in Acapulco's *mercado* may very well undercut those of sellers who are roving up and down the Costera.

Costera Miguel Alemán

In the early eighties, the Costera Miguel Alemán got a much-needed face-lift. The renovation included new shopping centers and modernization of the existing shops that sell stylish, famous-label resortwear and exotic gift items. The Costera's posh boutiques nicely complement the colorful outdoor stalls clustered along several segments of the Strip. All together, shops and stalls make for an entertaining shopping stroll.

You can encounter street vendors any time of day and late into the night. Shops, however, are usually open from 10 or 11 A.M. until 8 P.M. Some close for lunch from 2 to 4 P.M.

The Costera is several miles long. You might find it convenient and relaxing to shop-hop. Rent a car or jeep, and breeze along the Costera, stopping at shops that appeal. Caution: Don't leave purchases in the vehicle while you're in the stores. Most likely they'll be gone when you get back.

Finding Costera street numbers isn't easy. Buildings aren't clearly marked, and many shop attendants don't even know their exact addresses. In general, lower numbers are near Old Acapulco. A good landmark toward one end of the Costera Miguel Alemán is Hotel Paraíso Radisson (number 163). Near the other end is Hotel Fiesta Tortuga (number 3675). Mainly falling between these boundaries are many interesting shops, including the following:

Fiorucci (number 74) has exact copies (bearing Fiorucci labels) of amusing, trendy Italian clothes and accessories, including studded denim short skirts and jackets, the latest in torn and distressed jeans, stone-washed denim shirts, bathing suits, shorts, ties, knit dresses, and kids' T-shirts. The shop also offers unusual plastic sandals and shoes.

Daniel Hechter (number 115) has more conservative casual clothes, with attractive, stylish sweaters, cotton trousers, and shirts and jackets in brightly appealing solid colors and plaids. A handsome multipocketed flak jacket is fun and unusual.

Across the Costera, **Ralph Lauren**'s two Polo stores are filled with sophisticated casual clothes, plus some business suits and shirts. There are traditional V-neck sweaters with the Polo logo, cotton knit shirts in bright or pastel colors, cotton and corduroy trousers, ties, fabric belts with leather trim, and olive-drab jackets. Women's fashions, on the second floor, include knit shirts, sweaters, floor-length casual dresses in white or denim, skirts, and shorts.

Ocean Pacific (number 120) has a big picture window displaying colorful beachwear, shorts, sweat clothes, and other casuals with the OP logo, plus attractive shirts with flounces, and tank tops.

Nearby, **Guess?** (number 154) clothes have the company trademark (a question mark within a triangle) but are labeled "*Hecho en México.*" The prices may tempt you to overlook such details. There are denim jackets with leather patches and matching jeans, attractive denim multipocketed vests and matching miniskirts, plus attractive oversized cotton shirts and skimpy T-shirts.

Two additional clothes shops are numberless: **Jag** has knit jump suits in white and bright colors, in addition to cute tiered "Camp Beverly Hills" jean skirts with matching jackets. **Pasarela** sells unusual evening wear, including gowns heavily beaded with black jet or glittering silver, and slinky little silk sheaths with beaded trim.

Take a break from clothes to stop in at **Sergio Bustamente**'s charming gallery (number 711) and browse among his whimsical ceramic and brass animal and plant sculptures. You'll also find attractive animal prints by Howard Nordlund.

At number 1999 is **ACA Joe,** with popular clothes that sell in the United States at much higher prices. ACA Joe originated in this town, and the well-stocked local store sells stacks of colorful mix-and-match cotton shorts, shirts, sweat clothes, T-shirts, and other casual clothes.

Next door is **Ruben Torres,** another casual-clothes label, this one relatively unknown in the United States. Ruben Torres's styles are similar to ACA Joe's, but colors are softer and patterns a bit less bold. Prices for mix-and-match shorts, slacks, and shirts are about equal to those at ACA Joe. Ruben Torres's designs appeal to people who want to buy clothes that are not found easily at home.

Also at number 1999, **Mad Max** is a super children's shop with trendy togs for tots. Sizes run from 3 or 4 to 14. There are matching pants and jackets in bright, colored cotton with patchwork animal appliqués, and comfortable shirts and T-shirts. You don't have to spend a fortune here to have a fashionable child.

Nearby, **Ricardo**'s has heavy white ponchos with ornate trim, silkscreened cotton dresses, beach towels pretty enough to hang on the walls, giraffe-print jersey slacks and tunic tops, and stone-washed denim flared skirts.

Izod (number 4057) has exact copies of crocodile shirts, as well as copies of Calvin Klein men's shirts, trousers, underwear, and socks.

South of the Costera Miguel Alemán, high atop one of the cliffs along the Carretera Escénica, you'll find **La Vista Shopping Center,** a collection of exclusive boutiques with top Mexican designer labels. **Aries** has superb leather bags, accessories, and clothing. **Gucci** has leather goods, scarves, and clothing—much of it made in Mexico, but all bearing the Gucci label. **Armando's** has Girasol designer Gonzalo Bauer's colorful cotton clothes. These contemporary casuals are based on traditional Mexican regional costumes and come bedecked with ribbons and appliqué. The shops at La Vista are quite expensive, but browsing is free. And if you tire of that, you can always enjoy the splendid view of Acapulco and the bay.

Hotel shopping arcades are also quite expensive, but they are convenient. One of the best of these is at the Hyatt Regency, where you'll find boutiques belonging to **Tane** (for fine silver jewelry and home accessories); **Michel Domit** (great shoes and some leather clothing, beautiful silk ties and accessories); **Fiorucci** (chic and camp clothes for the young at heart and trendy in spirit); **Martha** (fine and colorful cotton clothes by Mexican designers, ranging from trendy to traditional—traditionally Mexican, that is); and **Gucci** (all designer-label articles, made in Mexico). In addition, most hotels have craft and souvenir shops that will spare you the trouble—or pleasure—of having to spend your time browsing along the Costera and elsewhere.

Acapulco's Mercado: Great Prices, Great Ambience

People who live in Acapulco say prices in shops along the Costera Miguel Alemán are so high because Americans come with fists full of dollars and seek relief from Acapulco's perpetual sun by shopping up a storm. They purchase bundles of casual clothes and handsome handicrafts, and drive prices up, well beyond the means of ordinary Acapulqueños.

But despite the strength of the dollar in Mexico, more and more American travelers are noticing sharp rises in the prices in shops along the Costera, and they're asking tour guides and hotel concierges to direct them to the shops where budget-

---

Handicrafts

Mexico abounds in fabulous handicrafts. Unfortunately, Acapulco isn't one of the most prolific producers of them. However, a large shop called **Artesanias Finas Acapulco** (Avenida Horacio Nelson, behind Baby'O) has an ample selection of baskets, embroidered clothes, tooled leather wallets and briefcases, onyx bowls and chess sets, papier-mâché animals, earthenware pottery, handblown glass, and more. Most of the merchandise comes from other parts of Mexico and costs more here than it would there. But prices are fixed and fairly reasonable, especially if you're not going to be shopping in other Mexican cities. Or . . . you can look for handicrafts in Acapulco's *mercado.*

---

conscious Acapulqueños buy their casual clothes, beachwear, and decorative items.

Acapulqueños shop mostly in the old section of town, where dozens of boutiques, specialty stores, supermarkets, and gift shops line narrow cluttered streets. These shops aren't fancy, but their merchandise costs about one-third less than it would on the Costera.

The best bargains of all are in the *mercado.* This mazelike triangular area has about four hundred selling stalls clustered around small, shaded octagonal parks with benches where vendors take time off for a siesta and where wandering cats scamper and stalk stray goods.

The market is bounded by Matamoros, Velasquez de Leon, and Parian streets. It's divided into two distinctive sections: Stalls numbered to the 280s offer traditional goods and handicrafts; stalls in the 290s and 300s sell foodstuffs, household goods, inexpensive clothing, electronic goods, shoes, and personal accessories.

Those who go to market are guaranteed an unusual and fun shopping experience, along with welcome savings. Of course, in the *mercado,* items don't have fixed prices. Many vendors assume that American tourists have vast quantities of money, and they hike up prices for *gringos.* This is especially true in the handicrafts section of the market.

What you pay depends upon the impression you make on the seller and on your bargaining skills. Here are some tips: Dress down for the occasion. Wear simple, neat, casual clothes, and leave jewelry and designer watches in the safety-deposit box at your hotel. Be friendly and polite, and assume that "private" conferences in English will be understood. Feign disinterest, especially if you really like something. Ask the prices of several items, including those you really like. Never accept the first price quoted. Comparison shop to price similar objects, and get vendors to bid competitively for your business. Look for discounts when you purchase several items; try to make several purchases in one shop. If you can't agree on an acceptable price, walk out. Often the vendor will follow you with a better offer.

Vendors quote prices in pesos; sometimes you can get a better deal if you pay in dollars. Know the daily exchange rate and round off dollar figures in your favor. Many vendors accept this practice because the peso has a steady, built-in daily rate of decline against the dollar.

If you have a Mexican friend who lives in Acapulco or is traveling with you, shop as a team. You go into the stall first, choose your merchandise, and ask prices. Then your friend enters independently, prices the same items (they'll be about 30 percent less), bargains them down further, and buys for you.

Bargaining is a game. In the *mercado,* you're playing with pros. Use your techniques to best advantage; take satisfaction in scoring some points. You have little chance of winning the match, but the experience is exhilarating and, in the case of bargaining, you can take home reasonably priced souvenirs.

These may include attractive straw baskets in a variety of sizes and shapes. **Stall Number 129** sells multicolored handwoven round barrel-shaped baskets with lids and handles, and rectangular bags decorated with straw flowers—both large enough to carry purchases home. Cute little shoulder bags made of a plastic-type material called raffia come in silver, gold, and pastel colors ideal for tropical evening wear.

Stall Number 265 has leather goods. Unusual carry-on luggage is made to look like distressed denim and has six convenient compartments. The same bag is available in tan or brown leather. There are also beautifully tooled leather golf bags, handbags, eyeglass cases with pen and pencil compartments, and change purses. Leather bomber jackets, belts, and sandals are good buys.

Stall Number 238 sells large, sturdy tube-shaped leather bags with tooling and darling tot-sized suede vests.

Onyx sculptures, table service, and chess sets are sold at **stall numbers 187** and **193.** Items range from decorative onyx fruit in an onyx bowl to functional onyx shot glasses on a tray. There are also onyx elephants and giraffes, Mexican peasants with large sombreros, and attractive onyx boxes, small and large. These stalls sell pretty papier-mâché parrots and colorful fruits and vegetables, plus dolls in traditional dress from the different regions of Mexico.

Rugs, blankets, and ponchos are sold throughout the market. **Stall Number 124** has pure-wool ponchos. **Stall Number 226** sells lovely rugs.

Silver and alpaca (nickel silver) jewelry and trinkets are good buys. Prices are calculated according to weight of the metal and complexity of the workmanship. **Stall Number 247** has beautiful modern-looking silver and lapis bracelets made in Taxco and diamond-cut silver bracelets made in Guadalajara. Alpaca and malachite bolo ties, engraved belt-buckle sets, and smooth and shiny evening bags are great gifts.

Acapulco souvenir T-shirts with elaborate sequined decorations, adults' and children's embroidered dresses and shirts, bathing suits and cover-ups, and lightweight cotton shirts for men hang from the rafters of many shops.

The part of the market where vendors sell foodstuffs, casual clothes, and electronic goods has some good buys too. There are pretty barrettes with colorful silk flowers, festive parrot earrings, women's cotton shorts and tops, and wind-up toys of all sorts.

The atmosphere in this part of the market is different. For one thing, prices quoted to Acapulqueños and *gringos* are similar here. And it is noisier. Rock-and-roll and salsa blare from cassette players that compete with one another in size and volume. Children dart across the crowded alleys, chasing rubber balls or each other. Some shopkeepers siesta on cardboard cartons; others snack or chat or rearrange their wares. Roving merchants wear stacks of hats on their heads or carry numerous birdcages filled with colorful and noisy parakeets. Here, merchandise is not so exotic as that found in the handicrafts section, but this area offers a fascinating glimpse into the local lifestyle.

ENTERTAINMENT

CLUBS

Every hotel in Acapulco has a nightclub, and most have live entertainment or dancing or both. One of the resort's most unusual night spots is **Tequila's Le Club** (Urdaneta 29; tel. 748-5-86-23), which presents "La Mágica de la Transformación Paris Vegas Show," a transvestite revue. There's an international show (with impersonators doing Ethel Merman, Diana Ross, Melissa Manchester, Madonna, and more) at 11:15 P.M. and a Latino show (Lupita D' Alessio, Rocio Durcal, Daniela Romo, Lucia Mendez, Pimpanela, etc.) at 1:30 A.M. Take your pick!

DISCOS

If you prefer to take the stage, you can pick from Acapulco's many discos. New names are added to the roster—and drop off it—with some regularity. Here's an abbreviated list of some of the better-established dance halls in town:

Baby'O
Costera Miguel Alemán
Tel. 748-4-74-74

Baby'O is one of Mexico's most famous discos, and its reputation extends around the globe. The building is an intriguing sight: a mound shaped to read "BABY'O," with lush plants growing from the round parts of the letters. Inside, the place is cavelike. Its brown walls have roots climbing up them, and there is a primordial feel about the environment. But the lighting and sound system are all high tech—perhaps the most sophisticated in Acapulco. Baby'O is special because it's different from the other glitter-and-glass discos that line the Strip. Always crowded, and the dancers most often stay to celebrate dawn with breakfast. Open 10:30 P.M.–sunrise.

Bocaccio
Costera Miguel Alemán
Tel. 748-4-19-01

Bocaccio is all pink-and-gray elegance, with lots of mirrors to reflect the strobing lights and twirling dancers. Behind the dance floor is a big peacock-shaped mirror. Run by Acapulco entrepreneur Aaron Fux, Bocaccio is one of the oldest and best-established discos on the Strip. Open 10:30 P.M.–4 A.M.

Le Dome
Costera Miguel Alemán
Tel. 748-4-11-90

The mosaic of mirrors as you walk down the entry hall creates glittering expectations of an exciting evening within. How disappointing to find a rather small dance floor surrounded by unremarkable decor! Still, the light show is flashy, and Le Dome's got a huge following of what seem to be young urban professional Mexicans. Open 10:30 P.M.–4 A.M.

Fantasy
Carretera Escénica at La Vista Shopping Center
No phone

The hot-pink exterior of Fantasy camouflages the club's coolly elegant interior. The walls are covered in black paper with star and galaxy tracings. Tables, on different tiers around the dance floor, are set with lacy clothes and real silver. Overhead, the laser-light effects tease your perceptions, and, best of all, the dance floor is situated in front of wraparound windows with a spectacular, panoramic view of Acapulco. At about 2 A.M. nightly there's the added excitement of a great fireworks display. This disco attracts an older, elegant, and monied crowd that likes to dress up for the dance. You should too—or you won't be let in. Open 10:30 P.M.–4 A.M. Fantasy is run by Ruben Fux, son of Aaron Fux of **Bocaccio** fame.

News
Costera Miguel Alemán
No phone

This big gray concrete building has one wall of windows through which you can see a gray high-tech interior. In the midst of it, there's a pink neon bar. The dance floor is beyond. The sound system and light show are as high tech as the decor. It's all very fashionable and very foxy. Popular with vacationing Mexican bigwigs. Open 10:30 P.M.–4 A.M.

Ixtapa-Zihuatanejo

During the 1960s, vacationers seeking unspoiled little towns surrounded by beautiful secluded beaches discovered the old fishing village of Zihuatanejo, on a bay about 150 miles up the coast from Acapulco. The sleepy, dusty port became a favorite hideaway for people who wanted to get away from it all. In the early 1970s, developers who had taken note of the spot decided to build a first-class resort six miles away on the beaches of the Bay of Palmar. In 1975, the first hotel (the Aristos, which was severely damaged in the 1985 earthquake and has still not reopened) was inaugurated in Ixtapa, the new resort town just six miles up the beach from Zihuatanejo. Ixtapa, an enclave of first-class services carved out of swampland (the surrounding area—and even Club Med at Playa Quieta—aren't connected to the public water system), has now become a pricey international playground, with a strip of luxury hotels and great restaurants and night spots. Zihuatanejo, too, has changed: The population has grown from about five thousand to more than forty thousand. There are now many more hotels, restaurants, and shops that cater to the tastes of tourists. However, Zihuatanejo has retained much of its charm, and its prices are still reasonable. Together the sister cities of Ixtapa and Zihuatanejo offer a varied and pleasing vacation experience.

CONNECTIONS

Mexicana and Aeromexico airlines have service to Ixtapa-Zihuatanejo from several U.S. cities, with stops in either Guadalajara, Puerto Vallarta, Manzanillo, Mazatlán, or Mexico City. Delta Airlines flies nonstop to Ixtapa-Zihuatanejo from LoAngeles. Both Mexicana and Aeromexico have several daily nonstop flights between Mexico City and Ixtapa-Zihuatanejo. Connecting flights on other international carriers, via Mexico City or Guadalajara, are easily scheduled.

The airport is about a 20-minute ride from Ixtapa, about 15 minutes from Zihuatanejo. The airport transfer service, Transportación Terrestre, has individual taxis and combis (group taxis) stationed at the airport to meet arriving flights. The ride costs about $8 in a van; $15 in a taxi, and you can buy a round-trip ticket if you choose, for $18. If you don't have a round-trip ticket and you want to reserve a return ride to the airport, you must call Transportación Terrestre (tel. 743-4-20-46) at least 24 hours before your departure time. Taxis stationed at the hotels charge about $18 for a one-way trip to the airport.

Both Ixtapa and Zihuatanejo are compact enough so that you can get around them on foot without much difficulty. They're about six miles apart, but there is frequent bus service between them. Taxis are plentiful, and the cab ride between Ixtapa and Zihuatanejo costs only several dollars.

A B C

1

Isla
Ixtapa

Isla De
A Pie

Playa Linda

Playa Quieta

Playa

■ Club Med Resort

Playa Cuata

Bahía

Del Palmar

■ Marina

IXTAPA

2

Los Moros

*Laguna de
Barra Potosí*

Playa del Palmar

Hotel Zone

■ La Puerta Shopping Center

Playa Vista Hermosa

**Palma Real
Golf and
Tennis Club**

■ Camino Real Resort

3

Playa Majahua

Federal Highway

San Esteban
Punta

Ixtapa Boulevard

5 de Mayo *Galeana*

Bravo

■ Pier

J. Alvarez

■ State Handicrafts Store

*Bahía
Zihuatanejo*

■ Public Market

*Playa
Madera*

Paseo Zihuatanejo

4

Playa La Ropa

ZIHUATANEJO

*Playa Las
Gatas*

■ *Airport*

N

IXTAPA/ZIHUATANEJO

| 0 miles | | 2 |
| 0 kilometers | | 2 |

5

Mexico City Playa Azul

Acapulco

Unless you plan to go back and forth between Ixtapa and Zihuatanejo several times a day and make long excursions along the coast or into the countryside, there's really no advantage to renting a car or jeep. However, if you do wish to rent a vehicle, the major rental agencies have offices at the airport and in several of Ixtapa's large hotels. Remember that you get a better rate on auto rentals if you make your reservations in the United States.

Recently, mopeds and bicycles have become popular with vacationers. If you're not used to strenuous pedaling, opt for the moped. Ixtapa is flat enough, but there are hilly areas in Zihuatanejo. You can rent mopeds and bikes at the Dorado Pacífico Hotel in Ixtapa.

You might also consider taking a guided tour to get an overview of the twin resorts. Tours are scheduled mornings and afternoons and take about three hours. You get a glimpse of the outlying beaches and all the panoramic views, and the locations of interesting restaurants and night spots are pointed out. The tour costs approximately $10 per person and can be booked through any local travel agency.

Beaches are the big attraction in Ixtapa-Zihuatanejo. The wide ribbon of sand in front of Ixtapa's luxury hotels is known as **Playa del Palmar.** It's a great beach for walking, frolicking, and sunbathing—the pretty white sands seem to stretch for miles. But swimmers are always cautioned about the strong undertow. To the west of Playa del Palmar, covering several miles beyond the borders of Ixtapa's hotel zone, are the undeveloped beaches **Playa Don Juan, Playa Rodrigo,** and **Playa Casablanca,** with private residences and estates. Just west of these, hidden from the road, is the secluded **Playa Cuata,** a favorite with nude sunbathers. Next, to the west, is **Playa Quieta,** the active beach belonging to Club Med.

At the eastern end of Palmar Bay is **Playa Vista Hermosa,** a beautiful and secluded beach backed by high rock cliffs. This is where the Camino Real is located.

Zihuatanejo's beaches are several miles east of Playa Vista Hermosa. **Playa Zihuatanejo,** the public beach, is tranquil and protected from the open sea. This is the area's best beach for swimming. Farther east are **Playa la Madera,** with brownish sand, and **Playa la Ropa,** a very popular white-sand beach. There are some tricky currents and undertow at both of these beaches. Farther east still is **Las Gatas,** a fairly isolated beach with coral reefs that are very popular with snorkelers and divers. You can get to Las Gatas via a narrow, somewhat treacherous path at the eastern end of Playa La Ropa or by boat from the docks near Playa Zihuatanejo. There are also organized tours that include lunch and sports activities. Ask your hotel concierge or local travel agent for details.

About 14 miles along the coast to the southeast is **Playa Blanca,** a primitive tropical paradise surrounded by mango plantations and coconut groves. Near this isolated beach is the fishing village of **La Barra de Potosi,** with some inexpensive *palapa*-covered seafood restaurants. This is really a day's excursion for adventurous nature lovers. Ask your hotel concierge for directions by bus, taxi, or jeep.

Ixtapa Island, about ten minutes by launch off the coast, has several protected beaches with excellent swimming, snorkeling, and scuba conditions, and a bird sanctuary. Bring a picnic lunch and binoculars. You can go to the island with an organized tour (Mexico Travel Advisers has one that lasts for five hours and costs $15, including lunch, hotel pickup, and boat ride from Playa Quieta; call 743-313-79 for scheduled departures and reservations) or by hiring a boat at the dock at Playa Zihuatanejo or at Playa Quieta.

Also popular are small game and deep-sea fishing excursions, which can be booked through Mexico Travel Advisers or any local travel agent, or negotiated independently with fishing boats docked at Playa Zihuatanejo. The tours last from five to seven hours and cost about $150 to $250 per person, covering bait and tackle and the advice, or instruction, of the ship's captain. The area's big-game fish include sailfish and marlin.

When you tire of the water, try golf for diversion. There's an 18-hole championship course opposite the Ixtapa Sheraton Hotel. You can rent clubs if you don't feel like bringing your own, but rental and greens fees are rather high. Make arrangements through your hotel concierge.

Both Ixtapa and Zihuatanejo offer good shopping. Along the strip, Ixtapa has posh shopping centers with sophisticated boutiques, jewelers, and charming crafts shops. At **Centro Comercial la Puerta,** visit **Florence** for fine handicrafts of all kinds, and **Creaciones Alberto** for jewelry. At **Galerías Ixtapa,** the **Fernando Huertos Boutique** has Mexican designer clothes of brightly colored cottons bedecked with appliqués. Down the strip, toward Zihuatanejo, **Tane,** in the Camino Real Hotel, is one of Mexico's best silver shops, with fine jewelry and lovely home accessories. In Zihuatanejo, head for the **Mercado,** a collection of small shops and stalls that sprawls over several blocks along Paseo del Cocotal and side streets, including several pedestrian-only streets near the *zócalo.* Here you'll find handicrafts, leather goods, clothing, silver and gems (beware of fakes!), and foodstuffs. For a good selection of textiles and embroidered clothing, try **El Embarcadero** (at Juan Alvarez and 5 de Mayo). For more Mexican designer clothes, visit **La Fuente** (at Cuauhtemoc and Ejido).

Ixtapa-Zihuatanejo doesn't have the nonstop activity of Acapulco. Nightlife here consists of dining out (see **Restau-**

rants, below), clubs, and discos—but it doesn't last all night long. Two of the most popular discos are along the strip: **Christine,** at the Krystal Ixtapa, has a good sound system and light show, and attracts a chic young crowd; and **Da Vinci,** at the Holiday Inn, caters to a more mature group.

🧳 HOTELS

Picking a hotel in Ixtapa-Zihuatanejo involves a clear-cut choice: Do you want to be surrounded by the glamour of a glittering resort area with luxury hotels, posh restaurants, and shops? Choose expensive Ixtapa. Do you want the quaint charm and atmosphere of a Mexican fishing village? Choose moderately priced Zihuatanejo. Both have good beaches, although Zihuatanejo's beaches are a bit better for swimming because Ixtapa's Playa del Palmar often has a strong undertow. But there is easy access between the two.

Bungalows Allec

Apdo. Postal 220, Playa la Madera, 40880
Tel. 743-4-20-02
A bungalow accommodating two to four persons, from $70, including breakfast

Ten charming little bungalows are stacked up against the hillside; each has a sitting area, kitchenette, and two bedrooms, each with two beds. All bungalows have ocean views and are surrounded by gardens. The place is run by Klaus and Nickolaus Errodt, who are German but speak perfect English. A great find for families or people who are traveling in a group of four. Free transportation to other beaches by boat. No credit cards.

Camino Real

Apdo. Postal 97, Playa Vista Hermosa, 40880
Tel. 743-3-21-21 or 800-228-3000
Doubles, from $165

Widely considered to be the best resort hotel in Ixtapa, the Camino Real is secluded from the rest of the strip. It is a dramatic structure, built down the side of a steep rock cliff. Each of its 450 spacious rooms has a private sundeck overlooking the sea and a pretty beach bordered by high rock formations on both ends. The rooms are decorated with bright colors, heavy wooden furniture, tiled floors, and other Mexican touches, plus servibar and color TV with eight satellite channels. Surrounding the hotel are lush terraced gardens and a remarkable series of pools connected by waterfalls. The hotel has four tennis courts, water sports, access to deep-sea fishing and golf, several excellent restaurants, including the new Portofino Italian bistro, plus bars and a disco. There's free transportation around the hotel grounds, but you'll need to take a taxi or rent a jeep to get to restaurants, night spots, or shops along the strip, or in Zihuatanejo. Credit cards: AE, DC, MC, V.

Club Med

Playa Quieta, 40880

Tel. 743-4-33-80, 743-4-34-52 or 800-CLUB MED

Two persons, two twin beds, from about $800 (depending on the month of travel) per week per person, including meals, wine, and most sports. Land/air packages available from many U.S. cities. Some long weekend packages also available during off-season

Club Med Ixtapa is located on Playa Quieta, a beautiful secluded cove about four miles west of Ixtapa. The village can house up to 750 "members" (guests) in three-story beige bungalows, clustered by the beach. All rooms are air-conditioned and have two twin beds (if you go alone, you'll be assigned a roommate), private bathroom (showers only), and ocean views. Club meals are sumptuous feasts, always with several entrées, a huge salad, heaps of fresh fruit, and lush desserts. Breakfast and lunch are buffets, and dinner is served family-style, around large tables that seat up to ten people. There's always a full carafe of house wine on the table. You can sit on the beach and soak up the sun; play tennis on 12 courts (four night-lit); wind surf; sail; do aerobics or water exercises; play golf on a Robert Trent Jones course or go deep-sea fishing (extra charge for both); or learn to paint on silk. Participate in or simply watch nightly shows, and disco until dawn.

Children are welcome. In fact, there's a "mini club" with supervised activities 9 A.M.–9 P.M. for kids from two to eleven, and at certain times of the year children aged two to seven stay free (limit two per family).

Club Med is a bit isolated but will arrange local tours (at an extra charge), or you can take a taxi into town and explore on your own. Credit cards: AE, DC, MC, V.

Dorado Pacifico

Apdo. Postal 15, Bulevar Ixtapa, 40880
Tel. 743-4-30-60
Doubles, from $135

In the center of the strip, this luxury high-rise hotel has two towers joined in the middle by an atrium lobby with fountains and windowed elevators. Most of the three hundred spacious and pleasantly decorated rooms have ocean views; the others overlook shopping centers and marshlands beyond. All have servibars and color TV with English-language channels. The pool area has an expansive patio with *palapas* and umbrellas, deck chairs, and bar, all surrounded by lush greenery. Tennis courts and water sports. Restaurants and bars are lively. Credit cards: AE, DC, MC, V.

Fiesta Mexicana

Apdo. Postal 4, Playa la Ropa, 40880
Tel. 743-4-37-76
Doubles, from $100 (Modified American Plan required in winter)

This small hotel has the sands of Playa la Ropa, one of Zihuatanejo's prime beaches, as its lobby. There are 35 pleasantly decorated rooms, arranged around the beach and the hotel's gardens. Most rooms have balconies. The pool is small. During high season, guests are required to pay for the Modified American Plan, which covers breakfast and dinner in the hotel's homey restaurant. Fiesta Mexicana provides free transportation to the Hotel Irma on La Madera Beach. Credit cards: AE, MC, V.

Holiday Inn Ixtapa
Bulevar Ixtapa, 40880
Tel. 743-3-11-86 or 800-HOLIDAY
Doubles, from $115

The pool area of this hotel is magnificent, with a spectacular free-form pool surrounded by a nicely landscaped patio. The 280 rooms are clean, well maintained, and pleasantly decorated. All have servibars and color TV with cable; some have ocean views. A restaurant, bar, and the popular **Da Vinci** disco are on the premises, but many guests prefer to use this hotel as a convenient base for going out to other restaurants and night spots along the strip. Credit cards: AE, CB, DC, MC, V.

Hotel Susy
Guerrero y Juan Alvarez, 40880
Tel. 743-4-23-39
Doubles, from $45

Susy is a reasonably priced little hotel with just 14 rooms (fans only), located on a busy corner in sleepy Zihuatanejo, just one block from the town beach. It's clean and friendly and filled with ambience—and very inexpensive—in short, just right for folks who are looking for the antithesis of the Ixtapa experience. Credit cards: MC, V.

Ixtapa Sheraton
Bulevar Ixtapa, 40880
Tel. 743-3-18-58, 800-334-8484 or 800-325-3535
Doubles, from $130

This beautiful hotel has two towers facing each other over a huge and airy lobby area, with an enormous angled skylight, and glass-enclosed elevators that sweep up and down the interior walls. About half of the 350 rooms have sea views; the others look out over a championship golf course and expansive marshlands beyond. All rooms are decorated with modern furniture and pastel color schemes and have servibars and color TV with English-language channels. The recreation area features a patio; snack and drinks bar; an enormous angular swimming pool and a smaller pool for children; an expansive beach; water sports; tennis courts; Ping-Pong and volley ball; plus outdoor cooking and crafts classes and special activities for children. The service is friendly and helpful. Three restaurants—including the lovely **Casa Real**—plus a lively bar complete the picture. Credit cards: AE, CB, DC, MC, V.

Krystal Ixtapa
Bulevar Ixtapa, 40880
Tel. 743-3-03-33 or 800-231-9860
Doubles, from $130

The Krystal is one of the most popular hotels in Ixtapa. It's conveniently located midway down the strip and has two of the town's biggest nighttime attractions, **Bogart's** restaurant and the **Christine** disco. The hotel's spacious lobby has a breezy, cool ambience—welcome relief from the steamy outdoors. The spacious rooms are given a tropical feel with palm tree–patterned bedspreads and curtains. Furnishings are modern. Rooms have color TVs with cable channels, servibars, and balconies with ocean views. The recreation and beach areas are spectacular. A huge patio with sundeck has an enormous free-form pool with a swim-up bar, volleyball net, bridges that create patches of welcome shade, and a large *palapa* bar. Around this is an expanse of lawn leading down to the beach. The hotel's pet deer are kept in a large enclosed pen. An outdoor stage for performances and ceremonies, backed by a series of graceful columns, is near the beach. The hotel has social activities for guests and special activities for children. Tennis courts, water sports, restaurants, and bars. Credit cards: AE, DC, MC, V.

Stouffer's Presidente Ixtapa

Bulevar Ixtapa, 40880
Tel. 743-3-00-18 or 800-472-2427
Doubles, from $125

The roadside facade of this high rise looks like a huge white monolith, with beautifully colored stained-glass windows. The ocean side, however, is a beehive of balconies, each belonging to one of the hotel's 450 rooms. The rooms are modern, clean, and comfortable, each with servibar and color TV broadcasting English-language programs, and there are pleasant restaurants and a bar on the premises. On Wed. night, the El Presidente presents a delightful Mexican fiesta (about $25 per person) with buffet dinner, Ballet Folklórico, and other entertainment. Credit cards: AE, DC, MC, V.

Sotavento and Catalina hotels

Playa la Ropa, 40880
Tel. 743-4-20-32 and 743-4-21-37
Doubles, from $75 (Modified American Plan required in winter)

Sister hotels perched side by side on a cliff overlooking Playa la Ropa offer terrific accommodations for those who prefer the Zihuatanejo ambience but still want the comforts and activity of a fairly large resort. The Sotavento has eighty rooms arranged on terraces going down the cliff toward the beach. The upper-level rooms are best, with large balcony areas furnished with cheerful yellow deck chairs and hammocks. Lower-level rooms are smaller, and some don't have very good views (and are less expensive, of course). The Catalina's 26 pleasant bungalows vary in size, amenities, and price. During the winter season, you must take the Modified American Plan, which includes breakfast and dinner in the hotel restaurant. One drawback: Few of the rooms have air-conditioning. But there are fans to create a cooling breeze. Credit cards: AE, MC, V.

🍽 RESTAURANTS

Seafood is the specialty in many Ixtapa-Zihuatanejo restaurants, but fine Mexican and international dishes are also served. Try the hotel restaurants, but don't be afraid to venture out into town for the additional pleasure of local atmosphere.

Bay Club
Scenic Drive, above La Madera Beach
Tel. 743-38-44

Bay Club provides a lovely setting overlooking the beach. The varied menu lists soups, salads, and entrées that range from homemade pasta to enchiladas, from grilled steaks to tempura, all prepared to taste—and tastefully served. There is also a pleasant bar, so you can enjoy the sunsets without dining. The unusual wine list offers vintages from small vineyards at big prices. Open Tues.–Sun. for dinner only, 7 P.M.–midnight. The bar opens at 5 P.M. The average price of a meal for two, including wine, is about $60. Reservations suggested. Credit cards: AE, MC, V.

Bogart's
Krystal Ixtapa Hotel
Bulevar Ixtapa (no number)
Tel. 743-3-03-33

The fanciest restaurant on the strip is a fantasy caravansary that makes an evening in Ixtapa feel like an Arabian Night. High domes of billowing white fabric, high-back rattan chairs, lush potted palms, candlelight, overhead fans, a long reflecting pool, and the hushed atmosphere create the impression that you've entered a sheik's tent. The effect is abetted by attentive teams of turban-clad waiters. Only the bar, lined with photos and posters of Humphrey Bogart, et al., and the piano man, playing somewhat jazzed up show tunes, suggest that this all might be slightly camp. For dinner, choose from Caribbean lobster, chicken Casablanca, Mediterranean seafood soup, or the wonderful giant shrimps Krystal, dressed with brandy, Pernod, and garlic, flambéed right at your table and spooned over homemade pasta. Desserts are equally extravagant. The extensive wine list offers domestic labels at reasonable prices, although the prices of imports are astronomical. Open daily for dinner: two seatings only, at 6:30 and 9:30 P.M. The average price of a meal for two, including wine, is about $80. Reservations required. Credit cards: AE, DC, MC, V.

Canaima
On the beach, just west of 5 de Mayo
No telephone

Be prepared to get sand in your shoes! You have to enter this little eatery, actually little more than a hut with bamboo walls around a wrought-iron frame, from the beach. But the fresh fish, especially the red snapper, oysters, and shrimp, are worth the extra effort. And if the taste doesn't keep you coming back for more, the prices will. A meal for two averages about $25. Open for lunch and early dinner. No reservations. No credit cards.

Carlos 'n Charlie's
Bulevar Ixtapa (no number)
Tel. 743-4-33-25

Located in a large mansion-like building fronted by an expansive lawn, this Carlos 'n Charlie's seems a bit more sedate than its sister restaurants of the Carlos Anderson chain. Still, the place has a roster of energetic waiters who love to kid around with the clientele, and all the elements that provide these eateries with a fun-house atmosphere. The menu offers ribs, steaks, and seafood, with a wide choice of soups, salads, and desserts. Very popular and usually crowded. Open for lunch and dinner. Go at off-hours—or make reservations. The average price of a meal for two, including wine, is about $50. Credit cards: MC, V.

Casa Real

Ixtapa Sheraton Hotel
Bulevar Ixtapa (no number)
Tel. 743-3-18-58

In one corner of the posh Ixtapa Sheraton lobby, this elegant eatery is decorated Mexican hacienda–style, with tiled fountains, grillwork, plenty of plants, and comfortably upholstered straight-back chairs. The menu features fresh fish and seafood, including smoked marlin, shrimp, scallops, and red snapper, all prepared with Mexican sauces or simply grilled. The dessert cart is laden with rich cakes. Good wine list. Open for lunch and dinner. The average price of a meal for two, including wine, is about $50. Reservations suggested. Credit cards: AE, MC, V.

Coconuts

Vicente Guerrero 4, near Alvarez
Tel. 743-4-25-18

A pleasant garden setting and fine seafood make Coconuts a favorite choice for dinner. For your entrée, select fried, sautéed, or poached red snapper or shrimp, or a thick steak, accompanied by a splendid fresh salad. And you can dawdle under the stars over a deliciously rich dessert or some fresh fruit. Open daily for dinner only, 6 P.M.–midnight. Good wine list. The average price of a meal for two, including wine, is about $60. Reservations suggested. Credit cards: AE, MC, V.

Los Garrobos

Juan N. Alvarez 52
Tel. 743-4-29-77

The decor is cheerful and Mexican, and the seafood is superb. The menu offers lobster, shrimp, oysters, squid, octopus, crawfish, and various fresh fish fillets—prepared with different sauces and seasonings, as you like them. Meat and chicken dishes are also available, as are spaghetti and paella. Limited wine list. Open for lunch and dinner. The average price of a meal for two, including wine, is about $40. Reservations suggested. Credit cards: AE, MC, V.

Hacienda del Sol

Bulevar Ixtapa (no number)
Tel. 743-4-24-06

The Hacienda features Mexican cuisine in a Mexican setting. Regional specialties include *pollo con mole* (chicken in a mole sauce) from Puebla and *pollo pibil* (barbecued chicken) from the Yucatán, as well as a wide range of dishes from every other area of Mexico. Good wine list with top domestic vintages. Open daily for dinner only, 6 P.M.–midnight. The average price of a meal for two, including wine, is about $50. Reservations suggested. Credit cards: AE, MC, V.

Kon Tiki
La Madera Beach
Tel. 743-4-24-71

The place may look Polynesian, and the bar mixes up many a tropical drink, but Kon Tiki's menu is anything but South Pacific: it offers pizza, pasta, hamburgers, and shish kebab, all tasty and served with a smile. Open 4 P.M.–midnight. The average price of a meal for two, without drinks, is about $20. No reservations. No credit cards.

La Mesa Del Capitan
Nicholas Bravo 18
Tel. 743-4-20-27

This unpretentious and very popular Zihuatanejo seafood restaurant offers a pleasant decor of dark wood furniture and red tablecloths, and an absolutely delightful garden. The menu offers fine seafood entrées, including lots of shrimp, lobster, and red snapper, plus meat and chicken for landlubbers. Reasonable wine list. Open for lunch and dinner. The average price of a meal for two, including wine, is about $40. Reservations suggested. Credit cards: AE, MC, V.

Villa Sakura
Centro Comercial la Puerta, Bulevar Ixtapa
Tel. 743-4-36-00

The sushi, sashimi, and tempura all put the area's fresh seafood and fish to good use, but the menu doesn't offer all the standard Japanese favorites. The restaurant has a peaceful Japanese garden and screen-clad interior. Open for lunch and dinner. Beer and saki served. The average price of a meal for two, including saki, is about $60. Reservations suggested. Credit cards: AE, MC, V.

Manzanillo

About 240 miles northwest of Ixtapa-Zihuatanejo is Manzanillo **(see map, Page 502),** the state of Colima's thriving commercial port and tourist resort. Manzanillo Bay was discovered by the Spanish in 1526 and became their embarkation point for expeditions to Baja California and the Orient. It was here that they built the ships that sailed to conquer the Philippines. Today, port activities still dominate Manzanillo: In fact, the town's beachfront is occupied by docks and railroad tracks, and the *zócalo* is surrounded by commercial buildings and warehouses, all generated by the port. Granted, this atmosphere is neither particularly pretty nor very relaxing. There are, however, some pretty scenic drives and lovely old homes in the hills behind Manzanillo; and just north of town, **Las**

Brisas, a beach area with small, relatively pleasant motels and inexpensive eateries, is a favorite vacation retreat for Mexican families. This is also a popular point of embarkation for deep-sea fishing excursions. Manzanillo and Las Brisas lie at the southern end of a seven-mile strip of beach called Playa Azul (not to be confused with the state of Michoacán's Playa Azul, about 175 miles southwest of Manzanillo). At the northern end of Manzanillo's Playa Azul is **Santiago Peninsula,** an exclusive resort area with luxury residences, pricey condos and time-shares, and deluxe hotels, including the famous Las Hadas resort, where the motion picture *10* was filmed. Santiago Peninsula is frequently used as a point of departure for hotel and resort hopping along the **Costo de Oro,** an eighty-mile stretch of pretty beaches and bays along the shore to the northwest. Starting at the southern end, Costa de Oro's treasures include **Playa de Oro; Bahía de Navidad** (with charming towns at Barra de Navidad and San Patricio, also known as Melaque); **Los Angeles Locos** (with hotel); **El Tecuan** (with hotel); **Costa de Careyes** (with hotel); and **Playa Blanca** (with Club Med). About 120 miles northwest of Playa Blanca is Puerto Vallarta.

CONNECTIONS

Manzanillo's airport is located 24 miles north of town. Mexicana has flights to Manzanillo from several U.S. cities via Dallas/Fort Worth, Los Angeles, Guadalajara, or Mexico City. Aeromexico has flights to Manzanillo from several American cities via Los Angeles. Connections on other international carriers flying into Mexico City can be made either via Mexicana or Aeromexico's flights (several each day) from Mexico City to Manzanillo.

Manzanillo's Transportación Terrestre operates individual taxis and combis (group taxis) between the airport and the major hotels. One-way combi service costs about $8; taxis are at least $15. If you want to take a combi, find one as soon as you get off the plane: combis fill up with passengers and leave the airport shortly after flights arrive. Once they've left, you're basically at the mercy of the taxi drivers and stuck with whatever rate they quote. Combis are also available for the return ride to the airport. Ask your hotel concierge to make reservations for you.

National (333-3-06-11) is among the auto-rental agencies that have offices at the airport. If you're staying around Santiago Peninsula or plan to explore the Costa de Oro, having a car is advisable. Rates are high, but taxis in Manzanillo don't have meters, and the drivers are merciless. And local bus service leaves a lot to be desired. Remember, you'll get lower rates with unlimited free mileage if you reserve your car in the United States rather than renting it on the spot in Mexico.

Estrella de Oro has first-class bus service between Manzanillo and Guadalajara, via Barra de Navidad. The whole trip takes about five hours; the segment of the trip from Barra de Navidad to Manzanillo takes about an hour and a half. There is also a daily train from Guadalajara—via Colima—that is supposed to take eight and a half hours but often takes longer.

🧳 HOTELS

Manzanillo is rather devoid of attractions, so you'll probably spend a lot of time at your hotel. Most of the hotels and time-share resorts offer a relaxing vacation yet provide enough activities to keep you entertained. Access to beach or boating is important. Here are some possibilities:

Club Maeva
Apdo. Postal 442 (on Santiago Peninsula), 28200
Tel. 333-3-01-41 or 800-525-1987
Doubles, from $130

This self-contained condominium resort village offers organized activities for adults and children. Club Maeva has 440 bungalows, all with kitchens, plus two huge swimming pools, 12 tennis courts, a beach club, several restaurants, a supermarket, and other shops. This is a great vacation spot for a family that basically wants to stay put by the beach. Credit cards: AE, DC, MC, V.

Fiesta Mexicana
Manzanillo–Santiago Hwy. (about 5 miles north of Manzanillo), 28200
Tel. 333-3-11-00
Doubles, from $85

A new colonial-style hotel, Fiesta Mexicana offers two hundred airy rooms decorated with lovely wicker and wood furniture, featuring both air-conditioning and overhead fans. Some rooms have ocean views. The rooms are off balcony corridors that surround a spacious central courtyard with a huge pool and bar area. There are two patio entrances to the beach, which is dotted with beach chairs and colorful umbrellas. The restaurant, open for breakfast through dinner, serves everything from seafood and Mexican specialties to burgers. The bar/disco has live music, which, fortunately, doesn't interfere with the quiet of the lobby or pool area. The staff is very helpful and accommodating. Credit cards: AE, MC, V.

Las Hadas
Apdo. Postal 158, Peninsula Santiago (about 10 miles north of Manzanillo), 28200
Tel. 333-3-00-00 or 800-228-3000
Doubles, from $210

This extravagant white caravansary in the middle of the jungle and overlooking the sea was built in the 1960s by Bolivian tin magnate Atenor Patino as a private beach hideaway club for his jet-set friends. Since this property has gone public, Las Hadas has become one of the most-photographed—and most famous—resorts in the world. In fact, the hotel's reputation got its biggest boost when Las Hadas was used as a backdrop for the film *10*. And now, almost every day of the year, there are fashion shoots or TV commercials in the works on-site. The place is big enough, however, so that these don't interfere with your privacy. There are 220 rooms and *casitas* arranged around little plazas and down cobbled streets. Most have private pools and views of the sea. The furnishings are sparsely elegant—white wicker in a setting of white marble, all cool and refreshing after the bright heat of the sun. No TVs—but lots of greenery. Little electric golf carts shuttle you around the grounds, 15 acres of scenic hillside dotted with restaurants, lounge areas, tennis courts, shopping arcade, swimming areas, and golf course. This is a place to indulge yourself and spend lavishly. The guests tend to be upper crust, and the excellent staff and management team treats everyone like visiting royalty. One drawback—or advantage, depending upon your point of view—is that you're far away from town and thus are limited to dining in Las Hadas's eateries, all fine and elegant but very expensive. You need to have a car, or rely on taxis, to get around to the off-the-premises sights, beaches, and restaurants. Credit cards: AE, DC, MC, V.

Hotel Colonial

Calle México 100 (near Gonzales Bocanegra), 28000
Tel. 333-2-10-80 or 333-4-35-19
Doubles, from $30

This hotel, a colonial extravaganza that's seen better days, used to be the best hotel in town. Now all the carved wood seems a bit dusty, the plush furnishings are worn, and the chandeliers need polishing. Still, the Hotel Colonial has a lot of history, and if you want to be in the center of Manzanillo, you can't get much closer than this. The hotel is just a block away from the *zócalo,* and the rooms are clean and very reasonably priced. Credit cards: AE, MC, V.

☕ RESTAURANTS

Manzanillo doesn't have as many fine restaurants (or night spots) as the other Pacific Coast resorts. In fact, in Manzanillo, most people dine in their hotels. In case you wish to wander out, however, here are several suggestions:

Bar Social

21 de Marzo, on the *zócalo*
No phone

Everyone stops in here at about 1 P.M. to order a beer or two and get a free lunch of ceviche and guacamole. In the evening, there are quesadillas and other inexpensive snacks. No credit cards. No reservations.

Carlos 'n Charlie's

Manzanillo–Santiago Hwy., north of Las Brisas
Tel. 333-3-11-50

One of Manzanillo's hot spots: at Carlos 'n Charlie's, the waiters keep the atmosphere festive and friendly, and decorative elements add to the fun-house atmosphere. The menu offers ribs, steaks, and seafood, with a wide choice of soups, salads, and desserts. Very popular and usually crowded. Open for lunch and dinner. The average price of a meal for two, including wine, is about $60. Reservations are suggested—unless you're going at an off-hour. Credit cards: MC, V.

Hotel Colonial

Calle México 100, near Gonzales Bocanegra
Tel. 333-2-10-80 or 333-4-35-19

Reliable, clean, and inexpensive, the Colonial offers fish and
seafood, as well as hamburgers and some Mexican specialties.
Open daily for breakfast through dinner. The average cost of a
dinner for two is about $30. No reservations. Credit cards: AE,
MC, V.

El Sombrero

At Las Brisas, off Manzanillo-Santiago Hwy., near the Naval
Hospital
No phone

A terrific and unpretentious little restaurant in a *palapa* hut.
The menu has Mexican dishes from quesadillas to *pozole* (a
kind of corn-and-grits soup), and it's all very inexpensive. Open
for dinner only, 7–11 P.M. The average cost of a meal for two is
about $25. No reservations. No credit cards.

El Vaquero

Manzanillo–Santiago Hwy.
No phone

Where's the beef? Right here,.behind El Vaquero's chuck-
wagon facade—ordered by the kilo, butchered, and charcoal-
grilled the way you like it. Grilled quail is also available. Open
2 P.M.–midnight. The average cost of a dinner for two is about
$35. No reservations. Credit cards: AE, MC, V.

EXCURSIONS

Deep-sea fishing expeditions can be arranged through local
travel agencies. By boat or land via coastal route MEX200,
you can head southeast to **Playa Azul,** the state of Michoacán's pretty beach resort, a tropical paradise with a dense
growth of palm trees and other vegetation. Tourist services
aren't developed here, however, and the fact that it's on the
open sea, rather than in a protective bay, makes for hazardous
swimming. If you head toward the northwest, you'll be on the
Costo de Oro, where there are several points of interest.
Within reach, for day trips or overnighting, are **Barra de
Navidad** and **San Patricio** (**Melaque**), two charming little
beach towns on the Bahía de Navidad, about forty miles northwest of Manzanillo. This is a good place for walking along the
beach, enjoying picnic lunches, and watching sunsets. The trip
takes about an hour and a half by bus or combi. There are
hotels in both towns should you decide to overnight. Farther
north, about sixty miles from Manzanillo, is **El Tecuan,**
where the isolated El Tecuan Hotel, amid groves of mango
trees, provides shelter. The sea is rough here, but there's a
lagoon for swimming and water sports, and you can hire
horses for lovely rides along the beach. **Costa de Careyes,**
about 74 miles northwest of Manzanillo, is a beautiful secluded resort area, with a dozen isolated beaches and cozy coves,

backed by lush tropical greenery. Hotel Plaza Careyes is a hacienda-style retreat with about one hundred rooms, suites, and *casitas,* attractively arranged around a central plaza. Through the hotel you can arrange fishing trips, diving expeditions, horseback riding, and other activities. The hotel's Mexico City office (at Amberes 43, 06600 México, D.F.; tel. 5-514-1208) takes reservations. Room rates are about $105 per night, double occupancy. Several miles away is beautiful **Playa Blanca,** with a large Club Med, which has recently undergone a $10 million makeover. Farther up the coast is Puerto Vallarta.

Puerto Vallarta

Charming Puerto Vallarta **(see map, Page 506),** is about 170 miles north of Manzanillo, on beautiful Bahía de Banderas (Bay of Flags), a 28-mile-long horseshoe-shaped section of the state of Jalisco's shoreline. Puerto Vallarta, or P.V. for short, doesn't have a very long history, as Mexican history goes. The town was founded in 1851, and its name became Puerto Vallarta in 1918, after Ignacio Luis Vallarta, then governor of the state of Jalisco. Puerto Vallarta was just another obscure little fishing village until 1963, when it became an overnight star thanks to *Night of the Iguana,* filmed at Mismaloya Beach. The celebrated romance of two of the film's other stars, Elizabeth Taylor and Richard Burton, who fell in love with the town as well as with each other, added to Puerto Vallarta's newfound fame. In 1968 a new road built to Puerto Vallarta from Tepic allowed the development needed to satisfy the ever-increasing number of tourists. Today, Puerto Vallarta is the third most popular tourist destination in Mexico (after Acapulco and Cancún).

But in spite of all the development and the perpetual influx of tourists, Puerto Vallarta has maintained its charm and special atmosphere. P.V. offers an appealing blend of beach life and town life. It is active and hip, friendly and chic—but never hyper, never aggressive, never frenetic.

Located about midway along the bay, Puerto Vallarta hugs the coast and goes only several blocks inland. The town is divided into three distinct zones. El Centro, P.V.'s urban center, is divided into northern and southern sections by the Cuale River. There are two bridges over the Cuale and an island in the middle of it. El Centro has lots of hotels, restaurants, and shops on both sides of the river and on the island. Up the river, toward the verdant hills that surround town, is Gringo Gulch, an influential enclave where the rich and famous (Liz Taylor tops the list), and many retirees, have splendid residences. Farther upriver are more modest dwellings belonging to townsfolk. The oldest part of town is south of the Cuale River, where you'll find Playa los Muertos, the popular town beach, rimmed with *palapa*-covered restaurants and bars serving fresh seafood and tropical drinks. North of the Cuale River is the Malecón, also known as Paseo Díaz Ordaz. This is the boardwalk and main drag, especially popular for evening strolls.

North of El Centro is a hotel zone, a strip of luxury high-rise beachfront hotels, with fancy recreation areas, restaurants, bars, and discos. At the northern end of this strip is the marina, the point of embarkation for most local water tours. This area is well served by public buses that travel along the Airport Highway between El Centro and the airport, which is four miles north of town. South of El Centro, a long stretch of scenic highway twists and turns past secluded beaches, along high cliffs overlooking the bay, all the way to Mismaloya Beach and beyond. This area has some exclusive hotels, a number of condos, and many expensive private homes. It is not so developed or so commercial as the northern hotel zone, and it is not so well served by public transportation.

CONNECTIONS

It's easiest to get to Puerto Vallarta by airplane. Mexicana Airlines flies to Puerto Vallarta nonstop from Chicago, Dallas/Fort Worth, Los Angeles, San Antonio, and San Francisco, and from various other U.S. cities with connections via the above, or through Guadalajara, Mexico City, Ixtapa-Zihuatanejo, or Mazatlán. Aeromexico flies to Puerto Vallarta from Los Angeles via La Paz. Continental Airlines has direct flights from Houston, and American Airlines has direct flights from Dallas/Fort Worth. Delta Airlines flies nonstop to Puerto Vallarta from Los Angeles and Phoenix. In addition, Mexicana has several nonstop flights daily from Mexico City and Guadalajara to Puerto Vallarta, and Aeromexico has nonstop service from La Paz, Guadalajara, and Tijuana.

Puerto Vallarta's airport is located about 4 miles north of town. Airport taxis and combis, operated by Transportación Terrestre, are plentiful. The combis charge about $5 to take you to the hotels north of Puerto Vallarta, slightly more for those in town, and more still for those to the south. Taxis cost about $8–$15. You can also walk the short distance to the highway and take an ordinary bus for about $.20. To get back to the airport, you can take a taxi stationed at your hotel, or you can walk out to the Airport Highway and hail the Transportación Terrestre combis as they pass by—or you can take the public bus.

National (tel. 332-2-12-26) is among the car-rental agencies represented at the airport, but rental rates in Puerto Vallarta are fairly high. Actually, in P.V. you can rely on public bus service, which is good if not fancy. Public buses run constantly along the Airport Highway, into Puerto Vallarta, along the Malecón, and out along the highway again. Farther inland, where the roads are too hilly or too narrow for buses, there are combis with regularly scheduled routes that go just about everywhere in town.

And taxis, which are plentiful and inexpensive, are another affordable alternative. However, if you're staying at a hotel that's south of town, you may want to rent a car because bus service in that area is less frequent, and taxis are more costly. Remember, you'll get lower rental rates with unlimited free mileage if you reserve your car in the United States rather than renting it on the spot in Mexico.

You can also get to Puerto Vallarta by first-class bus. There is frequent service from Guadalajara (the ride takes about seven hours), from Mazatlán (about six hours), and Manzanillo (about four hours). Buses leave you off at various terminals in downtown Puerto Vallarta.

When you first arrive in town, you might want to take a guided city tour. In three hours, you'll cover the highlights: the *zócalo;* church; Gringo Gulch; the Malecón; and beaches from the north to as far south as Mismaloya. You'll get a good overview that lets you know where you want to spend more time and where you don't. Several companies offer these tours. Mexico Travel Advisers (322-2-43-60) or other local travel agents can make reservations for you. Most tours pick you up at your hotel.

Puerto Vallarta has dozens of beaches to explore. From north to south along the Bahía de Banderas, some of the most important are the **Playa las Glorias, Las Palmas, Vallarta de Oro, Playa Olas Altas, Playa de los Muertos** (also known as **Playa del Sol**), **Las Amapas, Conchas Chinas, Las Estacas, Punta Negra, Palo Maria,** and **Gemelas.** Most of these beaches have fairly rough surf and are better for wading and surfing than for swimming. Farther south is **Mismaloya Beach,** where *Night of the Iguana* was filmed. In the jungle-like hills behind Mismaloya are **Chino's Paradise** and **El Eden** (see **Restaurants,** below), two eateries that serve fresh seafood and have waterfalls that fill natural swimming holes. You might want to take a boat tour to Mismaloya or to nearby **Los Arcos,** a cluster of three islands, all with natural arches, carved over the centuries by the tides. Los Arcos is a popular spot for snorkeling and scuba diving. You can rent equipment and sign up for a tour at Chico's Dive Shop in Puerto Vallarta. Other boat tours leave the marina (off the Airport Highway, north of El Centro) for **Playa las Animas** and **Yelapa.** These secluded beaches, south of Mismaloya, are surrounded by palms and lush tropical undergrowth. Yelapa has horseback riding along the shore. These and other tours operate daily. Reservations can be made through Mexico Travel Advisers (322-2-56-84) or other local travel agents. For sports enthusiasts, Puerto Vallarta offers, in addition to water sports and horseback riding, excellent tennis at the **John Newcombe Tennis Center** (at the Plaza Vallarta Fiesta Americana Hotel; see below) and golf at **Los Flamingos Golf Club** (north of the airport).

Downtown Puerto Vallarta has limited "sights"—no colonial architecture, no great museums—but there's plenty to do. Strolling along the **Malecón** and in the **zócalo** (Plaza de Armas) is a popular activity. Stop to see the **Church of Guadalupe,** with an unusual crownlike belfry. Farther inland is **Gringo Gulch,** with fancy private residences. And nearby, on Cuale Island, there's a small archaeological museum with pre-Hispanic artifacts.

Cuale Island also has lots of outdoor stalls and the colorful **Mercado Municipal** selling handicrafts of all sorts. All in all, Puerto Vallarta is a fabulous town for shopping. If you don't feel like leaving the hotel zone north of El Centro, the **Plaza Vallarta Shopping Center** (near the Plaza Vallarta and Plaza Las Glorias hotels) has dozens of handicraft and souvenir shops, jewelry and clothing boutiques, and even a huge supermarket. But El Centro has the better selection of excellent specialty boutiques: **Olinala** (on Lázaro Cárdenas) has great lacquerware chests, trays, and boxes from the town of Olinala. **Olé** (Juárez 500) sells textiles and embroidered clothing. **La Reja** (Juárez 201) has wonderful papier-mâché animals, figurines, fruit, and vegetables. **Galería Lepe** (Lázaro Cárdenas) has affordable silk-screened posters, while **Galería Uno** (Morelos 561) exhibits Mexican contemporary art. For jewelry, visit **Ric** (Juárez 207), with a large selection of distinctive gold and silver pieces set with semiprecious stones. **Tane** (Camino Real Hotel) has terrific Mexican designer silver jewelry and home accessories. For designer shoes and leather accessories, there's **Gucci** (Juárez and Iturbide). The source for terrific Mexican *huaraches* (traditional handmade sandals) is **Huaracheria Lety** (Juárez 478). **D'Karlo** (Augustin Rodriguez 270) has unusual cowboy boots in exotic leathers. Of course, there are dozens of shops with trendy and classic casual and beach attire. The best include **Ocean Pacific** (Morelos 660); **Piña Cólada** (Libertad 327); **ACA Joe** (Paseo Díaz Ordaz 588); and, next door, **Ruben Torres** (Paseo Díaz Ordaz 590). The last two shops are on the Malecón. This is a great place to begin an evening stroll, with stops at some of Puerto Vallarta's fine restaurants and night spots. Incidentally, there are several ways to approach P.V.'s nightlife: You can hop from place to place sampling the pleasures of all; you can find one place you like a lot and become a regular; or you can escape from it all with a sunset cruise that leaves from the marina nightly at about 5 P.M. Take your pick.

🧳 HOTELS

Because public transportation in Puerto Vallarta is easy and convenient, you can stay in the hotel zone north of town and still enjoy restaurants and nightlife in El Centro. Only with the hotels south of town do you have to think twice about moving around. So where you choose to stay will probably have more to do with budget than location. Do you want to pay the high price of luxury digs in the hotel zones to the north or south? Or will you settle for a centrally located, less expensive room and splurge more on food and drink?

Buenaventura
Apdo. Postal 8-B, Avenida México 1301, 48350
Tel. 322-2-37-37 or 800-223-6764
Doubles, from $60
   This hotel, privately owned and run and not frequently advertised, is a terrific find. The service is excellent, and the location can't be beat: You're right in Puerto Vallarta but still on the beach. The hotel is five stories tall, with a huge atrium lobby complete with an attractive thatched roof, a marvelous mobile-like chandelier, a small museum of archaeological finds, lots of potted palms, and very comfortable seating areas. There's also a delightful lobby bar. The 210 rooms and four suites are modern and spotlessly clean. Some have ocean views—but you must request these when you make your reservation. Otherwise, rooms are assigned randomly, and all rooms, ocean view or not, are the same price. Color TVs with cable channels are offered in fourth-floor rooms only. The patio area surrounds a pleasant pool, and there are small *tianguis* (markets) on the beach. The **Villa Ventura Restaurant** serves all day long, and the Mexican plate (around $5) makes a terrific lunch. Even if you're not staying at the hotel, you can stop in for lunch or drinks, or the Mexican fiesta the hotel puts on around the pool on Fri. nights (about $24 per person). Credit cards: AE, MC, V.

Buganvilias Sheraton
Carretera Aeropuerto 999, 48310 (U.S. sales office, Box 1168-274, Studio City, CA 91004)
Tel. 322-2-30-00 or 800-325-3535
Doubles, $125–$150 peak, $80–$100 off-peak (in summer)
   As you might imagine from its name, this modern luxury hotel on Las Glorias Beach, north of Puerto Vallarta, is bedecked with beautiful bougainvillea. It also has five hundred lovely rooms and suites with modern furnishings, TVs with cable channels, servi-bars, and lots of plants. A spacious lobby, large free-form swimming pool with swim-up bar and ample sundeck, illuminated tennis courts, four restaurants, and a shopping arcade complete the picture. The hotel's nightclub, **El Embarcadero,** is a very popular night spot. Credit cards: AE, DC, MC, V.

Camino Real
Apdo. Postal 95, Playa de las Estacas, 48300
Tel. 322-3-01-23 or 800-228-3000
Doubles, from $150
   Unquestionably one of the best resort hotels in Puerto Vallarta, the Camino Real is a self-contained complex on secluded Playa de las Estacas, south of the city. The hotel's architecture and decor are a pleasing blend of Mexican modern and Mexican colonial. You walk across a bridge over a stream to get from the breezy lobby area to your room in a modern high rise. The 250

rooms have brightly colored bedspreads, curtains, and accessories, plus folk art, cable TV, servibars, ocean views, and balconies. The recreation area overlooks a beach bordered by high rock cliffs at both ends. The pool is huge and irregularly shaped, surrounded by a sundeck with lounges, umbrellas, and palm trees. There are also a swim-up bar and terrace restaurant, tennis courts, and a playground for children. Other restaurants include **La Perla,** an exceptionally elegant formal room for dinner only, and **Azulejos,** a cafeteria that's open all day. The hotel has had many celebrity guests. Credit cards: AE, DC, MC, V.

Coral Grand Hotel

Apdo. 448, Km. 8.5, Carretera Mismaloya, 48300
Tel. 322-2-51-91 or 322-2-17-91 or 800-527-5315
Doubles, from $110

The Coral Grand is a new and lovely luxury hotel on the beaches south of Puerto Vallarta. It's a ten-story structure built on the side of a cliff, with the lobby at the top and rooms on lower floors. The 120 rooms and several palatial suites are beautifully furnished, and all have ocean views; some have whirlpools. There are two swimming pools, a game room, a gym with weight-training equipment, tennis courts, several restaurants, and a bar with live entertainment from 7:30 P.M.–midnight. Modified American Plans are available, as are honeymoon packages, and this resort is very popular with honeymooners. Credit cards: AE, DC, MC, V.

Fiesta Americana Puerto Vallarta

Apdo. Postal 270, Los Tules, 48300
Tel. 322-2-20-10 or 800-223-2332
Doubles, from $170

The Fiesta Americana Puerto Vallarta has traded its old colonial look for contemporary southwestern. The 291 rooms have been recently remodeled, with pastel floral bedspreads and drapes and blond-washed wood furniture, marble floors, and off-pink adobe walls. All rooms have cable TV and servibars; almost all have ocean views and balconies with lots of plants. The lobby is impressive: you drive up to a monumental *palapa,* and inside it's cool and breezy. The pool is enormous, with two islands, a large deck, and *palapa*-covered bars. The expansive beach area offers pretty white sand, palm trees, and—what else?—*palapas.* Tennis courts and instruction are available. There are good restaurants and a fun lobby bar on the premises. **Friday Lopez,** the on-premises disco, is one of P.V.'s best and most popular night spots. Credit cards: AE, DC, MC, V.

Hacienda Buenaventura

Apdo. Postal 95-B, Paseo de la Marina, 48300
Tel. 322-2-66-67 or 800-223-6764
Doubles, from $50

This new hotel, owned and run by the people who own and run the Buenaventura, has the same charming atmosphere and excellent service. The Hacienda Buenaventura has 155 rooms decorated in modified colonial style. Most of the rooms have small balconies. The swimming pool is surrounded by tropical gardens. The hotel is north of Puerto Vallarta, near the marina.

It is not on the beach, but guests have the use of and easy access to the beach at the Krystal Vallarta. Credit cards: AE, MC, V.

Holiday Inn Puerto Vallarta

Apdo. Postal 555, Carretera Aeropuerto and Ave. de las Garzas, 48300
Tel. 322-2-17-00 or 800-HOLIDAY
Doubles, from $130 (suites higher)
If you're from the United States, this hotel will remind you of home—but in a tropical setting. Architecture and decor are quite suited to U.S. tastes and expectations: there are two large beige-colored towers, one with 224 comfortable rooms, the other with 246 suites, each with wet bar. All rooms have color TV with cable channels, servibar, and angled ocean views. The pool area is sizable, with one bar on the patio and another on an island in the middle of the pool, plus children's pool and play area. The Holiday Inn also offers a large beach area; a health club with whirlpools, sauna, and exercise equipment; several excellent eateries; and lively lobby bar. Credit cards: AE, DC, MC, V.

Hotel Molino de Agua

Apdo. Postal 54, Ignacio L. Vallarta 130 (and Aquiles Serdan, at the Río Cuale), 48380
Tel. 322-2-19-07 or 800-826-9408
Doubles, from $50
This is an unexpected hideaway in the middle of Puerto Vallarta. On the banks of the Cuale River, in a tropical coconut grove, are a cluster of little cabins with double rooms or suites, all with colonial-style furnishings. A patio restaurant, swimming pool, and whirlpool are also on the premises. Charming and secluded, yet within walking distance of all the action in P.V. Credit cards: MC, V.

Krystal Vallarta

Avenida de las Garzas sin nombre, 48300
Tel. 322-2-14-59 or 800-231-9860
Doubles, from $140
Think of Krystal Vallarta as a village rather than a hotel. It covers about 12 square blocks of beachfront property and has several distinct sections of rooms, suites, and *casitas,* plus 48 (!) swimming pools (including one Olympic-sized, one free-form, two children's pools, and 38 private pools at the *casitas*); tennis courts (with resident tennis pro); nine restaurants (including those specializing in Mexican, Japanese, Argentinian, and a variety of other international cuisines) and bars (excluding room service and the snack areas at the pools and beach); conference facilities; a garden reserved for Mexican fiestas (Sun. evenings at 7 P.M.) and mini-bull fights—both the bull and the arena are under-sized (Wed. evenings at 7 P.M.); private banquet rooms; a colonial chapel and colonial aqueduct; shopping arcades; and grocery stores. Enough to keep you entertained? The rooms here are spacious and beautifully furnished in colonial style, complete with folk art. The gardens are lush. There are little carts to drive you around the grounds on cobblestone

roads. Krystal Vallarta is owned by one of Mexico's top soap-opera writers, and she has turned it into the kind of elegant and romantic setting where one of her own fantasies—and perhaps one of yours—could evolve. Credit cards: AE, DC, MC, V.

Las Palmas

Km. 2.5 Carretera Aeropuerto, Apdo. 55, 48300
Tel. 322-2-04-42
Doubles, from $55

This reasonably priced retreat is on the beach amid the pricey Puerto Vallarta palaces. The lobby may be smaller, but the 150 comfortable rooms have ocean views or surround a pleasant pool and patio area. You can dine at the restaurant here, or sample the many restaurants in nearby hotels. All in all, a very good buy. Credit cards: AE, MC, V.

Playa los Arcos

Olas Altas 380, 48380
Tel. 322-2-05-83
Doubles, from $60

If you want to stay in the center of town, in a moderately priced hotel, this is a good choice. There's not much atmosphere, but the 120 rooms are clean and cheerful. The best rooms have balconies and ocean views. These must be specially requested when you make your reservations. There's a large pool, along with access to Playa los Muertos, the town beach, and a rooftop tennis court. The hotel restaurant is reasonably priced, but one of the pleasures of being in the middle of town is proximity to P.V.'s fine array of eateries. Credit cards: AE, MC, V.

Playa de Oro

Apdo. Postal 78, Avenida de las Garzas, 48300
Tel. 322-2-68-68 or 800-421-0600
Doubles, from $55

This colonial-style hotel offers 390 comfortable rooms, many with views overlooking the ocean and nearby marina, and is very convenient if you want to rent a boat or take local water tours. There's a great beach, plus two pools and clay tennis courts. Three bars offer live entertainment, dancing, and Mexican fiestas. Credit cards: AE, MC, V.

Plaza las Glorias

Avenida de las Garzas, 48300
Tel. 322-2-22-24 or 800-342-AMIGO
Doubles, from $100

Plaza las Glorias, a colonial-style hotel on the beach of the same name, has 220 pleasantly decorated rooms with balconies and ocean views. All have cable TV and servibars. The pool is situated in an interior courtyard with plenty of palms and other greenery, and beyond this is lovely Playa las Palmas. The hotel also runs the villas across the street, comfortable units with sofas that convert to king-sized beds, and full kitchenettes. The villas are conveniently located next to the Villas Vallarta Shopping Center, with boutiques, gift shops, and a big supermarket. Credit cards: AE, MC, V.

Plaza Vallarta Fiesta Americana

Avenida de las Garzas (on Playa las Glorias), 48300
Tel. 322-2-44-48 or 800-223-2332
Doubles, from $115

The emphasis at the Plaza Vallarta is tennis, tennis, tennis. This is the location of the **John Newcombe Tennis Center,** with a dozen clay courts, daily clinics, and tournaments. In addition, the hotel has a wonderful beach and sizable pool, as well as a restaurant and bar. The four hundred spacious rooms have balconies, most with ocean views. Good location on Playa las Glorias, near the Plaza las Glorias complex and the Villas Vallarta Shopping Center. Credit cards: AE, DC, MC, V.

🍵 RESTAURANTS

This town is filled with fine dining spots specializing in seafood, Mexican, or international fare. Pick a mood and a type of cuisine, and off you go.

Los Arbolitos

Lázaro Cárdenas, at the end of the road, in front of Puente Colgante
No phone

Very much off the beaten path and a favorite with those who know Puerto Vallarta, this is a small restaurant with simple Mexican decor and a terrific menu featuring fresh fish and seafood prepared Mexican-style, plus meat and chicken dishes, soups, enchiladas, quesadillas, and salads. Beer and soft drinks are served. The food is fabulous, and so are the prices. A meal for two, with beverages, costs about $20. Open 8 A.M.–midnight every day except Thurs. No reservations. No credit cards.

Bogart's

Krystal Ixtapa, Airport Hwy.
Tel. 322-2-14-59 or 322-2-13-78

The newest and largest addition to the Krystal hotel chain's fancy restaurants bears considerable resemblance to the others. (See the **Bogart's** listing, **Restaurants, Ixtapa-Zihuatanejo,** above, for details.) Open daily for dinner; two seatings only, at 6:30 and 9:30 P.M. The average price of a meal for two, including wine, is about $70. Reservations required. Credit cards: AE, DC, MC, V.

Brazz

Galeana and Morelos
Tel. 322-2-03-24

This is the place for steaks and prime ribs or lobsters and shrimp in Puerto Vallarta. The restaurant, part of a Guadalajara-based chain, is enormously popular with tourists and locals. The decor is Mexican-style. The bar has live entertainment and is action-packed from about 9 P.M. until late at night. Good wine list. Open daily, noon–midnight. The average cost of a meal for two, with wine, is about $45. Reservations suggested. Credit cards: AE, MC, V.

Carlos O'Brien's

Díaz Ordaz 786, on the Malecón
Tel. 322-2-14-44

Located in the heart of things, on the Malecón, Carlos O'Brien's, the local link in the Carlos Anderson chain of fun eateries, is the happeningest scene in P.V. The young and young-in-spirit congregate here to swig and sway to the high-volume rock. A bar, large dining room, and balcony dining area are all done up with movie star photos, old newspaper front pages, and graffiti by thousands of patrons. Waiters do their shtick while serving ribs, steaks, seafood, soups, salads, and desserts. This very popular—and usually crowded—restaurant is open daily, noon–1 A.M. The average price of a meal for two, including wine, is about $50. Go at off-hours, or make reservations. Credit cards: MC, V.

Casa del Almendro

Galeana 180
Tel. 322-2-46-70

The Casa is a charming and romantic restaurant on a large and lovely Mexican patio shaded by a magnificent almond tree. The restaurant's food is its own tradition, with recipes drawn from family files. Excellent seafood is offered, of course, and there's a good wine list. Open for lunch and dinner. The average price of a meal for two, including wine, is about $50. Reservations suggested. Credit cards: AE, MC, V.

Las Cazuelas

Badillo 479
Tel. 322-2-16-58

Home cooking is what is promised here, and that's what you'll get. The menu is made up of daily specials, and everything is freshly cooked, mostly in earthenware (*cazuela* means earthenware pot). Open for dinner only, 6–11:30 P.M. Closed Mon. and during the summer. The place is small, and you must make reservations. The average price of a meal for two is about $30. No credit cards.

Chee Chee

Along the coast, south of Mismaloya Beach, at Boca de Tomatlán (mouth of the Tomatlán River), about 10 miles from Puerto Vallarta
Tel. 322-2-01-22

Chee Chee is carved out of the rock cliffs overlooking the spot where the Tomatlán River meets the sea. The restaurant's compound has several *palapa*-covered dining areas, sundecks with colorful umbrellas, swimming pools, sandy beaches, and a marina. You can get there by car (a taxi from P.V. costs about $10) or boat (Chee Chee has its own catamaran; call for rates and reservations). Fresh seafood, complemented by tropical drinks, is the specialty here. This is a lovely place to spend the day. Open 10 A.M.–7 P.M. The average cost of a meal for two, with drinks, is about $45. Reservations suggested. Credit cards: AE, MC, V.

Chino's Paraiso

At Mismaloya Beach (take the turn-off into the hills before you cross the bridge, and follow the signs to Chino's)
No phone

This hideaway in the hills behind Mismaloya Beach is a favorite stop for groups touring Puerto Vallarta. The restaurant is like a jungle compound, with a large thatched-roof hut in its center. There are pools for swimming and decks for sunning. The seafood is fresh and prepared to your taste. Beer and wine are served. Open 11 A.M.–6 P.M. The average price for a meal for two, with beer or wine, is about $40. No reservations. No credit cards.

El Eden

At Mismaloya Beach (take the turn-off into the hills before you cross the bridge, keep going past Chino's, and follow the signs to El Eden)
Tel. 322-15-37-23

El Eden, a tropical paradise deserving of its name, is hidden away in the jungle-like environs of the hills behind Mismaloya Beach. You drive up a steep, bumpy, unpaved road until you can go no farther. There you find the burnt-out shell of a crashed military helicopter, and a structure that looks like an abandoned mine shaft. These were used in a movie filmed here a short while ago. The restaurant is a quick walk through the brush, down a hill. There's a huge *palapa*-covered dining room, surrounded by sundecks. As you enter, you select your entrée from the fresh fish and seafood on display, and this is prepared to your taste. Beer and wine are served. A steep rock stairway leads farther down the hill to a grotto-like swimming area, with a natural waterfall that can be used as a water slide—or you can swing into the pool on ropes suspended from the sundecks. Open daily, 11 A.M.–6 P.M. The average cost of a meal for two, including beer or wine, is about $40. No reservations. No credit cards.

La Hacienda

Aguacate 274
Tel. 322-2-05-90

Seafood and meat dishes are delicately prepared and elegantly served in this attractive colonial-style setting. Try a nice fish fillet *en papillote* for a subtly flavored treat. The ceviche is especially fresh and delicious. Good wine list. Open 6 P.M.–midnight. Closed Mon. The average price of a meal for two, including wine, is about $40. Reservations suggested, especially for dinner. Credit cards: AE, DC, MC, V.

La Iguana

Lázaro Cárdenas 311
Tel. 322-2-01-05

The setting is a large Mexican patio, decorated with festive banners and balloons, and Chinese lanterns. This odd mixture is the invention of owner-chef-maître d' Gustavo Salazar, who hails from Hong Kong. Every Thurs. and Sat. night, Salazar serves as master of ceremonies for La Iguana's amazing *Fiesta Méxicana*. In between Ballet Folklórico and mariachi numbers, the audience is invited to the stage to dance to live rock music.

There are mostly tourists at this party, and they all have a terrific time, aided, perhaps, by the open bar. The food is a buffet of Mexican specialties, filling if not spectacularly tasty. One drawback: You have to line up for the buffet, and getting your food takes what seems like an eternity—especially if you haven't eaten any lunch so you could save room for dinner. On other nights, there's an à la carte menu with some of the same specialties, and international dishes too. The *Fiesta Méxicana* costs about $30 per person. Reservations required. No credit cards.

La Jolla de Mismaloya
On the cliffs above Mismaloya Beach
No telephone
Ideally situated on the cliffs overlooking Mismaloya Beach, this restaurant's large terrace is a popular hangout around sunset. La Jolla is a sizable establishment, with a bar and cocktail lounge and formal dining room, in addition to the terrace. Musicians entertain during dinner. The menu features fish and seafood, plus steaks and chops. The food is good, but the restaurant's biggest draw is its location. Good—but expensive—wine list. Open for lunch and dinner. The average cost of a meal for two, including wine, is about $50. Reservations suggested. Credit cards: AE, DC, MC, V.

La Langosta
Lázaro Cárdenas and Ignacio L. Vallarta
Tel. 322-2-06-76
Yes, the specialty here *is* lobster—large and luscious lobster, plus shrimp, oysters, octopus, squid, and fish of all species. All are grilled, fried, steamed, or stewed. The atmosphere is colorfully colonial, and there is live piano music. Open daily for lunch and dinner. During happy hour, 6–7 P.M., drinks are two for the price of one. The average price of a meal for two is about $40. Reservations suggested for dinner. Credit cards: AE, MC, V.

Mexican Joe's
Ecuador 1283, between Nicaragua and Honduras
Tel. 322-244-75
Don't be put off by the touristy name and look of this restaurant: The food is excellent. Fresh fish and succulent seafood top the menu, followed by a rich array of typical Mexican dishes. The hearty *charro* soup has been praised all over the world. Open for dinner only, 5–11 P.M. The average cost of a meal for two is about $35. Reservations suggested. Credit cards: AE, MC, V.

Moby Dick
31 de Octubre 182
Tel. 322-2-06-55
Excellent seafood of all sorts is prepared in a variety of ways here. The recipes are inventive (shrimp Moby Dick, for example, is blanketed in bacon and cheese) and traditional (*huachinango a la veracruzana,* for example, is a typical Mexican preparation of red snapper with a tomato-based sauce). Hearty soups make good appetizers, or constitute a meal in themselves. The atmosphere is as wholesome and bracing as the food. Open for lunch and dinner. Wine list with both domestics and imports. The aver-

age price of a meal for two, including wine, is about $50. Reservations suggested. Credit cards: AE, MC, V.

Ostion Feliz

Libertad 177
Tel. 322-2-25-08

You come here for the food rather than the decor. The name of this place means "Happy Oyster," and you'll be happy as a clam while you munch on lobster, shrimp, and other seafood delicacies—including oysters, prepared every way imaginable. Bouillabaisse and crab crêpes are specialties. Open noon–midnight. The average price of a meal for two is about $40. Credit cards: AE, MC, V. Another **Ostion Feliz** is at Las Americas 1301.

ENTERTAINMENT

Nighttime diversions in Puerto Vallarta are plentiful and varied. Restaurants are open late, and the dinner hour stretches into the wee hours. In addition, there are colorful Mexican fiestas every night of the week at different hotels and restaurants. Especially entertaining are those presented Thursday and Saturday nights at **La Iguana** (Lázaro Cárdenas 322; tel. 322-2-01-05) and those on Sunday nights at the **Krystal Vallarta** (Airport Highway; tel. 322-2-14-59 or 322-2-13-78).

At midnight, the Malecón is a parade of strollers enjoying the sounds of the waves in the cool of the night. **Oceano Bar** (at the Oceano Hotel, Galeana 103; tel. 322-2-13-22), a popular watering hole along the Malecón, is where strollers stop for a drink. Or they head for nearby **Carlos O'Brien's** (Díaz Ordaz 786; tel. 322-2-14-44), for drinks delivered by jovial waiters amid loud rock music. **Brazz** (Galeana and Morelos; tel. 322-2-03-24), off the Malecón but still on the beaten path, is another favorite for drinks and mariachi music.

The discos (in general open from 10 P.M. to 4 A.M.) are always packed, especially **The City Dump** (Ignacio L. Vallarta; tel. 322-2-07-19). This, the oldest disco in P.V., draws the young-and-single set, although it's easier for a single woman to get through the door than for a single man to do so. **Capriccio's** (Púlpito 170; tel. 322-2-15-93) has a more sophisticated atmosphere and, situated as it is atop a cliff, offers romantic vistas in addition to a racy light show. The other very popular disco is the Fiesta Americana's **Friday Lopez** (Airport Highway, in front of the hotel; tel. 322-2-20-10, ext. 1254), in the heart of the hotel strip to the north of town. Friday's has beveled-glass doors and an Old West interior—a bit bizarre for a disco, to be sure—and draws an older but still quick crowd. Also in the northern hotel zone, the Buganvilias Sheraton's **El Embarcadero** (Airport Highway 999, at the hotel; tel. 322-2-30-00) looks like a carefully constructed abandoned wharf. Don't ask what happens when you request "Sail Away With Me."

8

NORTHERN MEXICO

Much of Mexico is mountainous desert redeemed by thick green jungle and sparkling white-sand beaches. But the thick green jungle and sparkling white-sand beaches are east and west and south—northern Mexico gets most of the mountainous desert. As one traveler from Texas, who had just completed a bus tour west from Matamoros to Chihuahua, commented with surprise, "it's worse than West Texas!"—which is a lot for a Texan to say.

For the purpose of this chapter, which covers a lot of ground, northern Mexico consists of the states of Tamaulipas and Nuevo León east; Coahuila, Chihuahua, and Durango central; and Sonora and Sinaloa west. Except for the magnificent Cañon de Cobre (Copper Canyon) between Chihuahua and Los Mochis, there is not much of interest to the traveler in the miles of unpopulated space between the inhabited cities of **Matamoros, Nuevo Laredo,** and **Reynosa** in Tamaulipas along the Texas-Mexico border; **Monterrey,** capital of Nuevo León, and its neighbor **Saltillo** in the state of Coahuila; **Ciudad Juárez** and the city of **Chihuahua** in Chihuahua; **Nogales** and **Guaymas** in Sonora; **Los Mochis** and **Mazatlán** in Sinaloa; and **Durango,** capital of the state of Durango.

The country's mountainous center is edged with a thin green belt along the Gulf of Mexico on the East Coast and the Gulf of California (called the Sea of Cortés by the Mexicans) on the West. Cotton is grown along the East, and wheat and livestock in the West. In between, for more than fifteen hundred miles, the Sierra Madre Occidental range takes over the central Mexican plateau.

Climate varies, as is to be expected in such extremes of terrain. Both gulf coasts provide humid, almost tropical weather most of the year, with the East Coast prey to hurricanes during October and November when fierce tempests brew in the Gulf of Mexico. The West Coast is more fortunate, its gulf being protected by the long peninsula of Baja California bounding the Sea of Cortés to the west. Northeast Mexico is hot and arid, with desert cactus and mesquite climbing to the barren peaks of the Sierra Madre. Central Northern Mexico is generally dry and sunny, with an average temperature in the seventies in Chihuahua, Coahuila, Durango, and Sonora. September brings a few drops of rain, and in winter, lows in the high fifties and low sixties suggest the need for a light wrap in the mountains. Los Mochis and Mazatlán on the West Coast average in the seventies and eighties most of the year. **(Please note: throughout all the Northern Mexico chapter, hotels are air-conditioned unless otherwise noted.)**

CONNECTIONS

Transportation is best by air, with most cities served from Mexico City by Mexicana Airlines and the newly restructured Aeromexico. Northern Mexico is crossed by bus lines, but bear in mind that the road is long between most towns, and even on first-class lines the advertised air-conditioning and on-board toilet very often are not present. However, bus travel is very inexpensive. Gasoline is also very inexpensive (at this writing, under $.90 a gallon but sold by the liter), but if you drive away from the large towns, beware that this is primitive country, so follow several stringent rules for your own safety. Drive slowly and carefully, and always allow more time than you think you are going to need, as highways are generally two lanes, with hairpin curves in the mountains carrying a recommended speed of 31 miles per hour. Never under any circumstances drive at night; animals roam freely in the north central states, and just as disconcerting is the fact that many cars and trucks in Mexico drive without headlights on. Always top off your gas tank at each gas station along the way (Pemex is the national—and only—brand available, and it's best to buy premium grade); carry one or two days' supply of bottled water in desert or other regions in which there is a long stretch between settlements; and do not camp out in isolated areas unless you are with a large group. There have been recent reports of road incidents involving assaults and robberies, and, though infrequent, they are on the rise, so use the same precautions you would use in other unsettled areas of the world.

Particular caution should be exercised in two areas included in this guide: MEX15 along the coast in the states of Sinaloa and Sonora, and MEX40 between Mazatlán and Durango.

The main highways of Mexico are patrolled by the **Angeles Verdes,** the Green Angels, who operate a fleet of emergency-service trucks for minor road repairs. They change tires, give first aid, carry gasoline and oil, and are a source of road information. There is no charge except for fuel and parts.

Tamaulipas

The state of Tamaulipas, along the west shores of the Gulf of Mexico, stretches in a thin line up along the Texas border to include three popular border towns, Matamoros, Reynosa, and Nuevo Laredo, where shopping for Mexican arts and crafts is one of the pleasures of travel.

Matamoros

Here is the easternmost point of the United States–Mexico border, and to enter Mexico you merely have to cross the International Bridge in Brownsville, Texas, over the Rio Grande, called the Río Bravo del Norte in Mexico. Matamoros was founded in 1765 but was called Congregación del Refugio. Spanish merchants ignored the tiny settlement, funneling merchandise instead through the Port of Veracruz, although Refugio was just 32 miles from the mouth of the river, which empties into the Gulf of Mexico. But after the 1821 Mexican War of Independence the town was named H. (for Heroic) Matamoros after Father Mariano Matamoros, who was executed for leading the Mexican revolutionaries against the Spanish.

Matamoros has had a turbulent past, what with Apache and Comanche Indians raiding from the north, pirate raids, the Revolution, and the Mexican-American War, when it lost to Brownsville on the Texas side both the port and the bustling Mexican trade that was on the rise. Today Matamoros is content with perfect soil and weather for growing cotton. That crop, and industry in the form of clothing, chemicals, and electronics, have helped Matamoros grow into a city with a population of half a million.

🧳 HOTELS

Autel Nieto, Calle 10 1508, 87300; tel. 891-3-09-09. Doubles, from $22. Credit cards: AE, MC, V. Eighty-five huge guest rooms albeit with rather shabby hallways, and a restaurant. **Presidente Matamoros,** Alvaro Obregón 249, 87330; tel. 891-3-94-40. Doubles, from $57. Credit cards: AE, MC, V. A 122-room colonial hotel with swimming pool, restaurant and bar, and parking. All rooms are air-conditioned and offer cable TV. **Ritz,** Calle 7a 612 and Matamoros, 87300; tel. 2-11-90. Doubles, from $22. Credit cards: AE, MC, V. Remodeled and luxurious, with 92 air-conditioned rooms.

Life in Matamoros centers on **Plaza de Hidalgo,** with oleanders, azaleas, and palms framing the bandstand, the hub of a Mexican town square. Around the plaza, dining and drinking spots share space with rustic cantinas hiding within shaded brick patios. Four blocks from the plaza, on Calle 10, is the

Juárez Market, an enclosed mall of small shops and stalls where bargaining is an art form. The Old Juárez Market, on Calle 9, was gutted back in 1967 by a fire. Today the markets are surrounded by an open-air mall complete with benches and fountains.

Sights to see bordering on the plaza are the **Palacio Municipal** and the **Church of Our Lady of Refuge,** with high ceilings and twin towers. Also of interest is the **Casa Mata Museum in Old Fort Mata,** located off Lauro Villar on Calle Cuba, which still has the stone walls, cannon, and brick turrets—reminders of the city's warlike past. The **Mexican Tourist Office** is located on Puerta México, with English-speaking employees ready to help with maps and information. You can negotiate for taxis near Mexican customs at the International Bridge—or you can flag one down in the street.

🍵 RESTAURANTS

Dining in Matamoros is a delightful prospect, with a good choice of restaurants offering inexpensive but high-quality meals. Two classics are **Garcia's** (Avenida Obregón, one block from the International Bridge; tel. 891-3-15-66), and **The Drive Inn**—but not a drive-in!—(Hidalgo and Calle 6; tel. 891-2-00-22). The latter is elegantly formal with an orchestra and dance floor, while Garcia's offers strolling musicians and a second-story view of the bridge. There is a shopping emporium on the ground floor. Both Garcia's and The Drive Inn accept MC, V.

Reynosa

Reynosa is approximately one hundred miles west of Matamoros, and the International Bridge here is ten miles south of the Texas valley city of McAllen. There is plenty of parking if you want to leave your car on the U.S. side of the border. Just to your right across the bridge is Calle Allende, the beginning of the Pink Zone, always tourist territory in Mexico. Tried and true restaurants, bars, and shops here are enjoyed time and again by North American travelers crossing the Rio Grande to Reynosa, where you can shop and dine with ease even though your Spanish is limited, or altogether nonexistent. English is widely spoken, and U.S. currency is accepted all over Reynosa and the rest of the Tex.-Mex. border.

🏨 HOTELS

Engrei, Carretera A. Monterrey km 104, 88500; tel. 892-3-17-30. Doubles, $35. Credit cards: AE, MC, V. This 110-room hotel, on the road to Monterrey, offers swimming pool, restaurant and bar. **San Carlos,** Hidalgo N. 970, 88500; tel. 892-2-12-80. Doubles, $34.Credit cards: AE, MC, V. This 76-room hotel, a long-time favorite, offers an excellent restaurant, as well as bar service and parking. **Virreyes,** Hidalgo and Praxedis Balboa Pte.,

88500; tel. 892-3-10-50. Doubles, $37. Credit cards: AE, MC, V.
This newer hotel has 180 guest rooms in spacious gardens, a
swimming pool, and an excellent restaurant.

Plaza Principal, lined with trees and flowers, surrounded by
toy and food vendors and shoeshine stands, its benches filled
with people at leisure, is remarkable for its unusual cathedral:
A modern, cream-colored A-shaped building with two slender
towers has been grafted onto a lovely old colonial church.
Here are both Mexico old and Mexico new, happily blended
in Reynosa. **Hidalgo Street,** beyond the Plaza, is a pedestrian mall replete with sellers of serapes, pottery, piñatas, baskets, clothing, and souvenirs. It leads to a huge open-air fruit
and vegetable market. Along the way you'll encounter throngs
of shoppers, because this is where all Reynosa shops. Vendors hawk toys, souvenirs, balloons, cages of tropical birds.
If you plan to enter the United States, don't be coaxed into
bird buying; you are not permitted to bring live animals, fruit,
or vegetables across the border.

You will usually find just as many bargains in the Pink Zone
by the bridge as in the Zaragoza Market, a mile from the
bridge, but you'll miss a lot of local color if you miss browsing
in a Mexican *mercado.* If you get lost, stop and ask directions;
you'll find Mexicans are a courteous and friendly people. But
if you take a cab, settle the price beforehand.

☕ RESTAURANTS

Dining is delicious and inexpensive in Reynosa, with **Sam's
Place** (Allende Ote. 990; tel. 2-00-34) specializing in two-meat
main courses, such as a combination of wild game and seafood,
a specialty. Bean soup with cilantro, a Mexican herb, and *cabrito*
(kid) roasting on a spit, will make your mouth water. At
Trevino's (International Bridge; tel. 2-14-44), sip a margarita
and watch the waterfall; the keynote in Reynosa is relaxing.

Nuevo Laredo

Here is another place where stepping across the United
States–Mexico border is as easy as one-two-three. To walk,
it will take about five minutes and $.15 at the toll booth. If
you drive, it's $.75 a car, and you probably won't save any
time (unless of course you intend to head into the interior)
because with the yearly crossing count in the millions, there
can be a lot of traffic here.

Nuevo Laredo shares an interesting history with its sister
city of Laredo, Texas, with strong ties on either side. In the
beginning, both the Laredos were one, named Villa de San
Agustín de Laredo, after a town in Spain. Neglected equally
by both Mexican and Texas authorities after the birth of the
Texas Republic in 1826, the little community decided to de-

clare its independence from both countries. In 1839 it boldly
declared itself the Republic of the Rio Grande.

This was too much for General Santa Anna (the very same
who massacred Texans at the Alamo and suffered final defeat
at the Battle of San Jacinto), and he chased the little republic's
army until he caught it. It took him 283 days, time to earn
Laredo a seventh flag, one up on the six flags of the rest of
Texas. In Los Dos Laredos of today, everybody on both sides
of the border is related.

💼 HOTELS

Don Antonio, Gonzales 2435, 88000; tel. 871-2-11-40. Doubles, from $20. Credit cards: AE, MC, V. A reasonably priced 38-
room air-conditioned motel. **El Río,** Reforma and Toluca,
88000; tel. 871-4-36-66. Doubles, $46. Credit cards: AE, MC, V.
A motel south of town away from the International Bridge, El Rio
has 152 large units, two swimming pools, a restaurant and bar.
Hacienda, Prolongacion Avenida Reforma 5530, 88000; tel.
871-4-46-66. Doubles, $40. Credit cards: AE, MC, V. Another
motor hotel, the Hacienda features 74 units, swimming pool, and
restaurant and bar with entertainment. **Reforma Hotel,** Avenida Guerrero 822, 88000; tel. 871-2-62-50. Doubles, about $25.
Credit cards: AE, MC, V. This hotel, in the center of town just
south of the plaza, is an old favorite, offering 38 guest rooms
and one suite, all with TVs and telephones. Dining room and bar.

Nuevo Laredo has some of the best shops around if you're
looking for widely renowned Mexican handicrafts. You'll find
products from all the diverse states of the country: embroidered dresses from Oaxaca, *guayabera* shirts from Veracruz,
hand-blown glass from Guadalajara. And the prices are often
as good or better than they would be in the interior.

The main street, **Guerrero,** is a continuous shopping mall
up and down its entire length of several miles, but there are
enough shops and markets near the bridge to keep you happily occupied an entire day. **Maclovio Herrera Market,**
burned to the ground in 1980, set up shop across the plaza
the very next day and has been doing business as usual ever
since—only out in the open, like a proper Mexican *mercado.*
The old site is back in business, too, attracting additional vendors. The stacks of serapes, piles of pottery, piñatas, and baskets, the hangers full of embroidered dresses are all there for
the bargaining. (Bargain in the markets only; in the shops, the
general rule is, the cooler and more air-conditioned the establishment, the more fixed its prices.)

In Nuevo Laredo there is a sea of shops to drown in and
not come up for air for weeks. For more elegant designer
goods, **Marti's,** near the bridge, is the place to go. **Rafael's**

hand-made furniture on Reforma (an extension of Guerrero) is special too.

☕ RESTAURANTS

In Nuevo Laredo, next to shopping, food and drink are the biggest attractions. The **Cadillac Bar,** at O'Campo and Beldon; tel. 2-00-15, is to Nuevo Laredo what Harry's Bar is to Venice—an institution. In business since 1926, it's a border landmark second only to the Rio Grande itself. However, service is slow, and the food, with the menu in English, is no longer outstanding. Seafood and *cabrito* are specialties.

The **Winery Pub and Grill,** just behind the old marketplace, at Matamoros 308; tel. 2-08-95, has good Mexican dishes as well as standard U.S. fare—with a Mexican flavor. Good salad bar and steaks. **México Típico,** on Guerrero; tel. 2-15-25, is another favorite spot for travelers, with dining alfresco on the patio much preferred to a table inside. Happy patrons are entertained by wandering trios, and occasionally, a duet of guitar and voice by two very talented young boys in miniature mariachi costumes. Mexican cuisine, of course. All three restaurants accept all major credit cards.

Nuevo Leon

The road south crosses into the state of Nuevo León, and along the way you can see the low scrub and cactus give way to tall, oddly shaped yucca as the mountains begin to appear as blue shapes in the mist. The mist is likely to continue, because Monterrey, 140 miles south of Nuevo Laredo, is surrounded by steel and cement factories that cause a perpetual dust to envelope the west edges of town. About 25 miles south of Monterrey, near Santiago Village, are Cola de Caballo Falls, a mountain cascade plunging eighty feet down the green mountainside. The falls can be reached by leaving MEX85 at El Cercado and going four miles west to the falls. They are reached by walking the three-quarter-mile footpath or by hiring a horse or a burro. Beside the falls are the Three Graces, a triple cascade.

Monterrey

Monterrey was a colonial outpost around 1596 when it was named Monterey by Spaniard Don Diego de Montmayor (the second "r" was added later), and it had to be hardy—the early settlers were often attacked by Indians from the north. But the settlers dug in and finally prevailed, although the city is on a natural crossroads, which puts it in the path of anyone traveling either north or south. The War of Independence put the city alternately in Spanish and Mexican hands; the 1910 Revolution embroiled the citizens in battle; and during the Mexican-American War, U.S. troops were repulsed by can-

nons mounted on the Bishops' Palace, on Chepe Vera Hill on
the west side of town.

Monterrey is on the Santa Catarina River, a rather indifferent body of water, thanks to the La Boca Dam. For a large
commercial city, Monterrey offers a surprising number of
sights to catch the interest of travelers, described after **Hotels,** below.

CONNECTIONS

Mexicana Airlines flies to Monterrey from Chicago, Dallas/Fort
Worth, Kansas City, St. Louis, and San Antonio in the United
States, as well as from many gateways in Mexico. Taxis from
the airport run about $5 for the fixed-price yellow and white cabs.
Rides around town run about $2 to $3; always ask the price beforehand. Car rentals are available at the airport and major hotels.

**The government tourist office is off the Gran Plaza in front
of the Congreso del Estado building at calles Zaragoza and
Matamoros; tel.: 45-08-70 and 45-00-95.**

🧳 HOTELS

There is a wide choice of places to stay in Monterrey, with a wide
variety of rates as well. All hotels accept major credit cards unless otherwise noted.

Ambassador
Hidalgo and Carranza, 64000
Tel. 83-40-93-90; in the United States and Canada, 800-228-
3000
Doubles, from $90; executive suites, $140
   Now a Camino Real under the Westin banner, this 242-room,
beautifully renovated hotel has a restaurant, lobby bar, travel
agency, valet service, pool, sauna, gym, and jogging track.

Motel Chipinque
Meseta de la Sierra Madre, 64000
Tel. 83-78-13-38 and 78-66-00
Doubles, from $25
   Twenty km from the center of town, this picturesque 55-room
motel on a mesa beneath the mountains has swimming pool,
restaurant, bar, and two lighted tennis courts.

Gran Ancira
Hidalgo and Escobedo, 64000
Tel. 83-40-20-60
Doubles, $55–$70
   For more than 75 years this three-hundred room hotel with
a grand staircase ascending from the lobby has been a landmark in downtown Monterrey. You'll find a swimming pool, restaurant, soda fountain, bar and lobby bar with live music, shops,
and security.

Hotel Jandal
Avenida Cuauhtémoc 825 Nte., 64000
Tel. 83-72-46-06 and 72-30-07
Doubles, from $25
   Once evidently a more luxurious property, as the marble and mirrored lobby attest, this small but comfortable hotel has large rooms, a coffee shop, and private parking.

Hotel Jolet
Padre Mier Pte. 201, 64000
Tel. 83-40-55-00 and 09
Doubles, from $25
   With 120 guest rooms and 14 suites, a modern lobby and restaurant-bar and lobby bar, the Jolet is a comfortable and quiet place to stay.

Monterrey
Moreles 574 and Zaragoza, 64000
Tel. 83-43-51-20; in the United States 800-528-1234
Doubles, from $50
   Located downtown, near the Cathedral, this Best Western has 196 guest rooms, a dining room, a bar with nightly entertainment, and free parking for guests.

Monterrey Crowne Plaza
Avenida Constitución Ote. 300, 64000
Tel. 83-44-60-00; in the United States 800-HOLIDAY
Doubles, from $100
   This large 15-story 388-room hotel, part of the Holiday Inn chain, is next to the Palacio Municipal on a main boulevard. You'll find a concierge floor, heated indoor swimming pool, solarium and Jacuzzi, three restaurants, three bars, tennis courts, and a daily breakfast buffet.

Monterrey's Gran Plaza, bounded by Constitución, Zuazua, Zaragoza, and Padre Mier streets, is perhaps the largest civic square in the world, with almost one hundred acres of green park anchored on the north by the **Palacio del Gobierno** and on the south by the **cathedral.** Construction of the cathedral (at Zuazua and Ocampo) began in 1600, but the church, with its Catalonian bell tower and richly carved baroque facade, was not completed until the mid-19th century. There are interior murals. The Palacio del Gobierno (at Zaragoza and 5 de Mayo), built in 1908, is a pink sandstone temple that has eight Corinthian columns in the front, giving it a classic Hellenic look. The guns utilized to execute Emperor Maximilian are in the red reception room, and there is a plaque commemorating the meeting of U.S. President Franklin Delano Roosevelt with Mexican President Manuel Avila Camacho.

   Behind the Palacio del Gobierno is the **Palacio Federal,** the old city hall. There is a 16th-century courtyard and a central tower from which you can get an excellent view of the city. The new **Palacio Municipal** (city hall) to the west of the plaza (at Zaragoza and Ocampo) has a sculpture by Rufino Tamayo next to it, and a fine view of the Gran Plaza from the roof. Another interesting structure in the plaza is the pencil-thin, bright orange-red **Laser Beam Tower.**

The **Alameda Plaza** is another large green landscaped park, bounded by Avenida Pino Suárez, 5 de Mayo, Aramberri, and Carranza. This is a great place to stroll and watch the people of Monterrey at relaxation and play. To the west, **El Obispo,** the Bishops' Palace (on Chepe Vera Hill, by way of Padre Mier and Calle Mexico), was built in 1788 as a retirement home for high-ranking clergymen but has been a museum since 1956. High on a hill west of downtown, the palace also served as a fort—the French attacked it; Pancho Villa occupied it; and the cannons along the outside wall were used to fire on invading U.S. troops in the Mexican-American War. **Purísima Church** (Jalisco and Libertad) is an interesting architectural mix; Monterrey's patron saint, credited with saving the city from a river flood, is represented by a statue inside.

Two museums are of interest: The first is the **Centro Cultural Alpha** (Avenida Roberto Garza Sada 1000), in an unusual looking modern building that resembles a giant tin can tipped to pour out its contents. The centro features hands-on exhibits and a planetarium with a giant-screen Omnimax Theater. (Open 3 P.M. to 9:30 P.M. daily except Monday; free transportation from Alameda Park.) **Casa de la Cultura** (Colon Norte 400 and Carranza), housed in a Tudor-style train station, is for train aficionados and art lovers as well, since there are also changing exhibits of modern art. (Open daily.)

The **Arco de la Independencia** arches magnificently over Bulevar Francisco I. Madero at Pino Suárez. As for the **Cuauhtémoc Brewery** (Universidad at Mora), where both Bohemia and Carta Blanca beers are brewed, it is enhanced by paintings by some of Mexico's outstanding artists: Works by Rufino Tamayo, José Orozco, and David Siqueiros grace the brewery's huge bronze and copper vats. The Hall of Fame on the grounds honors national and international baseball greats, bullfighters, soccer stars, boxers, and cowboys. (Open daily except Monday.)

🍵 RESTAURANTS

In addition to the fine dining rooms in the Ambassador and Gran Ancira hotels, there are restaurants specializing in *norteño* (northern) Mexican cuisine, with emphasis on *cabrito* (kid) and charcoal-broiled steaks. *Harina* (flour) tortillas are more popular here than are the corn tortillas of the rest of the country. Approximate prices listed do not include drinks, wine, or tip. Major credit cards are accepted throughout unless otherwise noted.

El Gaucho

Arroyo Sur 100, south of the river
Tel. 58-24-18

The Argentine cuisine served here is popular in Monterrey and includes *carnes asadas* (grilled meats), *empanadas* (turnovers), *churrasco* (bean soup), and *alambre* (beef tips). A meal for two will cost about $20.

Luisana

Hidalgo Ote. 530
Tel. 43-15-61

A formal Continental-style restaurant, Luisana offers white linen napery, waiters in tuxedos, and live piano music in the background. Seafood a specialty. A meal for two will cost about $30.

El Palenque

Avenida Morones Prieto
Tel. 45-13-47

Cockfights are the dinner entertainment here, and are served along with the Mexican fare in this huge restaurant, where seven hundred can dine at once. This Mexican spectator sport is not for the faint-hearted. A meal for two will cost about $20.

El Pastor

Madero Pte. 1067
Tel. 74-04-80

The *cabrito* roasting in the window here is a real eye-catcher, and you can order the local specialty prepared several ways. A meal for two would cost about $10.

La Residence

Degollado Sur 605 and Matamoros
Tel: 42-72-30

This old-fashioned town house serves fine international cuisine, with prime rib a specialty. The Sun. *menú de degustación* is a wonderful sampling of seven special dishes. A meal for two will cost upwards of $30.

Sanborn's

Escobedo Sur 920, a half-block north of Plaza Hidalgo
Tel. 42-14-41

This branch of the classic House of Tiles is a must for homesick Americans who still want some Mexican flavor: Mexican dishes with American flair and generous portions. A meal for two will cost about $12.

SHOPPING

Leather goods are just about all that this area is known for, although, as is usual in Mexico, you can find crafts and handiwork from all over the country here. The **underground shopping center** (at Calle Hidalgo) beneath the Gran Plaza, the Plaza Morelos, and Plaza Dorada all have shops and restaurants. **Carapan,** at Hidalgo and Galeana, is good for handicrafts, and **Kristaluxus** (José María Vigil 400) a large glass factory outlet store, has good prices. The **pedestrian mall** beginning at Hidalgo and Carranza is entertaining to stroll around—there are often street entertainers doing their thing, as well as the usual street vendors outside the many shops (mainly shoe stores!).

SPORTS

Bullfights are held every Sunday at the **Plaza Monumental** at the north edge of Avenida Universidad. Tickets are sold at the bull ring. *Charreadas,* Mexican rodeos, are held almost every Sunday—check at your hotel desk for information. For cockfights (if you don't want to watch while you dine at El Palenque restaurant), check with your hotel desk. For golf, the **Club de Valle Golf Club** seven miles south has an 18-hole course; many of the hotels can arrange for temporary guest memberships. There are half a dozen other private courses, and again, temporary membership can often be arranged through the hotel travel desk.

Water sports take place on **La Boca Dam,** reached by Urban-Tourist Route 15, where the large manmade lake is fine for boating, wind surfing, and waterskiing. As for swimming, there is a large pool at the entrance of the García Caves, 13 miles west on the Saltillo highway and then 15 miles north to Villa de García. The caves, inside a mountain, are among Mexico's largest and most beautiful. There is a cable car to the cave entrance, and tours take 45 minutes. Closed Mondays.

ENTERTAINMENT

Mexican Independence Day begins with fireworks on the night of September 15, with parades all the next morning. December 12 is the **Day of Our Lady of Guadalupe,** celebrated by parades and dances that begin two weeks earlier. In different sections of the city, you will come upon groups of adults and children who seem to be following, Pied Piper–style, groups of dancers in gorgeous ethnic costumes, dancing down the street. Happy faces are split by wide grins, and the mood is contagious.

As for nightlife, you can enjoy regional music in the lobby bar of the elegant **Gran Ancira** and live music weekday evenings at the **Monterrey Plaza Hotel.** Popular discos are **Sahris,** at the Ramada Inn; **El Jaguar,** in the Holiday Inn, at Avenida Universidad 101 Nte; **Scaramouche,** at the Monterrey Crowne Plaza; **Sergeant Pepper's** (Orinoco Oriente 105); and the **White Rabbit Disco** (Matamoros Oriente 125). **La Milpa de Valerio** (Gomez Morin 200) plays Latin American folkloric music and serves dinner as well as drinks.

Coahuila

Highway 40 west enters the state of Coahuila, which at its northern edge shares a 590-kilometer border with the state of Texas, around the Big Bend of the Rio Grande. The highway, running alongside mountain ranges so high and flat they look like painted backdrops, leads to Saltillo, capital of the state of Coahuila and some fifty miles west of Monterrey. The mountain city, with an altitude of 5,245 feet in the Sierra Madre Oriental range, has gentle breezes and sunny days, making it one of Mexico's most pleasant climates.

Saltillo

The city was founded in 1575 by Captain Alberto del Canto, who had the happy idea of forming a teaching center for the Indians of the north by mingling then with the more "civilized" Tlascalan Indians of the Central Highlands. During the 18th and 19th centuries, Saltillo was the capital of an enormous area which extended across Texas all the way to Colorado. Today Saltillo, with a population of more than four hundred thousand, is an industrial center ranking first in Mexico in steel and nonmetallic mining, combined with agriculture, livestock, commerce, and tourism. Manufacturing plants produce pottery, silverware, and engine parts, and textile mills weave the fabric for serapes, for Saltillo is the center of this Mexican industry.

There is much to do in Saltillo, and the Saltillo tourist office in the new **Convention Center** (Highway 10 to Mexico City; tel. 5-58-11), itself something to see as a marvel of modern architecture, has tourist maps and brochures as well as hotel, restaurant, and activities information.

🛄 ACCOMMODATIONS

All hotels accept major credit cards unless otherwise noted.

Camino Real Saltillo
Bulevar los Fundadores 2000, km 865, 25000
Tel. 841-5-25-25; in the United States 800-228-3000
Doubles, from $73
This luxury resort, one of a chain of fine hotels in Mexico under the Westin banner, offers modern adobe decor within spacious landscaped grounds. There are 116 large and modern guest rooms, a restaurant, coffee shop, cocktail lounge with live music, swimming pool, two tennis courts, putting green, and children's playground.

Huisache
Bulevar V. Carranza 1746, 25000
Tel. 841-2-83-55
Doubles, from $23

An older motel on the outskirts of town in a pleasant green setting offers 53 comfortable rooms, swimming and wading pools, a restaurant, and a bar.

La Torre
Bulevar los Fundadores km 369, 25010
Tel. 841-5-33-33
Doubles, from $38
The new 12-story tower shares the grounds with the older colonial-style structure, making 118 guest rooms in all, with restaurant-bar, coffee shop, and two tennis courts.

In addition to hotels, Saltillo also offers the following RV parks: **Los Magueyes,** thirty spaces with services and a swimming pool, adjacent to Hotel La Torre, and **La Estrella;** tel. 5-00-11.

Saltillo's best colonial architecture consists of the **Catedral de Santiago** on the **Plaza de Armas; Iglesia de San Juan** (Escobido between Allende and Hidalgo), originally a chapel constructed in the 18th century for a private family; **El Templo de San Esteban** (calles Victoria and Padre Flores), constructed in the 16th century by the Franciscans, restored in this century but with the original facade; and the **Templo de San Juan Nepomuceno,** also constructed in the 18th century.

The Cathedral of Santiago, built between 1746 and 1801, is considered one of the finest examples of churrigueresque architecture on the North American continent. The style is named after a Spanish architect, José Churriguera (1665–1725) who was called the Spanish Michelangelo because he combined his art with both sculpture and painting. This baroque architectural style lasted from 1650 to 1740 in Europe. The cathedral, on the large Plaza de Armas and fronted by a fountain, has a tower that offers a fine view of Saltillo.

Also on the Plaza de Armas is the **Palacio de Gobierno,** the government palace where the then governor, Venustiano Carranza, recruited his army to combat the assassin of Francisco Madera, Mexico's first revolutionary president. Inside are murals of the political life of the state, painted by Salvador Almaraz y Tarazona.

More modern architecture is exemplified by the **Santuario de Guadalupe** (at Murguia and Perez Trevino), constructed in the 19th century in the Gothic style.

Plaza Manuel Acuña, on Allende between Perez Trevino and Aldama, is the city's busiest square where, on a typical day in Mexico, you will see street vendors selling sundries and tacos, shoe shiners busily polishing customers' boots, old men sitting and sunning on benches, women gossiping—in short, the daytime heartbeat of a Mexican city, where no one seems to stay at home.

Alameda Zaragoza (calles Carranza, Victoria, Aldama, and Arizpe) is a landscaped garden containing the Lago de la República (Lake of the Republic) in the shape of Mexico, and monuments dedicated to poets and national heros.

Museums include the **Museo de Arte Ruben Herrera** (Nicolas Bravo, open 9 A.M. to 1 P.M. and 3 to 7 P.M., Tuesday through Saturday); **Recinto de Juárez** (Juárez near Nicolas Bravo); and **Museo y Pinacoteca del Ateneo Fuente** (on the highway to Monterrey, open 8 A.M. to 2 P.M., Monday through Friday). The **Centro Cultural Vanguardia** (Hidalgo, just north of Plaza de Armas) was the family home of a French family, the Pourcells; today it has been converted into an art center with painting exhibitions (open 10 A.M. to 1 P.M. and 4 to 7 P.M., Monday through Friday; 10 A.M. to 1 P.M. Saturday and Sunday).

El Fortín de Carlota, the Fortress of Carlota, not far from the Plaza de Armas, is dedicated to Princess Charlotte of Belgium, wife of ill-fated Emperor Maximilian, both of whom history has decided were innocent pawns of ambitious Napoleon III of France. Carlota fled to France to beg for help against the Mexican anticolonial forces. When she heard of her husband's execution, she went mad and spent the remainder of her life in an asylum.

An interesting historical site is **La Angostura,** the battlefield where in 1847 General Santa Anna met General Zachary Taylor's forces during the Mexican-American War. Greatly outnumbering the U.S. forces, the Mexicans in two days captured most of Taylor's strongholds. Then, inexplicably, Santa Anna withdrew his troops, leaving the field to the United States.

▣ RESTAURANTS

Saltillo's most outstanding eateries are in such hotels as the Camino Real, but **La Canasta** at Bulevar Carranza 2486 (tel. 5-88-40) and **El Principal** at Allende Norte 702 (tel. 4-33-84) are well worth trying also. Both serve moderately priced Continental cuisine. For a pseudo-American fix, **Martin's** is a modern coffee shop on Francisco Coss at Calle Aguascalientes (tel. 6-26-33) across from a lineup of lovely pink government buildings housing the **Teatro de la Ciudad Fernando Soller, Palacio Municipal, Palacio de Justicia,** and **Palacio del Congresso;** the last three contain interesting murals.

SHOPPING

Saltillo is the center of the serape industry of Mexico, and at **El Saltillero** (Victoria 217 and Acuña) and **La Favorita** (Calle Bolivar 608), you can watch the entire process of spinning and carding the wool and cotton, dying it bright colors, and weaving it on handlooms. Calle Victoria is the main street for local crafts such as silver and leather goods. For silver, two *talleres de plateria* (silver workshops) offering a good variety are **Plateria Taxco,** Calle Victoria 428, and **Plateria Moeller,** nearby at Calle Victoria 404. **La Azteca,** Calle Acuña Nte. 159, has a wide assortment of leather goods such as billfolds, purses, and belts. The city market, Mercado Juárez (Acuña and Allende), has the Mexican blouses, curios, and serapes that make good souvenirs.

ENTERTAINMENT

Late summer and early fall are festival season in Saltillo and environs. **Fiesta del Santo Cristo,** based upon a legend of a donkey that collapsed under a box containing a figure of Christ, is celebrated by fireworks, bullfights, and **La Malinche,** a Huastec dance based upon another story, this of betrayal between brothers. Other festivals are the **Fiesta del Ojo de Agua,** which takes place the second week in September; **Fiesta Regional,** in June in the nearby town of General Cepeda; and **Feria de la Uva y del Vino,** in August in Parras de la Fuente, also west of Saltillo.

Chihuahua

The state of Chihuahua has some of Mexico's most spectacular scenery in the magnificent gorges of Barranca del Cobre, or Copper Canyon, one of a series of vast canyons that are wider, longer, and deeper than the Grand Canyon of the United States. A train that is an engineering feat (experts said it couldn't be done) makes it possible to cross the canyon from one end to the other.

Cascada de Basaseáchic is a spectacle, too, a waterfall plunging more than one thousand feet into a green pine forest. In addition to its two interesting towns, Ciudad Juárez and the city of Chihuahua, Chihuahua is the origin of the tiny hairless dogs *(perros chihuahuenos),* used by the Aztecs as hot-water bottles to warm their beds during cold desert nights. The dogs make up for their small size with an ear-piercing bark.

Ciudad Juárez

Ciudad Juárez is the fourth major city on the border that Mexico shares with Texas and—with a population of one million—the largest. Three bridges, one of them dubbed the Good Neighbor Bridge, make it easy to walk, ride, or catch a taxi either way with ease. Juárez shares with El Paso colorful mountain scenery, sunny climate (the sun has failed to shine only 38 days in the past twenty years), and an exciting history of cowboys, bandidos, and conquistadores, who called it El Paseo del Norte, the Pass to the North.

Like the rest of Mexico, Juárez echoes with its Spanish past. It was founded in 1659 by the Franciscan priest García de San Francisco y Zuñiga. He established the **Mission of Our Lady of Guadalupe** (Avenida Juárez and 16 de Septiembre), one of the popular sights to see in Juárez. It contains a beautifully hand-carved beamed ceiling with a story: Tradition has it that the beams, made of palm logs, were shipped from Spain. They were unloaded at the Port of Veracruz and carried all the way to El Paseo del Norte on the backs of Indians who had been converted to Christianity.

When President Benito Juárez fled to the city to escape the French soldiers of Emperor Maximilian, who had been put on the throne of Mexico by Napoleon III, Juárez became the temporary capital of Mexico, but it was not until 1888 that Paseo del Norte was renamed Juárez in his honor.

🧳 HOTELS

Major credit cards accepted unless otherwise noted.

Calinda Quality Inn
Avenida Hermanos Escobar 3535, 32310
Tel. 16-16-34-21; in the United States and Canada 800-228-5151/5152
Doubles, from $42
   This 111-room hotel, part of the pleasant and courteous Calinda chain, has suites with Jacuzzis, swimming pool, restaurant and lobby bar, and convention and meeting facilities.

Colonial Las Fuentes
Avenidas Lincoln and de las Americas, 32310
Tel. 16-13-50-50
Doubles, $46
   This excellent 190-room hotel north of ProNaf Center offers two swimming pools. For homesick Americans, there is a Denny's restaurant-bar next door with 24-hour service.

Presidente
Centro Comercial ProNaf, 2 km south of the Cordoba Bridge, 32310
Tel. 16-13-00-47
Doubles, about $50
   Luxurious 150-unit hotel offering rooms and suites features a swimming pool, restaurant, bars and cocktail lounges, shops, and a valet.

Sylvia's
16 de Septiembre, 1977
Tel. 16-15-04-42 and 16-15-04-98
Doubles, about $40

This oldie but goodie motel has recently been remodeled into 91 units with gardens, swimming pool, restaurant and bar, and enclosed parking. No credit cards.

Benito Juárez Plaza is the heart of local color, especially on Sundays, when the plaza is crowded with local families taking the air. Mexican fast food, toy vendors, musicians, shoeshine booths, strolling couples, and laughing children make every Sunday seem like carnival time in the square.

Juárez shares **Chamizal,** a 760-acre park, with El Paso, a triumph of diplomacy that solved a border dispute. The park has a sports stadium, fairgrounds, an archaeology museum, and a botanical garden. Just south of the park lies **ProNaf,** with the Centro Artesanal, a government-run craft store offering a wide selection of specialties of each Mexican state: native weavings, hand-blown glass, *guayabera* shirts, embroidered dresses, and silver and leather work, all crafted by fine Mexican artists.

Nearby, the **Museo del Arte y Historia** is well worth a stop. Mexican museum buildings in themselves are usually architecturally distinctive, and this is no exception. Light, bright, and airy, the museum combines Mexican art from Aztec and Toltec eras with traveling shows of contemporary Mexican work.

There are two bull rings in Juárez: the **Monumental,** on the east side just off Highway 45, and the older Juárez bullring, on the west side between avenidas Lerdo and Juárez, just a few blocks from the Good Neighbor and Del Norte bridges. Also, while you're here, try to catch a *charreada,* a Mexican rodeo, more decorative and less dusty than the traditional U.S. version. Every Sunday afternoon in the López Mateos Charro Arena, *charros* (cowboys) in gorgeous costumes perform daring feats on horseback. The arena is located off Avenida Charro, half a mile north of Avenida 16 de Septiembre.

The **Juárez Racetrack** is first-rate, featuring an elegant, glass-enclosed, and air-conditioned viewing stand, with greyhound racing Wednesday through Sunday all year, and Thoroughbred racing every Sunday afternoon at 1:30 P.M. May through September. There's off-track betting at the Foreign Book at the **Juárez Turf Club,** located a block north of the Del Norte Bridge on Avenida Juárez.

Although the **Mercado Juárez** is typical of every Mexican town of any size, part of the adventure is to walk through and see what's going on. Here, with the sky for a roof, lies the romance of the Mexican market, where bargaining is expected as a matter of course. Mexican curios, *huaraches,* serapes, jewelry, piñatas—it's all there on Avenida August Melgar at 16 de Septiembre. Different wares are to be found at **Cris-**

tales de Chihuahua, a glass factory located right downtown (Avenida 16 de Septiembre, east of the city market), with blown-glass lamps and other interesting items.

Serious shoppers will want to investigate **Casa Oppenheim,** which has a large selection of jewelry, glassware, furniture, clothing, sandals, perfume, crafts, and much more, on the west side of town on Avenida Juárez across from Guadalupe Mission. Another shopping bonanza is the **Rio Grande Shopping Center,** which contains more than sixty shops under one roof at Avenida 16 de Septiembre.

☕ RESTAURANTS

The restaurants listed below accept major credit cards and cost about $10–$20 for dinner for two.

Casa del Sol
In the arts-and-crafts center on the north side of ProNaf
Tel. 13-65-09
This excellent colonial-style restaurant offers international cuisine with black bass a specialty.

La Fogata
Avenida 16 de Septiembre, near downtown
Tel. 13-00-40
This colonial-style steakhouse features both steak and seafood specialties.

Chihuahua

Highway 45 south of Ciudad Juárez leads to the city that is the capital of the state and bears the same name. The city of Chihuahua, 223 miles south of Ciudad Juárez, sits on a plain five thousand feet high, and during the five-hour drive (by car or by bus; the only air service is from Mexico City or Mazatlán), you can feel the road climb gradually.

Chihuahua's history was pretty violent, since two of the Mexican Revolution's most renowned figures made their mark here. Father Miguel Hidalgo, who rang the church bell that began the Revolution, was executed here in 1811— murals in the State Capitol **(Palacio del Gobierno)** depict the story with broad strokes and vivid color. Pancho Villa, a bandido across the border and a patriot on his home ground, had his home here. The mansion is now a museum.

Silver was discovered in Chihuahua's hills by the Spanish in 1679, and the city is still one of the nation's leading producers. Its long formal name, San Felipe de Real de Chihuahuas, was bestowed in 1718, but after the Revolution it was shortened to Chihuahua, and Mexicans sometimes exclaim *"¡Ay, Chihuahua!"* as folks in the United States might say, "Good grief!"

Chihuahua, like Ciudad Juárez, was the capital of Mexico for a short time in 1864 and 1865, when President Benito Juárez was based there during the French invasion of Mexico.

TOURING

Tours of Chihuahua are offered by Rojo y Casavantes, S.A. This organization also offers excursions to the **Campos Menonitas,** a community of about 55,000 Mennonites, an interesting religious community that has kept to itself, clinging to old-fashioned ways. Tours provide an opportunity to buy handicrafts such as hand-embroidered scarves and the famous Mennonite cheese. (Rojo y Casavantes, Bolivar 1000-C; tel.: 12-60-30, 12-88-89, 15-46-36, 15-53-84, 15-58-15; there is also a branch in the Hotel Victoria lobby.)

HOTELS

There is a good choice of places to stay in Chihuahua in all price ranges. All hotels listed take major credit cards unless otherwise noted.

Castel Sicomoro
Bulevar Periférico Ortez Mena 411, 31230
Tel. 14-13-54-45
Doubles, from $75
The Sycamore Palace is a new two-story, 130-room luxury hotel, with swimming pool, restaurant and cafeteria, lobby and video bar, and a club with entertainment on Fri. and Sat. The only drawback is that the hotel is 3 miles from downtown.

Mirador
Avenida Universidad 1309, 31240
Tel. 14-13-22-05
Doubles, from $32
This 87-unit two-story motel has an excellent restaurant, as well as a swimming pool, bar, and enclosed parking. No credit cards.

Misión San Francisco
Avenida Victoria 409, 31000
Tel. 14-16-75-50 and 14-16-75-55
Doubles, from $64
A favorite downtown hotel just behind the cathedral on the plaza, this 150-room, five-story structure has a popular restaurant, busy at all hours, featuring Mexican and international cuisine, Sun. brunch, and buffet; a lobby bar; and live music in Los Primos Bar.

Palacio del Sol
Avenida Independencia 500, 31000
Tel. 14-16-60-00; in the United States 800-228-9000
Doubles, from $62
The pride of the city, this 15-story salmon-colored downtown skyscraper has two hundred deluxe rooms, 29 junior suites and

one presidential suite, two different views of the city, two restaurants, lobby bar, room service, travel agency, beauty salon, tobacco shop, and even a house physician.

Tierra Blanca
Camargo and Niños Héroes, 31000
Tel. 14-15-00-00
Doubles, $32

This downtown motel is hidden behind a white-walled courtyard without a sign, but it is worth the hunt, with its one hundred guest rooms, swimming pool, dining room, coffee shop, bar, and disco.

Victoria
Juárez and Colon (at the Juárez Monument), 31000
Tel. 14-12-88-93
Doubles, $32

An older, colonial-style hotel, the Victoria features 124 rooms spread around a huge lobby with a grand staircase. There's a lovely large Mexican-tiled swimming pool in a beautiful garden setting. You'll also find a restaurant, bar, tour agencies—and friendly service.

Chihuahua has several fascinating museums, and the one that most captures the imagination is **Quinta Luz** (Calle 10 Nte. 3014), once the home of Pancho Villa, hero of the Mexican Revolution of 1910. The guide relishes telling the tale of Villa's many "wives," the last of whom, Doña Luz Corral, ended up with the mansion, which has many rooms full of memorabilia surrounding several lovely green courtyards; the bullet-riddled car in which the general was assassinated is also on the grounds. Open 9 A.M. to 1 P.M. and 3 to 7 P.M. daily. Admission is 400 pesos.

Part of the legend of Pancho Villa is the extravagant mausoleum (in Revolución Park) he built in 1913 as his last resting place: an architectural extravaganza worth viewing, although Villa was buried where he was assassinated, two hundred miles to the south. His body was later moved to Mexico City.

Another interesting museum is **Quinta Gameros** (Bolivar 401), a magnificent mansion with an even more romantic history. Built by a wealthy architect on the whim of his intended, who then later changed her mind, the Art Nouveau building is decorated on the outside with a rose motif (her name was Rosa) and inside with Italian blown-glass chandeliers, much gold leaf, and a beautiful stained-glass window on the large landing of the staircase leading to the second story. The window cost $1,500 in 1907—today it is priceless. Open 10 A.M. to 2 P.M. and 4 to 7 P.M. Closed Mondays. Admission is 800 pesos.

Chihuahua's **cathedral** (Plaza de la Constitución), a magnificent baroque piece of work, was begun by the Jesuits in

1726 after the bishop decreed that the small existing church did not properly reflect the wealth of the city. The cathedral was finished by the Franciscans in 1825, and consequently dedicated to Saint Francis of Assisi, patron saint of the city. There is a **Museum of Sacred Art** at the west side of the cathedral (open 9:30 A.M. to 2:30 P.M. Monday through Friday; small admission charge). Even older—in fact, the oldest church in Chihuahua—is the smaller **Iglesia de San Francisco** (Plaza Zaragoza), built by the Franciscans in 1721. After Father Hidalgo's execution, his decapitated body was interred here, protected by the Franciscan fathers until Mexican independence was finally won in 1823. It was then exhumed and sent to Mexico City. A tablet in the chapel tells the story (in Spanish).

Murals beneath the arches along the courtyard of the **Palacio del Gobierno** tell the story of Father Hidalgo and the entire Mexican War of Independence in broad and colorful strokes. The leaders of the uprising against Spain were imprisoned and executed here. "Anyone would be executed who had anything to do with him [Hidalgo]—that's why you see the people of Chihuahua [in the mural] with stone faces," explained one guide. The building is on the north side of Plaza de Hidalgo, a lovely green place with, in its center, a wonderful monument to the priest and his fellow patriots. Across from the plaza is the **Palacio Federal,** in which the revolutionaries were confined during their trial.

Museo de Arte Popular (Reforma 5 and Independencia) has interesting displays of the Tarahumara Indian lifestyle, plus a shop that sells their crafts. The shy Tarahumara Indians, who live southwest of the city in the Sierra Madre, come to town only on market days and other occasions.

The **Aqueduct,** reminiscent of Roman ruins and begun in the 1700s of sandstone and mortar, was in use until 1985, when it could no longer carry enough water for a town of one million. The best portion to see is at Avenida Zarco and Calle 34.

☕ RESTAURANTS

Mexico is not generally known for good steaks, but Chihuahua is an exception. There is also a variety of other cuisines, and as usual, hotel restaurants are quite good. Major credit cards are accepted unless otherwise noted.

La Calesa
Juárez and Colon, at the Juárez Monument
Tel. 12-45-55 and 12-85-55
   An old carriage is mounted above the door of this steakhouse, which features baby sirloin served with salad and refried beans. The average cost of dinner for two is $12–$20.

Club de los Parados

Avenida Juárez 3901

Tel. 15-13-33 and 12-44-41

This is where *los paradors,* the "stand-ups," used to quaff their beer at the bar—but there are tables now! Good cold draft beer—the bar seats are shaped like saddles—and the Alexander porterhouse, a chicken mole, or fish fillet *a la veracruzana* are the best items to order. The average cost of dinner for two is $15–$20.

La Olla

Juárez 3333

Tel. 12-36-02 and 12-36-01

This picturesque old brewery specializes in seafood dishes such as *camarones al ajo* (shrimp with garlic) and *fuente de mariscos* (literally, large dish of seafood), as well as Caesar salad and steak. Dinner for two begins at $15.

Los Parados de Tony Vega

Avenida Juárez 3316

Tel. 15-13-13

Across the street from the Club de los Parados, housed in an old mansion, and under the same ownership as the club, Tony Vega's is the more formal of the two and offers specialties such as tournedos Mignonet, *pollo* cordon bleu, *helado* Alaska, and crêpes suzette all served in style. The average cost of dinner for two is $15–$25.

Salignac

Juárez 3309

Tel. 12-85-55 and 15-86-16

The French influence is celebrated here, with international food and live entertainment. The restaurant is also known for good beef and seafood, especially king crab and black bass. The average cost of dinner for two is $15–$20.

La Trufa

Avenida Independencia 500

Tel. 16-64-75

Specializing in Cajun food such as blackened red snapper, this upscale retreat also offers French, Italian, and seafood specialties. The average cost of dinner for two is $10–$20.

SHOPPING

There are two large **outdoor markets** on Calle Aldama and another *mercado* on Victoria Street (open 8 A.M.–1 P.M. and 3 P.M.–7 P.M.; 8 A.M.–noon Sundays). **Museo de Arte Popular** at Independencia and Reforma, and **Artesanias Mexicanas,** across from Quinta Luz, sell Mexican handicrafts. The latter sells rocks also.

ENTERTAINMENT

Like much of Mexico, the action is at the discos, with **La Mina** (avenidas Colon and Niños Heroes); **Medanos** in the Castel Sicomoro; and **Robin Hood** (Avenida Talavera) three of the best ones.

Copper Canyon

Called Mexico's Grand Canyon, spectacular Cañon de Cobre is even more of a show than is that other famous canyon in Arizona: deeper and longer, with more than a dozen gorges all branching off one another in a magnificent display of rugged grandeur. Unless you hire a plane or travel by horseback, the only way to see the canyons, which are west of Chihuahua, is to take the Ferrocarril de Chihuahua al Pacífico, the railway between Chihuahua and Los Mochis, a port in Sinaloa on the Sea of Cortés. (In Chihuahua, the station and ticket office are at Mendez and 24; for reservations, call 2-22-84 between the hours of 8 A.M. and 6 P.M. The ticket office (tel. 2-04-13) is open from 6 A.M. until 6 P.M.)

The ride is a 14-hour journey, and to see the six major canyons you must get off the train at several stops, spend the night, and take excursions. There are not too many adventures left on this continent, and Sanborn Tours (1007 Main Street, Bastrop, TX 78602; tel. 512-321-1131; 800-531-5440), pioneers of travel in Mexico and one of the primary providers of excursions to Copper Canyon, cautions that your enjoyment of the trip will depend greatly upon your expectations. Hotel accommodations, though not deluxe, are comfortable (except when there is no hot water!); train windows are rarely sparkling clean; air-conditioning or heating may break down; restrooms often are without paper—so you must go with the proper spirit of adventure when you embark upon one of the most fascinating tours on the North American continent.

The railway itself is an exceptional feat—in fact, many U.S. engineers told the Mexicans that it could not be built. But in 1872 U.S. engineer Albert Kinsey Owen determined to link the U.S. Midwest with the Pacific Coast from Norfolk, Virginia, to Topolobampo, on the Sea of Cortés. His dream was not realized until 1961, when with much drama the east and west lines were linked at Temoris, 3,365 feet above sea level. There, at one point, the roadbed descends by means of curves and loops, and three levels of the railroad and bright red bridges can be seen. The route, climbing from an altitude of four thousand feet at Chihuahua to more than eight thousand feet in the Sierra Madre, and down to sea level at Los Mochis, crossing the Continental Divide three times, takes a total of

39 bridges (some over gorges more than a mile high) and 86 tunnels (one more than a mile long).

One of the stops along the route is **Divisadero,** with scenery so spectacular that the train halts for 25 minutes to let passengers off to catch the view. Waiting in the open-air station are Tarahumara Indians with wares to sell. No bustling entrepreneurs here, soft sell is their trademark. They sit quietly on the ground amid their playful children and their handicrafts—very finely woven basketry is the specialty, as well as ethnic dolls, wooden carvings, and copper jewelry—waiting until excited tourists have finished rushing down the path to the overlook of Copper Canyon.

Two trains a day leave from both Chihuahua and Los Mochis (at 6 A.M. and 7 A.M.) and whichever arrives first at Divisadero has to wait for the other to pass. There are hotels at Divisadero, Creel, and Cerocáhui, comfortable but rustic, and the food, served family-style, is quite good. However, this is rugged adventure country, not for bon vivants; for instance, at Hotel Cabañas Divisadero-Barrancas, the bar closes at 9:30 P.M. and all outside lights go out at 10 P.M.

📷 HOTELS

All hotels listed below accept major credit cards unless otherwise noted. Prices include three meals daily.

CEROCÁHUI

Hotel Misión
c/o Hoteles Balderrama, Los Mochis, Sinaloa, 81200
Tel. 681-5-70-46 and 16-65-89
Doubles, $108
  For this you must get off the train at the Bahuichivo station, where the hotel bus meets the train daily, providing free transportation to Cerocáhui, 8 miles distant. The thirty-room one-story hotel, built around a courtyard, is attractive, rustic, Mexican—and serves delicious food. The neighboring mission was founded in 1690; the tiny town square has several very small shops; the hotel offers a tour to spectacular Urique Canyon. Kerosene lamps are provided in each room: The electricity goes off between 7:30 P.M. and dawn.

CREEL

Hotel Cabañas Cañon del Cobre
c/o Angelica Lerma, Hotel Victoria, Juárez and Colon, Chihuahua 31000
Tel. 14-12-88-93 and 15-82-14 (in Chihuahua)
Doubles, $102
  This twenty-room lodge is made of logs and adobe and located about 45 minutes from the Creel station. The rooms are large, with wood stoves and oil lamps; good meals are served family-style.

DIVISADERO

Hotel Cabañas Divisadero-Barrancas

c/o Aldama 407-C, Box 661, Chihuahua, 31000
Tel. 14- and 15-11-99 and, for reservations, in Chihuahua, 12-33-63

Doubles, $108

This is the only hotel on the brink of the canyon; there are 35 guest rooms and a dining room-lounge offering spectacular views of the canyons and the sunset. Activities offered are guided tours on foot or horseback around canyon rims and through forests of the Sierra Tarahumara, and visits to Tarahumara Indian caves. Three meals are included in the daily rate.

TOURING

Sanborn Tours offers eight-day, seven-night Copper Canyon round-trip tours or a five-day, four-night Copper Canyon one-way south or north tour from El Paso, Texas, with an extra day trip to the Cuauhtémoc/Mennonite Colony and extensions south to Mazatlán or west to La Paz and Los Cabos in Baja California Sur. (Contact Sanborn Tours, 1007 Main Street, Bastrop, TX 78602; tel. 512-321-1131; 800-531-5440.)

Lajitas Travel offers Copper Canyon tours from Oakland, California, and El Paso and Midland-Odessa, Texas, that include Texas destinations Fort Davis and Lajitas in Big Bend country. (Lajitas Travel is a division of the Mischer Corporation, 2727 North Loop West, Suite 200, Box 7479, Houston, TX 77008; tel.: 713-869-7800; 800-527-4078.)

Sinaloa: Los Mochis

There is not a great deal of interest for the traveler in this prosperous agricultural center in the state of Sinaloa on the West Coast; primarily it is a stepping-off point for La Paz, in Baja California Sur, or the resort of Mazatlán to the south, or for the Chihuahua al Pacífico Railway's eastbound trip, which many consider the best way to see Copper Canyon, especially if you only plan to go one-way, not round-trip. That's because the most spectacular part of the canyons is between Los Mochis and Divisadero, and consequently it is important to be there during daylight hours.

Los Mochis, out of the mountains and on the seacoast, and consequently with an average temperature of seventy to eighty degrees Fahrenheit, is home to one of the largest sugar refineries (founded in 1893 by an American family, the Benjamin Johnstons from Virginia) on the West Coast. The Johnstons cultivated sugarcane, built the sugar mill, laid out the town, built the first church, and constructed a lighthouse atop Cerra de la Memoria (Memory Hill) and, later, an airport. However, even before the advent of the Johnstons, a Utopian colony was founded here in 1872 by Albert Kinsey Owen, the man who conceived the idea of the railroad over the Sierra.

Los Mochis means "the turtles" in the Mayo (not to be confused with the Maya) Indian language, and acres of marigolds, fed to the chickens so that their egg yolks will have a brilliant hue, are grown here. There is good bird hunting in this area—duck, speckled geese, quail, white-tail dove are plentiful in the hunting season, from November 1 to February 15. (Arrangements can be made through your hotel.) Nearby **Topolobampo,** ten miles south, is a small fishing village known for its shrimp fleet and sport fishing—roosterfish, yellowtail, sailfish, and marlin. A new ferry now links Topolobampo to La Paz daily except Tuesdays. For reservations, call 5-82-62.

🧳 HOTELS

All hotels accept major credit cards unless otherwise noted.

Las Colinas
Carretera Internacional no. 15 and Bulevar M. Gaxiola, 83200
Tel. 681-2-01-01; in the United States 800-528-1234
Doubles, from $40
   A Best Western five-story, 121-room motor inn atop a hill, Las Colinas features a pool, restaurant, coffee shop, and bar-nightclub.

El Dorado
Avenidas G. Levya and H. Valdez, 81200
Tel. 681-5-11-11
Doubles, $28
   This 43-room, three-story hotel plus a fifty-unit, two-story motel offers a swimming pool, restaurant specializing in steaks, cafeteria, and enclosed parking.

Plaza Inn
Avenida G. Levya 701, 81200
Tel. 681-5-80-20
Doubles, $42
   Originally Chapman's, built by Dr. Chapman, the medical man for Johnston sugar company and the U.S. colony, the Plaza Inn has been recently remodeled, with 38 guest rooms, swimming pool, coffee shop, and a cafeteria next door.

Santa Anita
G. Levya and Hidalgo, 81200
Tel. 681-5-70-46
Doubles, $53
   Los Mochis's largest hotel, this is a five-story, 135-room downtown property with dining room, bar and nightclub, travel agency, and gift shop. Train tickets and hotel reservations to Copper Canyon, hunting and fishing, city tours, and cruises on Topolobampo Bay can all be arranged here.

Suites Florida
G. Levya and Ramirez, 81200
Tel. 681-2-12-00 and 2-14-83
Doubles, $23

This is a small 66-room hotel; some units have kitchenettes. You'll also find a coffee shop, bar, and disco.

☕ RESTAURANTS

Dinner for two at these establishments should cost no more than $15; lunch should be under $10. Both accept major credit cards. **El Farallon,** at Avenida Flores and Obregón, around the corner from the Santa Anita Hotel; tel. 2-14-28. The "Rocky Island" has nautical decor and seafood only. **La Parrilla Dorada,** Levya 222 Sur; tel. 2-26-03. Swiss cuisine, as well as *menudo* (tripe) and other Mexican dishes and charcoal-broiled steak are served in this converted old home.

SHOPPING

Downtown streets are filled with the ubiquitous shoe stores and *papelerias* (stationery stores), but there is also a *mercado* beginning one block parallel to Levya, where the Santa Anita Hotel is located. It's open from 8 A.M. to 8 P.M. and is filled with stalls offering everything from cookies and candy to clothing.

> The Pacific League, a professional football league, has a season in Los Mochis from October to January; ask at your hotel desk for information on obtaining tickets.

ENTERTAINMENT

There's not much nightlife in Los Mochis; a late drink and conversation are about the town speed, but there's dancing at **Bar las Bugambilias,** at the Suites Florida, G. Levya and Ramirez, tel. 2-12-00, and the adjoining **Scorpio's** disco. A cool drink can be enjoyed at the bar in the Santa Anita, G. Levya and Hidalgo, tel. 5-70-46 and at the **Fantasy Bar** in the Plaza Inn.

MAZATLÁN

Approximately 270 miles south of Los Mochis along Highway 15 lies Mazatlán **(see map, Page 503),** one of Mexico's most popular travelers' resorts, as well as one of the coast's finest ports. The city, situated on the West Coast just where the Sea of Cortés joins the Pacific Ocean, enjoys mild and sunny winters with an average temperature in the seventies, and not too much hotter in the summer—those looking for really hot and humid weather do better in the resorts farther south. There is very little rain here, however.

The Chibcha Indians were the early residents, and a few Spaniards settled in the early 1600s at the Presidio de Mazatlán, established in 1576 by order of Hernándo de Bazán, governor of the entire territory of northwest Mexico and the Californias. Pirates were plentiful back then, too, supposedly using coves and inlets to bury their treasure. The town was incorporated in 1806, had a municipal government by 1837, and by the end of the 19th century Mazatlán's port was involved with international trade all the way to China.

Mazatlán was not left untouched by the events that shaped the rest of the country: In the Mexican-American War, U.S. forces marching south from the border and north from Veracruz to Mexico City blockaded the port; the port was blockaded again in 1859 when the nation was divided between Juárez and the conservatives; in 1864 the French bombarded the city; and during the Revolution there was a blockade in effect from 1913 to 1914.

Mazatlán has one of Mexico's largest shrimp fleets; it is a popular port of call for cruise ships stopping along what is often called "the Mexican Riviera"; and it was popular with sun-and-sea sport enthusiasts in the know from the United States and Canada even before the resorts to the south were fully developed.

Mazatlán is accessible by road from north and south Highway 15 or from the east by Highway 40 to Durango. But highway travel must be accompanied by a warning due to recent incidents involving robberies of both motorists and bus passengers. Though one official remarked that crimes against the person are rare, having your money and jewelry removed at gunpoint is bound to be an unnerving experience, not to mention the inconvenience such an encounter is bound to cause monetarily. Best to arrive in Mazatlán by air or by sea. The daily ferry ride from La Paz takes approximately 17 hours, and fares run from 36,000 pesos (a little more than $14 at this writing) for a salon seat to 144,000 pesos (about $55) for a "Special class" berth. Mexicana Airlines flies to Mazatlán from many U.S. cities as well as Vancouver, British Columbia, Canada, and Mexican cities. Major carriers such as American, Continental, and Delta fly to Mexico City from major gateways, connecting with Aeromexico and Mexicana flights to Mazatlán.

Mazatlán curves around the warm blue water (75 degrees in summer, 68 degrees in winter) in a long 17-mile sweep of beautiful white beaches that can be seen to the best advantage from the hill above the city on the way to the lighthouse on Cerro del Crestón. Three islands visible from shore are characteristic of Mazatlán: Bird Island, Deer Island, and Wolf Island. In addition, sea lions migrate to a small island from

> The name Mazatlán is from a Nahuatl word meaning "place of
> the deer," but "place of the fish" would be more to the point,
> as Mazatlán is another of Mexico's great sport-fishing heavens.
> Sailfish, billfish, and marlin abound, as well as smaller but possibly
> "gamer" catch in inland lagoons.

October through May and can be seen by boat. While beaches
are a priority in Mazatlán, the busy port city also provides
plenty of excitement in shopping, sightseeing, and everyday
atmosphere.

CONNECTIONS

Minibus transportation from the airport costs 5,000 pesos; taxis
charge 20,000 pesos. In town there are two kinds of taxis, the
conventional ones—and always ask the fare beforehand—and
the *pulmonias,* small jeep-like vehicles that offer an open-air ride
for up to three people for about 4,000 pesos. There are several
bus lines found on the major streets, with destinations clearly
marked in front.

**The government tourist office is located at Paseo Olas Altas
1300, 2nd floor (tel. 2-12-20 and 2-12-22) and the Secretario
de Turismo is located at Rodolfo T. Loaiza 100 (tel. 4-02-22
and 3-25-45). The U.S. Consulate is at Circunvanción 120
and Carranza (tel. 5-22-05).**

🛍 HOTELS

There is a wide choice of places to stay in Mazatlán, and reservations are a good idea in this popular resort. All hotels take
major credit cards unless otherwise noted. Rates listed here are
for high season and drop as much as 50 percent in summer and
fall months.

Camino Real
Punta del Sábalo (about seven miles north of downtown), 82100
Tel. 678-3-11-11; in the United States 800-228-3000
Doubles, from $110
   This luxury resort, another under the Westin banner, is right
on the beach, with 170 guest rooms, swimming pool, restau-
rants, lobby bar and disco, a weekly Mexican fiesta, tennis, mas-
seuse, and social director.

El Cid
Sábalo Beach Road s/n (sin número), 82110
Tel. 678-3-33-33; in the United States 800-525-1925
Doubles, from $130
   Probably Mexico's largest resort so far, this six-hundred-room
extravaganza on the beach consists of two separate hotels, the
original Country Club section, with a marina soon to be con-

structed, and the new 17-story ocean tower, both connected by a pedestrian bridge. There are five swimming pools, sauna, children's recreational area, 11 restaurants and lounges, **El Caracol** tango palace, 17 lighted tennis courts, an 18-hole golf course, squash court, a Mexican fiesta every Sat. night, and all water sports including wind surfing, parasailing, snorkeling, and deep-sea fishing.

Holiday Inn Mazatlán

Calzada Camarón Sábalo 696, 82100
Tel. 678-3-22-22; 800-HOLIDAY
Doubles, from $120

A comfortable 208-room hotel on the beach with two swimming pools, the Holiday Inn offers two restaurants, lobby bar, beach-front bar, disco, water sports, drugstore, shops, and beauty salon.

Oceano Palace

Avenida Camarón Sábalo s/n (sin número), 82110
Tel. 678-3-06-66;
Doubles, from $109

A two-hundred-room hotel on the beach, the Palace offers two swimming pools with lifeguard, two restaurants, two bars with live music, golf and tennis at **Las Gaviotas** racquet club, sailing, parasailing, waterskiing, snorkeling, deep-sea fishing, travel desk, beauty salon, and shops.

Playa Mazatlán

Las Gaviotas Beach s/n (sin número), 82010
Tel. 678-3-44-55
Doubles, from $100

This 425-room hotel, a favorite of U.S. travelers, offers swimming pool, dining room, outdoor dancing, social director, water sports, and a great deal of excitement at all times.

Plaza Gaviotas

Avenida Camarón Gaviotas s/n (sin número), 82110
Tel. 678-3-43-22
Doubles, from $100

This seventy-room hotel, one block from Playa Camarón Sábalo beach, has no elevator but boasts nice-sized comfortable rooms and a good restaurant and bar.

Pueblo Bonito

Avenida Camarón Sábalo 2121, 82000
Tel. 678-4-37-00
Doubles, from $150

This new luxurious Mexican pink-adobe pueblo has 133 oceanview suites, elegantly furnished—with kitchenettes equipped with fine tableware—plus a free-form pool with swim-up bar, dining room, full doorman and valet service, concierge and travel/sightseeing desk, aerobics, and sportfishing, hunting, and tennis arrangements.

La Siesta

Paseo de Olas Altas 11
Tel. 678-1-26-40
Doubles, from $18

This small, modest but clean hotel on the Malecón offers nice service, has a sunny central-patio eatery, and is the home of the famous **El Shrimp Bucket** restaurant.

Los Sábalos

Rodolfo T. Loaiza 100, 82110
Tel. 678-3-53-33
Doubles, from $70

A beachfront hotel with 185 luxury rooms, Los Sábalos features wet bars and flower-filled balconies, three restaurants, a health club, and tennis courts.

Suites las Flores

Las Gaviotas Beach s/n (sin número), 82010
Tel. 678-3-51-00; in the United States 800-421-0767; in California, 800-252-0327
Doubles, about $54

This beachfront high-rise features 27 guest rooms and 95 apartments (with kitchenettes), swimming pool, restaurant, and bar. Tennis can also be arranged.

The **Malecón,** as in every Mexican seaside city, is the name given to the waterfront promenade, a pleasant place to stroll and enjoy the breezes off the water. Runners, bicyclists, and joggers take to the pavement too. The **Fisherman's Monument,** on the south end of the Malecón, is a Mazatlán landmark. It's a large sculpture depicting a standing fisherman, a supine woman, and underneath, three fish: a sailfish, a shark, and a dolphin. Local explanation: "A Mazatlán sailor, a Mazatlán woman, and the shark tries to catch the *delfín* [dolphin], but it is too fast."

The **Aquarium,** with 250 species of fish on display, gives another idea of what's in the waters of Mazatlán. In addition, there is an auditorium where educational films are shown. The adjacent Museum of the Sea contains sea objects and a souvenir shop, and the small botanical garden outside has plants from all over the world. (Both are open daily, 10 A.M. to 6 P.M., except Monday. Deportes 111; tel. 1-78-15.)

Along the Malecón at Olas Altas Beach and Paseo Claussen you'll see **El Mirador,** a large rock formation just offshore. What makes it noteworthy is that young divers use it as a high-dive, heading for a small clear spot in the rocky water below. They attract a small crowd and collect donations before they leap.

Mazatlán has quite a few hills that afford tremendous views of the city. **Cerro del Vigía** (Watchman's Hill), on the east side of town, was chosen by the first settlers as the place to establish Mazatlán, and today it is a residential area with beautiful views of the port and the sea. **Cerro de la Nevería** (Icebox Hill), above Bulevar Claussen, was so named because its cave was a cool place to preserve fish and other food. **Cerro de Crestón** is the craggy peak of land that, jutting out into the Pacific, separates the ocean from the harbor. At its very tip is **El Faro,** which stands five hundred feet above the water and is the second-highest lighthouse in the world. It's at the end of Centenario Drive, and on the way you will pass **Pergola Angela Peralta,** a Greek-style gazebo that's a popular trysting spot. (Angela Peralta was an internationally known opera singer who died in Mazatlán.) The pergola is landscaped with *amalpa,* a sweet-smelling shrub that you will see all over Mazatlán with yellow, orange, or pink flowers. The view overlooking Cerro del Crestón offers a double treat: To the right is the resort of Mazatlán on the ocean, with the curve of white-sand beaches fronting the resort hotels; to the left, the busy harbor with shrimpers and freighters tends to the business side of the town.

The **fishing docks** located at the base of El Faro are a good place to see the fishing that Mazatlán is really all about. Afternoons at about 2 P.M., the sport-fishing boats dock, and many a happy fisherman will display the day's catch: Be it marlin, sailfish, or sometimes shark, it will no doubt be a whopper.

The **cathedral** on the **Plaza República** was begun in 1875; it faces the **Palacio Municipal** (City Hall). The downtown architecture in Mazatlán reflects a German influence, along with Spanish and French influences (during the 19th century, Germans developed the port in order to import agricultural equipment). Another point of interest downtown is the **Teatro Angela Peralta,** named for the internationally renowned opera singer who died in Mazatlán.

The **Arts and Crafts Center,** a large shopping complex with many working artisans, contains the five-hundred-seat **Azteca Theater** (Rodolfo T. Loaiza 417; tel. 2-50-55), whose pyramided stage is the scene of folkloric and other cultural events several times a week. The **Yate Fiesta Cruise Mazatlán,** a three-hour cruise of the harbor and bay, is a good way to get a waterfront view of Mazatlán. It leaves from El Faro at about 11 A.M., and English-speaking guides are aboard (usually) to point out places of interest. The cruise passes the town and the harbor, the pirate *grutas* (caves) of Cerro del Crestón, and rocks where seals lounge in the sun. You will pay 16,000 pesos, and that includes tax and two soft drinks; children between five and 14 can go for half-price. Boarding is at the dock on the main road to the lighthouse; tel. 1-30-41 for information.

🍵 RESTAURANTS

As you would expect in a resort town, good dining choices abound, and your main difficulty may be in deciding where to go. *Chilorio,* a dish of well-seasoned pork, is a local specialty. Marlin and sailfish are also traditional dishes, and Mazatlán shrimp is the largest and tastiest in the world. Besides those (generally quite good) restaurants in major hotels, the following were chosen as among the best representatives of the great variety the city enjoys.

Although more expensive in a resort city like Mazatlán, food is still relatively reasonably priced. Prices do not include wine, drinks, tax, or tips. Easily obtainable beers here include Tecate, Corona, and Pacífico, as well as imported brews. Wines run $2 to $3 a glass, and approximately $10 to $14 a bottle, possibly even higher in an expensive restaurant, depending upon choice. Imported French wines are very expensive; Mexican wines such as Domec, Los Reyes, Quinta El Mirador, and Calafia Santo Tomás are served in the best restaurants. Domec wines, such as Riesling and blanc de blanc, and Los Reyes wines are considered better than those of Calafia, but all are products of Baja California and served with pride throughout Mexico. Other imported liquor is also expensive, so, as fun eatery **Señor Frog's** advises, "while in Mexico, drink rum and other domestic spirits; the prices of Scotch and Cognac are ridiculous!"

The following restaurants accept major credit cards unless otherwise noted.

Doney's
Mariano Escobedo 610, a block from the Palacio Municipal
Tel. 1-26-51

This family restaurant in a restored old house downtown has been a local favorite since 1959, serving home-style Mazatlán dishes, seafood, and steaks *(carnes),* as well as American banana splits. The average price of a dinner for two is $20.

Lobster Trap
Avenida Camarón Sábalo
Tel. 3-42-55

Lobster is of course the specialty here, but seafood and steaks are also served. The average price of a dinner for two is about $40. DC only.

Mamucas
Simon Bolivar 73
Tel. 1-34-90

Very popular for many years among the locals, this unpretentious downtown eatery has some of the best seafood in town. The name, one authority said, comes from a person who stuttered "a very bad word," but the "seafood explosive"—an order of squid, shrimp, *manchaca* (mashed shrimp), marlin, and octopus on a huge (12 inches by 15 inches) metal tray—is very, very good. The average price of a dinner for two is $30.

El Patio
Avenida del Mar 30
Tel. 1-73-01

Theme eatery on the oceanfront featuring a fun, festive atmosphere and a good selection of seafood and Mexican dishes. *Caldo xochitl,* a thick and nutritious soup, is recommended as a hangover solution—useful since among the specialties here are killer drinks. The average price of a dinner for two is $30.

Señor Frog's
Avenida del Mar
Tel. 2-82-70, 2-19-25, 5-11-10

This offshoot of the Carlos 'n Charlie's family is noisy and crazy (especially when cruise ships in port release their passengers) but a lot of fun, with people dancing between the tables as well as on the small dance floor. The huge menu is both entertaining and all-encompassing, and the barbecued ribs are outstanding, as is the *sarsuela de mariscos,* a rich, delicious concoction of sauced shellfish, and the bouillabaisse. Dinner for two costs about $30.

El Shrimp Bucket
Olas Altas Sur 11-126, in the La Siesta Hotel
Tel. 1-63-50 or 2-80-19

A waterfront classic on the south end of town, with seafood served to the beat of marimbas and mariachis. The average price of a dinner for two is about $40.

Tres Islas
Calzada Camarón Sábalo
Tel. 3-59-32

Some of the best seafood in town, right on the beach north of downtown, with a view of three islands (hence the name). The average price of a dinner for two is under $20.

BEACHES

While some of Mazatlán's beaches seem to be the private bailiwick of resorts, you need not be a guest to use them—there are no private beaches in Mexico, and thus the shores are open to everyone. **Sábalo Beach,** out north and fronted by the luxury resorts of Los Sábalos, Holiday Inn, Camino Real, and the new Pueblo Bonito, is sheltered, quiet, and chic but open to the public. **Las Gaviotas Beach,** often much more crowded, is a good place for swimming. **Playa Norte** has lockers for rent, as well as umbrellas and beach chairs; there are small restaurants, with mariachis, that are good for lunching. **Olas Altas Beach,** a good surfing beach on the south end of town, lives up to its name of "high waves." There are no lifeguards.

SHOPPING

Although Sinaloa is not known for much in the way of native handicrafts, an exception might be **Sea Shell City** (on Sábalos Gaviotas, across from Suites Las Flores), two floors of every conceivable item that can be made from shells (although many are imported). The shop is even decorated with shells—see the seashell mosaics on the second floor. Mazatlán also has a large selection of shopping centers selling goods from all over the country. **Mazatlán Arts and Crafts Center** (Rodolfo T. Loaiza 417) is a cooperative of some two dozen shops with craftspeople right on the scene. A large shopping center is also part of the Playa Mazatlán hotel complex. **Casa Pacífica** (far out on Avenida Camarón Cerritos, at number 335) and **Casa Roberto** (Playa Mazatlán) have exclusive gifts; for poking around local shopping spots, you might enjoy the busy downtown area around the *mercado*. **The Leather Factory** (Sábalo Beach) offers excellent Mexican leather wallets, purses, and clothing at good prices.

SPORTS

Water sports include water- and jet-skiing, parasailing, diving, sailing, snorkeling, wind surfing and surfing, kayaking, and water biking, available collectively at the following: **Chicos Beach Club** (tel. 4-07-77); **Ocean Sport Centers at Camino Real** (tel. 3-11-11); **Pueblo Bonito** (tel. 4-37-00); **Oceano Palace** (tel. 3-06-66); **El Cid** (tel. 3-33-33); **Caravelle Beach Club** (tel. 3-02-00); **Flota 233** (tel. 3-69-32); and **Los Sábalos** (tel. 3-53-33).

Hunting around Mazatlán centers on species of duck and pigeon, with facilities, transportation, and equipment, from boots to airplanes, available if necessary. Permits are required. Arrangements can be made through the government tourist office or the Mazatlán Chamber of Commerce (Avenida Miguel Alemán 914; tel. 678-1-20-68).

For anglers, ten fishing fleets provide more than 75 cruisers for two to six passengers. Fishing is good all year, although November to May is considered the best season for giant marlin, sailfish, billfish, bonita, tuna, sea bass, and red snapper. Arrangements can be made through your hotel. **Bill Heimpel's Star Fleet** (you can reserve by calling from the United States, 800-531-0084, or, in Texas, 800-531-0083) and **Mike's Sportfishing Marina** (call 1-28-24 or 2-49-77) at the Marina Flota Faro are reliable.

ENTERTAINMENT

Mazatlán's big **Carnaval** is a classic week-long affair, celebrated since 1898 from Wednesday to Tuesday prior to Ash

Wednesday. Prices often double during Carnaval, and you will probably need to reserve at least six months in advance.

On October 15, the official opening of the fishing season, there is a **procession to bless the fleet.** The **Feast of the Immaculate Conception** is on December 8, with fireworks and religious statues paraded through town.

As for nightlife, the disco scene is big in Mazatlán, with the leading hotels offering their own dance clubs and nightclubs (some with shows). But outstanding is **Valentino's** (tel. 3-62-12), a white Arabian palace high on a cliff above the sea at Punta el Camarón on the north end of the Malecón. Others are **Frankie O's** (Avenida del Mar; tel. 2-58-00); **Fandangos** (Las Palmas Shopping Center; tel. 3-67-67); and **El Carousel** (Avenida del Mar 720; tel. 2-46-07), one of those old-fashioned nightclubs with fun floor shows.

Mexican fiestas are held in the **Arts and Crafts Center's Teatro Azteca** (tel. 2-50-55) and in the leading hotels: **Hotel Playa Mazatlán** (tel. 3-44-44); **Holiday Inn** (tel. 3-22-22); **Oceano Palace** (tel. 3-00-66); and **El Cid** (tel. 3-33-33).

Durango

The city of Durango, the capital of the state of Durango, is up in the Sierra Madre between Saltillo on the east and Mazatlán to the west. It was founded in 1563 by Francisco de Ibarra, who first named it Nueva Viscaya. That was changed almost immediately to Durango, a name with Basque roots, meaning, "fertile lowland bathed by a river and encircled by mountains." Well, it certainly is that, and the circle of mountains has provided Durango with a glamorous image, for it has been the locale of many a Hollywood western. As recently as 1989, the mountains and the river became Los Alamos, New Mexico, circa 1945, for a Paul Newman film about the atom bomb, *Fat Man and Little Boy.* On the way to movie-locale country is **El Tecuan,** a beautiful national park.

Weather is changeable from one region of the state of Durango to another: It is warm in the plains and cold in the mountains, where it can be freezing in winter. Average temperatures in the city range from high fifties (degrees Fahrenheit) in winter to high sixties in the summer. None of this has put a damper on Durango's natural resources, which the Spanish discovered in the 16th century to be gold, silver, lead, copper, and iron. **Cerro del Mercado** (Market Hill), with a 65- to 70-percent iron content, is just north of the city.

Very little English is spoken in Durango, and so far there are only five hotels, two of which are motels, that could be considered comfortable travelers' accommodations. Tourism officials agree that Durango needs more hotels and more tourism promotion, but the city still offers many visitors' attractions.

CONNECTIONS

The best way to get to Durango is to fly, and Aeromexico flies there from Mexico City and Tijuana. Highway 40 (to Mazatlán on the West Coast and Saltillo toward the east) is not considered safe for motorists at this time, and it would be a good idea to ride buses with caution, although they now leave directly from the bus stations and do not stop for passengers on the road along the route. Information on all train routes is available from Ferrocarriles Nacionales de México, Estación Buena Vista, Depto. de Tráfico de Pasajeros, Insurgentes Norte and Avenida Mosqueta, México, D.F. 06358; tel. 5-547-1097 and 547-6939 (or consult the *Official Railway Guide* in your city library).

Within Durango itself, taxis are available, but they can be expensive: the ride from the airport to your hotel will run about 30,000 pesos if you are the only passenger, but can be split if there are several. In town, there are city buses, but you must know in advance which ones to take, and they are always very crowded. You will find very few English-speaking people to help you out.

The **tourist office** (Dirección Estatal de Turismo y Cinematografía) is located downtown at Calle Hidalgo Sur 408 (tel. 1-21-89), but you may not find anyone there who speaks English, so bring along a dictionary if you don't speak Spanish.

🧳 HOTELS

All the following take credit cards unless otherwise noted.

Campo Mexico Courts
Avenida 20 de Noviembre Ote., 34000
Tel. 181-1-55-60
Doubles, from $25
This comfortable motel, away from downtown toward the airport, landscaped around a large green area, offers large rooms, a swimming pool, children's play area, restaurant with live music and good food at reasonable prices, and a "ladies bar" (women welcome).

Casablanca
Avenida 20 de Noviembre Pte. 811, 34000
Tel. 181-1-35-99
Doubles, from $26
This 46-room hotel in the heart of downtown has a lovely lobby, reminiscent of past grandeur (the hotel is almost fifty

years old). Rooms badly need renovating, and such renovation is in the works. You'll find a restaurant and bar, and the management is very friendly.

Plaza Cathedral
Avenida Constitución Sur 103, 34000
Tel. 181-1-48-66
Doubles, from $18

Downtown alongside the cathedral, this charming old colonial hotel (the building is more than four hundred years old) has forty large rooms (some with refrigerators) and a restaurant. From the front rooms with balconies you might be able to see the ghost of the nun (see box, **Catedral de Durango**, below).

On the **Plaza de Armas,** a lovely green square in the center of downtown where Sunday concerts are played, you will find the **Catedral de Durango,** a splendid Mexican baroque edifice begun in 1695. The side facades are from the churrigueresque period dating from 1765. From one of the three towers (the east one), the ghost of the white nun is supposed to be visible. The legend originated in the colonial period and tells the story of a young woman who tended and fell in love with a young Spanish captain wounded in battle. When he recovered and left her, she entered a convent, but, the story goes, every night she would wait for her beloved in the east tower of the cathedral. Her vigil of undying love was rewarded in that her apparition appears on the nights of the full moon, and if you stand on Avenida Constitución and concentrate on that east tower, above the side door of the cathedral. . . .

Palacio de Gobierno (Calle 5 de Febrero and Zaragoza), once the Palacio Zambrano, was built in the 18th century by a rich mining magnate named Don José Zambrano and is now the seat of the state government. The palace has murals upstairs and down by Durango artists Francisco Montoya and Guillermo Bravo, and by De Lourdes from Aguascalientes. Legend has it that Zambrano was so rich that on his daughter's wedding day he laid a path of silver bars from his home to the door of the **Templo del Sagrado Corazón de Jesus** (Avenida Apartado between 5 de Febrero and 20 de Noviembre). (Zambrano also wanted to install window casings of solid silver, but the authorities persuaded him that this would be too much temptation for robbers.) Both facade and interior of the **Templo del Sagrado Corazón de Jesus,** without a silver pathway and looking rather like a feudal fortress, were carved in the quarry in Durango.

Parque Guadiana, on Highway 40 east toward Mazatlán, is another green area, a large park famous for its *Lago de los Patos* (Duck Lake) where black-bass fishing tournaments are held periodically. Originally the site was swampland, but now there are gardens and fountains. In the park is the **Escuela**

de las Artesanias (School of Painting, Sculpture, and Crafts), where you can observe textiles, blown glass, ceramics, and painted fabric in the making.

Cerro de Mercado, Market Hill, is that giant of a hill overlooking the city. It has been producing ore every day for centuries.

San Juan de Analco (two blocks south of Boulevard Dolores Del Rio) was Durango's first mission, built by Jesuits in 1558, but the Italians were later expelled from Mexico and the mission became the charge of Franciscans Diego de la Cadena and Geronimo de Mendoza.

Iglesia de los Remedios is a church atop a high hill (known as Los Remedios) west of downtown overlooking Durango. The church was built by the priests from the parish of San Antonio; the exact date is not known, but it was renovated in 1724. The simple small chapel was used by the hermits of Los Remedios, and consequently the use of jewels, gold, and silver was prohibited. The magnificent view from the courtyard reveals all of Durango.

Off Esplanada Insurgentes in the north section (Guadalupe) of town is the **Santuario de Guadalupe and Esplanada de los Insurgentes,** where lie the remains of priests who were executed in the nearby town of San Juan de Dios in 1812 for participating in the fight for Mexican independence. There is a monument on the walkway, and every December 12, the day of the Virgin of Guadalupe, dancers called *matachines* dance in an offering to the Virgin.

To see the **movie locations,** it is usually necessary to obtain a permit from the Turismo y Cinematografía office at Hidalgo Sur 408 (tel. 1-11-07 and 1-21-39), especially if there is filming under way at the time. However, a knowledge of Spanish, or a dictionary, is advisable for communication—you may not find anyone at the office who speaks English.

■ RESTAURANTS

The restaurant scene in Durango is so-so, but some of the regional specialties are worth a try. Typical local cuisine includes *caldillo durangueño* (meat soup); *chorizo* (sausage with chile); smoked pork loin; cheeses, such as *queso menonita;* sweets made with almonds and other nuts; and dried fruits with sugar. *Bebidas* (drinks) include *mezcal,* made with cactus juice; *membrillo* liquor; and apple and *tejocote* (a local fruit) wine. The **Hotel Casablanca restaurant** (Avenida 20 de Noviembre) is a popular spot, with moderate prices; **La Fogata** (Cuauhtémoc and Negrete) specializes in grilled meats and both local and imported wines; **La Bohemia** (Hidalgo at 20 de Noviembre) specializes in German dishes as well as Mexican; **La Majada** (20 de Noviembre) features beef and goat dishes; **La Venta** (20 de Noviembre Ote.1902) serves German and international food; and **Café y Arte Plaza Los Condes** (5 de Febrero Pte.

201) is a coffee shop with a variety of coffees served to musical accompaniment.

SHOPPING

Shopping, except for the fine wares from the Escuela des Artesanias (which you can buy in stalls along the **Plaza de Armas**), is mainly for souvenirs, with scorpions as the leitmotif of Durango. Dried-but-once-live scorpions are for sale under plastic and glass on ashtrays, key chains, and other such wares in the **Mercado Gomez Palacio** on 20 de Noviembre and 5 de Febrero.

Sonora

Sonora is the state that borders the United States on the West Coast of the Mexican mainland, and Nogales, Sonora, and Nogales, Arizona, are sister cities. The state has the highest wheat production in Mexico, and thirty percent of the country's annual output of soya beans, sesame seeds, alfalfa, and cotton is also grown here. The second most important industry is cattle, with steer raised for export. Silver, gold, lead, zinc, iron, coal, and clay are mined, with copper mined at La Caridad in Nacozari.

Before the Conquest, Sonora was populated by several Indian groups, mainly the Opata, Pima, Papago, Yaqui, Mayo, and Seri. The first Spaniards to arrive were victims of a shipwreck—they had been sent from Acapulco by Hernán Cortés. The state of Sonora was formed around 1767 and declared a free state in 1830, and ratified as such by the constitution of 1857. Three presidents of the Republic of Mexico were native sons: Plutarco Elías Calles, Alvaro Obregón, and Abelardo L. Rodríguez.

Hermosillo

Approximately 170 miles south of Nogales on Highway 15 is the larger city of Hermosillo, capital of the state. Particular caution should be exercised in driving Highway 15 along the coast in the states of Sinaloa and Sonora. When you learn that "Suicide Alley," full of ruts and potholes and slow trucks, has also earned the soubriquet, "the drug highway," you will understand why this road can be very unsafe for travelers— millions of dollars worth of poppy fields and marijuana are rumored to lie in the shrouded valleys of the Sierra Madre in Sonora. Safer transportation is provided by Mexicana Airlines, which flies to Hermosillo from Acapulco, Guadalajara, Mexicali, Oaxaca, Veracruz, and Villahermosa. The two major bus lines are Tres Estrellas de Oro and the second-class Transporte Norte de Sonora (TNS). (There have been rumored incidents of bandidos harassing bus passengers, and first-class buses no longer stop on the highway to pick up passengers.) A thorough train system operates along the northwest coast: contact Ferrocarriles Nacionales de México.

Originally called Santisima Trinidad del Potic, which means "confluence of rivers," Hermosillo was the center of the Pima Indian culture. It was founded as a Spanish town in 1700 by Juan Bautista Escalante, and eventually named after José María Gonzalez Hermosillo, a revolutionary hero of the Mexican War of Independence. Sometimes called "the city of oranges," Hermosillo has a main strip that is green with orange trees and palm trees along the median. Like Nogales to the north, there is not much of interest for the traveler here, but mention must be made of **Rodríguez Dam** and **Lake, Rodríguez Museum** and **Library,** and **Rodríguez Boulevard** leading into town, all named for President Abelardo Rodríguez, who served as Mexico's head of state from 1932 to 1934. He promoted industry for his home state, and the dam, which harnesses the waters of the Río Sonora, is one of the largest earthfill dams in Mexico, causing this desert region to blossom like a rose.

🧳 ACCOMMODATIONS

Hermosillo has half a dozen lodging places, including members of the Calinda and Holiday Inn chains. All hotels listed below take credit cards unless otherwise noted.

Bugambilia
Bulevar Padre Kino 712, 83150
Tel. 621-4-50-50
Doubles, $57
   This remodeled older motel with bungalows on neatly landscaped grounds has 82 units in its new section and 27 in the original section, plus a swimming pool and restaurant.

Calinda Hermosillo
Rosales and Morelia, 83000
Tel. 621-3-28-25; in the United States and Canada, 800-228-5151/52
Doubles, $60
   This downtown high-rise contains 115 comfortable guest rooms and suites, swimming pool, restaurant and cafeteria with Mexican and regional food, and lobby bar.

Gandara
Bulevar Padre Kino 1000, 83150
Tel. 621-4-44-14 and 4-42-41
Doubles, $47
   The 154 units here offer a choice of new hotel rooms or renovated bungalows. You'll also find a swimming pool, restaurant, coffee shop, cocktail lounge, and lobby bar.

Plaza Zaragoza in the center of town, with a fine cathedral, is the heart of the city, with both a flower garden and a Moorish kiosk. Statues there are of General Garcia Morales and General Ignacio Pesqueira. The state government building has murals depicting historical scenes. **Madero Park,** in the southeast section of town, has facilities for baseball, tennis, and handball, as well as statues of Francisco Madero and Jesus Garcia, the Hero of Nacozari. Four kilometers from town is the **Ecological Center,** a park built to preserve the area's flora and fauna. **La Campana** (the Bell) **Hill,** on the outskirts of town, affords a panoramic view of the city and Rodríguez Dam.

There is good hunting in season, with deer, coyote, rabbit, and duck the prey, and ninety miles east at Novillo Dam there is good bass fishing.

☕ RESTAURANTS

Although Hermosillo in general is certainly not a tourist town, the Holiday Inn and most of the hotels listed above have reliable restaurants. In addition, you can sample fine traditional Mexican food at the **Restaurant Villa Fiesta,** Yanez 33, tel. 2-18-40, open noon to midnight, which offers both cocktails and entertainment, in addition to food; and at **La Huerta,** San Lois Potosí 109, tel. 7-27-90, where seafood dominates the menu.

Two principal local celebrations are the Vendimia Fiesta, held in July, an industrial fair featuring a colorful parade of floats, and the typical Yaqui Holy Week, before Easter, when folk dances are performed in a section of town called El Coloso.

Guaymas

Many ports along the West Coast of Mexico are beautiful, but Guaymas might top them all, with the mountains and the desert coming right down to meet the cobalt-blue waters of the Sea of Cortés. Like many of Mexico's ocean ports, Guaymas was not so long ago an undiscovered haven. Today it is again two communities: the old city with its port, and the resort areas along Bacochibampo and San Carlos bays. Situated on the Sea of Cortés, which, teeming with fish, has been called "the largest fish trap in the world," Guaymas means big fishing in both sections of the town. The old city has a harbor lined with shrimp docks and filled with shrimp boats, freighters, and tankers, and the new resorts are filled with sportfishermen catching fish year-round.

Guaymas was explored by the Spanish as early as 1535, but the area was not settled until the 18th century, when in

1771 fathers Kino and Salvatierra founded the Jesuit mission San José de Guaymas. The port was called San Fernando de Guaymas, so the town had two identities from the beginning. San Fernando de Guaymas was opened as a trading post in 1841, serving as a Mexican-Spanish free port, an outlet for the rich mineral resources of Sonora.

Guaymas has had a busy history. In 1847, during the Mexican-American War, the port was attacked by U.S. naval forces and occupied until 1848. Again, in 1854, the port was attacked, this time by French pirate Count Gaston Raouset de Bourbon, who, with some four hundred buccaneers, tried to seize the city. Bourbon was captured and executed, but the French tried again 11 years later, under Emperor Maximilian, and took the port. During the U.S. Civil War, supplies for troops in Arizona were shipped through Guaymas from San Francisco and transported overland.

The downtown **Plaza de Pescador** has a large bronze sculpture of a fisherman with a giant fish underfoot, tribute to the town's main industry. Nearby is the white-domed 18th-century **Catedral de San Fernando** (calles 24a and 25a); other points of interest are the Moorish bandstand in **San Fernando Plaza;** the **Plaza of the Three Presidents,** honoring the men from Guaymas; the municipal palace and the facade of the municipal jail; and **Sagrado Corazón** (Sacred Heart) Church. Otherwise, there is not much of interest for the traveler in the old part of town.

Guaymas's two bays serve different tourist purposes. **Bacochibampo** is where the boats set out for sport fishing, bringing back marlin, sailfish, red snapper, yellowtail, and sea bass; **San Carlos** has the beautiful beaches that are making Guaymas one of Mexico's prime seaside resorts, rivaling Cancún, Cozumel, Mazatlán, Ixtapa, and Acapulco. Cortés and Miramar beaches have several good dive spots.

Special **sailing** events are scheduled throughout the year, with the Christopher Columbus competition for different classes of boats held the weekend closest to October 12. The **International Sports Fishing Tournament** is held in July, with sailfish, sawfish, swordfish, dorado, grouper, and barracuda the prize catches.

The pre-Lenten **Carnaval** is the principal fiesta. There is ferry service from Guaymas across the Sea of Cortés to Santa Rosalía in Baja California Sur.

🧳 ACCOMMODATIONS

All hotels listed below accept major credit cards unless otherwise noted.

Armida
Carretera Internacional Nte., 85400

Tel. 622-2-30-50
Doubles, $35–$85

With 85 moderately priced units, swimming pool, French restaurant, steakhouse and cafeteria, lobby bar, and video disco, this is a find. Arrangements can be made for water sports such as scuba diving and waterskiing, as well as fishing and tennis.

Club Med Guaymas

Playa de los Algodones, Apdo. Postal 198, 85400
Tel. 622-6-10-66 and 622-6-02-13; in the United States 800-CLUB-MED; in New York State 212-750-1687
Doubles, $90; many packages available

With its reputation as a wonderful all-inclusive resort preceding it, this adobe village offers a complete vacation, with two beaches (one on a lagoon) as well as a swimming pool, three outdoor Jacuzzis, two saunas, a gym, two restaurants, thirty tennis courts (15 lighted), all water sports, deep-sea fishing, rafting down the Yaqui River, and overnight horseback expeditions. Located 17 miles from Guaymas.

Playa de Cortés

Bahía de Bacochibampo, Apdo. Postal 66, 85400
Tel. 622-2-01-21
Doubles, $54

Built by the Southern Pacific Railroad back when it operated the Nogales–Guaymas–México route, this oldie but goodie has 133 guest rooms, swimming pool, restaurant, dancing, two tennis courts, and fishing. A villa-style local institution with extensive gardens, the Playa de Cortés has a lobby filled with interesting antiques. On Bacochibampo Bay 4 miles from town.

☕ RESTAURANTS

Restaurant del Mar

Avenida Serdan 206 and Calle 17
Tel. 2-02-26

Delicious seafood is served in a colonial setting. There is also a cocktail lounge with entertainment, and at this popular spot reservations are in order. The average cost of dinner for two is about $20.

Del Río

Avenida Serdan 417 and Calle 9
Tel. 2-74-00

Specializing in steaks and entertainment, Del Rio offers shows nightly at 9 P.M. The average cost of a dinner for two is about $22.

L'Club

Avenida Serdan and Calle 17
Tel. 6-00-07

True to its name, this restaurant is on the grounds of the Guaymas golf and tennis club. Reservations are recommended. The average cost of a dinner for two is about $20.

Playa de Cortés

Bahía de Bacochibampo
Tel. 2-01-35

The dinner menu changes nightly here; specialties include both traditional Mexican dishes and local seafood. Mariachis add to the charm of this classic restaurant, which has waiters who have served for more than thirty years. The average cost of a dinner for two is about $20.

SHOPPING

Sort of bringing coals to Newcastle is **La Casona** (Calle 24a no. 3), a shell shop with shells from Australia and the Philippines, among others, mingling with the native shells. The **Mercado Central** (Avenida Rodríguez between Calle 19a and Calle de Alemán) has the usual collection of fruit and vegetable stalls in with those selling clothing, sandals, and toys.

9

CENTRAL HIGHLANDS

Mexico's Central Highlands, the soaring peaks and fertile valleys between the western and eastern branches of the Sierra Madre, were the heart of colonial Mexico, and the birthplace of the movement for Mexican independence from Spain. The Central Highlands, comprised of (in alphabetical order) the states of Aguascalientes, Guanajuato, Jalisco, Michoacán, Querétaro, San Luis Potosí, and Zacatecas, have a range of altitude from about five thousand to 8,500 feet. The temperature is mild year-round, but locations at higher altitudes cool off considerably during the night. The countryside is varied and beautiful, with dense forests, lovely rivers and lakes, farmlands, and spectacular mountaintop views.

This is mining country, and it is Mexico's breadbasket. From the mountains, the Spanish extracted the silver, gold, and other precious ores that fed the coffers of the mother country while colonial mine owners became exceedingly rich. The fertile valleys supported large haciendas where colonial farmers and ranchers thrived while supplying local towns and mines, and all Mexico, with the necessary staples of life. Wealthy mine and hacienda owners built beautiful cities— Guanajuato, Morelia, Querétaro, San Miguel de Allende, Guadalajara, and others—with magnificent plazas and monuments, splendid cathedrals, and impressive mansions and palaces. Missions were built where masses of Tarascan, Aztec, Otomi, Huichol, Nahuatl, Chichimec, and other Indians were converted and became part of the faithful flock—and an excellent labor force.

The Mexican struggle for independence from Spain began in this area because the wealthy colonial *criollos* (people born in Mexico of Spanish forebears) were discontent with commercial and administrative restrictions placed on them by the crown. Most authority in local matters was held by *peninsulares* (colonials who had been born in Spain) and most manu-

MEXICO

pages

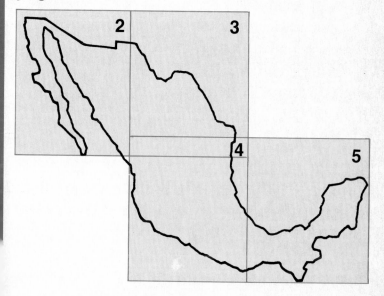

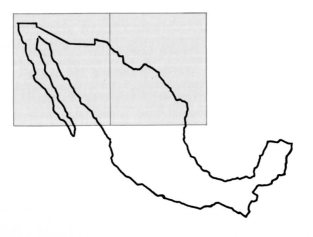

MEXICO

0 — Kilometers — 250

Miles — 200

N

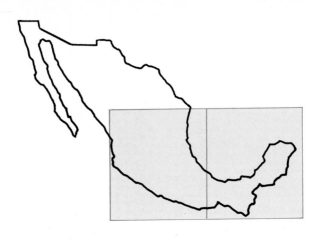

MEXICO

0	Kilometers	250
	Miles	200

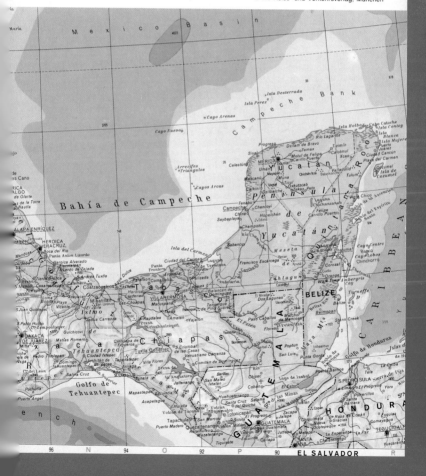

1

2

3

4

5

A

B

C

M. Av

Durango

Tepic

Guanajuato

Calz. de la Providencia

Zafiro

Carrasco

David Gutierrez

Jaime Nuno

I Ramirez

Nicholas Romero

Gregorio Davi

Mungu A

Jua

Boulevard Adolfo Lopez Mateos

Av. de las Americas

Pedro Castro

Reforma

Colina

Veracruz

Zacatecas

Sinaloa

Hidalgo

A Leon

Pedro Moreno

Justo Sierra

Avenida Juarez

Lopez Cotilla

Progresso

Morelos

Vallarta

Tepic

Veracruz

Av. Union

Marsella Sur

Chapultepec

Yucatan

Sonora

Sinaloa

Museum

Mexicalcingo

Vidrio

A

Av.

Circunvalacion

Santa Edu

Av. Ninos Heroe

Luna

Noche

Calz. de la Victoria

Hercules

Sol

Mexico
Morelia

Tepic

Fc. A. Tepic

Cip

Barra de Navidad

I

a
99 20
b

San Mateo Tecoloapan
Barrientos
Pirámide de Santa Cecilia

Atizapán de Zaragoza

99 10

1
Santa Ana Jilotzingo

San A. Atenco

Tlalnepàntla de Comonfort

San Nicolás Viejo

Río Tlalnepantla

Pirámide de Tenayuca

19 30

Vista Bella
Mirador

Ciudad Satelite
Ocipaco

San Juan Toltoltepec

REYNOSA TAMAULIPAS

E s t a d o   d e

Santiago Tepatlaxco

Ciudad de Naucalpan de Juárez

AZCAPOTZALCO
EL RECREO

Presa las Julianas

Santuario de los Remedios
El Molinito

Loma Linda

San Francisco Chimalpa

San Antonio Zomeyucan

Río Hondo

San Rafael

Toreo
Campo Militar

TACUBA

Colegio Militar

CU.

2
Chichicaspa

Hipódromo
Ode las
Americas

MIGUEL HIDALGO
Museo Nacional
de Antropología

Río Hondo

LOMAS CHAPULTEPEC

Jardín Zoológico
Bosque de Chapultepec

P.
Be

O Hipo

El Guarda

Acueducto de Lerma

Presa Los Jazmines

Observatorio

TACUBAYA

F
Na

UNIDAD SANTA FE

University of the Americas

SANTA FE

MIXCOAC

BENIT

Dos Rios

MOLINO D ROSAS

O

Ciudad de los Deportes

Presa de Mixcoac

ALPES

Cruz Manca

Presa Tarango

VILLA OBREGÓN

CHL

Cuajimalpa

Cañada de los Helechos

OLIVAR DE LOS PADRES

Huixquilucan de Degollado

San Mateo Tlaltenango

Universidad Militar Latino Americ.

TIZAPÁN

ROS

19 20

San Lorenzo Acopilco

San Bartolo Ameyalco

SAN JERÓNIMO LIDICE

Estadio Olímpico
Ciudad Universitaria

COY

Las Alicias

Parque

D   i   s   t   r   i   t   o

CIL
JA

La Marquesa

Nacional

3161 Cerro Campamento

La Magdalena Contreras

Pirámide de Cuicuilco

Esta
Azte

Parque Nacional

de los Leones

San Nicolás Totolapan

TLALPAN

Miguel Hidalgo

Cuarto Dinamo

Río de la Magdalena

San Pedro Mártir

San Andrés Totoltepec

MEXICO CITY

0   Kilometers   10

Miles   7.5

N

Cerro 2968
del Picacho

Sierra de
Guadalupe

UAUTEPEC
EL ALTO

JAUTEPEC
MADERO

ICOMÁN

uto
cnico
nal **h**

GUSTAVO
A. MADERO

Ecatepec
de Morelos

Santa Clara
Coatitla

Santa María
Tulpetlac

Planta de
Evaporación

El Caracol

Acuexcomac

El Contador

Río Hondo

San Petro Xalostoc

Canal del Desagüe

Guadalupe del Norte

SAN PETRO
ZACATENCO

JUAN GONZÁLEZ
ROMERO

NUEVA
ATZACOALCO

L a g o

d e   T e x c o c o

19 30

*Basílica de
Guadalupe*

SAN FELIPE
DE JESÚS

SAN JUAN DE ARAGÓN

HÉROES CHAPULTEPEC

Zoológico de
San Juan
de Aragón Bosque San Juan
de Aragón

M é x i c o

MOC MORELOS

*Palacio
Nacional*

CIUDAD DE MÉXICO

VENUSTIANO
CARRANZA

Aeropuerto

Central

JARDIN-
BALBUENA

San Juan
Chimalhuacan

San Pedro

Xochitenco

San Lorenzo

AGRÍCOLA
PANTIT-
LÁN

**CIUDAD
NETZAHUALCOYOTL**

Autódromo

Ciudad
Deportiva

AGRÍCOLA
ORIENTAL

JUAN ESCUTIA

IXTACALCO

TEPALCATES

La Magdalena
Atlipac

SAN ANDRÉS
TETEPILCO

ESCUADRÓN
201

SAN FELIPE
TERREMOTOS

SANTA
MARTHA ACATITLA

Los Reyes

HÉROES
DE CHURUBUSCO

IXTAPALAPA

SANTIAGO
ACAHUALTEPEC

Country
Club

LOS
REYES

LA
CANDELARIA

Cerro de
la Estrella
2460 *Parque Nac.
Cerro de la
Estrella*

SANTA CRUZ
MEYEHUALCO

SAN FRANCISCO
CULHUACÁN

AVANTE

Cerro
Peñon 2750

19 20

Santa Catarina
Yecahuizotl

F e d e r a l

EL
RELOJ

VILLA
COAPA

San Lorenzo
Tezonco

Sierra de Santa Catarina

San Francisco
Tlaltenco

TEPEPAN

L. de
Xochimilco

Jardines
Flotantes

Santiago
Zapotitlán

XOCHIMILCO

Tlahuac

Cerro Xico
2346
Xico Viejo

tiago
alcat-
an

Santa Cruz
Alcapixca

San Gregorio
Atlapulco

Tulyehualco

San Juan
Ixtayopan

Nativitas

© RV Reise - und Verkehrsverlag, Munchen

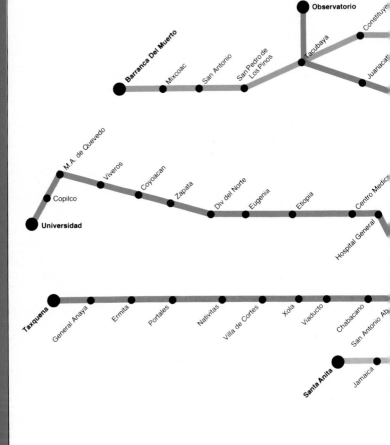

Observatorio

Constituye

Barranca Del Muerto

Mixcoac · San Antonio · San Pedro de Los Pinos · Tacubaya · Juanacath

M.A. de Quevedo

Viveros · Coyoacan · Zapata · Div del Norte · Eugenia · Etiopia · Centro Medic

Copilco

Universidad

Hospital General

Taxquena · General Anaya · Ermita · Portales · Nativitas · Villa de Cortes · Xola · Viaducto · Chabacano · San Antonio Ab

Santa Anita · Jamaica

Pantitlan — Observatorio
Taxquena — Quatro Caminos
Universidad — Indios Verdes
Santa Anita — Martin Carrera
Pantitlan — Politecnico
El Rosario — Martin Carrera
Tabuca — Barranca del Muerto

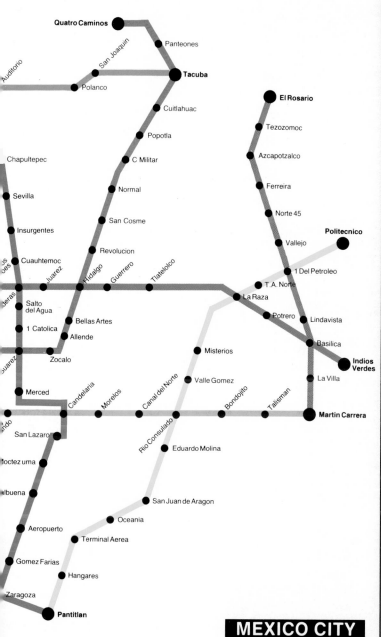

MEXICO CITY Metro

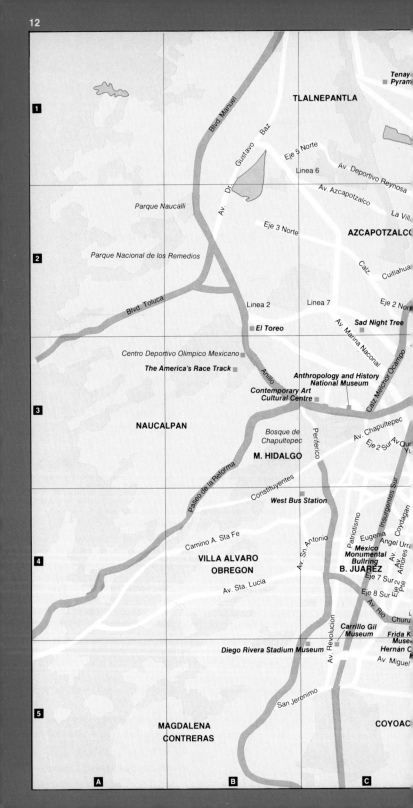

MEXICO CITY METROPOLITAN AREA

0 miles 3
0 kilometers 3

N

Linea 5

Politecnico National

Parque del Tepeyac

Av. Instituto

orth Bus Station

Insurgentes Norte

Our Lady of Guadalupe Basilica

Calz. Eduardo Molina

Av. San Juan de Aragon

Av. Talisman

Eje 4 Norte

nsulado

Tres Culturas Square (Tlatelolco)

nuel Gonzalez

V. CUSTAVO A. MADERO

Canal del Norte

Mosqueta

CUAUHTEMOC

Av. Oceania

East Bus Station

Eje 1 Norte

V. CARRANZA

v. Fray Servand

Banito Juárez International Airport

Via Tapo

Teresa de Nier

Av. Taller

Eje 3 Sur

Av. Rio Churubusco

Sports City Stadium

Hermanos Rodriguez Autodrome

Av. Central

ucto Miguel Aleman

Av. Francisco del Paso Troncoso

Elias Calles Eje 4 Sur

Rio Churubusco

Gomez

Calz. Ignacio Zaragoza

ardo Cardenas

Calz. de Tlalpan

Andres Molina Enriquez

Plutarco

Calz. de la Viga

IZTA CALCO

Rojo

Villa del Mar

Eje 5 Sur

Pie de La Cuesta

Eje 6 Sur

Eje I Ote

Eje 2 Ote

Eje 3 Ote

Av. Javier

icipio Libre

. Zapata

ocatepetl

South Bus Station

do

Av. Taxquena

Parque Cerro de la Estrella

Av. San Lorenzo Tezonco

Ermita

Iztapalapa

IZTAPALAPA

el Norte

Av. Canal de Miramontes

Calz. Tulyehualco

D

E

F

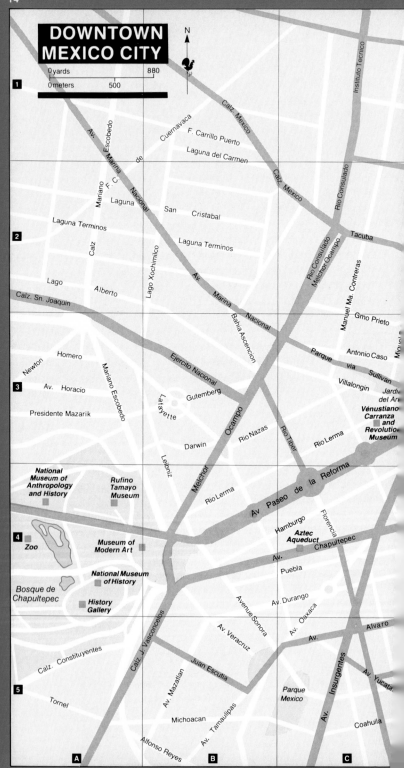

DOWNTOWN MEXICO CITY

0 yards 880
0 meters 500

1

2

3

4

5

N

Calz. Mexico

Av. Marina Escobedo

F. C. Nacional

de

Cuernavaca

F. Carrillo Puerto

Laguna del Carmen

Mariano

Laguna

San

Cristabal

Instituto Tecnico

Rio Consulado

Laguna Terminos

Calz

Laguna Terminos

Tacuba

Lago Xochimilco

Av. Marina Nacional

Rio Consulado

Melchor Ocampo

Manuel Ma. Contreras

Gmo Prieto

Lago

Alberto

Bahia Ascencion

Antonio Caso

Calz. Sn. Joaquin

Parque

via

Sullivan

Homero

Ejercito Nacional

Villalongin

Newton

Mariano Escobedo

Jardin del Ar

Av. Horacio

Gutemberg

Vénustiano Carranza and Revolution Museum

Presidente Mazarik

Lafayette

Darwin

Ocampo

Rio Nazas

Rio Tiber

Rio Lerma

Leibniz

National Museum of Anthropology and History

Melchor

Rio Lerma

Rufino Tamayo Museum

Av. Paseo de la Reforma

Zoo

Museum of Modern Art

Hamburgo

Aztec Aqueduct

Florencia

Chapultepec

Bosque de Chapultepec

National Museum of History

Av.

Puebla

History Gallery

Av. Durango

Calz. J. Vasconcelos

Avenue Sonora

Av. Veracruz

Av. Oaxaca

Av.

Alvaro

Calz. Constituyentes

Juan Escutia

Av. Insurgentes

Av. Yucata

Tornel

Av. Mazatlan

Parque Mexico

Av.

Michoacan

Av. Tamaulipas

Coahuila

Alfonso Reyes

A   **B**   **C**

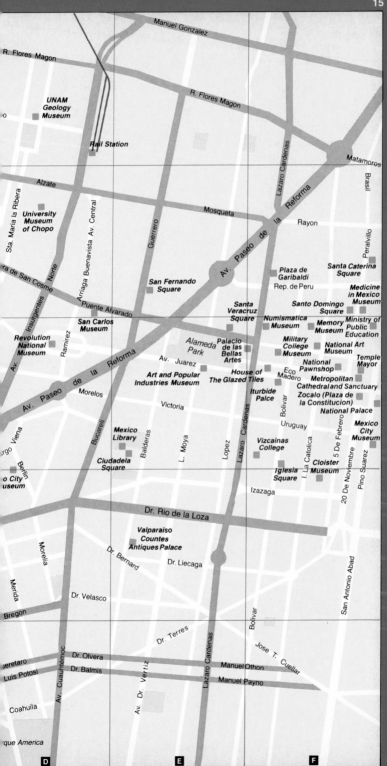

R. Flores Magon

Manuel Gonzalez

R. Flores Magon

UNAM
Geology
Museum

Rail Station

Matamoros

Alzate

Brasil

Lazaro Cardenas

Paseo de la Reforma

Mosqueta

Rayon

University
Museum
of Chopo

Sta. Maria la Ribera

Av. Central

Guerrero

Arriaga Buenavista

Norte

...ra de San Cosme

Puente Alvarado

San Fernando
Square

Av.

Plaza de
Garibaldi

Santa Caterina
Square

Peralvillo

Rep. de Peru

Medicine
in Mexico
Museum

Insurgentes

San Carlos
Museum

Santa
Veracruz
Square

Santo Domingo
Square

Numismatica
Museum

Memory
Museum

Ministry of
Public
Education

Ramirez

Revolution
National
Museum

Reforma

Alameda
Park

Palacio
de las
Bellas
Artes

Military
College
Museum

National Art
Museum

Av.

de la

Av. Juarez

National
Pawnshop

Temple
Mayor

Art and Popular
Industries Museum

House of
The Glazed Tiles

Eco
Madero

Metropolitan
Cathedral and Sanctuary

Av. Paseo

Morelos

Iturbide
Palce

Zocalo (Plaza de
la Constitucion)

Bolivar

National Palace

Victoria

Uruguay

Mexico
City
Museum

...rgo Viena

Bucareli

Mexico
Library

Balderas

L. Moya

Lopez

Lazaro Cardenas

Vizcainas
College

I. La Catolica

5 De Febrero

20 De Noviembre

Pino Suarez

Berlin

Ciudadela
Square

Cloister
Museum

...o City
...useum

Iglesia
Square

Izazaga

Dr. Rio de la Loza

Valparaiso
Countes
Antiques Palace

Morelia

Dr. Bernard

Dr. Liecaga

San Antonio Abad

Merida

Dr. Velasco

Bregon

Bolivar

Dr. Terres

Jose T. Cuellar

...queretaro

Dr. Olvera

Av. Cuauhtemoc

Dr. Balmis

Av. Dr. Vertiz

Lazaro Cardenas

Manuel Othon

Luis Potosi

Manuel Payno

Coahuila

...que America

D

E

F

ACAPULCO

0 miles

0 km

Zihuatanejo

A

Av. Mexico

Av. Ejido

LA FABRICA

Calz.

Pie de la Cuesta

Av. Pote. A. Ruiz Cortines

B. California

HORNOS
INSURGENTES

Av. Constitu Yentes

LA MIRA

Craftmanship Market

see inset

Av. Cuauhtemoc

Costera Miguel Aleman

Amusement Park

Paseo del Farallon

B

The Quebrada

La Quebrada

Playa la Angosta

Sky Diving

Playa Manzanillo

Playa Honda

Playa Marzanillo

Playa Tlacopanocha

Playa Dominguillo

Playa Noa-Noa Papagayo

Playa Hornos

Playa Condesa

Playa La Redonda

Playa Pdte. Kacos

C

Pacific
Ocean

Playas Caleta y Caletilla

Isla y Playa La Roqueta

Bahia de Acapulco

1

2

3

4

5

Inset

Guerrero

City Hall

La Quebrada

Aquiles Serdan

Tourist
Information

Av. Costera Miguel Aleman

Parque del Malecón

'San Diego' Fort

Bahia de Acapulco

LOMAS COSTA AZUL

L. del Mar

Archeological Museum

ICACOS

N

facturing was still, by law, done only in Spain. Independence movement leaders were planning a peaceful secession from Spain when the discovery of their conspiracy led to the outbreak of armed rebellion.

Today the Central Highlands' delightful colonial cities, so rich in architectural beauty and historical and cultural importance, are on what is known to travelers as the Independence Trail. It was in these cities that the heroes of Mexican independence were born, here they rebelled, and here they ultimately triumphed.

Although all the states in the Central Highlands have lovely and interesting sights and captivating scenery, the area is so vast that it is necessary to focus on several key cities and their surrounding regions. For most travelers, the cities of **Guadalajara, Guanajuato, Querétaro, San Miguel de Allende,** and **Morelia,** which may be visited individually or as a full Independence Trail tour, will satisfy either the need for pleasing colonial surroundings or an avid historical curiosity. These cities and the local excursions from them are featured in detail in this chapter.

CONNECTIONS

With the exception of a major international airport at Guadalajara, there are few airports in the colonial cities of the Central Highlands, largely because mountain locations don't permit landing strips or because the government doesn't feel there's enough traffic to warrant regular air service. The best way to get to and around this part of Mexico is by car. Roads are well maintained, although two-lane highways through mountain passes often require patience. Rain and fog make these roads treacherous, and the pervasiveness of trucks makes them slow-going.

Rental cars are readily available in both Mexico City and Guadalajara, the two major gateways to the Central Highlands cities. **National** (tel. 5-762-8250 at Mexico City airport or 36-35-84-05 at Guadalajara airport) and other rental companies have several convenient locations throughout both cities. And most car-rental companies will supply maps upon request.

Ferrocarriles Nacionales de México's Servicio Estrella de Pasajeros offers quite good and surprisingly inexpensive first-class train service between Mexico City and Guadalajara; Guanajuato; Morelia; and San Miguel de Allende via Querétaro. First-class bus service is available from Mexico City and these cities as well. Details are given in city sections below.

Guadalajara

Guadalajara. That musical name is celebrated in song, and it evokes images of colonial mansions, flower-filled gardens, singing mariachis, handsome *charros* (cowboys), lovely señoritas, and the Mexican hat dance. Guadalajara is gracious, genteel, and filled with tradition. People from these parts call themselves Tapatíos. Nobody seems to know the origin of that nickname, but it has come to signify the people of Guadalajara's pride in their heritage and their friendliness toward foreigners. Guadalajara, Mexico's second-largest city, is the culturally sophisticated capital of Jalisco, one of Mexico's largest and richest states.

The state of Jalisco has no major archaeological ruins, but this area was occupied from 250 B.C. to A.D. 600 by tribes that built deep shaft tombs for multiple burials, perhaps for several generations of one family. This type of tomb is not found elsewhere in Mexico but is quite common in the area between Panama and Peru. Archaeologists therefore believe that tribes who occupied the Central Highlands had extensive contact with civilizations to the south.

National Geographic magazine has reported that Guadalajara has the second-best climate in all the world; with approximately the same altitude as Denver, Guadalajara offers mild year-round temperatures. The city is a magnet for people who are tired of cold and snow. At present, there are thirty-five thousand Americans and five thousand Canadians living in and around Guadalajara, and the city is considered an excellent community in which to retire—or at least, spend the winter months. Nevertheless, the rapidly growing population does present this Eden with increasing problems of pollution, traffic jams, and property crimes. It isn't a good idea to walk around Guadalajara by yourself after 9 or 10 P.M., even in well-lighted downtown areas, and be sure to watch your wallet or handbag when you're in a crowd.

Guadalajara has some lovely colonial buildings and historical monuments, mostly concentrated in the downtown area, around the *zócalo,* and a series of pedestrian-only plazas that are very pleasant for strolling. Hotels are located both downtown and in the city's southwestern residential Zapopan district, where you'll also find some terrific restaurants. Suburban Tlaquepaque is terrific for shopping. Getting from area to area by public bus or taxi is easy, but you'll still want to wear comfortable shoes for walking from sight to sight. There's so much to see and do that you can easily be on the go all day.

CONNECTIONS

Both international and national flights connect at Guadalajara's busy airport. Continental Airlines flies nonstop to Guadalajara from Houston, with connecting flights from many other U.S. cities. American Airlines flies to Guadalajara from Dallas/Fort

Worth nonstop on Tues. and Thurs., and with a stop in Puerto Vallarta on Mon., Wed., and Fri. Mexicana offers direct flights to Guadalajara from Chicago, Dallas/Fort Worth, Los Angeles, and San Francisco, with connecting flights from many U.S. cities. In addition, Mexicana has at least nine nonstop flights to Guadalajara from Mexico City with international connections from other airlines, as well as direct flights from other Mexican cities. Aeromexico flies nonstop to Guadalajara from Los Angeles, direct from Tucson, and nonstop or direct from several Mexican cities.

The **airport** is about 10 miles from Guadalajara, along the highway to Lake Chapala. Transportación Terrestre operates flat-fee taxi and combi service to downtown hotels. The combi ride costs about $10; the taxi rate is slightly higher. Getting back to the airport from your hotel is a bit tricky, however. Because of an agreement between Transportación Terrestre and the taxi drivers stationed outside the hotels, airport combis cannot pick up passengers at hotels, nor can the hotel taxis pick up passengers at the airport. Yet the hotel taxis charge more for the same ride. The difference in rates is only about $5, but it is annoying nonetheless. Most people simply capitulate and pay. But if you haven't got a lot of luggage and you're not anxious about being late, simply walk into the street and hail a cruising cab. The price will be half the hotel taxi rate.

You can rent a car at the airport. However, rental rates in this part of Mexico are particularly high, and you really don't need a car in Guadalajara unless you're planning to take several day trips and perhaps visit other cities of the Central Highlands on the Independence Route.

Guadalajara has excellent first-class bus connections with the rest of Mexico, including Mexico City (about ten hours away), as well as nearby Guanajuato, Querétaro, San Miguel de Allende, and Morelia. The biggest operators are Tres Estrellas de Oro and Omnibus de México. The latter has connections to U.S. bus companies at the border. To ensure your place on the bus you want to take, make reservations and buy your ticket at least a day in advance. Guadalajara's **Central Camionera** (Bus Terminal) is located downtown at the end of Avenida de los Angeles, off Calzada Independencia Sur. You can get to your hotel by taxi or public bus.

The Ferrocarriles Nacionales de México's Servicio Estrella de Pasajeros first-class overnight train service from Mexico City to Guadalajara is superb. **El Tapatío,** as the train is known, leaves Mexico City at 8:40 P.M. and arrives in Guadalajara at 8:10 A.M. the next morning. The return train leaves Guadalajara at 8:55 P.M. and arrives in Mexico City at 8:08 A.M. the next morning. Single and double sleeperettes are available for about $30 and $60, respectively. And that price includes dinner and breakfast elegantly served in the train's dining car. Reservations are required. Telephone 36-12-51-86 in Guadalajara or 5-547-5819 in Mexico City for information and reservations. The Guadalajara train station is downtown at the end of Calzada Independencia Sur. You can get to your hotel by taxi or by public bus.

TOURING

Getting around Guadalajara is quite easy. Taxis are plentiful, and the public bus system is quite convenient. You'll probably find that two or three bus routes satisfy your needs. There are a number of buses, including the **Estación–San Juan de Dios** buses, that travel north and south along Calzada Independencia. These connect with **Par Vial** buses that run in a circular route: east along Avenida Hidalgo to Mercado Libertad and west along Avenida Juárez toward the Minerva Circle. At Minerva Circle, there are buses that run north and south along Avenida López Mateos. These three routes will get you between the high-rise hotels along Avenida López Mateos and downtown. Buses cost about $.30 per ride, and no transfers are available. Riding the buses is fun: The drivers and fellow passengers are usually friendly and polite, and they'll help by telling you when you've reached your stop. But if buses seem like too much of a hassle, you can take a taxi. As was mentioned previously, hotel taxis are fairly expensive, and you will therefore get a much less expensive ride if you walk out into the street and hail a cruising cab. Even so, negotiate the fare before you get into the taxi. To economize on time and pesos, try to plan your sightseeing so that you can sweep through an area. For example, take a day or two to visit places of interest near the *zócalo* before heading for Parque Azul or Tlaquepaque.

Guided tours will also help you to use your time efficiently. City tours cover the downtown area, with stops at the **cathedral, Teatro Degollado, Tapatía Plaza, Hospicio Cabañas,** and other major points of interest. There are also guided day tours to **Tlaquepaque, Lake Chapala, Tequila,** and other nearby destinations. Panoramex (tel. 36-10-50-05) is one of the largest group-tour operators in Guadalajara. Excellent individualized and group tours can also be arranged through Mexico Travel Advisers, tel. 36-14-72-72, ext. 138.

🛏 HOTELS

Guadalajara's excellent selection of hotels ranges from modern and efficient high-rises to quaint colonial mansions converted into intimate inns. Some hotels are located downtown near the *zócalo,* while others are in almost suburban residential areas— near Minerva Circle, for example. Public transportation in Guadalajara is quite good, so you needn't insist on a room in the thick of things. Base your choice on preferred ambience, rather than on location.

Hotel Aranzazu
Avenida Revolución 110, 44100
Tel. 36-13-32-32
Doubles, from $60
This modern, moderately priced hotel has two sections, across the street from each other, with a total of five hundred rooms. These are comfortably furnished and have cable TV; some have nice views of the city. The best thing about the Aran-

zazu aside from the price, is the location—just a short walk from the *zócalo* and all the downtown sights and shopping. You'll also find a decent restaurant, and a nightclub with entertainment. Credit cards: AE, MC, V.

Camino Real
Avenida Vallarta 5005, 45040
Tel 36-47-80-00 or 800-228-3000
Doubles, from $120
   This charming and quiet villa-like hotel offers 220 recently redecorated colonial-style rooms in motel-like units around small patios and gardens. The rooms are carpeted and have small balconies with views of gardens, patios, and pools. There are four swimming pools, lighted tennis courts, and a putting green. The restaurants are excellent, and the bar has evening entertainment. The Camino Real is located past the Minerva Circle in a quiet residential area. This is a good retreat from downtown bustle, but requires taxi or bus rides to get around. Credit cards: AE, MC, V.

Carlton Hotel
Niños Héroes 125 and Avenida 16 de Septiembre, 44100
Tel. 36-14-72-72
Doubles, from $90
   You can't beat the location of this hotel, about five minutes by taxi from Guadalajara's central downtown-plaza district and the lovely Parque Azul. The hotel is a twenty-story tower with 220 rooms, all with small balconies, views of downtown, servibars, and charming folk art murals. Good restaurants, nightclub, and disco. Credit cards: AE, MC, V.

Exelaris Hyatt Regency
Moctezuma 3515 and Avenida López Mateos Sur, 45050
Tel. 36-22-77-78 or 800-228-9000
Doubles, from $125
   This spectacular and sophisticated high-rise Hyatt hotel has 350 large modern, pastel-colored rooms with great views of the city, servibars, and other amenities. Two floors are given over to Regency Club service, with Continental breakfasts and daylong cocktails served in a private lounge. The lobby is a 14-story atrium with glass-enclosed elevators and manmade waterfall. The **Hacienda la Morena Restaurant** is one of the best eateries in Guadalajara, with a terrific Mexican buffet breakfast and wonderful à la carte lunch and dinner menus. The two-story shopping arcade, with superb designer shops, is built around an ice-skating rink—the only one in Mexico! Credit cards: AE, DC, MC, V.

Fiesta Americana
Aurelio Aceves 225 (Minerva Circle at avenidas Vallarta and López Mateos), 44100
Tel. 36-25-34-34 or 800-223-2332
Doubles, from $110
   This modern high-rise hotel offers 25 stories, atrium lobby, glass-enclosed elevators, and colorful Mexican-style decor in four hundred rooms that have views of the city. There's a de-

lightful supper club with a huge panoramic window covered by a curtain of lights, as well as a jazz club, shopping arcade, art gallery, rooftop tennis courts, and swimming pool—all of which make this a fine self-contained resort within the city proper, at the convenient crossroads of the Minerva Circle. Credit cards: AE, DC, MC, V.

Hotel Francés
Avenida Maestranza 35, 44100
Tel. 36-13-62-93
Doubles, from $45

This small hotel is very attractive and has a great location on a quiet street that's closed to traffic. There's a colonial-style lobby with a fountain, chandelier, and colonnades. The forty rooms are pleasantly decorated; some have small balconies. There is no air-conditioning, but Guadalajara's persistently pleasant weather allows you to do very nicely without it. Just off the *zócalo,* the Hotel Francés offers a lobby restaurant and bar, friendly service, and an unbeatable price. Credit cards: AE, MC, V.

Holiday Inn
Avenida López Mateos 2500, 45050
Tel. 36-31-55-66 or 800-465-4329
Doubles, from $110

The hotel takes up an entire city block and has both a tower and a garden section. There are 220 pleasantly furnished rooms offering, among other amenities, servibars and either terrific views of the city or small balconies and easy access to the hotel's pretty interior garden with swimming pool and putting green. On the top floor of the tower, there's a gourmet restaurant with an excellent view along with expensive and well-prepared French food. The lobby bar has nightly entertainment, and there's a Mexican-style coffee shop with 24-hour service. Credit cards: AE, DC, MC, V.

Plaza del Sol
Avenidas López Mateos Sur 2375, 45050
Tel. 36-21-05-15 or 800-421-0000
Doubles, from $60

This modern circular-shaped high-rise hotel is right next to Guadalajara's expansive Plaza del Sol Shopping Center. The hotel has 335 rooms in two towers. Rooms in the 12-story circular tower have excellent views, servibars, and cable TV—but private shower only. On executive-club floors, guests are served Continental breakfast and cocktails. The Plaza del Sol offers a large circular swimming pool and Jacuzzi, plus a restaurant and bar. Popular with shoppers for obvious reasons. Credit cards: AE, DC, MC, V.

Quinta Real
Avenida México 2727, 44680
Tel. 36-52-00-00
Doubles, from $160

A small and fabulously intimate hotel, Quinta Real features 45 luxuriously appointed suites and eight elegant standard rooms. Five of the suites have Jacuzzis, some are duplexes, and all have high beamed ceilings and antique furnishings, plus other amenities, including hair dryer and terry robe. The rooms, public areas, and lobby all look like illustrations from *Architectural Digest,* and original art and fresh flowers are everywhere. Rooms and suites are situated around an interior courtyard and garden with a small aqueduct, fountain, heated pool, and patio restaurant/bar. The gourmet restaurant serves exquisite international and Mexican dishes: luxury all the way! Credit cards: AE, DC, MC, V.

Hotel El Tapatío
Bulevar Aeropuetro 4275, 44100
Tel. 36-35-60-50 or 800-424-2440
Doubles, from $120

Located on a hilltop on the outskirts of town, on the road to the airport, El Tapatío is a luxurious self-contained resort with 120 charming and newly redecorated villa-like rooms and suites arranged around flower-filled patios and gardens. The hotel runs shuttle service between the rooms and the lobby area. El Tapatío offers the fabulous **Mesón del Chef** restaurant and a bar with a view overlooking all of Guadalajara, plus golf, ten tennis courts, stables and horseback riding, and a swimming pool. Colorful and entertaining Mexican fiestas are presented on Fri. nights, 7–10 P.M. El Tapatío is in the process of building a state-of-the-art spa and is planning to run a full spa program within the near future. The hotel is quite far from the center of town, so you'll wind up taking taxis at about $12 per ride. Credit cards: AE, MC, V.

Begin your tour at the Metropolitan Plaza area, a series of five pretty pedestrian-only plazas that stretch for several blocks. Four of these plazas form a cross with Guadalajara's **cathedral** (at Hidalgo and Alcalde) as the centerpiece. The cathedral was built between 1558 and 1616 and is eclectic in architectural style. Most interesting are the paintings showcased in the white-and-gold interior, especially Murillo's *Assumption of the Virgin,* as well as works by Cristobal de Villalpando and Miguel Cabrera. The wooden inlaid floor is particularly beautiful.

Directly in front of the cathedral, toward the west, is **Plaza de los Laureles,** with a large fountain and surrounded by attractive shops in shady arcades.

The south side of the cathedral is on the **zócalo,** or Plaza de Armas, with its wonderful turn-of-the-century **kiosk.** A present from France in 1907, the kiosk caused a scandal in Mexico because its columns are sculptures of women with bared breasts. On Sundays at 6 P.M., the kiosk offers a free band concert.

The **Palacio de Gobierno,** built in 1643, is on the east side of the *zócalo.* In 1810, Father Hidalgo proclaimed the end of slavery in Mexico from this building. Beginning in 1937, the great painter José Clemente Orozco, a native of Jalisco, decorated the interior of the palace with dramatic murals about the Mexican struggle for independence. The overwhelmingly large portrait of a stern and scolding Hidalgo greets you as you walk up the stairs. It is a powerful image and might actually be frightening for young children. The palace is open daily from 8 A.M. to 8 P.M. Notice that the clock on the outside of the building has a hole in it, from a bullet shot in 1915 by Jesus Medina, one of Pancho Villa's band.

To the north of the cathedral is the tree-lined **Park of the Illustrious Men,** also called the **Rotunda Plaza,** where a rotunda of Greek-style columns commemorates regional heroes, including the leaders of the independence movement, as well as painters, poets, and politicians.

Across the street to the east, on the corner of Hidalgo and Corona, is the **Museo Regional de Guadalajara.** Located in a former colonial seminary, the museum has a wide variety of exhibitions of local archaeology, ethnography, colonial portraits, religious art, old photographs and documents, and contemporary Mexican art and handicrafts. Open Tuesday through Sunday from 9 A.M. to 3:45 P.M. Admission is charged.

The **Plaza de la Liberación** is the fourth plaza, behind the cathedral to the east. This long open plaza offers a few trees and rose bushes, and two cooling fountains. At the end of it is **Teatro Degollado,** a neoclassical opera house built in 1866. The theater has an ornate lobby with beautiful crystal chandeliers and a vaulted ceiling decorated with a painting inspired by Canto 4 of Dante's *Divine Comedy.* This magnificent theater is still in use. Consult local newspapers or your hotel concierge for current performance schedules.

Behind the Teatro Degollado is **Founders' Square,** with a commemorative fountain titled *River Among the Rocks,* which depicts the original settlers, including Beatriz Hernandez. From Founders' Square there is a traffic-free promenade leading east to **Plaza Tapatía,** the fifth plaza, dominated by the **Fortune Sculpture** and **Quetzalcoatl Fountain.** Completed in 1982, the plaza is built over Calzada Independencia and a huge underground parking lot. Another traffic-free promenade leads to the **Hospicio Cabañas,** founded in 1801 as an orphanage and now home of the **Instituto Cultural Cabañas,** a superb arts center and academy. The institute has an excellent program of courses in fine and applied arts, dance, theater, and music taught on delightful patios and in history-filled rooms. But even if you don't intend to enroll, treat yourself to a thrilling view of the magnificent **Orozco Murals,** painted on the vaulted ceiling and dome of a large chapel. Benches are provided for viewers to lie down while they study the awe-inspiring paintings. Best of all is *Man of Fire,* a remarkable study in perspective that leaves viewers wondering whether the man on fire is falling into hell

or rising to heaven. Open Monday through Saturday from 10 A.M. to 6 P.M., Sunday from 10 A.M. to 3 P.M.

Near the Hospicio Cabañas, to the south, just off Calzada Independencia, is **Mercado Libertad,** reputedly the largest market in Mexico, with hundreds of stalls selling everything from shoes to toothpaste. (For more details, see **Shopping,** below.)

From Mercado Libertad you cross an overpass over Javier Mina to get to **Plaza de los Mariachis.** This small square, lined with the colorful umbrellas of sidewalk cafés, is the headquarters for Guadalajara's famous mariachis. These black-and-silver-clad musicians are the genuine article: Mariachi music originated in Guadalajara. The plaza closes down at about 11:30 P.M.

Further south along Calzada Independencia, near the bus terminal, is **Parque Azul,** a delightful recreation area with a lot of greenery and flower gardens, a zoo, a minitrain for kids, a house of mirrors, and other similar diversions. There is also the **Museo Arqueología de Occidente,** with pre-Hispanic ceramics from Jalisco, Colima, and Nayarit. Open Monday through Friday from 10 A.M. to 7 P.M.

At the entrance to the park is Guadalajara's **Flower Market,** a real delight for the senses. And nearby is the **Instituto de las Artesanias de Jalisco,** the government-run crafts shop with an exceptionally fine selection of handicrafts made in the state of Jalisco (see **Shopping,** below, for more details). Open Monday through Friday from 10 A.M. to 7 P.M., Saturday and Sunday from 10 A.M. to 2 P.M. Also near the park is the **Casa de la Cultura,** a museum of contemporary Mexican art, and the **Teatro Experimental de Jalisco,** with interesting avant-garde presentations in Spanish. Consult the daily newspaper or ask your concierge about current exhibitions and performances.

Guadalajara was the home of muralist José Clemente Orozco, whose work is represented in both the Palacio de Gobierno and Hospicio Cabañas. More murals are at the **University of Guadalajara**'s auditorium, at Vallarta 975. The paintings are eloquent reminders of the horrors of war. Accessible Monday through Friday, mornings and afternoons. Orozco's home and studio at Aurelio Aceves 27, near the Minerva Circle and Los Arcos, now house the **José Clemente Orozco Museum,** with about one hundred of his smaller works. Open Tuesday through Saturday from 10 A.M. to 2 P.M. and 3:30 to 6 P.M., Sunday from 10 A.M. to 2 P.M.

South of the Minerva Circle, along Avenida López Mateos, is the **Plaza del Sol Shopping Center,** a modern mall with dozens of shops selling everything from chic contemporary clothing to antique furniture. (See **Shopping,** below, for more details.)

But Guadalajara's best shopping is in **Tlaquepaque.** Although this charming artsy suburb is now well within city limits, you'll probably want to think of your visit to it as an excursion. You'll need a full day for wandering around this enclave of colonial buildings and for buying terrific clothes and handicrafts. (See **Excursions,** below, for more details.)

🍵 RESTAURANTS

Guadalajara has dozens of restaurants to suit every palate and every pocketbook. Local specialties feature grilled meats, including dishes made from innards, and *pozole,* a typical soup made from hominy and pork and garnished with onions, radishes, and cilantro. Hotel dining is popular in this city, and many of Guadalajara's finest restaurants are in the city's best hotels. Other popular dining spots reflect Guadalajara's international outlook by offering fine Mexican, French, Chinese, and even Japanese cuisine.

Baccarat
Avenida López Mateos Sur 2380
Tel. 36-21-72-76
Located near the high-rise hotels on Avenida López Mateos, Baccarat features high-tech decor, with lots of gray and pink accents, and nouvelle cuisine. The menu offers steaks and seafood, all with light and flavorful sauces, prettily presented. Dim lighting, jazz music 9 P.M.–midnight, and a well-dressed clientele complete the picture. Good wine list, with high-priced imports. Open daily, 1–4:30 P.M. and 6 P.M. to 1 A.M. The average price for a dinner for two, with domestic wine, is about $50. Reservations suggested. Credit cards: AE, MC, V.

La Copa de Leche
Avenida Juárez 414
Tel. 36-14-84-15
This restaurant in three sections is an all-in-one dining treasure. There's an upstairs dining room, **El Balcón,** with Mexican specialties and quiet music. On the ground floor is a pleasant outdoor café and bar with tasty light snacks, and an elegant dining room with fine steaks and seafood, grilled and sauced to perfection. Take your pick of tastes and ambience. Nice wine list. Open daily, 11 A.M.–midnight. The average price of dinner for two, with wine, is about $30. Reservations suggested. Credit cards: AE, MC, V.

Hacienda la Morena
Exelaris Hyatt Regency Hotel, Avenida López Mateos
Tel. 36-22-77-78
One of the best restaurants in Guadalajara, la Morena is housed in a reconstruction of an old hacienda's interior. A small central courtyard, complete with fountain, is used to set up the splendid breakfast buffet. Choose from freshly prepared custom-made omelets; bacon, ham, and sausage; scrambled eggs; all sorts of dry and hot cereals; rolls and breads, tortillas, refried beans, chilaquiles (made with broken tortilla chips, eggs, chiles,

cheese, and salsa, served with bits of chicken); sopa de menuda (tripe soup); fresh juices and fruit; and best of all, freshly prepared individual miniature open tacos, prepared on tortillas with any or all of the following: chicken, sausage, meat, chiles, pumpkin greens, onions, guacamole, refried beans, mushrooms, sour cream, grated cheese, and salsa. Lunch and dinner are à la carte, and the menu offers a rich variety of meat, chicken, and fish dishes, salads, soups, and pastas. Specialties include shrimp-filled tacos, oysters Rockefeller, giant shrimp in an avocado boat, fettuccine Alfredo, and fillet of sole with baby shrimps and mushroom sauce. Enjoy strong Mexican coffee prepared with orange and clove, and wonderful desserts, including almond pie and beautiful French pastries. The dining area is around the courtyard, on a small balcony and in several small dining rooms ideal for intimate or power lunches or dinners. You'll find gleaming table settings, candlelight, unimpeachable service, abundant floral bouquets, colonial art, and Mexican popular romantic music. Excellent wine list. Open daily, 8–10 A.M., noon–4:30 P.M., and 7–11 P.M. The average price of dinner for two, with wine, is about $70. Reservations suggested. Credit cards: AE, DC, MC, V.

Mesón del Chef

Hotel El Tapatío, Bulevar Aeropuerto 4275
Tel. 36-35-60-50

Be sure to get a window seat at El Tapatío's lovely gourmet restaurant: The view overlooking all of Guadalajara is spectacular. The decor is colonial with beamed ceilings, colonial art, and elegant silver and blue table service. A pianist entertains with show tunes. As El Tapatío inaugurates its new spa program, the current menu, offering steaks, seafood, fresh salads, and rich desserts, will be maintained, with the addition of a new spa menu offering light, low-calorie gourmet meals. Nonguests will still be welcome to dine and enjoy the view. Good wine list. Open Tues.–Sun., 8 P.M.–midnight. The average price of dinner for two, with wine, is about $60. Reservations suggested. Credit cards: AE, MC, V.

Palacio China

Corona 145
No telephone

Surprise! Delicious and quite authentic Cantonese food served by Mexicans! Go for one of the fixed-price meals that provides a sampling of several savory dishes, including wonton soup, pork fried rice, spare ribs, fried shrimp, chicken chop suey, dessert, and tea. The decor is plastic modern, with Chinese lanterns. Open noon–10 P.M. The average price of dinner for two is about $18. No credit cards.

Place de la Concorde

Fiesta Americana Hotel, Aurelio Aceves 225, at Minerva Circle
Tel. 36-25-34-34

The specialties of the house are escargots, onion soup, beef medallions with grapes, and lobster thermidor. The decor features multilevel seating for maximum privacy, and a lovely lounge area with comfortable overstuffed armchairs and banquettes. Enjoy a great view of the city from a panoramic window covered with sparkling lights. Excellent—and expensive—wine list. Open 1–5 P.M. and 7 P.M.–midnight. The average price of dinner for two, with wine, is about $70. Reservations suggested. Credit cards: AE, MC, V.

Recco
Avenida Libertad 1973
Tel. 36-25-07-34

A nice little touch of Italy in the heart of Guadalajara. Best known for its cannelloni, shrimp Casamona (made with garlic and oil), lasagna, and pepper steak, this versatile Italian restaurant also serves excellent seafood and a wide range of pastas. Good wine list. Open 1:30 P.M.–midnight. The average price of dinner for two, with wine, is about $48. Reservations suggested. Credit cards: AE, MC, V.

Restaurant los Cazadores
Golfo de México 606
Tel. 36-35-19-83
(another location at Avenida Union 405, tel. 36-15-97-10; also at Tlaquepaque, tel. 36-41-41-97)

Popular with large groups of people in a festive mood, los Cazadores offers a Mexican fiesta ambience. Outdoor garden dining is most popular, but there are colonial-style rooms in case you prefer them. The specialties are grilled meats and chicken served with Mexican-style garnishes. You can also order the standard enchiladas and tacos and a terrific *queso fundido* (cooked cheese). Cocktails are *very* expensive—ask for prices before you order, and specify that you want national brands. Open daily, 1–10 P.M. The average price of dinner for two is about $50. Reservations suggested. Credit cards: AE, MC, V.

La Rinconada
Plaza Tapatío
No telephone

This is a delightful and very popular downtown restaurant with an unpretentious and moderately priced menu and a pretty atmosphere. The setting is a colonial mansion, with high ceilings and dark woodwork framing cream-colored walls, overhead fans, lots of plants, etched-glass windows, and mariachis who sing while you dine on terrific salads, soups, and entrées of fish, chicken, or beef—all freshly grilled and garnished with excellent Mexican sauces and seasonings. Nice wine list. Open daily, 11 A.M.–9 P.M. There's a long wait for a table at lunch hour, so go very early or a little bit late. The average price for a dinner for two, with wine, is about $28. No reservations. Credit cards: AE, MC, V.

Suehiro
Avenida de La Paz 1701
Tel. 36-25-18-80

Featuring kimono-clad waitresses and full of show, Suehiro offers tempura, teriyaki, *teppanyaki* and other Japanese favorites. The food is surprisingly authentic, and the place is a fun change of pace. Saki, as well as Japanese beers, is served.

Open 1–11 P.M. The average price of dinner for two, with saki, is about $50. Reservations required. Credit cards: AE, MC, V.

La Vianda
Chapalita 120
Tel. 36-22-59-26

This is French cuisine with a creole accent—rich and savory. The menu includes meat, fish, chicken, and excellent salads. The decor features soft pastel colors and a lovely garden. Nice wine list. Open Mon.–Sat. 1–5 P.M. and 7 P.M.–midnight, and Sun. for lunch only. The average price of dinner for two, with wine, is about $60. Reservations suggested. Credit cards: AE, MC, V.

SHOPPING

Guadalajara is most definitely a shopper's town. There are terrific modern malls and arcades, and quaint villages filled with scores of superb boutiques and handicraft shops. Merchandise-wise, Jalisco is famous for ceramics. Especially lovely are blue-gray tableware, ranging from plates to pitchers, and decorative animals painted with pretty bird and flower motifs. The best of these are made by celebrated ceramicist **Jorge Wilmot,** whose studio is in Tonalá. Beautiful deep-red hand-blown glass tumblers, goblets, pitchers, and other objects are made in **Tlaquepaque.** Guadalajara also has an astonishing array of *huaraches,* the typical braided leather sandals made in a variety of styles and dyed or painted just about any color you could imagine, and very reasonably priced work boots. Leather clothing and accessories are also abundant and reasonably priced. Traditional Huichol Indian embroidered clothing and religious art, including beautifully beaded bowls and bags, yarn paintings, and the well-known Eye of God yarn decorations are also widely available. Local designer-clothing labels belong to **Irene Pulos** and **Josefa,** both of whom create beautiful modern adaptations, richly appliquéd and embroidered, of traditional Indian costumes.

In the downtown plaza area, dozens of attractive boutiques and several excellent department stores line pedestrian-only promenades, but your most colorful and affordable shopping experience will be at **Mercado Libertad,** reputedly the largest market in Mexico, with hundreds of stalls selling all sorts of typical handicrafts, plus clothing, shoes, and personal and home accessories. One of the market's largest sections is devoted to *huaraches* and boots: Thousands of pairs are displayed on open racks. They come in tiny sizes for tots and as boats big enough for giants, in a variety of styles with closed or open toes or backs, and in dozens of colors ranging from traditional brown to trendy aqua, pink, and green, and combos or plaids. And—they're dirt cheap.

Other stalls sell *charro* (cowboy) and pseudo-*charro* supplies, including iron or silver spurs, silver earrings shaped like spurs, leather crops, knife holders, all sorts of belts, hats, and horse belts intended to secure saddles but so colorful and decorative that a dozen other uses could be invented for them. You'll find lots of leather luggage, handbags, and briefcases, plus armadillo handbags and deerskin pouches, leather car seats, straw baskets, hand-woven blankets and serapes, *rebozos,* embroidered clothing, silver jewelry, and more. Prices are set by negotiation. If you're a good bargainer, you get a good deal. Otherwise, you'll probably pay much more than whatever you're buying is worth.

The second floor of the market has food stalls with tasty local specialties, such as *carnitas* and *pozole.* You get a hefty portion of fresh food for very little money. The stalls are clean, but if you've got a sensitive digestive system or are nervous about getting sick, stick to the regular restaurants.

Typical Jalisco handicrafts are also sold at **Casa de las Artesanias de Jalisco** (at the entrance to Parque Azul; open Monday through Friday from 10 A.M. to 7 P.M., Saturday and Sunday from 10 A.M. to 2 P.M.) and **El Instituto de las Artesanias Jaliscience** (Avenida Alcalde 1221; open Monday through Saturday from 10 A.M. to 7 P.M.). Both of these government-sponsored galleries and shops sell a good variety of unusually high-quality crafts, including ceramics, hand-blown glass, textiles and clothing, leather goods, and Huichol art, all from the state of Jalisco. The best selection of Huichol arts is found at **Artesania Huichol** (near the Basilica Zapopan, on Calzada Avila Camacho, about five miles from downtown). The shop is open daily from 9 A.M. to 1 P.M. and 4 to 7 P.M.

Also in the Zapopan area, along Avenida López Mateos, is **Plaza del Sol Shopping Center,** Guadalajara's modern shopping mall. It's enormous—one of the largest shopping complexes in Mexico. There are hundreds of contemporary clothing and personal-accessories boutiques, shops for gadgets and home accessories, book and record shops, and many food shops with Mexican food, gourmet cookies, and other quick eats. Plaza del Sol has dozens of shoe stores, and prices are low.

Some of Guadalajara's best shopping, however, is in **Tlaquepaque,** a charming self-contained village within city boundaries. You'll want to take a full day for wandering around the delightful cobblestone streets, ambling into colonial buildings that now house boutiques and ateliers offering terrific clothes and handicrafts. (See **Excursions,** below, for more details.)

ENTERTAINMENT

Guadalajara is a cultural capital. The town has two symphony orchestras and several chamber ensembles. There is constant activity at **Teatro Degollado,** where music, theater, and dance performances, including touring international stars, are presented. Shows are usually at 6 and 9 P.M. The **Teatro Experimental de Jalisco,** with interesting avant-garde presentations, usually in Spanish, is located near the entrance to Parque Azul. Consult the daily newspaper or ask your concierge about current schedules at both.

The **Instituto Cultural Cabañas** (Calle de Cabañas 8, Plaza Tapatía), the former orphanage where you'll find the magnificent Orozco murals, presents evening programs of foreign films and national Ballet Folklórico, as well as entertaining and educational classes and workshops in theater, dance, music, construction of musical instruments, sculpture, ceramics, and painting. All classes are quite reasonably priced and may be joined short-term. Special two-month study programs are scheduled for foreign students in July and August. The fee for these courses is less than $50. Enrollment is limited. The institute makes no provision for housing arrangements but sometimes has lists of local families with rooms to rent. For information on classes, contact the Department Escolar, Monday through Friday from 9 A.M. to 8 P.M., Saturdays from 9 A.M. to noon, by calling 36-18-60-03, ext. 22, 24, or 42.

Similarly, **Instituto Mexicano de Cultura Internacional** (Guadalajara Center, Chapultepec Sur 444) offers intensive small-group Spanish-study courses using texts, tapes, and constant conversation. Group classes begin on the first and 16th of each month; private classes can begin at any time. Fees depend upon the number of students in the group (the range is two to four per group) and the number of class hours per day (ranging from three to eight hours daily), with the highest fee less than $800 per month. Classes are held Monday through Friday, and the minimum course of study requires eighty hours. The institute has no housing facilities but will help students to find room and board with Mexican families for less than $400 per month per person in a double room. For more information, call 36-16-66-60.

Guadalajara's festive spirit clearly expresses itself at the popular **Plaza de los Mariachis,** at Calzada Independencia and Avenida Javier Mina. People celebrating anything from a birthday to a sales quota or a simple stroll at sunset gather here to sit at a sidewalk café and hire the famous mariachis to serenade them. The action usually begins at around 9 P.M. and ends at around 11:30 P.M.

Entertaining Mexican Fiestas, with Ballet Folklórico and other performers and sumptuous Mexican buffet dinners, are presented by various hotels and restaurants throughout Guadalajara on alternating nights of the week. Two of the best are at the **Fiesta Americana** (Aurelio Aceves 225, at Minerva Circle; tel. 36-25-48-48, ext. 3062, for reservations) on Thursdays at 7:30 P.M. and at **Hotel El Tapatío** (Bulevar Aeropuerto 4275; tel. 36-35-60-50 for reservations) on Friday nights from 7 to 10 P.M. Tickets to Mexican Fiestas average about $25 per person.

For ballroom dancing, you can't beat El Tapatío's **Memories Lounge,** a romantic, dimly lighted cocktail lounge with a panoramic view of Guadalajara, the soothing sounds of forties to sixties favorites, and a spacious dance floor. Open Tuesday through Sunday, from 7 P.M. to midnight. Guadalajara's big hotels have discos, and there's the trendy **Dady'O** (Avenida Chapultepec, open from 10 P.M. to 3 A.M.), a lookalike for Acapulco's famous Baby'O.

Tapatíos have two favorite spectator sports. Soccer is a passion: In fact, Guadalajara hosted the world-championship games in 1970 and 1986, at the Jalisco and 3 de Marzo stadiums. Game schedules are available in local newspapers or with your concierge. The second sport is the *Charreada,* a typical Mexican ridin'-'n'-ropin' rodeo. The horsemanship is superb, and the costumes for the grand promenade are spectacular. *Charreadas* are held at the Aceves Galindo Lienzo (a rodeo ring) on Sundays at noon.

Guadalajara's Fiestas de Octubre, held annually from October 1 to 16 at the **Núcleo Auditorio Benito Juárez** in Zapopan, is a huge state fair that serves as a national showcase for Mexican products and handicrafts. There are information booths for everything from travel to birth control, and stalls selling everything from regional sweets to rare books. Evening is show time, with performances by popular Mexican and Latin American singers, bands, dance groups, and comedians. This fiesta, very popular with the masses, produces the usual madhouse of activity. Check with your concierge for daily schedules during the month of October.

EXCURSIONS

Tlaquepaque

From the turn of the century to the 1950s, the little town of Tlaquepaque (TLA-kay-pah-kay; also known as San Pedro Tlaquepaque), about three miles southeast of downtown Guadalajara, was a suburban retreat for wealthy Tapatíos who wanted to escape the bustle of city life for idyllic country weekends and for artists who wanted to have space, privacy, and a peaceful environment in which to establish their studios. Although expanding Guadalajara engulfed Tlaquepaque decades ago, the town has retained its unique charm and calm and its pretty tree-lined streets and old pastel-colored buildings. During the mid-1970s buildings, parks, and streets were renovated, and several pedestrian-only promenades were established. Chic galleries and boutiques moved into converted colonial mansions, and Tlaquepaque became one of the most famous shopping districts in all of Mexico.

Tlaquepaque has more than two hundred shops, but the biggest concentration of interesting boutiques is on **Avenida Independencia,** a pedestrian-only street that extends for about five blocks between Niños Heroes and Obregón. Here you'll find clothing and crafts shops with beautiful and tempting displays. Lower street numbers are closer to **El Parián,** the *zócalo.* Here are some highlights:

Leo E Hijos (Independencia 150; tel. 36-35-18-21) sells terrific leather clothes and accessories, including soft leather trousers, bomber jackets, desert boots, wallets, and oversized carryalls, all at comparatively moderate prices. Craftsmanship is excellent, and the variety of styles and colors is impressive.

Caoba (Independencia 156; tel. 36-35-97-70) features fine home accessories, including unusual lizard-shaped vases, giant clay pots with a secret finish that makes them look like rusted metal, brown ceramics accented with a bright green glaze, and ceramic and carved napkin rings. There is also an appealing selection of rustic-looking furniture, including armoires, tables, and chairs.

Bazar Hecht (Independencia 158; tel. 36-35-22-41) sells a wide variety of clothes and personal accessories, as well as home accessories. Featured are Diane Martin's Opus One designer clothes in colorful cotton with contrasting appliqués of geometric and animal motifs, as well as traditional embroidered blouses and dresses. There are attractive Guatemalan-style woven carryalls and pretty beads, plus elaborate dolls, solid brass apples, and candlestick sets that stack into a tree for storage.

Mis Ochos Reales Bazar (Independencia 173; tel. 36-35-51-81) has terrific furniture. Beautifully upholstered sofas have hand-carved wooden frames with baroque floral motifs, or delicate rattan frames with lots of curlicues. Tables have hand-carved wooden bases that look like racing horses, and there are many green-glazed ceramic pineapple-shaped water jugs in various sizes.

Bazar Barrera (Independencia 205; tel. 36-35-19-61) is a menagerie of ceramic, brass, papier-mâché, straw, and wooden birds. Many species (including some fantasy breeds) are represented, but the parrot is clearly this shop's favorite feathered friend. The birds are realistic or stylized, very colorful, and attractive. Especially appealing are the brass and ceramic ducks, with pretty flowers painted on their ceramic wings.

Irene Pulos (Independencia 210B; tel. 36-57-84-99) designs and produces dramatic and colorful caftans, long and short dresses, and pantsuits with appliquéd flowers and embroidered geometric patterns. In addition, the shop's superb accessories include Tuya & Mia's hand-painted folk bracelets; embroidered pocketbooks; charming necklaces made of hundreds of tiny ceramic cups; and Huichol beaded bowls and bags. Pulos is a terrific find for anyone who likes distinctive and beautiful wearables.

Platería Tlaquepaque (Independencia 211; tel. 36-35-36-64) is a series of smaller silver shops with a good selection of inexpensive earrings, bracelets, and necklaces. There are also some picture frames, candlesticks, and platters. The styles are not that unusual, but the quality is good. You can also stop at this silver arcade for a free soft drink or tequila.

La Rosa de Cristal (Independencia 232; tel. 36-39-71-80) makes and sells hand-blown glass. The shop is filled with reasonably priced blue or red glass goblets and tumblers with matching pitchers. There are also dozens of glittering glass animals in all shapes and colors. The shop also carries stoneware dishes and serving bowls with pretty floral motifs.

Sergio Bustamente Gallery (Independencia 236; tel 36-39-55-19) shows this Mexican surrealist sculptor's latest works, in addition to the limited editions of his well-known pieces, including rabbits hatching out of eggs and lizards emerging from shells. This was Bustamente's first gallery and is his headquarters, with a more complete selection of his work than is available elsewhere.

Casa Canela (Independencia 258; tel. 36-35-37-17) is a gallery of exclusive and expensive colonial antiques, art, and hand-carved stone artifacts, as well as ceramics from Puebla and other regions of Mexico.

Casas de Mexico (Independencia 393; tel. 36-57-46-52) has its own line of Southwest-style furniture, including bed headboards, tables, chairs, chests, and armoires, with rough-finished blond wood. The shop designs and manufactures its own upholstery fabrics, mostly heavy handwoven cottons in pastel geometric patterns, also used to decorate traditional chairs made of logs with leather seats and backs.

A second shopping street, **Avenida Juárez,** runs parallel to and one block south of Independencia. However, traffic is often quite heavy on this street, so be careful when you zigzag from one side to the other to look in windows.

Tlaquepaque has attractions other than shopping. Both avenidas Independencia and Juárez begin (or end) at the lively *zócalo,* known as **El Parián.** This square is filled with activity, with children's games and mariachi music. El Parián is lined with sidewalk cafés and bars, all with moderately priced drinks and snack foods. There's activity in El Parián daily from about 11 A.M. to midnight, but the place is most fun in the evenings and Sunday afternoons. Nearby, **Templo Parroquial de San Pedro,** Tlaquepaque's principal church, a 17th-century structure, is noted for its Plateresque-style facade and for 17th-century religious paintings. The church borders **El Jardín,** a pretty tree-lined plaza with a new bandstand that's frequently used for well-attended and free outdoor concerts. Check with the nearby Tourist Information Office (Guillermo

Prieto 80; tel. 36-35-15-03) for a current performance schedule.

Tlaquepaque's **Museo Regional de la Cerámica** (Independencia 237; tel. 36-35-54-04) has excellent exhibits of Jalisco pottery dating from the 1850s to the present. You can see original pieces and photographs of highly acclaimed ceramicists at work. Huichol crafts are also shown. The museum is in a wonderful colonial building with a lovely courtyard and garden. Open Tuesday through Saturday from 10 A.M. to 4 P.M., Sunday from 10 A.M. to 1 P.M. No admission fee.

Tlaquepaque is also known for its cuisine. Guadalajara's **Restaurant los Cazadores** (see **Restaurants** above) has a branch in Tlaquepaque (tel. 36-41-41-97); a still-better bet is the **Restaurant with No Name** (Madero 80; tel. 36-35-45-20). Dining in this converted colonial mansion is a tradition. You choose to sit in a lovely garden or inside, in one of several colonial rooms. The atmosphere is festive, the food excellent. The menu is pure Mexican, with great homemade soups, mole, enchiladas, tacos, *carnitas,* tamales, quesadillas, and plates that provide a little bit of everything for satisfying sampling. Don't insult the singing waiters by refusing a tequila—after all, Jalisco is the birthplace of this national drink. Open from 11 A.M. to 9 P.M. No reservations. Credit cards: AE, MC, V. The average price of dinner for two is about $45. The Restaurant with No Name also offers individualized and five-day cooking classes on the restaurant terrace. One or both of the two entertaining owners, Dayton Herzog (a U.S. citizen) and Felix Carillo (a Mexican), are often on hand to greet guests.

It's quite easy to get to Tlaquepaque from downtown Guadalajara. Taxis are available, but public buses are almost as convenient and much cheaper. Buses marked "Tlaquepaque" or "San Juan de Dios–San Pedro–Tonalá" run along Calzada Independencia. The fare is about $.45, and the trip takes about half an hour, maximum. If you're driving, go south on Calzada Independencia Sur and turn left (east) on Avenida Revolucíon, which takes you into Tlaquepaque. There is a public parking garage at the corner of Obregón and Morelos, about a block away from the *zócalo.*

Guanajuato

Guanajuato is a mountainous state, the geographical center of Mexico, and the heart of the grain-producing Bajío region, Mexico's breadbasket. The city of Guanajuato, capital of the state, is a delightful colonial town, nestled in a long narrow valley between two high mountain ridges. Guanajuato's dozens of picturesque plazas and parks, narrow cobblestone streets, magnificent municipal buildings and baroque churches, and the panoramic views from nearby mountain drives, plus its excellent university, sophisticated cultural life, historical importance—and the annual International Cervantes Festival—make this town a favorite with travelers.

CONNECTIONS

Guanajuato has no airport. To get to Guanajuato by car from Mexico City, take toll road MEX57 to Querétaro (150 miles, three hours). At Querétaro, take toll road MEX45 through Celaya (about 29 miles), continuing until you connect with MEX110 into Guanajuato (about 75 miles from Querétaro).

There is excellent bus and train service to this mountain community. Flecha Amarilla is the biggest bus company in town, with 15 daily bus departures to and from Mexico City, 17 to and from Guadalajara, ten to and from San Miguel de Allende, and 15 to and from Querétaro. Flecha Amarilla has the most buses, but they're not all first-class. When taking longer trips, especially between Guanajuato and Mexico City, make sure you get on an express. Omnibus de México operates (less frequent) first-class buses to and from Guadalajara, San Miguel de Allende, and Querétaro.

The Ferrocarriles Nacionales de México's recently inaugurated Servicio Estrella de Pasajeros first-class train service from Mexico City to Guanajuato via Querétaro is excellent. Guanajuato is a branch stop on an already established route between Mexico City and San Miguel de Allende via Querétaro. *El Constitucionalista,* as the train is known, leaves Mexico City at 7:35 A.M. and arrives in Querétaro at 10:45 A.M., and in Guanajuato at about noon. Returning to Mexico City, the train leaves Guanajuato at 4:30 P.M. and arrives in Querétaro at 6 P.M., and in Mexico City at 9 P.M. First-class tickets cost about $12, and include a full breakfast, served in the train's pleasant dining car. Telephone 5-547-5819 in Mexico City for information and reservations.

In Guanajuato, take a taxi from the bus or train station to your hotel, and after that plan to walk as much as possible. Almost everything you want to see is within walking distance of the *zócalo.* Guanajuato's downtown streets are narrow one-way passages, and traffic can become mighty congested. There's nothing more frustrating than spending one of your precious hours in this gem of a town in the back seat of a fuming taxi stuck behind a smoking bus. Bring comfortable shoes, and plan to get some exercise scurrying up Guanajuato's charming, albeit steep, cobbled streets and alleyways. If you're not a very strong walker, you'll have to rely on taxis to get between hotels on the outskirts of town and the *zócalo.* Ask your concierge for the going rate, and negotiate with the cab driver before you take the ride.

🧳 HOTELS

Guanajuato's hotels are colonial-style and charming. In making your selection, you should decide whether you want to stay in the atmospheric center of town, within walking distance of all the sights, or on the outskirts, for more spaciousness, gardens, and some great panoramic views.

Hotel Castillo Santa Cecilia

Apdo. 44, 36000
Tel. 473-2-04-85
Doubles, from $60

Tall stone walls surround the pretty castle-like hotel and its lavish gardens. Is it colonial-style or medieval? A little of both, with touches of Disneyland. But the place is comfortable and luxurious. The one hundred rooms are spacious; some have fireplaces and wonderful views overlooking Guanajuato. You'll find a pleasant heated pool, a patio area, a chic restaurant and bar, and peacocks roaming around the garden. The private chapel is great for weddings. Credit cards: AE, MC, V.

Hotel Hacienda de Cobos

Calle Pare Hidalgo 3 and Juárez 153, 36000
Tel. 473-2-01-43
Doubles, from $45

The forty small but charming rooms here are in a wonderful old mansion hidden away behind a huge stone wall that used to be part of the 17th-century estate of a Guanajuato silver magnate. The restaurant and bar are delightfully quaint, with very pleasant service. The Hacienda de Cobos is near the bus station, but not too noisy. Credit cards: MC, V.

Hosteria del Frayle

Sopena 3, 36000
Tel. 473-2-11-79
Two persons, two beds, from $45

The Hosteria del Frayle's colonial charm is a bit frayed around the edges. The hotel occupies what was formerly the town's silver mint, and the colonial architecture and accents are all authentic. But furnishings in the 38 rooms are a bit run-down, and rooms facing the street are quite noisy. Despite this, the hotel's location is considered good, and the restaurant and bar are very pleasant. Credit cards: MC, V.

Hotel Parador del Convento

Calzada de Guadalupe 17, 36000
Tel. 473-2-25-24
Doubles, from $40

Quite off the beaten track, this intimate little hotel is located on the hill above the university. It's a bit of a hike from the Jardín Union or *zócalo* but will give you another perspective on Guanajuato. The rooms are small but spotlessly clean and pleasantly furnished. Some have splendid views of La Compañia and of El Pípila, all lit up at night. Credit cards: V.

Parador San Javier

Plaza Aldama No. 92, 36020
Tel. 473-2-06-50
Doubles, from $60

This colonial hacienda has been converted into a luxurious hotel with 120 rooms (some with great views, brick arched ceilings, and fireplaces) and lovely gardens, which incorporate the hacienda's old reservoir with a waterfall. The hacienda's high-ceilinged and beamed chapel now serves as a delightful Mexican-style restaurant. There's also a popular disco. San Javier is about one mile from the center of town, and you'll need a car or taxi to get around. Credit cards: AE, DC, V.

Hotel Paseo de la Presa

Carretera Panorámica (near El Pípila Monument), 36000
Tel. 473-2-30-21
Doubles, from $50

The 53 rooms of this modern mountaintop hotel have splendid views of Guanajuato. The rooms are spacious, comfortably furnished, and equipped with cable TV and servibars. The hotel lobby has a huge TV and big red armchairs. There's a lovely swimming pool with patio bar, and **La Cascada** restaurant has a terrific view and excellent Mexican food. The staff is friendly and very helpful. Credit cards: AE, MC, V.

Posada Santa Fe

Apdo. 101, 36000
Tel. 473-2-00-84
Doubles, from $40

In one corner of the Jardín Union (the *zócalo*) the Posada Santa Fe is *the* meeting place in Guanajuato: sooner or later everyone ambles by its sidewalk café and bar. Inside, the colonial-style architecture has much charm. Rooms vary in quality and size, but all are clean and comfortably furnished, and the location is terrific. Be sure to avoid rooms facing the street because they're quite noisy. The sidewalk café, which serves reliably good food, invites lingering—and you're never rushed by the waiters to vacate your table. Credit cards: AE, MC, V.

Hotel Real de Minas

Nejayote 17, 36000
Tel. 473-2-14-60
Doubles, from $60

Just as you enter Guanajuato via the road from Irapuato, you see the colonial-style Real de Minas on your left. It's a lovely hacienda-like building with all the modern conveniences. The 175 spacious rooms have colonial-style dark-wood furniture and beamed ceilings. You'll find lovely gardens and a pool, tennis court, restaurant, and bar. One caveat, however: You need a taxi to get into the center of town. Credit cards: AE, MC, V.

Hotel San Diego

Jardín Union 1, 36000
Tel. 473-2-13-00
Doubles, from $55

On the corner facing the *zócalo,* the San Diego is located in a former monastery. There are 55 rooms furnished colonial-style; all are pleasant and clean, but rooms facing the *zócalo* can be noisy. The second-story restaurant overlooks the *zócalo:* Get a window table for a prime view. A bar and a Jacuzzi are also on the premises. Credit cards: MC, V.

Guanajuato's Guide Kids

About a dozen years ago, a teacher in one of Guanajuato's secondary schools decided to try to do something to alleviate the problem of the town's many poor and homeless children. With the idea of giving Guanajuato's street kids a means of legitimately earning some money, he began giving free lessons teaching the kids the facts about Guanajuato's famous tourist attractions, so that they could conduct guided tours and get paid. The plan was successful. A lot of children enrolled in the classes and learned the history of their city and how to tell visitors local lore in an informative but entertaining way. Guanajuato now has dozens of guide kids. You won't have any trouble finding them: They're not the least bit shy about asking you to hire them, either to drive around with you or to tell you about one particular sight. These guides don't have a set fee but work for tips. The kids are darling and knowledgeable—and most of them really do need the income. Unfortunately, few of them speak any language other than Spanish, but if you can communicate at all, you'll get a good story—the basic facts with some elaboration for dramatic effect. If you don't want a guide, just wave them away politely. If they try to convince you that you really do need them, a firmer *"No, gracias"* will usually send them packing.

Guanajuato's **zócalo,** the lovely Jardín de la Union, is a small triangular square with wonderful old shade trees and a charming bandstand. On one side of the *zócalo* is **Teatro Juárez,** an ornate opera house with columns, friezes, and statues of the muses outside and a gilded interior. Teatro Juárez opened in 1903 with a performance of *Aida.* The building, a favorite of Porfirio Díaz's, is considered one of the most beautiful theaters in Mexico and is currently used for performances by outstanding national and international artists and ensembles, especially during the annual International Cervantes Festival (see **Entertainment,** below). Ask your concierge about current programs. Next to Teatro Juárez is the **Church of San Diego,** a lovely churrigueresque-style building constructed in 1633 and rebuilt during the 18th century.

Off the *zócalo,* **Avenida Benito Juárez** leads to **Plaza de la Paz,** where you'll find the baroque **Basilica de Nuestra Señora de Guanajuato,** built in the 17th century. Inside is a small statue of the Virgin of Guanajuato standing on a heavy and ornate silver base presented to the town in 1557 by King Philip II of Spain. Also in the Plaza is **Casa Rul y Valenciana,** a mansion built by architect Francisco Eduardo Tresguerras for the count of Rul, owner of a large silver mine.

Further along Avenida Juárez is **Plazuela de los Angeles** and the **Callejón del Beso** (Alley of the Kiss), a narrow street just about two feet and three inches wide. The street got its name from a local Romeo and Juliet–type legend about a young couple in love. The girl's father did not approve of the boy, so the couple used to meet secretly, standing on separate balconies over the *callejón,* and kiss.

Mercado Hidalgo is about one long block farther along Avenida Juárez. The huge market, constructed in 1910, has hundreds of stalls and stands. On the first floor are all sorts of fresh fruits and vegetables, meats, fish, and prepared foods. Guanajuato is known for its sweets, especially the candy skeletons and mummies gift-wrapped with cigarettes and tequila in colored cellophane. The market is where you buy these goodies. On the second floor, vendors display all kinds of leather clothing, *huaraches,* wallets and handbags, and other accessories. The *mercado* also has a lot of locally produced ceramics (Guanajuato has several large ceramics factories) and other handicrafts. As you go up the stairs, notice the pretty glass-encased statue of the Virgin, and all the flowers and offerings that are left there daily.

Across Avenida Juárez from the market is a narrow alley leading to the **Templo de Belén** (Bethlehem), a lovely churrigueresque church built in 1773.

One block north, in Calle de los Positos, is the **Alhóndiga de Granaditas,** an unadorned fortress-like structure. Built in 1799, the Alhóndiga was originally a granary, but later became a prison and fortress. In 1810, Guanajuato's hero, El Pípila, blew up the door to the Alhóndiga, thereby enabling Allende to capture Guanajuato for the independence movement, and it was at the Alhóndiga that the severed heads of Allende, Hidalgo, Jimenez, and Aldama were displayed for a decade. The Alhóndiga is now used as a museum, with terrific exhibitions of archaeological and historical artifacts, colonial furniture and arms, photographs by Romualdo Garcia, paintings by Hermansillo Bustos, and changing exhibitions of contemporary Mexican fine art and handicrafts. The main staircase to the balcony and second-floor exhibition halls has José Chávez Morado's marvelous murals, completed between 1955 and 1966. Open Tuesday through Saturday from 10 A.M. to 2 P.M. and 4 to 7 P.M., and Sunday from 10 A.M. to 2 P.M. Admission is charged. A large plaza adjacent to the Alhóndiga is used for free outdoor concerts and dance performances during the International Cervantes Festival.

Nearby, the **Diego Rivera Museum,** at Calle Positos 47, is the great muralist's birthplace. The house is filled with turn-of-the-century furniture and much memorabilia from Rivera's childhood, as well as his early paintings. Open Tuesday through Saturday from 10 A.M. to 2 P.M. and from 4 to 7 P.M., Sundays from 10 A.M. to 4 P.M. Admission is charged.

The **Museo del Pueblo,** Calle Positos 7, exhibits 18th- through 20th-century paintings, with an emphasis on religious art from the colonial period. There is also a collection of José

Chávez Morado paintings about the history of Guanajuato, and some fine folk art. The museum is in the former mansion of the marquis San Juan de Royas, which was built in 1776.

In the direction of the *zócalo,* and off a small side street to the right, is **Plaza San Roque,** where the 18th-century **Church of San Roque** forms a beautiful backdrop for outdoor performances of the *entremeses Cervantinos,* one-act plays by Miguel de Cervantes Saavedra (yes, the Cervantes of *Don Quixote* fame). The performances are presented by University of Guanajuato students during the **International Cervantes Festival.** From time to time Plaza San Roque is also used for outdoor concerts by *estudiantinas* (or *tunas,* as they are also called), a traditional type of choral group with a Spanish heritage.

The **University of Guanajuato** is at the top of a huge flight of stairs off Calle Positos. The main building is a castle-like colonial-style white stone structure, built in 1955, with a baroque and Moorish facade. The university has frequent film showings, public lectures, and other cultural programs. Ask the main office or your hotel concierge for current schedules.

Next to the university is the **Iglesia de la Compañía de Jesús,** built in the 18th century by the Jesuits. The church is churrigueresque in style, with ultra baroque altars and doors, a neoclassical dome, and two fine Miguel Cabrera paintings. Concerts are staged here during the International Cervantes Festival.

One of Guanajuato's most interesting sights is a subterranean road, **Calle Miguel Hidalgo,** or the **Subterráneo,** built on the bed of a river that was diverted away from Guanajuato because it frequently caused flooding in the town. The cavernous Subterráneo, used for southbound traffic (northbound traffic is routed on surface roads) provides a fascinatingly different perspective on Guanajuato. At various uncovered segments of the road, you can glance upward and see numerous wooden balconies, all prettily bedecked with flowers and plants.

Still another perspective on Guanajuato—and a beautiful one—may be had from the **Carretera Panorámica,** a road that skirts the town on surrounding mountaintops, providing exquisite overviews of this lovely old city. The Carretera Panorámica is the way to the **El Pípila Monument,** an enormous statue that depicts Juan José de los Reyes Martinez ready to charge at the door of the Alhóndiga. The statue towers over Guanajuato and can be seen from almost any location in the city. From the plaza around El Pípila you get a great view of the town.

Guanajuato's cemetery, the **Panteón Municipal,** on Calzada de Tepetapa, has a bizarre exhibition of **Las Momias,** the mummified remains of human corpses. These were ordinary citizens who were buried in local soil containing minerals that preserved their bodies. Some are clothed, others naked. There are old people and infants—even a mother and child. The mummies are displayed in glass cases. Whether viewers find them fascinating or gruesome, they do seem to have a profound effect on mood. Open daily from 9 A.M. to 6 P.M. Admission is charged. You can get to the Panteón by the public bus marked "Presa-Estación."

Three miles from Guanajuato on the road to Dolores Hidalgo, you'll find the fascinating **La Valenciana Mine,** discovered in 1788 by a miner named Antonio Obregón y Alconer, who later became the Count of Valenciana. In its heyday, this was the world's leading silver mine, with more than three thousand miners hauling silver ore from a depth of about five hundred feet. The mine was recently reopened after a forty-year hiatus, and it still has a sizable annual yield. Visitors can see the main shaft and mechanized trolley carts that are lowered into the earth empty and return to the surface filled with ore. There's a small shop selling hunks of silver-saturated rock, crystals, and other semiprecious minerals taken from La Valenciana and other mines in the area.

Nearby is the **Templo de San Cayetano,** the baroque church built by the Count of Valenciana and dedicated in 1788. The carved facade is purely churrigueresque, with Moorish-looking windows. Only one of the two planned towers was built, so the structure looks a bit unbalanced. Inside is a magnificent wood-and-ivory pulpit and gilded churrigueresque altars. You can get to the mine and Templo by the public bus marked "J. Perones-Marfill," with Valenciana written in white on the windshield.

Also on the outskirts of Guanajuato, about two miles from town on the road to Irapuato, is the **Museo Ex-Hacienda San Gabriel de la Barra,** a 17th-century hacienda in which you'll find a beautiful formal garden, formal rooms with lovely colonial furniture, and an ornate private chapel. Open daily from 9 A.M. to 6 P.M. There's a small admission fee.

☕ RESTAURANTS

With the enormous popularity that Guanajuato enjoys with travelers, you would expect it to have some first-rate gourmet restaurants with ambience and charm to match the town. Unfortunately, however, the restaurant selection is rather limited: Most places have tasty and reasonably priced food but little or no ambience. Perhaps the best idea is to eat quickly, for the most part—and then go for a nice long stroll to soak up local color.

Café el Retiro
Sopena 12, near the *zócalo*

Tel. 473-2-06-22

Conveniently located just off the *zócalo,* this homey restaurant has good home cooking, Mexican-style. There are stews, steaks, roast pork, rice prepared with cheese, soups, and good strong coffee. Open daily, 8 A.M.–10 P.M., and it's crowded at lunch time. The average cost of a meal for two is about $15. No reservations. No credit cards.

Casa Valadez
Jardín Union and Sopa
No telephone

Not much ambience, but the food is good and the service is fast at this restaurant. The menu includes Mexican quickies like quesadillas and tacos, plus steaks and grilled chicken breast. Good soups and salads. Open daily, 8 A.M.–midnight. Special lunch menu served 2–5 P.M. The average cost of a meal for two is about $16. No reservations. No credit cards.

Centro Nutricional Vegetariano
Aguilar 45
Tel. 473-2-11-91

Stir-fried vegetables, guacamole, refried beans, brown rice, and tofu are all on the internationally eclectic menu of this health-conscious restaurant. You might find that the chef uses a little more salt and oil than you're used to at home, but ask him to cut down on those ingredients in freshly prepared dishes, and he'll happily oblige. The Centro is distinguished by its excellent preparation and pleasant service. Open daily, 11 A.M.–9:30 P.M. The average cost of a meal for two is about $14. No reservations. No credit cards.

El Claustro
Jardín de la Reforma
No telephone

El Claustro actually offers a bit of atmosphere—a wine-cellar setting with original artwork on display. The steaks and grilled chicken breast served with rice and vegetables are especially recommended. Special lunch menu. Modest wine list. Open 1 P.M.–1 A.M. The average cost of a meal for two is about $20. No reservations. Credit cards: AE, MC, V.

El Granaro
Avenida Juárez 25
No telephone

Typical Mexican food is served in this family-style restaurant, which features excellent *pozole,* quesadillas, and *enchiladas con queso y crema.* The service is efficient if not fawning. You'll find good breakfasts of *huevos rancheros* and *huevos a la mexicana.* Open 8 A.M.–10 P.M. The average cost of a meal for two is about $15. No reservations. No credit cards.

Pizza Piazza
Plazuela San Fernando
Tel. 473-2-42-59

Outdoor tables on the plaza and an indoor dining room are pleasant places to enjoy an individual pizza prepared with your favorite toppings. Or you can get a pie for four—or six—or select from a list of pastas. Beer and sangría are served. Open noon–11 P.M. The average cost of a meal for two is about $12. No reservations. Credit cards: AE, MC, V.

Posada Santa Fe
Jardín Union
Tel. 473-2-00-84

This is *the* place for unhurried eating and people watching. The outdoor café is on the *zócalo,* separated from the sidewalk by low shrubbery. At lunch and dinner, large platters of tempting foods, including entrées of chicken, pork, and beef, are displayed on a large table. You can also have a light meal of *sopa* and quesadillas, or coffee and dessert. Modest wine list. Open 9 A.M.–midnight. The average cost of a meal for two, with wine, is about $30. No reservations. Credit cards: AE, MC, V.

Hotel San Diego
Jardín Union 1
Tel. 473-2-13-00

This second-floor restaurant has a charming colonial setting with the best tables overlooking the *zócalo.* The San Diego is a place to dine at leisure. The menu includes steaks, chicken, and fish, grilled or prepared with garlic. Excellent salads and soups, and a nice dessert tray are featured, along with a modest wine list. Open 8 A.M.–11 P.M. The average cost of a meal for two is about $35. Reservations suggested. Credit cards: AE, MC, V.

Tasca de los Santos
Plaza de la Paz 28
Tel. 473-2-23-20

This is a charming Spanish-style taverna. The menu, which features Spanish favorites, offers an especially excellent paella. The chicken with white wine is a delightful entrée, and cooked cheese with Spanish sausage *(queso fundido con chorizo)* is a very satisfying appetizer. Good wine list, with some expensive imported labels. Open 8 A.M.–midnight. The average cost of a meal for two, with wine, is about $38. No reservations. Credit cards: AE, MC, V.

ENTERTAINMENT

The **University of Guanajuato's** film and lecture series is worth noting: an interesting range of intellectual diversions throughout the year is offered.

But Guanajuato is best known for the **International Cervantes Festival,** held each year in October and November. The festival lasts for two weeks and presents hundreds of performances, concerts, and other events in venues throughout town, including the magnificent Teatro Juárez, La Compañía de Jesús, and the Alhóndiga de Granaditas. Classical, traditional (ethnic), and avant-garde theater, dance, and music ensembles from Mexico and around the world perform for audiences that have come to Guanajuato from far and wide to enjoy the festival. Some of the world's top artists have performed at the festival to sold-out houses. The schedules of upcoming festivals usually aren't finalized until the last minute, but tentative programs with dates and events should be available through the nearest Mexican Government Tourist Office. If you're planning to visit Guanajuato during the festival, make hotel reservations far in advance. Guanajuato is almost entirely booked up for the two weeks of the International Cervantes Festival.

During the festival and at other times of the year, Guanajuato's hotel bars are lively. The sidewalk café and bar at the **Posada Santa Fe,** on the *zócalo,* is a center of activity until late at night. Nearby, the **Hotel San Diego** has a charming wine cellar–like bar. **Parador San Javier's** disco is popular, and **Castillo Santa Cecilia's** bar has ballroom dancing Monday through Saturday from 9 P.M. to 1 A.M.

San Miguel de Allende

Everyone is enchanted by the charm of colonial San Miguel de Allende, a town that has been designated a national monument in order to preserve all its colonial mansions, baroque churches, plazas, and cobblestone streets. San Miguel de Allende's picturesque streets meander up the low slopes of a mountain overlooking a peaceful fertile valley, and there are splendid vistas.

The town's economy is based largely on tourism. People come to San Miguel de Allende from all over the world, and it is especially popular with U.S. and Canadian retirees who either settle here permanently or move in for the winter months. The weather is nearly perfect all year long. Strolling around town, stopping in the fabulous shops, and sipping a refreshing drink at an outdoor café are the most popular pastimes. San Miguel de Allende also has a thriving arts community. Many resident painters, writers, and musicians are affiliated with several outstanding art institutes. Most famous of these is the Instituto Allende, which offers courses of study in all the fine arts and crafts.

San Miguel de Allende has a relatively peaceful but interesting past. In pre-Hispanic times, the area was settled by Tarascan and Chichimec Indians. In 1542, the Franciscan friar Juan de San Miguel, who had been an influential missionary in Morelia, founded an Indian mission here, which he called San Miguel de los Chichimecas. The settlement grew fairly rapidly owing to Indian migrations from other, less peaceful, areas. During the 17th and 18th centuries, the town became a popular place for mine owners from Guanajuato and Zacatecas to establish family mansions. It was here that Ignacio de Allende, the Mexican independence hero, was born in 1779—and the town of San Miguel was renamed in his honor in 1862.

If you are driving north from Mexico City, after about four hours you reach a turn. If you miss the turn, you can go straight back to America in about ten hours flat. But if you leave that main road and turn left, toward the west in the direction of San Miguel, as I did one summer in what seems now like a long time ago, you enter a different world. The kind of world you might read about in the works of Latin American writers such as Fuentes, Rulfo, García Márquez. Macondo could be out there.

You come to the old Mexico, a lawless land. It is a landscape that could be ruled by bandits or serve as a backdrop for the classic Westerns, where all you expect the Mexicans to say is *"hombre"* and *"amigo"* and *"si, señor."* It is a land with colors. Desert colors. Sand and sienna, red clay and cactus green, scattered yellow flowers. The sky runs all the ranges of purple and scarlet and orange. You can see dust storms or rain moving toward you. Rainbows are frequent. The solitude is dramatic.

—Mary Morris
Nothing to Declare, 1988

CONNECTIONS

San Miguel de Allende has no commercial airport. You can easily drive from Mexico City on toll road MEX57, taking the bypass around Querétaro, and continuing until you see the signs for San Miguel de Allende, then continuing on a two-lane road into town. This way, you'll enter San Miguel de Allende via El Mirador, the scenic road with a spectacular panoramic view of the entire town and the lovely surrounding countryside. The distance from Mexico City is about 190 miles and should take about four hours.

Train service from Mexico City to San Miguel de Allende via Querétaro, is excellent. The Ferrocarriles Nacionales de México's Servicio Estrella de Pasajeros first-class train, known as *El Constitucionalista,* leaves Mexico City at 7:35 A.M. and arrives in Querétaro at 10:45 A.M., and in San Miguel de Allende at about noon. Returning to Mexico City, the train leaves San Miguel de Allende at 4:30 P.M. and arrives in Querétaro at 6 P.M., and in Mexico City at 9 P.M. First-class tickets cost about $12 and include a full breakfast, served in the train's pleasant dining car. Telephone 465-2-00-07, in San Miguel de Allende, or 5-547-5819, in Mexico City, for information and reservations.

Or you can take the bus: Flecha Amarilla has eight daily buses to and from Mexico City. Tres Estrellas de Oro operates one daily first-class bus between Mexico City and San Miguel de Allende, and two daily first-class buses between San Miguel de Allende and Guanajuato. Omnibus de México has two first-class buses daily between San Miguel de Allende and Mexico City, and one bus daily to and from Guadalajara, via Guanajuato.

Walking around town is one of the best things to do in San Miguel de Allende, so bring comfortable shoes. All the sights, shops, restaurants, and hotels are within walking distance of one another. If you're really tired, you can drive or take a taxi—but you'll be missing half the fun of being in this quaint little town.

What I saw as we drove into San Miguel bore little relation to what I'd thought I'd find. A dusty town rose out of a hill, with a salmon-pink church spire and pale stucco buildings. Buses were everywhere, idling near the center of town, sending up exhaust that would make me choke whenever I walked past. Their drivers shouted the names of destinations unknown to me—Celaya, Guanajuato, Dolores. Tortilla ladies and avocado ladies sold sandwiches near the buses as blind beggars and naked children, broken-spirited donkeys and starving dogs, filled the streets.

I was missing the fine points. Expectation does that to you. I missed the bougainvillea, the colonial buildings, the cobblestone streets. It is easy to miss all of that once the panic sets in. I only saw the dust and the donkeys and the strangers and a place that seemed so distant from anything I thought I could ever call home.

—Mary Morris
Nothing to Declare, 1988

🧳 HOTELS

San Miguel de Allende is full of small hotels that specialize in making a comfortable home away from home for travelers who may spend long vacations here each year. Hotels are in all price categories, but the best ones are run by owners who take a personal interest in the goings-on and the guests. Several of these, including the Casa de Sierra Nevada, Hacienda de las Flores, and Villa Jacaranda, are quite famous. If you can't afford to stay at one of these, treat yourself to lunch or dinner in their restaurants and savor the ambience as well as the food. And please note that all hotels listed below are air-conditioned unless otherwise noted.

Hotel Aristos
Ancha de San Antonio 30, 37700
Tel. 465-2-01-49 or 800-5-ARISTOS
Doubles, from $45; meal plans available at higher rates
This sixty-room colonial-style hotel, with cobblestone walkways, a rose garden with tiled fountain, and private bungalows, is on the grounds of an old hacienda, part of which is now occupied by the Instituto Allende. Rooms have large arched windows that overlook the gardens, dark-wood colonial-style furniture, servibars, and super-large bathrooms. The Aristos has a small pool with patio and an airy restaurant with lovely rose-garden views. Credit cards: AE, DC, MC, V.

Casa de Sierra Nevada

Calle Hospicio 35, 37700
Tel. 465-2-23-37
Doubles, from $100

Owned by Peter Wirth, the Casa is one of the most famous inns in Mexico. It occupies three colonial mansions, each with lovely gardens and a lot of original art in public areas. There are 22 units, including spacious double rooms and delightful home-like suites. Each is individually and imaginatively decorated; all have fireplaces, and some have private patios for sunning. The hotel's restaurant is the best in town. Make your reservations as early as possible because the Casa is usually full. No credit cards.

Hacienda de las Flores

Calle Hospicio 16, 37700
Tel. 465-2-18-08
Doubles, from $90

Hidden away behind an old iron gate, this intimate inn has 12 beautifully decorated junior suites, some with fireplaces. The bathrooms have pretty tile tubs. The rooms are arranged around a pretty flower-filled courtyard with a heated pool. The second-floor restaurant has a lovely view of town. Alicia Franyutti, who treats guests like friends of the family, supervises the very friendly and helpful staff. No credit cards.

Hacienda Taboada

Km 8 on the highway to Dolores Hidalgo, 37700
Tel. 465-2-08-50 or 5-559-9352 in Mexico City
Doubles, from $65

About five miles north of town, this newly constructed colonial-style resort has thermal sulphur springs for soaking and swimming. The place is family-oriented and has tennis, golf, and horseback-riding facilities. The one hundred rooms are large and decorated with colorful Mexican rugs and blankets. Bathrooms have huge sunken tubs and use thermal waters. All units have small balconies overlooking the pretty garden and pool area. The restaurant serves excellent buffets, and nonresidents may make reservations to use the pools and have lunch. A free shuttle bus takes guests to and from town. Credit cards: AE, DC, MC.

Posada de las Monjas

Canal 37, 37700
Tel. 465-2-01-71
Doubles, from $40

This ex-convent with rose-colored stone exterior offers sixty rooms, all on the small side, but comfortable. In addition, there's a newer section with larger, brighter rooms, some with fireplaces. Pretty patios are scattered throughout the property, as are colonial arches and colonnades. Credit cards: AE, MC, V.

Posada de San Francisco

Plaza Principal 2, 37700
Tel. 465-2-00-72

Doubles, from $45

Located in the center of town, right on the *zócalo,* this converted colonial mansion has a large plant-filled interior courtyard with a pretty fountain. Rooms are large and have high ceilings and beams. Although the colonial-style furniture has seen better days, the rooms—and halls—are clean. You'll find a pleasant courtyard restaurant and bar on the premises. Credit cards: AE, MC, V.

Posada la Ermita
Calle Pedro Vargas 64, 37700
Tel. 465-2-07-77
Doubles, from $40

Anyone who has enjoyed the performances of Cantinflas will love Posada la Ermita. The hotel belongs to the Mexican comedian and has lots of his memorabilia, including a huge mural of his celebrity friends and him. The setup is villa-like, with 24 junior suites and small individual patios arranged on a hillside overlooking San Miguel de Allende. There's also a very pleasant restaurant with an equally spectacular view of town. Credit cards: MC, V.

Villa Jacaranda
Calle Aldama 53, 37700
Tel. 465-2-08-11
Doubles, from $60

Gloria and Don Fenton welcome you to the Villa Jacaranda as though you were their personal houseguests. There are 12 full and junior suites, individually furnished with colorful Mexican crafts and original art. You can enjoy a delightful garden, and a fine, somewhat pricey, restaurant. Credit cards: MC, V.

Life in San Miguel de Allende centers around the charming **zócalo,** also called **El Jardín** or **Plaza de Allende.** The town's **Parroquía,** or parish church, was built in 1880 by the self-taught Indian architect Ceferino Gutiérrez, who modeled it after what he knew of the great European cathedrals. Inside, the **Capilla del Señor de la Conquista** houses a famous 16th-century statue, Cristo de la Conquista, made in Patzcuaro by the Indians out of corn paste and crushed orchid tubers. There are also beautiful wall paintings and works done by architect Francisco Eduardo Tresguerras, as well as tombs of several important Mexicans. Nearby is the lovely baroque 18th-century **Church of San Rafael.**

On the southwest corner of the *zócalo* is the **Museo de la Casa de Allende,** in the baroque mansion in which Ignacio de Allende was born. The museum has exhibitions of colonial furnishings and accessories and historical documents having to do with Allende and independence. Open Tuesday through Saturday from 10 A.M. to 4 P.M. and Sunday from 10 A.M. to 2 P.M. Across Plaza de Allende, on Calle Reloj, is the **Casa de los Conspiradores,** the house that had been occu-

I walked to the center of town, to a square lined with benches and trees, which in most parts of Mexico is called the *zócalo,* but in San Miguel is called the *jardín,* where an odd procession passed in front of me. A circle of girls walked in the clockwise direction around the perimeters of the jardín, perhaps half the distance of a square city block. There were at least a hundred of them. And encircling them, moving counterclockwise, was a group of young men. Hesitating, I cut through their circle and sat down on a bench, where I watched as the single men and women of the town encircled each other on and on into the darkness in this ritualized form of courtship—called the promenade—which would occur every night at the hour when the birds came home to rest in the trees of the jardín.

—Mary Morris
Nothing to Declare, 1988

pied by Allende's brother and where independence-movement meetings were held.

Casa del Mayorazgo de Canal, on the northwest corner of the *zócalo* at Calle Canal 6, is the former home of the Count of Canal. The mansion has a splendid inner courtyard and magnificently carved baroque wooden doors. Also on the *zócalo* are the **Posada San Francisco** and **Palacio Municipal,** both 18th-century buildings.

All around the *zócalo* and along **Calle Canal** are fabulous boutiques and gift shops with fine handicrafts, furniture, and clothing. San Miguel de Allende is one of Mexico's most famous shopping towns. (See **Shopping,** below, for more details.)

The **Convento de la Concepción,** on Calle Canal, was begun in the mid-18th century but was not completed until 1891. The beautiful church dome was designed by Gutiérrez. Inside are religious paintings by Miguel Cabrera. The convent is now used as the **Centro Cultural Ignacio Ramírez,** an arts school under the auspices of the Instituto Nacional de Bellas Artes. There are art exhibitions of works by instructors and students, and an unfinished mural by David Siqueiros.

The **Instituto Allende,** most famous of San Miguel de Allende's art schools, occupies an 18th-century mansion, formerly belonging to the family of the Count of Canal, at Ancha de San Antonio 20. The institute's studios surround several spacious flower-filled courtyards and gardens. There are also two art galleries, a theater, library, and coffee shop. (See **Entertainment,** below, for information about courses of study.)

Several churches are of special interest. One block northeast of the *zócalo,* the **Church of San Francisco,** surrounded by a park with a commemorative statue of Columbus, has an interior designed by Francisco Eduardo Tresguerras.

About two blocks north of the Church of San Francisco is the 18th-century **Oratorio de San Filipe Neri,** a baroque church constructed of pink cantera stone, in which there are a number of Miguel Cabrera paintings. The famous **Santa Casa de Loreto** chapel, sponsored by the Canal family, is located here. The chapel is a copy of the Italian original and houses a much-revered statue of the Virgin. In the octagonally shaped **Camarín** (dressing room), there are five baroque and one neoclassical altars. Statues of the Count of Canal and his wife stand over their tombs. Adjacent to the Oratorio is the mid-18th century **Iglesia de Nuestra Señora de la Salud,** with paintings by Miguel Cabrera and Antonio Torres, among others. An unusual feature on the facade is a carved conch with an Eye of God in its center.

The best overview of town and the surrounding countryside is from **El Mirador,** a lookout point, on Calle Pedro Vargas (named for the famous Mexican singer whose house is nearby), in front of **Posada la Ermita,** a hotel owned by the Mexican entertainer, Cantinflas. There are usually street vendors at El Mirador, with locally made crafts. It's quite a climb up to this spot, so if you don't like walking—or don't have much stamina—take a taxi.

▣ RESTAURANTS

San Miguel de Allende has dozens of eager-to-please restaurants. There's a vast variety of food served, but many of the finest eateries specialize in dishes with an international flavor served in a pure Mexican colonial ambience. The hotel restaurants at Casa de Sierra Nevada and Villa Jacaranda are world-famous.

Bugambilias
Hidalgo 42
Tel. 465-2-01-27

All the Mexican standards are prepared perfectly here, but Bugambilias is noted for its *sopa azteca,* a rich chicken broth with strips of crisp tortillas and pieces of avocado. The surroundings are pleasant too: a covered courtyard filled with tables and wicker chairs, walls of the surrounding buildings lined with beautiful bougainvillea. Open daily, 11 A.M.–10 P.M. The average cost of dinner for two, with wine, is about $30. No reservations. Credit cards: AE, MC, V.

Casa de Sierra Nevada
Calle Hospicio 35
Tel. 465-2-04-15

The menu at this famous restaurant is more French than Mexican, and the place has an international following. Guests come from far and wide to enjoy the beef brochette, tournedos with béarnaise sauce (lovely!), and other delicious specialties. The restaurant, off the courtyard lobby of the delightful Casa de Sierra Nevada hotel, has charm and elegance, with candlelight and exceptional service. Desserts—and the wine list—are especially noteworthy. Open daily (except Tues.), 1–4:30 P.M. and 8–10:30 P.M. Reservations a must—and call as far in advance as possible. The average cost of dinner for two, with wine, is about $60. Credit cards: MC, V.

La Casona
Canal 21
Tel. 465-2-10-65

The menu here offers everything from hamburgers to spaghetti Alfredo, so this is a good place for an alternative to traditional Mexican cuisine. The setting, however, is purely Mexican colonial. Good wine list. Open daily, 2–10:30 P.M. The average cost of dinner for two, with wine, is about $40. Reservations suggested. Credit cards: AE, MC, V.

La Dolce Vita
Canal 21
No telephone

The local pastry shop serves up terrific coffee and superb sweets, including homemade *gelato*. The fruit flavors are best. The average cost of coffee and dessert for two is about $8. No credit cards.

Hacienda de las Flores
Calle Hospicio 16
Tel. 465-2-18-01

Hotel owner Alicia Franyutti supervises this kitchen with loving care. The menu is made up of her personal recipes, and she will gladly accommodate guests with special requests. Chicken and fish in a variety of lovely sauces are specialties, and the homemade pasta is excellent. A wide variety of wines is offered. Breakfast is served to hotel guests only, and the restaurant is closed to nonguests all day on Mon. Otherwise, open for lunch, 1–5 P.M., and for dinner, 7–10 P.M. The average cost of dinner for two, with wine, is about $50. Reservations suggested. No credit cards.

Mamma Mia
Umuran 8
Tel. 465-2-20-63

This exceedingly popular pizza joint offers all sorts of combos prepared as individual pies, served in a covered colonial courtyard. The chic clientele comes for the crust—and for the musical entertainment, ranging from mariachi to Peruvian folk to modern jazz. Good fun. Salads and quesadillas also served. Modest wine list. Open daily, 11 A.M.–1 A.M. The average cost of dinner for two, with wine, is about $28. No reservations. Credit cards: AE, MC, V.

Señor Plato
Jesús 7
Tel. 465-2-06-26

U.S. visitors favor the prime ribs or barbecued spare ribs, but there are also Mexican standards on the menu. The restaurant is in an old courtyard; tables are set elegantly, surrounded by

blue canvas director's chairs. Good wine list. Open 1
P.M.–midnight. The average cost of dinner for two, with wine, is
about $25. No reservations. Credit cards: AE, MC, V.

Villa Jacaranda
Calle Aldama 53
Tel. 465-2-10-15

This hotel restaurant is famous for exquisitely prepared beef
with béarnaise sauce, rack of veal, and a variety of superb chick-
en dishes. The dining room, in the middle of a lovely old colonial
mansion, is equally exquisite. Fine wine list. Open Tues. through
Sun., 1–4:40 P.M. and 8–10:30 P.M. The average cost of dinner
for two, with wine, is about $55. Reservations a must. No credit
cards.

SHOPPING

San Miguel de Allende's shops cater to people who have an
eye for the finer things in life—and a pocketbook large enough
to acquire them. The town's elegant shops are filled with
beautiful objects, a stunning assortment of handicrafts made
locally or imported from other regions of Mexico. Most of the
shopkeepers have exquisite taste and have carefully assembled a most appealing collection of wearables, home accessories, gift items, and collectible art. Shopping San Miguel de
Allende could become a passion.

As you're wandering around the *zócalo,* you'll easily spot
shops of interest. Prices are fixed and it is not advisable to
bargain, unless you're negotiating for an antique or are buying
several items that amount to a substantial sale. Browse before
buying: in San Miguel de Allende, as elsewhere in Mexico,
sales are final. It would be a pity to make a purchase and then
find something you like better, or a very similar item at a better price. Here are some best bets:

Unión de las Artesanias (Plaza Principal 6; no telephone) shows the work of six local craftspeople. The shop
has woven metal baskets with hand-painted flowers, tin and
brass woven wastepaper baskets, large brass peacock mirrors, small pocketbook mirrors in brass cases, brass trivets,
large white hammocks, and beautiful white wool area rugs.

Artes de Tequis (Plaza Principal 20–24; tel. 465-2-03-54)
sells some attractive and quite reasonably priced gift and souvenir items. There are broad leather and cotton belts with
wild geometric patterns, ceramic pots (made in the state of
Michoacán) with pointillistic designs of birds and flowers, and
oversized mugs with pretty hand-painted designs. In the back
room, you'll find a terrific selection of hand-painted ceramic
lamp bases.

Casa Canal (Canal 3; no telephone) is one of San Miguel
de Allende's two most famous shops. In a colonial home-like
setting, the shop displays beautiful and very expensive colonial-style home furnishings, decorative craft items, and won-

derful fashions. Begin with the clothing boutique, featuring the wonderful creations of Josefa. These are dramatic long dresses, caftans, tastefully appliquéd ensembles bedecked with ribbons, and beautifully hued adaptations of traditional Indian clothing. The boutique also has clothes by Opus 1, with fringed caftans and other exotic items. The furniture galleries display hand-carved wooden sets for bedrooms and dining rooms, plus assorted individual chests, headboards, armoires, and cabinets. Smaller items include tableware, lamp bases, and brass and ceramic sculpture. All merchandise is quite expensive.

Joyería Monaco (Canal 13A; no telephone) is a delightful jewelry shop with unusual and reasonably priced pieces, including terrifically sleek and modern pendants made with silver and large polished sections of onyx, plus square- or dot-shaped silver ear posts with onyx, malachite, or turquoise. A stunning silver thick-link bracelet looks quite heavy but is light enough to wear with comfort.

Casa Maxwell (Canal 14 and Umaran 3; tel. 465-2-02-47) is the second of San Miguel de Allende's two most famous shops. It is a sprawling, multilevel mansion with room after room, section after section, and patios of fabulous antique furnishings and all sorts of contemporary Mexican decorative crafts and designer wearables. Take a good long browse through this shop to see the assortment, including hand-carved pine-wood chandeliers; headboards; wooden chests and dressers; carved hard-wood dolphins; colorful woolen area rugs and blankets; hand-blown glasses and pitchers with red, blue, or brown tints; and earthenware table settings from Guadalajara, Guanajuato, and Morelia. The shop also carries fine silver jewelry and designer clothing, including Judith Roberts's denim coats and Irene Pulos's dresses with ribbons, appliqué, and beading.

Platería Cerroblanco (Canal 17; tel. 465-2-05-02) is a family-owned and -run jewelry shop that designs and makes all its own fabulous pieces. The style is modern. There are large smoothed oval chunks of turquoise, onyx, and other semiprecious stones set into sleek square-shaped earrings and matching rings. The shop also specializes in silver and leather bracelets and mother-of-pearl earrings.

The arcade at Canal 21 has several lovely shops. **Tendencia Mexicana** has colorful cotton fashions with appliquéd flowers and birds. Across the patio, **Acento** has stuffed pigs, among other toy animals, made out of plaid, striped, and polka-dot fabrics. **Amanda Boutique** has coats made from handwoven serapes in red, white, and black, plus beaded gourds and masks, handmade leather and cotton shoes, and musician Jim Doney's unique handmade "monocrome" instruments and New Age cassette tapes.

Bazar Unicornio (San Francisco 1; tel. 465-2-13-06) is a vast showcase for home-decorating accessories, including carved wooden masks of devils, angels, monsters, and pirates, thick white woolen handloomed rugs, carved wooden doves perched on driftwood bases, and green metal tissue boxes with matching oval picture frames. There are baskets filled with *milagros* (the small silver medals that religious Mexicans pin beside statues of the saints to ask or give thanks for blessings) and black wooden crosses. The shop also has a large selection of crystals, fossils, and exquisite tooled leather handbags with silver clasps.

La Calandria (San Francisco 5; tel. 465-2-18-80), another home-decorating shop, has large tin chests with etched patterns of flowers and butterflies, hand-painted ceramics, antique wooden medicine cabinets, painted wooden chests, and hand-carved wooden benches with ornately sculpted bases. There are also sets of dishes and J&B bottles that have been cut and filed into sets of tumblers.

El Sombrero (San Francisco 14; no telephone) is a shop that's filled to the brim with hats—beautiful Mexican hats of all shapes, and mostly of straw or sisal. The best hats in the house are the Panama hats that actually hail from the town of Becal, in the state of Campeche. Some of these are so finely woven that you almost can't see the pattern of the weave; these will last forever. The coarser variety has the same basic shape but doesn't wear nearly so well. The shop offers a variety of bands for the hats, and also sells those big gaudy *charro* or mariachi hats, made of black or red felt embroidered with silver or gold thread.

ENTERTAINMENT

One of the centers of cultural life in San Miguel de Allende is the **Instituto Allende** (Ancha de San Antonio 20), which occupies an 18th-century hacienda, formerly the family seat of the Count of Canal. The institute has two art galleries, a theater, library, and café, plus ample studio space for workshops in drawing and painting, printmaking, multimedia sculpture, silver work and jewelry making, enameling, traditional Mexican weaving, textile design, and ceramics. Intensive Spanish courses are also given. Courses may be taken for undergraduate or graduate credit. The institute, which has a minimum attendance requirement of two weeks, makes no provision for housing but will refer students to hotels, apartments, and Mexican families offering room and board. Fees are quite reasonable. For more information on class schedules, special events, and fees, write to Instituto Allende, San Miguel de Allende, Guanajuato, Mexico C.P. 37700, or call 465-2-01-90.

For evening entertainment, San Miguel de Allende has several discos. Most popular is **The Ring** (Calle Hidalgo 25), in a converted cockfighting ring. Many of San Miguel de Allende's bars and restaurants have live music in the evenings. **Mamma Mia,** a pizza restaurant, features bands ranging from mariachi to Peruvian folk to modern jazz, plus good food. The music usually begins at around 9 P.M. and continues until closing at 1 A.M. **La Fragua** (Cuna de Allende 3) is San Miguel de Allende's salsa scene, with terrific bands and a small dance floor. **Pancho & Lefty's** (Calle Mesones 99) is a lively bar with a Western theme and loud live music.

Some of the hotels and restaurants in town have **cinema clubs** that periodically run theme series or retrospectives of the films of major directors or stars. Check with local newspapers or your concierge for current programs.

EXCURSIONS

Whether you're one of the travelers who is fortunate enough to be settling in San Miguel de Allende for several months, or is making the most of a brief visit, you'll want to make your way to the other towns along the Independence Trail. Dolores Hidalgo (the birthplace of Mexican independence), Guadalajara, Guanajuato, and Querétaro are all easily accessible.

Queretaro

The state of Querétaro, along with the state of Guanajuato, is the heart of Mexico's Central Highlands and of the Bajío, the fertile plateau that is the country's granary. Querétaro, located between the western and eastern ridges of the Sierra Madre, is hilly country, rich in minerals, most notably mercury and opals.

The city of Querétaro, capital of the state of Querétaro, is a regular stop on Mexico's Independence Trail, a popular tourist route that traces historical developments leading up to Mexico's independence from Spain. Querétaro is to Mexico what Concord and Lexington are to the United States. Mexican vacationers have been following the Independence Trail for years, and it is now catching on with foreigners who want to know more about Mexico's history and understand why Mexico's pantheon of heroes—Hidalgo, Allende, Morelos, Juárez, and others—is so revered.

Today Querétaro is an industrial city, but the factories have been built on the outskirts of town, and the charming colonial center, so filled with history, has been left intact. This is a delightful place for an entertaining and informative stroll.

CONNECTIONS

Querétaro has no commercial airport. You can drive here from Mexico City on toll road MEX57. The distance is about 150 miles and takes about three hours. To get to MEX57, take Paseo de la Reforma through Chapultepec Park to Periférico Norte. Traffic is very congested on this road during evening rush hours.

The Ferrocarriles Nacionales de México's Servicio Estrella de Pasajeros offers excellent first-class train service from Mexico City to Querétaro. *El Constitucionalista,* as the train is known, leaves Mexico City at 7:35 A.M. and arrives in Querétaro at 10:45 A.M. Returning to Mexico City, the train leaves Querétaro at 6 P.M. and arrives in Mexico City at 9 P.M. First-class tickets cost about $9 and include a full breakfast. Telephone 463-2-17-03, in Querétaro, or 5-547-5819, in Mexico City, for information and reservations.

Because Querétaro is on the main toll road from Mexico City, bus service is frequent and rapid. Flecha Amarilla buses leave Mexico City for Querétaro about every 15 minutes all day long. Other bus companies, including Tres Estrellas de Oro and Omnibus de México have less frequent service, but their buses are first-class—a distinct advantage on the three-hour trip.

🧳 HOTELS

As a regular stop on Mexico's Independence Trail, Querétaro has a number of excellent hotels in all price ranges. Querétaro's most important sights are rather spread out, and no hotel will put you within walking distance of everything you want to see. Choose a place where you can relax a bit, perhaps take a swim and some sun, before continuing on to explore the other colonial towns in the Central Highlands area. All hotels listed below are air-conditioned unless otherwise indicated.

Hacienda Jurica
Km 229 on MEX57 (going toward San Luis Potosí), 78000
Tel. 463-8-01-42
Doubles, from $55

Located about five miles north of Querétaro, this lovely hacienda-style, self-contained resort, run by the Camino Real chain, offers guests tennis, golf, horseback riding, swimming, and evening entertainment. The rooms are along colonnaded walkways surrounding pretty patios and delightful topiary gardens. Rooms are average-sized and have modern, cared-for furnishings. Excellent restaurant and bar with entertainment. Outdoor buffets are sometimes offered, especially for large groups or conventions. You need a car to get into town if you're staying here. Credit cards: AE, DC.

Holiday Inn
Carretera Constitución Sur 13, 76010
Tel. 463-6-02-02 or 800-465-4329
Doubles, from $65

From the outside, this Holiday Inn looks like a colonial hacienda, and that impression is carried through in the reception area, lobby restaurant, and bar. The rooms are attractively furnished with colonial-style furniture, canopy beds, servibars, and cable TV. The grounds offer gardens, a pool, and tennis courts, and the restaurant offers a good Mexican breakfast buffet. Credit cards: AE, DC, MC, V.

El Mesón de Santa Rosa
Pasteur Sur 17, Plaza de la Independencia, 76000
Tel. 463-4-56-23
Doubles, from $85

This distinctive and lovely hotel is a converted 18th-century town house. The 21 suites and duplexes, elegantly and individually decorated, are arranged around an attractive pastel-pink courtyard with a pretty blue-and-white tiled fountain. The hotel is located on a quiet, very pleasant plaza. Credit cards: AE, DC, V.

Hotel Real de Minas
Avenida Constituyentes Poniente 124, 76000
Tel. 463-6-04-44
Doubles, from $70

A very pleasant lobby with sturdy wicker furniture and high-beamed ceilings opens out to an interior courtyard with a large free-form geometric pool. A series of two-story hotel wings with cheerful and colorfully decorated rooms surrounds this area, and there's an enormous dining room with handsome fireplace and a breezy bar. You'll also find tennis courts and a game room. Credit cards: AE, DC, MC, V.

On the south side of the **zócalo,** known as **Plaza de la Constitución,** is the **Convent of San Antonio,** a lovely mid-16th-century building that now houses the **Museo Regional de Querétaro,** with a wonderful collection of colonial secular and religious paintings, plus fascinating historical documents and arms.

Nearby on Avenida 5 de Mayo is the **Palacio Municipal** (Town Hall), an 18th-century building with wrought-iron balconies, where independence leaders were meeting when they were warned that the Spanish had discovered their plot. Town Hall is also known as **Casa de la Corregidora,** in memory of Doña Josefa Ortiz de Dominguez, who warned of the discovery. The neighboring building, **Casa Municipal,** also has wrought-iron balconies.

On Avenida Venustiano Carranza, to the east of the *zócalo,* is the **Convento de la Cruz,** a sprawling baroque structure now only partially occupied by a museum containing wonderful historical paintings, furnishings, and documents. Most fascinating is the kitchen area, which contains huge ovens and some old cooking utensils. Founded in the 16th century but rebuilt in the 17th century, this baroque building is where

Maximilian had his headquarters in 1867 and where he was imprisoned in a small room with a narrow bed and small desk until the time of his trial and execution. In the **Convent Garden** is the Cross Tree, a much-revered pine tree with needles shaped like crosses.

Across the street is the **Capilla del Calvario,** a 17th-century church said to be the site of the first Spanish Mass in the area.

Two interesting colonial buildings are on Avenida Francisco Madero, southwest of the *zócalo*. On the left-hand side of the street is the **Hostería de la Marquesa,** built during the mid-1700s, and on the right-hand side of the street is the late-17th-century **Iglesia de San José de Gracia.** Farther along the street, at the corner of Madero and Allende, is a garden with the **Neptune Fountain,** built in 1797 by famous architect Francisco Eduardo Tresguerras. Adjacent to the garden is the **Church of Santa Clara.** The 16th-century facade is rather unadorned, but the interior is all fine churrigueresque artistry, with carved and gilded figures of the apostles and saints, cherubim and flowers, and leaf motifs. On the wooden choir screen is a beautiful figure of Christ.

On Calle Guerrero, the **Palacio Federal,** which began as an Augustinian convent dating from the early 18th century, was designed by Ignacio Mariano de las Casas. It has a fabulous baroque facade. Across the street is the 17th-century **Church of Santo Domingo,** with a handsome but plain facade, and the **Chapel of the Rosary,** built in 1760 by de las Casas in the baroque style. De las Casas's own house, called **Casa de los Perros** because of its doglike gargoyles, is around the corner on Calle Allende Sur. This 18th-century mansion has a lovely patio with a beautiful baroque fountain.

The **Iglesia de Santa Rosa de Viturbo,** around the corner on Avenida General de Arteaga, near Calle Ezequiel Montes, was also built by de las Casas. Completed in 1752 and later altered by architect Tresguerras, the church's most unusual detail is its heavy flying buttresses supported by large square columns. The interior is purely churrigueresque, adorned with colonial paintings, a magnificently carved confessional, and life-sized statues of the apostles at the Last Supper.

On the outskirts of town, to the west, is **Cerro de las Campañas** (Hill of the Bells), where Maximilian and his generals, Miramon and Mejia, were executed by shooting. The hill has two memorials. A small and lovely chapel, the **Capilla de Maximiliano,** was built in 1901 by Franz Joseph of Austria in memory of his brother, the ill-fated Maximilian. Standing on a plateau in front of the chapel is a monumental **Statue of Benito Juárez,** with stern expression and slogans from the reform movement. It is visible from all of Querétaro as a constant reminder to citizens of the important role their town played in the Mexican independence and reform movements.

🍵 RESTAURANTS

You'll find on the menus of many Querétaro restaurants two local favorites: goat (or kid), and rabbit, stewed or roasted. If those don't appeal to you, try some other Mexican standard. There are always enchiladas and quesadillas, all sorts of chicken dishes, and some fish.

Café Viena

Avenida 16 de Septiembre Poniente 8
No telephone

An unpretentious café and restaurant, with good food and low prices, Café Viena offers *vieja ropa* (which means "old clothes," but not to worry—in this case, it's a savory meat stew) as a specialty. Other Mexican favorites are available here as well. Open daily, 8 A.M.–10 P.M. The average price of dinner for two is about $15. No reservations. No credit cards.

La Estancia de Querétaro

On the road toward San Luis Potosí
Tel. 463-7-04-05

La Estancia is a delightful hacienda converted into a gourmet restaurant and bar. There are several dining rooms, all with stone walls and wood-beamed ceilings, fireplaces, and colonial art. The menu offers an excellent selection of typical Mexican dishes and grilled meats, chicken, and fish, and a good wine list. Music for dancing nightly. Open daily 1–4 P.M. and 6–10 P.M. The average cost of dinner for two, including wine, is about $50. Reservations suggested. Credit cards: AE, MC, V.

La Flor de Querétaro

Avenida Juárez Norte 5
Tel. 463-2-01-99

This convenient restaurant is one of the most popular in town, with locals and visitors alike. The menu offers a large selection of food, prepared mostly Mexican-style; homemade soups are the specialty. The simple and charming decor features old photos on wood-paneled walls. Open daily 9 A.M.–midnight. The average price of dinner for two is about $23. No reservations. Credit cards: AE, MC, V.

Fonda del Refugio

Jardín Corregidora 26
Tel. 463-2-07-55

Dine indoors or on the charming patio of this delightful restaurant that offers a large selection of typical Mexican dishes, including *carnitas* and enchiladas, as well as Chateaubriand and chops. Modest wine list. Open daily 1–10 P.M. The average price of dinner for two, with wine, is about $38. No reservations. Credit cards: AE, MC, V.

El Mesón de Santa Rosa
Pasteur Sur 17, Plaza de la Independencia
Tel. 463-4-57-81

This hotel restaurant is an elegant intimate eatery with fine Mexican and international fare, including beef, goat, rabbit, chicken, and fish dishes, plus quesadillas and other typical Mexican treats. The decor is colonial and charming, with stenciled walls and shell-shaped arches; the ambience is quiet and relaxing. Best tables are those with fountain views. Good wine list. Open daily, 7 A.M.–10 P.M., Sun. to 5 P.M. The average price of dinner for two, with wine, is about $45. Reservations suggested. Credit cards: AE, MC, V.

Restaurante los Balcones
Independencia Oriente 111
No telephone

Goat and rabbit are among the local specialties offered on the menu of this popular family-style restaurant, but if these don't appeal to you, you can get a lovely roasted chicken or a lighter meal of tacos or enchiladas. The food is fresh and reasonably priced. Open daily, 9 A.M.–9 P.M. The average price of dinner for two is about $15. No reservations. No credit cards.

Truchuelo
Calles de Juan Caballero y Ogio and Angela Peralto, one block from the *zócalo*
No telephone

A delightfully elegant bistro and bar features cheerful table settings of blue and white with fresh flowers. The menu offers well-prepared Mexican and international standards, and there's a wine list with good domestic labels. Open daily (except Tues.), 11 A.M.–3 P.M. and 7–10 P.M. The average price of dinner for two, with wine, is about $40. No reservations. Credit cards: AE, MC, V.

SHOPPING

Querétaro has its share of pleasant boutiques, but there's really only one reason to shop in this town: opals. Querétaro is one of the world's opal capitals. These fiery semiprecious gemstones are mined in the surrounding hills, refined at local factories, and sold in charming small jewelry shops. Opals are graded by color and fire. You'll find all grades of stones, loose or set, at very reasonable prices. Shops around the *zócalo* and on side streets are more or less equivalent to one another in quality, price, and reliability. If you are planning to go to Querétaro and are thinking about buying opals, ask your local jeweler for some tips about what indications of quality to look for, and get some sample prices. That way you'll be able to make an informed purchase and save yourself the heartache of paying a large sum for a stone of little value. Topaz and aquamarine are also mined in Querétaro and are reasonably priced in the town's jewelry shops.

ENTERTAINMENT

Querétaro's nightlife is relatively quiet. Restaurants are usually open until 10 or 11 P.M., and some of the hotel bars have live entertainment.

Theater performances are presented at the **Corral de Comedias** (Orgullo de Querétaro, Venustiano Carranza 39; tel. 463-2-01-65), a courtyard theater, with fun and inventive shows ranging from presentations of Volpone for adults to kiddie puppet extravaganzas. With the show comes a wine and cheese party. The schedule is irregular, so check with your concierge for current programs.

The **Casa Municipal de Cultura de Querétaro** (5 de Mayo 40; tel. 463-2-56-14), sponsored in part by Mexico's Instituto Nacional de Bellas Artes, is located in a lovely colonial building with a pretty courtyard. This municipal arts organization presents theater, Ballet Folklórico, and art exhibitions, many of which are the product of local talent. There are also workshops and classes. Check the Casa Municipal's bulletin board or ask your concierge for current schedules.

EXCURSIONS

Within the vicinity of Querétaro are five missions founded by Brother Junipero Serra, the Franciscan friar who later founded the missions that became Los Angeles and San Francisco. The missions in the Querétaro area are **Jalpan** (with a beautiful baroque church built between 1751 and 1758, dedicated to Saint James); **Concha** (24 miles from Jalpan); **Tilalco** (31 miles from Jalpan); **Landa** (13 miles from Jalpan); and **Tancoyol** (37 miles from Jalpan). You need a car to visit the missions, and your concierge can give you driving directions so that you can make a loop tour of all of them.

San Juan del Río, 34 miles east of Querétaro, is a little town noted for basketry and furniture making. It's fun to drive out here for a day of browsing and bargaining.

Tequisquiapan, 16 miles northeast of San Juan del Río (or about 47 miles direct from Querétaro on the toll road to Mexico City), is a popular weekend getaway for people who live in Querétaro. The town has great charm, with cobblestone streets lined with little craft boutiques. Around the end of May or the beginning of June, the town hosts the annual **Feria Nacional del Queso y el Vino,** a wine and cheese festival, with painting and craft exhibitions, *charreadas* (rodeos), and lots of wine sipping and cheese tasting. Popular throughout the year are Tequisquiapan's thermal hot springs (with radioactive water, said to have therapeutic powers against a wide variety of ailments).

Morelia

Morelia, capital of the state of Michoacán, is about halfway between Mexico City and Guadalajara. The city is on the banks of the Río Grande de Morelia, in a wide and fertile valley basin high in Mexico's Central Highlands, at an altitude of about 6,400 feet. In the area surrounding the city, Michoacán has a varied geography of plateaus, valleys, rivers, volcanoes, gorges, waterfalls, and mountains covered with dense forests. Michoacán is a beautiful state, and Morelia, with a touch of old-world Spanish elegance, is a beautiful city. The colonial buildings and ambience of the town are carefully preserved. Morelia's outstanding university is a leading center for studies in ethnology, as well as Mexican history and culture, and the city shows full support for the variety of local traditional handicrafts for which the state of Michoacán is famous.

CONNECTIONS

Morelia has an airport, but at press time, no major airline is flying there. The regional airline Aeromar (tel. 800-950-0747) offers service from Mexico City to Morelia.

There is excellent train service from Mexico City to Morelia on the Ferrocarriles Nacionales de México's Servicio Estrella de Pasajeros first-class overnight train *El Perepecha.* The train leaves Mexico City at 10 P.M. and arrives in Morelia the following morning at 6:30 A.M., with continuing service to Pátzcuaro (arrives at 8 A.M.) and Uruapan (arrives at 10:10 A.M.). Single and double sleeperettes are available for those bound for Morelia for about $15 and $25, respectively, with dinner in the train's dining car included. On the return trip, trains depart from Morelia at 11:05 P.M., and arrive in Mexico City the following morning at 7:20 A.M. For reservations call 5-547-5819 in Mexico City, 451-2-02-93 in Morelia.

There is frequent first-class bus service between Morelia and Guadalajara, Guanajuato, and Mexico City. Buses arrive at and leave from Morelia's Central Camionera at Valentin Gomez Farias and Eduardo Ruíz. Current schedules are available at the bus terminal.

If you're driving, you can make the trip between Mexico City and Morelia in about five and a half hours. Take MEX15 all the way. It's an incredibly scenic route, but there's a lot of twisting mountain road that can be dangerous, especially during the rainy season—so drive very carefully. You can also drive to Guanajuato and Guadalajara via MEX43 to Irapuato, then north to Guanajuato (about 96 miles) or west to Guadalajara (about 173 miles).

Morelia is a great city for strolling. Most of the interesting sights in Morelia are within walking distance of the *zócalo.* But a car is essential if you want to visit Michoacán's wonderful crafts towns. If you need to rent a car in Morelia, remember that you will save considerably on the daily rental fee and get unlimited free mileage only if you reserve your car in advance in the United States, if possible.

🧳 HOTELS

Morelia lives up to all accommodations expectations that one would have of a charming colonial town. The selections here also provide the modern comforts and amenities—and all are air-conditioned unless otherwise noted.

Hotel Calinda Morelia
MEX15 at Carretera 3466, 58000
Tel. 451-4-57-05 or 800-228-5151
Doubles, from $65

The Calinda Morelia, run by Quality Inn, is well kept and comfortable. There are 125 modern rooms with colonial motifs. The restaurant is reliable, the bar has entertainment, and there's a pool. The hotel is across the street from a shopping mall, but it's a bit far from the center of town. Credit cards: AE, DC, MC, V.

Posada de la Soledad
Zaragoza 86, 58000
Tel. 451-2-18-88
Doubles, from $60

This 18th-century building was the first inn in Morelia. In colonial times, it was an overnight hospice for Augustinian monks. Now the sixty rooms are completely modernized and charming, though they do vary greatly in size. Some rooms have fireplaces; double rooms on the main courtyard are the biggest and best. The colonial atmosphere has been maintained, and you'll find lovely arcades and a wonderful courtyard with a fountain. Good restaurant and lobby bar. Credit cards: AE, DC, MC, V.

Villa Montana
Santa Maria Hills, 58000
Tel. 451-4-02-31
Doubles, from $100

This self-contained resort hotel has 69 individual cottages arranged around landscaped gardens and patios. Each room or suite is decorated uniquely: Some are duplexes; others have fireplaces and private patios; most have spectacular views of Morelia. A heated pool, tennis courts, restaurant and bar with entertainment, crafts shop, and game room are all on the premises, which are unfortunately a bit far from the center of town: You'll need a car, or you'll have to rely on taxis. Credit cards: MC, V.

Hotel Virrey de Mendoza
Portal Matamoros 16, 58000
Tel. 451-2-06-33 or 800-528-1234
Doubles, from $55

Managed by Best Western, this converted colonial mansion has fifty charming rooms decorated with antique furniture arranged around a glass-covered courtyard enclosing the hotel's lobby and restaurant. Some of the rooms have terrific cityscape views of the cathedral. There's a bar with evening entertainment. Credit cards: AE, DC, MC, V.

Morelia's **zócalo,** the Plaza de los Mártires, is surrounded on three sides by arcades with shops and cafés, and on the east side is the **cathedral.** This brownish-pink stone structure was begun in the early 1600s and took about a century to complete. It has a magnificent tiled dome and two towers that are about two hundred feet tall, making this the tallest cathedral in Mexico. Inside there are paintings by Miguel Cabrera, José María Ibarra, and other leading religious artists of the colonial period, as well as a crucifix by Manuel Tolsa. This cathedral is considered to be one of the finest churrigue-resque-style buildings in Mexico.

In the center of the *zócalo* there is a pretty silver-domed **kiosk** used for public concerts. On the corner west of the cathedral is the **Hotel Virrey de Mendoza,** an 18th-century mansion now converted into an intimate hotel. The charming covered courtyard is worth a visit.

The **Government Palace,** across Avenida Madero, faces the cathedral. A baroque building constructed between 1732 and 1770, the palace contains huge murals by Alfredo Zalce that depict Mexican historical and social developments from the struggle for independence through the reform and Revolution.

On Avenida Madero Poniente is Morelia's famous **Mercado de Dulces** (Sweets Market), filled with stalls selling nothing but exotic sweets, including *ates* (a kind of fruit paste) made from guava or mango, crystallized tamarind, and fruit jellies. There are also all sorts of delicious nut brittles. These tend to be very, very sweet—so you don't need a great quantity.

On Calle Galeana and Avenida Madero Poniente is the **Colegio de San Nicolás,** the second-oldest college in North America (after the Colegio de Santa Cruz in Tlatelolco). It was founded by Bishop Vasco de Quiroga in Pátzcuaro in 1540 and later moved to the current site. Miguel Hidalgo was both a student and teacher at the college, which is now a part of the university. The beautiful building surrounds a large courtyard with two stories of baroque arcades.

Opposite the *colegio* is **La Biblioteca,** Morelia's library with an important collection of Jesuit manuscripts. It occupies the **Iglesia de la Compañía,** built between 1660 and 1681 and formerly a Jesuit church. Next to the church is the **Palacio Clavijero,** a 17th-century building that now houses the **tourist office** and other government offices.

On Madero Oriente is the **Palacio de Gobierno,** the state capitol, located in a former seminary from which José Morelos, Melchor Ocampo (a member of Juárez's cabinet), and

Augustín de Iturbide (briefly emperor of Mexico) were graduated. Muralist Alfredo Zalce has decorated the stairway and second floor with paintings of Mexican political heroes and villains. Open daily from 8 A.M. to 9 P.M.

Nearby, on the corner of calles Allende and Abasolo, is the **Museo Regional de Michoacán,** with a fine collection of pre-Hispanic artifacts, colonial furniture, arms, religious art, and magnificent frescoes by Alfredo Zalce and Frederico Cantu. The 18th-century building was the emperor Maximilian's residence in Michoacán. Open Tuesday through Saturday from 9 A.M. to 6 P.M., Sunday from 9 A.M. to 3 P.M.

A small and very pretty plaza at Santiago Tapia and Nigromante has bronze statues of Bishop de Quiroga and Miguel de Cervantes, and is dominated by the **Church of Santa Rosa,** built in the late 16th century with a lovely and unusual double doorway adorning a baroque facade. The inside is decorated with magnificent gilded and painted *retablos.*

Also on the plaza is the **Conservatory of Music,** one of the oldest music conservatories in the Americas and now the headquarters for the famous Children's Choir of Morelia. Check with the tourist office or local newspapers for current performance schedules. At the end of the plaza, at calles Santiago Tapia and Guillermo Prieto, is the **Museo del Estado,** a historical museum exhibiting documents and all sorts of artifacts having to do with the political and economic development of Michoacán. There are fascinating displays about the Tarascan culture and way of life. Open Monday through Friday from 9 A.M. to 2 P.M. and 4 to 8 P.M., Saturday and Sunday from 10 A.M. to 7 P.M.

Nearby, the **Museo de Arte Colonial** at Benito Juárez 240, has a famous collection of colonial religious art from the 16th to 18th centuries. One room is filled with exquisite paintings by Miguel Cabrera. Open Tuesday through Sunday from 10 A.M. to 2 P.M. and 4 to 8 P.M. Contemporary art is exhibited at the **Casa de la Cultura,** at Morelos Norte and Zapata.

Near the Museo del Estado, on Corregidora, is the **birthplace of Morelos,** now used as a library. The Mexican hero was born here on September 30, 1765. He later moved to another house at the corner of Morelos Sur and Aldama, just two blocks away. This colonial building is now a **Morelos Museum,** with memorabilia, documents, and furniture from the life and times of Morelos. On display is the blindfold Morelos wore when he was executed by a firing squad. Open daily from 9 A.M. to 7 P.M. Admission is charged.

At Plaza Valladolid, the **Church of San Francisco** is the oldest church in Morelia, built in 1540 with an impressive tiled dome. The adjacent convent buildings now house the **Palacio de Artesanias,** with superb displays of regional handicrafts (see **Shopping,** below).

A little bit outside the center of town, there are impressive 18th-century stone **aqueducts,** with 253 arches in a one-mile span. The aqueduct was built in 1785 to alleviate a two-year drought. The arches are dramatically spotlighted at night. In the vicinity of the aqueduct is the main campus of the **University of Michoacán** and **Bosque de Cuauhtémoc,** an expansive park with the **Museum of Contemporary Art,** which has a permanent collection of work by Alfredo Zalce and changing shows of Mexican modernists. Open Tuesday through Sunday from 10 A.M. to 2 P.M. and 4 to 7 P.M.

☕ RESTAURANTS

Morelia's hotel dining rooms are very popular with locals as well as with travelers, but there are several additional restaurants that are especially pleasant. While you're in this area, try the tasty Pátzcuaro trout. Other local specialties include roasted *cabrito* (kid) and wild boar.

Boca del Río
Santiago Tapia and Gomez Farias
No telephone

This local seafood stop offers terrific ceviche, shrimp with garlic, and Pátzcuaro trout, all very fresh and finely prepared. Modest wine list. Open daily, 8 A.M.–9 P.M. The average cost of dinner for two, with wine, is about $30. No reservations. Credit cards: AE, MC, V.

Las Bugambilias
Avenida Las Camelinas 514
Tel. 451-4-70-62

Roasted goat and wild boar are local favorites, and this is a good place to sample them. But if they seem too gamey for you, the menu has domesticated steaks and other dishes that will delight. Good wine list. Open daily, 1–10 P.M. The average cost of dinner for two, with wine, is about $45. No reservations. Credit cards: AE, MC, V.

Los Comensales
Zaragoza 148
No telephone

An unpretentious eatery with a fine menu of Mexican specialties, Los Comensales offers snack foods—quesadillas, *sopes* (tiny tortilla-based pizzas with refried beans, onion, chile, cheese, chicken or sausage, and cream), tamales—all delicious and, in combination, provide a satisfying meal. Open daily, 8 A.M.–10:30 P.M. The average cost of dinner for two, with wine, is about $28. No reservations. No credit cards.

La Fuente
Avenida Madero Oriente 493B
No telephone

Excellent vegetarian dishes ranging from stir-fries to curries are offered here, along with rice, tortillas, and salads. Open daily for lunch only, 1:30–5 P.M. The average cost of a meal for two is about $10. No reservations. No credit cards.

Grill de Enrique
Hidalgo 54
No telephone

One of the specialties of the house here is roasted quail, a local favorite; another is *cecina,* a type of dried and seasoned beef. The menu also offers steaks and chicken. Modest wine list. Open daily, 1–11 P.M. The average cost of dinner for two, with wine, is about $35. No reservations. Credit cards: AE, MC, V.

Las Morelianas
El Retajo 90
Tel. 451-4-08-91

A most unlikely edition of the Carlos Anderson chain of restaurants, Las Morelianas has a more formal atmosphere than the Carlos 'n Charlie's around Mexico. The menu is similar, however, with terrific barbecued ribs, seafood, soups, and salads, and a good wine list. Open daily, 11 A.M.–11 P.M. The average cost of dinner for two, with wine, is about $45. Reservations suggested. Credit cards: MC, V.

SHOPPING

Michoacán is famous for its fabulous handicrafts, produced in small towns throughout the state. There is superb lacquerware, copperware, ceramic figurines, green and brown pottery, straw figurines and baskets, handwoven serapes, guitars, and more. Some of the techniques used by the artisans predate the Spanish arrival in Mexico, and others are modern adaptations of ancient techniques.

As capital of Michoacán, Morelia has access to the best selection of state-wide handicrafts, and there are several shops that should not be missed. The **Casa de las Artesanias** (or El Palacio del Artesano) is a collector's paradise. This government-sponsored gallery and salesroom occupy the ex-convent of San Francisco, next to the San Francisco Church, at Plaza San Francisco near Avenida Bartolome de las Casas. The shop has two floors of rooms filled with wonderful objects from all the state's craft villages. There is also a splendid exhibit of antiques and contemporary pieces that are not for sale but are worth viewing—the workmanship is superb. The casa is open Tuesday through Sunday from 10 A.M. to 8 P.M. A smaller branch of the Casa de las Artesanias is located at the Morelia Convention Center on Ventura Poniente, about two miles from the center of town. Open Monday, and Wednesday through Saturday, from 10 A.M. to 2 P.M. and 4 to 8 P.M., and Sunday from 10 A.M. to 2 P.M. Both casas accept major credit cards. The shop will ship, but if at all possible, take your purchases with you.

Casa Cerda, at Zaragoza 163, is where you can find the unique hand-carved wooden dishes and platters made by the Cerda family. Esperanza Cerda is famous for her dishes, painted in gold and lacquered, in the style that originated in Pátzcuaro. Others in the family work with the lacquer *incrustado* method, now practiced by few artisans.

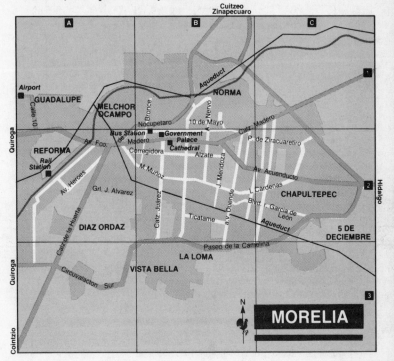

10

BAJA CALIFORNIA, NORTH AND SOUTH

Baja California is that long finger of land extending south from the U.S. state of California, bounded on the west by the waters of the Pacific Ocean and on the east by what the Mexicans call the Sea of Cortés, and the rest of the *norteamericanos* call the Gulf of California.

The name California, according to the state government, has two possible explanations, although there is insufficient data to interpret the meaning positively. Some sources believe it came from now-extinct native dialects, but the other version will give you a more descriptive idea of what sort of climate to expect. The alternate version attributes the name to the Latin words *calida* and *fornax,* meaning "hot oven," supposedly Hernán Cortés's baptism of the hot and arid territory. Yet a third explanation for the name is offered in La Paz at the museum in the old government palace, on the plaza opposite the cathedral. A large mural by artist Francisco Cota depicts Calafia, a mythical queen of a legendary island named California. It was inhabited only by females, and Cota depicts at Calafia's side a mythical beast with a lion's head and horse's ears, an eagle's beak and wings, and a mane like a fish fin. This myth was widely read in Spain during the conquest of the New World, and consequently, according to this version, the first white men to reach Baja named the place California. Calafia is one of the words you will see on Baja wine labels and as hotel names.

Baja has a mystique generated by its long isolation. If, like many of us, you expect the Baja to be one long stretch of sandy desert land, you'd be right except for the surprise of a backbone ridge, a spine of rocky mountains down the center, an extension of the San Jacinto range, which reaches a height of 10,069 feet at its high peak of La Encantada, and offers glorious glimpses of the blue Sea of Cortés. There is a theory, supported by shells found on the mountaintops, that in the distant past the land sank and rose several times.

Baja California is pretty much a land the rain gods forgot—sunny but arid, rocky and brown, mountainous in the center and sandy on the edges, with a wide range of desert vegetation. There are vast forests of giant cactus, heavy growths of barrel cactus, much yucca and ocotillo, as well as the strange-appearing elephant wood (*Veatchia discolor*). The gray cactus and dusty scrub are redeemed by the incredible blue of the Sea of Cortés. "Once in a while, though, the sea gets gray," an expatriate U.S. couple now settled in Santa Rosalía reports. "That's in the winter, when the winds from the north sweep down through Baja like it's a tunnel."

In Baja you wouldn't choose a city as a base and then go explore far afield—since the land is so deserted, the best bet is to see one city at a time, and then travel either up or down the peninsula to the next major stop. The long and often lonely stretch of land is divided, almost in half, at the 28th parallel, into the two states of **Baja California** and **Baja California Sur.** Isolated until 1973, when the Mexican government opened the 1,050-mile Transpeninsular Highway, the Baja is now attracting millions of travelers, but outside the cities the number of visitors does not make a dent in the immensity and desolation of the land. Only since the advent of the highway has Baja been truly open to tourism, and even so, many of the best fishing spots and the most picturesque areas are for the brave who trek or take their four-wheel-drive vehicles off the paved highway onto the treacherous sand.

But this is the place, nevertheless, for fabulous fishing, because Baja California is one of the fishing heavens of the world, with sea bass, dorado, bonito, yellowtail, marlin, sailfish, and tuna leading the list of native game fish. In fact, the Sea of Cortés has been called "the largest fish trap in the world," with its many small, secluded seaside fishing villages for solitude seekers. While these villages are reached only by isolated roads off the main highway, holiday seekers flock to the growing number of glittering resorts catering to land and water sports, as well as fishing.

CONNECTIONS

Mexicana Airlines flies to Los Cabos from Los Angeles, California, and there is some air service from the Mexican mainland to Tijuana, La Paz, and Cabo San Lucas, but the principal way to get around Baja is by car or bus. Mexicana, Aeromexico, and

The climate in **Baja California** is warm in the summer, averaging eighty degrees Fahrenheit, but more temperate in the winter, with winter nights sometimes chilly; a light wrap is a good idea. Dawn in winter can be foggy and arrive with a chill before the sun burns through by midday. **Baja Sur** is warm and dry almost all year, with temperatures usually in the eighties, although in winter, from November to February, they may drop to the sixties. Rarely does the thermometer reach a high of one hundred, and then only between April and October. Rain is extremely scarce along the entire peninsula.

Aero California serve some of the major tourist destinations. Transportation is no problem at the California-Mexico border at Tijuana, where you can simply walk across or take a taxi or bus from San Diego, California. Car-rental agencies have offices in the major cities. The alternative to driving into the interior is traveling by bus (Baja is served by Tres Estrellas de Oro), but bear in mind that the road is long between most towns, and that even on first-class lines the advertised air-conditioning and on-board toilet very often are not present. Both gasoline (as of this writing, less than $.90 a gallon) and bus fares are inexpensive. (The 14-hour bus ride between Ensenada and Loreto is approximately $15.) If you drive away from the large towns, be aware that this is primitive desert country, so follow several stringent rules for your own safety: Drive carefully—the highway is two lanes with mountainous curves; never drive at night; always top off your gas tank at each station along the way (Pemex is the national and only brand); carry one or two days' supply of bottled water (never drink any water but *agua purificado,* purified water, in Baja California); do not camp out in isolated areas unless you are in a large group—there have been recent reports of road incidents involving assaults and robberies, which, though infrequent, are on the rise, so use the same precautions you would use in other unsettled areas of the world. The main highways of Mexico are patrolled by the Angeles Verdes, the Green Angels, who operate a fleet of emergency-service trucks for minor road repairs. They change tires, give first aid, carry gasoline and oil, and are a source of road information. There is no charge except for fuel and parts.

Baja California (North)

The main travelers' destinations in the northern state of Baja California are, on the Pacific side of the peninsula, **Tijuana,** with nearby beaches in Rosarito; **Tecate,** forty miles to the east; and **Ensenada** and **San Quintín** to the south. Along the eastern side are the towns of **Mexicali** on the California–Mexico border, and **San Felipe** on the Sea of Cortés.

Before the two-lane, paved Transpeninsular Highway 1 was built, the only means of transportation from one isolated settlement to the next was on foot, following the shore, for the mountains are inaccessible, or by boat or plane. For centuries the land provided a desolate, inhospitable existence for the native Cochimi, Guaycura, and the Pericu Indians, indigenous peoples who survived by hunting, fishing, and gathering edible native plants. When Cortés arrived in 1535 there were about forty thousand Indians; by the 18th century the number had diminished considerably, with perhaps five thousand remaining; today they are mostly extinct. It was the Italian Jesuits in the 17th century who found the natives to be ripe for conversion. The first Jesuits were Francisco Eusebio Kino, Pedro Matiás Goni, and Friar Juan Mariá Salvatierra, the last founding a mission in Loreto in 1697. Today children play around a pedestal supporting a bust of the good father, facing the mission.

Half a century later, the Italian Jesuits were ousted from all New Spain, and the Franciscans took over their missions. In 1772 they were ousted in turn by the Dominicans, but on the whole the peninsula was ignored and forgotten. No one was interested in the bleak, isolated land, and many of the missionaries moved to the more fertile fields of California, abandoning both missions and Indians. Today's Baja Californians are predominantly descendants of mainland migrants, mixed with traces of early Russian, U.S., and Chinese settlers, the last possibly accounting for the numerous Chinese restaurants found in the larger cities.

It was only after the Mexican Revolution that Baja began to be settled. Prior to that, La Paz was considered an outpost, noted for fishing and pearls, and officials still smart from what they consider neglect by the central government. It was in 1888 that the Californias were divided along the 28th parallel into North and South, and each given its own government. In 1951 the northern half of the peninsula became a state, with the south remaining a federal territory. It was not until 1974 that Baja California Sur was raised, by presidential decree, from a territory to the status of a free and sovereign state. It makes for some confusion to find that the northern state took the name of Baja California, while the southern state calls itself Baja California Sur. Both Baja California and Baja California Sur have been declared duty-free ports in an effort, so far successful, by the government to boost the economy.

Tijuana

Since all Baja California is a duty-free port, it makes for attractive shopping, and along the California-Mexico border in Tijuana, which enjoys a great influx of visitors from California, U.S. dollars are accepted. Just 17 miles south of San Diego, Tijuana, which claims to be the foreign city visited by the most U.S. residents, is Baja California's most renowned city. But for years, Tijuana had suffered from a less-than-savory reputation, from the Prohibition era, when U.S. revelers crossed the border for the forbidden demon drink, to the present-day proximity of San Diego's naval bases. But no longer. In fact, the city could easily adopt the name of Nuevo Tijuana, so fast is it changing its image. In the past several years everything—hotels, restaurants, even the racetrack—has been in the throes of extensive remodeling and renovation, or is about to be remodeled and renovated.

Famed Avenida Revolución has replaced its honky-tonks with reputable stores, and even the red-light district on the east side is disappearing. There are new ways of dealing with visitors—a number of English-speaking police officers, trained specifically to work with travelers, no longer write tickets for minor traffic offenses or meter violations. (But rowdy behavior could produce the same treatment as it would anywhere else in the world, authorities warn.)

The city is pursuing a fresh image due in part to economic reform and the growth of a new machine industry. The city now boasts one of the highest per-capita incomes in Mexico and, with a population of 1.7 million, is the sixth-largest city in the country. The city's commercial and manufacturing boom has created a new middle class, providing so many jobs that Mexican citizens from the interior are pouring into Tijuana in search of work.

And no wonder, for Tijuana is a happy town, happy for and with its visitors, offering fine hotels, good food, lively nightlife, and exciting entertainment, especially in the form of the fast-paced game of jai alai or the faster-still pace at the Thoroughbred and greyhound track. And the ubiquitous sombrero-capped and zebra-striped burros along Avenida Revolución are still there, waiting to be photographed with visitors.

CONNECTIONS

Most visitors to the city usually come from California, with many spending only a few hours, and the Tijuana Trolley runs regularly between downtown San Diego and the border, collecting passengers along the way. Both Mexicoach (tel. 619-232-5049) and Greyhound (88-01-65 in Tijuana) run excursions to Tijuana from San Diego. If you drive a car from California, Mexican car insurance is required. If you don't want to bring your car into Mexico, it can be parked just north of the international line, and you can walk across or take a taxi downtown. Parking in Tijuana is a problem, as is the usually long line of cars waiting to cross back into California—the wait could easily take as long as an hour. Once in Tijuana, for local bus transportation information, there is a kiosk downtown on Avenida Revolución, guiding you, for instance, to the green-and-cream local buses to the racetrack. Taxi rates are both reasonable and not, so try to bargain if the quoted price seems too high. *Colectivos,* multicolored vans that pack in as many passengers as possible but only charge U.S. $.25 a head, run along the main boulevards. Mexicana has flights to Tijuana from Acapulco, Ixtapa-Zihuatanejo, Mexico City, Oaxaca, Villahermosa, and Zacatecas on the mainland.

Tourist information booths are located at both the Mexico–U.S. border and downtown on Avenida Revolución between calles 3 and 4. The Caseta de Información Turistica (tel. 81-73-33 or 84-05-37) is at Revolución and Calle 1. As both a reminder of Tijuana's past reputation and its desire to reform, a 24-hour legal-assistance service has been established, with a lawyer-ombudsman available to help tourists in trouble in Tijuana, Rosarito, Ensenada, Mexicali, and San Felipe. (In Tijuana, Via Oriente 1; tel. 84-21-81 or 84-21-38, 8 A.M. to 3 P.M. In Rosarito, Centro de Gobierno; tel. 2-02-00 or 2-11-21.) The U.S. consulate is located at Calle Tapachula 96, Colonia Hipodromo; tel. 86-10-06; the Canadian consulate is at German Gedovius 5-202, Zona del Río; tel. 84-04-61.

📮 HOTELS

There is a good choice of places to stay in Tijuana, and reservations are a good idea in this popular place. First, Tijuana hotels are listed, followed by those at Rosarito Beach. All are air-conditioned and take major credit cards unless otherwise noted.

Caesar Hotel
Avenida Revolución 827 (at Calle 5), 22000
Tel. 66-85-16-66 and 66-85-16-06
Doubles, about $40
This 1930s landmark in the heart of downtown lays claim to the invention of the Caesar salad. Now rather rundown, Caesar's still has a certain charm, with rooms named after matadors, who have their favorite units when in town. There are 75 rooms, a restaurant and bar, and shops.

El Conquistador
Bulevar Agua Caliente 1777, Apdo. Postal 2491, 22000
Tel. 66-81-79-55 and 66-86-20-10
Doubles, from $60
This 110-room, five-suite, four-star hotel across from the Fiesta Americana has been busy remodeling its rooms and restaurant, which is raising its rates. You'll also find a cocktail lounge, disco, swimming pool, and sauna.

Country Club Motor Hotel
Tapachula 1, Apdo. Postal 1602, 22000
Tel. 66-81-77-33
Doubles, from $43
Remodeled, and enlarged from one hundred guest rooms to 131, this hotel has a spacious glass-and-marble lobby dominated by a wonderful onyx sculpture by Francisco Suñiga. The hotel is a favorite with golfers; its gardens back onto the country club.

Fiesta Americana

Bulevar Agua Caliente 4500, 22420
Tel. 66-81-70-00

Doubles, from $82

This luxury hotel, rated as five-star property in the Mexican system, which takes into account such amenities as elevators and the number of restaurants, is a 22-floor tower with the upper guest rooms sometimes in the clouds on a foggy day. The 430 comfortable rooms each have a king-sized bed; there is the gourmet French restaurant, **Place de la Concorde,** a 24-hour cafeteria, **La Fiesta,** room service, a lobby bar, nightclub and disco, two lighted tennis courts, a Jacuzzi, outdoor swimming pool, gym, and spa. A Foreign Book (an area at which bets can be placed for local and U.S. races) is being added: A $50 fee gets you in, but then the money's for betting on the horses.

Lucerna

Paseo de los Héroes 10902, Apdo. Postal 2552, 22320
Tel. 66-84-01-15

Doubles, from about $60

A modern six-story structure with 168 rooms, Lucerna offers a good restaurant, a disco, and a bar around a beautifully land-scaped courtyard with a lovely swimming pool. A bridge over the pool leads to a large domed convention hall, among other meeting spaces.

Palacio Azteca

Avenida 16 de Septiembre 213
Tel. 66-81-81-00

Doubles, from $50

This is one of the oldest hotels in town, with a dedicated clientele that keeps returning for the good service provided by private owner Mauro Chávez. Added to that are a beautiful palm-fringed pool, two excellent restaurants, two bars, and live music by the same group that has played here for the hotel's 19 years.

Radisson Paraíso Tijuana

Bulevar Agua Caliente 1; send mail inquiries to Box 1588, San Ysidro, California 92073
Tel. 66-81-72-00

Doubles, from about $55

This two-hundred-room hotel next to the country club has undergone a transformation from its past life as a Calinda and an El Presidente, and offers an outdoor swimming pool, Jacuzzi, lobby bar, and two restaurants.

ROSARITO BEACH

Plaza del Mar

Carretera Tijuana-Ensenada km 58, 22000
Tel. 800-528-1234, 423-8835, and 621-0852 in the United States; 85-91-52 in Mexico

Doubles from $55

This Best Western, halfway between Rosarito and Ensenada, has 140 guest rooms, beach and swimming pool, restaurants, disco and bar, and tennis club and spa.

Quinta del Mar

Playas de Rosarito, Apdo. Postal 184, 92073
Tel. 661-2-13-00
Doubles, from $50

This resort has guest rooms, condominiums, and beachfront houses for rent. Featured are a sandy beach, three swimming pools, Jacuzzi, steam baths, spa and massage center, two tennis courts (including one on the hotel's eighth floor), basketball and volleyball courts, three restaurants, three bars including one on the beach, disco, and the Quinta Plaza for shopping.

Rosarito Beach Hotel

Tijuana-Ensenada Hwy. km 27.5; send mail inquiries to Box 145, 92073
Tel. 661-2-11-06 and 2-11-26
Doubles, from $50

This 1926 classic, right on the water's edge, has been recently remodeled. The quaint 135 rooms and suites have catered to many a famous personality. In addition to the beach, you'll find an Olympic swimming pool, exercise center, restaurant and piano bar, Foreign Book, and Ballet Folklórico shows.

It's hard to ignore a **border,** always a romantic sight in any country, especially if seen for the first time, and here the holes in the border fence give pause for reflection. The fence runs along the Tijuana-Ensenada Highway and leads to a beach where a small monument and flag mark what is the southwesternmost point of the United States.

There's nothing like competition to get the blood racing, and Tijuana's biggest excitement centers on the racetrack and the jai alai games. **Agua Caliente Race Track** (Bulevar Agua Caliente; tel. 81-78-11), a bright orange Moorish palace, harbors both horse- and greyhound-racing tracks. Computer technology makes it possible to use any window to wager any amount ($2 minimum) in any combo at any track; there are two Foreign Books. The well-landscaped, almost picturesque track is surrounded by, and peppered with, duck ponds and geese, which appear quite unperturbed by the commotion around them. The huge multilevel glass-enclosed clubhouse houses the Jockey Club, Turf Club, and **La Cupula** restaurant. The year-round racing schedule features greyhounds nightly (except Tuesday) and Thoroughbreds Saturday and Sunday, with Tuesday races from July to September.

The **Jai Alai Palace** (also called **Frontón Palacio;** Avenida Revolución, between calles 7 and 8), features one of Mexico's most exciting sports. Similar to lacrosse and handball but much faster (the rock-hard balls have been clocked at 182 m.p.h.), jai alai originated in the Basque provinces of northern Spain about two hundred years ago. The betting is in dollars, the announcer speaks in English, and there is action every night except Thursdays. The restaurant has a view of the games, and is also open for lunch. Dress can be either informal sports clothes or party attire, depending upon how much of an occasion you want this to be.

Centro Cultural (Paseo de los Héroes at Mina; tel. 84-11-11), is a museum that definitely lives up to its offer of a spectacular view of Mexico. The building itself *is* spectacular, an ultramodern complex centered on a giant round ball of a building. There's plenty to keep adults and children entranced for hours: an Omnimax Theater; a museum offering Mexican symbols on a specially designed ramp; constantly changing temporary exhibits colorfully and imaginatively displayed; a technologically advanced one-thousand-seat theater presenting ballets, concerts, plays (only in Spanish), and traditional Mexican dances; and seasonal outdoor entertainment. Museum hours are 11 A.M. to 8 P.M. daily.

To get the flavor of Tijuana, you'll want to stroll along both **Avenida Revolución** and **Bulevar Agua Caliente.** The first is the prime shopping section in the heart of downtown, extending between calles 1 and 8, where there's action day and night. Many vendors may slightly overdo the insistent invitation to come in and browse, but a quick smile and a "No, gracias," is enough to keep you on your way. Agua Caliente, an extension of Avenida Revolución, has some of the better hotels and restaurants, as well as the racetrack and country club.

Drive or ride a bus along the **Paseo de los Héroes,** where towering statues are planted in the center of landscaped traffic circles. There's a terribly tall Cuauhtémoc, last of the Aztec chieftains; slender and tall Abraham Lincoln, who holds a broken chain to symbolize emancipation; and yet another tall and slender work, this one a modern sculpture in front of the Centro Cultural. Locally dubbed "The Scissors," this piece commemorates the joining of Mexico and the United States in the making of a canal from Tijuana's river.

Plaza Santa Cecelia is a small corner at the bottom of Avenida Revolución, and this is where the mariachis are to be found, garbed in the traditional gold-trimmed black tight pants, matador jackets, and fringed sombreros. These musicians stand around with their instruments, waiting to be hired. But, sad to say, though some attempt has been made to brighten up the plaza, you will find it somewhat tawdry.

Not for the fainthearted are Tijuana's two **bull rings,** and you can choose from larger and lesser spectacles. The best matadors appear at the **Bull Ring by the Sea,** officially known as **Plaza Monumental,** west of town along the Pacific Ocean. The smaller **Toreo de Tijuana** has lesser spectacles, but for both the season runs from May through September, with *corridas* (bullfights) scheduled on Sunday afternoons at one or the other. Tickets are available at the bullring gates or at the entrance to the Sonia Arcade alongside Caesar's Hotel on Avenida Revolución at Calle 5.

A different rousing spectacle is the **Charreada,** a Mexican rodeo, held almost every Sunday at several rings. Two of them are **Misión del Sol** and **Hacienda Arroyo** in Las Playas de Tijuana. Tourist information booths have up-to-date information.

☕ RESTAURANTS

Tijuana offers many good restaurants, some of which are located in hotels. The following were also chosen as among the best representatives of the great variety the city enjoys. As mentioned earlier, Tijuana lays claim, via Caesar's Hotel, to the famous Caesar salad as its contribution to world gastronomy. Unfortunately, too many restaurants list it on the menu, and many drown it in too much of a good thing: the dressing. Food is relatively reasonably priced in Mexico, but prices listed do not include wine, drinks, tax, or tips. Beers include Tecate, Corona, and Pacífico, as well as imported brews. Wines run approximately $2–$3 a glass and approximately $9–$13 a bottle, but could be more in an expensive restaurant. Imported French wines are very expensive; Mexican wines such as Domec, Los Reyes, Quinta El Mirador, and Calafia Santo Tomás are served in the best restaurants. Domec wines, such as Riesling and Blanc de Blanc, and Los Reyes wines are considered better than Calafia wines, but all are products of Baja California served with pride throughout Mexico. And please note that all establishments accept major credit cards unless otherwise noted.

Boccaccio's Nueva Mariana

Bulevar Agua Caliente 2500, across from the country club
Tel. 86-22-66

A favorite for many years, Boccaccio's serves international dishes with emphasis on the Italian, and especially, fine pastas. The average price of a dinner for two is about $35.

Bol Corona

Avenida Revolución 520
Tel. 85-47-08

Here the burritos are the most famous in all Tijuana, and the soups are special, too. The atmosphere in this large emporium is that of an old-time cantina. Open 7 A.M.–4 A.M. The average cost of a dinner for two is about $20.

Carnitas Uruapán

Bulevar Díaz Ordaz 550
Tel. 81-61-81

The specialty here is *carnitas,* cubes of tender roast pork. Mariachis begin to play at about 3 P.M. The average cost of a dinner for two is $20.

Chikky Jai

Avenida Revolución and Calle 7

Tel. 85-49-55

This unusual tiny restaurant serves Basque food, perhaps in homage to the Basque game of jai alai so popular in Tijuana. The average cost of a dinner for two is about $20.

Dragon Plaza
Paseo de los Héroes E-17
Tel. 84-19-63

Chinese food is conveniently served in the Plaza Río shopping mall. The decor in the large, multi-roomed restaurant is worth a quick tour. The average cost of a dinner for two is $12–$14.

La Fonda Roberto
In the Hotel la Sierra, Avenida 16 de Septiembre
Tel. 86-46-87

For award-winning gourmet Mexican food, this is the place. Specialties from Puebla and southern Mexico, such as crêpes with *huitlacoche* (black corn mushrooms) or squash-blossom crêpes in a cream sauce; mole *poblano* (chicken with seven varieties of chile, chocolate, and roasted sesame seeds); *conchinita pibil* (juicy shredded pork seasoned with achiote seeds, cumin, and garlic); *puntas de filete al chipotle* (tenderloin beef tips with adobo sauce served with onions and avocado slices); and *pipián rojo* (with tongue and *nopalitos,* or edible cactus) will make you think you've died and gone to Mexican heaven. The average cost of a dinner for two is about $30.

Margaritas Village
Avenida Revolución 702
Tel. 85-73-62

This lively downstairs Mexican restaurant serves up Ballet Folklórico performances on its stage along with such fine Mexican dishes as *asada azteca.* There's a bar as well, with live music. The average cost of a dinner for two is about $20.

Mr. Fish
Bulevar Agua Caliente 6000, in the center of its own parking lot
Tel. 86-36-03

A thatched hut serving a wide variety of seafood, this restaurant offers clam chowder and shrimp with mango and steamed or fried whole fish as specialties.

Pedrin's
On the corner of Avenida Revolución and Calle 7
Tel. 85-40-62

Specializing in seafood, from lobster thermidor to *huachinanga a la veracruzana,* Pedrin's is another classic. The second floor has large windows overlooking the action on Avenida Revolución, and the restaurant is always packed, upstairs and down. The average cost of a dinner for two is about $25.

Place de la Concorde
Bulevar Agua Caliente 4500
Tel. 81-70-00

A great dining experience in the French manner, with spotless napery, sparkling crystal, and waiters in formal dress, is offered here. The menu is international, and the wine list extensive. The average cost of a dinner for two is upwards of $30.

BEACHES

Tijuana is almost the only city in Baja California not on the water (Tecate and Mexicali are the others), but nearby **Rosarito Beach,** 18 miles south of Tijuana, is a fast-growing resort featuring swimming, surfing, horseback riding, camping, and both newly built and recently remodeled resort hotels. There are many great small seafood restaurants and some outstanding interior design and jewelry shops. **Puerto Nuevo** is famous for lobster, beginning with lobster burritos, "which you *must* stop for," counsel the locals.

SPORTS

Tijuana is not much of a participation-sports town, but the **Club Campestre** (Country Club; tel. 81-78-51) is open to the public and has a restaurant as well as golf greens. The **Fiesta Americana Hotel,** next door (on Bulevar Agua Caliente), has two lighted tennis courts.

SHOPPING

Although **Avenida Revolución** is still the main shopping drag (it even boasts a chrome-and-glass drug store), there are several new shopping malls, such as the **Plaza Río** on Paseo de los Héroes, and the charming new **Plaza Fiesta,** a colonial mall across from the Centro Cultural, with specialty shops and restaurants whose bright awnings give it a European flair. Others off the beaten track are **Dorian's** in the Plaza Río, a Mexican department-store experience if ever there was one, with clothing for men and women; Mexican blown glass at **El Toreo** in front of the bullring at Bulevar Agua Caliente 677; and handbags and leather goods at **Castillo,** a saddle shop at Díaz Miron 2044. Since Tijuana is a free port, European crystal, porcelain, perfumes, and fashions vie with Mexican handicrafts for exposure, especially in the many shops along Avenida Revolución. Fixed prices are set for all imports, and the U.S. dollar is used more than pesos. Store hours generally are from 10 A.M. to 7 P.M., and some shops are closed on Sunday.

ENTERTAINMENT

Tijuana parties all year long as well as day and night, but worth a special mention is August's **Gran Feria de las Californias,** a three-week-long show promoting export goods. And **Mexican Independence Day** (which always falls on September 15, but celebrations for which begin the weekend before) invariably attracts large crowds.

Tijuana is even more alive after dark, and most dance clubs are open Thursday through Sunday nights. In addition to the various hotel bars and discos, there are several that are considered special. **OH!,** the laser-light club in Paseo de los Héroes, attracts thousands because, according to a Tijuana expert, "it's rated internationally as one of the third or fourth best in the world." **Tequila Circo** (tel. 85-02-75) specializes in American music, the **Aloha-Aloha** (tel. 85-46-10) in Latin. **El Torito's** (tel. 85-98-30) dubious distinction lies within the potency of their drinks: Says one regular patron, "one drink of El Toro and you are drunk." Two old favorites are the **London Club** (Bulevar Agua Caliente 3401; tel. 86-54-17), which plays European and American music, and **Marko Disco** downtown, just off Avenida Revolución (Gobernador Balarezo 2000; tel. 86-29-25). Nightclubs **La Cueva del Dragon** (Bulevar Agua Caliente 1698; tel. 86-49-88) and **Charlie's New Chile** (Calle 7, Number 701; tel. 85-80-75) have dancing; **Flamingo's** (Tijuana–Ensenada Highway km 6.5; tel. 84-42-72) has shows; and **Mike's** (Avenida Revolución 1000; tel. 85-35-34) has live disco and rock music.

West to Tecate

Its location on MEX 2, forty miles east of Tijuana, has begun to make smaller Tecate (population thirty-four thousand) an alternative border crossing for cars wishing to avoid Tijuana's long lines. Together with California's small Tecate, Tecate has not become a "border town," instead remaining a typical quiet Mexican community with life centering on the tree-shaded plaza with its roses and bandstand. Every Saturday night, from May to September, the city holds fiestas in the plaza, organized by the Department of Tourism.

Tecate is most famous for its brewery (you wondered where that beer came from!), but there is not much here for the traveler, who usually comes by car, which, with walking, is about the best way to get around. The **tourist office** is at Callejón Libertad 305, and the government-sponsored **FONART Centro Artesania,** on MEX 3 a mile south of MEX 2, sells handicrafts made on the spot as well as folk art from other parts of Mexico. Another popular spot is **El Mejor Pan,** at which you can sample delicious bread and rolls—but otherwise, there is not much to do.

Farmers in the 19th century were attracted to this area's abundant water and fertile soil, unusual in Baja, and the productive region yields grapes, olives, and grain. Lately, industry in the form of instant coffee and beer (brewery tours Monday through Friday) is bringing continuing prosperity to the town.

One exciting aspect of quiet Tecate, however, is **Rancho La Puerta,** a fitness spa on one hundred acres three miles west of town. The exclusive spa offers an all-inclusive rate that covers three healthful meals per day plus snacks, six tennis courts, four swimming pools, two whirlpools and three saunas, and a choice of more than thirty exercise courses as well as a Vita Parcours track with twenty exercise stations. Dating from 1940, when Tecate had four hundred residents, the ranch still boasts the same smogless, fogless climate amid Tecate's quiet foothills and purple mountains. For reservations, call (in the United States) 619-744-4222.

South to Ensenada

South of Tijuana on a secluded beach off the highway between Tijuana and Ensenada, **Outdoor Resorts of Baja** is a new resort for RVers. Amenities include spacious patios and concrete drives for the 280 full-service sites; twenty-thousand-square-foot clubhouse with large recreation, game, and reading rooms; full-service restaurant and Cantina Lounge; two lighted tennis courts; ocean-view swimming pool and spa; locker rooms, showers, sauna, and steamroom; volleyball court and horseshoe pit; full-service laundry room; convenience store; satellite-TV hookups; safety deposit boxes; guarded entry and 24-hour security within resort walls; toll-free message service center. Tennis and fishing, horseback riding, golf at a nearby course, and buffets and theme parties complete the resort life here. At Tijuana-Ensenada Highway km 72. For reservations, contact 4650 Border Village Road, Suite 208, San Ysidro, California 92073. Tel. 619-428-8787 in California; 800-982-2252, also in California; and 800-356-2252 in the rest of the United States.

Ensenada

Sun, sea, and participant sports on pleasant Pacific beaches make low-key Ensenada the perfect complement to Tijuana, with its relentless shopping and extensive spectator-sports scene. Ensenadans tend to view Tijuana as too hectic. But in Ensenada, the oldest community in the state, there's all the time in the world to cater to the great number of visitors delighted to find so many well-run hotels and resorts, excellent restaurants, shops with good bargains, bright nightlife, fine fishing, and good beach playgrounds on the way down Baja's highway. Reached from the deserts of the south by the Transpeninsular Highway and from Tijuana on the north by a four-lane road (with a toll of a little more than $1.50), Ensenada is a pleasant place to pause for a while. The toll road is very scenic, curving around cliffs high above the Pacific Ocean. It follows the coastline most of the way between the two cities.

Portuguese explorer Juan Cabrillo thought Ensenada was worthwhile, too, as early as 1542, when he stopped for six days to claim the land for Spain before moving north to San Diego. Ensenada's bay, Bahía Todos Santos (All Saints Bay) was named by Sebastián Vizcáino in 1602, and it became a small harbor when the town grew into a small trading town for area ranchers and a supply town for some of the missions.

Wine production began about two hundred years ago when Dominican friars first introduced mission grapes into the Santo Tomás Valley, forty kilometers south of Ensenada. It continued to thrive in the Mediterranean climate of this section of Mexico, and the valley, with its cool mountain breezes, warm sun, and abundant mountain streams, now produces the highest quality of varietal grapes in Mexico. The local wines are distributed with pride throughout the country, with plans for export soon.

In 1870 gold was discovered in nearby Real de Castillo, and the gold rush that followed turned Ensenada into the territorial capital. When the gold played out, the capital was moved to Mexicali, and Ensenada went into a decline. During the Mexican-American War, U.S. troops landed at Ensenada, but Mexican troops drove them off.

American Prohibition revived the town: Bahía Todos Santos became a safe harbor for rum runners. Today it's a thriving port, and the one hundred twenty-five thousand citizens of Ensenada mainly make their living through fishing, canneries (Chicken-of-the-Sea tuna), leather-processing plants, and three wineries. In fact, Ensenada is "first in tuna," according to a local spokesperson, with a record capture of one hundred twenty thousand tons of tuna, as well as a record two hundred tons of lobster. (You can enjoy a lobster dinner here for about $12 to $17.)

CONNECTIONS

Many of the hotels and restaurants are within walking distance of one another. This is especially desirable since, although taxis are plentiful, they are expensive—$4.50 for a short ride from the bus terminal to La Pinta hotel; $15–$20 round-trip to Estero Beach. Viajes Guaycura (Avenida López Mateos 1089; tel. 8-37-18) runs a three-and-a-half-hour tour of the city and outskirts several times a week, but otherwise city buses are not of much use. Hertz (avenidas Alvarado and López Mateos, tel. 8-37-76); Scorpio (Avenida Alvarado 95, Number 2, tel. 8-32-85); and Ensenada (Avenida Alvarado 95, Number 1, tel. 8-32-85) Rent-A-Car are all conveniently located.

🛏 HOTELS

Ensenada has a wide variety of accommodations, from inner-city hotels and motels to luxury hotels and resorts a short way out of town. Reservations are always a good idea, but especially

The **tourist information office** is located at Avenida López Mateos 1350 (tel. 6-22-22), next to the office of the **state attorney for protection of tourists** at López Mateos 1350-12B (tel. 6-36-86). The **Chamber of Commerce** (tel. 4-09-96) and the **Convention and Visitors Bureau** (tel. 6-43-10), where López Mateos and Bulevar Costera y la Riviera meet, are open long hours and are very helpful. The Chamber of Commerce has a booklet of discount coupons for merchandise and drinks in local establishments.

so during the big weekends of the Baja 500 and Baja 1000 off-road races, when the town fills up. All hotels are air-conditioned and accept major credit cards except where otherwise noted.

Casa del Sol
Avenida López Mateos 1001, 22800
Tel. 667-8-15-70
Doubles, about $55
In the heart of town, one block from the beach, this Best Western has 43 guest rooms, a restaurant, bar, and gift shop—and claims the largest swimming pool in Ensenada.

Cortez Motor Hotel
Avenida López Mateos 1089, Apdo. Postal 396, 22800
Tel. 667-8-23-07
Doubles, about $60
This Best Western next to the Civic Center and Riviera Convention Center is remodeling. It offers 82 comfortable guest rooms, swimming pool, restaurant and cocktail lounge, meeting rooms, and underground security parking.

El Cid
Avenida López Mateos 993, 22800
Tel. 667-8-24-01
Doubles, from $65
A small 52-room (plus two suites, each with Jacuzzi) Mediterranean-style hotel, El Cid names each of its rooms for a Mexican city and then decorates it with appropriate handicrafts. An on-premises shop sells more of the works of specially selected artisans. Restaurant, bar, disco with lighted dance floor, live music, and weekend poolside breakfast complete the picture.

Estero Beach Hotel Resort
Apdo. Postal 86, 22800
Tel. 667-6-62-25, 6-62-30, 6-62-35
Doubles, from $60
For sports enthusiasts who want everything, this resort offers volleyball, tennis, biking, horseback riding, sailing, waterskiing, wind surfing, kayaking, snorkeling and skin diving, jet skiing, and fishing. With recent remodeling, thirty rooms were added to the original 84. Guest rooms, cottages, and suites have private terrace-patios overlooking Estero Bay, which enjoys its own white-sand beach. Amenities include a children's playground, recre-

ation/meeting room, an exclusive RV park, and a boat ramp. Award-winning **Las Terrazas** restaurant specializes in lobster and Mexican cuisine; there is a museum with pre-Columbian exhibits, and a gift shop, on the premises.

La Pinta

Apdo. Postal 292 Bucaneros s/n, 22800
Tel. 667-6-26-01
Doubles, about $50

Part of the La Pinta/Stouffer Presidente chain of lovely colonial inns at major stops down the peninsula (with the same menu in each restaurant), this 52-room hotel has a comfortable ambience, with very helpful personnel. Included are a restaurant, bar, disco, and live entertainment.

Punta Morro Hotel-Suites

Tijuana-Ensenada Hwy., km 106, 22800
Tel. 667-8-35-07, 4-44-90
Doubles, from $60

This new all-suite hotel has studio and one-, two-, and three-bedroom accommodations, all with kitchen, fireplace, and terrace overlooking the ocean. Heated swimming pool and Jacuzzi are on the premises.

Quintas Papagayo Beach and Tennis Resort

Tijuana-Ensenada Hwy., km 103, Apdo. Postal 150, 22800
Tel. 667-4-45-75 and 4-41-55
Doubles, about $45

Choose from villas, bungalows, and luxury suites, all with fully equipped kitchens, on the ocean. Some have fireplaces, and there are sheltered patios for barbecues. Swimming pool and Jacuzzi, two tennis courts, and **Hussong's Pelicano** restaurant and bar complete the picture.

Las Rosas by the Sea

Apdo. Postal 316, Tijuana-Ensenada Hwy.
Tel. 667-4-43-10
Doubles, from $80

Ensenada's newest luxury property, actually two miles north of town, of pretty pink adobe, is the only hotel in town right on the water. Each of the 31 guest rooms has a balcony and ocean view. The restaurant features seafood, Continental cuisine, and a Sun. brunch created by a chef from Acapulco. Also featured are a piano bar, sauna, spa with Jacuzzi, and two swimming pools right on the brink of the ocean, all with a magnificent view of the sunset. Guests like to go crab fishing on the shores.

San Nicolas

Avenida López Mateos and Guadalupe, 22800
Tel. 667-6-19-01
Doubles, from $80

This fun fantasy of a hotel (recently remodeled) was created by owner Nico Saad. The facade is covered with Aztec murals, the 145 guest rooms are decorated in colonial style, and the huge Temple of the Gods swimming pool, scene of the annual Miss Ensenada International Beauty Contest, must be seen to be believed. You'll also find a smaller pool, restaurant, coffee shop/cafeteria open 24 hours, bar, disco, and meeting rooms.

Villa Marina

Avenida López Mateos and Blancarte 130, 22800
Tel. 667-8-33-21

Doubles, about $88

Recently remodeled, the Villa Marina has added a new high-rise, along with a building that will eventually harbor shops and a travel agency. This hotel offers a fine view of Ensenada, the harbor, and both sunrise and sunset. Cafeteria, 12th-floor restaurant, and new swimming pool are also on the premises.

Since leisure is the mode in Ensenada, take a stroll along the *malecón,* as every waterfront boulevard in Mexico is called. The wide boulevard is pleasant and European in feeling, with restaurants and shops on the landward side. Next, walk over to the briskness of **Avenida López Mateos** (also known as **Calle 1**), **avenidas Juárez** and **Ruíz,** and **Boulevard Costero,** where most of the shops and the throngs of visitors are.

Or, be lazy—those charming horse-and-carriage conveyances, the **calandrias** are back, and you can take a tour of the city to the leisurely clip-clop of horses' hooves. Catch a buggy near the Civic Plaza at Bulevar Costero and Avenida Macheras. Rent-A-Moto D'Baja also rents scooters for a visit to the hilltops behind the city. From **Chapultepec Hill,** there's a good view of Ensenada, the harbor, the bay with Isla Todos Santos on the horizon, and the half-circle of sand that is Ensenada's beach.

The **Riviera del Pacífico,** on Bulevar Cardenas at Avenida Riviera, is now a convention center, but this white-domed palace began life as a gambling casino. It was built in the 1920s and managed by pugilist Jack Dempsey, who brought in planeloads of his movie-star friends to drink and gamble. Another interesting stop right in town is **Bodegas de Santo Tomás** (Avenida Miramar 666, between calles 6 and 7; tel. 667-8-25-09), a winery established in 1888 in the Santo Tomás Valley. Now moved into the center of Ensenada, the winery offers tours and wine tastings all week long at 11 A.M. and 1 and 3 P.M., with groups at any hour by appointment. The half-hour tour ($1.50 per person) by a bilingual guide includes wine sampling and assorted breads and cheeses.

An interesting outing is to **La Bufadora,** a dramatic sea geyser located at Punta Banda on the southern arm of the bay, about half-an-hour's drive from town. You'll have to cover some unpaved terrain, so wear comfortable shoes. (There's so much dust in Baja, anyway, that closed and comfortable shoes are the sensible way to go regardless of whether it's along a city street or out in the countryside.)

☕ RESTAURANTS

Ensenada, between the ocean and the mountains, has many good restaurants, including hotel restaurants, specializing in seafood and game. Gastronomic specialties therefore are abalone, Pacific lobster, and quail. The following were chosen as among the best representatives of the great variety the city enjoys. In fact, two that are considered among the best restaurants in all Mexico are in Ensenada: the award-winning **El Rey Sol,** in the center of town, and **La Cueva de los Tigres,** on a dead-end dirt road to the beach. Prices listed do not include wine, drinks, tips, or tax. Beers available include Tecate, Corona, and Pacífico, as well as imported brews. Wines run $2–$3 a glass and approximately $9–$13 a bottle, possibly more in an expensive restaurant. Imported French wines are very expensive; Mexican wines such as Domec, Quinta El Mirador, and Calafia are served even in the best restaurants. All restaurants accept major credit cards unless otherwise indicated.

La Cueva de los Tigres

Avenida Acapulco, off MEX1 (a mile and a half south of town by car—there's a sign)
Tel. 6-64-50

The other of Ensenada's best-known restaurants faces the ocean, and the view matches the caliber of the cuisine. The "Tiger's Cave" specializes in such seafood as abalone topped with shredded crab, served in the glow of a magnificent sunset. The average cost of a dinner for two is about $40.

Dragon Mandarin

Bulevar Costero 263
Tel. 8-13-28

If you need a Chinese fix, this is *the* place for lobster Cantonese or abalone with black mushrooms, but the menu includes seafood, Mexican and American cuisine, plus inexpensive breakfasts (from $2 for eggs with bacon to $6 for eggs and lobster). The average cost of a meal for two is about $15.

Ensenada Grill

Bulevar Costero 915
Tel. 4-00-22

If you get hungry for American food, this is the place—but the seafood and Mexican dishes are also good. The average cost of a dinner for two is about $22.

La Ermita

Avenida Balboa 213
Tel. 6-32-61

This fine Mexican restaurant serves *chiles en ahogada* and a good lamb barbecue. The average cost of a dinner for two is about $18.

El Rey Sol

Avenidas López Mateos and Blancarte

Tel. 8-23-51

This Ensenada legend takes honors every year at the *Feria Internacional del Pescado y el Marisco,* and you can indulge your taste buds in such prize winners as abalone in shrimp sauce, and mussel soup Baja California. Duck in mango sauce, quail in Madame Geffroy's special sauce, salmon in crayfish sauce, and pork with kiwi are but a few of the gastronomical delights served in the formal French restaurant begun more than thirty years ago by the French-Mexican family of Joseph Geffroy. Live music. The average cost of a dinner for two is about $50.

BEACHES

For swimmers and other water-sports enthusiasts, there are four beaches nearby: **Estero, La Jolla, Mona Lisa,** and **El Faro.** Estero, just south of downtown, is the favorite, although at high tide there is an undertow. Surfers go to **San Miguel,** eight miles north of Ensenada. The best facilities for waterskiing are at the **Estero Beach Hotel Resort,** where guests from other hotels are also welcome.

SPORTS

Sport fishing is big, as it is all over Baja, and there are facilities on shore for icing and smoking the results of a day's angling, or obtaining canned yellowtail, which is the big catch here. Both charter boats and open-ticket vessels are available. The Convention and Visitors Bureau and the Tourist Information Office have a list and will know the going rates, which, at press time, range from $280 to $1,000 to charter a boat; climbing aboard an open-ticket vessel will run about $20 less currently. North of town, **Emilio López Zamora Dam** has good angling; south, there's good surf fishing.

As for golf, **Estero Beach Hotel Resort** has a driving range. Otherwise, the closest course is **Bajamer,** an 18-hole course, featuring fine facilities, twenty miles to the north. The **Baja Tennis Club** is private, but reservations for the five lighted courts can be made by hotel guests through their hotels. Facilities may also be available at the Estero Beach Hotel Resort and Bajamer. Horseback riding, available at **Playa Hermosa, Mona Lisa,** and **La Bufadora,** will cost about $10 per hour. There is good hunting in the hills, with dove, quail, and duck in season. Hunters must bring their weapons with them, which entails much red tape. Obtain a permit from a Mexican consulate and report the weapon at customs. The Ministry of Urban Development and Ecology (SEDUE), at Avenida López Mateos 1350-A, takes reservations for **Elido Uruapan,** a hunting ranch 26 miles south of Ensenada.

SHOPPING

Ensenada, like Tijuana and the rest of Baja, is a free port, and items are imported untaxed. Along Avenida López Mateos (Calle 1), avenidas Juárez and Ruíz, and Bulevar Costero, where many hotels and restaurants are located, are shops loaded with both Mexican and imported goods. **Plazablanca,** at Alvarado and Calle 1, is a group of shops specializing in leather jewelry and accessories; gold, silver, brass, and copper jewelry; pottery; designer clothes; and Mexican handicrafts. Ensenada as a rule has good prices and quality merchandise. **FONART,** a government shop next to the tourist office at López Mateos 1350, has choice crafts from all over Mexico.

ENTERTAINMENT

Ensenada considers itself a "sports capital" and is indeed famous for its off-road racing, with such classics as the June **Baja 500** and the November **Baja 1000,** which begins in Ensenada and finishes in Los Cabos. Other special events include a pre-Lenten **Carnival,** and the **Fun Bicycle Race** in March. Late April or early June brings a **sailing regatta,** when thousands of yachts set off from Ensenada for Newport Beach, California. July is a big party month with **Antojitos Fair,** a food festival featuring Mexican finger foods, and **Fiesta Mexicana,** a spirited mariachi, dance, and piñata-breaking party. September brings **Feria Internacional del Pescado y Marisco,** an international seafood fair, and there's more food in October at the **International Chili Cook-Off.** In November, in addition to the Baja 1000, there is a large travel and handicrafts show.

Most of the action after dark takes place at hotel discos; popular are those in the **San Nicolás** and **El Cid** hotels, and the former offers Ballet Folklórico performances Saturday nights. Live music until the wee hours can be found at **Tony's, San Nicolás, La Nina, Anthony's,** and **El Muelle 5,** all off Costero or López Mateos. **Hussongs,** at Avenida Ruíz 113, is a wild and wooly cow-town saloon à la the gold rush days. There are shows at the nightclub **Señorial** at López Mateos 639; tel. 8-33-55.

Along the Highway South

The Transpeninsular Highway all along the length of Baja California seems such a long and desolate ribbon of road that the temptation is to speed along as fast as possible to get to a civilized destination; this is what the buses try to do. But if you are into exploring, and have your own transportation, there are several interesting stops along the way, including quite a few missions or mission sites giving evidence of the European influence on the Indian culture. But this is primitive desert country, so to reiterate: If you drive, never drive at night; fill up your gas tank at every opportunity; carry one or two days' supply of bottled water (and again, never drink any water but *agua purificado,* purified water, in Baja California); and unless you are part of a large group, do not camp out in isolated areas, as there have been recent reports of road incidents involving assaults and robberies. Though infrequent, they are on the rise, so use the same precautions you would use in other unsettled areas of the world. And remember that the main highways of Mexico are patrolled by the Angeles Verdes (Green Angels), who operate a fleet of emergency-service trucks for minor road repairs, change tires, give first aid, carry gasoline and oil, and are a source of road information. There is no charge except for fuel and parts.

Small restaurants in small towns sometimes are a delightful find, other times rather a disaster. For the unadventurous, hotel restaurants, especially in the Baja, are usually among the best in town. A safe rule for Baja (and indeed for all of Mexico), in addition to not drinking tap water, is to eat only vegetables that you feel confident have been washed (or cooked) before being served, and only fruit that has to be peeled. A preventive measure that works for many is Pepto-Bismol, taken before meals (when in doubt about the local cuisine; usually not necessary in hotels and restaurants that cater to tourists). The tablet form available in the United States is very convenient; it can be found only in bottled form in much of Mexico.

Over the mountains 27 miles south of Ensenada, MEX 1 intersects the road to Puerto Santo Tomás and La Bocana. Stop there, and you can enjoy both the **Santo Tomás Valley** and **La Bocana,** which has intertidal areas to explore if you take a boat out for a day of fishing. The refurbished motel, **El Palomar,** overlooks the valley made famous for the wines, still enjoyed today, begun by the padres of the past. The motel has a restaurant that critics have discovered, as well as a store selling a variety of seashells. There is also an RV park with a swimming pool in a pleasant setting.

There's hunting in "them thar hills" too, with an abundance of quail and dove in season. Remember, however, that there are a tremendous number of restrictions applying to hunters in Mexico, including the necessity for special licenses for both guns and ammunition.

The first mission you come to is **Santo Tomás de Aquino Mission,** 29 miles south of Ensenada. It was founded April 24, 1791, by friars Crisóstomo Gómez and José Lorrente. The **San Vicente Ferrer Mission,** 23 miles farther south, stands by the shores of the San Vicente River. Founded October 12, 1780, by the Dominican preaching friars Miguel Sales, Miguel Gallegos, and Tomás de Valdellón, it was the third mission installed in Baja California. Architecturally the most important of the Baja missions because of its fortifications, San Vicente Ferrer was the administration center of the Dominican order in the territory.

Rosario de Viñadaco Mission, located 109 miles south of San Vicente Ferrer Mission, was founded in 1774. Originally headquartered in a place called Rosario de Arriba, it was relocated in 1802 to a site closer to the beach. Unfortunately, ruins are all that are left at both sites.

The only Franciscan mission built in this territory is **San Fernando Velicata,** 42 miles from Rosario de Viñadaco. Founded in 1769, San Fernando was incorporated into the Catholic church a year later. Interesting artifacts still exist. **San Francisco de Borja Adac Mission,** 22 miles from El Rosario, was the first chapel the Dominican missionaries built in Baja California. Originally, there was a church and a warehouse; a stone building was begun later but left unfinished. All the same, this is considered the best example of architecture from Mexico's Viceroy period (the 16th through the 18th ,centuries).

Near the border of Baja California Sur, 114 miles south of San Francisco de Borja Adac, is **Santa Gertrudis la Magna Mission,** located quite close to the Sea of Cortés. Built in the 17th century by Jesuit Jorgé Retz, the mission was originally constructed of adobe and only later of stone. One of the best preserved missions along the route, it has a bell tower separate from the chapel.

The remains of the last mission founded by the Jesuits in Baja California is **Santa Maria de los Angeles,** in Cataviña, 116 miles south of San Quintín. Cataviña's more interesting claim to fame, however, lies in the prehistoric cave paintings of geometric and zoomorphic figures found there. (There is a good exhibition of the paintings in La Paz at the Anthropological Museum; see below.)

 Cataviña's **Hotel La Pinta** is one of the La Pinta/Stouffer Presidente chain, with thirty colonial-style rooms, a swimming pool, restaurant, bar, hunting, and excursions into the desert to the site of prehistoric carved rocks and paintings; tel. 667-6-26-01, 800-262-2656 in the United States. **Doubles, from $60.** Credit cards: AE, MC, V.

East to Mexicali

The citizens of this prosperous agricultural center on the California–Mexico border call themselves *cachanillas,* after the name of a desert plant native to the area. The city of Mexicali, the state capital of Baja California, has embarked upon a development program to encourage more tourism. The keystone is the construction of a Civic Center immediately adjacent to the city's Zona Rosa, where there are plans for a handsome neighborhood of traditional Spanish buildings, which will ultimately house five hundred shops to lure visitors. At present, a short walk from the border, which Mexacali shares with the small farming community of Calexico, California, leads to the **Melgar Street Mall,** a pedestrian mall, where merchants sponsor band concerts on the weekends to keep shoppers happy.

The recently created **Mexicali Tourism and Convention Bureau** (Bulevar López Mateos and Calle Camelias) offers assistance with hotel reservations as well as a 24-hour telephone service (52-57-44) for any tourist problem, be it medical, legal, or auto. "Soft sell" is the Mexicali motto, and even traffic tickets are bilingual, to make the English-speaking visitor feel more at ease, evidence of the Mexicali wish to make tourists welcome even when they may be infringing on local laws.

Although on the border, Mexicali considers itself the gateway to the Sea of Cortés. The town lays claim, by virtue of its Highway 5 down to San Felipe on the water, to being one of the world's premier deep-sea fishing areas.

Though there has been a lack of major tourist hotels, that is changing with the influx of more tourists. Several new hotels are on the drawing board, and the existing four-star, 124-room **Holiday Inn** (Bulevar Benito Juárez 2220; tel. 65-566-1300; doubles, from $70; all major credit cards) and the 192-room **Hotel Lucerna** (Bulevar Benito Juárez 2151; tel. 65-566-1000; doubles, from $52; credit cards: AE, DC, V) offer the usual desired amenities of comfortable rooms, restaurants, bars, swimming pools, and many other services. Ten minutes from downtown and catering more to the business trade with its newly completed Las Joyas Convention Center is the recently expanded **Calafia** (Calzada Justo Sierra 1495, Fracciomiento Los Pinos, 21230; reserve through Amex Hotels Ltd., 7462B La Jolla Boulevard, La Jolla, California 92038; tel. 800-262-2656, 65-68-33-11 in Mexico; doubles, from $50; credit cards: AE, CB, V), now with 173 spacious rooms, a 24-hour coffee shop, **Los Tules** restaurant with salad bar and Mexican specialties, a lobby bar with live entertainment, and swimming pool with sundeck. The **Mexicali Country Sports Club at Laguna Campestre** has an 18-hole golf course and a pro.

There are several excellent restaurants, including the newest Chinese restaurant, **El Dragon** (Bulevar Benito Juárez 1830; tel. 6-20-20), revealing the presence of a large Chinese population. Mexicali's Chinese food is so famous that there's a special festival dedicated to the preparation and tasting of many Chinese dishes. Other recommended restaurants include

Bum Bum (pronounced "Boom-Boom"; Avenida Reforma 1300, Margarita Building; tel. 2-20-65), with Continental cuisine. Both **Casino de Mexicali** (Avenida Pino Suarez and Calle L; tel. 4-17-51) and **Dino's** (Bulevar Justo Sierra 900; tel. 8-29-66) offer fine Continental cuisine, along with live and recorded music.

Sports City, on the site of the pre-1975 airport, is an eighty-acre sports and recreation complex. Centered on a 12,000-seat baseball stadium are soccer fields; swimming pools; basketball, handball, and tennis courts; and track-and-field facilities—all available to residents and visitors alike, without cost. (Open 6 A.M. until 10 P.M.)

San Felipe

One of Baja's major fishing centers and winter resorts is small-town (population 5,000) San Felipe, 302 miles south of Mexicali on MEX5. **Los Arcos,** the Arches, a sculpture on the highway into town, forms a pleasant introduction to this rapidly growing resort area. San Felipe faces east toward the shimmering blue waters of the Sea of Cortés, just below the place where the mainland and the peninsula part. To the west across the sandy coastal plain is the steep eastern wall of the **Sierra de San Pedro Mártir,** the highest range in Baja California. **Punta San Felipe,** 940 feet high, towers over the town, providing a rugged headland that shelters boats in shallow Bahía San Felipe. The coastline swings southward with long white sandy beaches, down to Punta Estrella 12 miles distant. A natural phenomenom in the bay is an extreme tidal range, which can reach more than twenty feet. For sailors inexperienced in these waters, boating can be hazardous.

Modest dwellings, sandy streets, and not much vegetation on the shores of the forbidding desert characterize San Felipe. Although nomadic fishermen were attracted to the teeming waters of the sea, the town did not become a permanent settlement until 1920. It was during World War II that large-scale fishing began, but San Felipe was not discovered by U.S. sports enthusiasts until the advent of the paved highway from Mexicali in 1951. However, it did not take long for word of the five hundred species of fish, including white sea bass, cabrilla, corbina sierra, swordfish, and sailfish, as well as other species, to get out. A specialty here is the sweet-tasting game fish totoaba. Today, especially on holidays such as Washington's Birthday, Easter week, Memorial Day, Labor Day, Thanksgiving, and Christmas, San Felipe can become extremely crowded. Undeterred by the summer days when daytime temperatures sometimes exceed 120 degrees Fahrenheit, and despite the average annual rainfall being less than two inches, the crowds come, bringing their own excitement, counting on the usually refreshingly cool nights to dispel the heat of the day. The port is the scene of many sports events, from regattas to triathlons and cycling competitions. There are almost a dozen handicrafts shops selling a good assortment of Mexican goods.

Tourist information and assistance can be obtained at the **Delegación de Turismo del Estado,** avenidas Mar de Cortés and Manzanillo; tel. 7-11-55; and **Delegación Municipal,** Avenida Mar Blanco; tel. 7-10-21. The attorney general for the protection of tourists can be reached through the state office also, at 7-11-21.

🧳 HOTELS

All establishments listed below accept major credit cards and are air-conditioned unless otherwise indicated.

Las Misiones Hotel

Justo Sierra 1495, Fraccionamiento los Pinos, 21000
Tel. 656-7-12-80

Cafeteria, disco, swimming pool and bar, two lighted tennis courts, volleyball court, meeting room, and gift shop are all on the premises.

El Pescador

Avenida Mar de Cortés and Bulevar Chetumal
Tel. 657-7-10-44

There are 24 additional rooms under construction in this (currently) 12-room motel, which has heat as well as air-conditioning, laundry, safety deposit boxes, and a liquor store on the premises.

Villa del Mar Suites

Fraccionamiento Playas de San Felipe, 21100
Tel. 657-7-13-33; in Mexicali call 65-52-40-16

Across from Las Misiones Hotel, Villa del Mar offers eight one-bedroom suites and one two-bedroom suite, all plain but clean and comfortable, each with a large terrace, living room with convertible sofa, and fully equipped kitchen. In addition, you'll find daily maid service, a swimming pool, and an outdoor barbecue area.

There are a baker's dozen **trailer-RV parks** in San Felipe, attesting to the proliferation of fishermen. One of the newest is **Parque Mar del Sol** (Paseo de las Misiones; reserve in the United States through Mexico Resorts International, 664 Broadway, Suite G, Chula Vista, California, tel. 619-422-6900 or 800-336-5454; reserve in Mexico at Avenida Reforma 1232, Mexicali, tel. 65-52-65-28). Five minutes away from San Felipe, Mar del Sol has 120 spaces with complete RV hookups, paved streets, tennis courts, swimming pool and Jacuzzi, a gourmet restaurant, coin-operated washers and dryers, and a grocery store nearby.

🍵 RESTAURANTS

Both seafood and Mexican cuisine, not surprisingly, are the specialties in the restaurants of San Felipe, with the exception of **Puerto Padre** (Avenida Mar de Cortés), which specializes in Cuban food, and **El Nido** (Avenida Mar de Cortés), which in addition to seafood and Mexican dishes, also specializes in steak. Almost all the action, both in restaurants and bars, can be found on Avenida Mar de Cortés along the waterfront, and in general the hotel restaurants are also recommended.

ENTERTAINMENT

There's more going on after dark in San Felipe than you would imagine, considering that all those fishermen have to rise at dawn for the next day's sport. In addition to what some of the hotels have to offer in the way of evening entertainment, there is also **Club Miramar,** with a dance floor, open 8 P.M. to 2 A.M.; **Club Bar Plaza,** with live music, open 9 P.M. to 2 A.M.; and **Perro Neto,** open noon to 2 A.M. In addition, **El Faro,** on the airport road, is open 10 A.M. to 7 P.M. Monday through Thursday, and 10 A.M. to 10 P.M. Friday through Sunday.

Baja California Sur

Baja California Sur is, at first, merely an extension of the mountainous desert that has come before, and, as such, the scenery does not change a great deal—until you come to land's end at San José del Cabo and Cabo San Lucas. The two towns have been developed by FONATUR, the Mexican government's tourist development arm, into a major resort area called Los Cabos, meaning "the capes." In the works is the same treatment for Loreto, where much of the infrastructure for a major resort has already been constructed.

As you cross into Baja's southern state, you will be in **Guerrero Negro,** just below the state line. Nearby is **Scammon's Lagoon,** famous for whale migrations. Along the route are prehistoric cave paintings, the source of which has not yet been discovered: figures of humans and animals painted in red, yellow, and black, some of them as high as forty feet above the floor of the cave. Unfortunately, most of the caves are difficult to get to, requiring a four-wheel-drive vehicle.

Other important destinations in this state are Santa Rosalía, Mulegé, Loreto, and La Paz, along with of course the aforementioned sea, sun, and sand resort areas of Los Cabos.

It's a long ride down the peninsula—from Ensenada to Loreto, it's 14 hours on a first-class Tres Estrellas de Oro bus, with Mexican music playing loudly all the way. But there are stops every two or three hours at restaurants or Pemex gas stations for bathrooms (not always clean, and come prepared with your own tissue), snacks, and soft drinks or beer. Resorts Air flies from Los Angeles, Orange County, and San Diego, California, and from Phoenix, Arizona, to Loreto, La Paz, and Los Cabos. Aeromexico has resumed its service to Baja California Sur—call 800-237-6639 within the United States for information; Aero California flies from Tijuana to La Paz.

Guerrero Negro

Salt is what keeps the economy of this town on the 28th parallel in good shape. The enormous salt mines are the largest in the world, and huge blocks of salt can be seen from afar. The salt is transported in small vessels to the island of Cedros, and from there exported to the United States and Japan. Permits to visit the salt flats may be obtained by applying in advance to Exportada de Sal, S.A., B.C.; on-the-spot permits may be obtained at Avenida Carranza, Guerrero Negro, B.C.S.

But visitors are mainly interested in the gray whales that migrate to lagoons off the Bahía San Sebastián Vizcaíno and the protected Bahía Ojo de Liebre every winter to have their young. The area has been designated a wildlife preserve, and whales usually can be seen from November to late March in both **Scammon's Lagoon** and the adjoining **Guerrero Negro Lagoon** and nearby **San Ignacio Lagoon.** The area is reached by a fairly well-marked 17-mile dirt road, passing the salt flats. During the season when the mammals arrive, navigation in the waters is controlled and recorded, but visitors can observe the whales from lookouts posted along the coastline; special permission is required to take a boat into the lagoons during the season. The mammals are naturally protective of their young, so although they are not violent, their very size makes it safer to view them from afar. Best viewing times are dawn, between 6 and 9 A.M., and sunset at 5 P.M., when the whales come right to the pier. Small planes are for hire to view the whales from above, and naturalist tours to whale-watching sites are available from several California outfits. (Two are Oceanic Society Expeditions, Fort Mason Center, Building E, San Francisco, CA 94123, tel. 415-441-1106; and Baja Adventures, 16000 Ventura Boulevard, Encino, CA 91436, tel. 800-345-BAJA in California, 800-543-BAJA elsewhere in the United States.)

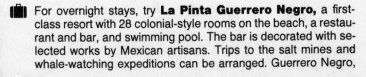 For overnight stays, try **La Pinta Guerrero Negro,** a first-class resort with 28 colonial-style rooms on the beach, a restaurant and bar, and swimming pool. The bar is decorated with selected works by Mexican artisans. Trips to the salt mines and whale-watching expeditions can be arranged. Guerrero Negro,

23940; tel. 667-6-26-01 in Ensenada, 800-262-2656 in the United States. Doubles, from $58. Credit cards: AE, MC, V.

Santa Rosalía

This ancient copper-mining center was at the height of its glory at the end of the 19th century. Today it concentrates on its port and boat building to serve the coastal fishing industry, which creates the demand. Ships unite the peninsula with Guaymas across on the mainland—the Baja terminus of the ferry to Guaymas also is here. Santa Rosalía is unexpectedly picturesque, with quaint **Old West wooden buildings** and the even more unexpected **Misión de Santa Rosalía.** This tiny church has two unusual claims to fame: not only was it the first prefabricated construction in Mexico, it was built by engineer Alexandre Gustave Eiffel, creator of Paris's Eiffel Tower. The church was transported piece by piece from Europe by a director of the French mining company El Boleo (no longer in existence). The town in those days was divided into Mesa Francía, where the French executives of the mining company lived; Mesa México, locale of the local government offices; and La Playa, where the mine workers lived. (As a result of the French occupation, Santa Rosalía is also known today for its French bread!) The rugged landscape and the beautiful blue Sea of Cortés make this a favorite destination.

A side road several miles south of town leads to the **caves of San Borjita,** site of the oldest cave paintings found in Baja California. Life-sized humans are depicted at war and hunting, with lions, deer, rabbits, and fish painted in colors still bright to this day.

🧳 HOTELS

Frances
11 de Julio 30, 23920
Tel. 685-2-08-29
Doubles, from $20
This three-star property, recently in the throes of remodeling, offers a fine restaurant, pool, and bar. All major credit cards.

El Morro
Carretera al Sur km 1.5, 23920
Tel. 685-2-04-14
Doubles, from $25
One of Santa Rosalía's two three-star hotels is a twenty-room motel just one mile south of town, with restaurant, bar, and swimming pool. All major credit cards.

The highway south of Santa Rosalía through Mulegé (pronounced Moo-luh-HAY) to Loreto is characterized by hairpin turns through the mountains, accounting for the length of time it takes to get through it relative to the actual number of miles

---
Restaurants

In addition to those offered by your hotel, there are several good restaurants in Santa Rosalía, including **Las Brisas** (Transpeninsular Hwy.) and **California** (Transpeninsular Hwy.), featuring Mexican cuisine.

---

you are covering. On the bus you will find yourself tossed back and forth on the seat, but if you drive you can certainly exercise greater restraint. In addition to the height and the curves, the brief bright glimpses of the incredibly blue Sea of Cortés make the drive an exciting one.

Mulegé

Another oasis in the mountainous desert is this small town (population thirty-five hundred) at the mouth of Río Santa Rosalía, more commonly referred to as the Mulegé River. The word *mulegé* is Indian, meaning "wide river, white water," and fishing and swimming in it is the delight of both residents and visitors. Across the river is the **Mission of Santa Rosalía,** built in 1705 by Jesuit Juan de Ugarte. The mission, on top of a hill facing the river, has two naves and stone walls. Date palms and fruit trees provide green shade, and just south of town is **Bahía Concepción,** a sheltered body of water just right for aquatic sports. New in Mulegé is scuba diving; check with **Mulegé Divers** on Calle Madero. Good bathing beaches are found on the north side of the river mouth, in front of the hill **El Sombrerito,** named for the hat-shaped lighthouse on top, as well as at the **Serenidad Hotel.**

👜 HOTELS

All properties listed below are air-conditioned and accept major credit cards.

Serenidad
Barrio el Cacheno, 23900
Tel. 685-3-01-11
Doubles, from $40
   This beachfront hotel has fifty guest rooms, a restaurant, bar, swimming pool, tennis court, scuba gear rental, an airstrip, and 35 trailer hookups. In addition, owner Don Johnson (no, not *that* Don Johnson; this one is the U.S. vice-counsul) offers a pork barbecue every Sat. night, and a Mexican fiesta on Wed. nights.

Vista Hermosa
Camino el Faro, 23900
Tel. 685-3-02-33
Doubles, from $50

Overlooking the river, the former **Mulegé** has been renovated and renamed, with 21 guest rooms, a restaurant, poolside cookouts, live music on Sat. nights, waterskiing, diving, snorkeling, and an airstrip.

Other overnight possibilities are the two-star **Terrazas,** calles Zaragoza and Moctezuma, tel. 685-3-01-01; and two economy motels, **Las Casitas,** with a seafood restaurant, at Madero 50, tel. 685-3-00-19; and **Vieja Hacienda,** Madero 3, tel. 685-3-00-20.

BEACHES

Bahía Concepción, south of Mulegé, has beautiful beaches with crystalline waters wonderful for swimming, diving, and fishing—for clams in particular. The main beaches are **Santispac, El Requesón,** and **El Coyote.** Baja in general is full of surprises, not the least of which is El Coyote's rock painting of an attacking coyote, for which the beach is named. There is also an RV park on the beautiful bay, **Posada Concepción,** with eighty spaces, and services.

RESTAURANTS

In addition to the fine restaurants in the **Serenidad** and **Villa Hermosa** hotels, try **El Michoacano** (Transpeninsular Hwy. and Ortega), and **Las Casitas** (Madero 50; tel. 3-02-19).

Loreto

The oldest known human settlement on the peninsula is Loreto, caught between the desert and the deep blue sea. Called "the Mother of the Californias," because Jesuit Juan María Salvatierra began the Catholic missionary work of the Baja here, the town today has a population of about twelve thousand, nestled amid date palms and fig and olive trees. The lovely green bit of a **town plaza** is bordered by the city hall, with languid policemen hanging around outside, since law-enforcement work is understandably limited in this pleasant small town. Around the corner, the **Misión de Nuestra Señora de Loreto,** founded in 1697, still has its original bells: they ring on Saturday to call to catechism the boys playing ball in front of the church and the girls jumping rope in the cool side yard. The area around the plaza, that in front of the church and the block or two surrounding, is paved with cobblestones, while the remaining streets are dirt, so wear appropriate shoes. In extreme contrast are the wide paved boulevards surrounding the town, built by FONATUR, the governmental tourism development agency, in preparation for turning peaceful Loreto into a major tourist resort.

The **Museo de las Misiones Californias,** a series of carved stone rooms with wood-beam ceilings, surrounds a garden courtyard with square columns and arches next door to the church. The displays of artifacts and manuscripts have been well organized by personnel from Mexico City's National Museum of Anthropology.

The cobblestone area around the plaza and the mission is lined with small chic boutiques, which have attractive clothing and fine Mexican handicrafts. **El Palomar,** two blocks south of the plaza, has the best collection of Guadalajara pottery.

Beaches in town are not very attractive; the sand is more like fine gray dust, and the shores are littered with trash, dead fish, and even an occasional dead bird, but . . . the sunrise is lovely, with the *pangas* (outboard-motor skiffs for fishing, $70 for seven hours and $7 for tackle) silhouetted against the orange sky as they set out for the day's catch. Both fishing and tennis are the main sports of Loreto. Found all year round are roosterfish and other fighting fish, with record catches of roosterfish and dorado. Throughout June and July and from September until November, sailfish and marlin are the main attraction. Nearby **Isla Coronado** is populated with dolphins, sea lions, pelicans, and frigate birds.

For tennis, the **Centro Tenistico de Loreto** ($12 per hour to use the facilities, extra charge to use lighted court at night; $25 per hour for lessons) offers year-round clinics and hosts a week-long tournament in late October or early November, when the days have cooled down and the nights are downright breezy.

The beaches are better south at **Nopoló Point,** where FONATUR plans the newest in a complete resort along the lines of the successful resorts of Cancún, Ixtapa, the Bays of Huatulco, and Los Cabos. Three separate areas totaling 25,300 acres will include areas from the town of Loreto, the Bay of Nopoló, and the harbor of Puerto Escondido. Three luxury hotels, an **Intercontinental,** the **Paraíso Radisson,** and the **Concorde,** are expected to open at Nopoló sometime in the 1990s, and a golf course and marina are planned. **Puerto Escondido** (not to be confused with the budding resort village of the same name in Oaxaca), a natural port, is being developed as a first-class nautical village and a 120-space trailer park. The yacht-oriented resort will have hotels, canalside homes, a low-rise condotel, and condominiums on small islands connected by bridges. Sailing excursions on the Sea of Cortés are offered by **The Moorings** (tel. 800-535-7289 in the United States), a charter-boat company based in Clearwater, Florida, charged with management of the Puerto Escondido marina facility.

CONNECTIONS

First-class Tres Estrellas de Oro bus fares between Loreto and La Paz run about $5 for the six-hour trip. Taxis are a viable way

> Loreto has two large, modern supermarkets, a pleasant find for food and sundries after the long haul down the peninsula: **Super Mercado** at Plaza Loreto, is open from 7 A.M. to 10 P.M. And **Super Pescado,** two blocks away, is open from 7 A.M. to 9 P.M.

of getting around town, and they are not expensive—about $2 to an in-town destination and $5 out to Nopoló and the tennis club.

📖 ACCOMMODATIONS

All properties listed below (with the exception of the Tripui RV Resort) are air-conditioned and accept major credit cards.

Misión de Loreto
Bulevar López Mateos 1, Apdo. Postal 49, 23880
Tel. 683-3-00-48
Doubles, from $30
The 54 guest rooms here are available on either the European or Modified American Plan. You'll find a restaurant and bar, as well as a swimming pool. Boating, hunting, fishing, and scuba diving can be arranged at the hotel.

Oasis
Bulevar López Mateos, Apdo. Postal 17, 23880
Tel. 683-3-02-11 and 3-01-12
Doubles, from $70 (three meals included daily)
A haven for dyed-in-the-wool fishermen, this stone- and shell-encrusted 35-room motel is both near downtown and along the waterfront, with restaurant, bar, swimming pool, professional tennis court, fishing arrangements, and gift shop.

La Pinta Loreto
Francisco I. Madero, 23880
Tel. 3-00-25; 667-6-26-01 in Ensenada
Doubles, from $40
This comfortable hotel with 48 extra-large rooms right on the beach offers a restaurant and bar; swimming pool; two lighted tennis courts; and volleyball, game room, and shuffleboard—all this, and only six blocks from the plaza.

Stouffer Presidente Loreto
Bulevar Misión de Loreto, 23880
Tel. 683-3-07-00; 800-GRACIAS in the United States
Doubles, $250 per person per night; includes three meals daily, airport transfers, and all sports activities; four- and seven-day packages available
This complete resort on beautiful Nopoló Beach has 250 terraced guest rooms, two swimming pools, three restaurants, two bars, a disco, tennis courts, horseback riding, a shopping center, a water-sports center (scuba diving, sailing, and fishing), and travel and car-rental agencies, as well as special seafood buffets and Mexican fiestas.

In addition to the above-mentioned hotels, you'll find the **Tripui RV Resort** at Puerto Escondido, 15 miles south of Loreto, with 116 full hookups, restaurant and bar, swimming pool, lighted tennis court, Laundromat, hot showers, and boat-launch ramp. Box 100, Loreto, B.C., Mexico 23880; tel. 683-3-04-13 and 3-05-19.

🍽 RESTAURANTS

Some of the finest are in the hotels, but other recommended restaurants include **Cesar** (Zapata and Juárez; tel. 3-02-03), which serves fish and seafood, and has a daily happy hour 5–7 P.M. The average cost of dinner for two is $15–$20. All major credit cards. Also try **El Nido Steak House** (Avenida Salvatierra 152; tel. 3-02-84), one of a chain of restaurants with branches in Rosarito, San Felipe, Mulegé, and now newly opened in Loreto. The specialties are steak and lobster, and the chef will cook your catch if you bring it along. The average cost of dinner for two is about $20. No credit cards. **Playa Blanca** (Madera and Hidalgo; tel. 3-04-28), offers live music, a huge whale skeleton hanging overhead in the downstairs room, and a whale-bone banister upstairs, where there is a view of Loreto—in addition to succulent garlic-spiked clams and American-style baked potatoes. The average cost of dinner for two is under $20. No credit cards.

From Loreto, MEX1 crosses the mountains and heads west to Ejido Insurgentes and south through Ciudad Constitución to La Paz. There is not much of interest for the traveler in either Insurgentes or Constitución, except for dirt roads leading west to fishing villages along the Pacific Coast, where abalone and lobster are plentiful. In Ciudad Constitución, **RV Park La Pila** provides 32 spaces and all services.

From Ciudad Constitución, MEX22 leads west to Puerto San Carlos, on Bahiá Magdelena, the largest in Baja. Isla Santa Margarita, in the bay, is a major shelter for sea lions. Puerto San Carlos has an **RV park** that makes arrangements for whale-watching excursions: **Pueblito Magdalena,** with 14 spaces, cabanas, and services.

La Paz

The capital of the state of Baja California Sur, La Paz is a bustling city of one hundred fifty thousand, situated at a deep inlet on the Sea of Cortés. Long summers and mild winters, coupled with the blue-green sea and white-sand beaches, make La Paz a prime tourist destination. It was once a prime pearl-fishing locale—in fact, John Steinbeck's novel *The Pearl* was set here—and La Paz pink and black pearls found their way into many a European crown jewel. But finally some sort of plague decimated the oyster beds, and today they are no longer part of La Paz.

Although the morning was young, the hazy mirage was up. The uncertain air that magnified some things and blotted out others hung over the whole Gulf so that all sights were unreal and vision could not be trusted; so that sea and land had the sharp clarities and the vagueness of a dream. Thus it might be that the people of the Gulf trust things of the spirit and things of the imagination, but they do not trust their eyes to show them distance or clear outline or any optical exactness. Across the estuary from the town one section of mangroves stood clear and telescopically defined, while another mangrove clump was a hazy black-green blob. Part of the far shore disappeared into a shimmer that looked like water. There was no certainty in seeing, no proof that what you saw was there or was not there. And the people of the Gulf expected all places were that way, and it was not strange to them.

—John Steinbeck
The Pearl, 1945

La Paz had to survive not only the failure of the pearl industry, but the silver-mining industry too (at El Triunfo and San Antonio, south of town, you can still find entrances to some of the mine shafts), as well as years of unsuccessful attempts at colonization. The settlement did not become official until 1720, when the Cathedral Nuestra Señora de La Paz was built by Father Juan Ugarte, who hoped to found a mission. The Baja Indians revolted, killing many whites, including some of the priests. The mission was abandoned around 1749, and eventually the harbor began to be used as a supply point for the more successful missions in Southern Baja, but there were no inhabitants on the shores of Bahía de La Paz. Finally, in 1811 Juan José Espinosa settled here, with more colonists arriving after the Mexican War of Independence, and La Paz was formally declared a city, becoming the territorial capital in 1830.

Well, the oysters and the pearls might be gone, but sport fishing is what mostly draws visitors to the area: the rich catch in the bay includes sailfish, marlin, roosterfish, swordfish, yellowtail, dolphin fish, cabrillas, tuna, and sierras. March through September is the best season for deep-sea fishing, and rentals of fishing gear and boat charters can be arranged through all the leading hotels. Two top sport-fishing outfits are the **Jack Velez Marlin Fleet** (in the lobbies of Gran Hotel Baja and Los Arcos Hotel) and **La Paz Sport Fishing Fleet** (Paseo Obregón and Puerta). Both offer experienced crews and seaworthy boats ranging from 21 to thirty feet in length, with sanitary facilities.

CONNECTIONS

Mexicana flies to La Paz from Mexico City and Tijuana; Aero California flies to La Paz from Los Mochis and Tijuana. Taxis, though plentiful in town, are expensive. Car rentals, available at the La Paz International Airport, include Hertz (2-53-00); Avis (2-18-13); Budget (2-10-97); and Auto Renta Sol (2-27-44).

TOURING

Viajes Coromuel (Hotel Los Arcos lobby; reservations 2-27-44) offers a two-hour city tour and a four-hour tour of the city and Pichilingue Beach.

Reina Calafia (Hotel Los Arcos lobby; tel. 2-27-44, ext. 608) offers four glass-bottom boat tours: (1) To Pichilingue and Puerta Balandra beaches; includes snorkeling equipment, beer, and soft drinks. (2) A one-hour cruise to see fish and coral formations, plus two hours at Pichilingue Beach. (3) A cruise to Isla Espíritu Santo and Los Islotes, offering fishing, snorkeling, and swimming; includes lunch, beer, and soft drinks, snorkeling and fishing equipment. (4) City tour to Pichilingue Beach, with a boat ride to Gaviota and San Rafaelito, and bird watching at sunset.

From the United States, veteran **Sanborn Tours** (Box 761, Bastrop, TX 78602; tel. 800-531-5440 in the United States) offers a three-day La Paz and Los Cabos tour as an extension of their Northern Mexico Copper Canyon tour. Included is airfare to La Paz from Los Mochis; three nights in a hotel; a day-long bus tour to Los Cabos for a glass-bottom boat tour and lunch and swimming at a waterfront restaurant; a day to explore La Paz; and transfers to and from the airport.

> The state **tourism office** has moved to the Transpeninsular Hwy. km al Norte (tel. 2-11-99 and 2-79-75) but has kept the information booth on the Malecón at Paseo Alvaro Obregón and 16 de Septiembre. Open 9 A.M. to 1 P.M. and 4 to 7 P.M.

🧳 ACCOMMODATIONS

The following properties take major credit cards and are air-conditioned unless otherwise noted.

Los Arcos
Avenida Obregón 498, 23000
Tel. 682-2-27-44; 800-347-2252 in the United States
Doubles, from $55

A La Paz landmark, this popular Spanish-colonial hotel, featuring 130 guest rooms with balconies, is downtown on the Malecón facing the bay, with swimming pool, saunas and massage, restaurant and cafeteria, bar, disco with live music, boutiques, and touring and fishing facilities. Each guest gets a complimentary margarita on registration.

Las Arenas

Bahía de la Ventana, for reservations, write to Box 3766, Santa Fe Springs, CA 90670
Tel. 800-423-4785 in the United States
Doubles, from $125

This deluxe forty-room resort is 40 miles east of La Paz on a secluded beach on Bahía de la Ventana, across from Isla Cerralvo. Elegant dining room, two bars, tennis, fishing arrangements, and an airstrip complete the picture.

La Concha Beach Resort

Carretera A. Pichilingue km 5, Apdo. Postal 607, 23010
Tel. 682-2-24-44; 800-999-BAJA in the United States
Doubles, from $55

This All-Seasons Inn has 109 guest rooms with ocean view, private beach, swimming pool, restaurant, lobby bar, beach bar, two professional tennis courts, gift shop, meeting and banquet facilities, and water sports—scuba diving, snorkeling, wind surfing, waterskiing, parasailing, and canoeing.

Misiones de La Paz

Playa el Mogote, Apdo. Postal 152, 23000
Tel. 682-2-06-63 and 2-40-11
Doubles, from $50

Located on Mogote, the sand pit visible from the waterfront, this 25-room hotel can only be reached by boat service (departing from La Posada Hotel, 7 A.M.–3 A.M.). Misiones de La Paz offers a swimming pool, restaurant, bar, fishing arrangements, and jet skis for rent.

Palmira

Carretera A. Pichilingue km 2.5, Bulevar Alberto Alvarado Aramburu s/n, 23010
Tel. 682-2-40-00; 800-423-8835 in California; 800-262-2656 in the rest of the United States
Doubles, from $45

This motor inn and convention center in a lush garden setting is on a beach on the west side of town. There are 120 guest rooms, swimming pool, restaurant, piano bar, and the most popular disco in town, as well as lighted tennis court, separate playground for children, gift shop, travel agency, and car-rental facilities.

La Posada de La Paz

Reforma and Playa Sur, Box 152, 23090
Tel. 682-2-40-11
Doubles, from $30

This small 25-room colonial hotel on the north end of town includes cottages with kitchens, swimming pool, restaurant and bar, gift shop, and fishing arrangements. The boat leaves from here for Misiones de La Paz (see above).

Be sure to walk around the cobblestone streets of the **old section of town,** under magnificent old trees up toward the plaza from the waterfront. There are many charming shops to pop into while strolling through this lovely part of La Paz.

Two museums are well worth a visit. Plan to spend some time in the **Agora de La Paz** (avenidas 5 de Mayo and Altamirano; tel. 2-01-62), a well-designed museum containing geological and anthropological exhibits depicting the history of the peninsula, with fossils and fascinating renditions of the mysterious prehistoric cave paintings of Baja. The paintings of both humans and animals, some found as high as forty feet above the floor of the caves, are so far inexplicable, which makes them even more fascinating. Open 9 A.M. to 1 P.M. and 4 to 7 P.M.; closed Mondays.

The other museum of note is the **Biblioteca de las Californias** (on Madero and Avenida 5 de Mayo), which contains volumes of cultural and historical data of the three Californias. Interesting paintings describe the history of the missionaries and Spanish colonization, and there is a large mural of Calafia, the legendary queen of the Californias.

The **Cathedral of Our Lady of La Paz** (on Constitution Square—the Plaza—Revolución between 5 de Mayo and Avenida Indepencia), though built in 1720, no longer has its original facade. The interest in the **Government Palace** (Isabel la Catolica, between avenidas Bravo and Allende) is largely on the outside, where a carved mural depicts Mexico's history.

As always, the **Malecón** is a great place for strolling along the sea to see the surf. It is a favorite, too, with the runners and joggers who are out at sunrise, which can be spectacular. Unusual is the **Ciudad de los Niños y Niñas** (5 de Febrero, between Avenida Serdan and Revolución), an orphanage where the youngsters are trained in printing and carpentry skills. Visitors are welcome.

☕ RESTAURANTS

Some delicacies of La Paz are turtle (*caguama*) stew, shark-fin soup, prawn broth (in Mexico a broth, or caldo, is a thick soup) and prawn cakes, lobster, abalone, dried shredded fish, and cured meat with egg. Here are some places to find them. All establishments take major credit cards unless otherwise noted, and at each, dinner for two should come to no more than $20.

Bermejo
Avenida Alvaro Obregón, Number 498
Tel. 2-39-00
This establishment, located in the Hotel Los Arcos, offers fine steaks, along with such culinary delights as lobster in garlic

sauce, and the house specialty, a heaping seafood platter of shrimp, clams, scallops, and lobster.

Las Brisas
Avenida Obregón and Calle Militar
Tel. 2-14-65

This popular restaurant on the waterfront toward Pichilingue offers a good selection of steaks, lobster, salads, and soups, such as *sopa de los mariscos* (seafood soup). As one La Paz resident said about Las Brisas, "It's ugly and needs remodeling, but the food is delicious!"

La Pazlapa
Avenida Obregón, where the Malecón begins
Tel. 2-60-25

Another thatched-roof *palapa,* this one specializing in fresh abalone steak and *caguama* (turtle) soup, La Pazlapa is popular with locals and tourists alike.

La Terraza
Avenida Alvaro Obregón, Number 1570
Tel. 2-07-77

This local meeting-and-greeting spot has a bar famous for its view of the La Paz sunset. Enjoy great frozen margaritas, seafood dinners, and hearty breakfasts of omelets and *huevos rancheros* (spicy ranch-style eggs).

BEACHES

La Paz has more than a dozen beaches, but they are on the outskirts of town. **Coromuel,** three miles from downtown, is the closest. Other special beaches with such services as restaurant, bar, bathrooms, and shaded areas are **Tesaro, El Calmancito, Las Cruces,** and **Pichilingue.** The last also houses the ferry terminal with service across the Sea of Cortés to Mazatlán and Topolobampo in the state of Sinaloa. **El Tecolote, El Coyote, Punta Arenas,** and **Balandra** are beautiful but have no services. Ask at your hotel desk to find out how to reach any of the above. **Isla Espíritu Santo** has no facilities, but the island is great for water sports and fishing, with wild fauna and natural pools of clear water. Tour service of this island from La Paz is offered by Yate Trinidad, at Esplanada de Malecón; tel. 2-09-96. **Isla Cerralvo,** with wonderful beaches, plentiful fishing, and wild fauna, is reached by boat from the Hotel Las Arenas beach or from La Paz.

The Lower Peninsula

Both San José del Cabo and Cabo San Lucas, 14 miles apart at the tip of the peninsula 118 miles south of La Paz, are grouped together as Los Cabos (The Capes). FONATUR, the Mexican government tourist development agency, has begun an extensive 4,310-acre resort project with the intention of making Los Cabos as popular a tourist destination as Cancún and Ixtapa. The locale is both dramatic and spectacular—there are great rock formations along the southern tip where seals and pelicans roost; below, the ultramarine blue waters of the Sea of Cortés meet with the crashing surf of the Pacific Ocean.

There are two routes south to Los Cabos: the scenic inland route of MEX1, still mountainous—"We thought this would be all flat sandy desert!" exclaimed a group of both German and U.S. tourists on their first ride—and MEX19 along the Pacific, approximately half an hour shorter. The south tip of Baja is not nearly so desolate as the upper regions, and along the way are several small communities with varying degrees of interest.

Following Highway 1 about 33 miles south of La Paz, the road leads to **El Triunfo,** in the past a mining town. You can still see entrances to some of the shafts. But the main attractions now are seashell arts and crafts, with delicately worked flowers and crucifixes. Wicker, liana, and rattan furniture is also made here. **San Antonio** and **San Bartolo,** tiny towns about eight miles farther south and a mile apart, are two more of those surprising oases that turn up in this arid land. San Antonio is noted for springs and a diversity of vegetation, while San Bartolo is known for mango and papaya preserves, as well as *ates,* a type of fruit pudding.

Buenavista, 28 miles farther, on the calm waters of Bahía de Palmas, is famous for angling tournaments. **Club Spa Buenavista** is a 21-room fishing resort with restaurant, bar, swimming pool, tennis, fishing boats, and a natural spa famous for thermal waters. (Closed during August; tel. 213-703-0939 in the United States; no credit cards.) **Rancho Buena Vista** is a popular, well-operated 52-room fishing camp on a nice beach a short way off the highway. Seven rooms are not air-conditioned, however. Restaurant, bar, swimming pool, tennis, shuffleboard, landing strip, and fishing boats are all on the premises. (Closed during August and September; tel. 818-300-1517 in the United States; no credit cards.) There is an RV park also, **Vista del Mar,** with 25 spaces and all services.

Santiago, nine miles farther south, has a small zoo with quite a variety of animals, with the secretary bird, lioness, and black bear of particular interest. Signs are in both Spanish and English.

Miraflores, nine miles farther toward Los Cabos, is famed for leather goods, such as belts combined with snakeskin, as well as reed handicrafts.

The Pacific route on the west leads through **Todos Santos** and down the coastline to Los Cabos, with tempting views of the ocean along the way. Todos Santos was one of the last of the Baja missions of the Jesuits—it was built in 1733. The original settlement was destroyed by the Indians a few years afterward. **Santa Rosa Mission** is of some interest, as is the theater of **Manuel Márquez de Leon,** colonial-style although built in 1944. Good beaches nearby are **San Pedrito, Los Esteros, Punta Lobos,** and **Los Cerritos.** El Batequito is a good surfing spot.

Los Cabos

With a record 360 sunny days a year and a shoreline of unspoiled white-sand beaches, it is not surprising to learn that a record number of visitors descend upon Los Cabos (consisting of San José del Cabo and Cabo San Lucas) every year. After centuries of obscurity, the Capes are coming into their own not just for fishermen but also as delightful sun, sand, and sea destinations for holiday seekers.

Historians once labeled the land here desolate, and at one time only the truly adventurous, looking for solitude and nature, ventured down the unpopulated peninsula to the Capes. Now there are both scheduled and charter flights available, landing visitors at the airport, 15 minutes from San José and 45 from Cabo San Lucas. The area has become a major cruise stop, with more than 150 calls a year, and ferry service from Puerto Vallarta stops here twice a week. The twin towns already rank fourth in Mexican tourism, barely trailing the established tourism meccas of Acapulco, Cancún, and Puerto Vallarta.

CONNECTIONS

Taxis are stationed in both San José and San Lucas; in San José there is a taxi stand in Plaza Mijares, facing the church, but in San Lucas you must hail taxis downtown on the street. A one-way ride between the two towns runs about $7. Fares from the airport to San José are approximately $12, while vans and *colectivos* charge $1.50 a head. From San José's Hotel Zone into town is $1; taxis to Palmilla Beach are about $2.50 one-way. The bus station is a storefront, with buses making nine trips daily between San José and San Lucas for about $.50. (Buses run between 7 A.M. and 10 P.M.) There are eight daily bus departures to La Paz from Los Cabos; a one-way trip runs about $3. Most hotels have tour desks arranging for tours between Cabo San Lucas and San José. For convenience and perhaps economy, a rental car is a good way to get around, and there are major car-rental agencies at the airport: Hertz (3-02-11); Budget (3-02-41); and Servitur (3-03-09). **Vespa Easy Tour** on Bulevar Marine and Madero rents motorcycles; **Vagabundo's** on Bulevar Costero, in front of the Presidente Hotel, rents mopeds; both are in San José.

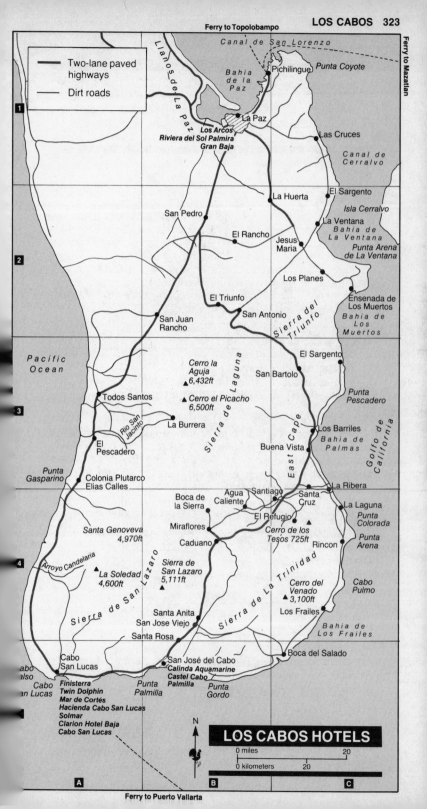

Ferry to Mazatlan

Canal de San Lorenzo

Punta Coyote

Pichilingue

Bahia de la Paz

La Paz

Los Arcos
Riviera del Sol Palmira
Gran Baja

Las Cruces

Canal de Cerralvo

Two-lane paved highways

Dirt roads

Llanos de La Paz

1

La Huerta

El Sargento

Isla Cerralvo

San Pedro

El Rancho

Jesus Maria

La Ventana

Bahia de La Ventana

Punta Arena de La Ventana

2

Los Planes

El Triunfo

San Antonio

Ensenada de Los Muertos

Bahia de Los Muertos

San Juan Rancho

Sierra del Triunfo

Pacific Ocean

Cerro la Aguja
▲ 6,432ft

El Sargento

San Bartolo

Punta Pescadero

Cerro el Picacho
6,500ft

Todos Santos

3

Rio San Jacinto

La Burrera

Sierra de Laguna

Los Barriles

Buena Vista

Bahia de Palmas

Golfo de California

El Pescadero

East Cape

Punta Gasparino

Colonia Plutarco Elias Calles

Boca de la Sierra

Agua Caliente

Santiago

Santa Cruz

La Ribera

Santa Genoveva
4,970ft

Miraflores

El Refugio

Cerro de los Tesos 725ft

La Laguna

Punta Colorada

Arroyo Candelaria

▲ *La Soledad*
4,600ft

Sierra de San Lazaro
5,111ft

Caduano

Punta Arena

Rincon

4

▲

Cerro del Venado
▲ 3,100ft

Cabo Pulmo

Sierra de San Lazaro

Santa Anita
San Jose Viejo

Sierra de La Trinidad

Los Frailes

Bahia de Los Frailes

Santa Rosa

Cabo San Lucas

Boca del Salado

Cabo Falso

Cabo San Lucas

San José del Cabo
Calinda Aquamarine
Castel Cabo
Palmilla

Punta Palmilla

Punta Gordo

Finisterra
Twin Dolphin
Mar de Cortés
Hacienda Cabo San Lucas
Solmar
Clarion Hotel Baja
Cabo San Lucas

N

LOS CABOS HOTELS

0 miles   20

0 kilometers   20

A   **B**   **C**

The **tourist office** is in the Municipal Palace in San José del Cabo (tel. 2-03-77), and hotel desks are helpful also. The offices of FONATUR, on MEX1 around the corner from the Hotel Zone in San José and at the marina beside the outdoor market in San Lucas, can provide maps, as can the car-rental agencies.

📖 HOTELS

Divided between San José del Cabo and Cabo San Lucas are perhaps a dozen good hotels, all with extensive water-sport facilities and tour desks. It is necessary to reserve several months ahead for the high season of Nov. through May and even longer for the Christmas-New Year's holiday time. Resorts in Los Cabos are generally more expensive than are accommodations in the rest of Baja. Hotels below accept major credit cards and are air-conditioned unless otherwise noted.

SAN JOSÉ DEL CABO

Calinda Aquamarina
Bulevar Mijares s/n, Apdo. Postal 53, 23400
Tel. 684-2-01-10; 800-228-5151/2 in the United States and Canada
Doubles, from $55
   This 140-room Comfort Inn, recently remodeled, is surrounded by beautiful desert gardens alongside one of Baja's sandy beaches stretching for miles. The swimming pool has a *palapa* bar, and you'll also find a restaurant; open-air lobby bar with live music; horseback riding, skin diving, snorkeling, and fishing; and car rentals.

Fiesta Inn
Bulevar Malecón San José, Apdo. Postal 124, 23400
Tel. 684-2-07-01; 800-223-2332 in the United States
Doubles, from $90
   This 159-room hotel has a swimming pool, restaurant and snack bar, pool and lobby bars, boutique and travel agency, laundry and valet service, and offers deep-sea fishing, snorkeling, wind surfing and surfing, parasailing, and both nine- and 18-hole golf.

Palmilla
Carretera Transpeninsular (MEX1), Apdo. Postal 52; reserve through 4577 Viewridge Ave., San Diego, California 92123
Tel. 684-2-05-82/3; 800-854-2608 in the United States; 800-542-6082 in California; 800-854-6742 in Canada
Doubles, from $180
   This luxurious 62-room hotel has suites and villas, a restaurant, bar, Fri.-night Mexican fiesta and Sun. brunch, live entertainment nightly, swimming pool, tennis, horses, airstrip—and the Palmilla Fishing Fleet, with six 31-foot cruisers.

Stouffer Presidente Los Cabos

Bulevar Mijares, Apdo. Postal 2, 23400
Tel. 684-2-00-38; 800-472-2427 in the United States; 800-843-9633 in California
Doubles, from $85

A social center that never stops, this 250-room hotel built of native stone has balconies overlooking the sea. Features include a pool with swim-up bar, restaurants, coffee shop, bar, a video disco open until 3 A.M., water sports, marina, lobby and poolside games, horseback riding, paddleboating on adjacent lagoon and bird sanctuary, and tennis instruction.

CABO SAN LUCAS

Cabo San Lucas

Carretera Transpeninsular, 23410
No on-site phone; 800-421-0777 in the United States
Doubles, from $100

This very pleasant beachfront hotel offers one hundred rooms and 25 villas on secluded Chileno Bay; there are two- and three-bedroom, three-bath villas, which accommodate up to six persons, plus several seven-bedroom, six-bath villas accommodating up to 14. Three swimming pools, a restaurant, two tennis courts, putting green, gift shop, skeet shooting, and landing strip complete the picture. No credit cards.

Clarion Hotel Baja

Carretera Transpeninsular km 4.5 Apdo. Postal 12, 23410
Tel. 684-3-00-44; 800-228-5151/2 in the United States and Canada
Doubles, from $125

A dramatic red-brown adobe on the edge of a cliff, with a view of Land's End, this 125-room establishment has three swimming pools, a sauna, restaurant, bar, two lighted tennis courts, and meeting rooms.

Finisterra

Apdo. Postal 1, 23410
Tel. 684-3-01-00; 800-347-2252 in the United States
Doubles, from $90

An architectural masterpiece of tile, rock, and mahogany, this impressive hotel has 58 guest rooms, swimming pool, restaurant and bar, two tennis courts, a boutique, and fishing. Perched on a hilltop, the Finisterra offers a wide view of the town, the marina, and the ocean.

Hacienda Cabo San Lucas

Carretera Transpeninsular, Apdo. Postal 34, 23410
Tel. 684-3-06-65; 800-421-0645 in the United States
Doubles, from $100

This delightful property offers 118 rooms (with more planned) laid out in seven buildings on secluded, three-tiered grounds, with swimming pool, as well as the only swimming beach on Medano Beach in downtown Cabo San Lucas. Indoor-outdoor restaurant, tennis, gift shop, and fishing are also offered. No credit cards.

Solmar
Playa Finisterra, Apdo. Postal 8, 23410
Tel. 684-3-00-22
Doubles, from $100

The name means "sun and sea," appropriate for a beachfront (but too rough for swimming) property on the southernmost tip of Baja. Seventy guest rooms, pool with swim-up bar, restaurant, and a curio-and-bazaar shop are on the premises. Modified American and American Plans during Easter, Thanksgiving, and Christmas holidays.

Twin Dolphin
Send mail inquiries to 1625 West Olympic Blvd., Suite 1005, Los Angeles, California 90015
No on-site phone, 800-421-8925 in the United States
Doubles, from $100

This deluxe 56-suite resort is on the Sea of Cortés, two miles south of Hotel Cabo San Lucas. Swimming pool, restaurant, two tennis courts, putting green, horseback riding, fishing, water sports, and a boutique. No credit cards.

In San José del Cabo, the **Cathedral,** completed in 1940 on the site of a mission built in 1734, offers eye-catching painted tiles over the door. **On Plaza Mijares.**

The yellow colonial **Municipal Palace** has a 1730 inscription on its tower, commemorating the town's inception. **On Bulevar Mijares between Zaragoza and Manuel Doblado.**

The Estuary, which marks the mouth of the San José River, is a bird sanctuary where more than one hundred species of birds flock. The first and longest finger of water leads to a picturesque view of the church tower. In dry season the estuary can disappear, but it always comes back with the rains. Canoes and paddleboats rent for $7 an hour. **Beside the Stouffer Presidente Hotel.**

In Cabo San Lucas, you'll find **Land's End,** with its fantastic and majestic rock formations, where the Sea of Cortés and the Pacific Ocean mingle. Each formation is more awesome than the next, with **El Arco,** the Arch, the most outstanding. A seal colony lives there, sunning on the rocks with the pelicans. This has to be seen by boat, and glass-bottom boats and trimarans have frequent departures for a variety of cruises ranging one and a half hours to longer sunset cruises. Some allow for several hours of swimming at Lovers' Beach (Playa del Amor), or cruise between San José and San Lucas. Boats depart from the dock next to the ferry pier, from the marina, and from the beach in front of Las Palmas Restaurant in San Lucas.

🍵 RESTAURANTS

As you would expect, food in Los Cabos, as in the rest of Baja, centers on *pescados* and *mariscos,* fish and seafood. Lobster, clams, crayfish, shrimp, squid, abalone, bonita, mackerel, tuna, red snapper, sardine, and shark form just part of the list of the fruits of the sea. In addition, there is a choice of Mexican, Italian, French, Japanese, and Continental cuisine, as well as house specialties and the delicious fast food of tacos and *tortas,* the Mexican sandwich. The local liqueur, *damiana,* is purported to have aphrodisiac propensities.

The choice of eating places is large—open-air patios, ocean-view or rooftop dining rooms—and is growing every season. (Although this is a resort area, beachwear and swimwear are not acceptable for dinner.) Here are some suggestions, all of which accept credit cards unless otherwise indicated.

SAN JOSÉ DEL CABO

Anuiti
Bulevar Costera
Tel. 2-01-03
The super margarita house of San José serves steaks, fish, and seafood to live music alongside the lagoon. Dinner for two starts at $25.

Los Cabos Grill
At the golf course clubhouse by the sea
Tel. 2-09-04
Prime steaks and international food and Sun. champagne brunch are all offered by the owners of Anuiti. Dinner for two starts at $25.

Damiana
Bulevar Mijares, downtown
Tel. 2-04-99
Named for the local liqueur, *damiana,* rumored to be an aphrodisiac, this restored 18th-century house serves Mexican and seafood specialties. Dinner for two starts at $15.

D'Georgio
MEX1, km 25 (overlooking the Sea of Cortés)
Tel. 2-08-30
An Italian restaurant, a Cabos pioneer, D'Georgio offers ravioli, lasagna, linguini, and scampi cooked with Old Country flair—and you can watch it being prepared. Dinner for two starts at $30.

Pepe's Restaurant
Palmillas Beach
No phone

Breakfast, lunch, and dinner are served by the ocean, with live music at night. Lobster and shrimp are the specialties: and the chef will cook your catch, if you bring it. (Pepe's also advertises "the best snorkeling area around," with free rental gear for lunch guests.) Lunch or dinner for two will cost between $10 and $20.

Las Terrazas del Mar

Carretera Transpeninsular km 31
Tel. 3-08-30

A romantic bamboo-strewn garden is the setting for lobster and other seafood specialties. Exotic tropical drinks are also featured. Dinner for two starts at $25.

CABO SAN LUCAS

La Balandra

Morelos and 16 de Septiembre, a short block off the hwy. at the north end
Tel. 3-01-12

The oldest restaurant in town, La Balandra specializes in seafood and familiar Mexican dishes. Popular with home folks and visitors alike. Dinner for two starts at $15.

El Galeon

Bulevar Marina (across from the ferry terminal)
Tel. 3-04-43

Enjoy Mexican dishes and seafood on a balcony overlooking the bay (there's a dining room, too). Dinner for two starts at $25.

Las Palmas

Playa Medano
Tel. 3-04-47

International cuisine and seafood are offered, along with quail and frog's legs in season. Live music and a folklórico show are featured three days a week. Dinner for two starts at $25.

BEACHES

In the San José area, **Palmilla Beach,** four miles south of San José, is convenient for renting sports equipment and fishing boats. White sand, good shade, diving, boat charters, and marlin, dolphin, and sierra for the catching, constitute the attractions here. There's swimming, too, but there are better beaches, such as **Costa Azul,** which attracts hundreds of surf lovers yearly. **Cabo Pulmo,** about thirty miles west of town by a dirt road, is ideal for diving (some of the best coral in the Pacific littoral); fishing for shark, black bass, and snapper; and seal watching.

In the Cabo San Lucas vicinity, **Playa del Amor** (Love Beach) is at El Arco, the point where the waters of the Sea of Cortés meet and mingle with the Pacific Ocean; it can be reached only by boat or by cliff climbing. The underwater **Submarine Sand Falls** are located nearby, but the sight is only for experienced divers. **Puerto Chileno** is located between San Lucas and San José. A deep downward slope and rough waves characterize this beach, which is good for diving. There are boat charters, with marlin, dolphin fish, and sierra the main catches here.

SHOPPING

Although most visitors do not come to Los Cabos to shop, wandering around both small towns is part of the fun. The best streets in San José are **bulevars Zaragoza** and **Doblado,** where everything, including traditional Mexican clothing, gold and silver jewelry, handicrafts, beachwear, footwear, wood carvings, and woven rugs are for sale in a variety of shops. In Cabo San Lucas, **Cardenas** and **Hidalgo** are the main shopping streets, although the *palapa*-covered open-air market beside the marina has booth after booth of silver jewelry, as well as other Mexican merchandise at excellent prices.

11

THE YUCATÁN PENINSULA

If you think of Mexico as a large cornucopia positioned so that its mouth is opening into the United States, you'll find the Yucatán Peninsula at its other end, curving to the north, into the Gulf of Mexico. The peninsula is a large flat plateau of land that differs geologically and historically from the rest of Mexico. Even today, when modern means of communication and transportation create instant links between all regions of Mexico, the Yucatán still has a personality all its own.

For travelers, the Yucatán Peninsula is a superb combination of spectacular resorts, some of the world's best beaches, and an array of fascinating ancient Mayan ruins that constitute some of the world's most important archaeological zones. There are also splendid cities that are too often overlooked as tourists rush from shores to ruins to shores to ruins.

> The Yucatán's resorts at Cancún, Cozumel, and Isla Mujeres are among the world's most appealing and accommodating beach destinations. Prospective travelers to these points were understandably apprehensive about the damage wreaked by Hurricane Gilbert in fall 1988. But the news is good: As of winter 1990 nearly all damaged hotels have been rebuilt, with their accompanying services restored. And while it is true that nature (in the form of beaches and coral reefs) is more difficult and time-consuming to repair than are buildings, the situation, aided by Mother Nature herself, is steadily improving.

At present, the Yucatán Peninsula is divided into three Mexican states, and each occupies an uneven third of the land mass. Smallest but most highly developed is the state of Yucatán, a triangular wedge with one side formed by the peninsula's northern coast and the other two sides angling inward to a point just about in the center of the peninsula. Mérida, the most important city in the Yucatán, is the state of Yucatán's capital. It's located in the northwestern region of the state, fairly near the coast. Most people think of Mérida and the Yucatán, in general, as farther south than Mexico City. Wrong. Most of the Yucatán Peninsula is actually farther north than Mexico City. Mérida is about nine hundred miles northeast of Mexico City.

The state of Quintana Roo, where the great resorts of Cancún and Cozumel are located, is another triangular wedge, on the eastern coast of the Yucatán Peninsula. Quintana Roo was an autonomous state governed by the Mayan Indians until the beginning of this century. Its capital is Chetumal.

Biggest is the state of Campeche, another triangular wedge, to the west of the state of Yucatán. The city of Campeche was the first Spanish settlement on the Yucatán Peninsula, but the state, from the standpoint of travelers, is the least developed of the Yucatecan states.

Geology and geography have had a great deal to do with the Yucatán Peninsula's distinctive development. Much of Mexico's land is dominated by the great Sierra Madre chains that create high fertile valleys and plateaus, with many rivers and lakes, but the Yucatán Peninsula is a low-lying plateau with very few hills or rivers and very little topsoil. Basically, most of the Yucatán Peninsula is one very huge limestone rock, so porous that rainwater seeps through to form underground rivers and lakes; and in general the only surface water is found in large natural cisterns, called *cenotes*. There are exceptions, however; the state of Yucatán has a section of low hills (it is beautiful country!) known as the Puuc region. And Campeche has a large tropical rain forest.

Climate-wise, the Yucatán Peninsula is in the tropical zone, like most of Mexico. But the region's inland heat and humidity aren't modified by altitude, as they are elsewhere in Mexico. The temperature can hover at around ninety degrees Fahrenheit for weeks on end. In the rainy season, especially in November, there are downpours so torrential that Noah himself might have flinched. The rains come daily, but they usually don't last for more than an hour or so at a time and leave the air clean and fresh. On the coasts, however, sea breezes keep heat and humidity in check.

Geographically, the Yucatán Peninsula is separated from the rest of Mexico by dense tropical rain forests in the southern sections of the peninsula, and by steep mountains beyond the rain forests. Good roads to connect Yucatecan cities effectively with other Mexican cities (and with one another, for that matter) were not constructed until the 1950s and later. Small wonder, then, that the region developed from ancient times until quite recently as a unit separate from mainstream Mexico.

Historically, the Yucatán has been inhabited since about 800 B.C. by several distinct lowland branches of the great Mayan civilization that flourished in areas now occupied by the Mexican state of Chiapas, as well as Belize, Guatemala, and Honduras. The various Mayan settlements had different dialects and customs, but there were great cultural similarities that unified them too.

But the Mayan civilization was quite distinct in culture and customs from the civilizations of the Aztecs and other Indians who lived and ruled in the central Mexican highlands. Our knowledge about the ancient Maya comes from excavations of the great Mayan ceremonial and administrative centers at Chichén Itzá, Mayapan, Uxmal and other sites that have yielded glyphic writings, sculptures, and other artifacts that indicate dates, customs and rituals, theology, and other aspects of their lives. For example, we know that the distinctive Mayan standards of beauty included a flattened head and crossed eyes, and that mothers would tie boards to their babies' heads to shape them, and suspend beads down the center of their foreheads to train their eyes to cross. We know of ritual ball games that resulted in the sacrifice of the highly honored winner. We know of their impressive knowledge of astronomy and of their complicated and symbol-laden calendar. But because the evidence is so sketchy, there is much about Mayan history and accomplishment that is a matter of pure speculation.

Archaeologists do know, however, that the Maya were very independent. Evidence shows there was extensive trade between the Maya and the Central Highlands civilizations, including much contact with the Aztecs. However, the Central Highlands cultures never ruled the Maya, nor did the Maya pay tribute to them. The intercultural interaction did influence Mayan culture, though, especially in the late-Classic period (from A.D. 600 to 900). This period of great trade throughout Mexico seems to have affected the development of new styles of Yucatecan architecture and art. Uxmal, Kabáh, Sayil, and other examples of the Puuc-style (meaning hill, and referring to the Yucatán's small and only hilly region) of architecture were constructed during this period, with some stylistic elements that were apparently adapted from central Mexican models. Some archaeologists believe that this development came about through Mayan contact with the Toltecs.

During the latter part of the late-Classic period and just following it, a seagoing Mayan subgroup called the Putun Maya (Chontal Maya, or Itza) developed trade routes into the Central Highlands and around the Yucatán Peninsula to as far away as Honduras to sell cacao beans (then used as currency), obsidian, salt, cotton, and metals to other Mayan and central Mexican settlements. The Putun Maya's commercial success translated to political power, and it is believed that they exerted their influence over Palenque and other important inland Mayan ceremonial centers, and that they eventually took over Chichén Itzá and made it the most powerful city in the Yucatán during the post-Classical period from A.D. 900 to 1200. The extensive construction and decoration done in Chichén Itzá during this period show the influence of contact with the Mexican highland civilizations. Some archaeologists believe that the Toltecs invaded and conquered Chichén Itzá in A.D. 987; others believe that style and ideas were imported from the highlands by the Putun Maya. Either way, Chichén Itzá's influence declined after A.D. 1200. The Maya continued to use Chichén Itzá as a place of worship until the time of the Conquest, but after A.D. 1200, political and economic power shifted to Mayapan, one of the largest and the last of the great cities built by the Maya. Mayapan dominated the Yucatán and all its 12 provinces until around 1450. Artistically, the settlement never achieved the greatness of Chichén Itzá. Some archaeologists contend that this may be because in Mayapan, the élite were more concerned with secular life than with religion, and most of the fine decorative art is found around the residences of the rich and powerful, rather than around the temples. There are more than thirty-six hundred structures in the city, and of these only 140 are for religious purposes, a very small percentage compared with other Mayan cities. Mayapan's dominance ended in 1440, when other Mayan cities rebelled against Mayapan's centralized authority. Thereafter, Mayan settlements continued to flourish, to study astronomy and practice astrology, to worship their gods and write chronicles of their history—but there were no longer any predominant groups that built mighty cities of stone.

Nevertheless, the Spanish found thriving Mayan cities, larger than most European cities, when they came to Yucatán. At first the Spanish thought the peninsula was an island. As far as they could tell, it had no gold or silver, or anything else that mattered to them. Nor were the Maya friendly. So the Spanish focused their attention—and their greed—on the "mainland" cities of the wealthy Aztecs.

The Spanish effort to conquer the Yucatán was made by Francisco de Montejo, of whom there were actually two—a father and son. Montejo the Elder was one of Cortés's captains. He was independently wealthy and petitioned for permission to finance the conquest of the Yucatán and then set himself up there as governor. In 1527 his first attempt failed miserably. In 1530, he succeeded in establishing one small settlement at Campeche and another at Chichén Itzá. And eventually—in 1542—Mérida became the first Spanish city established in the Yucatán.

But after their hard-earned conquest of the Yucatán, the Spanish didn't seem to find much use for most of the peninsula. They built and lived in additional cities at Campeche and

Valladolid, and not much more. Administratively and economically, they related directly to Spain rather than through Mexico City. Communication with and transportation to and from Mexico City was more difficult than it was with Spain and with France. So the Spanish colonials in Yucatán had little to do with central Mexico.

The conquered Maya were forced to leave their farmlands and move into Spanish towns where they could be more closely supervised. In 1562, Friar Diego de Landa, who later became bishop of the Yucatán, burned all but three of the Mayan codices, destroying all traces of written Mayan history and information. The burning of these source books not only cut the Maya off from their roots, it has also kept generations of archaeologists and historians from knowing about one of the great human civilizations.

Some of the conquered Maya escaped to unsettled regions of the Yucatán, or to Guatemala, but most became virtual slaves of the Spanish. And they died in great numbers. By 1700, the Mayan population was reduced to less than half of what it had been at the time of the Conquest.

The Yucatán didn't much participate in Mexico's War for Independence, but in 1821 the peninsula found itself independent from Spain anyway, as a result of that revolution. The area very quickly developed a terrifically profitable export economy, based upon an extensive plantation system that produced henequen (a type of fiber also known as sisal) and sugarcane, two crops that flourish in the poor soil and irrigation conditions that prevail on the peninsula. By the 1840s, Yucatecan plantation owners had become phenomenally wealthy. They set up remote palaces out in the bush and built extravagant mansions along fashionable streets in Mérida, which became a cultured and sophisticated city that attracted European travelers and traders.

Throughout this period, influential Yucatecans could never quite decide whether they wanted to be part of Mexico or not. The Yucatán joined Mexico in 1823, then seceded, then joined again, then seceded again. In 1847, while Mexico and the United States were doing battle over Texas, rival factions in the Yucatán did battle over whether to join Mexico again or not. The Maya, most of whom had by now become indentured and impoverished plantation workers, were not consulted about whether the Yucatán should join Mexico, but in a way, they decided the issue. During the civil confusion caused by the "to join or not to join" politics, the Maya began to rebel and demand their own lands. This situation quickly escalated into a bloody and racial conflict, the Caste War of the Yucatán.

Since the Mayan defeat by the Spanish, the Maya had preserved their culture, religion, and pride as much as possible. They had, however, also been trained by the Spanish in the use of arms and in European techniques of warfare. By 1848, the rebel Maya had taken control of most of the Yucatán, and most of the Spanish had fled from the cities of Campeche and Mérida. The governor of Yucatán was about to give an order for all Spanish to leave—when the Maya left the battlefield in order to plant their crops.

As soon as the Spanish Yucatecans were thus reprieved, they sought aid from the United States, Cuba, and Spain—offering in return to be a colony of the country that helped them to end the war. But it was the Mexican government that sent support in 1849, after the war with the United States had ended. By 1855 the Caste War was more or less over. The Maya had been pushed back to remote regions in the eastern Yucatán and established Chan Santa Cruz as their capital. The Maya maintained an autonomous state until the beginning of this century, when the federal government of Mexico took control of what is now the state of Quintana Roo.

Following the Caste War, the Yucatán went back to its plantation economy. The sugarcane crops had been ruined forever, but production of henequen was never better. The economy continued to grow until it reached an all-time high during World War I, when rope made from the fiber was crucial. The demand for henequen was so great that little land was used for other crops. Food had to be imported at very high prices, and many workers became indentured, nearly slaves to plantation owners. This eventually led to demands for land reform, and to the Revolution of 1910, which addressed those demands.

Henequen is still the Yucatán's biggest crop. Since the 1940s, synthetic fibers have much diminished the demand for rope made from the fibers. Nevertheless, about thirty percent of the Yucatán's work force is employed in the henequen industry, either growing the plants, processing the fibers, making rope, or weaving baskets, hammocks, or hats. Other sources of income are fishing, the oil industry, and shipping (in Campeche). And during the past decade, the region has been experiencing a boom in the tourism trade. The Yucatán Peninsula is Mexico's second-most-popular tourist destination, attracting fun and sun seekers with its fine resorts and magnificent beaches and fascinating foreigners from around the world with the mysteries of its archaeological wonders.

The Yucatán Peninsula is one of Mexico's most distinctive regions, with charming colonial cities, terrific beaches and resorts, and an extraordinary collection of ancient Mayan ruins. Any vacation should, as much as possible, combine all three of these elements, which, despite the expansiveness of the peninsula, can be done without too much difficulty. Plan to use one of the cities as a base for touring to nearby beaches and ruins—or settle into a resort and take day trips to the city and ruins. The following is a list of what you would want to see if you could see it all. Following that, you'll find in-depth descriptions of the Yucatán's most important and popular cities and resorts, with suggested convenient excursions.

THE CITIES

MÉRIDA
State of Yucatán

Mérida, capital of the state of Yucatán and the largest city on the Yucatán Peninsula, is a delightful colonial town with a lovely tree-lined *zócalo* (with unusual *confidenciales* benches, shaped like loveseats), the wonderful **Parque Cepeda Peraza,** and other pretty parks with colorful flowers, beautiful old buildings including the famous **Palacio Montejo** and **Government Palace,** a grand **Cathedral** and marvelous churches, including **Jesus Church** and **Ermita de Santa Isabela.** There are excellent museums of archaeology and local handicrafts, as well as a **Zoo** and the **Botanical Gardens.** Mérida's excellent reputation for friendliness and fine Yucatecan food has been earned by some terrific hotels and restaurants, and, considering the quality and service, these are very reasonably priced. Because the city is so clean and most of its citizens walk around in spotless and sparkling white clothes, Mérida has been known, since the 18th century, as the "White City." Many tourists just overnight in Mérida on their way to the ruins or the beaches, but this charming city deserves a longer visit.

CAMPECHE
State of Campeche

This charming old port city is located on the west coast of the peninsula, overlooking the Gulf of Mexico. Campeche was the first Spanish settlement in the Yucatán, and the city center is dominated by the beautiful old **Fuerte San Carlos** and thick stone city walls and bastions, including **Baluarte de la Soledad,** that once protected Campechaños from the repeated raids of the gulf's worst pirates. Campeche has beautiful colonial buildings and churches, and an excellent **Museum of Archaeology.** The **Mercado** has hundreds of colorful stalls. The fresh seafood is fabulous and incredibly inexpensive. There are no luxury hotels, but accommodations are clean and comfortable and very inexpensive. Campeche, about 125 miles southwest of Mérida, is a good base for visiting the Mayan ruins at Edzna. The pace of life here is slow and relaxed, and the city has a fantasy-land quality about it, especially around the bulwarks and forts—but there are never tons of tourists around.

Yucatecan food is among the most famous of all Mexico's regional cuisines, and there is no place like the source to sample typical delicious dishes. Common ingredients in the Yucatán include *pavo* (turkey) and *venado* (venison), both of which are native to the peninsula. For typically Yucatecan dishes, the most characteristic spice is *achiote,* a bright red seasoning made from the crushed seeds of the annatto tree. Favorite sauces include *de pepita* (pumpkinseed); *pibil* (barbecue sauce); and *escabeche* (a pickling marinade). The Yucatecan chile *habanero* is one of the hottest chiles around, but it is used sparingly, and will usually arrive on the side, if you request it. Just in case you have the unforgettable experience of biting into one, try a Yucatecan beer. The region's popular brands include Carta Blance and Montejo (both lagers), and Leon Negro (dark). And the local liquor is Xtabentun, a traditional elixir made from fermented honey flavored with anise. It comes dry (*seco*) or sweet (*crema*) and is very, very strong. The following list will help you to figure out a typical Yucatecan menu:

Cocinita pibil is suckling pig that has been marinated with *achiote* and the juice of a sour orange (*naranja agria*), as well as other flavorings, then wrapped in banana leaves and baked in a pit with heated stones (although some restaurants now steam it) for a long period of time. It is tender and delicious. If you don't eat pork, this method of preparation is also applied to *pollo* (chicken), with great results.

Huevos motuleños is a breakfast dish (but it tastes good at lunch too) of eggs on top of a thick corn tortilla and garnished with re-fried beans, peas, crumbled sausage, diced ham, and grated cheese. Cream and onions are optional.

Panuchos are made of small thick corn tortillas fried and topped with refried beans, onions, and *cochinita* or *pollo pibil* or *pollo en escabeche.*

Papadzules are corn tortillas stuffed with chopped hard-boiled eggs and either sunflower or cucumber seeds—or both—and served with a rich tomato and pumpkinseed sauce, and green oil made from pumpkinseeds. A chile sauce comes on the side.

Pavo relleno negro is turkey that's been stuffed with spicy chopped pork and beef and cooked in a savory dark sauce made from scorched chiles (they have a sort of bitter taste, rather than a hot one); *pavo relleno blanco* is stuffed turkey with a creamy, mild white sauce with olives, capers, and almonds.

Poc Chuc is thinly sliced, grilled pork that's served with a sauce of sour orange juice, tomatoes, onions, and spices.

Sopa de lima is a rich and slightly tart broth made of chicken stock and flavored with the juice of limes or sour oranges.

When you get to the coast and the resorts, the typical menu includes much more fresh fish and seafood, for obvious reasons, and these dishes are often prepared with tomato-based sauces from Veracruz, grilled with garlic, or served breaded and fried in the style of Campeche. But some of the Yucatecan sauces are also used. As they say in Mexico, *¡buen provecho!* Enjoy!

THE RESORTS

CANCÚN
State of Quintana Roo

On the Yucatán's Caribbean coast, glittering and glamorous Cancún is the second-most-popular tourist destination in Mexico. It is a modern mainland town offering an island resort strip with pricey luxury hotels, terrific restaurants, good nightlife and shopping, and superb beaches. This resort was initiated by the Mexican government in 1974, based on a computer study that evaluated several locations for potential development. Cancún was found to have the perfect location (at the northeastern tip of the Yucatán Peninsula, about an hour and a quarter flying time from Miami, and an hour and three quarters flying time from Mexico City); good weather (with infrequent rain); ideal temperature (averages eighty degrees Fahrenheit); and wonderful surf conditions, among other factors. Cancún's high season is from mid-December to mid-April, but travelers visit the place year round. Cancún offers all types of water sports, plus golf and tennis, and excursions to the resort islands of Isla Mujeres or Cozumel and to nearby archaeological sites at Tulúm and Cobá, among others.

COZUMEL
State of Quintana Roo

The island of Cozumel is a tropical paradise, located about twelve miles off the eastern coast of the Yucatán Peninsula, in the beautiful turquoise waters of the Caribbean Sea, almost directly across the water from the beach town of Playa del Carmen. Cozumel was made for swimmers, sailors, snorkelers, scuba divers, and other water-sports enthusiasts. Topographically it is almost flat, about 28 miles long and 11 miles wide (about 189 square miles, in total). The island has one small town, San Miguel de Cozumel, on the western coast. The atmosphere is friendly and casual. Cozumel has luxury resort hotels, but prices are much lower than those at Cancún. There's little glitter here; the emphasis is on sun and surf rather than on nightlife. Popular activities include bicycling from one end of the island to the other, and boating to one of Cozumel's many lovely coves and inlets. Secluded beaches, with their brilliant blankets of white sand and cooling groves of palm trees, are perfect backdrops for intimate picnics or beach parties. Excursions to the mainland to Playa del Carmen or the ruins at Tulúm and Cobá are easily arranged.

ISLA MUJERES
State of Quintana Roo

Isla Mujeres (Island of Women) is the least developed, least expensive, and most casual of the Yucatán Peninsula's three major beach resorts. Located about five miles north of

Cancún, across the Bahía de Mujeres, Isla Mujeres is a little island, just about five miles long and about one-half mile wide. It has a sleepy little fishing village at its northern end and pretty white-sand beaches all around it—and not much else. Surf on the seaward side of the island is too rough for swimming, but the bayside waters are serene. The coral reef at El Garrafón Beach is very much favored by snorkelers and scuba divers. Some people think of Isla Mujeres as a day trip from Cancún, but others choose the island's relaxing atmosphere as their perfect getaway. Most of the hotels are a bit rustic but clean and comfortable. Day cruises to nearby Contoy Island Wildlife Preserve for bird watching and snorkeling are very popular.

THE RUINS

CHICHÉN ITZÁ
State of Yucatán

One of the largest and best-restored archaeological sites in Mexico, the awesome city of Chichén Itzá, 75 miles east of Mérida, was founded by the Maya in about A.D. 450 and reached the height of its influence from A.D. 900 to 1200. The site covers miles and includes the fabulous **Pyramid of Kukulcan,** which is almost one hundred feet tall, with a temple at its summit. The pyramid is situated so precisely that on the equinoxes (about March 21 and September 23), the sun causes shadows in the shape of a serpent that seems to be descending down the pyramid from the heavens. The additional pyramids, palaces, ball courts, the **Temple of the Warriors** and the **Group of the Thousand Columns,** along with other structures, are decorated with bas-relief and sculpted serpents' heads. There is also a **Sacred Cenote** where, it is believed, human sacrifices were made.

COBÁ
State of Quintana Roo

Cobá, about thirty miles west of Tulúm, is one of the largest Mayan ceremonial centers. Dating from around A.D. 900 to 1200, Cobá wasn't discovered until 1891. Some excavation work has been done, especially on the pyramid known as **The Church,** which is about eighty feet tall and offers a terrific view from the top. Another pyramid, **El Castillo,** is the tallest pyramid in the Yucatán, at almost 140 feet. There are also many interesting stelae and some fascinating frescoes. But much of Cobá is still completely grown over, and paths between the various structures can be difficult to follow.

TULÚM
State of Quintana Roo

Preparing for the Ruins

The Yucatán's great archaeological zones were once thriving metropolitan centers, but today they're ruins in the middle of the tropical jungle. Most of them have a staff of caretakers and guards, and there are guides available, but remember that you're essentially going into the wilderness, so prepare accordingly.

A pair of good walking shoes with thick treads is essential. Smooth-soled shoes can easily slip on rock stairs that have been polished and worn by the ages. You'll appreciate the grip of some waffling when you scurry up those pyramids.

Wear a broad-brimmed hat and bring sunscreen: The tropical sun can be brutal, especially in the afternoon. If you want to survive a full day of sightseeing, protect yourself in every way possible. Similarly, wear sunglasses to protect your eyes from the glare of the sun reflected off the rock buildings and stone walkways.

Carry a plastic bottle filled with purified or mineral water with you. Most of the refreshment stands at the ruins sell only sweetened soft drinks and these are not as thirst-quenching as water.

Although the terrific heat and humidity will tempt you to wear shorts and sleeveless shirts, you're much better off with long pants and sleeves for protection—not only against the sun, but also against insects and thorny brush.

Douse yourself with an insect repellent that is effective against mosquitoes.

It's fun to explore on your own, but there can be some danger involved. Especially in the less extensively excavated ruins, try to follow trails that are marked or otherwise obvious. Be especially careful after a heavy rainfall, when the snakes and scorpions (yes!) tend to wash into the open. At any time, think twice about turning over rocks or reaching into rock crevices with ungloved hands. You'll probably encounter a number of iguanas. These fierce-looking creatures are essentially harmless. Leave them alone, and they'll leave you alone.

When did it consciously begin, this delight in decayed or wrecked buildings? Very early, it seems. Since down the ages men have meditated before ruins, rhapsodized before them, mourned pleasurably over their ruination, it is interesting to speculate on the various strands in this complex enjoyment, on how much of it is admiration for the ruin as it was in its prime. . . how much esthetic pleasure in its present appearance. . . how much is association, historical or literary, what part is played by morbid pleasure in decay. . . .

—Rose Macaulay
Pleasure of Ruins, 1953

Beautiful Tulúm is located about 82 miles south of Cancún, on a cliff overlooking the Caribbean. This is the only known Mayan fortified town on the coast, and the landward side is completely surrounded by a protective **stone wall.** It was a late settlement and was apparently still occupied when the Spanish conquered the area in 1544. During the Caste War, rebel Mayan Indians fled to this site. The most interesting buildings are the **Temple of the Frescoes,** with traces of original paintings on inner walls; the **Castillo,** perched on the edge of the cliffs; and the **Temple of the Diving God,** depicted with wings and a bird's tail.

UXMAL
State of Yucatán

One of the most beautiful and best restored of the Mayan sites in Mexico is Uxmal, about fifty miles south of Mérida. Uxmal was probably founded during the sixth century A.D., perhaps by a group of Maya from the Peten region of Guatemala. Uxmal represents Mayan architecture in its purest form. The **Pyramid of the Magician,** with its rounded base, is really five structures built one on top of another, and each is decorated with Chac masks and other relief sculpture. The **Nunnery Quadrangle** has small chambers, friezes with geometric patterns, Mayan huts, coiled serpents, and masks. The **Governor's Palace** has vaulted corridors, friezes, and an altar. The **Great Pyramid** has nine levels and a summit that was occupied by a group of four small buildings. The **Dovecote** is built around a quadrangle and gets its name from its unusual roof, made of a series of triangular structures with small openings resembling a series of pigeonholes. Uxmal has numerous other structures not yet excavated.

We took another road, and emerging suddenly from the woods, to my astonishment came at once upon a large open field strewed with mounds of ruins, and vast buildings on terraces, and pyramidal structures, grand and in good preservation, richly ornamented, without a bush to obstruct the view, and in picturesque effect almost equal to the ruins of Thebes. . . .

The place of which I am now speaking was beyond all doubt once a large, populous, and highly civilized city, and the reader can nowhere find one word of it on any page of history. Who built it, why it was located on that spot, away from water or any of those natural advantages which have determined the sites of cities whose histories are known, what led to its abandonment and destruction, no man can tell.

—John Stephens
Incidents of Travel in Central America, Chiapas and Yucatan,
1841

CONNECTIONS

While the Yucatán was once an isolated region, it is now very well connected with the rest of Mexico and the rest of the world. Arrive by air at international airports at Mérida, Cancún, and Cozumel; national airports at Campeche and Ciudad del Carmen (Campeche); and smaller airports at Isla Mujeres, Chichén Itzá, Uxmal, and some of the other ruins.

If you are planning to tour various cities, beach resorts, and ruins, it's most convenient and comfortable to rent a car. Rental fees are on the high side, but you can cut costs by booking your car in advance from the United States, if that's where you'll be coming from: The rates are several dollars lower per day, or per week, and you'll get unlimited free mileage. If you reserve your car while you're in Mexico, you'll have to pay a per-mile charge, in addition to the higher fees. The large car-rental companies have offices in Mérida, Cancún, and Cozumel. National (tel. 800-328-4567 in the United States, 99-4-17-64 in Mérida, 988-4-18-51 in Cancún, and 987-2-12-12 in Cozumel) is more reliable than most and has a convenient no-drop-off-fee policy that allows you to rent a car in one city and leave it in another without having to pay extra charges. The company is also helpful with directions.

If you need to economize, you can rent a car selectively to see several ruins in one day (for example, to visit Tulúm and Cobá, with Cancún as your base) while using first-class buses to travel long distances between major cities and resorts (between Mérida and Cancún, for example, which is a five- or six-hour trip). The main highways on the Yucatán Peninsula are well paved and carefully maintained and are usually relatively free of heavy traffic. They are, however, narrow (two lanes only) and shoulderless, and you'll sometimes need a good deal of patience if you get behind a slow-moving truck when there's oncoming traffic. On the other hand, when there's no traffic, you can really speed along. But always be on the lookout for unmarked *topes* (speed bumps placed across the road). These dreadful devices are usually placed at the entrances and exits to towns along the road. They're intended to slow traffic, and they're very effective. If you hit them while traveling at any speed greater than 20 miles an hour, you're likely to be stopped permanently. Driving at night is not recommended: The roads are unlit and deserted.

The Yucatán Peninsula, and especially Mérida, has good first-class bus service. There are regular routes with frequent service between Mérida and Cancún, Puerto Juárez, Chichén Itzá, Uxmal, Valladolid, Mayapan, Campeche, Chetumal, and other destinations. ADO is the biggest and most reliable bus line in the region. Check with your travel agent for current schedules and costs. Buses are definitely preferable to trains, which in this part of Mexico are usually pretty run-down and not very reliable.

The Yucatán's sophisticated tourist industry offers many well-organized and convenient guided tours throughout the peninsula. If you don't mind traveling with a group, these are wonderful, hassle-free solutions to the problems of getting around to see the sights in a short period of time. Consult your travel agent.

Mérida

The delightful colonial city of Mérida **(see map, Page 504),** capital of the state of Yucatán and the largest city in the Yucatán Peninsula, is located in the northwestern corner of the peninsula, about twenty miles inland from the Gulf Coast. It is a clean, friendly, and bustling town, with colonial buildings, many pretty parks, and a rich cultural life. Mérida is an excellent base for travelers who wish to visit the nearby ancient Mayan ruins or travel to the Yucatán's beach resorts, and many of the people who arrive with the intention of just passing through town decide to stay longer and enjoy the relaxed and easy charm of the city.

For years, Mérida has been known as the "White City." The nickname comes from the dazzling impression of cleanliness Mérida has made on visitors. The sight of its citizens scurrying about town in dazzlingly white *huipiles* and *guayaberas* creates a pleasant and lasting image of brightness. Even in busy downtown areas, Mérida is swept, scrubbed, and spotless. The streets are lined with light-colored colonial buildings, churches, and monuments.

It's quite easy to find your way around town. Streets are narrow, straight, and laid out in a gridlike pattern. Most of the streets have numbers rather than names. Streets that run from north to south have even numbers, those that run from east to west have odd numbers. The *zócalo* is bounded by calles 60, 61, 62, and 63. Streets decrease in number as you go north, or east. Tourist maps are given out in most hotels, and they're very easy to follow. And don't hesitate to ask directions: Even someone who seems to be in a hurry will take time out to help a stranger. Mérida is that kind of town.

Mérida's very pretty tree-shaded **zócalo** (known alternately as Plaza Mayor, Plaza de la Constitución, Plaza de la Independencia, Plaza de Armas, Plaza Grande, and Plaza Principal) is famous for its *confidenciales,* a series of unique S-shaped benches ideal for intimate conversations, and for its well-kept sculpted shrubbery.

On the east side of the *zócalo* is the **cathedral.** It was built from 1561 to 1598, with the stones taken from buildings in the former Mayan city of Tiho, which the Spanish razed and used as a base for Mérida. The cathedral looks very much like a fortress and, indeed, doubled as one during the times of Mayan attacks on Mérida. Inside is the famous **Christ of the Blisters,** a wooden statue that survived a fire that completely burned the small town church of Ichmul. The statue blistered, but was not destroyed. Look also for a painting of Ah Kukum Tutul Xiu, the famous Mayan chief who converted to Christianity, and a life-sized diorama of the Last Supper. Next to the cathedral is the former **Archbishop's Palace,** which now houses government offices and shops.

On the south side of the *zócalo* is **Palacio Montejo,** the home of Montejo the Younger, who founded Mérida in 1541, and of all his heirs until the 1970s. The building is now occupied by a branch bank belonging to Banamex, so you can see the interior during banking hours, from Monday to Friday from 9:30 A.M. to 1:30 P.M. But take a good look at the interesting facade, with its huge family coat of arms flanked by two conquistadores standing on the heads of Mayan Indians. The palace was built by Mayan artisans in 1549.

The **Palacio Municipal** (City Hall) is on the west side of the *zócalo.* It was originally the town clock tower and jail when it was built in 1542, and it sat on top of a Mayan pyramid. But in 1735, the pyramid was removed to allow for expansion of the city to the west, and the building was reconstructed. The current structure dates from the 1850s, and has a Moorish look to it.

The **Palacio de Gobierno** (Government Palace), on the north side of the *zócalo,* dates from 1892 and contains Fernando Castro Pachecho's interesting murals (1971 to 1974) about the Maya, the history of Mérida, and of Mexico.

Walk along Calle 60 north of the *zócalo* to get to **Parque Cepeda Peraza** (also known as Parque Hidalgo). This lovely little plaza has shaded benches, an outdoor café, a hotel, several shops, several *calesas* (horse-drawn buggies) waiting for passengers, and the **Jesus Church** (also known as Church of the Third Order), built in 1618 by the Jesuits. Near the church, at the corner of calles 60 and 59, is the **Pinacoteca Gamboa Guzman,** with 19th- and 20th-century portraits and religious paintings by Gamboa Guzman.

Farther north on Calle 60 is the **Parque de la Madre** (also known as Parque Morelos), named for its modern *Madonna and Child,* a copy of a famous statue in the Luxembourg Gardens in Paris.

Past Parque de la Madre, at Calle 57, is **Teatro Peón Contreras,** a large yellow structure with a marble interior built by Italian architects at the turn of the century. The theater was originally intended to bring culture to Mérida and, after a restoration completed in 1982, still does. This is where visiting musical ensembles and dance companies perform. Check with your hotel concierge for current schedules.

Nearby, the **University of Yucatán** occupies buildings constructed by the Jesuits in 1618, as part of their own university.

Along Calle 60, farther north, at the corner of Calle 55, is **Parque Santa Lucia,** a small park with the 16th-century **Santa Lucia Church,** originally a segregated church built by the Spanish for use by their black and mulatto slaves. Parque Santa Lucia is surrounded by a colonial arcade. This was Mérida's original stagecoach terminal. It is now used for **open-air concerts,** presented free of charge on Thursday evenings at nine. On Sunday afternoons, there's also a **flea market** and **crafts fair** here.

About two blocks away, running parallel to Calle 60, is **Paseo de Montejo,** Mérida's grand boulevard. The elegance and grandeur of this millionaire's row, lined on both sides by fabulous mansions, testifies to the riches that the henequen trade brought to Mérida. Paseo de Montejo is now a favorite evening stroll. Many of the mansions have been converted to restaurants, sidewalk cafés, shops, and offices.

Mérida's **Museo Regional de Arqueología** is in a particularly ornate mansion at Paseo de Montejo and Calle 43. The building, known as the Palacio Canton, dates from the turn of the century. It was built as a private residence but was later used as the official residence of the governor of Yucatán. The museum collection contains fine stone carvings, jade figurines, and other artifacts from Chichén Itzá and other Mayan sites. There are also exhibitions about early Mayan plastic surgery, which show how Mayan mothers tied planks to their babies' heads to shape them, and filed their teeth to form points. The museum is open from Tuesday through Saturday from 8 A.M. to 8 P.M. and on Sunday from 8 A.M. to 2 P.M. Admission is charged.

The 18th-century **Ermita de Santa Isabela,** at the corner of calles 66 and 67, is a former hermitage used for prayer by pilgrims traveling to and from Campeche. The grounds are exceptionally beautiful and well-cared-for gardens with Mayan statuary.

Near the Ermita de Santa Isabela, at calles 64 and 69, is one of three **colonial arches.** The three are all that remain of a protective wall the Spanish built around Mérida in the 17th century. The arches were entrances to the city. The other two are on Calle 50, at the cross streets of Calle 61 and Calle 63.

Parque Centenario, at Calle 59 and Avenida de los Itzaes, is Mérida's outdoor recreation center, with a small zoo that features Yucatecan birds, deer, and other wildlife, plus a botanical garden with Yucatecan flora, and an amusement park. It's fun, especially for children. Admission is charged.

Mérida's **Mercado Municipal,** just south of the *zócalo,* is a good place to shop for locally made hammocks, Panama hats (called *jipis*), embroidered blouses and shirts, and other local craft items, as well as fresh fruits and vegetables and household paraphernalia.

CONNECTIONS

Air service into Mérida is frequent and good. Mexicana Airlines has daily nonstop flights from Dallas/Fort Worth via Cozumel and from Miami via Cozumel (with connecting service from Atlanta, Baltimore, Washington, Charlotte, Cleveland, Columbus, Dayton, Jacksonville, Memphis, Orlando, Raleigh-Durham, St. Louis, and Tallahassee). In addition, Mexicana has several nonstop flights per day to Mérida from Mexico City (with connecting flights from Chicago, Los Angeles, San Antonio, San Francisco, and Seattle, as well as Guadalajara, Mazatlán, Puerto Vallarta, Monterrey, and other Mexican cities). Aeromexico flies to Mérida nonstop from Miami, and has connecting flights from Los Angeles and New York via Mexico City and Villahermosa, plus one daily nonstop flight from Mexico City. Connections from other international carriers may be made through Mexico City or Guadalajara.

Mérida's airport is located about 15 miles from town, and Transportación Terrestre operates flat-rate taxis and combis from the airport to the hotels. One-way by combi costs less than $10. There is also an airport bus that operates according to an erratic schedule between 5 A.M. and midnight and drops you off in the center of town, at calles 60 and 67. The fare is less than $1. To get a taxi back to the airport, ask your concierge to call the local *sitio* (taxi stand) for you. If your departure time is very early in the morning or late at night, you might want to book your cab in advance. This system has proved most reliable. The taxi should cost less than $15.

Renting a car at the airport to get into the city is also an option. You may not have much need of a car in town because most of the sights are downtown within walking distance of the best hotels, but a car will save you time and energy in making short excursions to the ruins, the beaches and resorts, or other Yucatecan cities. Driving conditions on the Yucatán Peninsula, despite the narrow roads, are quite good: The roads are new and not congested. However, beware of the many unmarked *topes* (speed bumps) along the highways, especially in rural areas just before you enter or leave small towns along the road. To drive to Cancún, take MEX180 east via Chichén Itzá and Valladolid. To drive to Campeche, take MEX180 west.

You can also get to and from Mérida by first-class bus. There is daily service between Mérida and Mexico City, Villahermosa, and Campeche, as well as frequent service to and from Cancún, Palenque, Playa del Carmen, Puerto Juárez, Chetumal, Chichén Itzá, Progreso, and other nearby places of interest. The bus terminal is on Calle 69 between calles 68 and 70.

To get around town, walk as much as possible. Mérida is a great city for walking. The main sights are within walking distance, and the city is very pretty and quite safe, even at night. If the heat and humidity make walking difficult, take taxis. They're inexpensive and are much more comfortable than the hot and crowded local buses.

📖 HOTELS

There's no shortage of hotels in Mérida, with many hostelries located in the downtown area, close to the *zócalo*. Choice is determined by your budget, though most Mérida hotels are quite reasonable, and what style you prefer: Choices range from completely modern high-rise buildings to charming converted colonial mansions. Mérida is a friendly town, and service personnel in most hotels are pleasant and accommodating.

Hotel los Aluxes
Calle 60, Number 444, 97000
Tel. 99-24-21-99
Doubles, from $60; suites from $70

This modern six-story structure is on one of Mérida's main drags, several blocks from the *zócalo*. You leave the busy street and enter a quiet circular driveway, right in front of the reception area. The cool lobby provides a welcome relief from Mérida's heat. The rooms are painted a pleasant dusty pink, have shag rugs and modern furniture, plus color TVs with English-language channels. A large rooftop pool offers a nice sundeck and *palapa*-covered bar. The lobby opens onto a pretty outdoor patio area with lush plants. The hotel restaurant has wood-paneled walls with mirrors and serves international-style steak and chicken dishes. Credit cards: AE, MC, V.

Hotel Calinda Panamericana
Calle 59, Number 455, 97000
Tel. 99-23-91-11 or 800-228-5151
Doubles, from $65

This elegant older hotel was recently acquired and refurbished by Quality Inn. Its lobby, offices, and special-function rooms occupy an old mansion, replete with ornate stucco friezes and flowing fountains. The 110 rooms are in more modern high-rise wings. The hotel has a large pool and an open-air restaurant, plus folkloric shows for evening entertainment, and is conveniently located just four and a half blocks from the *zócalo*. Credit cards: AE, DC, MC, V.

Casa del Balam
Calle 60, Number 488, 97000
Tel. 99-24-88-44
Doubles, from $60

Located conveniently near the Plaza de la Independencia (the *zócalo*), Casa del Balam is a charming six-story colonial-style hotel with 54 air-conditioned rooms arranged around a central atrium with a very pretty fountain. Both lobby and rooms are pleasantly decorated with local handicrafts. Rooms with windows on the street can be noisy. The swimming pool is surrounded by a private, quiet garden patio. There are shops and a restaurant and bar on the premises. Credit cards: AE, MC, V.

Hotel el Castellano
Calle 57, Number 513, 97000

Tel. 99-23-01-00
Doubles, from $40

This 12-story white high-rise with 170 rooms is Mérida's most modern hotel. Rooms are spacious and air-conditioned; some upper-story rooms have spectacular views. The hotel has a large swimming pool, boutiques, and a tour desk, plus restaurant and bar with nightly entertainment. El Castellano is about three blocks from the *zócalo* and is popular with businesspeople. Credit cards: AE, MC, V.

Gran Hotel

Calle 60, Number 496, 97000
Tel. 99-24-76-22
Doubles, from $45

This wonderful old hotel had been all but forgotten until new management decided to refurbish it. They've done a brilliant job of preserving the Victorian charm of the place, while freshening paint and adding amenities. The courtyard lobby is decorated with a forest of potted plants and a treasury of antique objects of all sorts—armchairs, desks, tables, Victrolas, radios, typewriters, sewing machines, hat racks with old hats and umbrellas. The rooms have high ceilings and antique furniture, doors are of heavy carved wood, and antique overhead fans create cooling breezes. Some of the rooms have air-conditioning too. There's no elevator here: you walk up a grand staircase to second-story rooms. The hotel is off the Parque Cepeda Peraza, within walking distance of the *zócalo*. Next door, on Parque Cepeda Peraza, there's a pleasant and inexpensive outdoor restaurant that opens early and stays open late. Credit cards: MC, V.

Holiday Inn

Avenida Colón 498, 97000
Tel. 99-25-68-77 or 800-465-4329
Doubles, from $80

This neocolonial hotel differs in style from most Holiday Inns. All the 211 rooms and suites have color TVs with cable channels, telephones, and air-conditioning, and many have their own balconies overlooking a charming little plaza replete with fountain and gnarled old shade trees. There's a big swimming pool with a swim-up bar, plus tennis courts and an entertaining disco. **La Veranda** restaurant offers fine food for lunch and dinner. **Las Guacamayas** serves a fabulous Mexican buffet breakfast with *huevos motuleños; chilaquiles;* chicken with mole; and even venison. This great sampler costs about $10 per person. The bar has entertainment in the evening. Close proximity to the American consulate makes this a good bet for business travelers. The hotel also has a laundry service and travel agency. Credit cards: AE, DC, MC, V.

Hotel María del Carmen

Calle 63, Number 550, 97000
Tel. 99-23-91-33 or 800-528-1234
Doubles, from $55

Recently brought under the Best Western umbrella, the María del Carmen is a modest modern hotel with 94 carpeted rooms, all of which have air-conditioning, color TV, and pleasant furnishings. The lobby's rattan furniture is attractive and comfortable. The hotel's large pool is in an interior courtyard, with an attractive sundeck and bar area. There's a pleasant breakfast room off the pool area, and a formal restaurant offers international cuisine. Credit cards: AE, DC, MC, V.

Hotel Mérida Misión
Calle 60, Number 491, 97000
Tel. 99-23-95-00
Doubles, from $65

This eleven-story hotel has an attractive white-walled lobby with high arched ceilings, dark wooden beams, and some stone artifacts and many potted plants. The lobby is actually in an old mansion, separate from the tower building in which the rooms are located. The terrace bar surrounds a large pool in an enclosed flower garden with bubbling fountains. There are 148 air-conditioned spotlessly clean rooms with red tile floors and modern blond wood and straw furniture. A touch of Mexican decoration is added with colorfully enameled metal mirrors shaped like flowers. Rooms have showers only. The hotel is several blocks from the *zócalo* and offers a popular restaurant and terrace bar, glassed-in and air-conditioned patio, nightclub, and an attractive heavy wooden front door with a great blue stained-glass canopy above. Credit cards: AE, DC, MC, V.

Hotel Montejo Palace
Paseo de Montejo 483, 97000
Tel. 99-24-76-44
Doubles, from $45

Away from the *zócalo,* the Montejo Palace is located on what is still one of Mérida's very fashionable streets, although most of its grand mansions, which once belonged to local plantation owners, are now used for commercial and public offices. The hotel is an eight-story colonial-modern structure with ninety comfortable rooms, many with small balconies with impressive views. Rooms have color TVs and servibars. There's a garden patio with a small swimming pool. The rooftop nightclub has nightly entertainment, which sometimes creates a disturbing background din in upper-floor rooms. **Las Farolas** is a favorite for Mexican and Spanish cuisine. The larger rooms, although they have sitting areas, are not recommended, since the air-conditioning is more effective in the smaller rooms. Credit cards: AE, MC, V.

⬛ RESTAURANTS

Mérida is a great place to sample and savor the Yucatecan style of cooking, which includes such specialties as *poc chuc, pollo pibil, papadzules, cocinita, pavo relleno, sopa de lima,* and other delicacies. If you tire of these or long for something more familiar, there are plenty of restaurants with fine international cuisine or the simple pleasures—like hamburgers.

Alberto's Continental Patio

Calle 64, Number 482, near Calle 57
Tel. 21-22-98

Alberto's is set in an 18th-century town house with a beautiful shaded interior courtyard. You choose to be seated in the air-conditioned dining rooms or on the open-air patio. The menu offers excellent Lebanese dishes, ranging from tabbouleh to shish kebab, and Mexican dishes, including a great *pollo pibil.* Fine wine list, with domestic labels less costly than imported ones. Open daily 11 A.M.–11 P.M. The average cost of a meal for two, with wine, is about $45. Reservations suggested. Credit cards: AE, MC, V.

Los Almendros

Calle 50A, Number 493
Tel. 23-70-91

The original Los Almendros is at Ticul, near Uxmal, in the heart of the Maya territory where Yucatecan regional cuisine was invented. With branches in Mérida and Cancún, Los Almendros has become *the* place where tourists stop to sample local specialties, including *poc-chuc* (a dish that Los Almendros supposedly created); *pavo relleno negro; pollo pibil;* and other delicacies. The restaurant is family-style and casual. Open daily, 11 A.M.–10 P.M. The average cost of a meal for two is about $20. No reservations. Credit cards: AE, MC, V.

La Casona

Calle 60, Number 434
Tel. 23-83-48

One of Mérida's elegant restaurants, La Casona occupies a lovely old courtyard and features antique furniture and beautiful tableware. The menu offers fine Italian dishes, with a splendid selection of pastas, including linguine, fettucine, manicotti, cannelloni, and lasagna. There are also fine seafood and chicken dishes, some prepared with a Yucatecan Italian accent. Good wine list with expensive imported and domestic labels. Open daily 1 P.M.–midnight. The average cost of a meal for two, with wine, is about $40. Reservations suggested. Credit cards: AE, MC, V.

Cedro de Líbano

Calle 59, Number 529, between calles 57 and 59
Tel. 23-75-31

A terrific Lebanese menu includes tabbouleh, kibbe, kefta, and other standards, plus delicious specialties such as chicken with chick-peas and yogurt. Cedro de Líbano offers unpretentious decor and excellent service, and if you don't know much about Lebanese food, the waiters willingly inform you about the ingredients and preparation of specific dishes. Open daily 11:30 A.M.–11 P.M. The average price of a meal for two is about $18. No reservations. No credit cards.

Le Gourmet

Avenida Ponce Pérez, Number 109A
Tel. 27-19-70

When this restaurant bills itself as "international," it isn't exaggerating. The menu has steaks and seafood, Mexican regional specialties, plus egg rolls and chow mein. The wine list is international too. The ambience is relaxed and service is unrushed, making this a wise choice for a long lunch. Open Mon.–Sat., noon–midnight. The average cost of a meal for two, with wine, is about $40. Reservations suggested. Credit cards: AE, MC, V.

El Mesón

Calle 59, Number 500
Tel. 21-92-32

This popular outdoor restaurant near Parque Cepeda Peraza is usually packed: the wrought-iron tables are pushed together, as large groups converse over lunch or dinner or late-night snacks. The food is good, and inexpensive. A different set meal is served daily from lunchtime until closing—or you can choose from a list of sandwiches and Mexican standards such as enchiladas. Open daily 7 A.M.–midnight. The average price of a meal for two is about $15. No reservations. No credit cards.

Las Palomas

Calle 56, Number 481, near Calle 55
Tel. 23-15-45

Diners at Las Palomas enjoy the lovely ambience of a beautifully restored colonial mansion, an ideal setting for sampling typical Yucatecan cuisine. Specialties include *pollo pibil* and an excellent assortment of *antojitos* and seafood dishes. Personalized service makes for a pleasant dining experience. Good wine list. Open daily 11 A.M.–11 P.M. The average cost of a meal for two, with wine, is about $45. Reservations suggested. Credit cards: AE, MC, V.

Pop Café

Calle 57, between calles 60 and 62, near the university
Tel. 21-68-44

This place is a favorite with university students who want tasty fast food at bargain prices. Pop prepares top hamburgers, french fries, and apple pie. The coffee is also very good. Open daily, 10 A.M.–10 P.M. The average cost of a meal for two is about $12. No reservations. No credit cards.

Pórtico del Peregrino

Calle 57, Number 501, between calles 60 and 62
Tel. 21-68-44

When you walk through the Pórtico del Peregrino, you're entering another era. The restaurant evokes the ambience of 19th-century Mexico with antique furnishings and elegant old-fashioned service. The international menu includes fish fillets and beef brochettes, as well as Yucatecan dishes and delightful desserts. Open daily, noon–3 P.M. and 6–11 P.M. The average cost of a meal for two, with wine, is about $50. Reservations suggested. Credit cards: AE, MC, V.

Restaurante and Café Express

Calles 60 and 59, near Parque Cepeda Peraza

Tel. 21-37-38

This, Mérida's traditional sidewalk café, busy all day long, is where you can sit for hours over a cup of coffee and watch the world go by. In addition, the café serves terrific regional food, including an excellent *pollo pibil,* and desserts. Open daily 6 A.M.–1 A.M. The average cost of a meal for two is about $15. No reservations. No credit cards.

Soberanis

Calle 60, Number 483, between calles 55 and 57
Tel. 23-98-72

This local chain of family-style seafood restaurants has several branches, all of which serve exceptionally fresh seafood and fish dishes prepared Yucatecan style. The decor is unpretentious, the atmosphere is friendly, and the service is good. Open daily 11 A.M.–10 P.M. The average cost of a meal for two is about $22. No reservations. Credit cards: AE, MC, V.

SHOPPING

Mérida is a mecca for certain hand-crafted goods. Tops among these are hammocks and Panama hats, both of which are made superbly in the Yucatán. In addition, there are *huipiles* (loose cotton shifts with embroidered necklines, sleeves, and hems worn by the Indian women); *guayaberas* (loose cotton shirts with tucked fronts and some embroidery, worn by most men in place of jackets and ties in these tropical climes); *huaraches* (the attractive Yucatecan version of these comfortable leather sandals are made with cut-up old tires for soles); henequen and palm handbags and baskets; tortoiseshell combs and bracelets (before you buy these, consider that U.S. Customs prohibits their import because tortoises are on the endangered-species list); ceramics; and reproductions of Mayan artifacts.

These items are sold in dozens of shops around the *zócalo* and throughout the downtown, and by street vendors stationed outside the hotels and around places of interest frequented by travelers. There is also Mérida's huge **mercado,** located southwest of the *zócalo* in an area bounded by calles 63 to 69 and 62 to 64, with hundreds of stalls selling handicrafts as well as foodstuffs, household supplies, and clothing. The profusion of goods can be confusing, especially when it comes to hammocks and Panama hats, which at first glance all look very much alike. But there are vast differences in quality and in price. Perhaps the following guidelines will help:

Hammocks (or *hamacas*), the Mayan traditional hanging beds, are made and sold throughout the Yucatán. They are woven of cotton, silk, or nylon string in one or many colors, and come in various lengths and widths. Fiber-wise, silk is the most expensive, and nylon is the most durable. Most people buy cotton because it is natural, attractive, and reasonably priced. With any of the three fibers, you should examine the string to see that it is tightly knit, not fraying, and that the weave pattern of the hammock is tightly knotted and without irregularities. The woven part of the hammock should be firmly attached to the end loops, without any loose or frayed strands. Length-wise, the body of the hammock should be a little bit longer than your body; otherwise you'll find lying in it uncomfortable. Maya tend to be short—and so are their hammocks. You must check length carefully before buying. Hold one end of the hammock level with the top of your head and let the hammock fall to your feet. If the other end of the hammock isn't lying on the floor, the hammock is too short for you. Even though you need this length, you lie in a hammock diagonally. So width is important too. The width of a hammock is determined by the number of strings used to make it. The single (*sencillo*) has fifty pairs of end strings; the double (*doble*) has one hundred pairs of end strings; the "matrimonial" has 150 pairs of end strings; and the "special matrimonial" (*matrimonial especial* or *hamaca de cuarto cajas*) has at least 175 pairs of end strings. A person of average height and girth can make do with a double, but the wider hammocks are definitely more comfortable. So buy the widest hammock you can afford.

You can get a hammock of reasonable quality at a very good price from street vendors. But you may feel uncomfortable about standing in the middle of the *zócalo* measuring length, counting strings, and inspecting weave, and the uninitiated may end up with low-quality weave anyway. The *mercado* has reasonably priced hammocks, and so do many of the craft shops. The best hammock shop in town is **La Poblana** (Calle 65, Number 492, between calles 60 and 62; tel. 21-65-03), with two floors filled with an incredible stock of hammocks of all fibers, colors, lengths, widths, and price categories. The staff will patiently help you make your selection. This is not the place to bargain. Prices are marked, and they're fair.

While you're wandering around the Yucatán, you'll want a sun hat. Panama hats are the hats of choice. Much of the world's supply of these is made in the town of Becal, in the neighboring state of Campeche. The name Panama became associated with the hats after they became popular during the building of the Panama Canal. Actually, the local name for them is *jipis*—because they were and still are made with the pliant fibers of the jipijapa plant, although they are sometimes now made with pliant palm fibers as well. The jipijapa fibers must be kept moist to retain their pliability, so the hats are woven in dank caves and grottoes.

You can go to Becal to see this process and make a purchase, or you can buy your jipis in Mérida. They're to be found in the *mercado* and all the shops, and some street vendors look like human hat racks. However, the best hat shop in town is **La Casa de los Jipis** (Calle 56, Number 526, near Calle

65, no telephone), with huge stacks of hats to choose from. Ask to see the *finos,* a higher grade of hat with a weave so fine it is almost undiscernable. The quality of this type of hat is amazing: You can crush it, roll it up, and shove it into your suitcase or handbag, and take it out, shake it out, and it's fine for wearing. These hats, while expensive, wear forever, and the style is a classic. Those in the middle price range are also perfectly acceptable. However, don't bother with the really inexpensive hats: The weave is quite coarse, and they will fall apart or get crushed quickly, perhaps even before you leave for home. La Casa de los Jipis is a good place to learn about the finer points of well-made *jipi* hats. Even if you eventually wind up buying a hat from the head of a street vendor, browse here first for information. And while you're at it, take note in the *zócalo* of the unusual statue depicting several huge concrete Panama hats stacked against each other.

There are several especially reliable and pleasant sources for other Yucatecan handicrafts. The **Agora Fonapas Crafts Center** (Calle 63, Number 503, between calles 64 and 66, no telephone) is a government-sponsored shop with wonderful *huipiles, guayaberas,* baskets, leather goods, ceramics, and lots of toys. **Sonrisa del Sol** (second floor at Calle 62, Number 500, between calles 59 and 61, no telephone) has a lot of papier-mâché, silver, and other craft items from other regions of Mexico, plus paintings by local artists, and a small outdoor terrace restaurant with good and inexpensive breakfasts, snacks, and coffee. These days, most of the embroidery on *huipiles* is done by machine, but the boutique at the **Hotel Casa del Balam** (Calle 60, Number 488, no telephone) has remarkable old-fashioned hand-embroidered *huipiles,* and they are gorgeous. They can cost up to six times as much as the machine-embroidered garments, but work like this is very hard to find and is worth every peso. The shop also has unique woven handbags, great *rebozos,* unusual dolls, and other items, all from the state of Chiapas. For quality *guayaberas,* visit **Jack** (Calle 59, Number 505) or **Camiseria Canul** (Calle 59, Number 496B), where you can get made-to-order shirts at very reasonable prices. **Perla Maya** (Calle 60, Number 485) has locally crafted jewelry, especially filigree. At the *mercado,* look for **Curios Lucy** (tel. 21-93-41) for a range of inexpensive *huipiles, guayaberas,* embroidered tablecloths, sandals, and some items made of onyx.

ENTERTAINMENT

People promenade around the *zócalo* and downtown streets of Mérida until quite late at night. This is when the air is balmy. People enjoy being out, sitting on the *zócalo's confidenciales* or around tables at outdoor cafés, and socializing.

The city organizes popular nightly entertainment at nine in various parks and plazas, performed free of charge. Especially well attended are the Yucatecan **folk dancing** in the *zócalo* on Sundays; the **mariachis** at Plaza Santa Lucia on Thursdays; and the **choral groups** at the Ermita de Santa Isabela on Fridays. Check with your hotel concierge for nightly schedules and locations.

Romantic **seranata** music (sort of Yucatecan torch songs) is an enormously popular local tradition and can be heard in many local bars, including the Holiday Inn's **Maya Bar** and **El Trovador Bohemio** (Calle 55, Number 504, music from 9 P.M. to 2 A.M.).

Los Tulipanes (Calle 43, Number 462A, tel. 27-20-09) puts on a very touristy but fun dinner show nightly at 8:30. This is sort of a folkloric cabaret with Maya-inspired dances and ceremonies, including a mock sacrifice. The à la carte menu offers Yucatecan dishes, priced at about $12 per entrée, and there's a cover charge of about $10. Reservations suggested. Credit cards: AE, DC, MC, V.

Teatro Peon Contreras (Calle 60, near Calle 57, no telephone) presents cultural events, including visiting musical ensembles, dance groups, and theater companies, plus the state of Yucatán's own **Ballet Folklórico,** which performs here on some Sunday mornings at 11. Check with your hotel concierge for current performance schedules.

EXCURSIONS

Mérida is a pleasant and convenient base for exploring other areas of the Yucatán Peninsula by car, bus, or guided tour. The following excursions are of special interest. Hotel and restaurant information is given for sites that might warrant overnighting.

Chichén Itzá

The awesome Mayan city of Chichén Itzá is one of the largest and best-restored ancient cities in Mexico, with a complex of buildings that astonishes and confounds archaeologists. It is believed that the city was founded by the Maya as early as A.D. 450, had a period of development under Mayan rule from A.D. 600 to 900, and reached its heyday from A.D. 900 to 1200, after it had been conquered (in 987) by Toltecs from the city of Tollan, near modern day Tula (state of Hidalgo). The story of this conquest was told to the Spanish by the Aztecs, and it has to do with the legend of Quetzalcoatl, the god of creation, the arts, and learning. The Aztecs believed that Quetzalcoatl was a Toltec king who had ruled in Tollan but was then exiled from that city. According to one story, the exiled Quetzalcoatl then became the morning star. But a second version of the story is that Quetzalcoatl sailed off to the east, where he supposedly conquered Chichén Itzá and built a new Toltec capital adjacent to the conquered city. Quetzalcoatl is known to the Maya as Kukulcan; both incarnations take the form of plumed serpents. The theory of the Toltec conquest of Chichén Itzá, believed valid for years, was used to explain evident Toltec architectural influences on the structures built in one section of Chichén Itzá after the year 1000. But recently, further excavations and archaeologists' dating techniques have revealed that there are Toltec influences in structures found beneath buildings that had been built long before 987, when the Toltecs supposedly arrived. Chichén Itzá therefore remains a great unsolved mystery.

> There is no rudeness or barbarity in the design or proportions; on the contrary, the whole wears an air of architectural symmetry and grandeur; and as the stranger ascends the steps and casts a bewildered eye along its open and desolate doors, it is hard to believe that he sees before him the work of a race in whose epitaph, as written by historians, they are called ignorant of art, and said to have perished in the rudeness of savage life. If it stood at this day on its grand artificial terrace in Hyde Park or the Garden of the Tuileries, it would form a new order, I do not say equalling, but not unworthy to stand side by side with the remains of Egyptian, Grecian, and Roman art.
>
> —John Stephens
> *Incidents of Travel in Central America, Chiapas and Yucatan,*
> 1841

The site covers an area that's about two miles long and half a mile wide, and includes three basic groupings of buildings. The north section is called **Toltec Chichén Itzá,** because this is the area where buildings show the greatest Toltec influence. Included are **El Castillo,** a pyramid about one hundred feet tall, with a temple to Kukulcan at its summit. The pyramid's construction is evidence of the Mayan preoccupation with time and the calendar. There are exactly 365 steps on the pyramid (one for every day of the year), and it is situated precisely so that on the days of the equinoxes (about March 21 and September 23), the noon sun casts shadows in the shape of a serpent seemingly descending from the heavens, down the sides of the pyramid directly to carved serpents' heads at the pyramid's base. You can climb the top of El Castillo to get a spectacular overview of Chichén Itzá, or go inside El Castillo (not if you're claustrophobic) and climb to the top of a smaller pyramid that had been covered over when El Castillo was constructed. The north group also has a **ball court,** with bas-relief panels showing the ritual game, costumes, and human sacrifice of players. The **Upper Temple of the Jaguars** has huge serpent columns supporting the temple's lintel. There are friezes depicting jaguars' heads and feathered serpents. Inside are the traces of paintings that show warriors throwing spears. The **Lower Temple of the Jaguars** has bas-relief of birds, fish, and plants, and at the entrance is a throne carved in the shape of a jaguar. The **Temple of the Warriors** resembles a similar temple in Tollan: it has carved columns that look like warriors and were used to support lintels and thatched roofs. There are also masks of Chac (the rain god); a Chacmool statue (shaped like a man lying on his back, knees and elbows raised, head turned sharply to his side, and stomach flat; archaeologists think the statue was used as an offering platter for hearts obtained from human sacrifices); and Atlantean figures. The **Group of the Thousand Columns** was originally surrounded by colonnades with bas-relief, and the ruins of the market. There is also a **sacbe** (ceremonial road) leading to the **Sacred Cenote,** the excavation of which yielded human and animal skeletons, and gold and other artifacts believed to have been sacrifices to the gods.

The south section is **Mayan Chichén Itzá,** an older group of buildings believed to have been more purely Mayan in influence and style, and similar to the Puuc-style buildings found at Uxmal and other sites dating from the late-Classic period from A.D. 600 to 900. The **High Priest's Grave,** or **Osario,** is a pyramid that covered a burial chamber where human skeletons, jade, rock crystal, shells, copper, and other offerings were found. **Casa Colorada** is a pyramid (with rounded corners like Uxmal) that has a comb-roof and a ball court. The **Caracol** (literally meaning snail) is an ancient observatory with a circular tower. An interior winding snaillike staircase leads to an upper chamber with three window slits situated for close observation of Venus (the Maya believed that when Venus sets, the planet loops through the Underworld where it may pick up evil energies, and that it may be dangerous when it first rises again). The **Nunnery,** a two-story building with many small chambers, has a facade entirely covered with carved masks of the rain god Chac. The **Templo de los Retablos** has traces of carvings on its walls, and an interesting assortment of pieces of columns and sculptures.

A third section, **Chichén Itzá Viejo,** is largely unexcavated and unrestored. You'll find this section overgrown and deserted, but there are some interesting structures and carvings to be seen, especially the **Temple of the Three Lintels,** with beautiful carvings of the rain god Chac.

The ruins of Chichén Itzá are open daily from 8 A.M. to 5 P.M. Admission is charged. There is a light-and-sound show at 7:15 P.M. (narrated in Spanish) and at 9 P.M. (in English). You'll find a small museum with artifacts from the site, a gift shop with a good selection of books on archaeology and Mexico, a restaurant, and rest rooms. Chichén Itzá is 75 miles east of Mérida on MEX180 (or two hundred miles west of Cancún on MEX180). You can drive yourself, use the frequent first-class bus service, or rely on excellent guided tours.

🧳 HOTELS AND RESTAURANTS

Chichén Itzá is a good place to overnight. You're quite likely to find that you want to spend a second day exploring the ruins, or that you're too exhausted to drive all the way back to Mérida. There are several hotels at Chichén Itzá that offer thoroughly delightful accommodations. The best food and service are at the hotel restaurants. They offer daily specials and fixed-price menus, with a meal for two averaging about $25. All take AE, MC, and V, with the exception of the restaurant at Villa Arqueológica, which takes no credit cards (as opposed to the hotel there, which accepts AE, MC, and V) and charges about $10 or less per meal. In general, lunch in Chichén Itzá restaurants is served from 12:30–3 P.M. and dinner from 7:30–9:30 P.M.

Hacienda Chichén

East Access Road; for reservations, Avenida Colón 502, numbers 60 and 62, Mérida 97000
Tel. 99-25-21-22 or 99-25-21-33 (both in Mérida)
Doubles, from $60
The Hacienda has a history of its own. Archaeologist Edward Thompson, who first dredged Chichén Itzá's Sacred Cenote, bought this place at the turn of the century (for $75!) to use as his base camp. He lived in the hacienda, now used as the hotel lobby, common rooms, and restaurant, and housed his crew in 18 cabins, now restored as hotel rooms. Parts of the grounds actually overlap Chichén Itzá Viejo. There are gardens and a pool. Some of the rooms have fans only. Open from Nov. through Easter. Credit cards: AE, MC, V.

Hotel Mayaland

East Access Road; for reservations, Avenida Colón 502, numbers 60 and 62, Mérida 97000
Tel. 99-25-21-22 or 99-25-21-33 (both in Mérida)
Doubles, from $65
The Mayaland is a delightful compound of pools, lush gardens, fountains, individual cabins with thatched roofs, and a central hotel building with a charming lobby, additional guest rooms, and a restaurant. The entire place is a movie-set's version of an Art Deco treasure. The sixty rooms have built-in cabinets, and furniture of inlaid wood with Art Deco designs. The rooms are cooled by overhead fans and have louvered doors and windows. Some of the rooms have views of the ruins. Credit cards: AE, MC, V.

Hotel Misión Chichén Itzá

Calle 60, Number 491, Piste 97000
Tel. 99-23-95-00, in Mérida

Doubles, from $70 (including breakfast and lunch or dinner)
A fairly new and very modern hotel with colonial-style decor and pleasant service. There are 45 comfortable rooms with air-conditioning. Located about three miles from the ruins, in the small town of Piste. Guests are required to take the Modified American Plan, with breakfast and lunch or dinner included in the room rate. Credit cards: AE, MC, V.

Villa Arqueológica
Carretera Mérida-Cancún, Apdo. Postal 495
Tel. 5-203-3833 (in Mexico City) or 800-528-3100 (in the United States)
$50 per person
Club Med's Villa Arqueológica offers easy access to the ruins, plus an excellent library filled with reference material. For relaxation, there are tennis courts and a pool. Each room has two single beds and a private shower. If you arrive alone, you may be assigned a roommate. Excellent meals, including a fine breakfast buffet, are very inexpensive (about $5 or $6 each) but are not included in the price of the room. Since the Villa fills up early, it's best to book and pay in advance if possible; otherwise you might not be able to get a room. (Please note that if you do book a room on the spot, you'll have to pay cash—in pesos.) Credit cards: AE, DC, MC, V.

Cave of Balankanche

Balankanche means "hidden throne," and that's the name the Maya gave to this cave that had been sealed for about one thousand years: the Maya believed there was something astounding inside of it. When explorers actually managed to wriggle through narrow passageways into the cavern, they found two beautiful chambers, one with a column-like formation made when a stalactite joined with a stalagmite, and the other with a crystal-clear lake with blind fish. Votive offerings were found in both chambers. The cave is located about three miles east of the ruins at Chichén Itzá. You, too, can wriggle in to see the treasures, by guided tour only, leaving every half-hour from 8 to 11 A.M. and 2 to 4 P.M. Admission is charged. You will want to avoid this place if you are the least bit claustrophobic.

Valladolid

The town of Valladolid, about 26 miles east of Chichén Itzá on MEX180, was founded by the Montejo family in 1543. The Spanish who settled here would not allow Maya or mestizos to live in the town. Valladolid was one of the first cities attacked during the Caste War in 1847. The town was practically destroyed, but several lovely colonial buildings survived. Look for the lovely Church of **San Bernardo,** founded by the Franciscans in 1552. The town also has some interesting

cenotes, where you can swim while you wonder about geology.

For overnighting, Valladolid's **Hotel el Méson dei Marques** (Calle 39, Number 203, 97780; tel. 985-6-20-73. Credit cards: MC, V; doubles, from $30) and **Hotel San Clemente** (Calle 41, Number 206, 97780; tel. 985-6-22-08; no credit cards; doubles, from $30) are friendly and accommodating, and much less costly than the hotels at Chichén Itzá. Both hotels have decent and moderately priced restaurants.

Uxmal

The Puuc region, a hilly area to the south of Mérida, must have been very densely populated during the late-Classic period, from A.D. 600 to 900 for there are an astonishing number of Mayan archaeological ruins in that area dating from that time. Of these, Uxmal is the most extensively excavated and best restored. It is a beautiful, majestic place with pyramids, colonnaded buildings, temples, and other structures adorned with finely cut stone-mosaic patterns and carvings of serpents' heads, monsters, and masks of the rain god Chac, with huge noses that look like elephant trunks.

The site is dominated by the extraordinary **Pyramid of the Magician,** so named because, according to legend, the structure was erected overnight by a dwarf with magical powers. Actually, excavation has revealed that the pyramid is the product of several phases of construction over a period of about three hundred years, and that there are several different pyramids superimposed on each other. The overall shape of the pyramid is unusual in that it has an elliptical rather than square base. The various levels of the pyramid have beautifully carved Chac and monster masks and decorative lattice designs.

The **Nunnery** is a quadrangle of buildings, each of a different height and with distinct decorative details and a beautiful arched entryway. Curiously, the walls of these buildings slope outward. In the quadrangle, the **North Building,** thought to be the oldest, has two temples with friezes, lattice design, Chac masks, sculptures of nude male prisoners, and niches containing carvings that show traditional Mayan thatched huts. The **East Building,** least ornate, has Chac masks over the central doorway and at the corners, and carvings of double-headed serpents. The **South Building** contains more carvings of Mayan huts. The **West Building** was last constructed and is most ornate. There are three-dimensional sculptures and geometric bas-relief with serpents' heads as a motif.

The **Casa de la Tortugas** (House of the Turtles) has turtles carved all along the upper molding, and each has a differ-

There is, then, no resemblance in these remains to those of the Egyptians; and, failing here, we look elsewhere in vain. They are different from the works of any other known people, of a new order, and entirely and absolutely anomalous: they stand alone.

I invite to this subject the special attention of those familiar with the arts of other countries; for, unless I am wrong, we have a conclusion far more interesting and wonderful than that of connecting the builders of these cities with the Egyptians or any other people. It is the spectacle of a people skilled in architecture, sculpture, and drawing, and, beyond doubt, other more perishable arts, and possessing the cultivation and refinement attendant upon these, not derived from the Old World, but originating and growing up here, without models or masters, having a distinct, separate, independent existence; like the plants and fruits of the soil, indigenous.

—John Stephens
Incidents of Travel in Central America, Chiapas and Yucatan,
1841

ent geometric pattern on its back. This building is considered one of the finest examples of the type of Puuc-style architecture found throughout this region.

The **Great Pyramid** and **Dovecote** have been only partially restored, but you can see the great palace structure built on top. The palace is decorated with carvings of parrots and Chac masks (on some of these, the trunklike nose serves as a step). The Dovecote is in ruins, but you can see what remains of it to the west of the pyramid.

The **Palacio del Gobernador** is situated on an enormous manmade platform about fifty feet higher than the other areas in Uxmal. It is about 330 feet long and has three wings connected by typical corbel arches. The building is covered with an incredibly intricate frieze of geometric patterns, Chac masks, and serpents. It is thought that the palace was also an observatory situated for watching the planet Venus as it rose over the pyramid at nearby Nohpat (between Uxmal and Kabáh), supposedly after a journey through the evil Underworld.

Uxmal was connected to Kabáh by a *sacbe,* or sacred road, and the **archway** leading to that road is located in the southernmost area of the Uxmal archaeological zone.

Uxmal is open daily from 8 A.M. to 5 P.M. There is an admission fee. A light-and-sound show is offered, narrated at 7:15 P.M. in Spanish and 9 P.M. in English. There is also a small museum with artifacts discovered during the excavations, along with a gift shop and refreshment stand.

Uxmal is about fifty miles south of Mérida on MEX261. You can get there by car or by first-class bus. Bus service is frequent, but the last public bus leaves the site after the Spanish light-and-sound show. If you want to see the English version, you'll have to arrange other transportation back to Mérida. Or you can take a guided tour, which includes the English light-and-sound show, and can be arranged through Aviomar (tel. 99-24-60-99 in Mérida).

📻 HOTELS

There are three very pleasant hotels at Uxmal, and it may be a very good idea for you to stay overnight for a second day of touring this archaeological zone—or to get a fresh start in going on to nearby Kabáh, Sayil, Xlapak, and Labna. If you're looking for a good meal, stick with the hotel dining rooms. They're the best and most reliable.

Hacienda Uxmal
On MEX261, across from the ruins; for reservations, Avenida Colón 502, numbers 60 and 62, 97000
Tel. 99-25-21-22 or 99-25-21-33 (both in Mérida)
Doubles, from $55
This is a very beautiful hacienda-like hotel with lovely shaded patios and lush gardens surrounded by an old-fashioned veranda with comfortable cane chairs and rockers. There's a large, well-kept pool. The 82 rooms are colonial-style, clean, and recently refurnished, with overhead fans for cooling. The dining room is large and airy, and has a patio extension. The menu offers typical Yucatecan dishes, plus traditional Mexican favorites and standard international fare. The restaurant serves wine and mixed drinks. The average cost of a meal for two, with wine, is about $32. Both the hotel and the restaurant take AE, MC, V.

Hotel Misión Uxmal
Carretera Mérida-Campeche km 78, 97000
Tel. 99-24-73-08 (in Mérida)
Doubles, from $60
The Misión is an attractive modern building with colonial-style furnishings in its spacious lobby and fifty air-conditioned rooms. Some of the rooms have balconies with views overlooking the ruins. A pleasant pool and landscaped grounds are also offered. The on-premises restaurant offers an international menu, some Yucatecan favorites, and a wine list. The average cost of a meal for two, with wine, is about $30. Again, both the hotel and the restaurant take AE, DC, MC, V.

Villa Arqueológica
Apdo. Postal 449
Tel. 5-203-3833 (in Mexico City), 800-528-3100 (in the United States)
$50 per person
Another of Club Med's excellent Villas Arqueológicas, this one offers easy access to the ruins, a library filled with fine background material, and a pool and tennis too. The rooms come with two single beds and a private shower. If you arrive alone, you may be assigned a roommate. The meals, as at Club Med's

vacation villages, are excellent; though inexpensive (about $5 or $6 each), however, they are not included in the price of the room. If you don't book and pay in advance, you'll have to take your chances when you get there—and you'll have to pay cash (pesos). Otherwise, AE, MC, V.

Yaxcopoil

One of the advantages of traveling to Uxmal by car is that you can stop at Yaxcopoil, a fabulous 17th-century hacienda that has been restored to the period of the great henequen boom in the 1880s—and the place really gives you a good idea of what the life of a wealthy plantation owner was like. Wandering through the living rooms, bedrooms, office, dining room, kitchen, pantry, and bathroom of this hacienda is like reading the owner's personal diary. There are photos of the owners, old books and documents, cane and wood rockers, rifles, hooks on the walls from which hammocks were suspended (even the wealthy preferred to sleep in hammocks in this heat and humidity), mirrors, rolltop desks topped with open record books, oil lamps, a private chapel, a porcelain toilet made in England, ceramics and silverware, and more. The place is usually deserted, except for a few children chasing pigs around the large courtyard, and the delightful caretaker who knows every nook and cranny of this place and will take care to share with you all sorts of interesting anecdotes. The hacienda is easy to find: Just keep an eye on the right side of the road for an incredibly beautiful double Moorish arch. That's the gate. It's about 20 miles south of Mérida on MEX261. Open Monday through Saturday from 8 A.M. to sunset. Admission fee charged.

Campeche and Edzna

Instead of returning to Mérida, you might choose to continue to Campeche (about 120 miles from Mérida, about seventy miles from Uxmal), perhaps with a stop at the Mayan ruins at Edzna. Campeche, a charming old port city on the west coast of the Yucatán Peninsula overlooking the Gulf of Mexico, was the first Spanish settlement in the Yucatán. The city is still dominated by the beautiful old thick stone walls, bulwarks, and forts built to protect Campechaños from the repeated raids of the Gulf Coast's worst pirates. Campeche has beautiful colonial buildings and a fine *zócalo*. The fresh seafood is fabulous—and incredibly inexpensive. There are clean, comfortable, and moderately priced accommodations. It takes about three hours to get from Mérida to Campeche by car or bus, along MEX180. That makes it a reasonable excursion from Mérida, but Campeche is a delightful destination in its own right. (For more information, see **Campeche,** below.)

A visit to Mérida is often combined with stops at the Caribbean resorts of Cancún and Cozumel. Both of these resorts are covered as separate destinations, below.

Cancun

The Mayan royalty who visited this Caribbean island, beginning at about A.D. 250, named the place Cancún, meaning "pot of gold." That name may well have been a prophecy, for today Cancún is the second-most-important tourist destination in Mexico (after Acapulco) and is a tremendous source of foreign revenue for the country.

But centuries passed between Mayan settlement on the island and the foundation of modern resort Cancún in 1974. During all that time, little of consequence occurred on this island. Cancún, you see, has very little history.

This city and resort are the progeny of finance and logistics, an invention of the computer age. The plan for development of Cancún was decided upon by the Mexican government through computer analysis of such factors as location (at the northeastern tip of the Yucatán Peninsula, about an hour and a quarter flying time from Miami and an hour and three-quarters flying time from Mexico City); humidity (it rarely rains here); temperature (average is eighty degrees Fahrenheit); and surf conditions (excellent). Apparently, the computer was right. At least the tourists think so, and they flock to Cancún year-round. This resort is truly a pot of gold for Mexico.

Cancún has two sections, the hotel resort zone (Zona Hotelera) and the town. The resort zone is on a 14-mile-long and very narrow island that's shaped like the number seven, with the top line of the seven at the northern end, facing the **Bahía de Mujeres** (Bay of Women) and the **Isla Mujeres** (see below). At the bend in the seven, on the seaward side, is **Punta Cancún.** And the downstroke of the seven runs from north to south and faces the beautiful turquoise Caribbean Sea. There are luxury resort hotels along both the North and East shores. On the western side of the island are **Laguna Nichupte,** an expansive lagoon, and **Laguna Bojórequez,** a small lagoon formed inside Laguna Nichupte (near the bend in the seven by a spit of land and a small island on which the **Pok-ta-Pok** golf course is located.

Cancún Island has been joined to the mainland by bridges at both ends, and Kukulcan Boulevard runs the length of the island, from the mainland at one end and back onto the mainland at the other. Cancún City is located on the mainland, across from the westernmost end of the top of the seven. It is a modern town, with banks, bus terminal, government offices, restaurants, shops, and less expensive hotels. The core of the city is an area of about 12 square blocks, and the main street for shopping—and everything else—is **Avenida Tulúm.** It's easy to get around this compact area on foot, but you need some form of transportation to get to town from the hotel zone, or to get around the hotel zone itself.

The first thing anyone does when they arrive in Cancún is head for the **beaches.** On the island, the beautiful beaches on the **North Shore,** including **Playa Langosta, Playa Tortuga,** and **Playa Caracol,** face the Bahía de Mujeres, and have calm and shallow waters with little surf. Along the **East Shore** of the island, the beaches, including **Playa Gaviota, Playa Chacmool,** and **Playa del Rey,** face the Caribbean Sea and have beautiful turquoise water, strong surf, and sometimes dangerous undertow (always heed warning flags on the beaches!). Some of the best swimming and most interesting diving is around **Punta Cancún,** where the North and East shores meet. These shores are dominated by luxury hotels, but you do not have to be staying at a hotel to enjoy its beachfront. In Mexico, all beaches are public by law, so don't be intimidated about setting down your towel on any beach on the island. You can also go to the mainland beaches, including **Playa las Perlas, Playa Juventud,** and **Playa Linda,** all of which have decent swimming, but not much of the glamour of the island beaches in the hotel zone.

Cancún abounds in **water sports,** including swimming, snorkeling, scuba diving, wind surfing, waterskiing, sailing, and lagoon and deep-sea fishing. Punta Cancún and Playa Tortuga are most popular for snorkeling and scuba diving. The lagoons are favored for wind surfing and waterskiing. At several marinas, you can hire boats for sailing or fishing. There are also convenient fishing or diving package tours and day cruises to nearby **Isla Mujeres** or slightly farther to the island of **Cozumel** for a combination of swimming and sightseeing. You can get current schedules of tours and cruises and book reservations through Aviomar (tel. 988-4-68-46).

Other sports include **golf** at the 18-hole Robert Trent Jones **Pok-ta-Pok Golf Course** (tel. 988-3-08-71 or 988-3-12-30), where one of the hazards at the 12th hole is a genuine Mayan ruin. Pok-ta-Pok and most of the resort hotels have **tennis** courts and instruction. And if you consider **shopping** a sport, you'll find the island's superb malls a champion-caliber challenge.

Although Cancún began its modern incarnation in 1974, the island has Mayan ruins at **El Rey,** along the East Shore near Punta Nizuc. The ruins are of minor importance, but it's fun to climb over the platforms and see the temple. This ceremonial center was apparently established in ancient times, abandoned, and then used again from about 1200 to around the time of the Conquest. The ruins are open daily from 8 A.M. to 5 P.M. A small admission fee is charged.

There is also the **Museo Arqueológico de Cancún,** with a small but interesting collection of Mayan artifacts found at Cancún and at sites throughout Quintana Roo. There are bowls, tools, and some jewelry, mostly dating from around the time of the Conquest. The museum is open Tuesday through Saturday from 10 A.M. to 5 P.M. There is an admission fee.

If you are interested in further exploring the ancient Mayan civilization, you can easily use Cancún as a base from which to take a variety of day trips to the significant ruins at **Chichén Itzá** (see above), **Tulúm,** or **Cobá** (see below).

CONNECTIONS

Cancún's international airport has nonstop or direct flights from several U.S. cities: Continental Airlines has nonstop flights to Cancún from Houston, and direct flights from Denver, with connecting flights from other U.S. cities. American Airlines flies nonstop to Cancún from Dallas; United Airlines does likewise from Chicago; and both have connecting flights from other U.S. cities. Mexicana, in addition to flying nonstop to Cancún from Baltimore, and offering connecting flights from many U.S. cities, also has nonstop flights daily from Mexico City with connecting flights from San Francisco, and from Guadalajara with connecting flights from Los Angeles. Aeromexico has nonstop flights to Cancún from Houston and New York, as well as a daily nonstop flight from Mexico City. Regional Aero Caribe and Aero Cozumel fly between Cancún and Cozumel or Chichén Itzá.

The airport is about 12 miles from the beginning of the hotel zone. The best way to get to your hotel is to take a flat-fee combi operated by Transportación Terrestre. The one-way fare is less than $10. You can also pick up a rental car at the airport from any one of a number of agencies with airport offices. This is a good idea, as Cancún is spread out, and a car is very useful in getting around the resort zone, into town, and for day trips to fascinating archaeological sites in the area. If you're driving to Cancún from Mérida, take MEX180 via Chichén Itzá. Cancún is an island, but there is no problem getting there by car: The island is connected to the mainland at both ends by bridges.

Regular first-class buses run between Cancún and Mérida, Mexico City, Tulúm, and Playa del Carmen (where you can get a passenger ferry to Cozumel). Cancún's bus terminal is at avenidas Tulúm and Uxmal.

Taxis are available for getting around town, but these can be expensive. Always negotiate the fee for a ride to your destination before you get into the taxi. The public buses are both inexpensive and crowded. If you want your own means of transportation, but find the car-rental fees exorbitant, you might opt for a moped. At the dozen or so moped-rental agencies, rates and conditions of the scooters vary significantly. Check several before choosing the one you're going to do business with. Also available are *calesas* (although most calesas are horse-drawn, these are horseless buggies with two or four seats), that are a little more expensive than a moped but less costly than a car. Both mopeds and *calesas* are convenient for getting from the hotel zone into town and back, but you have to be very cautious about potholes in the roads, and you really cannot use either as a means of transportation to the ruins or anywhere outside of Cancún proper.

🧳 HOTELS

Cancún has two categories of hotels. Beach hotels are located in the hotel zone on the island. These are exclusive and expensive resorts, with all the amenities, right on the beach and near the fancy—and pricey—resort zone restaurants and shops. All the big resort hotel chains have properties in Cancún. If you favor the Sheraton or Krystal or one of the other big names, you might as well reside with them. There are smaller chains and independents in the hotel zone too. These have the posh location, can usually provide excellent service, and tend to be somewhat less expensive. The second category of hotels is located downtown, and they are much less expensive than the resort hotels in the hotel zone. These are smaller hotels, which means that in some of them you get highly personalized service, while others seem quite lax. If you stay downtown, you can get to the hotel zone easily and use all the beaches there (according to Mexican law, all beaches are public). And you benefit by being closer to many of Cancún's better and reasonably priced restaurants.

Both beach resort and downtown hotels have two seasons. High season is from mid-Dec. to mid-Apr., when the snowbirds fly south to vacation in Mexico's warmth. Room prices are highest during this period—as much as double what they are during the off-season. In Cancún, rooms are booked year-round because the weather during summer rarely becomes unbearably hot, and there isn't usually enough rain to ruin a beach vacation.

If you're booking a hotel for a week-long vacation during the high season, your best bet for luxury and economy is to take a package tour that includes airfare and accommodations at one of the beach resort hotels. If you're going to spend just a few nights in Cancún during the high season, you're probably better off booking in a downtown hotel. During the low season, especially if you're only planning to stay a few days, you will find even the more luxurious resort hotels affordable. And once again, please note that at press time, post-Hurricane Gilbert paranoia will enable you to find Cancún bargains in the unlikeliest of places.

BEACH RESORT HOTELS

Hotel Calinda Cancún
Paseo Kukulcan, 77500
Tel. 988-3-16-00 or 800-228-5151

Doubles, from $130

The architecture here is modern Mayan pyramid, with two wings. There are 280 rooms with views of the Caribbean or of Laguna Nichupte. All rooms have cable TVs and servibars; some have spacious balconies. The pool has a *palapa*-covered bar and broad sundeck. There are restaurants, bars with live entertainment, and on-premises dive shop. Credit cards: AE, DC, MC, V.

Hotel Camino Real

Punta Cancún, Apdo. 14, 77500
Tel. 988-3-01-00 or 800-228-3000
Doubles, from $210

Camino Real's building covers several acres of prime property on the tip of the Yucatán Peninsula, looking out to the Isla Mujeres. The hotel is surrounded by sea and lagoon—thus a lovely vista wherever you look. Delightful gardens and patio areas create a sense of seclusion, even when the resort is full. There are 291 rooms and suites, accented with colorful Mexican folk-art decorations and equipped with cable TVs and servibars. The rooms have furnished balconies with great views. Four lighted tennis courts, large pool with swim-up bar, two secluded beaches, and organized water sports complete the picture. Credit cards: AE, DC, MC, V.

Cancún Sheraton

Paseo Kukulcan, Apdo. 834, 77500
Tel. 988-3-19-88 or 800-325-3535
Doubles, from $130

This beautiful hotel has a spacious, gleaming marble lobby that opens into an enormous recreation area with patios, sundecks and pool, poolside bar, tennis courts, and several beautiful gardens. On the grounds is a small Mayan ruin, very beautiful and exotic. You climb up a hill to see it and get, as a bonus, a panorama of the sea and lagoon. The 325 spacious rooms have views too—of either the ocean (most expensive) or bay. Some of the rooms have Jacuzzis; all have cable TV and servibars. The hotel has several restaurants and bars, a lively disco, and game rooms for adults, teenagers, and toddlers. Luxury all the way, and a very pleasant staff. Credit cards: AE, DC, MC, V.

Hotel Casa Maya

Paseo Kukulcan km 5, 77500
Tel. 988-3-05-55 or 800-262-2656
Doubles, from $130

The hotel has two eight-story tower buildings. Around the top of each is a bas-relief with a Mayan motif. Inside, the lobby has a large waterfall. There are 140 rooms and 160 suites with sea views. The suites have kitchen and dining areas, and all rooms have cable TVs and refrigerators. The kidney-shaped pool is large, and there is a smaller pool for children. The beach is broad and pretty, and there is an excellent beachfront seafood restaurant. Credit cards: AE, DC, MC, V.

Club Med

Punta Nizuc, 77500

Tel. 988-4-20-90 or 800-528-3100

Weekly package (Sun.–Sat.), per person, including meals and wine, and most sports and other organized activities, from $1,000 (land/air packages also available)

Club Med Cancún is located on Punta Nizuc, at the farthest end of the island resort zone. This is a beautiful spot. The main building surrounds a huge atrium with a bar, restaurant, and theater. In front of it is the large pool, sundeck, poolside bar and lounge, and disco. The accommodations are typically Club Med, with two twin beds (if you go alone, you'll be assigned a roommate), small sitting area, and bath with private shower. Some rooms have small balconies. Club meals are sumptuous feasts, always with several entrées, a huge salad, heaps of fresh fruit, and lush desserts. Breakfast and lunch are buffets, and dinner is served family-style, around large tables that seat up to ten people. There's always a full carafe of house wine on the table. You can sit on the beach and soak up the sun, play tennis, wind surf, sail, do aerobics or water exercises, or hang out in the arts-and-crafts center and be creative. Participate in or simply watch nightly shows, and dance until dawn. Credit cards: AE, DC, MC, V.

Exelaris Hyatt Cancún Caribe

Paseo Kukulcan, Apdo. 353, 77500

Tel. 988-3-00-44 or 800-228-9000

Doubles, from $135

The older of Hyatt's two Cancún properties is a semicircular structure with 202 comfortable modern rooms with balconies, and higher-priced beachfront villas—all overlooking a lovely white-sand beach and turquoise sea. Rooms have cable TV and servibars and are decorated in pleasing pastel colors. The lobby incorporates a waterfall into its decor. The hotel's large pool is surrounded by a pleasant sundeck and lawn area. You'll find a poolside bar and tennis courts, plus restaurants and disco. Credit cards: AE, DC, MC, V.

Exelaris Hyatt Regency Cancún

Hotel Zone 1201, 77500

Tel. 988-3-09-66 or 800-228-9000

Doubles, from $135

The hotel's architecture revolves around a 14-story central atrium with landscaped interior balconies that look like hanging gardens. There are three hundred rooms with colorful furnishings, cable TVs, and servibars. Rooms have small balconies, some with views of the sea. There are two Regency Club floors with their own concierge, private lobby, and other amenities. Three restaurants offer international and Italian cuisine and seafood. The very large pool (complete with waterfall) is shaped like a peanut and is surrounded by a sundeck. The hotel's beachfront, however, is small and often crowded. Credit cards: AE, DC, MC, V.

Fiesta Americana Cancún
Bulevar Cancún, 77500
Tel. 988-3-14-00 or 800-223-2332
Doubles, from $180

The unusual village-like architecture is a welcome change from the soaring white towers that crowd Cancún's shores. The ambience of the place is definitely colorful, filled with energy and activity. The 286 rooms have ocean views and balconies, as well as cable TV and servibars. Great social life in the restaurants, bars, disco, and at the pool, which has a cooling waterfall and warming sundeck. Credit cards: AE, DC, MC, V.

Fiesta Americana Plaza Cancún and Villas
Paseo Kukulcan km 11, 77500
Tel. 988-3-10-22 or 800-223-2332
Doubles, from $170

This exciting resort complex is very pretty and very large, with a plaza section and a villa section, along 1,350 feet of Cancún's beach. In all, there are 636 rooms and suites, all housed in a pink-and-white building, and all featuring soothing beige-and-pastel decor. Most rooms are split-level, with sitting area and bedroom separated by several stairs. All rooms have cable TVs and servibars. There are pools, restaurants, bars, and recreational areas throughout the property. Credit cards: AE, DC, MC, V.

Krystal Cancún
Paseo Kukulcan, Number 9, Punta Cancún, 77500
Tel. 988-3-11-33 or 800-231-9860
Doubles, from $220

The overall architectural style of this hotel isn't very inspired, but the landscaping is thrilling. The super-sized pool meanders through a patio and has a cooling waterfall and several bridges above. There's an outdoor stage area backed by seven columns, with the sea in the background, used for fiestas, entertainment, and ceremonies (great place for a wedding!). Many sun chairs are gathered around the patio, and some areas are shaded by *palapa* huts. One drawback: the beachfront is narrow, especially at high tide. For an indoor workout, there's a gym with weight-training equipment. The 322 rooms are pleasantly furnished with beige, browns, and earth tones, all have cable TVs and servibars, and most have sea views and small balconies. The pretty lobby is decorated with blue tiles and stucco. The Krystal has excellent restaurants, including **Bogart's** (see **Restaurants,** below), and lively bars, and the disco **Christine** is one of the best in Cancún. Credit cards: AE, DC, MC, V.

Stouffer's Presidente
Bulevar Cancún 7, 77500
Tel. 988-3-02-00 or 800-447-6147
Doubles, from $220

The hotel is a modern tower with several wings and a pleasant lobby. There are 294 rooms with at least partial ocean views. One of the two pools offers five Jacuzzi jets and a swim-up bar. This is a great base for the sports-minded: Water activities include scuba, snorkeling, waterskiing, sailing, wind surfing, and deep-sea fishing. There are lighted tennis courts and a nearby 18-hole golf course. Credit cards: AE, DC, MC, V.

Villas Tacul

Playa Langosta, Apdo. 290, 77500
Tel. 988-3-03-49
Doubles, from $180

This unusual hideaway offers 25 private villas with two or more bedrooms, all with ocean views, arranged around a free-form swimming pool and garden-like patio. There are lighted tennis courts on the premises. Restaurant. Continental breakfast is served in your villa each morning. Credit cards: AE, MC, V.

HOTELS IN TOWN

Hotel America

Avenidas Tulúm and Brisa, 77500
Tel. 988-4-15-00
Doubles, from $70

This modern high-rise hotel has two hundred colorfully decorated rooms, with orange walls, wicker furniture, wall-to-wall carpeting, and cable TV. There's a pool on the premises, and a terrific beach club and tennis courts are five minutes away by free shuttle bus. Pleasant service, coffee shop, and bar. Credit cards: AE, MC, V.

Hotel María de Lourdes

Avenida Yaxchilan, 77500
Tel. 988-4-47-44
Doubles, from $55

The Hotel María de Lourdes won't win any points for decor, but the lobby and 51 rooms are clean, and the staff is pleasant. And the hotel's price and excellent location, at the beginning of the Zona Hotelera, make it a good choice for budget-conscious vacationers who plan to spend most of their time on the beach or at the discos anyway. The hotel's pool is very pleasant, and the restaurant serves typical Mexican dishes at reasonable prices. Credit cards: AE, MC, V.

Hotel Plaza Kokai

Uxmal 26, 77500
Tel. 988-4-36-66
Doubles, from $65

This place is a real find! Forty-eight comfortable and tastefully decorated rooms are tucked away in a modern building. The lobby is cool marble, with a wonderful swirling mural painted on the ceiling. Rooms have pleasant wicker furniture, cable TV, and small balconies. There's a rooftop sundeck with a great view of Cancún, along with a pretty pool, bar, restaurant, and lovely stretch of beach. The Plaza Kokai offers well-maintained accommodations and good service at an unbeatable price. Credit cards: AE, MC, V.

Hotel Plaza del Sol
Avenida Yaxchilan 31, 77500
Tel. 988-4-38-88
Doubles, from $80

The 87-room colonial-style hotel has a lively lobby bar and active shopping arcade. The rooms, however, are quiet and have soothing indirect lighting, festive decor, and color TV. The large swimming pool is in the middle of a pleasant patio with lounge chairs and palm trees—and you're about seven minutes from the beaches. All in all, a good buy. Credit cards: AE, MC, V.

☕ RESTAURANTS

Cancún has restaurants to please every palate. Most restaurants offer both seafood and meat dishes, and menus tend to combine Mexican and international styles of preparation. The regional cuisine popular throughout the Yucatán Peninsula is also served in Cancún. So try to sample some *poc chuc* (pork grilled with onions and beans); *sopa de lima* (lime soup); and *venado tzic* (venison with a vinaigrette), among other specialties. But if you tire of these, you'll have no difficulty locating good hamburgers and pizza.

Los Almendros
Avenida Bonampak and Calle Sail
Tel. 988-4-08-07

The original Los Almendros is at Ticul, near Uxmal, in the heart of the Mayan territory where Yucatecan regional cuisine was invented, and there's another branch in Mérida. Los Almendros has become a favorite for travelers to sample Yucatecan specialties, including *poc chuc* (a dish that Los Almendros supposedly created), *pavo relleno negro, pollo pibil,* and other delicacies. The restaurant is family-style and casual. Open daily, 11 A.M.–10 P.M. The average cost of a meal for two is about $28. No reservations. Credit cards: AE, MC, V.

Blackbeard's Taberna
Avenida Tulúm 29, near Claveles
Tel. 988-4-16-59

This casual sidewalk café is very popular (and usually packed) because its atmosphere is freewheeling and festive, and because the food is quite good. The menu ranges from ceviche, shrimp, and lobster to brochettes of beef or chicken. There's also an indoor dining room, with generic maritime decorations, a bit on the rustic side, and a nice house wine. Open daily, 11 A.M.–midnight. The average cost of a meal for two, with house wine, is about $35. No reservations. Credit cards: AE, MC, V.

Bogart's
Krystal Cancún
Paseo Kukulcan (no number), Punta Cancún
Tel. 988-3-11-33

The most elaborate restaurant in Cancún's hotel zone features domes of billowing white fabric, high-backed rattan chairs, lush potted palms, candlelight, overhead fans, a long reflecting pool, and a hushed atmosphere; all this, abetted by attentive teams of turban-clad waiters, adds to the fantasy that you've just entered a sheik's tent. There are photos and posters of Humphrey Bogart and his co-stars, and a piano player (Sam?) tickles the keys with show tunes. The menu is varied: choose from Caribbean lobster, chicken Casablanca, Mediterranean seafood soup, or giant shrimps Krystal, dressed with brandy, Pernod, and garlic. Preparation at your table is quite an attention-getting show. Desserts are daringly extravagant. The extensive wine list offers domestic labels at reasonable prices, but the prices of imports are astronomical. Open daily for dinner, two seatings only, at 6:30 and 9:30 P.M. The average price of a meal for two, including wine, is about $80. Reservations required. Credit cards: AE, MC, V.

Cafeteria Pop
Avenida Tulúm 26
Tel. 988-4-19-91

This coffeehouse has the same relaxed—and relaxing—atmosphere that you find in the original Pop Café in Mérida. It's a popular hangout for the young and young-at-heart. The dining room is pleasant and air-conditioned, but the emphasis is on food rather than on decor. Good light Mexican meals, excellent breakfasts, and superb coffee any time of the day. Open daily, 9 A.M.–10 P.M. The average cost of a meal for two is about $18. No reservations. No credit cards.

El Campanario
Avenida Cobá 12, near Avenida Tulúm
Tel. 988-4-41-80

El Campanario's menu offers more than Mexican food. It promises a full meal of Mexican culture—a fiesta and extravaganza with regional folk dancing, music, and all sorts of entertainment. It's fun and festive, and the food is quite a good sampling of regional dishes from throughout Mexico. The show starts at 7 P.M. The average cost of a meal for two, with the show, is about $60. Reservations suggested. Credit cards: AE, MC, V.

Cancún 1900
Cancún Convention Center, in the heart of the hotel zone
Tel. 988-3-00-38

The setting is Mexican Victoriana—turn-of-the-century furnishings and photos, all bringing you back to a time in history when Cancún didn't exist. It's fun, and the fare is satisfying—good steaks and seafood, grilled or done up with some Mexican touches. And the service is very pleasant. Decent wine list, with some reasonable prices. Open daily, 8 A.M.–11 P.M. The average cost of dinner for two, with wine, is about $50. Reservations suggested. Credit cards: AE, MC, V.

Carlos 'n Charlie's
Paseo Kukulcan, across from Casa Maya Hotel
Tel. 988-3-08-46

If you've seen one, have you seen them all? No. Every Carlos 'n Charlie's in the famous Carlos Anderson chain has its own zany charm and appeal. Still, all have the energetic waiters who love to kid around with the clientele, and the menu offers the same ribs, steaks, and seafood, with a wide choice of soups, salads, and desserts. These places are reliable—that's why they're very popular and usually crowded. Open daily, noon–1 A.M. Go at off-hours (from about 3–7 P.M.), or make reservations. The average cost of a meal for two, including wine, is about $50. Credit cards: MC, V.

Casa Salsa
Plaza Caracol
Tel. 988-3-11-14

This shopping-mall restaurant serves some of the best traditional Mexican food in Cancún. The menu lists the mainstream dishes, like enchiladas and quesadillas, and adds a terrific *pollo chipotle* (chicken with a spicy *chipotle* chile sauce) and some Yucatecan specialties. This is a good place to order several different dishes and pass them around: portions are large. You can sit in the outdoor terrace dining area and avoid some of the mall-like atmosphere. Sometimes mariachis stroll by at lunchtime. Open daily, 10 A.M.–10 P.M. The average cost of a meal for two, with house wine, is about $30. No reservations. Credit cards: AE, MC, V.

Chacmool
East Shore, near Playa Chacmool
Tel. 988-3-11-07

A very scenic beachfront location sets the romantic mood in this restaurant. Candlelight and lovely classical music accompany dinners of fresh fish and seafood, steaks, and other international fare. Pasta dishes are excellent, but the wine list, though good, is on the pricey side. Open daily, noon–4 P.M. and 6 P.M.–midnight. The average cost of a meal for two, with wine, is about $70. Reservations suggested, and request a table near the sea. Credit cards: AE, MC, V.

Chocko's and Tere
Claveles 7, just off Avenida Tulúm
Tel. 988-4-13-94

The atmosphere is on the rowdy side here—intentionally so. Just think of it as background activity for a dining experience in which food plays a relatively minor role. There's graffiti on the walls (you're welcome to add some of your own) and loud music (you're welcome to sing along), along with mariachis, *charros,* and other performers who whoop things up. Food-wise, the fish and seafood are fresh, and the steaks prepared as you like them. Open daily, 7 P.M.–midnight. The average cost of a meal for two, with beer, is about $34, including a 15 percent surcharge for entertainment. Credit cards: AE, MC, V.

La Habichuela
Tierra 15
Tel. 988-4-31-29

One of the old favorites in Cancún, La Habichuela serves a surf-and-turf cuisine that has been satisfying locals and travelers for years. The garden-like ambience is casual and very pleasant, and it's possible to get a table with some degree of privacy.

Open daily, 10 A.M.–7 P.M. The average cost of a meal for two is about $20. No reservations. Credit cards: AE, MC, V.

Hard Rock Café
Plaza Lagunas Shopping Center
Tel. 988-3-20-24

Not as large as the state-side Hard Rocks, but with the same level of enthusiasm for rock-and-roll music and memorabilia, and the same satisfying menu of hamburgers and Tex-Mex. Open daily, 1 P.M.–1 A.M. The average cost of a meal for two is about $35. No reservations. Credit cards: AE, MC, V.

La Mansión
Costa Blanca Shopping Center
Tel. 988-4-12-72

A hacienda-style restaurant with Mexican decor and cuisine. This is a showplace, where you're served by Mayan maidens. The average cost of a meal for two is about $40. No reservations. Credit cards: AE, MC, V.

Maxime
Pez Volador 8, next to Hotel Casa Maya
Tel. 988-3-07-04

This fancy French restaurant is located in a lovely mansion, formerly the official residence of the mayor of Cancún. The elegant interior reflects the building's former function. Fine furnishings and paintings abound, and the floors are covered with Oriental rugs. The cuisine is a little too heavy to be really *haute*. Good wine list and great desserts—rich cakes and tarts, excellent mousse. Open daily for dinner only, 6–11 P.M., and for Sun. brunch, 10 A.M.–2 P.M. The average cost of a meal for two, with wine, is about $70. Reservations a must. Credit cards: AE, MC, V.

Perico's
Avenida Yaxchilan 71
Tel. 988-4-31-52

Despite the fact that Perico's is built to look like a traditional Mayan twig house with thatched roof, the decor of this Mexican-style seafood and steak house is Western, with saddles, lassos, and other cowboy paraphernalia. It's an odd blend of influences, but somehow it works, and this place is very popular. Open daily for dinner only, 6–11 P.M. The average cost of a meal for two is about $38. No reservations. Credit cards: MC, V.

El Pescador
Tulipanes 5
Tel. 988-4-26-73

There's usually a line to get in, but El Pescador is worth the wait. There is no better seafood—and reasonably priced, at that—in Cancún. Shrimp and lobster are prepared in a variety of ways, but *a la criolla* (creole-style) is the specialty. The gigantic shrimp stuffed with cheese and wrapped in bacon is also wonderful. While the emphasis is on food, the decor, sort of maritime casual, is pleasant enough. Open Tues.–Sun., 6–11 P.M.

The average cost of dinner for two is about $28. No reservations. No credit cards.

Pizza Rolandi
Avenida Cobá 12
Tel. 988-4-40-47

Great pizza and homemade pasta with rich sauces offer a nice change from Mexican cuisine. Seating is on an outdoor terrace or in a cooled dining room. Very popular—and usually crowded. There's another Pizza Rolandi in Cozumel. Open daily, noon–midnight. The average cost of a meal for two, with beer, is about $20. No reservations. No credit cards.

Soberanis
Avenida Cobá 5 to 7
Tel. 988-4-11-25

Typical Yucatecan preparations of fresh seafood, plus pork, chicken, and beef are served in this family-style restaurant, a good choice for sampling *poc chuc, sopa de lima,* and other regional specialties. Soberanis is part of a chain of unpretentious and reasonably priced restaurants popular with locals as well as travelers. The average cost of a meal for two is about $30. No reservations. Credit cards: AE, MC, V.

SHOPPING

Cancún's many terrific shops feature men's and women's beach, casual, and dressy clothing; leather goods; silver jewelry; and gift and souvenir items. Shops are conveniently located. Most of the resort hotels have their own arcades with boutiques and gift shops, and there are a number of modern shopping malls on the lagoon-side of the hotel zone. In fact, that strip of land is rapidly being developed into one very long, continuous modern shopping mall, with hundreds of shops, all geared for the visitor. Prices on clothing and gift items, especially in the hotel arcades, are higher than they are elsewhere in Mexico, but during the off-season, shoppers are likely to find sales with up to fifty percent discounts. Cancún is also a duty-free port, so prices on perfume and other typically high-duty items tend to be lower than they are elsewhere in Mexico, but they are often still higher than they are in the United States.

In general, stores open at 9:30 or 10 A.M. and close about 10 P.M., with a long lunch break from about 2 to 4 or 5 P.M. Most stores are closed on Sunday.

The mall thought to be biggest and best is the marble-walled **Plaza Caracol** (near the Cancún Convention Center), with 63 shops and restaurants. This is a great place to shop for beach and casual clothes, carried by many of the boutiques. Start with **ACA Joe,** whose colorful cotton sweatpants and tops and shorts and jerseys are always attractive. Credit cards: AE, MC, V.

Some of the shops offer Mexican handicrafts, but the selection usually isn't very good. One exception is **Victor** (in front of the Cancún Convention Center), owned and run by Victor Fosado, the son of one of Mexico City's finest dealers of modern and antique handicrafts. This shop sells Indian jewelry and excellent reproductions of Mayan ceramics, plus some hand-embroidered cotton blouses and shirts, among other garments. Stock varies, but the quality is good, and you might just come upon a treasure. No credit cards accepted.

Mexican surrealist sculptor **Sergio Bustamente** has his Cancún gallery in the **Plaza Nautilus** (across from the Playa Blanca Hotel). Bustamente's unusual pieces (well, they're less unusual now than they used to be, before Bustamente made so many of them, and before they were copied by other artists) include rabbits springing from huge eggs, and roosters peering out of the windows of miniature houses. The gallery is fun—for browsing and for buying. Credit cards: AE, MC, V. Another interesting gallery, **BMG Galería,** is also found in Plaza Nautilus. Here you'll see exhibitions of contemporary Mexican art and prints and find a fine selection of expensive art books. Also in Plaza Nautilus is **William Sprattling,** a silver shop featuring the jewelry and home accessories made by the American designer who regenerated the silver industry in the city of Taxco. Jewelry offerings here range from Indian-style pieces with geometric patterns to simple bangles with modern sleek lines. Items made for the home include traditional tea tray and service, modern-looking platters with rosewood handles (a trademark!), and beautiful silver goblets. Credit cards: AE, MC, V.

Another superb silver shop, **Los Castillos,** is in **Costa Blanca Shopping Center** (near **La Mansión** restaurant). This famous Taxco silver atelier offers a wide range of unusual jewelry but specializes in three-tone decorative items, such as mirror frames and cream-and-sugar sets, made from a combination of silver, copper, and brass, and in silver plaques and platters with cutout designs that have been filled with colorful bird's feathers and then coated with clear resins to prevent deterioration. Credit cards: AE, MC, V. Two excellent leather shops are also in Costa Blanca Shopping Center. **Charles Jourdan** sells expensive (almost as expensive here as they are state-side) and stylish shoes, handbags, and other leather accessories. Credit cards: AE, MC, V. **Via Veneto** has fine wallets, handbags, briefcases, luggage, and more. Credit cards: AE, MC, V. For an excellent selection of Mexican designer-label wearables, including Girasol's dresses, skirts, blouses, and caftans in colorful cottons with embroidery and appliqué, or Escalera silk-screened silk clothing and fabrics, go to **Charbelle,** also in the Costa Blanca Shopping Center.

In Cancún's many downtown shops, you'll find much more reasonable prices, but the shops and their merchandise are also less stylish. Avenida Tulúm is the main shopping street, and here you'll find, tucked in among a lot of less interesting boutiques, another **ACA Joe** and an **Ocean Pacific,** ACA Joe's rival in the casual clothes world. A truly dedicated shopper will want to stop in at the **San Francisco de Asisi** department store (Avenida Tulúm) just to get a feel for what local shopping is really like. (Think of this place as a museum of contemporary lifestyle for many Mexicans.) Next door is **Mercado Ki-Huic** (Centro de Artesanias), where you'll find dozens of stalls with embroidered clothing, blankets, *rebozos,* ceramic and onyx figurines and bowls, and other curios. This is a good source for handicrafts, and you are almost required to bargain the prices down to a reasonable level. At the corner of avenidas Tulúm and Uxmal is **Mercado Plaza Garibaldi,** another market with dozens of stalls selling typical clothing, baskets, ceramics, and leather goods.

ENTERTAINMENT

Cancún's nightlife consists of dining, dancing, and drinking— and there's plenty of that to be done, until the wee hours of the morning. Most of Cancún's restaurants (see above) stay open until 11 P.M., and late dinners are very much in vogue. Many of the big hotels feature **Mexican fiestas,** a pay-per-person (usually about $28 each) party that includes dinner and a show with folkloric ballet, mariachis and marimbas, *charros,* and sometimes cockfights. The hotels present their fiestas on different nights of the week, so check with your concierge or a local travel agent (who can make reservations for you and sell you the tickets) for the current schedule. There is also a **Ballet Folklórico** dinner and show at the Cancún Convention Center Auditorium (tel. 988-3-01-99) held nightly except Sunday beginning at 7 P.M. This is an extravaganza with more than thirty dancers and musicians, much more elaborate than the hotel shows. The main concentration of popular bars and discos is in the resort hotel zone. Of the many hotel bars, those in the **Sheraton, Presidente,** and **Cancún Viva** are most popular and highly recommended. If you're interested in discos, both the Hotel Krystal's **Christine** and the Camino Real's **Aquarius** have lively pulsing music, good sound systems, and terrific light shows. The ballroom dancing at the **Exelaris Hyatt Regency's** Wednesday-night Moonlight Serenade is more sedate. Country-and-western fans will want to stampede to the **Lone Star Bar,** at the María del Lourdes Hotel, in town near the beginning of the hotel zone. There are also lovely **sunset cruises** to Isla Mujeres, with dinner and dancing daily except Sunday. This is great fun, especially if you're with a group of friends. The cost is about $30 per person. Make reservations through your hotel concierge or travel agency.

Tulum

About eighty miles south of Cancún and 150 miles north of Chetumal, is **Tulúm,** the fascinating post-Classic (1200 to the Conquest) walled city that sits high atop a forty-foot cliff overlooking the beautiful Caribbean Sea. Tulúm's great location and unusual architecture make it a favorite archaeological visit for tourists.

A stone wall (11 to 17 feet tall) surrounds the ruins on three sides, and the fourth side is the cliff with a sheer drop down to the sea. Archaeologists debate whether this wall was built to protect the settlement, or whether it was used to contain the city's temple area. But another wall built within the surrounding wall was almost surely used to protect the sacred precinct.

The **Temple of the Frescoes** has traces of original paintings on its inner walls. Archaeologists find these odd because they show Mayan symbols of rain, fertility, and creation but are painted in the style of the Central Highlands. You have to look at them through protective bars. The temple also has a carved diving-god figure with wings and a bird's tail, and god masks on the corners of the building with traces of original paint.

The **Castillo,** perched on the very edge of the cliff, has a temple built on a palace base. Carvings include a diving god and standing figure, plus columns that look like serpents with their heads toward the ground. You can walk around the sides of the castillo for a wonderful view of the beach below the cliffs.

The niche over the door of the **Temple of the Diving God** has a carving of a diving god with wings and a bird's tail. The walls of this unusual building actually slope inward toward the ground.

Tulúm is open from 8 A.M. to 5 P.M. Admission is charged. And it's possible to walk down to the beach below the castillo for a cooling swim in the clear blue waters of the Caribbean.

You can also get to Tulúm by small airplane from Cancún and Cozumel aboard Aero Caribe or from Playa del Carmen and Cozumel aboard Aero Cozumel. First-class bus service is operated from Cancún by the ADO lines. If you don't have a car, you can get from Tulúm to Cobá by taxi. Flights, bus tickets, and excellent guided tours from Cancún to Tulúm and Cobá can be booked through your hotel concierge or travel agency.

 If you decide to overnight in the area, you can stay at the rustic **Cabanas Chacmool** (about 3 miles from the ruins), where you sleep in thatched huts with hammock-like beds, mosquito netting, and candlelight (no telephone, no credit cards, about $20

per night), or you can travel on to Cobá, where there are more luxurious accommodations.

Cobá

Located about thirty miles west of Tulúm, **Cobá** was a huge Mayan city that flourished during the late-Classic period (from A.D. 600 to 900). The city had lofty pyramids and buildings that bear some resemblance to those found farther south at Tikal (Guatemala). It is thought that Cobá was a major trading center to which southern Maya bought salt and honey from the north. Cobá probably had a population of about forty thousand, and was connected by *sacbes* (ceremonial roads) to about 16 other cities in the area. One of the *sacbes* extended for more than sixty miles, was thirty feet wide, and was elevated about two to eight feet.

Cobá, which was apparently never known to the conquistadores, was discovered in 1891, and has undergone only limited excavation. There are four groups of buildings in the vicinity of five lakes. The **Cobá Group** has a nine-level pyramid that stands about 78 feet high and has a now-empty tomb. The pyramid is in a plaza with an unrestored ball court. The **Macanxoc Group** has a number of stelae, scattered throughout several overgrown fields, depicting women rulers who carry ceremonial scepters and are standing on their captives. The **Conjunto de las Pinturas** has the **Temple of the Painted Lintel,** with traces of black, red, and blue paint and a 12-foot-high stele showing a ruler and captives. **Nohoch Mul** has a pyramid that stands 120 feet tall and resembles the structures at Tikal. The temple that stands on the top was evidently added at a later time and has carvings of a diving god, plus stelae of a male ruler with a ceremonial scepter, flanked by two smaller men with bound hands.

Cobá is open from 8 A.M. to 5 P.M. Admission is charged. You have three options for getting to Cobá from Tulúm: private car, taxi, or guided tour bus.

 If you want to overnight, the best accommodations in this area are at **Club Med's Villa Arqueológica** (tel. 5-203-3833 in Mexico City or 800-528-3100 in the United States; see **Villa Arqueológica, Chichén Itzá,** above, for details).

South to Chetumal

Continuing south on MEX307, there are scattered beaches and coves along the 150-mile stretch between Tulúm and **Chetumal,** the tropical capital of Quintana Roo, on the border of Mexico and Belize. In ancient times Chetumal was a Mayan shipping port, but the modern town was founded (under the name of Playa Obispo) in 1898 as a customs out-post to stop the smuggling of arms to Maya who were still fighting the Caste War. The town was renamed Chetumal in 1936. In 1955 it was destroyed by a hurricane, and the rebuilt version is what you see today. It is, for the most part, peaceful and quiet, but like all border towns it has its honky-tonk sections.

Chetumal is a duty-free port and is thus a popular destination for travelers on shopping sprees. There are dozens of shops along **Avenida de los Heroes,** Chetumal's main street, that are filled with imported goods—everything from electronics to dry-roasted peanuts—priced lower here than elsewhere in Mexico. Also along Avenida de los Heroes are several pleasant sidewalk cafés and the **mercado,** a good source for Yucatecan hammocks and other locally made handicrafts.

Near Chetumal are three fabulous secluded swimming holes. **Laguna Milagros** (nine miles from town) is an isolated lake with crystal-clear waters (great for swimmers), surrounded by a wonderful rain forest in which you find colorful wild parrots and toucans (great for bird watchers and nature lovers). **Laguna Bacalar** (about 22 miles from town), nicknamed the Lagoon of Seven Colors, is a beautiful large lake with almost transparent waters that are perfect for swimming. There's also an early 18th-century fort built here by the Spanish to fend off English pirates. **Cenote Azul** is a natural cistern with an estimated depth of five hundred feet. The water is cool and clear and fabulous. Visit this place on weekdays to avoid weekend crowds.

If you're really fascinated by the ruins, there are more to visit around Chetumal. **Kohunlich** (37 miles from town) has a lovely Pyramid of the Masks, surrounded by date palms. **Xpujil** has an unusual group of almost *trompe l'oeil* structures with shallow relief sculptures that look exactly like stairways and temple facades without interior chambers. Becan, Chicanna, and **Calakmul,** known as the Rio Bec Group, were discovered recently and are the subject of a Mexican TV documentary. There are plans for future excavation and restoration here.

Accommodations in Chetumal are best at the similarly priced **Hotel Presidente** (tel. 983-2-05-42) and **Hotel Continental Caribe** (tel. 983-2-11-00), located near each other on the Avenida de los Heroes. Both have comfortable air-conditioned rooms, pools, fine restaurants (where about $25 will buy dinner for two), and bars with entertainment. (In both, rates begin at $65 per night, double occupancy. Credit cards: AE, MC, V.)

Chetumal is connected to Cancún by MEX307. If you don't have a car, you can take one of a dozen daily first-class buses that stop in Puerto Morelos, Playa del Carmen, and Tulúm en route to Chetumal. Aeromexico has a daily flight between Chetumal and Mérida, with connections to other Mexican cities.

Isla Mujeres

Some people think of Isla Mujeres as a day trip from Cancún, but others consider this rustic, windswept island a delightful and relaxing vacation destination in its own right. Of Mexico's three Caribbean resort areas, Isla Mujeres is the least developed and expensive, and the most casual. Located about five miles north of Cancún, across the Bahía de Mujeres, Isla Mujeres is a little island, just about five miles long and about one-half mile wide, with a sleepy little fishing town at its northern end and pretty white-sand beaches all around it—and not much else.

In pre-Hispanic times, the Maya called their settlement here Zazil-ha, meaning "luminous waters." Apparently the island was a ceremonial center dedicated to Ix Chel, the goddess of fertility, and women came here to pray for babies. The name Isla Mujeres came from Francisco Hernandez de Córdoba, who discovered the island by accident in 1517. The Spanish explorer was on an expedition from Cuba to capture slaves when, during a terrible storm, his ships drifted off course and came into view of this island. When the sailors went ashore, they found the dozens of votive female statues and figurines that had been left by female worshipers: hence the name Isla Mujeres (or Women's Island).

The town of Isla Mujeres is just about four blocks wide and eight blocks long. There are docks and the *zócalo,* with a modern church, government buildings, and lots of kids playing soccer. The streets are narrow, and some are unpaved. The rest of the town is composed of several hotels, some very pleasant restaurants, a bank, a post office, a theater where local musicians often play, and the **Casablanca** nightclub, with good drinks and dancing.

But **beaches** and **water sports** are the most important aspect of a traveler's life on Isla Mujeres. The island is surrounded by beaches, but those on the north and west sides are protected from the open sea and are best for swimming and water sports. Beaches on the east side of the island face the Caribbean and can be too rough for swimmers. The island's southern tip is the meeting point for sea currents. Swimming here can be tricky, if not downright dangerous. Beware!

The most popular beach for swimming is **Playa los Cocos** (also called North Beach), near town at the northern end of the island. The beach has powdery white sand, little *palapa*-hut refreshment stands for shade, and wind-surfing equipment for rent. This is one of the best spots on the island to watch a beautiful sunset. The most popular beach for snorkeling is **El Garrafón,** about four miles from the center of town, on the southern end of the western side of the island. There is a coral reef just about six feet from the beach, and you can see schools of angel fish, a coral-encrusted anchor, and several cannons. South of El Garrafón, at the southern end of the island where swimming is dangerous, is a Mayan ruin believed to have been the temple dedicated to Ix Chel, the goddess of the moon and of fertility. Near the ruins, you'll find the island's fairly deserted lighthouse.

Playa Lancheros, on the west side of the island, has excellent swimming. Trees on the beach create very pleasant patches of shade, and there is a turtle pen where you can ride the backs of giant turtles. Isla Mujeres is a great place to relax. You don't have to do anything, and you don't feel like you're missing anything.

Near Playa Lancheros is the **Mundaca Fortress,** built by the pirate and slaver Fermin Mundaca de Marechaja. He planned to retire here from life on the high seas, and to marry a young woman known as *La Trigueña* (the Brown-haired One), with whom he had fallen madly in love. Unfortunately, she loved another young man, and when she married him and bore him child after child, Mundaca slowly went mad. The stone mansion surrounded by gardens was abandoned. Today it is a ruin, and the romantic story probably is, unfortunately, more interesting than the site.

CONNECTIONS

Aero Cozumel (tel. 988-2-02-39 in Isla Mujeres; 988-4-21-11 or 988-4-36-83 in Cancún; 987-2-05-03 or 987-2-09-28 in Cozumel) operates air taxi service between Isla Mujeres and Cozumel via Cancún, with one morning and one evening flight daily.

There is passenger-ferry service to Isla Mujeres from Puerto Juárez (about 10 miles north of Cancún), and passenger- and car-ferry service from Punta Sam (about 3½ miles north of Puerto Juárez), with several crossings daily from both ports. Check at the docks for current schedules, which change frequently. The crossing takes about forty minutes. One-way fare from Puerto Juárez is about $1 per person, from Punta Sam about $.50 per person. These ferries are quite crowded during the high season, so get to the dock early and be prepared to wait for the next boat if need be. Ferries do not run on Mon. mornings, when maintenance work is done.

To get to either Puerto Juárez or Punta Sam, you can take a bus (Route 8, which runs along Avenida Tulúm or Avenida

Cancún) from Cancún. You can also take a taxi (the fare to Punta Sam, which is farther away, is less than $5).

Some of the first-class ADO buses from Mérida to Cancún stop at the Puerto Juárez ferry dock.

There are also guided tour excursions to Isla Mujeres from Cancún and Cozumel. Check with your hotel concierge or travel agency for current tour schedules and rates.

Once you're on the island, it's quite easy to get around. The town is small enough so that you can walk everywhere. To get to the outlying beaches, you can take a taxi or rent a moped or bicycle. Rates are reasonable but varied, so check with several agencies before renting.

🧳 HOTELS

Like the island itself, Isla Mujeres's hotels are simple and *simpático* in nature. No glitz and glamour—the emphasis here is on comfort and casual charm. Most of the hotels have small lobby bars, some have restaurants, but you won't find the elaborate service that exists in luxury hotels in Cancún or Cozumel. Hotel space on Isla Mujeres is quite limited, and during the high season (from mid-Dec. to mid-Apr.), rooms are usually completely booked. So reserve space as much in advance as possible. And be sure to arrive at your hotel early in the day to ensure that your booked room is not given away to another guest.

Hotel Berny
Avenidas Juárez and Abasolo, 77400
Tel. 988-2-00-25
Doubles, from $40
This 41-room hotel is in a modern stucco building with a pleasant tiled patio and a pretty free-form swimming pool. Each room has one double bed and one single bed, floors are tiled, and there are overhead fans. Some rooms have balconies; all are spotlessly clean and offer pleasant service. Credit cards: MC, V.

Hotel Posada del Mar
Rueda Medina 15 (the *malecón*), 77400
Tel. 988-2-02-12
Doubles, from $55
This popular modern hotel offers fifty comfortable rooms, all air-conditioned and most with balconies and sea views. The hotel has a nice courtyard patio and pool, surrounded by garden greenery. There's a pleasant restaurant and bar area; and the location on the *malecón* is very convenient. Credit cards: AE, DC, MC, V.

Hotel Presidente Caribe
North Beach, 77400
Tel. 988-2-00-29 or 800-782-9639
Doubles, from $60
This hotel is on a small island, just off North Beach, and the setting is lovely, but you'll have to take a taxi to get to and from town via the causeway from North Beach. There are two hundred rooms with air-conditioning and sea views. The beach is

relatively secluded but too shallow for serious swimming. There is a fine swimming pool, nice restaurant, and bar. The Presidente, while a tad more luxurious than the island's other hotels, still does not offer all the amenities you find in the Presidente hotels in other resort areas. Credit cards: AE, MC, V.

Hotel Roca Mar
Avenidas Guerrero and Bravo, 77400
Tel. 988-2-01-01
Doubles, from $50
This, one of the island's most popular hotels, is on the edge of town, perched on a high cliff overlooking the sea, and the rooms have terrific views and the lovely lulling sounds of surf against rocks. The Roca Mar has thirty rooms and a common patio—but, alas, there's no swimming pool. There's no air-conditioning either, but overhead fans and sea breezes are an adequate cooling system. The rooms are smallish but comfortable, and the conch shells used as headboard lamps are a very nice decorative touch. Credit cards: MC, V.

Hotel Rocas del Caribe
Madero 2, 77400
Tel. 988-2-00-11
Doubles, from $45
Located on the Caribbean side of the island, where the waters are too rough for swimming but the views are truly lovely, the Rocas del Caribe has two wings. The older rooms are quite spacious but cooled only by overhead fans. The newer rooms are smaller, but have air-conditioning. Furnishings are comfortable in both. The hotel has a nice pool—important because the beach is really for sunning only. Credit cards: AE, MC, V.

☕ RESTAURANTS

The ambience of the restaurants on Isla Mujeres is in keeping with the style of the rest of the island: casual. You don't have to dress up. You don't even have to wear shoes. The restaurants all specialize in great seafood, but most of them also serve meat and chicken dishes. Restaurants are inexpensive, and service is friendly, if a little slow-paced.

Brisas del Caribe
Avenida Rueda Medina, near the *malecón*
Tel. 988-2-03-72
This large restaurant is a popular waterfront standard. The menu offers fish and seafood prepared Mexican-style or grilled—very tasty, very fresh, and reasonably priced. The atmosphere is casual, the decor simple. Open daily, 8 A.M.–10 P.M. The average cost of a meal for two is about $18. No reservations. Credit cards: AE, MC, V.

El Bucanero
Avenida Hidalgo between Madero and Abasolo
Tel. 988-2-02-36
An outdoor tiled terrace with individual *palapas* for shade is the setting for this charming restaurant that serves fresh and de-

licious seafood and traditional Mexican cooking. The *camarones al mojo de ajo* (garlic shrimp) are big, tender, and perfectly seasoned. You can also get good steaks and chicken dishes here. Service can be a little slow, but the fact that everything is freshly prepared makes the wait worthwhile. And while you wait, you can play with two darling and friendly pet monkeys. Reasonably priced wine list. Open daily, 11 A.M.–10 P.M. The average cost of a meal for two is about $20. No reservations. Credit cards: AE, MC, V.

Ciro's Lobster House

Avenida Matamoros 11
Tel. 988-2-01-02

One of Isla Mujeres's fancier restaurants, Ciro's has air-conditioning! It also serves terrific lobster and shrimp, plus turtle, meat and chicken dishes, and omelets. Good wine list. Open daily, 11 A.M.–11 P.M. The average cost of a meal for two is about $25. Reservations suggested. Credit cards: AE, MC, V.

Maria's

Near El Garrafón, about 4 miles from town
Tel. 988-2-00-15 (or, from Cancún, 988-3-14-20)

Recognized as Isla Mujeres's premier gourmet restaurant, Maria's has a special appeal evident in the atmosphere as well as the food. The menus are painted on woven mats, the decor is home-like, surrounding gardens are lush, and guests are given bouquets. Fresh fish and seafood are prepared with delectable sauces with a slightly French accent. Good wine list. Open daily, 1–5 P.M. and 7–10 P.M. You'll need to take a taxi from town, and if you decide you don't want to leave, you may be able to arrange to stay overnight in one of the five guest rooms (around $60 per night). Maria's also has a 36-foot yacht to pick up dinner and overnight guests in Cancún. The average cost of a meal for two, with wine, is about $50. Reservations a must. Credit cards: AE, DC, MC, V.

Miramar

Avenida Rueda Medina, next to the main pier
Tel. 988-2-03-63

It's nice to stop in at this popular restaurant, conveniently located on the *malecón,* for lunch, a refreshing cool drink, or coffee. The waterfront vistas are very pretty and peaceful. The menu is varied, but seafood and fresh fish are the best choices, especially the delicious *camarones al mojo de ajo.* Open daily, 8 A.M.–10 P.M. The average cost of a meal for two is about $18. No reservations. Credit cards: AE, MC, V.

Pizza Rolandi

Avenida Hidalgo between Madero and Abasolo
Tel. 988-2-04-30

Individual pizzas, eight inches in diameter, are topped with big black olives, ham, cheese, tomatoes, and asparagus. There are festive red-and-white checked tablecloths and comfortable red deck chairs set on a patio. Pizzas cost about $5 and up. There are also great spaghetti and lasagna dishes, with freshly made pasta. Rolandi serves wine, beer, and mixed drinks. Open daily, noon–midnight. The average cost of a meal for two, with beer, is about $18. No credit cards.

Restaurante Gomar
Avenidas Hidalgo and Madero
Tel. 988-2-01-42

The delightful Mexican decor is accented by pink walls, large stuffed parrots, overhead tulip-shaped fans, and serapes used as tablecloths. The specialty is fish, but the menu also offers meat and chicken prepared Yucatecan-style. The food is fresh and delicious. Modest wine list. The average cost of a meal for two is about $20. No reservations. Credit cards: AE, MC, V.

EXCURSIONS

You can hire boats to take you **deep-sea fishing** or **diving.** One popular destination for experienced divers is the **Caves of the Sleeping Sharks,** an underwater cavern about three miles northeast of Isla Mujeres, seventy feet down, where there are sharks in a trance-like or sleeping state. You need a guide for this dive: Check with your concierge for names. You can also cruise to **Contoy Island,** a nearby unspoiled island nature preserve where there are flocks of exotic wild birds. This is also a great place for snorkeling. Contoy tours usually last all day and include lunch. Ask your hotel concierge for schedules.

If you are using Isla Mujeres as your Caribbean vacation home base, you can also make excursions to Cancún, Cozumel, or the nearby ruins of Tulúm.

Cozumel

The island of Cozumel, often billed as Mexico's Caribbean island, was made for swimmers, sailors, snorkelers, scuba divers, and other water-sports enthusiasts. This tropical paradise is located about 12 miles off the eastern coast of the Yucatán Peninsula, in the state of Quintana Roo. Cozumel is almost directly across the water from the beach town of Playa del Carmen and is surrounded by the exquisite blue-green waters of the Caribbean. The island is about 28 miles long and 11 miles wide (about 189 square miles, in total), and it is one of Mexico's largest islands. Topographically, it is almost flat. Bicycling from one end of the island to the other is a popular pastime. But even more popular are bicycling, driving, and boating to one of Cozumel's many coves and inlets for a day of spectacular snorkeling or scuba diving, amid the island's famous complement of exotic aquatic creatures. Secluded beaches, with their brilliant blankets of white sand and cooling groves of palm trees, are perfect backdrops for intimate picnics or beach parties.

Cozumel was important long before it captured the attention of surf and sea buffs. The island had significance during the post-Classic period of the Mayan civilization, particularly between the years A.D. 1000 and 1200. Originally called *Ah-Cuzamil* ("land of the swallows" in Mayan), the island may have served as a place of worship for the rising sun and, perhaps, for Ix Chel, the goddess of fertility, medicine, and weaving. The Spanish discovered Cozumel when Juan de Grijalva landed here in 1518, soon to be followed by Cortés in 1519. The island was reported to have about forty thousand inhabitants at that time.

Subsequently, Montejo the Younger, the founder of Mérida, used Cozumel as a base in his efforts to conquer the Yucatán. From the 17th to the 19th centuries, the island was a hideout for pirates and smugglers, including Jean Lafitte and Henry Morgan, among others. Renegade Indians fleeing the Caste War, which occurred on the mainland during the second half of the 19th century, used Cozumel as a place of refuge.

In this century, the old town of San Miguel was destroyed during World War II in order to make room for construction of a strategic American air base. Since the 1950s, when the island was discovered by scuba divers and snorkelers, Cozumel has constantly gained in popularity as a quiet retreat from the mainland.

Cozumel's population is currently about thirty-two thousand. Its main dock is where ferries and tender boats servicing visiting cruise ships discharge their passengers. There are several pleasant restaurants and many shops in the single-story pastel-colored buildings surrounding the *zócalo*. A cab stand and ticket offices for local tours and ferries are conveniently located here as well.

Cozumel's main street, **Avenida Rafael Melgar** (also known as El Malecón), runs along the waterfront on the western shore of the island. The rest of the streets are laid out in a grid, and almost everything is within walking distance. *Avenidas* run north-south, and for some peculiar reason they are numbered by fives: 5a Avenida, 10a Avenida, 15a Avenida, and so forth. One exception to the numbering rule is Avenida Juárez, a principal east-west thoroughfare that runs from the main dock across town and further inland, and divides the town into north and south sections. *Calles* run east-west. North of Avenida Juárez, they are numbered evenly (2a Norte, 4a Norte, 6a Norte, and so on), and south of Avenida Juárez, they are given odd numbers (1a Sur, 3a Sur, 5a Sur, etc.).

Most travelers come to Cozumel for the island's magnificent **beaches,** and the wide variety of in- or on-the-water activities, including swimming, diving, snorkeling, and sailing. The beaches, alternatingly long strips of gleaming white powder sand and low rocky ledges that meet the sea, are located along the western shore of the island, on the side closest to the mainland. Scenery on the eastern side of the island, along the shores of the Caribbean, is more dramatic, especially when seen from the sea. The terrain is rocky, and the windswept beaches, backed by jungle landscapes, are great for walking, but water currents are known to be treacherous. Swimming isn't prohibited, probably because the area is too expansive to be properly policed. But beware!

The island's best resort hotels are located to the south or north of the town. They have their own beaches, as well as their own bars, restaurants, discos, tennis courts, dive shops and instruction, and marinas. It's possible to settle yourself in one of these modern resorts and never leave the property. But that would be a shame because there is much to do on the island.

Beach hopping is obviously a popular pursuit here. All the beaches in Cozumel (and throughout Mexico, for that matter) are public property, so you can swim or bask in the sun at any and all hotel beaches, regardless of where you're registered. In addition, several outlying beaches are musts. To the south of town, about one mile past the big hotels, is **Chankanaab** (Mayan for "Little Sea") **Nature Preserve,** with a small freshwater lake with underground water channels to the sea. This unusual combination of fresh and salt water has created a rare environment for sea life, and the variety of tropical fish found here is astonishingly colorful. Crystal-clear waters make observation easy. You don't even have to go into the water to see the rainbow swimming beneath the surface, and the snorkeling is, of course, superb here. You'll find changing rooms, equipment rental, and a breezy restaurant for food or liquid refreshments. Just beyond Chankanaab is **Playa Maya,** where you can rent paddle boats and catamarans.

About ten miles to the south are **Playa San Francisco,** a popular beach with a lively bar, and **Playa Palancar,** with its famous **Palancar Reef,** the source for black coral, among other types. Until black coral was discovered here (by Jacques Cousteau, about twenty years ago), it was thought that all its sources (in the Indian Ocean and Red Sea) had been exhausted. It is rare and carefully protected, and breaking it off the reef is prohibited. If you feel you must take some home, buy a trinket or some jewelry in one of the hotel shops or in town.

At the southern tip of the island, beyond Playa Palancar and past an expansive and rather unappealing stretch of jungle, is **Punta Celerain,** the island's lighthouse. Usually deserted, Punta Celerain is a good place to get away from it all. But toward the end of the journey, the road is all sand, and you really need a car to travel to the end of it.

El Cedral, El Caracol, El Castillo Real, and San Gervasio, Cozumel's Mayan ruins, are of minor interest compared with the Yucatán Peninsula's other archaeological zones. Cozumel's ruins are hidden away in the jungle and are a bit difficult to get to. Frankly, many tourists just skip them, but the ruins are another aspect of Cozumel and are a great change of pace if you tire of beach antics.

Back in the town of San Miguel de Cozumel, life centers on the zócalo. This is not an impressive plaza with colonial buildings and monuments, but there are some enjoyable restaurants (see listings below) with seafood and Mexican cuisine, and colorful shops featuring beach and diving gear, jewelry and sculptures made of black coral found deep in Cozumel's waters, and hammocks woven on the island. A crafts market, El Mercado de Artesanias, is on Calle 1a Sur, one block south of the zócalo. There is one movie house that screens contemporary Spanish-language films, and an occasional English title. Cozumel's Tourist Information Office is on Avenida Rafael Melgar, about half a mile south of the zócalo. The island has a small museum of local social and natural history, the Museo de la Isla de Cozumel, located on the waterfront, on Avenida Rafael Melgar between calles 4a and 6a Norte.

CONNECTIONS

Cozumel has an international airport with nonstop and direct flights from several American cities. Continental Airlines flies nonstop to Cozumel from Houston, with connecting flights from other U.S. cities. American Airlines flies nonstop to Cozumel from Dallas/Fort Worth and from Raleigh/Durham, with connecting flights from other U.S. cities. Mexicana Airlines operates daily nonstop flights to Cozumel from Dallas/Fort Worth and Miami. In addition, Mexicana has daily nonstop flights to Cozumel from Mexico City (with connecting flights from Chicago, Los Angeles, and San Francisco, as well as from the Mexican city of Guadalajara). Aero Caribe, a regional airline, operates small planes on short runs between Cozumel and Cancún, and to nearby ruins.

Cozumel's airport is about 15 minutes from town. Take a flat-fee taxi to your hotel. Once you've settled in, transportation into town is probably best by bicycle. The land is flat, and peddling is relatively easy, but if stamina is a problem, you can rent a moped, jeep, or car to get around. Rental agencies have their offices in town. You can get a list from your concierge if you haven't made transportation arrangements from home. There are also plenty of taxis available for short trips into or around town, or to the outlying beaches and sights. And tour boats cruise to some beaches and coves. For tour schedules and fees, consult your hotel concierge or travel agency.

You can also get to and from Cozumel by ferry. Fastest is the half-hour trip aboard the Water Jet Mexico to and from Playa del Carmen, a beach town on the mainland. *Water Jet Mexico,* a high-speed computerized hydrofoil, makes eight round-trips daily, has video entertainment and refreshments, and costs about $6 one-way. Buy tickets at the dock one hour before departure. When waters are rough, the ride is bumpy enough to make some people sick. For the smoothest ride possible, sit as far back in the middle section as you can.

Regular ferries take an hour and 15 minutes to make the crossing from Playa del Carmen to Cozumel. These are safe, though hardly elegant. They run frequently, and the fare is about $2. Buy tickets on the dock one hour before departure.

The car ferry to and from Puerto Morelos departs from and arrives at the international dock in front of the Sol Caribe Hotel. The trip takes four and a half hours and costs about $4 one-way. Call 987-2-09-50 or go by the pier for current schedules, which change frequently.

🧳 HOTELS

Cozumel's best hotels are, in general, located to the south or north of town, on the beaches that line the western coast of the island. These luxury resort complexes have their own restaurants, bars, discos, pools, tennis courts, dive shops, and tour desks, and many of them are located close enough to one another for you to stay at one hotel and visit neighbors for dining, diving, and disco. These are the most expensive accommodations on the island, but prices are relatively low even in high season and especially in comparison to the posher and pricier Cancún. If you can afford to do so, it's advisable to stay at one of the beachfront hotels. Otherwise, there are pleasant downtown pensiones that are less expensive.

HOTELS ON THE BEACH

Casa del Mar
Zona Hostelera Sur, 77600
Tel. 987-2-16-65
Doubles, from $110

This three-story yellow-stucco hotel, with 98 rooms and eight cabanas, is across the road from the beach, but rooms and lobby restaurant have a lovely view of the sea. Of all the luxury hotels, Casa del Mar is located closest to town. Most units have two double beds with yellow-tile headboards, overhead fans, air-conditioning, and small balconies overlooking the sea. A driveway paved with fossil-containing rocks leads up to a central triangular courtyard with a pretty fountain and rustic wooden benches. The spacious restaurant is covered by the traditional thatched *palapa* roof and has many overhead fans to circulate the air and create a cooling breeze. An open-air snack-and-drinks bar is also covered with a *palapa* and is conveniently close to the hotel's swimming pool. Service is conscientious, and the staff quite cordial. The hotel services a section of beach across the road, and its dive shop is well stocked with everything you'll need to buy or rent for snorkeling or diving in the island's many interesting coves. Credit cards: AE, DC, MC, V.

La Ceiba Beach Hotel
Apdo. Postal 284, 77600
Tel. 987-2-08-44
Doubles, from $150

The expansive lobby of this Mexican modern hotel has wide picture windows overlooking a tiled deck and the pool, with the sparkling blue sea beyond. One lobby area is devoted to a nautical bar designed to look like a pirate ship; the bar is called Lafitte, after the famous Jean, a pirate who plied the waters of Cozumel and has become part of its legend. The hotel's nooks are beautifully decorated with heavily carved dark-wood furniture, and there are display cabinets with artifacts resembling those in the local anthropological museums. The 103 comfortable rooms distributed over eleven floors feature king-sized beds, sitting areas, servibars, and small balconies. Many rooms have sea views. The penthouse, suitable for a vacationing family, has wraparound views, plus living room, two bedrooms, and kitchenette. The hotel also has a tennis court, shops, and a small steamroom and Jacuzzi. Credit cards: AE, DC, MC, V.

Hotel Mayan Plaza
Santa Pilar Beach, Apdo. 9, 77600
Tel. 987-2-04-11
Doubles, from $170

The unusual decor of this modern ten-story hotel complex, managed by Best Western, has a distinctive and exotic Mayan motif, both in the public areas and in the one hundred spacious rooms. Most rooms have ocean views and balconies. The attractive and airy wood-beamed lobby has a sunken seating area with comfortable sofas. The hotel's pool and patio area is accommodating, with a large, irregularly shaped pool, comfortable deck chairs, and shaded areas. You'll also find tennis courts, a dive shop, and a cocktail lounge featuring live evening entertainment. Credit cards: AE, DC, MC, V.

Stouffer Presidente Cozumel
Carretera Chankanaab km 6.5, 77600
Tel. 987-2-03-22 or 800-472-2427
Doubles, from $190

On the beach side of the road, a palm-lined drive leads up to a low white modern building with 154 rooms, divided between a five-story tower and a two-story wing. The lobby features an unusual dolphin sculpture, and the hotel's square-shaped pool is in a lovely patio setting with an open-air *palapa* restaurant. Spacious rooms with tropical decor have two twin beds; each room has one wall painted a hot Mexican pink, and that color is used freely for decorative accents. The bathrooms are large; baskets of shampoo and shaving paraphernalia sit on marble sink rims. The TV offers ESPN and other cable channels in English. Diversions include a video bar, tennis courts, Fri.-night fiestas with Mexican buffet and folkloric dances, and excursions to nearby Chankanaab Nature Preserve. Credit cards: AE, DC, MC, V.

Hotel Sol Caribe
Playa Paraíso (Paradise Beach), 77600
Tel. 987-2-07-00 or 800-223-2332
Doubles, from $150

The grand-scale lobby has a profusion of plants and a waterfall with a statue of the Mayan god Chacmool. Stairs lead past the waterfall to a multilevel garden, with areas for sitting and visiting. The pool is ample, and there is a nearby bar covered by a shady *palapa*. The Sol Caribe, a Fiesta Americana resort, has 220 rooms and is planning a new wing that will increase the number of rooms to three hundred. Rooms have attractive wicker sunburst-shaped headboards. Three lighted tennis courts are exclusively for guests' use. The hotel's **Maya 2,000** disco, built of heavy stone and with high wooden beams and a *palapa* roof, is a lively and popular night spot. Credit cards: AE, DC, MC, V.

HOTELS IN TOWN

Hotel Aguilar
5a Avenida Sur and Calle 3a Sur, 77600
Tel. 987-2-03-07
Doubles, from $50

This attractive and inexpensive small hotel offers interior gardens in full bloom, surrounding a filtered swimming pool. The air-conditioned rooms are small but comfortable. Furnishings are comfortable as well, though not new. No credit cards.

Hotel Elizabeth
Calle Salas 44, Apdo. 70, 77600
Tel. 987-2-03-30
Doubles, from $70

The choice of accommodations *chez* Elizabeth includes suites with living room, bedroom, and fully equipped kitchen, and double rooms—totaling 17 units in all. The brochure promises that you'll feel as "comfortable as in your own home" while you're here—but some rooms are outfitted with fan only. The place is clean, tidy, and quiet, however, even though it is located just about a half-block away from the *zócalo*. No credit cards.

Hotel Mary Carmen
5a Avenida Sur (one block south of the *zócalo*), 77600
Tel. 987-2-03-56 or 987-2-05-81
Doubles, from $60

The owners of this 28-room, two-story hotel carefully preserve its air of elegance. There are handsome brocaded sofas in the lobby; the pleasantly decorated air-conditioned rooms are set around a charming interior courtyard with a huge mamay tree; and the place is kept spotlessly clean. Credit cards: MC, V.

RESTAURANTS

Cozumel's beachfront resort hotels have excellent restaurants. If you're staying in the hotel zone, you can eat perfectly well by table hopping from one hotel restaurant to another. But to experience another side of Cozumel, venture into the fine and fun eateries in town.

El Acuario
Avenida Melgar, near Avenida Circunvalación, south of town
Tel. 987-2-10-97

This dining emporium and popular dance parlor features an underwater theme. There are fish swimming around in an aquarium, while some of their more unfortunate compatriots find their way into intricate preparations on patrons' plates. Or you can get into the swim yourself by joining the nighttime dancing at the Neptune disco. Open daily, 5 P.M.–midnight. The average cost of a meal for two, with wine, is about $35. Reservations suggested. Credit cards: AE, MC, V.

BBQ's
Avenida Melgar, between calles 4a Norte and 6a Norte
Tel. 987-2-15-69

Beautifully barbecued ribs, chicken, and roast beef are the main attraction, but diners love the atmosphere here too. The wood-beamed interior is decorated with old wagon wheels and Wild West memorabilia. Lest you begin to think you're in Texas instead of Cozumel, just look out the window at the lovely sea view. The menu is in English, and prices range between $5 and $10 for entrées. Live music—mostly tropical—is featured. Open daily, 11 A.M.–10 P.M. No reservations. Credit cards: AE, MC, V.

Carlos 'n Charlie's and Jimmy's
Avenida Melgar, near Calle 2a Norte
Tel. 987-2-01-91

This, the Cozumel branch of the famous chain of popular Mexi-Continental bistros, offers steaks and seafood, ample drinks, and great desserts. The menus make for fun reading, and the waiters love to joke irreverently with patrons. Open daily, 5 P.M.–midnight. The average cost of a meal for two, with wine, is about $45. No reservations. Credit cards: MC, V.

Casa Denis
Calle 1a Sur, west of the zócalo
Tel. 987-2-00-67

Cozumel's little secret, Casa Denis is known only to the very "in," including some of the rich and famous trendsetters. The casa is a private house with just several tables set up under a shade tree in the courtyard. Denis and his wife prepare and serve the set menu of the evening. Open daily for dinner only, 7–10 P.M. The average cost of a meal for two is about $30. Reservations required at least a day in advance. No credit cards.

La Laguna
Chankanaab Nature Preserve
No telephone

This beachfront *palapa* at Chankanaab is very popular with snorkelers who come to the nature preserve for sport and stay for a late lunch. The menu features wonderful fresh seafood and fish, served mostly Mexican-style. Try the lobster for a special treat. Liquid refreshment includes wine, beer, mixed drinks, and tasty fresh fruit *líquidos.* La Laguna opens at 11:30 A.M. and closes when Chankanaab closes at 5 P.M. The average cost of a meal for two, with beer, is about $20. No reservations. No credit cards.

Morgan's
Central Plaza
Tel. 987-2-05-84

One of the best and most elegant of Cozumel's restaurants, Morgan's is named after the famous pirate who crashed (colloquially speaking) on the island between raids. The restaurant's decor has a nautical theme, with dark-wood paneling and polished brass fittings. Roast beef, steaks, and chicken are on the menu, as well as seafood specialties, including superb lobster. Morgan's is slightly more expensive than Cozumel's other restaurants—but definitely worth the difference. Open daily, noon–3 P.M. and 6–11 P.M. The average cost of a meal for two, with wine, is about $50. No reservations. Credit cards: AE, DC, MC, V.

Las Palmeras
Avenida Melgar, across from the main dock
Tel. 987-2-05-32

At any hour of the day, this centrally located patio restaurant is a meeting place for hungry and thirsty people in search of good conversation, excellent food, and a good perch from which to watch the endless parade of promenaders amble by. The open-air setting, with a bouquet of colorful umbrellas to protect diners from the sun, is festive and fun. Service is efficient and pleasant. Breakfasts of eggs as you like them, bacon, fresh rolls, and strong coffee are an excellent way to start the day. Lunch features a full Mexican menu of enchiladas, tacos, and super guacamole, with the delicious combination of cheese and guava paste for dessert. Dinner promises a variety of meats, but best are the fresh fish and seafood, including sea bass, red snapper, shrimp, and lobster, prepared with Mexican or Continental accents. Open daily, 8 A.M.–11 P.M. The average cost of a meal for two, with wine, is about $30. No reservations. Credit cards: AE, MC, V.

Pepe's Grill
Avenida Melgar, south of the *zócalo*
Tel. 987-2-02-13

Pepe's is a luxurious dinner-only bistro, open daily from 5 P.M.–midnight. Its dim lights, quiet music, fresh sea breezes, and a delightful ocean view give the place a decidely romantic air. The menu is not extensive but does include a variety of excellent possibilities, including dramatic flambés, down-to-earth surf and turf, healthful salads, and Mexican combination plates. The fact that Pepe's is relatively expensive has not diminished its popularity. The average cost of a meal for two, with wine, is about $45. Reservations a must. Credit cards: AE, MC, V.

Pizza Rolandi
Avenida Melgar, four blocks north of the *zócalo*
Tel. 987-2-04-30

(See **Pizza Rolandi**, Isla Mujeres Restaurants, above, for details.)

Soberanis

Avenida Melgar, near Calle 5a Sur
Tel. 987-2-02-46

Excellent seafood, pork, chicken, and beef dishes are offered here, all prepared typical Yucatecan-style. This is a good place to sample *poc chuc, sopa de lima,* and other regional specialties. Soberanis, part of a chain of unpretentious, reasonably priced family-style restaurants, is popular with locals as well as travelers. The average cost of a meal for two is about $25. No reservations. Credit cards: AE, MC, V.

The Sports Page

Avenida 5, corner of Calle 2 Norte
Tel. 987-2-11-99

The latest sports action from the States is available here, thanks to the restaurant's rooftop satellite dish. The decor reflects the sports theme: Team pennants and caps and sports photos abound. The menu features hamburgers and other U.S. specialties. All-you-can-eat nights are reasonably priced and particularly popular. The Sports Page, a good place to socialize, is open 10 A.M.–2 A.M. The average cost of a meal for two, with wine, is about $30. No reservations. Credit cards: AE, MC, V.

SHOPPING

Most of the island's shops are located along El Malecón (waterfront boulevard). Browsing is fun, and you'll find all the typical Mexican beach souvenirs and some attractive locally made handicrafts.

Cozumel's **Mercado de Artesanias,** located on Calle 1a Sur, about a block away from the *zócalo,* is a good source for handicrafts from the island and elsewhere in Mexico, including baskets, beadwork, embroidered clothes, and other colorful items.

The **Flea Market,** located on Avenida 5a, near Calle 2a Norte, has an odd and interesting group of collectibles, including photos from the Mexican Revolution, arrowheads, fossils, old coins and bills, ceremonial masks, erotic Mayan figurines, and Cuban cigars.

ACA Joe, on Avenida Melgar near Calle 2a Norte, has great casual and beach clothes in bright colors and stylish cuts. **Los Cincos Soles,** on Avenida Melgar near Calle 8a Norte, sells Mexican designer clothes bearing the Girasol label, among others, as well as a good choice of crafts. The shop is more expensive than the *mercado,* but the selection is more sophisticated and offers better quality.

Cozumel is a great place to buy hammocks. They're sold in most of the town's shops, and you can't sit in an open-air restaurant or café or bask on the beach without being approached by someone selling hammocks. Of course, they're nice souvenirs, but buy wisely. If you can afford to do so, buy the *grande* size. It's much more comfortable than the smaller sizes. Cotton and silk wear well, but check to see that the loops are secure and that the weave has no irregularities that might tear with use. One reliable and reasonable source for hammocks is **Mañuel Asveta,** found at Calle 4, Number 198, at the corner of Avenida 5 Norte. Very often you can see hammocks being woven on the house's small patio. Heavy-weight cotton hammocks in large sizes sell for about $25; those with silk threads are slightly more expensive. The workmanship is excellent, and Asveta's hammocks should last through many seasons. Special orders can usually be filled within ten days.

Another good buy on Cozumel is jewelry made from black coral found at Palancar Reef, one of the off-coast reefs that make for the island's fabulous diving. Cozumel's best-known jeweler, Roberto Carlos Franco, has his shop, **Roberto's,** in the center of town; this is an excellent source for interesting necklaces, bracelets, pendants, and other pieces of jewelry. You can see artisans cutting and setting in the shop. The range of prices is broad enough to appeal to a wide range of customers.

ENTERTAINMENT

The tourists who come to Cozumel primarily for sun and surf, scuba diving, snorkeling, and sailing tend to retire early. A night on the town probably means dinner at a nice restaurant and home to bed by 10 P.M. The island's one and only movie house, **Cine Cozumel,** is located on Avenida Melgar between 2a Norte and 4a Norte. The show is usually in Spanish, but look for the occasional English-language film. Most of the hotels have dance clubs and bars with live entertainment. One of the most popular and lively is the Hotel Sol Caribe's **Maya 2,000,** with a good sound system and light show.

Campeche

Campeche is a wonderful old colonial city that has been largely overlooked by travelers and pays little attention to them when they get there. That doesn't mean that travelers are shunned. Campeche is friendly and welcoming, but people are shy with strangers and quite low-key. Not many people speak English, but those who do are very happy to have the opportunity to converse. There's really something quite delightfully naive in this rather old-fashioned city that hasn't yet been trampled by the tourist trade.

Campeche is a charming old port located on the west coast of the Yucatán Peninsula, overlooking the Gulf of Mexico, about 125 miles southwest of Mérida. The first Spaniard to land here was Francisco Hernandez de Córdoba in 1517. Ten years later, this is where Montejo the Elder launched his first attempt to conquer the Yucatán Peninsula, and where he established the first (short-lived) Spanish settlement on the Yucatán Peninsula in 1530. Montejo the Younger came back to build a city here in 1540. Named after the Mayan settlement of Ah-kin-pech, Campeche became the most important port of the Yucatán, and was repeatedly raided by famous and much feared pirates, including William Park, Diego the Mulatto, and Lorencillo, among others.

During these attacks, women and children hid out in underground passages until, between 1686 and 1704, a thick fortified stone wall was built around the town to protect it from raids. The wall was defended by eight massive forts. In 1777, King Charles III of Spain granted Campeche a city charter. In 1867, it became capital of the state of Campeche.

The town is still dominated by the beautiful old **Fuerte San Miguel,** one of the original protective forts, located high on a windy hilltop overlooking Campeche and the sea. The fort has old cannons still pointed toward the sea, and a small museum filled with wooden models of different types of ships used by the Mexican navy from the days of independence to the present, as well as colonial artifacts. The views from Fuerte San Miguel are spectacular, and the place is particularly romantic at dusk. Open Tuesday through Sunday from 8 A.M. to 8 P.M. Admission is charged.

Sections of the thick stone city walls and bastions still stand, including two portals to the city: **La Puerta del Mar** (Door of the Sea) is at Avenida 16 de Septiembre and Calle 59, and **La Puerta de la Tierra** (Door of the Land) is at the other end of Calle 59. The dramatic **Baluarte de la Soledad,** on the **zócalo,** is an indication of the powerful impression this walled town must have made in the olden days. This bastion now houses the **Museum of Archaeology,** with pre-Hispanic artifacts taken from the ruins at Edzna, as well as ancient documents, costumes, and musical and mariner's instruments that were important in Campeche's history. The museum is open from Tuesday through Saturday from 9 A.M. to 2 P.M. and 3 to 7 P.M., and Sunday from 9 A.M. to 1 P.M. Admission is charged.

Also around the *zócalo* are beautiful colonial buildings, including the **Cathedral de la Concepción,** begun in 1540 but not completed until 1705! Nearby, along the **Malecón,** is the **Church of San Francisco,** built in 1540 on the site said to have been where Hernandez de Córdoba and his crew celebrated the first Mass on the American continent.

Baluarte San Pedro, another beautiful stone bulwark, is near the bustling **Mercado** (on Avenida Circuito Baluartes Este), which has hundreds of colorful stalls. Handicrafts including hammocks, hats, and *huipiles* can be found at the **Centro de Artesanias** in the **Baluarte San Carlos** at calles 8 and 65. This is also the **Museum of Applied Arts,** open Tuesday through Saturday from 9 A.M. to 6 P.M., for which admission is charged.

CONNECTIONS

Aeromexico flies daily from Mexico City to Campeche. There is frequent first-class bus service to Campeche from Mérida, Chetumal, and Villahermosa. The ride from Mérida takes about three hours, and the 356-mile trip from Villahermosa takes about eight or nine hours. The roads have two lanes and a lot of heavy truck traffic. You can drive yourself, but it is tiring, and the roads are not lighted, so avoid night driving. You're really much better off taking the bus.

Campeche is a quite small and compact city, and you can walk to almost all the sights. However, you'll need a taxi to get to Fuerte San Miguel, overlooking the town.

🧳 HOTELS

Campeche has no deluxe hotels, but accommodations are clean and comfortable—and very inexpensive. The best bets are the following:

Hotel Baluartes
Avenida Ruiz Cortinez (no number; on the Malecón), 24000
Tel. 981-6-39-11
Doubles, from $70
   A charming older hotel with 104 rooms, the Baluartes offers delightful front rooms overlooking the gulf. Less appealing are the back rooms that overlook the parking lot. Not all rooms are air-conditioned, so make your requirements clear when you make your reservations. The lobby, restaurant, and pool area are all pleasant, and service is friendly. Credit cards: AE, DC.

Ramada Inn
Avenida Ruiz Cortinez 51 (on the Malecón), 24000
Tel. 981-6-22-33 or in the U.S. 800-228-2828
Doubles, from $45
   This is Campeche's most luxurious hotel, with 120 comfortable rooms, all with balconies and views overlooking the gulf. You'll find a pool, good restaurant, and a nightclub with entertainment. Credit cards: AE, DC, MC, V.

☕ RESTAURANTS

The decor in most Campeche restaurants is simple and unpretentious. Seafood is the specialty, and it's prepared with local Yucatecan recipes.

Restaurante del Parque
Calle 57 and the *zócalo*

No telephone

This brightly lighted and spotlessly clean family-style restaurant on the *zócalo* serves excellent shrimp and fish, plus standards like enchiladas and quesadillas. Open 8 A.M.–10 P.M. Excellent thick fish soup too. The average cost of a meal for two is about $20. No reservations. No credit cards.

Restaurante Miramar

Calles 8 and 61

Tel. 981-6-28-83

Generally considered to be the best restaurant in town, the Miramar serves terrific seafood prepared the Campeche way. Shrimp and fish are breaded and fried, served with rice and fresh vegetables. Excellent ceviche, calamari, and stone crabs. The ambience is pleasant, though by no means formal. Conveniently located near the Baluartes and Presidente hotels. The average cost of a meal for two is about $30. No reservations. Credit cards: AE, MC, V.

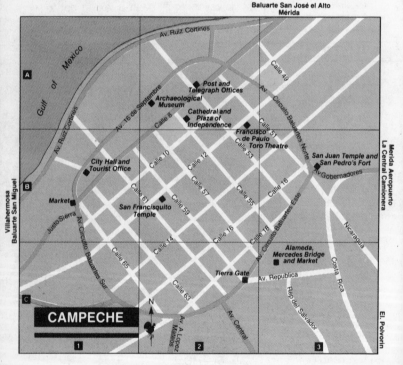

12

OAXACA

Oaxaceños may tell you that if their state were to be ironed flat, its territory would be equal in size to all of Mexico. While no method exists for testing the validity of their claim, it is certainly true that most of Mexico's fifth-largest state is wild, mountainous country that comparatively few sealed roads penetrate. The forested peaks of the Sierra Madre del Sur, their jagged summits rising to more than nine thousand feet above sea level, erupt over much of Oaxaca's 38,822 square miles, dropping off just short of the palm-fringed beaches of the Pacific Coast. Terrain like this would seem to pose an insurmountable challenge to travelers who have not completed Mountaineering 101. Happily, however, that is far from the truth. With all of its manifold attractions tightly compressed into two easy-to-explore regions of relatively level landscape—the tropical Pacific coastline and the highland Oaxaca Valley—the state of Oaxaca is tailor-made for touring.

The heart and soul of Oaxaca, and one of the most popular tourist destinations in Mexico, is the **Oaxaca Valley** in the center of the state. The enchanting capital city, Oaxaca de Juárez, often referred to simply as Oaxaca (it will be called Oaxaca City in this chapter for clarification's sake), along with an array of ancient ruins and bustling Indian villages, lies on this five-thousand-foot-high plateau encircled by the towering peaks of the Sierra Madre.

Any sojourn in the Oaxaca Valley will include visits to the villages, where tourists can observe artisans, using methods handed down for centuries, create the intricately patterned carpets, black pottery, lavishly embroidered regional costumes, delicate handloomed fabrics, lustrous silver and gold jewelry, and the other handicrafts for which the state is so famous. Among the most intriguing of the dozens of villages lying within a 25-mile radius of the city are **Teotitlán del Valle,** where Zapotec weavers have been turning out magnificent handloomed carpets for centuries, and **San Bartolo Coyotepec,** birthplace of Oaxaca's celebrated black pottery.

"There was no place I so much desired to live . . . as Oaxaca."

English friar Thomas Gage was referring to the city of Oaxaca and the valley surrounding it, and though his words were written more than three centuries ago, they echo sentiments expressed by countless travelers today. Oaxaca's unique character is a mixture of indigenous Indian, Spanish colonial, and the ancient, pre-Conquest past; nowhere else in Mexico do these three ingredients meet and embrace with more mesmerizing result than in the Oaxaca Valley.

The vast majority of the state's 3.7 million inhabitants are Indian—a polyglot ethnic potpourri of 18 distinct groups, each clinging to rich and intricate traditions that date back centuries. In the tiny villages that dot the Oaxaca Valley, the descendants of the great Zapotec civilization that ruled the valley for one thousand years from its mighty mountaintop capital of Monte Alban still converse with each other in pre-Conquest languages rather than Spanish (half a million Oaxaceños do not even speak Spanish); favor handloomed, colorfully embroidered apparel over denim and drip dries; and seek out local *curanderos,* who rely on herbal remedies rather than antibiotics when illness strikes.

In *Under the Volcano* Malcolm Lowry describes Oaxaca as "the saddest sound in the world." What he omits to describe is the pronunciation of this sound. I tried it out while reading Lowry's book. "O-ax-aka, Oh axe acka," it did not sound so sad. Then I discovered that it was pronounced "Wa-hah-ka." That did sound sad, and the town was better still. Here, after the forthright, brassy Mexicans of the capital and the north, one is suddenly among Indians. But not the familiar village Indians of "underdevelopment." These people are Indians of an Indian city. Oaxaca has a population of 180,000 [1985] which must make it one of the largest settlements of AmerIndians in the world. It is certainly an improvement on the pathetic reservation settlements of the Indians of Canada and the United States. In Oaxaca, Mexico is right to be proud of its Indian heritage. At its centre is the most beautiful plaza or zócalo, cool and roomy, a handsome bandstand shaded by tall trees and, in the evenings, a military band playing Strauss and Mozart.

— Patrick Marnham
So Far From God, 1985

Also on the sightseeing agenda will be the weekly markets that transform sleepy Indian hamlets into bustling open-air bazaars of exotic sights and smells. And on Saturdays, enjoy the largest and most colorful Indian market in all of Mexico: Thousands of indigenous Oaxaceños clad in extravagant ethnic costumes—beribboned *huipiles* and fringed *rebozos*—stream into the capital city to buy and sell everything from fried grasshoppers to foam-rubber mattresses.

Oaxaca City was founded by the Spaniards in the 16th century, an era that still endures along the cobbled streets lined with aristocratic mansions, gold-encrusted churches, and brooding convents and monasteries. For this rich trove of 16th- and 17th-century architectural wealth, Oaxaca's Centro district has been declared a national monument by the Mexican government.

Inhabited long before the Spanish arrived to found Oaxaca City, the valley was the cradle of the great Zapotec culture, one of the most advanced in Mesoamerica. The valley, in addition to the ruins of Monte Albán, offers more than two hundred archaeological sites that lie within an hour of the city, comprising a compelling legacy of the ancient past that allows us to travel back in time and glimpse the glories that were pre-Conquest Mexico.

Despite its population of almost 200,000, Oaxaca City retains a tranquillity reminiscent more of a large town than a prosperous provincial capital and major tourist center. The city's relaxed atmosphere, along with its bevy of fine museums, dozens of churches, outdoor cafés, and markets and shops that have earned it a well-deserved reputation as a purchaser's paradise, invites lingering. With a comprehensive selection of resort hotels and intimate colonial inns, Oaxaca City is an ideal base for exploring the surrounding valley and its attractions.

At 5,071 feet above sea level, Oaxaca is a city of perpetual spring. Except during the June-through-September rainy season, when afternoons—and sometimes mornings as well—bring brief thundershowers, skies are generally cloudless, and strong sunlight keeps daytime temperatures hovering between seventy and eighty degrees, even in the rainy months. At night, the mercury drops only to the sixties, and even in the coldest months of December and January, no garments warmer than thick sweaters and light woolen jackets are required.

After a stay in the valley, the coast beckons. Oaxaca's Pacific shoreline is a 298-mile-long succession of unending lengths of ivory sand pounded by Pacific breakers, tranquil coves sheltered by rocky headlands, and tracts of steamy jungle sliced by the wide mouths of slow-moving rivers. Mexico's most idyllic and unspoiled coastline was, until recently, a secret known only to surfers and sophisticated sunseekers, but all that is changing rapidly now that construction has begun on the massive development project known as the Bahías de Huatulco.

Two decades ago, Puerto Angel and Puerto Escondido were tiny fishing hamlets offering only rustic accommodations in thatched *enramadas,* where visitors slung up hammocks and slumbered under the stars. Today Puerto Angel boasts many small guesthouses and moderately priced hotels, but its tranquil atmosphere remains virtually unchanged, despite the legions of mostly young visitors attracted to its glorious beaches and laid-back ambience. Puerto Escondido offers accommodations of all types, ranging from luxury hotels to beach cabanas that cost only several dollars a night. Midway in its development between an unknown fishing village and a big-name resort, Puerto Escondido offers perhaps the best base for taking in the beaches and scenic splendors of the Oaxaca coast. From here, it's just one hour south to Puerto Angel, and only 45 minutes south from Puerto Angel to the newly emerging Bays of Huatulco development, where four hotels opened in December 1989.

Oaxaca City

ORIENTING YOURSELF

Bounded by the Periférico (highway) that encircles it, Oaxaca City's downtown area is a joy for walkers, who can traverse it from one end to the other in less than one hour. The cobblestone streets in this area run east to west and north to south, following the trademark grid pattern laid out by its original Spanish planners, which makes it practically impossible to lose your way. But carry a map anyway, since some streets change their names as they pass the *zócalo,* the city's main square and the heart and soul of Oaxaca City. (The tourist office at the corner of Morelos and 5 de Mayo will supply you with a free map, superior to most of those given out by hotels.)

Shaded by towering laurels and flowering jacarandas, this enchanting main square, with its splashing fountains and lacy white bandstand-gazebo, is the loveliest and liveliest in all of Mexico. Probably the Number One attraction in the state is the drama that unfolds before your eyes from a seat at one of the sidewalk tables of the cafés that ring the square. Another leafy square, dominated by the cathedral, adjoins the *zócalo* on the northwest edge, and although it is officially part of the *zócalo,* it's not commonly referred to as such. To the north of the *zócalo* lie most of the major sights, along with the better hotels and shops; to further enhance the pleasure of walking in Oaxaca City, many of the streets to the north of the square are closed to traffic much of the day and evening. To the south of the *zócalo,* you'll find the main Juárez market and, along the slightly raffish streets surrounding it, budget hotels and eateries, all manner of shops, and the red-light district.

Southwest of the *zócalo* on the far side of the Periférico, the Saturday Abastos Market is the only city attraction outside the downtown area. Also outside downtown, by the way, are several of Oaxaca's better hotels, which lie on the city's northern fringe.

CONNECTIONS

Mexico City and Oaxaca City are linked by road, rail, and air; flying is by far the most convenient option. Mexicana and Aeromexico both offer several daily departures in either direction. The flight, which takes fifty minutes, offers breathtaking aerial views of the Popocatépetl and Ixtaccíhuatl volcanoes.

By road there are two direct routes from the capital to Oaxaca City. The 340-mile drive through spectacular mountain terrain on MEX190 via Cuautla is a difficult one and takes about nine hours. Less arduous—and only slightly less scenic—the 313-mile route along MEX150 and MEX131 winds through mountain forests and cactus-covered desert hills, passing the cities of Puebla and Tehuacan; driving time is about eight hours.

The journey takes about ten hours on the first-class buses of the ADO line, with more than twenty daily departures in both directions between Mexico City's south terminal and the Oaxaca ADO station at the north edge of the city, at Niños Heroes de Chapultepec 1036. Seats should be reserved a day in advance.

Train service between the two cities has been upgraded; overnight trains depart daily in both directions in late afternoon, arriving the next morning about 9 A.M.

Public buses crisscross the city and, from the main second-class terminal at the southwest edge of the city off Calle Trujano, depart frequently for all nearby towns, as well as more distant destinations such as Mexico City. Connections are excellent within the valley: There are, for example, 36 daily buses to Teotitlán del Valle. All service within the valley is second-class, with no air-conditioning.

Taxis are plentiful, but unless you are staying in one of the outlying hotels, in which case you will likely take taxis to and from downtown, it is probable that you will do much of your sightseeing on foot within the city. Taxis do not use meters, so settle on a fare beforehand—and remember that no ride within the city should cost more than 5,000 pesos (about two dollars), and only if you summon a taxi by phone from one of the outlying luxury hotels should the rate be even that high. Within the downtown area, figure 4,000 pesos maximum (less than two dollars) a ride.

You can also hire a taxi by the hour or by the day for a price negotiated and split between three or four passengers. Before setting off for an excursion, make sure your driver's English is adequate if your Spanish is not.

There are branches of Avis (6-50-30), Budget (6-06-11), and Hertz (6-54-78), as well as local rent-a-car firms, in town and at the airport.

TOURING

Many travel agencies offer guided tours to nearby archaeological sites and craft villages and markets. One with an excellent reputation is **Viajes Convento** (6-57-91), in the Presidente Oaxaca Hotel, which offers daily tours to Monte Albán at 3 P.M. and to Mitla at 10 A.M. Viajes Convento will also arrange individual tours following an itinerary tailored to your interests—to the craft villages, perhaps, or to less-frequented archaeological sites. Up to six passengers can share the $15 cost per hour, which includes transportation in a new combi van and the services of an English-speaking driver-guide. One guide who is highly recommended is Eugenio Cruz Castaneda; fluent in English, this former U.S. resident can be contacted through Viajes Convento.

Since the one and a half hours allotted to Monte Albán on the standard guided tours is insufficient time for all but the most cursory view, you may choose to return for a more extensive visit. **Autobuses Turísticos** runs bus service departing four times a day from the Hotel Mesón del Angel, corner of Mina and Díaz Ordaz (6-53-27); the round trip is a very reasonable 2,500 pesos (about one dollar)—but departure times vary, so check beforehand with the hotel or with the tourist office. Ask, too, about the same company's economical guided tours to Mitla.

📖 HOTELS

As befits so popular a tourist mecca, Oaxaca City abounds with accommodations in all price categories. Rates are far lower than those in Mexico City or at the major beach resorts; none of the city's five luxury hotels charges more than $80 per night for a double room.

Although a few "international-style" properties have recently sprouted on the northern outskirts of the city, the central district remains unmarred by towering modern monoliths. Instead, small-scale *posada*-type properties, many occupying restored colonial residences, are the norm here.

Reservations, always advisable, are essential for the weeks preceding both Christmas and Easter, when the better hotels may be fully booked months in advance. If you've failed to book ahead, time your arrival for early in the day, when chances of finding a vacant room are best.

Each of the following five-star properties scores high marks for comfort and convenience, although, with the exception of the Stouffer's Presidente Oaxaca, none is located within the downtown area. Remember that in this colonial city, amenities such as satellite television and servibars are not ubiquitous even in the best hotels; if you want a television in your room, let this be known when you check in.

Fortín Plaza
Avenida Venus 118, 68070
Tel. 951-5-77-77
Doubles, $37; junior suites, $52
North of the city on the highway to Mexico City, this six-story hostelry recalls an upscale "chain" property back in the States; its one hundred rooms net low marks for regional charm but A-pluses for comfort. There are three bars, two restaurants, and a pool. Front rooms overlook the city—and the highway; light sleepers should forego the awesome views and request one of

the rear rooms. The suites offer better value than the double rooms. Credit cards: AE, DC, MC, V.

Hotel Calesa Real
García Vigil 306, 68000
Tel. 951-6-55-44
Doubles, $25; singles, $20

Hand-painted tiles, burnished wood paneling, ceramic floors, and ceiling beams lend vintage charm to the public areas; only the 77 guest rooms betray the relative youth of this inviting hostelry superbly located a few blocks north of the *zócalo,* in prime shopping territory. The contemporary rooms are clean and comfortable, if less than spacious. A rooftop terrace, an enclosed courtyard garden with a small tiled swimming pool, and a bar-restaurant renowned for its low-priced regional fare are on the premises. Based on the twin virtues of location and low prices, this is one of the best addresses in the city. Credit cards: AE, DC, MC, V.

Hotel Misión de Los Angeles
Calzado P. Díaz 102, 68080
Tel. 951-5-15-00
Doubles, $37; singles, $30

An ensemble of low-rise modern stucco units and tile-roofed bungalows set on sweeping, tree-shaded lawns, this 125-room property is a veritable self-contained resort, only a five-minute drive north from the *zócalo,* replete with a vast pool, tennis courts, a game room, as well as a good restaurant, a disco, and a piano bar. Credit cards: AE, DC, MC, V.

Hotel Victoria
Pan American Highway km 545, 68070
Tel. 951-5-26-33
Doubles, $48–$72; singles, $30

High on a steep hillside overlooking the city, the Victoria's salmon-hued multistory main buildings and one-story bungalows cluster around a large heated pool on parklike grounds abloom with purple bougainvillea and roses. Just ten minutes away by car or a half hour on foot from the *zócalo,* this local landmark suggests a tranquil country resort and is, in fact, a popular honeymoon spot. Many of the 151 rooms—which vary greatly in decor—have superb views of the city. Plushest rooms are the junior suites in the annex; simply furnished bungalows offer superb views and a secluded romantic setting but are a bit of a hike from the main building (a five-minute climb with many steps). The most convenient rooms, in the main building, can be sterile. Along with tennis courts, a disco, and a lobby bar with live guitar or piano music, the lovely **El Tule** restaurant turns out fine regional and international fare. Breakfast buffets daily are recommended (from 7 A.M.). Bring sunglasses if you dine here in the morning. Credit cards: AE, DC, MC, V.

Marqués del Valle
Portal de Clavería 1, 68000
Tel. 951-6-32-95

Doubles, $25; singles, $20

If you select a hotel according to the old real estate axiom "location, location, location," you need look no farther than this five-story local favorite smack in the center of the action on the *zócalo*. In contrast to the lively onyx-paneled lobby and ever-popular sidewalk café, the 160 rooms are simple and sedate—and very clean. Quietest rooms face the atrium; larger and far more in demand, those with *zócalo* views can be noisy, but there is no better vantage point for observing the unfolding drama of Oaxaca. Credit cards: AE, DC, MC, V.

San Felipe Misión

Avenida Jalisco, 15 Sur, San Felipe del Agua, 68000
Tel. 951-5-01-00
Doubles, $50; singles, $30

The newest star in Oaxaca's luxury-hotel galaxy, a member of the respected Misión group, is somewhat removed from the city in the historic suburb of San Felipe. A minibus shuttle to and from downtown lessens the inconvenience of the location, a ten-minute drive from the *zócalo*. If you can forgo colonial ambience, you'll find amenities few city hotels can match: Each of the 160 rooms is equipped with a minibar, television, telephone, and private terrace overlooking the swimming pool with swim-up bar. Room decor is understated and elegant. There are two restaurants, a disco, and a piano bar, and on-site parking. Credit cards: AE, DC, MC, V.

Señorial

Portal de Flores 6, 68000
Tel. 951-6-39-33
Doubles, $18–$26; singles, $20

What it lacks in charm this modern commercial-type hotel makes up for in location. The 127 rooms tend to be small and rather nondescript (and noisy)—but also comfortable and clean. And who needs decor when you have the *zócalo* out your window? There is a roof garden and bar, a small swimming pool, and an indoor-outdoor restaurant on the square. Parking is available for a fee. No credit cards.

Stouffer Presidente Oaxaca

Calle 5 de Mayo 300, 68000
Tel. 951-6-06-11 or 800-GRACIAS
Doubles, from $80

One of Oaxaca's most enchanting historic edifices houses the city's most celebrated accommodation, which, despite its affiliation, represents the antithesis of the stereotypical "chain" hotel. A 16th-century flavor still suffuses this former convent—a labyrinthine stone maze that meanders around flower-laden courtyards, one with a swimming pool and bar. The 91 rooms on two levels open off arched passageways; enhanced with colonial-style furnishings, textured fabrics, and glazed ceramic tiles, the rooms vary greatly in size and appeal (a few are dark and cramped), so have a look before checking in, if possible. You'll find there a restaurant and bar. Credit cards: AE, DC, MC, V.

Oaxaca City is not a sports town, but there are tennis courts—open to nonguests for a fee—at the Hotel Victoria and the Hotel Misión de los Angeles.

An ideal starting point for your sightseeing sojourn in Oaxaca City is the **Regional Museum of Oaxaca,** Mexico's loveliest small museum, housed in a former 16th-century Dominican convent. Plan to spend at least two hours here. The folkways of Oaxaca's principal ethnic groups are revealed through displays of colorful hand-embroidered regional clothing and exhibits explaining fiestas, household rituals, indigenous religion, traditional medical practices, and the use of hallucinogenic mushrooms. The main draw, however, is the upstairs sanctuary, sheltering the dazzling horde discovered in Tomb 7 at Monte Albán in 1932. The sparkling trove of objects fashioned by the Mixtec includes alabaster drinking vessels; ivory combs; a skull inlaid with turquoise; headdresses, earrings, and necklaces, all of jade, silver, and mother-of-pearl; and an array of gold jewelry attesting to a level of sophistication of design and workmanship that astonishes even today.
Calles M. Alcala and Gurrión. Open Tues.–Fri. 10 A.M.–6 P.M.; Sat. and Sun. 10 A.M.–5 P.M. Admission 950 pesos.

After the dazzle of the Monte Albán horde, you'd expect the sights that follow to pale by comparison. The **Church of Santo Domingo de Guzman,** next door to the museum, appears to support that notion from the outside. The formidable facade makes the interior all the more breathtaking. Completed in 1666, this baroque extravaganza is lavished with polychrome stucco saints, choirs of angels, and voluptuous ornamental carvings encrusted with layer upon layer of gold. The richest church in Mexico, it is best visited in late afternoon, when the gold sanctuary shimmers with amber light pouring through the stained-glass windows.
Calles M. Alcala and Gurrión. Open Mon.–Sat. 6 A.M.–1 P.M., 4–8 P.M.; Sun. 6–8 A.M. and for Mass. Donation requested.

The Tamayo Museum of Pre-Hispanic Art offers a trove of pre-Columbian art assembled by celebrated Mexican painter Rufino Tamayo, beautifully displayed in an 18th-century mansion wrapped around a courtyard lush with roses, bougainvillea, and exotic blooms. This collection, donated to Tamayo's native Oaxaca, spans the centuries from the Olmec era through the pre-Conquest years.
Morelos 503. Open 10 A.M.–2 P.M. and 4 P.M. –6 P.M. daily except Tues. Admission 5,000 pesos.

The Basílica de la Soledad, a 17th-century baroque church, is the sanctuary of the city's patron saint, the Virgin of Solitude, who is purported to have supernatural healing powers. Garbed in a jewel-studded black robe, her image, which today occupies a gilded shrine, was found in the pack of a stray mule on this site. The church was constructed to commemorate this event, which is viewed as a miracle by the devout, who crawl on their knees for many miles to pay tribute to the Virgin. Behind the church is a museum with an array of votive paintings dedicated to the Virgin.

Independencia and Galeana. Open Mon.–Sat. 10 A.M.–2 P.M., Sun. noon–2 P.M. Donation requested.

The poor Zapotec boy who would later become president of Mexico, Benito Juárez, spent ten years in the house that is now the **Benito Juárez Museum** with a wealthy family who later adopted him and encouraged and paid for his education as a lawyer. Aside from some memorabilia and portraits, the main interest here lies in the insight the house and its furnishings provide into the life of an upper-middle-class Oaxaceño family of the 19th century.

García Vigil 609. Open Tues.–Sat. 10 A.M.–1 P.M. and 4–7 P.M. Admission 550 pesos.

☕ RESTAURANTS

Oaxacan cuisine reflects the character of the surrounding valley, a blend of Spanish and indigenous. The area is known as the Land of the Seven Moles, after the piquant, chocolate-based sauce that appears in innumerable permutations on restaurant menus, combined with grilled beef, chicken, pork, or *enmoladas,* fried tortillas folded and soaked in black mole and garnished with onions and fresh cheese. The valley is renowned for its avocados, which yield another popular *plato,* guacamole. Other favored fare includes barbecued meat, fresh mozzarella-like Oaxacan cheese, tamales, and seafood trucked in fresh from the coast. Unless otherwise noted, plan to pay about $10 for a multicourse meal for one, including tax, at the following establishments:

El Asador Vasco
Portal de Flores 11
Tel. 6-97-19

This local landmark—with balconies opening onto the *zócalo*—enjoys a well-earned reputation for epicurean excellence. In a relaxed yet elegant (for Oaxaca) setting, you can savor traditional Mexican fare, regional dishes, and, as the name indicates, specialties from Spain's Basque provinces. Recommended are grilled meats, chicken dishes, fish soup, and *gambas al ajillo*—prawns bathed in a garlicky sauce. The wine list encompasses domestic and imported selections. Strolling musicians enhance the atmosphere in the evenings. Open daily, 1:30–11:30 P.M. Credit cards: AE, DC, MC, V.

Mi Casita
Avenida Hidalgo 616
Tel. 6-92-56

You'll be greeted by the sight of a sideboard laden with traditional Oaxacan *platos*—a preview of good things to come—as you enter the second-floor dining room of this *simpático* eatery on a corner of the *zócalo.* Open only for the midday meal, this is the best place in the city to acquaint yourself with the local gastronomic glossary. Stuffed chiles, chicken in mole sauce, creamed soups, and—for adventurous epicures—fried grasshoppers appear often on the menu, which changes daily. The *plato oaxaceño* provides a sampling of eight or nine specialties. Window tables offer fine views of the main square. Open daily, 1–6 P.M. Credit cards: AE, DC, MC, V.

La Catedral
García Vigil 105
Tel. 6-32-85

Not surprisingly, carnivorous fare dominates the menu at this watering hole, popular with residents and travelers alike, that dubs itself "The House of Fillets." Seated beside a sparkling fountain, you can order a meal beginning with mushrooms *al ajillo* (with garlic) or one of the savory cream soups, followed by charcoal-broiled rib-eye or pepper steak, or spicy fillet *ranchero*-style. One of the few dining spots open past midnight (till 1 A.M., in fact), La Catedral offers live music each evening. Open daily for lunch and dinner. Credit cards: AE, DC, MC, V.

El Guajiro
Alcala 303
No phone

Coral walls and stone columns that once enclosed a Spanish convent now create a dramatic backdrop for this *au courant* bar-restaurant well-known for its nightly salsa concerts that draw a lively, stylish audience. More of a surprise is the high quality of the food turned out by the kitchen. Pasta dishes, salads, and grilled meats dominate the limited menu, which is highlighted by various chicken dishes—the brochette of chicken is especially recommended, as is, for dessert, *crepa de cajeta* (caramel crêpe). Open for dinner daily until 1 A.M. No credit cards.

Del Vitral
Guerrero 201
Tel. 6-31-24

One of Oaxaca's most majestic 19th-century dwellings shelters the city's most elegant restaurant, which draws its name from the stained-glass mural imported from Germany that greets you as you ascend the sweeping stairway to the high-ceilinged coral-hued dining room. Embellished with ornately carved woodwork, the hushed and elegant room is more reminiscent of a grand European hotel dining room than a Mexican restaurant in a provincial capital. Not surprisingly, international standards dominate the menu's repertoire; these include chicken Kiev, Chateaubriand, and Caesar salad. But better bets are the offerings from the sea—oysters Rockefeller, shrimp brochette, red snapper. Dinner for two, with a selection from the wine cellar, can lost as little as $50, or run to $100, depending on your selections. Open daily for lunch and dinner. Credit cards: MC, V.

Memorable more for their ambience than for culinary excellence, the sidewalk cafés sheltered by the arches encircling the *zócalo* offer a wide range of edibles to suit every taste. Examples, appearing on most café menus, are eggs in various incarnations, club sandwiches, chicken mole, enchiladas, seafood cocktails, fruit juices, beer, and mixed drinks. All the cafés have similar menus, service that tends to be slow, and the same irresistible atmosphere. Among the most popular cafés surrounding the *zócalo* are **El Marqués,** in the Marqués del Valle Hotel, slightly more elegant and expensive than the others; **Guelatao,** recommended for breakfast; **Del Jardín,** open until 1 A.M.; and **Del Portal,** which is known for its tasty chicken mole.

If you want to venture off the tourist track, head north to the Reforma area, near the Hotel Victoria, where you will find two eateries favored by local folk, **Playa del Carmen** and **Los Pacos.** Seated under a *palapa* roof at Los Pacos (B. Domínguez no. 108, tel. 5-35-73), you can feast on grilled steaks, spicy *chorizo* sausage, barbecued ribs, or other carnivorous fare, preceded by fine guacamole and platters of local quesadilla cheese and sausages. The menu is in Spanish only, but the amiable English-speaking proprietor will be happy to translate and offer suggestions. Open daily for lunch and dinner. No credit cards.

A few blocks away, you'll find **Playa del Carmen** (B. Domínguez 225, tel. 5-16-60), where affluent local families and businesspeople gather when the craving for seafood strikes. Start with a briny fresh cocktail of oysters, octopus, or shrimp, followed by either grilled red snapper or garlicky lobster *al mojo de ajo,* accompanied by a frosty Corona beer. Open daily for midday meal. Credit cards: MC, V.

The dining situation in Oaxaca's hotels is far more appealing than in many places. Among hotel restaurants, **El Tule,** in the Hotel Victoria, enjoys favor with affluent locals as well as travelers; the menu is international and the open-air dining room serves lunch and dinner overlooking the city. For lunch, local businesspeople gather at the **Hotel Calesa Real** for the economical fixed-price daily meal featuring regional specialties.

You may be repulsed by the mere sight of them; on the other hand, you may declare them to be *soooo* good that, just like potato chips, you are unable to eat just one. But one thing is for certain—of all the strange wares you'll see in Oaxaca's market, the strangest of all will be *chapulines.* Fried to a crisp and sold in little plastic bags or on a sheet of old newspaper for a few cents, these inch-long relatives of the U.S. grasshopper are beloved snacks in Oaxaca, where they're eaten straight from the bag, heavily laced with salt, or combined with other ingredients such as cheese and guacamole and rolled up into a tasty tortilla.

SHOPPING

The clacking of looms and the slap of hands against wet clay are sounds that have been heard for centuries in the Oaxaca Valley, one of Latin America's legendary craft capitals. For aficionados of handicrafts and folk art, the area comprises Mexico's most fertile shopping terrain. The silversmiths of Yalalag, the carpet weavers of Teotitlán, the potters of Coyotepec and Atzompa, the basket makers of Ocotlán, among many others, turn out wares that find their way into collections and galleries around the world. Many of these products can be purchased at their source, in the villages close to Oaxaca City (see **Craft Villages and Markets,** below), as well as in the markets and shops of the city, where prices are usually higher. The following shops are mini-department stores of regional crafts, good places to acquaint yourself with the enticements Oaxaca has to offer. Prices are marked and fixed, so you can get an idea of costs before venturing into the markets—where hard bargaining is in order.

Its name stands for "Popular Arts and Industries of Oaxaca," and ARIPO (García Vigil 809), a spacious government-run emporium, overflows with an outpouring of arts and crafts from every region of the state. Prices and quality are relatively high, but since none of these objects is expensive to begin with, you won't dent your budget too much. ARIPO is particularly good for fabrics—cotton table linens and handwoven cottons in vivid colors sold by the meter (bring measurements from home if you plan to buy, and remember that Mexico uses the metric system); wooden ceremonial masks; whimsical painted animals carved from wood; straw pocketbooks and baskets; terra-cotta ceramics; and knives with folk sayings incised on their blades. There is a wide selection of folkloric music on records and cassettes, and literature on the indigenous ethnic groups of the state.

Yalalag (Calle M. Alcala 104) is a rambling warren of rooms arranged around a courtyard garden. This enticing gallery brims with handicrafts from all over Mexico—hand-blown glass from Jalisco, string bags from Chiapas, lacquer from the state of Guerrero. But the highlights here, of course, are the Oaxacan wares; you'll find excellent displays of black pottery (enough to fill an entire room from floor to ceiling); regional clothing, including rare handloomed white *huipiles* from the village of Yalalag; silver crosses from the same village; contemporary womenswear in vibrant handloomed cottons; painted tin Christmas ornaments; and delightful ceramic garden ornaments.

Among the many factors determining the cost of a naturally dyed carpet is color; carpets with extensive areas of deep wine red will always command higher prices than their equivalents in other colors. This rich red is cochineal, a natural dye made from the pulverized bodies of *Coccus cacti,* an insect that can be found clinging to certain varieties of cacti in the tropical lowlands of Oaxaca. The flourishing world market for cochineal brought wealth to the coffers of the Spanish crown during the colonial era. It was cochineal, for example, that colored the famous red coats worn by British soldiers during the American Revolution. The introduction of chemical dyes lessened the demand for cochineal, but throughout the world a dwindling number of weavers who cling to traditional methods still depend on this odd insect to impart the distinctive hue that is impossible to replicate with synthetic dye. Many Zapotec weavers of Teotitlán still foray into the lowlands on cochineal-collecting expeditions. And it is the difficulty of picking each tiny insect off the cactus by hand that is reflected in the high cost of any cochineal-dyed carpet.

If you're after an even more indigenous experience, Oaxaca's famous Saturday market, officially known as the **Abastos Market,** is a vast mercantile extravaganza that sprawls over an area of many square blocks in the concrete-block market hall on the southwest fringe of the city. A few hours spent roaming the aisles here will be one of the highlights of your stay in Oaxaca. The action continues nonstop from sunup to sundown as Indians from throughout the valley, and mestizos as well, haggle over the price of a bunch of calla lilies or a live turkey, and vendors hawk goods ranging from Pink Floyd cassettes to herbal cures guaranteed to alleviate everything from hangovers and heartburn to impotence and ingrown toenails.

Since the market is geared to locals rather than travelers, the selection of handicrafts is far outweighed by the displays of mundane household items and fresh foods. But among the plastic colanders and polyurethane containers, you may spot some inexpensive items that will make fine gifts back home. These include carved wooden spoons, chocolate whippers, and straw tortilla baskets—all of which epitomize the blending of form and function.

If you plan on purchasing or have purchased pottery, this is a good place to pick up some baskets in which to cart your purchases home. You'll find several aisles of basket sellers, as well as pottery vendors. Bring a flashlight if you plan on buying pottery here, since the pottery is located in a dark area of the market. And be sure to leave valuables in your hotel safe and carry cash in your front pocket when shopping in this or any other market.

If you miss the Saturday market, be sure to check out the city's daily market a few blocks south of the *zócalo,* where buying and selling go on from dawn to dusk daily. The **Benito Juárez Market,** smaller and far more manageable than the Saturday market, also caters to local folk. Inside the market building and along adjacent side streets, stalls beckon with incised leather belts, woven *huarache* sandals, straw goods, embroidered cotton blouses, and on and on.

Far more tranquil than the larger markets, the tourist-oriented **Artisan's Market** on Calle Zaragoza near the Juárez Market is a cavernous warehouse-type structure crammed with stalls where you can pick up traditional pottery, hand- and machine-embroidered clothing, inexpensive jewelry, woven cotton shawls and tableware, and much more. Prices are usually midway between those asked at the craft villages and those charged at the city's better shops.

Along Calle 20 de Noviembre south of the Juárez Market, you'll find a row of sidewalk stalls where painted tin ornaments, mirror frames, and boxes cost less than half what they do at the fine shops nearby. A few steps away, you can pick up straw bags and baskets to haul your booty.

Continue strolling south along Calle 20 de Noviembre and you will come to **Porfiria Gatica Hernández,** a minuscule shop crammed to the ceiling with black pottery from Coyotepec. The proprietor is charming, the quality of the design and craftsmanship is above average, and the prices are so low that bargaining is unnecessary.

ENTERTAINMENT

Oaxaca's most popular nighttime rendezvous is the **zócalo,** and each evening the sidewalk cafés nestled under the arched portals ringing the square pulsate with life as travelers and local residents, young and old, gather over frosty cold *cervezas* and steaming mugs of hot chocolate and sandwiches. For the price of a drink, you can sit until closing time (most cafés close between 11:30 P.M. and midnight), people watching, listening to roving musicians, and perusing the wares of ambulatory Indian vendors who meander from table to table, laden with handwoven rugs, braided wrist bracelets and belts, fringed shawls, carved wooden letter openers, and other ephemera. From here, too, you can listen to the music played in the bandstand, where concerts are held beginning at 7:30 P.M. on Mondays, Wednesdays, Fridays, and Saturdays.

On Friday evenings, the **Stouffer's Presidente Hotel** holds *Guelaguetza,* a Oaxacan fiesta featuring a dinner comprised of regional specialties and folkloric dances from different regions of the state, performed by a local troupe garbed in colorful, exotic costumes.

Oaxaca's bohemian night spot, the atmospheric **Café El Sol y La Luna,** at Murguia 105 (tel. 6-24-33)—around the corner from the Presidente Hotel—serves drinks and light fare. Live guitar or folk music draws a lively, late-evening crowd to this dimly lighted, greenery-laden domain dominated by a centuries-old tree that grows through the roof.

EXCURSIONS

CRAFT VILLAGES AND MARKETS

No shopping sojourn in Oaxaca City is complete without a visit to one or all of the villages below, where you will have an opportunity to watch artisans at work and to buy handicrafts for the lowest possible prices. Bargaining is accepted, and expected, both at the marketplaces and with the craftspeople themselves. Note that no plastic is accepted in these outlying towns, and while some places will accept traveler's checks, it's best to bring cash—preferably Mexican pesos—if you plan to do any buying. You will not find many enticing eating places in any of these villages, so have your meal before you leave, or bring a picnic lunch and drinks. Many tour operators run excursions to most of these towns; the Tlacolula Sunday market, for example, is always included on Sunday group tours to Mitla. Or you can arrange for either a private tour (Viajes Convento in the Stouffer's Presidente Hotel offers tours to the craft villages in a private minibus with an English-speaking guide, for example) or a taxi. All of these villages and towns are accessible from Oaxaca City by second-class bus departing from the main terminal southwest of downtown. There are many departures daily.

Teotitlán del Valle

Known as the town of three thousand weavers, Teotitlán has been renowned since pre-colonial times for its handloomed fabrics once demanded as a tribute by Zapotec overlords. Today the master artisans of Teotitlán still follow the formulas of their ancestors to make natural dyes from plants and the rare cochineal insect. The weavers welcome visitors and will give demonstrations of the spinning, dyeing, and weaving processes. All have a selection of rugs and runners for sale, and most will accept custom orders. If you plan to buy a carpet, it is helpful to bring measurements from home to help you choose the correct size. As you drive through town you will see dozens of signs indicating the homes of carpet weavers; you can stop at random. The following are among the town's most respected craftsmen (you will pay more for their products, but the quality is far higher than average): **Isaac Vasquez,** Avenida Juárez 44; **Hermanos Mendoza,** Carranza 2. Anyone in town can give you directions to their homes, identified by signs out front. Teotitlán is at the end of a dirt

Black Beauties—Pottery of Coyotepec

Any mention of Oaxacan crafts sparks images of the lustrous black pottery from the village of San Bartolo Coyotepec. Shaped into bowls, pots, figurines, ashtrays, and lanterns, the pottery fills shop shelves and crowds market stalls throughout the city of Oaxaca. Surprisingly, unlike many other Oaxacan handicrafts that have been produced for centuries, Mexico's most distinctive pottery had its genesis less than forty years ago in the workshop of the now legendary **Rosa Real de Nieto,** of San Bartolo Coyotepec. Accustomed to working with the gray clay of the area, Doña Rosa tried burnishing a clay pot with a piece of quartz before firing, a procedure that lent a satiny patina to the finished product. And, as she later learned, a shortened firing time would yield the then unusual black pottery.

Today in the village of San Bartolo Coyotepec, 7½ miles south of Oaxaca City on Route 175, where most families are in the pottery business, Doña Rosa's son, Valente, oversees the family workshop and showroom, where visitors can watch him at work and select from a wealth of signed objects. Prices are low, but remember that the clay is porous and can be used neither for holding water nor for serving food. Doña Rosa's is open from 9 A.M. to 5 P.M.; follow signs on the highway that will direct you to it.

Doña Rosa's is the most renowned workshop, but it's far from the only one in this village, where as you walk through the dusty streets you'll see signs identifying homes where pottery is produced. A knock at the door will gain entrance. Among the other potters in town, **Simon Reyes,** on the same street as Doña Rosa's, excels in animals, figurines, and small pieces more ornate than those of the Doña Rosa workshop.

track off the highway between Oaxaca City and Mitla. A sign on the highway indicates the turnoff to Teotitlán. You can also get there by bus; one leaves every 2 ½ hours beginning at 8 A.M. from the corner of Calle M. Cabrera and Calle Mina in Oaxaca City. The trip by bus takes less than one hour. More conveniently, taxis may be hired for the round trip to Teotitlán from Oaxaca City; inquire as to the approximate fare at your hotel desk before negotiating the price with a driver. The town's streets are unpaved and dusty, so dress accordingly. Bring Mexican money or U.S. dollars with you if you plan to buy.

Santo Tomás Jalietza

This is a tiny village reached via a dirt road off the Oaxaca–Ocotlán highway. Cotton weaving is the dominant occupation of the women here, and it is common to see four generations gathered together in the courtyards of their tin-roofed adobe houses, busily working back-strap looms. The local weavers' cooperative has set up a series of stalls in the main plaza where you can purchase tablecloths, placemat-and-napkin sets, leather belts with embroidered panels, and shawls for about half the price asked in the city's shops. The village is a bit out of the way, and there's little else of interest here, so decide if the potential savings is worth the cost in time and expense to get here. Buses for Santo Tomás depart frequently throughout the day from the second-class terminal in Oaxaca City. Or hire a taxi for the round trip for a negotiable price—probably about $20—which will include the driver's waiting time while you shop.

Atzompa

North of Oaxaca off Route 131, this small village with a market on Tuesday is famous for its rustic-looking pottery glazed a deep green. Prices are extremely low. Note, however, that the glaze contains lead and the wares are therefore not recommended for eating or serving. Look instead for decorative objects, especially figurines, miniature toys, and whistles fashioned in animal shapes.

Ocotlán

Every Friday morning, thousands of Indians pour into Ocotlán and set up their stalls, turning this large town into a giant open-air bazaar. There is also a separate animal market on the edge of town where, perhaps, you can haggle over the price of plow-trained oxen. Known for the straw sombreros woven by the inmates of a local prison, Ocotlán is also the home of the four Aguilla sisters, famous throughout Mexico for their whimsical, painted clay figures and Nativity crèches. Watch for signs identifying these sisters' homes and workshops, located close to one another on the main road north of town. Prices are very low—about half of what they are in the city.

Tlacolula

This large town, twenty miles southeast of Oaxaca, is known for its ornate 16th-century church—and for its Sunday market that is included on tours to Mitla on that day. Apart from a few craft stalls offering carpets from Teotitlán and clothing and shawls from Mitla, however, the market caters to the local populace rather than to travelers. The best buy in Tlacolula is *mezcal,* which is made nearby and is considered to be far superior to the commercial brands sold in Oaxaca's liquor shops. At the shop here known as **La Favorita,** you can buy *mezcal* in many varieties, including orange flavored. Bags of dried and salted worms are sold here too; these might make quite a hit at cocktail parties back home. Displayed in the shop are the business cards of many well-known customers, including Fidel Castro. Prices, however, reflect the shop's fame.

Other markets that you can visit with a tour group or via taxi or bus are held at **Etla,** which has a Wednesday market, and **Zaachila** and **Ejutla,** both of which have Thursday markets.

MONTE ALBÁN

Among the most important archaeological sites in the hemisphere and the Number One attraction in the state of Oaxaca, Monte Albán, six miles southwest of Oaxaca City, is believed to have been built originally by the Olmec as a medical center about two thousand years ago. Stones incised with anatomical drawings depicting breech birth, dwarfism, and other conditions were later incorporated by the Zapotec into their ceremonial center beginning around the time of the birth of Christ. Atop a sun-baked plateau on a mountain whose peak was leveled without the aid of the wheel or of domestic animals, the maze of stone temples, palaces, pyramids, and a ball court that covered 15 square miles rose up around a vast central plaza, where ten thousand subjects once danced for their priests. Under construction for about one thousand years, Monte Albán reached its most voluptuous flowering around the time of the fall of Rome, in A.D. 410, before being invaded in about A.D. 1200 by the Mixtec, who turned it into a vast funeral site, with hundreds of tombs, including the famed Number 7 that yielded the horde in the Oaxaca Museum. Near the entrance to the archaeological site, a shiny new building (open 10 A.M. to 5 P.M.; the rest of the site is open from 9 A.M. to 6 P.M.) houses a small museum, along with a pleasant cafeteria and several fine shops.

MITLA

Unlike most Zapotec and Mixtec centers in Oaxaca, Mitla, 24 miles southeast of Oaxaca City, was still flourishing at the time the Spanish arrived and was all but decimated by them. The remaining ruins are far smaller than Monte Albán and can be easily digested in a couple of hours. The main lure here is the two excavated buildings renowned for the geometric mosaics with which they are sheathed inside and out. Unique to Mitla, these are composed of tens of thousands of pieces of stone cut without metal tools and affixed without mortar. Fitted so tightly that they appear to be carved from a single block of stone, they rank with the marvels of Mesoamerican decorative arts.

Contemporary Mitla is a textile-producing center, and, at the entrance to the ruins, the giant parking lot is encircled by tiny stalls crammed with woven shawls, *huipiles,* and contemporary blouses, embroidered dresses, and children's clothes—all produced for the tourist market. The ruins are open 9 A.M. to 6 P.M. daily.

In the town of Mitla, about a mile and a half from the ruins, the **Frissel Museum** (open 9 A.M. to 6 P.M. daily; donation requested) enshrines thousands of figurines found at Mitla and other Mixtec sites in the valley.

In the museum courtyard, the lovely **La Sorpresa Restaurant** (Avenida Independencía 4; tel. 0-00-04) is by far the best lunch place between here and Oaxaca City.

> Note: Mitla is packed with tour groups on Sundays, especially between 10 A.M. and noon, when tour buses stop here before continuing on to the Tlacolula market.

The 24 miles along MEX190 between Mitla and Oaxaca bristles with enticements, especially for the archaeology buff. A brochure describing the route is available (in Spanish) from the tourist office in Oaxaca. In addition to Tlacolula (see **Craft Villages and Markets**, above) you can make the following stops.

EL TULE

As you head south to Mitla, six miles from Oaxaca, in a churchyard on your left, is the colossal cypress tree known as El Tule. Among the oldest living things in the Americas, it was already more than fifteen hundred years old when Cortés and his men allegedly sought its shade before striking out for Honduras. You'll need a super-wide lens to capture this giant creature. Now more than 160 feet in girth and still widening, the world's largest tree has already given rise to several offspring and will soon force the road to be moved in order to accommodate its vast underground root network.

DAINZU

Just off the highway ten miles southeast of Oaxaca, this partially excavated site is highlighted by magnificent relief carvings, affixed to the base of its tallest monument, of ballplayers in motion.

LAMBITYECO

Visible from the highway 17 miles southeast of Oaxaca, this Zapotec site rose to its zenith while Monte Albán was in decline, from about A.D. 700 to 900. The complex of structures is known for the small house with fine friezes and carved stucco heads that were found buried beneath it.

ZAACHILA

The Thursday market here is a popular stop on the tourist trail, but as interesting are the remains of what was the last Zapotec political capital. Locals, mindful of keeping their heritage preserved intact, prohibited exploration of the site until 1962; the small area that has been scrutinized thus far has already yielded several pyramids and a pair of tombs piled with gold, bone, jade, and turquoise artifacts, most of which are on display in Mexico City's Museum of Anthropology. To get to Zaachila by car, turn off the highway to Mitla (MEX190) onto the road to Xoxocatlan; signs indicate the turn-off. Zaachila is easily reached by second-class bus departing from the Oaxaca City terminal.

YAGUL

The remains of this ceremonial center lie 22 miles from Oaxaca City, off the highway to Mitla. Tombs, palaces, and the largest ball court in the Americas spill down the side of a fortified hill that provides a magnificent view of the valley from its summit.

Oaxaca Beaches

To most foreign tourists, the name Oaxaca calls to mind cobblestone streets lined with aristocratic colonial mansions, baroque churches dripping with gold leaf, stone pyramids rising from a sun-baked plain, and Indian markets bursting with gleaming chiles, black pottery, and lavishly embroidered textiles.

Oaxaca's coast, however, is another world. Unlike the Oaxaca Valley, one of Mexico's most popular tourist regions, the Pacific shoreline has been, until now, very much off the beaten path. Isolated from the rest of the state by the rugged ranges of the Sierra Madre del Sur, this realm of sun-soaked sands, where the only footprints are those of shore birds, offers tourmaline waters, rocky coves, palm trees, and rustic thatch-roofed eateries serving ceviche and *camarones* rather than chicken mole and *chiles rellenos.*

North of Acapulco, Mexico's Pacific Coast is dotted with resorts. Soon to be added is the most glittering of all—Bahías de Huatulco, the Bays of Huatulco, which within a decade's time will be Mexico's largest and most extravagant resort. Four hotels are open, but Huatulco's bays and its commercial center, Santa Cruz Huatulco, are still very much in the construction stage. While this glittering jewel is being polished, then, perhaps your best base for exploring the charms of this enchanting stretch of shoreline is Puerto Escondido, an hour and three quarters' drive north of Huatulco along the Pacific Coast Highway, Route 200. Two years ago, mention of Puerto Escondido was likely to have elicited a blank response from your local travel agent. Until recently, this out-of-the-way fishing hamlet was known only to surfers lured by Escondido's legendary breakers, and footloose young travelers who rented hammocks for a dollar a night at rustic beachfront restaurants and kept their backpacks stashed behind the bar. But just as the opening of Ixtapa revealed to the world the charms of a little-known fishing village named Zihuatanejo, so has the creation of Huatulco cast the international spotlight on Puerto Escondido (and to some extent its even lesser-known neighbor to the southeast, Puerto Angel), which is quickly evolving from a sleepy seaport to a bona-fide tourist destination. The airport outside town receives daily commercial flights from Mexico City and the city of Oaxaca. A trio of luxury hotels has sprouted on the bluffs of Bacocho Beach outside town, and glossy shops and seafood restaurants are springing up as fast as jungle vines along Puerto Escondido's main street, Avenida Perez Gasga, which has recently been paved. Group tours have begun to descend, but for the moment, Puerto Escondido's relaxed atmosphere and slow-moving pace remain unaltered. With these, and scenery seemingly lifted straight from the movie *South Pacific,* you couldn't ask for a more alluring spot with which to cap off your wanderings in Oaxaca.

The tiny fishing village of Puerto Angel, wrapped around the curve of a wide bay, is slowly, slowly emerging from obscurity, but it still lies a long way off the beaten tourist trail. Popular with free-spirited European and American travelers, many of whom stay for months on end, Puerto Angel will appeal to most visitors as a day trip from Puerto Escondido. But for those who want to linger, there are many inexpensive guest houses and one moderately priced hotel.

Puerto Escondido

Unlike most Mexican communities, Puerto Escondido is not laid out around a *zócalo.* Instead, this fishing village-turned-resort sprang up in fits and starts along the main drag, Avenida Perez Gasga. Paved only during the past few years (much of the town still lacks sealed roads), Perez Gasga runs parallel to the main town beach for about a half-mile before climbing uphill to meet the main Pacific highway, MEX200.

The ramshackle T-shirt shops, modest hotels, trendy bars, down-home seafood spots, and glossy silver emporia that hug both sides of Perez Gasga at its beach end constitute downtown Puerto Escondido, as far as tourists are concerned. (The market area, which most visitors never see, lies on the inland side of MEX200; follow Perez Gasga uphill and across the highway, and you will come to the market.)

In the evenings when it's closed to traffic, sleepy Perez Gasga swells with sun-bronzed surfers, local families, and travelers of every nationality and age group that converge to stalk the street, to stare, and to be stared at.

Preferred daytime pursuits are swimming and sunning, and several options exist. The most popular mecca is the main town beach, steps from Perez Gasga. To this mile-long crescent of palm-fringed sand lapped by tame waves, the local fishermen return and unload their hauls of tuna, red snapper, and sailfish each morning at about nine or ten, when a huge crowd of tourists gathers, welcoming the break in the daily routine.

When the town beach gets too crowded, or when you tire of the scene here, walk along the sand in the direction of the Santa Fe Hotel; make your way through the giant boulders strewn on the shoreline, and then you will see, stretching in front of you, stretching for miles in the distance, the golden sands of **Zikatela Beach,** a legendary name in the surfing lexicon. If you make it out here between the hours of 7 A.M. and 10 A.M., you can watch these aficionados with their boards try to master breakers that often swell to a massive ten feet in height. Most surfers drift away before noon, so after that you may find yourself sharing Zikatela's miles of sand with only a flock of gulls.

In Puerto Escondido you can play tennis at the Posada Real Hotel in the Bacocho area, between town and the airport.

A public launch from the main beach, or a bone-jarring drive along the dirt road from town, will transport you to **Puerto Angelito** (not to be confused with Puerto Angel), a set director's dream of a tropical Eden. Shaded by towering palms and strewn with giant boulders, this small cove has a seafood restaurant and hammocks that you can rent for the day. Stay away on Sundays, when hordes of families with many, many children descend.

Flocks of tropical birds nest in the luxuriant jungle flora that hugs the Manialtepec lagoon, 15 miles west of Puerto Escondido. You'll see many of these feathered friends if you join one of the inexpensive one-and-a-half-hour launch cruises that depart from the docks of several restaurants. (Look for signs along the highway, MEX200.) The García Rendon Agency (Avenida Perez Gasga; tel. 2-01-14) runs more extensive tours from Puerto Escondido.

CONNECTIONS

The best way to reach Oaxaca's beaches is by air; there is service from Mexico City to both Puerto Escondido and Huatulco. From Oaxaca City, it's a short flight to Puerto Escondido aboard daily flights of Aerovias Oaxaceñas; their offices in Oaxaca City are at Armenta y Lopez 209 (tel. 6-38-33) and on Avenida Perez Gasga in Puerto Escondido. Aeromexico also flies from Oaxaca to both Puerto Escondido and Huatulco.

The drive from Oaxaca to the coast is a grueling one along narrow, winding MEX175 through the Sierra; figure seven hours by car from Oaxaca to Puerto Escondido via Pochutla. The direct road from Oaxaca to Puerto Escondido that you see on the maps is only partially sealed and can be impassable during the rains. By bus from Oaxaca to Puerto Escondido is a journey of nine to ten hours; there is also service from Oaxaca to both

Puerto Angel and Huatulco, but you will have to transfer in Pochutla to reach these towns. Buses to the coast are second-class only, and there are several departures daily in both directions.

It's 230 miles from Acapulco to Puerto Escondido over fairly good—and mostly flat—MEX200. By car, figure five hours, a bit longer on the second-class buses of the Flecha Roja line; bus service on this route is efficient, and equipment is generally comfortable. There is no first-class service in this neck of the woods. When driving between Acapulco and Puerto Escondido during the rainy season, anticipate washouts and other delays on the highway.

TOURING

Mexico's Pacific Coast Highway runs through Puerto Escondido. You can travel south from there by bus to Pochutla, where connections can be made to Puerto Angel and Huatulco. By taxi, the one-and-three-quarter-hour trip between Puerto Escondido and Huatulco, one-way, costs about $35.

The best way of exploring the coast is by car; taxis can be rented for negotiable hourly rates. Avis, Hertz, and Budget car-rental agencies have branches on Avenida Perez Gasga in Puerto Escondido.

Viajes García Rendon, in Puerto Escondido on the main street, operates sightseeing excursions by private car or minibus to Huatulco, Puerto Angel, and the Manialtepec lagoon.

🧳 HOTELS

Puerto Escondido, with its fishing village/low-key resort ambience, makes the best base for exploring the attractions of the Oaxacan coast. Most hotels in the center of town, with the notable exceptions of the pair described below, are rather basic Mexican variations on the budget beachside motel, the major charms of which are low rates and proximity to the beach. The best of the dozen or so accommodations in this category, all on the main street, Perez Gasga (and all with postal code 71980), are **Hotel Nayar** (407; tel. 958-2-01-13); **Hotel Loren** (958-2-00-57); **Castillo de Reyes** (sin/número; tel. 958-2-04-42); the popular **Rincon del Pacífico** (900; tel. 953-200-93); and—directly on the beach—a long-running local landmark **Las Palmas** (sin/número; tel. 958-2-02-30). Each charges $10–$12 for a double room except Rincon del Pacifíco, where a double room with ocean view costs $33; all but Rincon del Pacifíco, which takes no cards, accept MC and V. **Note for light sleepers:** Bring earplugs to Las Palmas or you'll risk being jarred awake by the daily 5 A.M. reveille from the nearby naval base.

Campers have two choices: the busy and noisy **Neptuno** campground on the main beach in the center of the action, or the secluded, splendidly situated **Trailer Park Carizalillo** (tel. 2-00-77), outside town overlooking Carizalillo Beach, a beautiful, often-deserted rocky cove reached via a steep path.

The two hotels described below cost twice as much as the budget properties, but their unique charm makes them well worth the added pesos.

Hotel Santa Fe

Calle del Morro, sin/número, Apdo. Postal 96, Puerto Escondido, 71980
Tel. 958-2-01-70
Doubles, about $34

Often booked far in advance by a mostly American and Canadian clientele that includes many return visitors, the American-owned Santa Fe is one of a breed that is all too rare on Mexico's Pacific Coast—a beachfront *posada* that is both enchanting and inexpensive. Situated behind the boulders that separate the tranquil waters of the town beach from the mighty breakers of Zikatela Beach, this rambling terra-cotta–hued complex embellished by hand-painted tiles and iron grillwork encircles a flower-filled courtyard with a small swimming pool. Regional fabrics and handicrafts highlight the 34 spacious and very handsome guest rooms with both air-conditioning and ceiling fans, kept spick-and-span by the amiable and accommodating staff. Shaded by a *palapa* roof, the open-air restaurant overlooking the beach is the best in town. Credit cards: MC, V.

Paraíso Escondido

Calle Andador Union 10, Puerto Escondido, 71980
Tel. 958-2-04-44
Reservations: Apdo. 20–187, Mexico City 20, D.F.; Tel. 5-604-0834
Singles, about $22; doubles, about $28

The name means "hidden paradise," and it befits this unique inn, set back from the main street on a hill overlooking town. The idiosyncratic two-story brick structure looks as if it grew in fits and starts—and it probably did. The hotel was designed by the European-born owner-manager, whose love of Mexico shines throughout this maze of tiled patios, courtyards rich with stone sculpture and masses of flowers, and culs-de-sac brimming with Mexican folk art. An inviting alfresco bar-restaurant ajoins the small swimming pool. The twenty whitewashed air-conditioned guest rooms with colonial-style furnishings and modern fittings open off long, long passageways that snake through the rambling building; second-floor rooms have sea views. Mexicans and Europeans make up a majority of the clientele. Credit cards: MC, V.

A five-minute drive north of town toward the airport, **Fraccionamiento Bacocho** is Puerto Escondido's luxury hotel and residential zone. Several new hotels are scheduled to join the two described below. Each of these has four stars, but none is quite up to the par of similarly classed properties in more developed resorts of the country. Note that the beach here, while long and scenic, is dangerous for swimming due to rough surf and strong currents.

Fiesta Mexicana

Bulevar Benito Juárez, Puerto Escondido, 71980
Tel. 958-2-01-15 or 958-2-01-50
Singles, about $40; doubles, about $45

A few steps from the Posada Real (see below), the two-story pink stucco buildings of the more sedate Fiesta Mexicana are strung around a free-form pool and a small, *palapa*-roofed restaurant. Cheerful floral-patterned fabrics enliven the sixty glossy white guest rooms; double beds are gracefully draped with mosquito netting—most welcome in this climate. Credit cards: AE, MC, V.

Posada Real

Bulevar Benito Juárez Number 11, Puerto Escondido, 71980
Tel. 958-2-01-33 or 958-2-01-85 or 800-528-1234
Doubles, about $55

A member of the Best Western chain, this is Puerto Escondido's most elaborate hotel, with restaurants, bars, tennis courts, two pools, and all the expected first-class resort amenities. The low-rise main building, with one hundred motel-modern rooms, sits high on a bluff overlooking a long stretch of deserted beach. A lovely swimming pool, with a flower-filled island in the center, awaits at beach level; here, too, is **Coco's Restaurant and Bar,** with a seafood-dominated menu and live salsa music nightly. A minibus shuttles guests between the lobby and the beach level. Credit cards: AE, MC, V.

Puerto Angel offers the following hotels:

Hotel Angel del Mar

Cerro de la Playa Panteón, Puerto Angel, 71980
Tel. 958-4-03-97
Doubles, $20

Atop a high promontory at the end of a steep, winding dirt road from town, a stark modern concrete structure shelters 42 spacious and airy rooms with unpretentious decor and splendid sea views from private terraces. A bar, restaurant, and pool are also on the premises. The beach lies beyond easy walking distance, but taxis are plentiful and inexpensive. Credit cards: MC, V.

Not officially, but in practice, the north end of a six-mile-long beach that is a 15-minute drive from Puerto Angel (over dreadful roads) is Oaxaca's best-known nude bathing spot: **Zipolite.** There are no facilities apart from a few palm-thatched eateries and very rustic guesthouses, so pack a picnic lunch and plenty of suntan lotion, and take extreme caution when swimming in the rough surf.

Posada Cañon de Vata

Apdo. Postal 74, Puerto Angel, Pochutla
No phone

Suzanne and Mateo Lopez, she from the United States, he from Mexico, preside over this simple inn hidden away on a wooded site, a five-minute walk from the town's best beach, Playa Panteón. Often booked far in advance, the Cañon de Vata appeals to an eclectic international clientele of self-sufficient travelers eager to escape the prices and the "plastic character" of traditional resort hotels. Indeed, the ambience here suggests a private home more than a hotel, with only a handful of simple but comfortable rooms (most with private bath) and three bungalows. The top level, shaded by a thatch roof, is an inviting breezy lair where guests laze away the hours in hammocks. Fish dishes, vegetarian fare, and homemade breads highlight the offerings of the restaurant, where service is family-style. No credit cards.

And these properties are located in Huatulco:

Club Med
Bahía Tangolunda, Huatulco, Pochutla
Tel. 958-1-00-55 or 1-800-CLUBMED
Weekly package, excluding airfare, from $780–$1,350 per person; varies seasonally; packages including airfare also available

One of the prettiest of all the Club Meds, this is an enchanted village of rose, apricot, and sky-blue buildings spilling down a hillside to a postcard-perfect beach of dazzling white sand and edged by the iridescent waters of Tangolunda Bay. Although the club sprawls over hilly terrain, fringed surreys ply the trails so that minimal walking is required. Each unit contains a double room, which may be partially divided for privacy, and a shared tiled bathroom with shower and two sinks. Diversions offered free of charge range from aerobics to volleyball and include launch excursions to deserted beaches and prime snorkeling sites. The main restaurant presents buffets of mind-boggling proportions, and there are four other restaurants, one each offering seafood, steak, Moroccan and Italian cuisine. Credit cards: AE, DC, MC, V.

Huatulco Sheraton
Bahía Tangolunda, Huatulco, Pochutla
Tel. 958-4-03-40 or 800-325-3535
Doubles, $80–$120 ocean view, $95 pool view

One of the most luxurious hotels in the state of Oaxaca, the Sheraton is only partially opened, but the forecast looks excellent. The sprawling low-rise rose-hued structure blends in well with its surroundings of staggering beauty. A large pool augments the superb swimming offered in Tangolunda Bay. Three on-premises restaurants, **Cardinale** (Italian), **Casa Real** (Mexican), and **La Tortuga** (a beachfront eatery with bar), satisfy a wide variety of appetites. You'll also find a health and fitness center with sauna and steamroom, and lighted tennis courts, and a golf course is planned. Credit cards: AE, DC, EC (Euro-Card), MC, V.

Posada Binniguenda
Bahía Santa Cruz, Huatulco, Pochutla, Oaxaca
Tel. 958-4-00-77
Doubles, $50

Santa Cruz, the commercial center of the Bahías de Huatulco project, offers first-rate accommodations at this four-star contemporary update of a colonial inn, located five minutes by taxi from the town beach. Both public areas and the large, handsome guest rooms in this pink stucco structure derive substantial charm from their use of natural materials—tile floors, regional folk art, period-style furnishings. A lovely large pool, a restaurant, and a bar are also offered.

More than twenty centuries have elapsed since the Zapotec of the Oaxaca Valley embarked on one of the most awesome construction projects ever undertaken in this hemisphere—the building of Monte Albán. And now once again, 229 miles south of Monte Albán, history is being written in Oaxaca with brick and stone as the Mexican Tourist Development Foundation (FONATUR) transforms an idyllic—and up until two years ago, isolated—18-mile swath of shoreline indented with nine sparkling bays into what promises to be the country's most resplendent resort community, **Bahías de Huatulco.** Incredible as it may seem, it is predicted that by the year 2018 there will be three hundred thousand people living in Huatulco, which is now home to less than ten thousand. Taking care not to create a mini-Acapulco, or even another Cancún, FONATUR has mapped out a master plan with a strict set of architectural guidelines that must be followed. All new construction, for example, must employ local materials and be built with thick exterior walls and slanting roofs of terracotta tiles, thatch, or brick, in a style harmonious with the surrounding environment. The visitor to Huatulco has the sense of looking on as the map of Mexico is rewritten to include the result of what must be the largest construction project since the creation of Monte Albán. Just as Monte Albán transports us back through the centuries, the Bays of Huatulco lend a telescope through which we can glimpse the Mexico of the 21st century.

Huatulco offers a considerable amount of sports activity, including tennis at the Sheraton Hotel's lighted tennis courts. A golf course is scheduled to open soon at the Sheraton and will be available to nonguests for a daily fee. Snorkeling equipment can be rented from stands on the beach in the town of Santa Cruz Huatulco.

🍴 RESTAURANTS

In Puerto Escondido, there are several hotel restaurants worthy of note. The best dining in town is at the **Hotel Santa Fe**'s open-air restaurant, overlooking the crashing breakers of Zikatela Beach. The *palapa*-roofed open-air building is *the* place to be for breakfast. Lunch and dinner possibilities from the large menu include grilled lobster and other fare from the sea, tempura, meatless lasagna, and a host of vegetarian dishes. About $17 per person for lunch or dinner. Credit cards: MC, V.

Jungle murals and colorful animal masks create an exotic tropical backdrop for the beach-level **Coco's** at the Hotel Posada Real. Highlights of the menus, printed on surfboards, are octopus in garlic sauce, grilled shrimp, steaks, and salads. A salsa combo plays each evening. Open daily for lunch and dinner; meal service until 10:30 P.M. Lunch or dinner for two should come to about $30. Credit cards: AE, MC, V.

Main courses at the following nonhotel eateries range from $5–$20 (for a half-kilo lobster—equivalent to about 1.1 pound); service tends to be amiable but slow.

Two standouts among the dozens of seafood spots in town, both on Avenida Perez Gasga, are **La Sardina de Plata,** offering economical daily set menus along with à la carte seafood in a multitude of variations. Try to sit near the front; the heat from the open kitchen envelops the rear tables. Credit cards: MC, V.

From the main street, a staircase descends to the beach, where the romantic candlelit rendezvous **Los Crotos** awaits on the edge of the sands. Service is *very* slow at night, when many tourists converge, but the red snapper stuffed with shrimp and the day's catch are worth waiting for. Credit cards: MC, V.

You'll find the best *cucina Italiana* south of Acapulco at the **Spaghetti House** on Perez Gasga. At tables clad with blue-and-white checked cloths in either the fan-cooled main room or on the breezy upstairs terrace, you can sample daily specials rare in these parts: prosciutto and melon, oysters Florentine, and spaghetti with mussels. Credit cards: MC, V.

The restaurant scene in Puerto Angel includes the attractive stucco-and-tile restaurant of the **Angel del Mar Hotel,** recommended for breakfast, lunch, or dinner. Regional specialties are your best bet here. Credit cards: MC, V. On Playa Panteón, the town's prettiest beach, a cluster of thatched-palm enclosures serve up the catch of the day according to your preference. Among the several establishments here, the best regarded is **Bricio and Cordelia,** open 8 A.M.–10 P.M. As custom here dictates, the price of a meal (less than $10 per person)—or even a cold beer—entitles you to a lounge chair for the entire day. No credit cards. **Beto's,** on the dirt road leading uphill from Playa Panteón, is an inviting gathering place also specializing in seafood. Cocktails are served, and prices are reasonable (under $10 per person for dinner). Open 10 A.M.–10 P.M. No cards.

ENTERTAINMENT

Evening action here is centered in Puerto Escondido's discos, whose popularity waxes and wanes with the seasons. Current hot spots are **Macumba,** on the main drag, popular with young locals and the surfing crowd, and **Le Dome,** which presents live music for a mixed gay and heterosexual crowd in a dramatic setting high on a hilltop overlooking town. (To get there, walk up the long, long staircase from the main street.) **Bacocho's,** in the area of the same name, is Escondido's *beau monde* night spot. And, in what may be the prettiest setting in town, **Coco's** in the Posada Real presents nightly live salsa music in an alfresco beachside bar adorned with leopard-patterned fabrics and vibrant-green jungle motifs.

Tehuantepec

San Felipe del Agua

Huajuapan de León

Seven Regions Fountain

REFORMA
AMERICA
MORELOS
SN. JOSE LA NORIA

H. Escuela Naval
Sabinos
B. Domínguez
Calz. Niños Héroes de Chapultepec

Lic. E Vasconcelos
Periférico

RIO BLANCO
DIAZ ORDAZ
J. López Alvarez
Av. Juárez
Convent
INDEPENDENCIA
Melchor Ocampo
Calz Lázaro Cárdenas

Calz. Niños Héroes
Porfirio Díaz
B. Díaz Ordaz
Convent
C. Bustamante
20 de Noviembre
I. Izazaga
Nuño Mexicapan

SN. FRANCISCO
PASAJUEGO
CERRO DEL FORTIN
Observatory
STA. MARÍA
Div. de Orient

see inset

Calz. Madero
LIBERTAD
VICENTE SUAREZ
Río Xoayo
SN. MARTIN MEXICAPAN
Av. Mexicapan
Antigua Carretera A. Monte Alban
ROSARIO
ANITA

Prolongación Gpe. Victoria
Calz. V. Trujano
Calz. V. Trujillano

MONTE ALBAN

N

OAXACA

— Inset 1 —

Tourist Information
Av. Juárez
Mariano Matamoros
Av. Morelos
Museum
Cathedral
V. Guerrero
Archaeological Site
City Hall
Av. Independencia
Main Place
Av. Hidalgo
V. Trujano
C. Bustamante
I. López Rayón
Las Casas
20 de Nov
L. Aldama de
Mina

13

CHIAPAS

Chiapas is a world unto itself. Until a few decades ago, the lack of paved roads kept its lush emerald jungles and pine-forested highlands off-limits to all but a few ardent adventurers. The most Indian of Mexico's states, Chiapas is the land of the Maya. Cut off from the outside world until recently, the more than one million Maya in Chiapas keep their indigenous culture flourishing more richly than anywhere else in the country. In thatched-roof hamlets and picture-postcard colonial villages, these descendants of the ancient Maya speak pre-Conquest languages and wear colorful, lavishly embroidered costumes unique to their communities. For travelers eager to venture off the beaten track and willing to endure traveling on gravel roads and in small aircraft, Chiapas offers an unforgettable opportunity to explore an exotic outpost of an all but vanished world where Indians barely emerged from the Stone Age deck themselves in ornaments made from wild bird feathers and hold ceremonies at ancient shrines enveloped by jungle foliage; where Indian priests recite Mass in Mayan inside baroque churches shimmering with gold leaf; and where shamans practice healing rituals to exorcise evil spirits from the ailing.

Wedged between Guatemala and Oaxaca, bordered by Veracruz, Tabasco, and Campeche on the north and the Pacific Ocean on the south, Chiapas (33,732 square miles) comprises a kaleidoscope of contrasting environments. From the sunscorched beaches and lush groves of palm and banana trees edging the Pacific, the coastal plain slopes upward to the undulating hills of the Soconusco, a fertile agricultural region blanketed with plantations of coffee, cotton, tobacco, rubber, and sugarcane that yield much of Chiapas's wealth. The pine-forested Sierra Madre range sweeps through the interior of the state, its evergreen-clad peaks rising to enfold cool, cloud-shrouded valleys checkered with fields of corn and chains of sparkling highlands lakes. The mountains tumble down to meet tropical rain forests and unexplored jungles teeming with exotic vegetation and wild game that spread across the northeast and dip south along the Guatemalan border. Highlighting this panorama of primeval splendor are some of Mexico's most spectacular scenic marvels: the Agua Azul falls, where more than five hundred waterfalls thunder down into turquoise pools carved out of the bedrock below; the colossal Sumidero Canyon, whose ocher walls rise to a height of three thousand feet and stretch for 23 miles on either side of the Grijalva River; the Montebello Lakes, their waters shimmering turquoise, azure, and violet against the lush green foliage of the Montebello National Park.

Nature has indeed blessed Chiapas, but it is the legacy left by man than endows it with so much of its allure for visitors. Echoes of the past resonate throughout this varied and voluptuous landscape, richly strewn with the vestiges of two great civilizations that shaped the course of Chiapas's history and its character today.

A woman with crossed eyes and a flat head isn't likely to land on the cover of *Vogue* magazine today, but she would not have lacked suitors among the ancient Maya, to whom crossed eyes and flat heads were the ultimate marks of beauty. Not only were Mayan ideals of beauty different from our own, but the lengths to which the Maya went in attaining them seem extreme even in this era of tooth bonding and tummy tucks.

Small objects dangled on strings in front of infants' heads resulted in crossed eyes. Newborn infants, too, were made to wear a head press made from two boards, which flattened the forehead and pushed the nose area forward into the desirable silhouette. Adult males wore nosepieces to further exaggerate the size of the nose, large noses being considered the mark of nobility. Spanish historian Antonio de Herrera observed in 1615 that the faces of the Mayan men were "without beards, for they scorched them when young, that they might not grow." Designs were then cut into the cheeks with a sharp stick and dirt was rubbed into the incision to encourage infection, which would result in decorative scarring. And the smiles of both men and women would reveal teeth that had been filed into unusual shapes or inlaid with jade or turquoise.

—Erica Kleine

In the deepest reaches of the jungle, more than one hundred Mayan sites, many of them accessible only by helicopter, have been unearthed so far, granting testimony to the legendary empire of the lowland Maya that flourished in the humid jungle stretching from Chiapas eastward through the Peten in Guatemala to northern Honduras and north throughout the Yucatán Peninsula, before being abruptly abandoned in the tenth century for reasons not yet understood. No Mayan site better embodies the mystery and majesty of this enigmatic empire than Palenque, one of Chiapas's two primary tourist destinations. Seduced by the fairy-tale allure of this fabled "lost city in the jungle," a long line of archaeologists, explorers, and intrepid travelers has hacked its way through the dense tropical vegetation, risked malaria and snakebite, and endured an excruciatingly arduous journey of many days on muleback to reach this ruined ancient city, regarded by many as the ultimate artistic achievement in all of Mexico. The situation is much easier today. Small airplanes, paved roads, and a railroad penetrate the jungle, allowing today's travelers easy access to Palenque. From there, adventurous types can continue on to a pair of even more remote Mayan sites and indigenous villages sequestered in the deepest reaches of the jungle.

Along with Palenque, Chiapas's other "must" is one of the oldest Spanish settlements in Mexico, San Cristóbal de las Casas, a colonial jewel of a town whose cobblestone streets, little changed since the 1500s, echo with the footsteps of the conquistadores. San Cristóbal and its surroundings present a unique opportunity to glimpse the vivid indigenous culture that flourishes in the highlands.

The Chiapas rain forest is hot and humid all year, especially so from March through September. The months from June through September are the rainy season, when showers and sometimes torrential downpours fall during the afternoons. Traveling in this season has its consolations, though. The tropical foliage turns brilliant green, and the forest—blooming with exotic flowers—is at its most beautiful. Bring an umbrella for the rains and light cotton clothing for daytime all year long; a jacket or light sweater may be useful at night from December through February. Sturdy shoes are essential for tramping through the ruins, and hiking boots would be a good idea if you plan an overland expedition from Palenque to other Mayan sites deeper into the jungle. You'll want a flashlight, or torch, as well as a canteen for toting drinking water to off-the-beaten-trail sites where there are no facilities. And most important, bring insect repellent with a high percentage of the ingredient diethyl toluamide, or DEET; one such brand, Autan, is available in Mexico. The Chiapas rain forest is considered a malarial area, and although the incidence of the disease is low, you should begin a course of antimalarial tablets before you arrive. Check with your physician for more information.

The weather in the highlands is far different. You'll want a light sweater or jacket for evenings all year round and for daytime wear December through February. Light clothing will suffice in the daytime during the rest of the year, along with a raincoat or cover-up for summer showers. No dressy attire is needed anywhere in Chiapas; casual wear, even jeans, is appropriate even for the finest restaurants in the capital.

Chiapas's two principal regions then, from a traveler's perspective, are the rain forest or jungle and the highlands. Palenque is an ideal base for touring the former, while the highlands region is best explored from San Cristóbal de las Casas. This chapter, therefore, focuses on these two destinations. Since neither San Cristóbal nor Palenque is served by commercial airliner, your point of entry, if you arrive by air, will probably be Tuxtla Gutiérrez, the capital and transportation hub of the state. For travelers arriving overland from the north, Tuxtla is the first city inside the Chiapas border on the Pan American Highway, the main route from Mexico City and other points north. Once you've taken in the attractions of Tuxtla, your next destination will likely be San Cristóbal, less than two hours away by car. This is the route we follow here. To reach Palenque from San Cristóbal, a number of options exist; for those who make the trip overland, we reveal a little-known Mayan site, **Tonina,** that provides an excellent break in the journey.

The most complete information on Chiapas can be obtained through the Chiapas delegation of the Mexican Secretariat of Tourism; to contact it by mail, write Delegación en Chiapas, Secretaría de Turismo, Avenida Central Poniente 1454, C.P. 29030, Tuxtla Gutiérrez, Chiapas, México; or call 91-961-2-45-35 or 91-961-2-55-09.

Tuxtla Gutiérrez

Shiny new commercial buildings, sparkling shopping plazas, and late-model cars lined up on the street reflect the new-found wealth that the discovery of oil in Chiapas has brought to this already prosperous coffee-growing center and state capital. Tuxtla is the portal through which most visitors pass on their way to San Cristóbal de las Casas, and though lacking in architectural or historic interest, this relaxed and friendly sprawling modern boom town of three hundred thousand merits a stopover for the fascinating contrast it presents with the highlands to the east.

Tuxtla is not a place for foreigners. . . . It is like an unnecessary postscript to Chiapas, which should be all wild mountain and old churches and swallowed ruins and the Indians plodding by or watching from their mud towers the mule tracks from the north.
—Graham Greene
The Lawless Roads, 1939

CONNECTIONS

Tuxtla Gutiérrez, the capital of Chiapas and the jumping-off point for trips to the highlands and the Chiapas rain forest, lies some 620 miles south of Mexico City on the Pan American Highway. Driving time is about 18 hours. The stretch from Oaxaca to Tuxtla—among the most scenic drives in the country—takes ten hours, but will feel like ten days to anyone prone to motion sickness.

There are daily flights from Mexico City to Tuxtla, but currently no direct flights from Oaxaca; to reach Tuxtla from Oaxaca you must return to Mexico City and switch to the Tuxtla-bound flight. The Tuxtla airport is a forty-minute drive north of the city; it has a good restaurant on the second floor of the terminal, which does a booming business since departures are often delayed due to fog. Keep this in mind, and leave extra time when booking connecting flights out of Tuxtla.

🧳 HOTELS

Hotel Bonampak

Bulevar Belisario Domínguez, Number 181, Tuxtla Gutiérrez, 29030
Tel. 961-3-20-48 or 961-3-20-50
Doubles, $37

A lovely pool area and gardens span the space between the main four-story building and 26 private bungalows in the rear. The location on a busy thoroughfare, and the character of the modern air-conditioned rooms with closed-circuit television—long on comfort, low on charm—lend a commercial quality to the Bonampak, a long-standing landmark that has recently undergone a much-needed face-lift. There are tennis courts, a sauna, and a good restaurant, popular with guests as well as local businesspeople. Even if you don't stay here, stop in to see the murals copied from—and in far better condition than—the originals at the Mayan site of Bonampak in the jungle. Credit cards: AE, DC, V.

Hotel Flamboyant

Bulevar Belisario Domínguez, km 1081, Tuxtla Gutiérrez, 29000
Tel. 961-2-92-59 or 961-2-93-51.
Doubles, $69; singles, $55

Ten minutes from the city center on the road to the airport, this is by far Tuxtla's plushest property and the city's lone five-star hotel. Sparkling clean, airy air-conditioned rooms with television, modern tiled bathrooms (with shower), and simple contemporary decor occupy a two-level vaguely Moorish structure separated from the bustling lobby area by a large pool surrounded by lawns with lounge chairs. There are two bars, a restaurant, and a pretty coffee shop with hanging plants and wrought-iron tables and chairs, as well as a glitzy disco considered one of the chicest night spots in the city. Two tennis courts complete the diversions. Credit cards: AE, CB, DC, MC, V.

Real de Tuxtla
Carretera Panamericana, km 1088, Tuxtla Gutiérrez, 29040
Tel. 961-2-59-58
Doubles, $37; singles, $30
At the south end of town on the highway leading to San Cristóbal, this sprawling motel-like property is a good bet for those taking off early the following morning for San Cristóbal; you won't
have to negotiate the surprisingly heavy traffic in the center of
town. Ninety-six carpeted rooms with television and closed-
circuit movies occupy a series of two-level units that appear
slightly run-down. The grounds are, however, lovely; there are
two swimming pools surrounded by gardens, and an inviting alfresco restaurant (one of two in the hotel), with an adjacent bar
shaded by mango trees and a *palapa* roof—a romantic setting
for dancing at night. There are tennis courts and a putting green.
Recommended for families with children. Credit cards: AE, CB,
DC, MC, V.

The state tourist office on B. Domínguez 950, on the second
floor (tel. 961-3-30-79), is open Mon.–Fri., 8 A.M.–3 P.M. and 5–8
P.M.; the amiable English-speaking staff can provide you with maps
and answer any questions you may have on the city and your
upcoming destinations in Chiapas.

Highlighting Tuxtla's brief list of tourist attractions is this trio
of worthwhile sights:

Zoológico Miguel Alvarez del Toro
Parque Madero (in the northeast part of the city), intersection
11 Ote. and 5 Nte.
Open Tues.–Sun., 8 A.M.–5:30 P.M.
This is Tuxtla's principal attraction, regarded as the finest zoo
in Latin America. Animals and birds indigenous to Chiapas—
including the puma, coypu, jaguar, anteater, iguana, ocelot, and
a vast array of snakes, parrots, monkeys, and deer—are exhibited in cool wooded surroundings that approximate the animals'
native habitat. There is a cafeteria and picnic area.

Regional Museum of Chiapas
Open Tues.–Sun., 9 A.M.–4 P.M.
This museum, located in Madero Park, houses an extensive
collection of Mayan artifacts unearthed in Chiapas that complement the interesting exhibits devoted to the history and peoples
of the state, also on display here.

Botanical Museum
Open Mon.–Fri., 9 A.M.–2 P.M.; Sat., 9 A.M.–1 P.M.
The Botanical Museum, also in Madero Park, features intriguing displays presenting the regional flora of the state, highlighted
by exhibits of native woods, medicinal plants and their uses, and
a special display of corn that explains the various types and their
importance in indigenous culture. The live species are on display
at the Botanical Garden and Orchidarium next door to the museum. The Botanical Garden is open Tues.–Sun., 9 A.M.–4 P.M.; the
Orchidarium, Tues.–Sun., 9 A.M.–1 P.M.

🍴 RESTAURANTS

Even if you can read Spanish, you may not understand the menus placed before you in Chiapas. You're not alone—most Mexicans from outside the state are also unfamiliar with the contents of the *Chiapaneco* culinary compendium, which reflects the strong influence of its Mayan heritage.

Indigenous *platos* are generally less piquant than traditional Mexican fare; chiles, rather than being mixed in, are usually served on the side in Chiapas. Corn finds its way into many regional offerings ranging from *sopa de chipilin,* a chicken-based soup with cornmeal balls floating on top, to *pozol,* a refreshing drink from pre-Hispanic times made from cocoa beans and corn kernels. Another staple is tamales, which come in scores of intriguing variations, such as the popular tamale *juacane,* with a filling of dried shrimp, beans, and pumpkinseeds wrapped in the leaves of a local plant, *yierba santa.*

A good place to get acquainted with the unique gastronomy of Chiapas is **La Selva,** located between the city of Tuxtla and the airport at Bulevar Belisario Domínguez 1360 (tel. 2-62-51). Let the amiable owner plan your menu for you while you sit back and admire the airy dining room filled with palms and jungle artifacts. With live marimba music playing in the background (1–5 P.M.), you can feast on such local favorites as bread soup, stuffed chiles, succulent roast baby pig in barbecue sauce, and *plato grande,* beef in a piquant sauce. Credit cards: MC, V.

Another local landmark serving regional fare is **Las Pichanchas,** Avenida 14 de Septiembre, Oriente 837 (tel. 2-53-51), with live marimba music in a rustic open-air setting. Credit cards: MC, V.

For grilled meats try **Mesón El Paraje,** Calle 2 Sur, Oriente 170 (tel. 2-42-95). Credit cards: MC, V.

En Route to the Highlands

The fifty-mile drive along the Pan American Highway from Tuxtla Gutiérrez to San Cristóbal de las Casas provides a series of dramatic contrasts, rising in the space of less than two hours from 1,800 feet to a height of more than 7,000 feet, from a sweltering tropical plateau thick with palm and banana trees to the cool, cloud-draped highlands carpeted with forests of oak and pine, where the smoke from wood-burning fires wafts through the nighttime air, even in summer. You'll leave the 20th century far behind when you depart the bustle of Tuxtla, with its honking horns and clanging cash registers, and set off for the tranquil realm of the highlands, where time seems to have ground to a halt centuries ago. Ten miles east of Tuxtla you'll come to the picturesque town of **Chiapa de Corzo,** laden with architectural treasures from the colonial era. The centerpiece of Chiapa's **zócalo** is the famous Moorish-style brick fountain inspired by the crown of the kings of Spain that was erected in 1562 in order to supply the town with fresh

A road traveling northeast from Tuxtla climbs up the side of a steep mountain past the entrance to the Sumidero National Park and continues skirting the edge of the **Sumidero Canyon,** a magnificent 23-mile-long chasm cut by the Grijalva River, one of the scenic splendors of Mexico. Five lookout points along the road through the park offer spectacular vistas of the canyon walls towering to a height of up to three thousand feet and stretching as far as the eye can see on either side of the winding narrow river below. Perhaps you can hear a mournful wailing: The canyon is said to be haunted by the ghosts of one thousand Indians—men, women, and children—who leaped off the canyon rim rather than submit to slavery at the hands of the Spanish conquistadores. There is a simple restaurant at La Atalaya lookout serving good tamales, refreshing chocolate drinks, and other specialties of the region. Taxis charge about $20 for a 1½-hour tour of the park from Tuxtla; there is also a bus to the lookout points departing from the corner of 11 Ote. Nte. and 14 de Septiembre in Tuxtla.

drinking water during an epidemic that was raging at the time. Chiapa de Corzo is famous for its lacquerwork, and you can see lovely examples of this craft at the town's **Museum of Lacquer** (Museo de la Laca) on the *zócalo,* open from Tuesday through Saturday, from 9 A.M. to 1 P.M. and 4 to 6 P.M. Along with the wares from Chiapas, the museum showcases lacquerwork from other areas of Mexico—Olinala in Guerrero, and Uruapan in Michoacán, among others—allowing you to compare the differences between the various styles. From 10 A.M. to 1 P.M. during the week, you can watch artisans at work in the museum courtyard and even try your hand at this painstaking craft. The museum usually offers a few items for sale, and you can find an array of lacquerware products at the handful of curio shops overlooking the *zócalo.*

The Highlands

Soon after leaving Chiapa de Corzo, the two-lane Pan American Highway begins to wind its way upward, twisting and turning through a series of dizzying hairpin bends as it enters the Sierra de Chiapas range. If the ride seems a bit harrowing, think what it must have been like for author Graham Greene several decades ago, when the trip, which takes two hours today, was a 12-hour odyssey over a road that was ". . . more a mule track than a road, cut by crevices two feet deep and sprinkled with boulders. In the rains it is impassable. . . ."

The vista, though, remains the same as it has been for centuries: dark evergreen forests stretch toward the horizon, and steep hillsides rising up from the road are terraced with fields of corn. The richly embroidered costumes of the highlands

From 8 A.M. to 4 P.M. every day, ten-passenger motor launches depart from Chiapa de Corzo's embarcadero, or dock, on Calle Vicente Lopez, for the two-hour cruise up the Grijalva River that will bring you underneath plunging waterfalls and into giant watery caverns before passing through the Sumidero Canyon. The perspective from the bottom of this narrow chasm, with the chiseled bluffs rising straight up to a height of three thousand feet on either side, allows you to fully appreciate the majestic dimensions of this scenic tour de force. The river and its banks are home to an assortment of fauna, and along the way you're likely to spot ducks, turtles, crocodiles, and various exotic birds. Although the mist from the falls provides relief, the strong sun reflecting off the water makes the ride a hot one in the middle of the day; try to depart early in the morning. The trip is most spectacular during and after the summer rainy season, when the waterfalls are cascading with their full strength.

Indians are bright splashes of color that stand out against the gold and green landscape. You'll feel yourself slipping farther and farther back in time as you pass clusters of thatch-roofed Indian houses clinging to the mountain slopes, and women and children walking along the roadside, single file, balancing huge jugs of water on their heads. At makeshift stands piled high with apples and pears, young Indian boys wave their arms frantically to attract passing motorists. Rickety local buses rumble by, crammed to the bursting point with Indians returning from market, who hang on to the sides and crouch atop the roof between gargantuan sacks of grain, stacks of firewood, and bleating goats.

The highlands surrounding San Cristóbal de las Casas are home to some two hundred thousand Tzotzil and Tzeltal Indians, descended from the ancient Maya, who follow patterns of a traditional culture that traces back more than one thousand years. Each of the two groups is divided into two or three dozen communities, whose members speak a distinct dialect, wear a costume unique to the community, and consider themselves relatives. Each community consists of villages and outlying farms. Civil and religious officials live in the villages, while most community members reside close to their farms in the surrounding hills, returning to the village on Sundays and fiesta days to attend church, exchange gossip, and stock up at the local market. The religion of the highlands is a blend of Catholicism and indigenous belief; the Indians venerate Christ but also pay homage to a pantheon of supernatural deities, such as the goddess of earth and the god of corn—the element around which life in the highlands has revolved since time immemorial.

As you drive along the road you may notice crosses dotting the fields; these are placed by the Indians to indicate the dwelling places of ancestral gods. Rituals honoring the gods are held at these sites, and offerings of candles, food, incense, and alcohol are left beside the crosses in tribute.

Less than two hours of driving time will have elapsed when the road starts winding down into the valley of Hueyzacatlán and the red-tile roofs of San Cristóbal come into view. Graham Greene wrote in *The Lawless Roads,* "Suddenly we came out of the forest onto the mountain edge, and there below us were the lights of the town. . . . It was extraordinarily dramatic to come on a city like this, eight thousand feet up, at the end of a mule track, a city with . . . a score of churches, after the hairpin bends round the mountainside, after the precipices and foot wide tracks, the climbs and the descents. It was like an adventure of Rider Haggard—coming so unexpectedly out of the forest above this city, once the capital of Chiapas and the home of Las Casas, a place with one rough road, impassable in the rains, running down to Tuxtla and the coast, and only a mule track for the traveller from the north."

San Cristóbal de las Casas

The colonial jewel of Chiapas, San Cristóbal de las Casas nestles in a forested valley encircled by the cloud-shrouded peaks of the Sierra de Chiapas, which rise to more than eight thousand feet above sea level. This picture-postcard town of low-lying pink, lemon, and sky-blue houses capped by red-tile roofs and colonnaded mansions wrapped around flowering courtyards was founded in 1524 by the Spanish conquistadores and remained shut off from the rest of the world until the 1950s, when the roads into town were first paved. When the Pan American Highway came slicing through the Chiapas highlands, San Cristóbal suddenly found itself astride the tourist trail. But unlike most of Mexico's better-known "quaint colonial towns," chockablock with trendy art galleries, fashionable cafés, and real estate agencies selling colonial-style condominiums to retired Americans, San Cristóbal remains untainted by the arrival of the 20th—or even the 19th—century. Its cobblestone streets and tree-shaded plazas with lacy wrought-iron benches appear much as they did during the 16th and 17th centuries, when Ciudad Real, as the town was then known, was a provincial capital of the Spanish empire. This status is reflected in a wealth of courtly residences, arcaded palaces, and gilt-encrusted baroque churches that includes some of the oldest Spanish buildings in the Americas.

Architecture is only part of San Cristóbal's allure. The town is a commercial center for the indigenous peoples who have inhabited the surrounding hills and valleys since long before the arrival of the Spaniards. It is these descendants of the ancient Maya, speaking their own languages and wearing their traditional ethnic finery, that lend the town such color and character as they stride through its narrow streets barefoot, hauling immense sacks of grain or pairs of live chickens tied together at the feet, reenacting scenes that have taken place for centuries.

CONNECTIONS

San Cristóbal lies in the highlands of Chiapas, south of Tuxtla Gutiérrez, a one-and-a-half to two-hour drive along the Pan American Highway by car. Taxis charge about $40 for the trip and may be hired at the airport in Tuxtla or in the city itself. Hotels in Tuxtla can make travel arrangements for you. First-class buses depart every half-hour or so from the Cristóbal Colon terminal in Tuxtla at Calle 2 Norte, Pte. 268; by bus, the trip from Tuxtla to San Cristóbal takes two hours. If you prefer to do the driving yourself, you can rent a car at the airport in Tuxtla, where Hertz, Budget, and two local companies have offices.

TOURING

With the exception of Casa Na Balom, the major sights in San Cristóbal are located within easy walking distance of the *zócalo*. Should your feet give way, you'll find taxis cruising the streets; there is also a taxi stand on the north side of the *zócalo*. Taxi fares are fixed within town but are negotiable for excursions to more distant locales.

The **Municipal Tourist Office,** next to the cathedral on the *zócalo,* will provide you with information on the surrounding highlands region; the office frequently organizes excursions to nearby villages. Office hours are 8 A.M.–8 P.M. weekdays; 8 A.M.–1 P.M. and 3–7 P.M. Sat. Tel. 8-04-14.

For excursions to the surrounding villages and points of interest, there are several options apart from taxis. The least expensive, and probably the most interesting, are the local **buses and minibuses** that depart frequently for all Indian villages from the bus lot one block past the market. This method of transport is long on local color, short on comfort.

High on comfort and in expense, rental cars are available through the agent for Budget, **Auto Rental Yaxchilán** in the Posada Diego de Mazariegos on Calle M.A. Flores, San Cristóbal's only car-rental service. The telephone number is 8-18-71. Prices are very high, about $70 a day minimum.

⨐ HOTELS

San Cristóbal appears on the itineraries of many European group tours, placing rooms at the better hotels at a premium and making reservations essential. The busiest dates coincide with the annual Feria de Primavera, the Spring Fair, just before Easter, when foreign visitors and Indians from throughout Chiapas pack San Cristóbal to the bursting point and hotel rates rise accordingly.

The back of a horse is a delightful vantage point from which to view the pastoral panorama around San Cristóbal. The villages of Zinacantán and San Juan Chamula lie within easy trotting distance; the route follows the paved road before veering off onto a trail that cuts through rolling fields and takes you past clusters of thatch-roofed Indian houses. Reserve a mount, and a guide as well if you wish, a day in advance at the **Anfitriónes Turistícos de Chiapas** agency in the Posada Diego de Mazariegos, or check with the tourist office to see if any guided group excursions are planned.

Hotel Bonampak
Calzada México 5, 29200
Tel. 967-8-16-21
Doubles, $30; singles, $24

This motel-style modern establishment ten minutes by car from the *zócalo* presents an attractive alternative to in-town hotels for those arriving by private car; on-site free parking is available. Clean and comfortable contemporary rooms have modern bathrooms and satellite television; rooms open onto an atrium lobby area with plush seating. Amenities include an indoor swimming pool, tennis courts, and bicycle rentals (handy for exploring the town and surrounding countryside). Trailer hook-ups are available. Credit cards: AE, CB, DC, MC, V.

Hotel Ciudad Real
Plaza 31 de Marzo 10, 29200
Tel. 967-8-01-87
Doubles, $29; singles, $22

Opening onto arched passageways that ring a pretty courtyard with a fountain, the 31 small rooms in this elegant colonial dwelling afford adequate comfort, although they are less than spacious and rather poorly lit. A crackling fire in the stone hearth warms the courtyard restaurant, a favorite gathering spot for both guests and outsiders, offering regional and international fare at moderate cost. Ideally located in the town center, the Ciudad Real is affiliated with the **Parador Ciudad Real** (tel. 967-8-18-86), at the entrance to town, a good bet for those with autos. Credit cards: AE, MC, V.

Hotel Español
Avenida 1 de Marzo 16, 29200
Tel. 967-8-00-45
Doubles, $21; singles, $17

Opened in 1907, this was the first—and for many years the only—hotel in town. Two tiers of guest rooms—thirty in all—surround a flowery patio with quiet nooks for reading and relaxing. (Author Graham Greene mentions in his book *The Lawless Roads* that he wrote several magazine articles while seated on the patio in the 1930s.) Guest rooms of various sizes, each with modern bathroom and fireplace, are clean and attractive. The overall atmosphere is most appealing. There is a garage and restaurant. The Español is two blocks north of the *zócalo*. Credit cards: AE, MC, V.

Hotel Mansion del Valle

Calle Diego de Mazariegos 39, 29240
Tel. 967-8-25-81
Doubles, $21; singles, $17

A handsome colonial-style facade belies the crisp, contemporary interior of this two-year-old hotel located three blocks west of the *zócalo*. Clean, carpeted rooms, contemporary in style, have tiled bathrooms with showers, television, and simple wood furnishings; each opens onto an interior atrium. You'll find a restaurant and a cafeteria, as well as parking garage, on the premises. Credit cards: AE, MC, V.

Molino de la Alborada

Apdo. Postal 50 Periférico Sur
Tel. 967-8-09-35
Doubles, from $19; singles, from $15

If you have a car and plan to spend several days in the area, you might consider this United States–owned country retreat, two miles from town, where you can rent horses to explore the enchanting landscapes and villages nearby. Perched on a wooded hillside overlooking San Cristóbal, it has ten large, cozy rooms with fireplaces and private baths inside separate cottages. Trailer hook-ups are also available. U.S. home cooking is served six days a week in the on-premises dining room/bar (Mexican food is offered the remaining night). Adjacent to the hotel is a nine-hole golf course. Credit cards: MC, V.

Posada Diego de Mazariegos

Calle M. A. Flores 2, 29200
Tel. 967-8-18-25
Doubles, $25, singles, $22

Considered the town's premier property, the Diego de Mazariegos consists of two separate buildings whose handsome ocher and scarlet facades each open onto charming courtyards with hand-hewn pillars, fountains, and wrought-iron tables and chairs nestling amid exuberant tropical foliage. Public areas—a bar, cozy colonial-style restaurant offering good regional fare, and an old-fashioned coffee bar—are atmospheric and inviting. The eighty guest rooms are less consistent: some are dark and cramped with little visual appeal. Others, far more commodious, have fireplaces, which are a most welcome feature in this climate. Request a look before checking in. Located a block from the *zócalo*, the hotel is very popular with group tours and is often booked in advance. Credit cards: AE, CB, DC, MC, V.

Santa Clara

Plaza Central 1, 29200
Tel. 967-8-11-40
Doubles, $21; singles, $17

In an unbeatable location directly on the *zócalo*, this tile-roofed stone mansion, once home to the conquistador Diego de Mazariegos, founder of San Cristóbal, retains much of its original 16th-century appearance. Beamed ceilings and period-style furnishings imbue the guest rooms and cozy bar/restaurant with a colonial flavor. You'll find free parking, as well as a swimming pool. Credit cards: AE, V.

With most streets well marked and neatly laid out in the familiar Spanish grid pattern, San Cristóbal is ideal for walking, and its small size makes it likely that you'll do most of your exploring on foot. Strolling the streets and people watching are the main pleasures in this highlands town; also on the visitor's agenda are the market and a handful of churches, along with a very special museum.

Directly on the *zócalo* (main plaza) is the immense 16th-century **Cathedral,** with an imposing Tuscan-style facade. Inside, an elaborately carved wooden ceiling supported by rows of graceful columns rises over the pulpit shimmering with gold leaf and a striking baroque altarpiece depicting San José, or Saint Joseph.

One of the most lavish churches in Mexico is the **Church of Santo Domingo,** on 20 de Noviembre north of the *zócalo.* Embellished with statues of the apostles and the coat of arms of the Spanish king Charles V, the rose-colored facade seems rather sedate in comparison with the exuberantly carved and gilded baroque interior filled with *retablos* and other religious paintings. Huddled in front of the dazzling pulpit, groups of Indian worshipers are often encountered, immersed in devotional rites, their faces illuminated by the flicker of candles.

At V. Guerrero 33, you will find one of Mexico's most unique museums. Open from 4 P.M. to 6 P.M. only, from Tuesday through Sunday, **Casa Na Balom** is the charming home of Mrs. Gertrude Blom, who with her late husband, Franz, settled here in the 1920s and devoted her life to preserving the indigenous culture of Chiapas. The Bloms are credited with singlehandedly saving the Lacandon tribe of the Chiapas jungle from extinction. The colonial residence serves as a library, research institute, guest house for visiting anthropologists, and museum of Mayan and Lacandon art; guided tours, conducted by volunteers studying at the institute, are given every day at 4:30 P.M.

The market in San Cristóbal is open every morning except Sunday. While devoted mostly to edibles, it offers a small selection of regional handicrafts and is fascinating for the slice-of-life portrait of the Chiapas highlands that it presents.

🍽 RESTAURANTS

Multicourse *comidas corridas* that are as bountiful as they are inexpensive bring crowds of locals and travelers at lunchtime to **Restaurant Tuluc,** Insurgentes 5 (tel. 8-20-90). A more tranquil atmosphere reigns at night, when the kitchen turns out well-prepared grilled meats and fresh fish dishes. The house special-

The Chiapas highlands are one of the few areas left in Mexico where indigenous peoples still maintain their traditional mode of dress; each community has its own unique costumes for men and women that are worn by all members of the community.

Among the most elaborate and colorful in Latin America, these costumes are sewn and embroidered by hand by the women of the household from cloth that is woven at home. Among the costumes you will recognize in and around San Cristóbal are these:

Zinacantecan males wear the most flamboyant plumage of any in the region. Their wide cotton pants, cropped below the knee to show off what are said to be the most beautiful legs in the world, are topped by shocking-pink embroidered ponchos with dangling tassels. The flat straw sombreros are festooned with multicolored ribbons tied primly by married men and left loose to blow in the breeze by bachelors. The women are no less colorful in deep-blue long skirts secured by glossy sashes and turquoise or violet shawls draped over white wool *huipiles,* or traditional rectangularly cut blouses. Entwined in their black braids are brightly colored ribbons.

Chamula males sport black or ivory wool ponchos over white tunics and white calf-length pants. Ten-gallon-style sombreros complete the outfit. Black wool skirts that skim the ground and cotton *huipiles* with dangling red tassels distinguish the women, who tie their braids with ribbons and wear their shawls folded into squares on top of their heads.

Huistecan males wear an intriguing costume consisting of white diaper-like pants fastened with braided sashes, and white cotton shirts embroidered at the shoulders. Their flat straw sombreros with turned-up brims are tied under the chin with red ribbons. Women wear richly embroidered *huipiles* over dark blue skirts tied with red-and-black striped wool waistbands. Like most highlands women, they customarily go barefoot.

—Erica Kleine

ty is grilled fillet wrapped in bacon and garnished with spinach and cheese. Credit cards: AE, DC, MC, V.

Pass through the tiny shop selling high-quality textiles and clothing from Chiapas and Guatemala, and you will come to the entrance of the handsome dining room of **El Unicornio,** Insurgentes 33 (tel. 8-07-32). Here the coral-colored walls are decorated with framed Frida Kahlo prints and the tables are likely to be filled by members of San Cristóbal's *beau monde.* The menu lists pizzas and such exotic (in these parts) fare as New York–cut steak, fried chicken breast, and rib-eye roll. Credit cards: AE, DC, MC, V.

A popular retreat among locals, **La Parrilla** is a cozy, fireplace-warmed warren of rooms where you can feast on inexpensive grilled meats. Calle del Cecyt 92 (tel. 8-22-20). Credit cards: MC, V.

SHOPPING

Handwoven clothing and accessories worn by Chiapas's indigenous inhabitants is the primary acquisitory enticement in the Highlands. The trouble, however, lies in finding these items; since most families make their own clothing at home, the goods sold in the shops tend to be less attractive variations of the originals, made expressly for the tourist trade. Along San Cristóbal's main shopping artery, Calle Real de Guadalupe, a string of unpretentious curio shops overflows with all sorts of items, from duffel bags to dirndl skirts adorned with the distinctive embroidered motifs of the region. You'll find a few tempting buys, but on the whole, the price tags tend to be high and the quality fairly low—stitching is by Singer rather than fingers, and fabrics are often synthetic rather than handloomed natural fibers. The situation at the market is much the same, although you can pick up the beribboned straw hats worn by Zinacantecan men and handy leather-strapped pouches of woven cotton toted by many Highlands men; each item should cost under $10.

By contrast, a selection of exquisite regional offerings awaits at **Sna Jolobil,** a cooperative of more than six hundred indigenous craftspeople dedicated to preserving traditional Mayan textile art. From cotton and wool woven on backstrap looms and dyed with natural pigments, the artisans fashion flowing skirts, richly embroidered *huipiles,* and delicate fringed shawls, ponchos, and other traditional garments that may be worn or displayed on a wall at home as artwork. Augmenting the textiles are string bags, leather handbags and purses, and baskets of all shapes and sizes. The quality of all the items is high, and prices are fixed. Sna Jolobil, which means "weaver's house" in Tzotzil Maya, is in the former Convent of Santo Domingo, next to the church of the same name on Avenida 20 de Noviembre, and is open daily from 9 A.M. to 2 P.M. and from 4 to 6 P.M.

EXCURSIONS

The bucolic beauty of the surrounding countryside, checkered with yellow and green fields and blossoming with apple and pear orchards that stretch toward forested hillsides revered by *indígenas* as the homes of ancestral gods, encourages hiking, horseback riding, and excursions by car or taxi. Scattered in the hills around San Cristóbal are many tiny Indian villages that are popular destinations for day-trippers. The two closest villages, San Juan Chamula and Zinacantán, appear on the itinerary of every tour group that comes through town, and the villagers appear to be growing weary of the nonstop invasion of foreigners. Expect to be greeted with indifference if you go, and above all, heed warnings prohibiting photography in certain villages, including Zinacantán. After ignoring repeated warnings to stop snapping photographs inside the church, two foreigners were stoned to death by an outraged crowd of villagers in San Juan Chamula several years ago.

SAN JUAN CHAMULA

A paved road or a two-hour hike through the cornfields will bring you to this village of 25,000 inhabitants, nine miles from San Cristóbal. The political and ceremonial center of the Chamula Indians consists of a collection of adobe houses scattered around a central plaza that is dominated by an enchanting whitewashed church painted with colorful flowers. A ticket purchased from the adjacent tourist office will permit you to enter the church, and if you are lucky you may happen upon a healing ceremony, a ritual that traces its origins to the ancient Maya. Pine needles will cover the floor, and the air will hang heavy with incense—attempts to attract the gods of healing. A tight knot of onlookers will be gathered around the shaman and his patient, watching intently as the two engage in time-honored practices designed to banish evil spirits that are causing the malady. Mirrors are often hung around the necks of statues of saints in order to lure the spirits into captivity. Otherwise, however, you will find little of interest in San Juan Chamula except on Sundays, when colorful stalls spring up across the plaza, and highlands Indians from villages up to ten miles distant make the journey on foot to buy and sell and exchange gossip.

ZINACANTÁN

This tiny one-street hamlet close to San Juan Chamula is renowned for the exotic costumes worn by its male residents, especially the flat-topped straw hats festooned with multicolored ribbon streamers. (A favorite souvenir among foreign visitors, these can be purchased in almost every handicraft store in San Cristóbal.)

Like most villages in the region, Zinacantán is quiet during the week, when most families are away from the village and instead remain in their houses close to the fields. (Only village officials reside here then.) When the villagers return for church and the market on Sunday morning, dressed in their most flamboyant finery, this once-desolate village becomes a swirl of color and movement. The market usually breaks up about 11 A.M., so try to visit early Sunday morning. Tourists are usually welcome at services in the whitewashed church, provided they ask permission first; more interesting may be the pre-Hispanic rites held at the convent nearby. Ask permission before entering. Be sure to dress respectably, and above all, remember that photography is taboo throughout this village.

> We had come to a valley surrounded by jutting cliffs covered with green, their peaks obscured by a mist. From the heights of the cliffs, I saw what looked like a maypole of colors, living streamers of yellow and blue, of brilliant orange and green, weaving their way down the steep mountain paths until each color wrapped itself into the next color. The indigenous peoples of southern Chiapas, along with their sheep and their goats, wended their way from their mountain villages—wearing their village colors—to this valley where the trails met. They came from Chamula and Tenejapa and other small villages, climbing down the craggy paths on foot, some leading ponies or burros. From the cliff tops they made their way out of the mist.
>
> It seemed as though they were descending from heaven into a valley of light. We stood in silence, watching the Indians, like ghosts of another time, in their silent walk. In the heart of the valley it illumined the trees and the clay road that opened before us. It illumined the procession of the souls down the mountains. Its rays emblazoned the town of Zinacantán, to which we rode like pilgrims to Jerusalem.
>
> —Mary Morris
> *Nothing to Declare*, 1988

Perhaps because they receive fewer visitors than do those closer to San Cristóbal, the villages a bit farther afield tend to bestow a warmer welcome on travelers and should be considered as alternatives to the less-friendly San Juan Chamula and Zinacantán. While they offer no facilities for travelers, each may be easily visited in a half-day excursion.

San Andres Larrainzar is only about 12 miles northwest of San Cristóbal, but the rutted road extends driving time to one hour. A small but well-stocked market is open for business each morning. There are infrequent buses and minibuses from San Cristóbal to the village.

Chenalho, an hour's drive north from San Cristóbal, has a market on Sunday mornings.

Tenejapa (northeast of San Cristóbal, on an unpaved road that eventually leads to Cancuc) holds a market every morning where it is sometimes possible to purchase the hand-loomed textiles for which the village is celebrated. The lavishly embroidered scarlet *huipiles* worn by the women here are among the most striking in the highlands. Frequent buses from San Cristóbal make the trip here in one hour or less.

MONTEBELLO LAKES

A two-hour drive southeast along the Pan American Highway will bring you the 84 miles to the turn-off for the Montebello National Park, ten miles south of the town of Comitán, next to the Guatemalan border. Nestled in vivid tropical vegetation are more than sixty lakes whose sparkling waters range in

A strong belief in the powers of the supernatural influences the behavior of highlands *indígenas,* who tend to be reserved toward outsiders and united in their abhorrence of cameras, fearing that by photographing a person you will rob him of his soul. Photography is not permitted inside village churches and is totally prohibited anywhere within the village of Zinacantán. You will allay suspicions if you do not carry a camera at all when visiting the Indian communities near San Cristóbal.

color from pale aqua to deep violet. The lakes, which reportedly offer some of Mexico's finest freshwater fishing, take their color from the calcareous bedrock below the surface of the water—similar to the rock that underlies the *cenotes* of Yucatán.

If you arrive by bus, it will drop you off past the park entrance beside Monte Azul or Lake Montebello, where you'll find a parking lot, restaurants, and a picnic area. From here you can continue through the park by following the road that winds through the woods and skirts the shores of some of the lakes. If you've arrived by bus, you can hire a taxi to tour the park; you'll find them waiting near the restaurants. Bring a bathing suit for cooling off in the brisk lake waters, and hiking shoes if you want to set off on the trails that run through the woods.

There are no accommodations in the park other than a youth hostel, but if you'd like to linger in the area overnight you can find pleasant lodging in the town of Comitán at the hotel **Real Balún Canan,** La Poniente Sur 5; tel. 2-10-94.

Chiapas Rain Forest

Here were the remains of a cultivated, polished, and peculiar people, who had passed through all the stages incident to the rise and fall of nations; reached their golden age, and perished, entirely unknown. The links which connected them with the human family were severed and lost, and these were the only memorials of their footsteps upon earth.

—John Stephens
Incidents of Travel in Central America, Chiapas and Yucatan,
1841

The tropical rain forest of Chiapas, extending east across the Usumacinta River to the Peten jungle in Guatemala, is a vivid green wonderland of cedar, mahogany, and kapok trees entangled by liana vines, teeming with wild boar, jungle deer, and bands of howler monkeys. Shafts of sunlight streaming through the tree canopy illuminate iridescent butterflies and rainbow-hued hummingbirds, and in the farthest reaches of the forest, jaguar, ocelot, and puma prowl. This jungle realm is littered with ruined Mayan cities, crumbling pyramids, overgrown temples, and bits of stelae—all that remain of the lowland Mayan civilization, the most advanced in pre-Columbian Mesoamerica. From its heartland in the Guatemalan Peten stretching westward across the Usumacinta River to Palenque and eastward to Copán in northern Honduras, the lowland Mayan empire rose in the centuries before the birth of Christ and reached its full flowering from about A.D. 250 to 900. While Europe languished in the Dark Ages, the Maya were constructing vast stone cities without the aid of pack animals or metal tools. Composed of thousands of buildings built of precisely joined stones, the Maya cities were linked by causeways of gleaming white stone that stretched for hundreds of miles through the jungle.

No Mayan city better embodies the artistic grace and architectural sophistication attained by this enigmatic culture than Palenque, the architectural jewel of the Mayan empire and one of the most enchanting ruined cities in the Americas.

One of the first foreigners to visit the site, John Stephens, who hacked his way through the jungle in the 1830s and 1840s, wrote, "In the romance of the world's history nothing ever impressed me more forcibly than the spectacle of this once great and lovely city, overturned, desolate, and lost . . . overgrown with trees for miles around. . . ."

Palenque was all but inaccessible as recently as forty years ago. For author Graham Greene, who visited in the 1930s, the trip was a six-day odyssey on the back of a mule from San Cristóbal following a guide who sliced a trail through the vegetation with his machete.

Today's traveler has it quite a bit easier. A rail line from Mexico City was laid in the 1950s, and there are buses and small planes linking Palenque with Villahermosa, Tuxtla, and San Cristóbal.

From Palenque you can venture deeper into the jungle to two other Mayan sites that lie close to the Usumacinta River on the border with Guatemala. **Yaxchilán** can be reached by charter airplane or by a rough nine-hour jeep ride from Palenque followed by an hour's trip along the Usumacinta River. **Bonampak** is accessible by plane or by a drive of seven hours followed by either a two-hour trek through the jungle or a ride on the river.

Palenque

ORIENTATION

Santo Domingo is its official name, but the small village several miles from the Palenque ruins is commonly referred to as Palenque. The increasing number of tourists visiting the ruins over the past decade has transformed this former backwater jungle hamlet into a bona fide tourist town, bursting at the seams with hotels, cafés, restaurants, curio shops, and two banks—quite a different scene from the one Graham Greene encountered when he visited the ruins back in the 1930s. The village Greene saw was ". . . a collection of round mud huts thatched with banana leaves as poor as anything I ever saw in West Africa. We rode through the huts and came into a long wide street of bigger huts . . . and at the head of the street on a little hill a big plain ruined church." Nor will you have the problem quenching your thirst that Greene did; ". . . in the store near the church they had three bottles of beer only . . . at the other end of the village was the only other store . . . they sold no beer at all: all we could get was mineral water coloured pink and flavoured with some sweet chemical."

Most of the hotels in town cater to backpackers and lower-budget travelers; the upper-bracket hotels can be found outside town, mostly on the road to the ruins.

There is taxi and minibus (*colectivo*) service from town to the ruins, known as the *zona archeológica.*

The tourist office, in the Palacio Municipal on the *zócalo,* will answer your questions and provide help in arranging trips to the waterfalls and to the other Mayan sites deeper into the jungle. The office is open from Monday through Saturday from 8 A.M. to 2 P.M. and from 5 P.M. to 8 P.M., and every other Sunday from 9 A.M. to 12 noon.

CONNECTIONS

From Mexico City: The quickest way to Palenque from Mexico City is to fly to Villahermosa—both Mexicana and Aeromexico have scheduled service—and then take a scheduled flight on one of the small planes operated by local airlines including Aviacsa (tel. 5-02-10) to Palenque's airfield two miles from town. Travelers who want to avoid small planes can cover the 90 miles from Villahermosa to Palenque by taxi or first-class ADO bus in less than two hours; second-class buses take twice as long. Specify your destination to the driver: either Palenque *centro* for the village or *zona archeológica* or *ruinas* for the ruins.

A train stopping at Palenque departs every evening from Mexico City. According to the schedule, the trip takes 24 hours, but the frequent delays often stretch the ride to thirty hours or more. Cleanliness and comfort are less than top-notch, and robberies are not uncommon on this route.

From San Cristóbal: Aero Chiapas flies nine-passenger planes from both Tuxtla and San Cristóbal to Palenque for about $200 round-trip. But since the San Cristóbal airport is often closed, you may have to depart from Ocosingo, more than two hours away, or Comitán, about an hour and a half away. Inquire upon arriving in San Cristóbal; the telephone number is 8-00-37 in San Cristóbal; 3-09-78 in Tuxtla.

The road between San Cristóbal and Palenque (MEX199) is now paved, but washouts frequently occur during the rainy season. Second-class buses run by Autotransportes Tuxtla make this trip in six hours under normal driving conditions; there are several departures daily. By car the ride via Ocosingo takes five hours and offers two worthwhile stopovers en route. The first is described below; the second, the **Agua Azul** waterfalls, is described under **Excursions** from Palenque later in this chapter.

Viajes Pakal (tel. 8-28-19) operates a one-day trip that departs San Cristóbal early in the morning and takes you in a new minibus combi to the Aqua Azul waterfalls for a brief stay before continuing on to Palenque, where you are given a guided tour of the ruins and then dropped off at your hotel in Palenque. For more information, write to Viajes Pakal at Cuauhtemoc 6B, San Cristóbal de las Casas, Chiapas 29200; the telex is 78154 PAKAME.

The Ruins of Tonina

The large colonial town of Ocosingo lies on the road to Palenque, 56 miles north of San Cristóbal. From here, a half-hour drive over a dirt road will bring you to one of Mexico's least-visited archaeological sites, the Mayan religious and governmental center of Tonina.

Built on a seven-tiered mountain dominated by the massive Pyramid of War, Tonina is larger and more impressive than many better-known sites, and its substantial amount of well-preserved artwork makes it well worth the trip.

Ocosingo itself, famous for its *queso de bola,* cheese made from cow's milk, has many clean, inexpensive hotels. One of the best of these is the **Central,** Avenida Central 1 (tel. 967-3-00-24), in a white colonnaded building on the *zócalo.* The fan-cooled rooms have private tiled bathrooms. Doubles begin at $8. Taxis and buses can bring you to the ruins from town if you are not driving your own car. Bring drinks with you, as it gets hot and there are no facilities at the site.

🛄 HOTELS

La Cañada
Calle Canada 14, 29900
Tel. 934-5-01-02
Doubles, from $25

A budget standard, La Cañada is about a mile outside Palenque, on a dirt road leading from town. Nestled in a lovely garden setting, thatched-roof bungalows shelter simple fan-cooled rooms with private bathrooms. The management is especially amiable, and the restaurant, **La Selva,** is among the better eating spots in the area. Credit cards: MC, V.

Hotel Misión Palenque

Rancho San Martín de Porres, 29660
Tel. 934-5-02-41 or 5-533-5953 in Mexico City or 800-431-2138
Doubles, $48

First-class comforts, and even a touch of luxury, now await deep in the rain forest at this newest member of the Misión hotel group. Surrounded by lush tropical vegetation on the outskirts of the village, the hotel's low stone buildings shelter 160 handsome air-conditioned rooms furnished in contemporary Mexican style with natural materials; each overlooks the pool from a terrace. There is an attractive bar, and the on-premises restaurant serves Mexican and international dishes. The hotel provides transportation to the ruins and to the Villahermosa airport. Credit cards: AE, DC, MC, V.

Hotel Palenque

5 de Mayo 15, 29960
Tel. 934-5-01-03
Doubles, about $15

On the Parque Central in the village of Palenque, this long-standing older hotel has housed many an anthropologist and archaeologist in its day. Although no longer one of the only hotels in town, the Hotel Palenque is still one of the best choices for travelers on a budget. The two-story structure built around a courtyard has twenty rooms that are simple and clean, if far from luxurious. All are cooled by ceiling fans; some have air-conditioning as well, for a supplemental charge. All rooms have private baths, but, as is the case with most hotels in the village, hot water is not always available. You'll find a small swimming pool and a very basic restaurant on the second floor. Credit cards: AE, CB, MC.

In the midst of desolation and ruin we looked back to the past, cleared away the gloomy forest, and fancied every building perfect, with its terraces and pyramids, its sculptured and painted ornaments, grand, lofty, and imposing, and overlooking an immense inhabited plain; we called back into life the strange people who gazed at us in sadness from the walls; pictured them, in fanciful costumes and adorned with plumes of feathers, ascending the terraces of the palace and the steps leading to the temples; and often we imagined a scene of unique and gorgeous beauty and magnificence, realizing the creations of Oriental poets. . . .

—John Stephens
Incidents of Travel in Central America, Chiapas and Yucatan,
1841

The westernmost point in the Mayan empire, the ceremonial center of Palenque rose to its full flowering in the sixth and seventh centuries A.D., under the reign of King Pakal. Renowned for its delicate architectural proportions and for its eloquent stucco bas-reliefs, Palenque is widely regarded as the most beautiful Mayan site in the world and the most intriguing of Mexico's ancient ruins.

The temples, pyramids, houses, and other buildings are linked by causeways and sprawl over an area of about four square miles, hemmed in by the luxuriant foliage of the forest. The cleared area represents only a fraction of Palenque's total size; together with the unexcavated area, the entire city is believed to cover about 25 square miles.

Dominating the site is the Palace, a complex of temples sheathed with fine examples of the detailed stucco reliefs for which Palenque is celebrated. From the observation tower rising in their midst, you will have a fine view of the buildings and the reliefs.

> **The Palenque ruins are open daily from 8 A.M. to 5 P.M.; Temple of the Inscriptions, open from 8 A.M. to 4 P.M.**

Next to the Palace, a steep pyramid inscribed with details from the Mayan calendar is crowned by Palenque's most famous sight, the **Temple of the Inscriptions,** reached via a steep climb up 69 steps. The discovery here, in 1952, of a burial chamber at the end of a long tunnel laid to rest the conventional theory that pyramids in the Americas were never used as burial places. Inside the chamber is an elaborately carved sarcophagus whose lid alone weighs five tons; discovered inside were the remains of King Pakal, the principal builder of Palenque, surrounded by jewelry, a crown, and piles of jade. The skeletons of five servants sacrificed to serve their ruler on his voyage through death were also discovered. The skeletons and the jewels are now on display in Mexico City's National Museum of Anthropology.

Across the stream behind the pyramid are four other important buildings: **Temple of the Sun, Temple of the Cross, Temple 14,** and **Temple of the Foliated Cross,** the last with carved decorations that bear great resemblance to those found at Angkor Wat in Kampuchea.

There is also a small museum exhibiting a few of the artifacts unearthed during the excavations of Palenque.

EXCURSIONS

AGUA AZUL

It's hard to imagine a more spectacular swimming site than the Agua Azul waterfalls, less than an hour and a half from Palenque on the road to San Cristóbal. More than five hundred separate waterfalls cascade down to crystalline pools of placid and rushing water carved out of the bedrock below. The turquoise color of the water, set against the vivid green foliage surrounding the falls, creates a scene that will take your breath away. Strong currents cause treacherous swimming conditions in some sections, so inquire or look for posted signs before you take the plunge. Note: The scene loses much of its appeal during, and directly after, rainy season, when run-off muddies the water considerably. There are picnic grounds and a rather basic camping area.

Taxis and private cars can reach the falls, but if you arrive by bus, be prepared for a long hike down from the bus stop on the highway to the waterfalls.

MISOL-HA FALLS

Closer to Palenque than the Agua Azul falls, although only a fraction of their size, Misol-Ha offers fine swimming in a natural pool beneath the cascade. There is a small restaurant with a limited menu.

BONAMPAK AND YAXCHILÁN

The ruined Mayan cities of Bonampak and Yaxchilán, two of the most remote destinations in Mexico, lie deep in the Lacandon jungle near the Guatemalan border in eastern Chiapas. Both sites may be reached by charter four-passenger airplane from Palenque; Aviación de Chiapas has a round-trip excursion flight that stops at both places long enough to allow you a brief visit, and then returns to Palenque the same day. The price is approximately $250 per person. Aviación's office in Palenque is on Avenida B. Juárez. In the dry season, you can arrange overland transport with independent drivers in Palenque; the price is negotiable, so check first with the Tourist Office to get an idea of the going rate. The Tourist Office will also help you arrange to rent a four-wheel-drive vehicle if you want to go it alone. Keep in mind, however, that the gravel road goes only as far as Frontera Echeverría; from there you will have to hike through the jungle for two to three hours to reach Bonampak. From Frontera Echeverría you can take a one-hour launch trip up the river to Yaxchilán. The trip from Palenque to Frontera Echeverría takes about seven hours.

Viajes Pakal in San Cristóbal offers a two-day, one-night tour from Palenque to Bonampak and Yaxchilán that brings you overland to a Lacandon village, where you will begin a two-hour trek through the jungle to Bonampak. After a picnic among the ruins, you'll tour the site with a guide and, after admiring the famous frescoes, begin the trek back to the village, where you'll sleep in a tent with the sounds of the jungle all around. The second day brings you up the Usumacinta River to Yaxchilán, where you'll spend a couple of hours before embarking on the journey through the wilderness back to Palenque. For more information, contact Viajes Pakal at Cuauhtemoc 6B, San Cristóbal de las Casas, Chiapas 29200; tel. (9)67-8-28-19; telex 78154 PAKAME.

Far Flung Adventures (Box 31, Terlingua, Texas; tel. 915-371-2489) operates rugged ten-day Lacandon jungle expeditions that visit Palenque and Bonampak, followed by six days of rafting along the Usumacinta River past canyons and chasms and through swirling rapids and white water. Tours of two important Mayan sites along the river, Yaxchilán and Piedras Negras (on the Guatemalan side) are included. Nights are spent in simple hotels and in campsites in Lacandon villages and along the riverbank. The trips depart from Villahermosa and the price is $1,400, excluding airfare.

Sanborn Tours (1007 Main Street, Bastrop, Texas 78602; tel. 800-531-5440) offers a far less rugged tour, "Rain Forests and Mayan Cities," which covers all of the principal tourist destinations in Chiapas, including Tuxtla Gutiérrez, San Cristóbal, the Montebello Lakes, and the Mayan sites of Palenque, Yaxchilán, and Bonampak. Accommodations are in the finest hotels in each locale, except for three nights of camping in the Lacandon jungle near Bonampak and Yaxchilán. The 12-day tour, which departs from Tuxtla Gutiérrez, costs from $918 to $1,089 exclusive of airfare.

The ruins of **Bonampak,** a seventh- and eighth-century Mayan ceremonial center, were unknown to the outside world until 1946, when a young American was led here by Lacandon Indians who lived in the jungle nearby. Highlighting this "City of Painted Walls" are the outstanding murals that cover the walls of three separate rooms in the **Temple of the Frescoes,** known as the "Sistine Chapel of the Americas." Considered the finest Mayan frescoes uncovered to date, the life-sized drawings of rulers, servants, soldiers, sacrifice victims, musicians—a cross-section of the society of the day—provide tremendous insight into the daily life of the Maya. Much of the original color and detail have been lost, however, during the process of restoration, rendering the site less compelling than it was formerly. Regardless of whether or not you make the trip, stop in and see the replicas at the Hotel Bonampak in Tuxtla Gutiérrez.

There are no accommodations or facilities at Bonampak, so at least bring a water canteen along with you.

The Mayan ceremonial center of **Yaxchilán,** which reached its full flowering in the eighth century, sprawls over a vast area on the steep banks of the Usumacinta River on the border with Guatemala. Yaxchilán is located midway between the great cities of Palenque and Tikal, in the Guatemalan Peten region, and the influence of both these sites is reflected in the design of its temples and monuments, arranged to conform with the contours of the hilly, rocky site. Far more interesting than Bonampak, Yaxchilán has a tremendous amount of well-preserved artwork; wall panels and glyphs are carved with the images of the rain god and of the two powerful governors, Escudo (Shield) Jaguar and his son, Pájaro (Bird) Jaguar, who reigned during the eighth century. Other carvings depict the conquests and battles of these two rulers. Yaxchilán's large size makes it unlikely that you will cover all of it during the two hours or so that are allotted on guided tours. Be sure, though, not to miss buildings numbered 41, 20, and 21, which are adorned with magnificent carvings. The delicate stucco roof combs surmounting many of Yaxchilán's temples are regarded as the apogee of Mayan architectural embellishment. Yaxchilán is a sacred site for the Lacandon tribe, who consider it the dwelling place of their god, Atchayum.

The death of the last Lacandon will bring the apocalypse, says a legend of the Lacandon tribe, for with no one left to perform the intricate rituals to honor the sun and moon, these deities will fall to earth, causing a massive earthquake that will destroy the world. Happily, that will not happen anytime soon, for the Lacandon population, which was teetering on the brink of extinction several decades ago, is increasing and is now estimated to number about four hundred.

Among the least assimilated indigenous groups in the Americas, these descendants of the ancient Maya live deep in the jungle of Chiapas in the basin of the Usumacinta River next to the Guatemalan border. They survive by fishing and hunting and by selling timber rights to lumber companies, a practice that has made them one of Mexico's wealthiest Indian groups.

With their unshorn and uncombed hair, sacklike white tunics, and bird-feather ornaments, the Lacandon appear exotic even to other *indígenas,* when the Lacandons' rare contacts with the outside world bring them to Palenque, where they sell carvings and bows and arrows at the archaeological site and load up on supplies at the village.

Naja and Lacanja, two Lacandon hamlets on the edge of the rain forest, may be reached by four-wheel-drive vehicle from Palenque and also by infrequent bus. There are no accommodations at either place, but camping is possible. A visit to **Casa Na Balom** in San Cristóbal will supply you with information and an excellent map; speak with someone there about arranging a trip.

14

TRAVEL ARRANGEMENTS

Good travel agents are excellent sources of information about Mexico, but you can also get brochures, maps, and other useful items from Mexican Government Tourism offices located in the following cities:

New York
405 Park Ave., Suite 1002
New York, NY 10022
Tel. (212) 755-7261

Washington, DC
1615 L St. NW
Washington, DC 20036
Tel. (202) 659-8730

Chicago
70 East Lake St., Suite 1413
Chicago, IL 60601
Tel. (312) 565-2786

Los Angeles
10100 Santa Monica Blvd.,
Suite 224
Los Angeles, CA 90067
Tel. (213) 203-8191

Houston
2707 N. Loop W., Suite 450
Houston, TX 77008
Tel. (713) 880-5135

Miami
11522 S. W. 81 Rd.
Miami, FL 33156
Tel. (305) 252-1440

Montreal
1 Place Ville Marie, Suite 2409
Montreal, Quebec H3B 3M9,
Canada
Tel. (514) 871-1052

Toronto
2 Bloor St. W., Suite 1801
Toronto, Ontario M4W 3E2,
Canada
Tel. (416) 925-0704

London
60-61 Trafalgar Square
London WC2 1PB England
Tel. (441) 734-1058/9

Paris
4, rue Notre-Dame des Vic-
toires
75002 Paris, France
Tel. (331) 40-20-07-34 or
(331) 42-61-51-80

Rome
Via Barberini 3, 7th fl.
00187 Rome, Italy
Tel. (396) 474-2986

Madrid
Calle Velásquez 126
Madrid 28006, Spain
Tel. (341) 261-1827 or (341) 261-3120

Frankfurt
Wiesenhuttenplatz 26
D 6000 Frankfurt am Main, Germany
Tel. (4969) 25-35-41 or (4969) 25-34-13

Tour packagers specializing in travel to Mexico are also good sources of information. Literature you receive from them can help you determine a preferred destination within Mexico and give you a better idea of possible costs. By prebooking blocks of air and hotel space, these agencies are able to get good rates, which they pass on to their customers. Very often, these air and land packages offer substantial savings over the best prices you could get if you were to make reservations for individual travel. The packagers organize group travel to leading Mexican tourist destinations, including capitals, historical and cultural cities, and resort areas. When you're considering which package deals might be most economically advantageous for you, check whether items such as land transfers, gratuities, airport departure taxes, breakfasts, and group outings are included in the package price, or whether you've got these additional costs to consider.

Contact the package-tour operators for brochures describing their various destinations, travel arrangements, hotels, optional tours, and prices. Your travel agent may not have material from all these package-tour operators, but any travel agent can book their tours. According to the Mexican Government Tourism office, the major packagers of tours to Mexico (in alphabetical order) include the following:

Adventure Tours
111 Avenue Rd., 5th fl.
Toronto, Ontario M5R 3J8, Canada
Tel. (416) 967-1510
Tours to Acapulco, Cancún, Ciudad del Carmen, Cozumel, Ixtapa

Apple Vacations
606 E. Baltimore Pike
Media, PA 19063
Tel. (215) 565-7890
Tours to Acapulco, Cancún, Ixtapa, Puerto Vallarta

Asti Tours, Inc.
21 E. 40th St.
New York, NY 10016
Tel. (212) 684-3040 or (800) 535-3711
Tours to Acapulco, Cancún, Mexico City, Puerto Vallarta, Taxco

Club America Vacations
3379 Peachtree Rd., Suite 625
Atlanta, GA 30326
Tel. (404) 237-6002 or (800) 628-9045
Tours to Acapulco, Cancún, Cozumel, Ixtapa

Friendly Holidays
118-21 Queens Blvd.
Forest Hills, NY 11373
Tel. (718) 268-1420 or (800) 422-1312
Tours to Acapulco, Cabo San Lucas, Cancún, Cozumel, Guadalajara, Guanajuato, Ixtapa, Manzanillo, Mazatlán, Mérida, Mexico City, Puerto Vallarta, Taxco

GWV International
300 First Ave.
Needham, MA 02194

Tel. (617) 449-5460 or (800) 225-5498

Tours to Acapulco, Cancún, Cozumel, Manzanillo, Mazatlán, Puerto Vallarta

Jet Vacances
20 rue St. Paul Ouest, #101
Montreal, Quebec H2Y 1Y7, Canada
Tel. (514) 288-7832
Tours to Acapulco, Cancún, Mazatlán, Puerto Vallarta

Liberty Travel/Gogo Tours
69 Spring St.
Ramsey, NJ 07446
Tel. (201) 934-3500
Tours to Acapulco, Cabo San Lucas, Cancún, Cozumel, Guadalajara, Ixtapa, Manzanillo, Mazatlán, Mérida, Mexico City, Oaxaca, Puerto Vallarta

Magnatours, Inc.
325 E. 75 St.
New York, NY 10021
Tel. (212) 517-7770 or 800-223-04761
Tours to Acapulco, Cancún, Cozumel, Ixtapa, Mérida, Mexico City, Puerto Vallarta

Mexico Travel Advisers
1717 North Highland Ave., 11th fl.
Los Angeles, CA 90028
Tel. (213) 642-6444 or 800-876-4682
Tours to Acapulco, Cancún, Cozumel, Guadalajara, Ixtapa, La Paz, Loreto, Los Cabos, Manzanillo, Mazatlán, Mérida, Mexico City, Monterrey, Oaxaca, Palenque, Puerto Escondido, Puerto Vallarta, Taxco, Veracruz, Zihuatanejo, plus special interest tours, including colonial Mexico, religious Mexico, and "Mayaland"

Mexico Tourism Consultants
246 South Robertson Blvd.
Beverly Hills, CA 91324
Tel. (213) 854-8500
Tours to Acapulco, Cancún, Cozumel, Guadalajara, Puerto Vallarta

Thomson Vacations
6299 Airport Rd., Suite 407
Mississauga, Ontario L4V 1W3, Canada
Tel. (416) 673-8777
Tours to Acapulco, Cancún, Ixtapa, Manzanillo, Puerto Vallarta

Tours Mont-Royal
6767 Cote-des-Neiges
Montreal, Quebec H3S 2T6, Canada
Tel. (514) 342-4511
Tours to Acapulco, Cancún, Mazatlán, Puerto Vallarta

Trade Winds Tours
11 Grace Ave.
Great Neck, NY 11021
Tel. (516) 466-6920
Tours to Acapulco, Cabo San Lucas, Cancún, Cozumel, Guadalajara, Huatulco, Ixtapa, Mérida, Mexico City, Manzanillo, Mazatlán, Puerto Vallarta, Villahermosa

RECOMMENDED READING

Beyond the brochures or guidebooks that outline the basics about various destinations in Mexico and give practical information about organizing an itinerary, there's a wealth of wonderful source material, reference books, and literature that delves into Mexico's deepest mysteries and explores the imagination and soul of the Mexican people. Any well-informed librarian will be able to give you a list of excellent titles, which will undoubtedly include the following books:

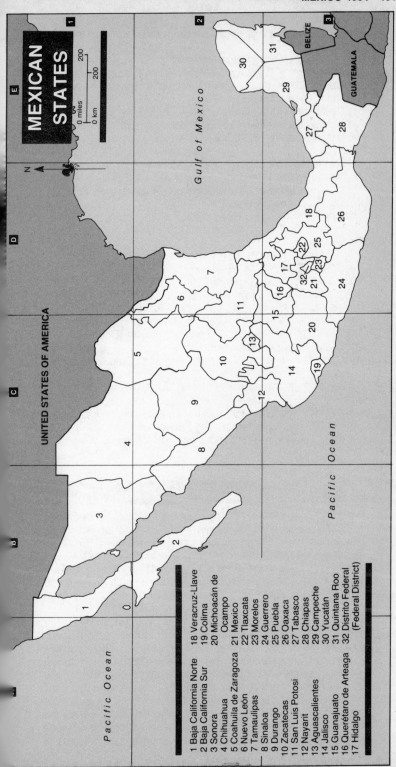

MEXICAN STATES

0 km 200
0 miles 200

UNITED STATES OF AMERICA

Pacific Ocean

Gulf of Mexico

Pacific Ocean

BELIZE

GUATEMALA

1 Baja California Norte
2 Baja California Sur
3 Sonora
4 Chihuahua
5 Coahuila de Zaragoza
6 Nuevo León
7 Tamaulipas
8 Sinaloa
9 Durango
10 Zacatecas
11 San Luis Potosi
12 Nayarit
13 Aguascalientes
14 Jalisco
15 Guanajuato
16 Querétaro de Arteaga
17 Hidalgo
18 Veracruz-Llave
19 Colima
20 Michoacán de Ocampo
21 Mexico
22 Tlaxcala
23 Morelos
24 Guerrero
25 Puebla
26 Oaxaca
27 Tabasco
28 Chiapas
29 Campeche
30 Yucatán
31 Quintana Roo
32 Distrito Federal (Federal District)

The Caste War of the Yucatán, Nelson Reed (Stanford University Press)

The Conquest of New Spain, Bernal Diaz del Castillo (Penguin)

The Conquest of the Yucatán, Frans Blom (Houghton Mifflin)

The Course of Mexican History, Michael Meyer and William L. Sherman (Oxford University Press)

The Death of Artemio Cruz, Carlos Fuentes (Penguin)

Distant Neighbors, Alan Riding (Alfred A. Knopf)

Frida: A Biography of Frida Kahlo, Hayden Herrera (Harper & Row)

A Guide to Ancient Maya Ruins, C. Bruce Hunter (University of Oklahoma Press)

Incidents of Travel in Central America, Chiapas, and Yucatan, John L. Stephens (Dutton)

Insurgent Mexico, John Reed (Simon & Schuster)

Labyrinth of Solitude: Life and Thought in Mexico, Octavio Paz (Grove Press)

Life in Mexico, Frances E. I. Calderon de la Barca (Dutton)

The Maya, Michael Coe (Praeger)

Mexico, Michael Coe (Praeger)

Nothing to Declare, Mary Morris (Houghton Mifflin)

The Plumed Serpent, D. H. Lawrence (Penguin)

The Power and the Glory, Graham Greene (Penguin)

A Short History of Mexico, J. Patrick McHenry (Doubleday)

Under the Volcano, Malcolm Lowry (Penguin)

Yucatán: Before and After the Conquest, Diego de Landa (Dover)

Zapata and the Mexican Revolution, John Womack (Random House)

Many of these titles will also be available in Mexican bookstores that cater to travelers. The Sanborn's chain, with outlets throughout Mexico, is a good place to look for English titles about Mexico.

Telephones

Using the telephone in Mexico can be an ordeal; the system is hopelessly antiquated. In theory, it shouldn't be too difficult to make local calls. Street phones are fairly prevalent, and, because of the recent changes in the value and shape of Mexican money, pay phones are generally free. But very often local lines are glutted with calls, and you cannot get a dial tone, or if you do get a tone, your dialing is interrupted by a constant fast-paced busy signal.

You cannot make long-distance calls on these phones. You cannot even reach a long-distance operator. Special long-distance public phones are few and far between. They're at the airport and other places you're not likely to be on a daily basis, and they require hundred-peso coins to pay for connection fees on credit-card and collect long-distance calls. By the way, whether you're calling from the street, your hotel, or a friend's house, you're better off, rate-wise, calling collect. The Mexican phone company charges an exorbitant amount for long-distance station to station and person-to-person calls, whether they're dialed direct (through what's known as the LADA direct-dial area code system) or with operator assistance. The difference in price is noticeable. For example, a call that might cost $10 from Mexico to the United States if you call collect might cost $25 if you dial direct.

You can call long-distance from most hotels, but if you do, be prepared to pay a connection fee for all long-distance calls, whether you reverse the charges or not, whether the phone at the other end is answered or not, and whether the party you're calling person to person is there or not. This hotel connection fee averages $3–$5 per call, and sometimes it's even higher. Most hotels, however, do not charge for local calls. If you want to spare your pocketbook the burden of connection fees on long-distance calls, you can call from any private phone—at a friend's house or office. There are no long-distance connection fees on private phones. Or you can go to the telephone company office, where there are private cubicles for callers. These offices are not hard to find. Ask your concierge for the address of the nearest one.

Of course, calling collect from a private phone requires capturing the attention of long-distance operators, and sometimes their phones ring twenty, fifty, one hundred times before they answer. Perhaps it's because these operators are overworked. But the wait can be excruciating. Ring. Ring. Ring. Chinese water torture.

One obvious solution, of course, is to arrange for family, friends, and business colleagues at home to phone you at prearranged times.

Language

It takes a bit of courage to speak a foreign tongue. But the effort is well worth it, because in doing so you break through the wall of language that can isolate you from the country you are visiting. Of course, you are bound to make mistakes and suffer embarrassing moments. Mexicans are likely to laugh good-naturedly at your errors, but you will encounter many who are helpful. And their laughter usually will be accompanied by good-will and appreciation for your effort.

If you're bound for any of the major tourist regions, you'll discover that English is spoken widely. The more adventurous you are in your travels, the more adventurous you'll need to be in speaking Spanish. Wander into an outlying Indian village, and you're likely to encounter villagers whose primary tongue is one of the many Indian languages spoken in rural Mexico, and such natives may have only a rudimentary knowledge of Spanish themselves.

Wherever you go, you'll find a few key Spanish phrases useful. And they're easy to learn. You'll quickly grasp how to ask important questions. More challenging will be deciphering the answers, frequently issued rapid-fire. That's where patience and creative sign language will come in handy.

The following are key phrases and words that will help you in your quest to understand and be understood. With them and

By American standards, Mexicans can be almost tediously polite. Friends who haven't seen each other for five minutes exchange several greetings, countergreetings, handshakes and assorted pleasantries.

The tourist often wonders if his Mexican acquaintance isn't putting him on with the apparent intensity of his feeling at each casual meeting. *"¡Qué milagro!"* (What a miracle!) the Mexican cries, though they had met just as usual in their regular *cantina*. With a warm handshake he inquiries after his friend's family and health, though he'd done exactly the same for day after day.

Although these pleasantries may seem superficial or unnecessary, their importance cannot be discounted. To a Mexican these formalities all add up to an American "Hi!" and their absence is as noticeable as a cold silent stare.

Effusive greetings between strangers are common and there's hardly any Mexican so impassive that he won't instinctively respond to a polite expression.

Don't worry about such common errors as saying, "Good afternoon" instead of "Good morning" (*Buenas tardes* vs. *Buenos días*). No one expects you to speak Spanish perfectly, but they do expect to hear something, even if it's incorrect. A mistake is much better than a nervous or impolite silence.

—Carl Franz
The People's Guide to Mexico, 1972

patience and a sense of humor as your allies, you'll enrich your Mexican adventure.

Useful Words and Expressions

Yes.	Sí. (see)
No.	No. (noh)
I don't know.	No sé. (noh SAY)
Please.	Por favor. (pour fah-VOR)
Thank you.	Gracias. (GRAAH-see-ahs)
You're welcome.	De nada. (day NAH-dah)
Excuse me.	Con permiso. (kohn pair-MEE-so)
I am sorry.	Lo siento. (loh see-EN-toh)
It's not important.	No importa. (no eem-POUR-tah)
I understand.	Yo entiendo. (yo en-tee-EN-doh)
I don't understand.	No entiendo. (no en-tee-EN-doh)
Please speak more slowly.	Habla más despacio, por favor. (AH-blah mahs day-SPAH-see-oh pour fah-VOR)
Please repeat that.	Repítelo por favor. (ray-PEE-tay-lo pour fah-VOR)
What?	¿Cómo? (KOH-moh)

What does that mean?	¿Qué quiere decir eso? (kay kee-AIR-ray day-SEER ES-oh)
How do you say in Spanish . . . ?	¿Cómo se dice en español . . . ? (KOH-moh say DEE-say en es-pahn-YOL)
I don't speak Spanish.	No hablo español. (no AH-blow es-pahn-YOL)
Do you speak English?	¿Habla usted inglés? (AH-blah ooh-STED een-GLAYS?)
Hello.	Hola. (OH-la)
Good morning.	Buenos días. (BWAYNE-os DEE-as)
Good afternoon.	Buenas tardes. (BWAYNE-nahs TAHR-days)
Good evening.	Buenas noches. (BWAYNE-nahs NO-chase)
Goodbye.	Adiós. (ah-dee-OHS)
See you later.	Hasta luego. (ahs-TAH loo-AY-go)
See you tomorrow.	Hasta mañana. (ahs-TAH man-YAN-nah)
Mr./Sir	Señor (sen-YOUR)
Mrs./Madam	Señora (sen-YOUR-ah)
Miss	Señorita (sen-your-EEH-tah)
I don't feel well.	No me siento bien. (noh may see-EN-toh bee-EN)

At Customs

Customs	La aduana (la ah-DWAH-nah)
Immigration	Inmigración (een-mee-grah-see-OWN)
I am a U.S. citizen.	Soy ciudadano/a de Los Estados Unidos. (Soy see-ooh-dah-DAH-noh/nah day los es-TAH-dos ooh-NEE-dohs.)
Here is my passport.	Aquí está mi pasaporte. (Ah-KEE es-TAH mee pah-sah-POUR-tay)
Birth certificate	Certificado de nacimiento (Sair-tee-fee-KAH-doh day nah-see-mee-EN-toh)
Tourist card	Tarjeta de turismo (tarr-HAY-tah day tourr-EES-moh)
I am a tourist.	Soy turista. (Soy tourr-EES-tah.)
I am here on business.	Vengo en vías de trabajo. (VEHN-go en BEE-ahs day trah-BAH-ho)

At the Airport

Airplane	El avión (el ah-vee-OWN)

Airport	El aeropuerto (el eye-ray-oh-PWAIR-toh)
I want a round-trip ticket to . . .	Quiero un boleto de ida y vuelta a . . . (key-AIR-oh OOH-na boh-LAY-toh day EE-dah ee VWEL-tah ah . . .)
One-way ticket	Boleto sencillo (boh-LAY-toh sen-SEE-yo)
First class	Primera clase (pree-MAIR-ah CLAH-say)
Second class	Segunda clase (say-GOON-dah CLAH-say)
Reservation	La reservación (la ray-sair-vah-see-OWN)
Flight number	Número de vuelo (NEW-mair-oh day VWAY-loh)
What time does the flight leave?	¿qué hora sale el vuelo? (ah kay OR-rah SAH-lay el VWAY-loh)
What time does the plane arrive?	¿A qué hora llega el avión? (ah kay OR-rah YEA-gah el ah-vee-OWN)
Do I need to confirm the return flight?	¿Hay que confirmar el vuelo de regreso? (eye kay kohn-FEER-mar el VWAY-loh day ray-GREH-so)
Smoking/No-smoking	Fumar/No fumar (foo-MAR/no foo-MAR)
On the aisle	En el pasillo (en el pah-SEE-yo)
By the window	Al lado de la ventana (ahl LAH-doh day la ben-TAH-nah)
Can you help with my bags?	¿Me puede ayudar con mi equipaje? (may PWAY-day eye-u-DAHR kohn mee eh-key-PAH-hay)

Getting Around

I'm lost.	Estoy perdido/a. (es-TOY pair-DEE-doh/dah)
Can you help me?	¿Me puede ayudar? (may PWAY-day eye-you-DAHR)
Can you tell me how to get to . . . ?	¿Me puede decir como llegar a . . . ? (may PWAY-day day-SEER KOH-moh yea-GAHR ah . . .)
Which way?	¿Por dónde? (pour DOHN-day)
Is it far? . . . near?	¿Está muy lejos? (es-TAH mwee lay-HOS) . . . cerca? (SAIR-kah)
Taxi	Taxi (TAHX-zee)

How much does it cost to go to . . . ?	¿Cuánto cuesta ir a . . . ? (KWAHN-toh KWEHS-tah eer ah . . .)
Stop here, please.	Pare aquí, por favor. (PAH-ray ah-KEY pour fah-VOR)
Train station	Estación de ferrocarriles (eh-stah-see-OWN day fair-rroh-kah-REE-lace)
Train	El tren (el trrehn)
Subway	El metro (el MEH-troh)
Bus	Camión (kah-mee-OWN)
Where is the bus stop?	¿Dónde está la parada de camiones? (DOHN-day es-TAH la pah-RAH-dah day kah-mee-OWN-ehs)
. . . the bank?	. . . el banco? (el BAHN-koh)
. . . a drugstore?	. . . una farmacia? (ooh-nah far-MAH-see-ah)
. . . a women's restroom?	. . . un sanitario de damas? (oon sah-nee-TAH-ree-oh day DAH-mahs)
. . . a men's restroom?	. . . un sanitario de hombres? (oon sah-nee-TAH-ree-oh day OHM-brays)
. . . the museum?	. . . el museo? (el moo-SAY-oh)
. . . the post office?	. . . el correo? (el kohr-RRAY-oh)
. . . the tourism office?	. . . la oficina de turismo? (la oh-fee-SEE-nah day tour-EES-moh)
. . . a telephone?	. . . un teléfono? (oon teh-LAY-foh-noh)

At the Hotel

I'd like a single room.	Quiero un cuarto sencillo. (key-AIR-roh oon KWAR-toh sen-SEE-yo)
Double bed	Cama matrimonial (KAH-mah mah-tree-moan-ee-AHL)
Twin beds	Camas gemelas (KAH-mas hay-MAY-lahs)
Air-conditioning	Aire acondicionado (EYE-ray ah-kohn-dee-see-oh-NAH-do)
With bath	Con baño (kohn BAHN-yo)
What is the nightly rate?	¿Cuánto cuesta por noche? (KWAN-toh KWES-tah pour NOH-chay)
One night	Una noche (OOH-na NOH-chay)
Two nights	Dos noches (dohs NOH-chase)

A week	Una semana (OOH-na say-MAH-nah)
I have a reservation.	Tengo una reservación. (TEHN-go OOH-nah ray-sehrr-bah-see-OWN)
The key	La llave (la YAH-vay)
Where is the restaurant?	¿Dónde está el restaurante? (DOHN-day es-TAH el rehs-toh-RAHN-tay)
Is there a pool?	¿Hay alberca? (eye ahl-BEAR-kah)
Please wake me at 7 A.M.	Despiérteme a las siete por la mañana, por favor. (des-pee-AIR-tay-may ah lahs see-EH-tay pour la mahn-YAH-nah, pour fah-VOR)

At the Restaurant

Waiter	Mesero/a (may-SAIR-roh/rah)
Please bring me a menu.	Tráigame el menú, por favor. (TRRY-gah-may el may-NEW, pour fah-VOR)
We want to order.	Queremos pedir. (kay-RAY-mohs pay-DEER)
The check	La cuenta (la KWEN-tah)
Is it spicy?	¿Es picante? (es pee-KAHN-tay)
Breakfast	Desayuno (dehs-eye-OO-noh)
Lunch	Almuerzo (ahl-MWEHR-soh)
Dinner	Cena (SAY-nah)
Appetizer	Aperitivo (ah-peh-ree-TEE-voh)
Entrée	Entrada (en-TRAH-dah)
Dessert	Postre (POHS-tray)
A bottle of white wine	Una botella de vino blanco (OOH-nah boh-TAY-yah day VEE-noh BLAHN-koh)
A glass of red wine	Un vaso con vino tinto (oon BAH-so kohn VEE-noh TEEN-toh)
Beer	Cerveza (sair-VAY-sah)
Mineral water	Agua mineral (AH-gwah meen-err-AHL)
Carbonated	Con gas (kohn gahs)
Uncarbonated	Sin gas (seen gahs)
Soft drink	Refresco (ray-FRES-koh)
Coffee	Café (kah-FAY)
With milk	Con leche (kohn LAY-chay)
Tea	Té (tay)
Bread	Pan (pahn)
Salad	Ensalada (en-sah-LAH-dah)
Fruit	Fruta (FROO-tah)

I need a knife.	Necesito un cuchillo. (neh-seh-SEE-toh oon koo-CHEE-yo)
. . . fork	. . . tenedor (ten-ay-DOHR)
. . . spoon	. . . cuchara (koo-CHAR-ah)
. . . napkin	. . . servieta (sehr-BEE-eh-tah)
. . . a clean glass	. . . un vaso limpio (oon bah-soh LEEM-pee-oh)
. . . an ashtray	. . . un cenicero (oon seh-nee-SEHR-oh)

Going Shopping

Where can I change money?	¿Dónde se puede cambiar dinero? (DOHN-day say PWAY-day kahm-bee-AHR dee-NAIR-oh)
Do you accept credit cards?	¿Se acepta tarjetas de crédito? (say ah-SEHP-tah tahr-HAY-tahs day KREH-dee-toh)
Traveler's check	Cheque de viajero (CHEH-kay day bee-ah-HAIR-oh)
The marketplace	El mercado (el mair-KAH-doh)
How much does it cost?	¿Cuánto cuesta? (KWAN-to KWEHS-tah)
It's very expensive	Está muy caro. (es-TAH mwee KAH-row)
Can you lower the price?	¿Puede usted bajar el precio? (PWAY-day ooh-STED bah-HAR el PRAY-see-oh)
Do you have . . . ?	¿Tiene usted . . . ? (tee-EN-ay ooh-STED)
Please show me another one.	Muéstreme otro, por favor. (MWAY-stray-may OH-tro pour fah-VOR)
I like it.	Me gusta. (may GOO-stah)
I don't like it.	No me gusta. (noh may GOO-stah)
Pretty	Bonito (boh-NEE-toh)
Ugly	Feo (FAY-oh)

Basic Conversation

How are you?	¿Cómo está usted? (KOH-moh es-TAH oo-STED)
I'm fine, thank you. And you?	Estoy bien, gracias. ¿Y usted? (es-TOY bee-EN GRAH-see-ahs. Ee ooh-STED)
What is your name?	¿Cómo se llama usted? (KOH-moh say YAH-mah ooh-STED)
My name is . . .	Me llamo . . . (may YAH-moh . . .)

It's nice to meet you.	Mucho gusto a conocerle. (MOO-cho GOO-stoh ah koh-noh-SAIR-lay)
Where are you from?	¿De dónde es usted? (day DOHN-day es ooh-STED)
I'm from the United States.	Soy de los Estados Unidos. (soy day los es-TAH-dohs ooh-NEE-dohs)
What do you do?	¿En qué trabaja usted? (en kay tra-BAH-ha ooh-STED)
I am a businessperson.	Soy comerciante. (soy koh-mair-see-AHN-tay)
I am a student.	Soy estudiante. (soy es-too-dee-AHN-tay)
I am a housewife.	Soy ama de casa. (soy AH-mah day KAH-sah)

Time

When?	¿Cuándo? (KWAHN-doh)
In the morning	Por la mañana (pour la mahn-YAH-nah)
In the afternoon	En la tarde (en la TAHR-day)
At night	En la noche (en la NOH-chay)
What time is it?	¿Qué hora es? (kay AW-rah es?)
Noon	Mediodía (may-dee-oh-DEE-ah)
Midnight	Medianoche (may-dee-ah-NOH-chay)
It's one o'clock.	Es la una. (es la OOH-nah)
It's two o'clock.	Son las dos. (sohn lahs dohs)
It's three fifteen.	Son las tres y cuarto. (sohn lahs trrays ee KWAR-toh)
It's four thirty.	Son las cuatro y media. (sohn lahs KWAH-troh ee MAY-dee-ah)
It's twenty to five.	Son las cinco menos veinte. (sohn lahs SEEN-koh MAY-nohs BAIN-tay)
Is it late?	¿Es tarde? (es TAHR-day)
Early	Temprano (tehm-PRAH-noh)
Yesterday	Ayer (eye-YAIR)
Today	Hoy (oy)
Tomorrow	Mañana (man-YAN-na)
Next week	La semana próxima (la say-MAH-nah PROHX-ee-mah)
Last month	El mes pasado (el mayse pah-SAH-doh)

Numbers

1	Uno (OOH-noh)
2	Dos (dohs)

3	Tres (trrays)
4	Cuatro (KWAH-troh)
5	Cinco (SEEN-koh)
6	Seis (sayce)
7	Siete (see-EH-tay)
8	Ocho (OH-cho)
9	Nueve (new-AVE-ay)
10	Diez (dee-ES)
11	Once (OWN-say)
12	Doce (DOH-say)
13	Trece (TRRAY-say)
14	Catorce (Kah-TOHR-say)
15	Quince (KEEN-say)
16	Dieciseis (dee-ES-ee-SAYCE)
17	Diecisiete (dee-ES-ee-see-EH-tay)
18	Dieciocho (dee-ES-ee-OH-cho)
19	Diecinueve (dee-ES-ee-new-AVE-ay)
20	Veinte (BAIN-tay)
21	Veintiuno (BAIN-tee-OOH-no)
30	Treinta (TRAIN-tah)
40	Cuarenta (kwah-REN-tah)
50	Cincuenta (seen-KWEN-tah)
60	Sesenta (say-SEHN-tah)
70	Setenta (say-TEHN-tah)
80	Ochenta (oh-CHEN-tah)
90	Noventa (noh-VEHN-tah)
100	Cien (see-EN)
1,000	Mil (meel)
20,000	Veinte mil (BAIN-tay meel)
100,000	Cien mil (see-EN meel)
500,000	Quinientos mil (key-nee-EN-tos meel)
1,000,000	Un millón (oon meel-YON)

The Seasons in Mexico

Mexico is an attractive destination year-round, but there is a definite high season, when it's difficult to find hotel rooms, and prices are as much as fifty percent higher. Basically, the tourist seasons coincide with the weather.

The dry season, which lasts from Nov. through Apr., is the most popular season for travel. During this period, temperatures at beach resorts average around eighty degrees Fahrenheit, and the climate is still quite humid. In the highlands, however, temperatures can be quite cool, especially at night. Mexico City in Dec. and Jan., for example, averages about sixty degrees Fahrenheit by day, with the readings falling into the thirties or forties during the night. This drop in temperature is characteristic of cities at an altitude of more than seven thousand feet, and travelers to such destinations are advised to bring sweaters or coats during the winter months. Cities in the four-thousand to six-thousand-foot range in altitude usually have milder weather, with an average temperature of about 66 degrees Fahrenheit, and with less difference between day and nighttime readings.

City	Average Yearly Rainfall (inches)	Temperature (°F) Max.	Min.
Acapulco	59	102	62
Aguascalientes	21	97	42
Cabo San Lucas	28	107	43
Campeche	47	100	53
Cancún	40	110	36
Ciudad Juárez	11	107	33
Colima	35	108	40
Córdoba	90	93	57
Cozumel	56	110	42
Cuautla	33	92	46
Cuernavaca	41	102	36
Chihuahua	16	102	34
Dolores Hidalgo	12	114	32
Durango	16	95	35
Ensenada	14	102	40
Fortín de las Flores	88	102	32
Guadalajara	38	95	34
Guanajuato	30	97	36
Guaymas	11	112	46
Hermosillo	10	112	32
Ixtapa-Zihuatanejo	50	97	50
Ixtapan de la Sal	41	100	49
Jalapa	62	96	40
La Paz	29	107	50
Loreto	27	106	46
Manzanillo	35	107	48
Matamoros	31	108	30
Mazatlán	33	94	54
Mérida	36	108	50
Mexicali	1	116	28
Mexico City	24	90	34
Monterrey	29	108	50
Morelia	33	89	40
Nuevo Laredo	17	110	25
Nogales	16	102	28
Nopoló	27	91	46
Oaxaca	24	102	37
Pátzcuaro	44	100	50
Puebla	33	88	30
Puerto Angel	30	111	54
Puerto Escondido	30	109	53
Puerto Vallarta	32	95	53
Querétaro	20	100	30
Saltillo	14	102	48
San Felipe	16	118	32
San José del Cabo	28	107	66
San José Purúa	37	95	45
San Miguel de Allende	21	100	34

City	Average Yearly Rainfall (inches)	Temperature (°F) Max.	Min.
Taxco	58	89	49
Tijuana	8	97	32
Veracruz	64	100	51

The rainy season lasts from May through Oct. During this period there may be daily downpours. These are quite intense, even torrential, but they are usually of short duration. Quite often, they clean and freshen the air, and a lot of people find this a very pleasant time to visit Mexico, especially in the highland cities. May is, in general, the hottest month. Temperatures in Mexico City in May, for example, hover at around ninety degrees Fahrenheit by day but often drop into the sixties at night. Again, cities at more moderate altitudes are usually milder, with average summertime temperatures of about eighty degrees Fahrenheit and, again, with less difference between daytime and nighttime temperatures. In the Yucatán Peninsula, the weather is usually hot and humid, but during the summer rainy season, particularly from May through Sept., temperatures rarely drop below ninety degrees Fahrenheit and often soar into the one-hundreds, and heavy rains can last, astonishingly, for hours. The Pacific Coast, too, is hot and humid, with summertime temperatures averaging between 75 and one hundred degrees Fahrenheit and rains heaviest from June through Oct.

High season at the Pacific Coast and Yucatán Peninsula beach resorts lasts from mid-Dec. until mid-Apr. Christmas, New Year's, and Easter are always very heavily booked by Mexican and foreign visitors, and it is advisable to book as far in advance as possible and to arrive early in the day with your written confirmation in hand. Even so, with overbooking problems in many hotels, you may find yourself shifted into another hotel. This is more likely to happen during the high season, but it has been known to happen year-round.

Formalities

The formal procedures for entering and leaving Mexico are fairly simple. Everyone entering the country needs to fill out a **Tourist Card** and present some form of official identification that indicates citizenship. Passport, birth certificate, or voter registration will do for identification. For naturalized citizens of the United States, naturalization papers are sufficient; however, naturalized Canadian citizens must present passports.

Tourist Cards are free and are obtainable from travel agents, airlines at the time of ticketing or check-in, Mexican Government Tourism offices, or immigration authorities at any border-control checkpoint. You must sign the Tourist Card in the presence of a Mexican official upon entering the country. The Tourist Card is then split. Officials keep the original, and you keep a carbon copy that must be presented, along with your passport or other form of identification, when you leave the country. Theoretically (according to Mexican law), you must keep your copy of the Tourist Card with you at all times while you're in Mexico. You must also be sure not to lose it, as getting out of the country without your Tourist Card is impossible, and replacing a lost Tourist Card is a grim and frustrating bureaucratic ordeal. If, by any chance, you have the misfortune to lose yours, contact your embassy or consulate immediately and report the loss to the closest office of the Mexican Immigration Office, under the Secretaria de Gobernación. Be prepared to spend a lot of time and some money to get the matter sorted out. Tourist Cards are for single entry into Mexico, and they're good for up to ninety days, with a possible extension of another ninety days upon application to the Mexican Immigration Office.

Children under the age of 15 years who are traveling alone must present, in addition to the Tourist Card and identification, an affidavit, in duplicate, of permission to enter Mexico, signed by their parents or legal guardians. This must be notarized and signed by an official of the Mexican consulate. Foreign students who plan to stay in Mexico for longer than six months must present, in addition to Tourist Card and identification, a letter of acceptance from the school they will be attending, plus proof of financial security during their stay in Mexico.

ENTERING BY CAR

Tourists entering Mexico by car need an automobile permit, which may be obtained at the border crossing upon proof of ownership of the vehicle. **Tourists who enter Mexico with a car must leave Mexico with a car.** If your car is stolen or damaged while you are in Mexico, contact your embassy or consulate immediately in addition to reporting the incident to local authorities and to the Mexican Immigration Office at the Secretaria de Gobernación. You must also have Mexican insurance for your vehicle. If you have the misfortune of getting into an accident and cannot prove on the spot that you can financially cover damages, you may very well wind up in jail until you can provide proof of your financial resources. Having Mexican insurance can nip this flowering situation in the bud. It is best to bear the expense and avoid the hassle.

If you're just visiting Mexican border towns for 72 hours or less, you don't need a tourist card, and, most often, you won't be required to have an auto permit. However, it's still a good idea to purchase Mexican auto insurance, which is available at all border crossings.

AVOIDING HASSLES

Mexico does not require any immunization shots, nor are there any health checks upon entry. However, you may be searched upon your arrival in Mexico. The standard procedure is that your bags are X-rayed, but you may also have the pleasure of experiencing a random hand check, in which an official paws through all your personals. This is indelicate, to say the least. Explaining that you're only a tourist doesn't help, and stronger complaints only exacerbate the problem. What are the officials looking for? Mexican customs does not allow any fruit or plants to be brought into the country, and officials also look for "extra" or duplicated personal appliances (hair dryers, shavers, cassette decks, and other items) that, they surmise, you may be importing for resale. If these are found, they may be confiscated—or you may be approached for a bribe. So bring only what's essential. You are permitted to bring in one still camera as well as one 8-mm movie camera, plus 12 rolls of film. You may also bring in one carton of cigarettes, fifty cigars, and one liter of alcohol. If you have a CB, you must register it with the Mexican consulate and obtain a permit. Firearms for recreational use are permitted into the country but must be registered and cleared with the Mexican consulate (this is a complicated procedure, and may take months).

If you're driving into Mexico, be prepared to have your vehicle searched. Arrive at the border before 9 P.M.; otherwise you may have to wait while officials are summoned. This can take hours. Also, there are two checkpoints at border crossings, so leave the customs official's seal intact until you've passed the second control point—or you may have to be reinspected.

If you take prescription drugs and have a supply with you, bring along the prescription. Many prescription drugs are available over the counter in Mexico, and you'll need the prescription for re-entry into the United States. Needless to say, the penalties for attempting to bring controlled substances over the border in either direction are severe, but Mexican law is based on the Napoleonic Code, which basically presumes you are guilty until proved innocent. Nobody wants to tangle with that.

Pets may be brought across the border, but you need a veterinarian's certification of the animal's good health issued fewer than 72 hours in advance of the border crossing, and the vet's statement must be registered with and stamped at the nearest Mexican consulate. Pets must also have certification of vaccination against rabies, hepatitis, leptospirosis, and pip. If you're planning to keep your pet in Mexico for thirty days or more, U.S. customs requires certification of inoculation against rabies before the pet will be allowed to re-enter the United States.

TAXES AND DUTIES

Upon leaving Mexico, you're required to pay an airport departure tax of $10 per person, payable in pesos or dollars. Be sure to reserve enough money to pay this tax, or you'll not be allowed to leave.

The Mexicans impose no currency restrictions. However, U.S. customs requires that you declare sums of cash, traveler's checks, or negotiable bonds in excess of $5,000.

If you have been out of the United States for 48 hours or more, you receive an exemption from duty and federal tax on the first $400 worth—fair retail value where acquired—of all personal and household items you obtain abroad and carry back with you. You may include one hundred cigars (Cuban cigars are not permitted unless they are imported directly from Cuba), regardless of your age, and one liter (33.8 fluid ounces) of alcoholic beverage, if you are at least 21 years of age. You may claim this $400 exemption only once in thirty days. If you've been outside the United States for less than 48 hours, or do not meet the thirty-day eligibility, you may bring back items totaling $25; however, you must have no more than $25 worth of goods to declare or you must pay duty on all dutiable items without exemption. Exemptions do not include items mailed to the United States. There will be no duties applied to "unsolicited gifts," provided that the declared value of the package is $50 or less. Alcoholic beverages may not be mailed into the United States.

You may orally declare every item acquired abroad and brought back with you (whether purchased or given to you), if the total value of the items is not more than $1,400. State the price actually paid for the item in U.S. or foreign currency. Repairs to articles newly acquired or taken abroad with you must also be declared, whether paid for or provided free of charge.

If your acquisitions exceed $1,400, if you have exceeded the tobacco or alcohol exemptions, if you bring in items for business purposes or for someone else, or if you are asked to do so by a customs inspector, you must declare your acquisitions in writing.

If your purchases exceed the alcohol limit, you must pay duty, internal revenue tax, and possibly state tax, on the excess. Duty for distilled spirits, wine, and beer is usually ten percent of their value. Internal revenue tax is $10.50 per proof gallon on distilled spirits, or $.17–$10.50 per proof gallon for wine, and $.29 per gallon for beer. Customs enforces the laws of the state into which you are entering, and state regulations regarding personal import, possession, and shipment of liquor differ. Some states do not allow individuals to import more liquor than the federally established limit, even by paying tax.

If you have exceeded the $400 exemption, the next $1,000 in items is generally dutiable at a flat ten percent rate. That means that the total possible duty on purchases valued at $1,400 per person will be $100. Families living in the same household and returning together may combine their purchases on a joint declaration and multiply their exemptions accordingly.

For a more complete explanation of what is and is not dutiable, contact your district customs office, or the Department of the Treasury.

Any article not declared or one that is misrepresented may lead to civil or criminal penalties, in addition to confiscation of goods. Certain products are not allowed into the United States at all. These include items made of ivory and tortoiseshell, and fruits, meats, plants, food (with some exceptions), birds, soil, snails, and other living organisms. Get the complete list from customs, and abide by it.

If you owe duty, you must pay it on the spot. Customs will accept cash or a personal check drawn on a national or state bank or trust company of the United States, and made payable to U.S. Customs.

Money Matters

The basic monetary unit in Mexico is the peso, which comes in various denominations of coins and paper currency. The symbol for the peso is $. Price tags are usually marked in pesos, unless otherwise specified. Coins (or *moneda*) are available in twenty-, fifty-, one-hundred-, five-hundred-, and five-thousand-peso units. At present, the coin system is being redesigned. Coins in denominations of less than one hundred pesos are being phased out of use, while coins of five hundred and one thousand pesos are increasingly replacing bills of those denominations. The new coins are confusing even to the Mexicans. In handling them, you had best read the coins before spending them. That way you won't be embarrassed or overpay. Notes (or *billetes*) are available in one-hundred-, five-hundred-, one-thousand-, two-thousand-, five-thousand-, ten-thousand-, twenty-thousand-, and fifty-thousand-peso denominations. You will probably not see many one-hundred- or five-hundred-peso notes, which are quickly being phased out of circulation, and one- and two-thousand-peso notes are becoming increasingly rare.

The increased use of coins may be desirable from the standpoint of the mint (they last longer than the notes), but walking around with a pocket full of change can weigh you down considerably. However, many small shops, taxis, and restaurants rarely have change. So if you want to save time and avoid having to overpay, you'll carry the coins.

Technically, the peso is comprised of one hundred centavos. Although centavo coins have little monetary significance, they are frequently used in pricing, especially in supermarkets where items ranging from cheese to underwear always seem to have 25 centavos or 95 centavos included in the price. Centavos are written after a decimal, and often in slightly smaller numbers. For example, two hundred and thirty pesos and ninety-five centavos is written $230.95. Sometimes the centavo units will be underlined, as well. If the price is two hundred and thirty pesos and no centavos, it is written $230.00. When your bill is tallied, there will probably be some centavos in the final figure. These will always be rounded off to the next-highest peso, or five- or ten-peso figure. Although this difference is minimal to each shopper, it amounts to huge overcharges for the supermarkets. If you object to this practice, you can ask for your change. You'll get a lot of dirty looks—but you'll also get your change.

You'll notice that twenty-centavo coins are required for local calls from public telephones. The phones instruct you to deposit the coins before attempting to dial your party. But if you don't have a twenty-centavo coin, and most people do not, you simply dial and the call goes through, free of charge. Phones now being installed require a one-hundred-peso coin, but by the time all the new phones are in, the one-hundred-peso coin may be obsolete and local calls may again be free of charge.

The reason for these changes in the monetary system is that the peso has been drastically devalued over the past seven or eight years. During the presidency of José Lopez Portillo (from 1976 to 1982), the exchange rate was about 23 pesos to one U.S. dollar. The rate at the time of this writing is about 2,600 pesos to one U.S. dollar; 3,250 pesos to one Australian dollar; 2,262 pesos to one Canadian dollar; and 4,160 pesos to óne British pound. And further devaluation is anticipated. As the devaluation has occurred, inflation has risen, and there is therefore no longer a great need for small denominations of money. At this time in Mexico's development, the one-thousand-peso note that used to be worth about four dollars in U.S. currency is now worth about fifty cents. The difference in peso value and prices is most noticeable to the Mexicans. For foreign travelers, the devaluation has certainly been an advantage, although the inflation that has been rising to combat it has made the devaluation less of an advantage to foreign visitors than the Mexican government would like them to believe it is. Mexico, especially resorts like Acapulco and Cancún, and Mexico City, can be quite an expensive destination. Still, meals and entertainment are usually less costly here than they would be at comparable destinations elsewhere.

CHANGING MONEY

When you travel in Mexico, it is advisable to keep about ten or twenty U.S. one-dollar bills with you for emergency tips (or bribes!); the remainder of your money can be in traveler's checks. The rate of exchange is usually equal for cash and traveler's checks, although occasionally traveler's checks have the advantage. It's best to carry traveler's checks in U.S. dollars. In Mexico City and other major resorts it isn't difficult to cash traveler's checks in Canadian dollars, for example, but elsewhere you may have difficulty and wind up with an unfair rate of exchange. It is also best to use smaller denominations of traveler's checks and to cash them as you need them; if you change large sums of money and don't spend it, you will lose money in reconverting the pesos to dollars. And you may have to wait until after you've cleared Mexican immigration at the airport before you're permitted to reconvert pesos, which sometimes involves waiting on long lines. Except at the airports, banks and change bureaus usually do not charge a commission for changing money, so you can use their services as often as you'd like without losing a dollar here and a dollar there.

If, however, you have your choice of changing money at a bank or at the *casa de cambio* (change house), choose the latter. The rate of exchange is, surprisingly, usually slightly better (maybe 25 to 50 pesos per dollar), lines are usually shorter, and the office hours are much longer. Banks, if you need them, are usually open Mon.–Fri., 9 A.M.–1:30 P.M.; *casas de cambio* are usually open daily 8:30 A.M.–6 P.M. Always count your money before leaving the window, and always get a receipt indicating the exchange rate. Make sure that this exchange rate coincides with the one that's posted. Exchange rates will vary from city to city, from resort to resort, and from house to house. If you're in an area with a cluster of *casas de cambio,* you should compare rates before changing your money. Sometimes you can actually up the exchange rate by saying that the bureau down the block offered you more. If at all possible, avoid cashing traveler's checks or changing money in hotels. The rate of exchange is usually quite a bit lower than at banks or *casas de cambio.*

CHECKS AND CREDIT CARDS

Personal checks are not accepted as a form of payment in Mexico, but credit cards are accepted in most places. American Express, however, is not the best card to bring if you're only bringing one; Visa and MasterCard are much more widely accepted.

TIPPING AND HANDOUTS

It seems that almost everyone in Mexico is angling for a piece of your action, in the form of tips or handouts or bribes. How you respond to this constant prompting is between you, your conscience, and your pocketbook. Tipping is appropriate in Mexico. The guidelines are similar to those elsewhere. On restaurant or bar bills, it's customary to add a 15 percent tip, depending, of course, on the kind of service you've received. If a service charge is included in the bill, and you've had an exceptionally good waiter, you might want to add another ten percent. In addition, the following tips are generally expected: bellhops, about 500 pesos per bag; hotel maids or valets, about 1,000 pesos per day; barbers and manicurists, about 1,500 pesos; group tour guides, about two U.S. dollars per person depending upon service received; parking-lot attendants, about 500 pesos. When you park on the street, old men or boys will often materialize to guide you into the space and guard your car. They expect a tip. You can wave them away, but you may find a mirror missing when you return. Most Mexicans simply pay them a few hundred pesos to avoid the confrontation. Whether this counts as a tip or a bribe is a matter of definition. However, bribes, or *mordidas,* are very much a part of the Mexican economy. You may have to pay them to police who stop you for some imaginary infraction of the law, or to customs officials, or to hotel receptionists who can't seem to locate your reservation. Here's where those single dollar bills come in handy. Of course, you can always refuse to pay, and you'll probably be able to work the situation out. But it will take time and may be unpleasant.

With regard to handouts, you'll notice that most *Mexicans* simply walk by the women and children who are begging on the street. These huddled, pathetic creatures can tug at your heartstrings, wrench your gut—and cost you a lot of money. Beggars are everywhere, and most of them do not have other means of support. However, unless you're a millionaire, you cannot give to all of them. Where you draw the line is up to you.

Safety

The sorry state of the Mexican economy has caused an increase in the country's crime rate, mostly in crimes of property. There are now many more holdups, robberies, purse snatchings, and picked pockets than there used to be. The police don't seem to be very effective in dealing with this situation; some people, in fact, have even suggested that they may be part of the problem. If you are traveling in Mexico, you should take basic, and obvious, precautions to ensure safety of limb and property. First of all, try to travel only with essentials and, whenever possible, leave expensive jewelry and gadgets at home. If you must have these things with you, leave them in the hotel safety-deposit boxes as soon as you arrive and whenever you're not wearing or using them. Put the bulk of your money as well as your tickets and passport in the safety box. You're supposed to carry your Tourist Card with you at all times, but since it's unlikely that you'll ever be asked for it, you may want to leave it in the safety-deposit box, too.

It is most unfortunate, but property—ranging from tape recorders to cassette tapes, from underwear (yes!) to silk shirts—does disappear from hotel rooms. To best safeguard your belongings, leave most of your things in a locked suitcase. If you find that too unbearably inconvenient, at least make sure that you've arranged everything neatly and in such a way that anything missing would be obvious immediately.

Never carry with you more money than you need for a given outing. You're safest with traveler's checks that can be replaced if stolen. Report any thefts or losses immediately.

Be discreet about how much money you've got. It is unwise to flash a fistful of dollars or dangle a diamond-studded Rolex watch in front of the masses. If, by any chance, you are the victim of a holdup, you are generally most likely to avoid violence if you hand over the money rather than resist.

To safeguard yourself, don't walk alone late at night or in secluded areas. This is true in posh residential areas in Mexico City and Guadalajara as well as beach resorts on the Pacific Coast or Caribbean, where purse snatchings, robberies, and other nonviolent street crimes have increased lately. Try to remain aware at all times of who's around you. If you see a person or group of people who seem to be suspicious, avoid them by going in another direction where there are crowds of people.

When you're in crowds of people, there may be pickpockets on the loose. Be aware of your wallet and pocketbook. Don't carry your wallet in your rear pants pocket or let your shoulder bag hang down your back. Be especially mindful on crowded buses and subways, where the normal jostling of people may provide pickpockets with greater opportunity to get the goods and get away.

Don't drive at night, especially in the more deserted areas. Country roads are usually unlit. There are unmarked *topes* (metal bumps on the roads), narrow shoulders, and other conditions that make driving conditions hazardous, but there have also been quite a few cases of highway robbery. If you are on the road, day or night, and you see another car by the side of the road, seemingly in distress, don't stop. You may seem heartless—but it could be a setup.

On the other hand, make sure that your vehicle is in fine functioning condition and filled with gas, so that you don't get stuck on the road, vulnerable to robbers. If, even with these precautions, you do get stuck, stay inside your locked car and open up only for the Green Angels, a group of official bilingual mechanics in green trucks who patrol Mexico's highways in search of distressed motorists. These mechanics are generally reliable and honest, although if you need an automobile part, you might have to pay fees that amount to highway robbery. Otherwise, the Green Angels service is free of charge.

Highway robberies have taken place throughout Mexico during the day as well as at night. Unfortunately, there have even been holdups of entire buses. Most of the robberies have occurred along the roads in and through Durango, in some areas of Jalisco, and along the Pacific Coast. Before setting off on a trip along one of these routes, check with the AAA or the nearest consulate to learn about current conditions or travel advisories. Again, if anything does occur, report it immediately to the local authorities and to the nearest consulate.

HEALTH

The most common health complaint during travel to Mexico is *la turista,* also known as "Moctezuma's Revenge" or "the Aztec two-step." All these are slang names for the diarrhea, weakness, and fever brought on as frequently by the sudden change of diet as by the presence of amoebas or unfriendly germs. To avoid this very common and annoying ailment, you should drink only purified or bottled water *(agua purificada* or *agua mineral)* with or without gas *(con gas* or *sin gas),* without ice *(sin hielo).* Of course, you can also drink bottled sodas *(refrescos)* or beer *(cerveza)* or other bottled, processed drinks, including juices *(jugos)* or milk *(leche)*. Avoid eating unpeeled fruits, uncooked vegetables, raw seafood, and very rare meats. Most of the larger hotels and more expensive restaurants purify all their water and disinfect all their fruits and vegetables; so, if you have a sensitive stomach, you're best dining at these establishments. Even so, avoid indulging in overly rich, greasy, spicy, or salty foods to which your system is not accustomed, and more important, don't consume excesses of anything. Many buffets and Mexican fiestas serve unlimited margaritas. If you're not used to drinking large quantities of tequila, these can lead to serious digestive ailments.

If you do get diarrhea, try a standard remedy such as Pepto-Bismol. If you don't have any with you, the pink liquid is sold in most hotel shops and all pharmacies *(farmacias),* including Sanborn's. In every city, there is at least one 24-hour pharmacy. Ask your concierge where it is. If the Pepto-Bismol doesn't relieve your symptoms, you might have to try something stronger, such as Lomotil or Imodium, both of which require prescriptions in the United States but are sold over the counter in Mexico. These are strong "antimotility" medicines and may have contraindications. Just to be on the safe side, ask your own physician whether you should take either of these, and, if not, get a prescription for another medicine that he or she recommends. It is generally agreed that you should not take Lomotil or Imodium for more than two full days. If your diarrhea persists, you may need an antibiotic. Bactrim F (made by Roche, sold by prescription in the United States and over the counter in Mexico) is frequently prescribed. Mexican pharmacists and physicians are very well practiced in dealing with *la turista,* and you can generally rely on them for good advice. Nevertheless, many travelers feel more confident knowing that they've sought the opinion of their own physician.

MEDICATIONS

If you have favorite brands of over-the-counter drugs or vitamins or toiletries, bring a small supply of them with you. Most generic medicines and cosmetic preparations are readily available throughout Mexico, but some of the brand names differ, so you might want to bring your own.

If you are traveling with prescription drugs, always bring the prescription with you. This will enable you to be certain that you're replacing empty or misplaced vials of necessary medicines with the same formula, and it will facilitate your re-entry into the United States. If you wear contact lenses or glasses, always bring an extra pair of either with you, as well as a copy of your prescription—just in case. And even if you're a veteran contact lens user, bring a pair of glasses with you: The air in different regions of Mexico is sometimes dry and dusty, and even you may have problems with your lenses under these conditions.

If you suffer from any serious ailment, such as diabetes or a heart condition, carry some form of medical identification with you at all times. This should also indicate medications you take regularly and any drug allergies you may have.

WARNINGS

Travelers to Mexico City and other urban centers at altitudes above 7,000 feet often suffer adverse effects from the high altitude. If you have any heart, blood pressure, or respiratory problems, you should consult your physician before traveling to these altitudes, and especially before visiting Mexico City, where the effects of the high altitude are exacerbated by a brutal degree of air pollution. Even those in perfect health sometimes gasp for breath, or they feel dizzy, weak, and exhausted in Mexico City. If you do spend time in any high-altitude destination, be certain to give yourself a day or two to adjust to the difference in air pressure and lack of oxygen before you go out jogging, or even walking extensively.

At high altitudes you should also try to adjust your eating habits so that you consume your biggest meal of the day in the afternoon. In general, the digestive system works slower at higher altitudes, and if you eat large meals late at night, as many Mexicans do, you're likely to wake up in the morning feeling full and bloated—and very tired.

You should also take precautions against sunburn, especially if you're taking antibiotics (some can make the skin very sensitive) for *la turista* or another ailment. The sun is unexpectedly strong at high altitudes. You should always wear sunblock and/or hats to avoid sizzling. That is also true at the beaches, ruins, and any place you're likely to be exposed to the sun for long periods of time. A tan may seem like a desirable souvenir of your vacation south of the border, but the long-term effects of fried skin may produce less-than-pleasant memories of the naive folly of fun in the sun.

When you're out in the jungle, exploring the ruins or following a nature trail, bring plenty of insect repellent and wear clothes that cover you sufficiently to protect you against insect bites, sunburn, and thorny plants. Unless you're quite experienced at surviving in the wilds, don't go off on your own. There are poisonous snakes, scorpions, and other dangerous critters in them thar hills. The beasties are surely as frightened of you as you are of them, and aren't intentionally aggressive. But they can hurt you. So make sure you have an experienced guide with you on the trails. If by any chance you do get bitten or stung, see a doctor as quickly as possible.

There are tropical diseases to which you may be exposed, but simple precautions will probably prevent infection. Mosquitoes transmit malaria (high fever, chills, headache, anemia, jaundice) and dengue fever (high fever, headache, joint and muscle aches, skin rash). Wear a lot of insect repellent in mosquito-infested areas. Schistosomiasis is a parasitic worm transmitted by freshwater snail larvae that can pass through unbroken human skin. You can be exposed by swimming or wading in stagnant freshwater pools, including Yucatecan *cenotes*. With infection comes fever, weight loss, joint and muscle aches, nausea and diarrhea. It usually takes about two months to diagnose this disease, but treatment with prescribed medicines is effective and relatively simple. Be careful about wading in stagnant pools or snail-infested streams, and if you think you've been exposed, wash yourself thoroughly with rubbing alcohol. Typhus is transmitted by lice, but the risk of infection is low unless you're staying in unclean lodgings in remote towns. Antibiotics cure typhus rapidly. Typhoid fever can be picked up from contaminated food. It causes severe diarrhea—much more severe than *la turista*. If you think you have typhoid fever, see a doctor immediately. If you do have it, you'll probably have to be hospitalized for some period of time. Viral hepatitis is also spread through contaminated food or through intimate contact with an infected person. Take common-sense precautions to avoid infection.

FINDING A DOCTOR

If you do need a doctor, you should have no difficulty in locating a reliable and knowledgeable Mexican physician who speaks English well enough to treat you. Ask your hotel concierge or contact the nearest consulate for a referral to an English-speaking doctor. In Mexico City, you'll undoubtedly be referred to the American-British-Cowdray Hospital (tel. 5-515-8359, 5-277-5000, or 5-277-7881), also known as the ABC and the Hospital Ingles, an excellent bilingual hospital connected with Baylor University Medical Center and a member of the American Hospital Association. The ABC can also refer you to English-speaking physicians, including specialists, in other Mexican cities and tourist resorts.

In case you need emergency dental work, ask the nearest consulate for a referral to an English-speaking dentist.

American Express offers Global Assist, an excellent medical referral service, to cardholders. You're given a collect number to call for a list of English-speaking physicians and hospitals anywhere in the world. The service will also make arrangements for necessary hospitalization or transportation, and will guarantee you the right to charge up to $5,000 for your medical bills. The referral service is free of charge; any monies advanced must be repaid according to your regular contract with American Express. For further information, call Global Assist at 800-554-AMEX or American Express at 800-528-4800 or 212-477-5700.

Women Travelers on Their Own

Apart from the fact that it can be downright depressing for single travelers of either sex to visit Mexico's beach resorts during heavy honeymoon weeks, women alone will find traveling in Mexico no more difficult than anywhere else. In general, Mexicans are not aggressive toward women traveling alone—they ignore them. This can be disconcerting when you are next in line for a table at a restaurant or for attention at an airline ticket counter, and are shuffled to one side while two men who arrived much later than you did are served. But any woman who has traveled alone anywhere has probably experienced this, and thus knows for herself whether she finds it more comfortable and dignified to politely say something (such as, "I believe I was next") or to let it pass without comment.

If you take common-sense precautions—not walking alone at night, not taking rides into the countryside with strangers—you should be quite safe in Mexico. However, Mexican men, in general, assume that you want company if you're alone at a bar or disco. If you don't want to be bothered, try to find someone else to hang out with. Two women at a bar or disco are much less likely to be hassled, or if they are, they can negotiate their way out of unpleasant situations more easily. So try to meet other traveling women or friendly couples with whom you can socialize. Many of the hotels, especially those at the beach resorts, organize sports activities or social events so guests can meet one another. Mexican fiestas, popular in most tourist destinations, are also good places to meet other vacationers. Or, if you're traveling on business, try to organize social activities with colleagues who live in town. Organized tours may also offer comfortable alternatives to trying to get around the countryside on your own, unless you're an experienced traveler and are used to fending for yourself.

Transportation

GETTING TO MEXICO

By Plane

Most travelers arrive in Mexico by air, and the country has excellent airports in most major cities. Mexico City is the primary hub for incoming international flights, but several international carriers have nonstop or direct flights from U.S. cities to Acapulco, Cancún, Cozumel, Guadalajara, Ixtapa-Zihuatanejo, Los Cabos, Manzanillo, Mazatlán, Mérida, Monterrey, and Puerto Vallarta. Other major Mexican cities have airports served by only domestic flights, but connections from international flights via Mexico City or Guadalajara are usually convenient. Mexicana Airlines has the largest number of international and domestic flights, and the most complete schedule of connecting flights within Mexico. U.S. carriers that fly into Mexico include American, Continental, Delta, Pan Am, and United. Aeromexico, which was reorganized following bankruptcy, has resumed both international and domestic flights.

For travelers from Canada, neither Air Canada nor Canadian Airlines International has regularly scheduled flights to Mexico at this time. Air transportation from most Canadian cities to Mexico City, Acapulco, Cancún, Cozumel, Guadalajara, Ixtapa-Zihuatanejo, Los Cabos, Manzanillo, Mazatlán, Mérida, Monterrey, and Puerto Vallarta can be arranged with connecting flights in U.S. cities.

From the British Isles, British Airways does not fly into Mexico at this time, but the airline will book passengers on connecting flights on other international carriers via Dallas/Fort Worth and Miami, along with other U.S. cities. However, at present all British Airways connections require an overnight stopover. Better connections are available on U.S. carriers, or European travelers may prefer to fly to Mexico City on KLM from Amsterdam with a stop in Houston; on Lufthansa from Frankfurt via Dallas; or on Air France from Paris via Houston.

There are at present no direct flights between Australia and Mexico. Qantas flies Mexico-bound passengers to Los Angeles with connecting flights on Mexicana or other carriers to Mexico City and other Mexican destinations.

By Sea

Several cruise-ship lines pull into ports along Mexico's Pacific (Cabo San Lucas, Mazatlán, Puerto Vallarta, Ixtapa, and Acapulco) and Caribbean (Cancún, Cozumel, Playa del Carmen) coasts. The ships are usually in port for about eight to ten hours at most. You don't really get to know much about Mexico if you're a cruise passenger, but this is a fun way to beach-hop. Princess Cruises (800-421-0522), of "Love Boat" fame, offers both Pacific Coast and Caribbean cruises. Chandris Fantasy ships (212-750-0044 or 800-432-4132) cruise into Mexico's Caribbean ports. For additional cruise suggestions, contact your travel agent.

GETTING AROUND MEXICO

By Train

Taking the train is not a particularly good choice for getting to Mexico, but the Ferrocarriles Nacionales de México (National Railway of Mexico) offers excellent first-class Servicio Estrella de Pasajeros, a pleasant, efficient and inexpensive way of getting around the country. At present, there are 14 routes:

El Centauro del Norte, from Zacatecas to Durango, via Fresnillo, about six and one-half hours, daytime.

El Coalhuilense, from Saltillo to Piedras Negras via Ciudad Frontera and Barroteran, about seven and one-half hours, daytime.

El Colimense, from Guadalajara to Manzanillo via Ciudad Guzman and Colima, about seven hours, daytime.

El Constitutionalista, from Mexico City to San Miguel de Allende or Guanajuato via Querétaro, about five and one-half hours, daytime.

El Tamaulipeco, from Monterrey to Matamoros via Reynosa, about five hours, daytime.

El Regiomontano, from Mexico City to Nuevo Laredo via San Luis Potosí, Saltillo, and Monterrey, about 18 hours, overnight with sleeperettes.

El Tapatío, from Mexico City to Guadalajara nonstop, about 12 hours, overnight with sleeperettes.

El San Marqueno-Zacatecano, from Mexico City to Zacatecas via Irapuato, León (Guanajuato), Lagos de Moreno, and Aguascalientes, about 12 and one-half hours, overnight with sleeperettes.

El Jarocho, from Mexico to Veracruz via Orizaba, Fortín, and Córdoba, about nine and one-half hours, overnight with sleeperettes.

El Nuevo Chihuahua-Pacífico, from Chihuahua to Los Mochis via Creel, Divisadero Barrancas, Bahuichivo, and Sufragio, about 12 hours, overnight with sleeperettes.

El Oaxaqueño, from Mexico City to Oaxaca via Puebla and Tehuacán, about 14 and one-half hours, overnight with sleeperettes.

El Purepecha, from Mexico to Uruapan via Morelia and Pátzcuaro, about 12 hours, overnight with sleeperettes.

El Rápido de la Frontera, from Chihuahua to Ciudad Juárez, nonstop, about four hours, daytime.

El Hidalguense, from Mexico City to Pachuca, nonstop, about two hours, four times daily.

Additional routes are planned for Mexico City to Ciudad Juárez, Mexico City to Mexicali via Guadalajara, Mexico City to Mazatlán via Guadalajara, Mexico City to Nogales via Guadalajara, Mexico City to Mérida, and San Luis Potosí to Tampico. The train fares are remarkably inexpensive, and include hot meals served in the train's dining car. For more information, call Ferrocarriles Nacionales de México at 5-547-59-19, 5-547-31-90 or 5-547-41-14, or ask your travel agent.

By Bus

Mexico has thousands of bus routes connecting all the major cities, resorts, and little hamlets that are of interest to travelers. Should you decide to travel by bus, you'll find it more comfortable, in general, on shorter trips.

Bus is a most convenient way to get from city to city within one region of Mexico (for example, from Guanajuato to San Miguel de Allende to Querétaro, and around the highland colonial cities) and to take short excursions from your Mexican base of operations (for example, visiting the ruins at Chichén Itzá or Uxmal from your base in Mérida).

For longer journeys (between Mexico City and Mérida, for example), you'll be better off flying if there are direct flights (there are, in this instance) and your budget permits you to do so.

Whenever possible, or unless absolutely necessary to do otherwise, take first-class buses with reserved seats. Second-class buses are for the birds—and chickens and sheep and (sometimes unwashed) masses. The difference in fares isn't that great, and unless you're absolutely poverty-stricken, you can't afford to travel second class.

Specific information on bus routes and best first-class bus lines is included in the chapters on various cities and resorts. But routes and schedules change fairly frequently, so if you plan to travel by bus, pick up current schedules at the local bus terminal as soon as you get into town. Make your reservations as early as possible.

By Car

Driving in Mexico has its pluses and minuses. On the positive side, please note the following:

Driving is convenient: You can arrive and leave when you want to, stop when you want to, change plans, or detour at a whim.

The roads between major Mexican cities and tourist destinations throughout the country are generally well maintained.

The Mexican government's "Green Angels"—repair trucks operated by bilingual mechanics who carry spare parts and can make minor repairs on the spot—patrol the road to help motorists in distress. The service is free; you pay for necessary parts.

You get to see Mexico close-up and at your own pace.

You don't need any special permits; your own driver's license from home is sufficient.

Gas is inexpensive in Mexico.

However. . . .

Many of the roads are two lanes only, with narrow or no shoulders. They are heavily traveled, and slow-moving trucks may cause backups that stretch for miles.

Most country roads are unlighted, so night driving is not recommended.

There has been a recent increase in highway robberies, especially along the Pacific Coast roads and on highways through and around Durango. The presence of the Green Angels is supposed to deter highwaymen, but the Angels are not always around when you need them.

Parking can be a real problem, especially in Mexico City and other major urban centers, and even along the Costera Miguel Aleman in Acapulco. You don't want to park illegally. If you do and your car is towed, you'll experience enormous fines and a staggering tangle of bureaucracy; if the car isn't towed, the license plates will be removed and taken to police headquarters (ditto). This may also be your opportunity to experience the *mordida* (bribe). Retrieving your car or plates can take days, but the entire process can be sped up to hours if you grease the wheels of bureaucracy with a couple of bucks. Be prepared. You'll easily recognize the pitch. When the police officer stands in front of you, shuffling slightly and not saying anything for five or ten minutes, reach for your billfold.

You may unfortunately have other opportunities for *mordidas.* There are lots of cases where motorists, Mexican or foreign, are stopped for imaginary infractions of the law. Be prepared to spread around some paper, or be detained for hours trying to argue about your rights.

If you do decide to drive in Mexico, here are some additional tips:

Car-rental fees in Mexico are, in general, rather high. You can minimize costs by booking in advance in the United States, if possible. For some reason reservations made in the United States lower daily rates by several dollars and allow for free, unlimited mileage. If you rent a car on the spot in Mexico, you pay a per-mile charge in addition to the higher daily rate. All major rental companies have offices throughout Mexico. National has a particularly good Mexican operation, with offices at all major airports and in all cities. Rental rates are comparable, and National's no-fee drop-off policy allows you to return your car in a city other than the one in which you picked it up, without charge. Phone numbers for National's offices are given in the chapters of specific destinations.

Make sure that you have good automobile insurance that covers you in Mexico. If by any chance you get into an accident, whether it's your fault or not, you have to provide on-the-spot proof of your financial ability to cover damage costs. If you don't have this proof, you'll be carted off to jail.

Make sure you keep your tank full of gas. Although Mexico is a big oil producer, there are long stretches of country road without gas stations. Fill 'er up, whenever possible.

Equip yourself with as many maps as possible. These are obtainable from the Mexican Government Tourism offices, from the AAA at home, in travel bookstores, in guidebooks such as this one, and in English-language bookstores in Mexico, including most Sanborn's.

Place all your belongings in the trunk of the car. Bags or packages on the back seat of a parked car are an invitation for thieves.

Park legally, and, if possible, in a garage. If you park on the street, you'll probably be approached by an old man or a gang of street urchins. They guide you into the parking space and offer to guard your car. In return, they expect a *propina* (tip). Give them several hundred pesos—that's cheaper than replacing a broken tail light or slashed tire.

Watch out for *topes*—these metal or concrete humps in the road are intended to keep you from speeding. Either you slow down for them or crack your axle. These are usually placed on country roads before and at the end of small towns, or in the cities at unusually busy intersections. Warning of them is usually posted by the side of the road, several feet in advance. The sign may just be several black humps in the middle of a yellow square. Problem is, some *topes* are unmarked.

If you are on the road, day or night, and you see another car by the side of the road, seemingly in distress, don't stop.

If you get stuck, stay inside your locked car and open up only for the Green Angels.

If you're driving from the state of Quintana Roo into any other state in Mexico, you'll have to stop for a vehicle inspection. That's because Quintana Roo is a duty-free area, and a lot of Mexicans go there to shop. The inspection is for dutiable items. If you're carrying with you an unusual amount of electronic equipment or cameras you should also be carrying some form of proof that these were not bought in Quintana Roo for resale in other parts of Mexico. Receipts with serial numbers from stores at home, or U.S. Customs registration forms, will do.

Try not to arrive at the Mexican border after 9 P.M., or before 6 A.M. If you do, inspectors may have to be called in from home. This can take a long time, and the inspectors tend to be quite grumpy. Problems. Avoid them whenever possible.

If you are driving your own vehicle into Mexico, in addition to the tips in the **Avoiding Hassles** section, above, please note the following:

When you cross the border into Mexico, your car will be inspected and your trunk will be sealed. Do not unseal the trunk until after you've passed the second border checkpoint. Otherwise, your car will be inspected all over again, and this is a tremendous waste of time.

Be prepared for lengthy waits at border crossings back into the United States, if that's where you're going. Inspectors thoroughly search suspicious-looking vehicles for drugs and other illegal substances. Be prepared to have your car, whether suspicious-looking or not, searched too.

Business Brief

The word *mañana* dominates the Mexican calendar, business or otherwise. If you're going to do business in Mexico, mastering the patience to deal with the Mexican notion of time is essential. *Mañana* means that scheduled business appointments begin late, or sometimes not at all; it means that workers arrive late, and that products are delivered late, *most of the time.* The Mexicans themselves are aware of this, and they often make jokes about it. If you can't keep smiling, maybe doing business in Mexico is not for you.

Still, there are many reasons why one would wish to do business in Mexico. The country, economic difficulties notwithstanding, is a huge marketplace, with millions of people eager to purchase as much as they possibly can. Mexico's large population also promises vast quantities of inexpensive labor, becoming more skilled as time goes on and always eager to please, if not always efficient. Businesspeople who sell in Mexico find the country rewarding. Those who manufacture in Mexico for sale elsewhere say that they are, in general, quite satisfied with their situation but must keep a close and constant quality and time check on production to make sure things go right.

Mexican business protocol might appear to be absolutely baroque when compared with some other cultures. Yet if you want to do business successfully in Mexico, it's best to know what to expect. Here are some tips:

- A great show of friendship and camaraderie usually embellishes business deals; from first introductions through breakfasts and luncheons, compliments are spread as thick and sweet as whipped cream. Gifts are also often given. It is very important to show tremendous enthusiasm for projects and colleagues whenever the opportunity arises.

- Looking important is essential to being taken seriously in Mexican business circles. Obviously, you have to dress the part and display a certain bravado, but you'll be even more successful if you work with reinforcements. Having people around to do your bidding gives you an aura of authority. Rarely do you see a Mexican approach a business meeting alone. If you cannot travel to Mexico with an entourage, you can employ locals for this purpose. Even simply having a regular driver helps you create the right impression. And having a Mexican agent, representative, or partner establishes your stature, facilitates your entry into the local business scene, and helps you through Mexico's incredibly complicated bureaucratic barriers.

- It also helps to have a good grounding in Mexican law and the tax system. These are so incredibly complicated that it often takes major debates on minute points before disputes can be settled. Books on Mexican law and taxes geared for foreign businesspeople are invaluable.

- Knowing the right people counts for a great deal anywhere, but in Mexico it is absolutely essential. This is a country where one key person can make an entire program that's been dragging its heels for ages fall immediately into place. How do you get to the right person? Your agent or Mexican partner should be able to help, but often it's a matter of trial and error and dogged persistence.

- It's quite difficult to get a straight answer in Mexico. The Mexicans like to please, and that means never saying a direct "No." So even if it is impossible from the outset for a business colleague to do your bidding, he usually won't say so. Instead, he'll keep putting you off. Your best protection against finding yourself in this situation is to take every promise made in Mexico with a grain of salt, and to hedge your bets with plan B, plan C, and, perhaps, plan D.

- Mexicans have many cultural sensitivities. One of these is to the phrase "I'm an American." If you're from the United States and you want to identify your citizenship, say "I'm North American." Many Mexicans feel that people from the United States have monopolized "being American," and they take offense. Whether this makes sense to you or not, you'll get along a lot better with Mexicans if you remember this small point.

- Although quite a few bank branches, among other offices in Mexico, now have women managers, Mexicans are not really accustomed to doing business with women in high executive positions. They're especially not used to women whose behavior might be characterized as businesslike and direct as opposed to charming and attractive. Mexican businessmen in particular seem to be most responsive to women who are very "feminine," rather coquettish, and quite done up.

- While contracts and other business formalities are important in Mexico, goodwill is equally significant. It is essential to put agreements in writing, to get formal letters of authorization or credit, and to document transactions. However, despite your good business practices, you'll probably find yourself in a situation where the terms of some agreement are simply not being met to the letter. How much should be allowed to slip by? Your best bet is probably some form of compromise, just to maintain goodwill—because without it, you won't be able to accomplish anything in Mexico.

CULTURAL TIMELINE

	the coast of the Yucatán Peninsula and of the Gulf of Mexico
1519	Hernán Cortés imprisons Moctezuma II in Tenochtitlán
1520	Moctezuma is deposed and then killed; Cortés defeats the Aztecs
1521	Cortés takes Tenochtitlán and completely razes the Aztec capital
1522–1821	**During this period of Spanish colonial rule, Spanish, Indians, and Africans intermarry and give birth to _la Raza,_ the Mexican people**
1522	As governor of New Spain, Cortés rebuilds Tenochtitlán as his colonial capital, to be known as México
1522–1524	Conquistadores under the command of Cortés take most of the territories ruled by the Aztecs
1526–1555	Period of greatest influence by Catholic missionaries
1527	New Spain is now governed by the Audiencia, a five-man panel with military and civil authority
1531	The Virgin of Guadalupe becomes the patron saint of the Mexican Indians
1535	Antonio de Mendoza is appointed viceroy of New Spain by Charles V
1535–1565	Spanish conquistadores target territories to the north and vastly expand New Spain
1547	Cortés dies in Spain
1551	The first university in the New World is established in Mexico City
1571	The Sancta Inquisición comes to Mexico City
c. 1600	The Spanish conquerors have established their rule over all the territory now occupied by present-day Mexico
1697	Last independent Indian center of Itza Maya is conquered by Tayasal (Peten)
1700	Charles II, last Hapsburg king of Spain, dies, and the Bourbons ascend to the Spanish throne
1767	Jesuits are expelled from Spain and from Mexico
c. 1800	New Spain, at the height of its expansion, is about 1,500,000 square miles in size
1803–1804	As the crown expropriates church property in Mexico, many _criollos_ (Creoles) and churchmen abandon their loyalty to Spain
1810–1821	**War of Independence**
1811	The independence forces are defeated; Miguel Hidalgo and Ignacio Allende are executed
1813	At Chilpancingo, the insurgents write a Declaration of Independence

1820   The movement for independence in New Spain is strengthened by the *liberales* revolution in Spain

1821   General Augustín de Iturbide presents the "Iguala Plan" for Mexican Independence; on August 24, Iturbide and the viceroy sign the Treaty of Córdoba, giving Mexico national sovereignty

1822   The Treaty of Córdoba is rejected by the Spanish parliament; Iturbide is elected emperor by Congress, assumes the title of Augustín I

1823   Iturbide abdicates; the Monarchy is abolished; the Central American provinces declare their independence as the United States of Central America, which remains a political union until 1939

1824   A constitutional government takes office; Guadalupe Victoria is the first president of the republic; Iturbide is court-martialed and executed

1825–1828   North Americans begin to settle Texas, then an underpopulated Mexican province

1833   General Antonio López de Santa Anna, a revolutionary republican leader now supported by the liberals, becomes president and later dictator of Mexico; tensions rise between North Americans and Mexicans in Texas

1836   Texas secedes from Mexico and becomes the Lone Star Republic

1845   Texas is annexed by the United States and becomes its 28th state

1846–1848   War between the United States and Mexico follows the Texas annexation; the Treaty of Guadalupe Hidalgo forces Mexico to relinquish claims to Texas and cede Northern California, Arizona, and New Mexico in exchange for $18,250,000, thereby reducing Mexican territory by more than half

1847   Beginning of the War of the Castes, the Mayan uprising in the Yucatán, that lasts until the start of the 20th century

1856–1857   Reform laws are enacted by the liberals who, led by Ignacio Comonfort, Benito Juárez, and Sebastián Lerdo de Tejada, take over the government

1858–1861   Civil War erupts

1861   The liberals take Mexico City, and Juárez returns with his government to the capital; Juárez freezes repayments of Mexico's external debts for two years; Britain, France, and Spain move to enforce payment by allied military action, and they land at Veracruz in December

1862–1867	**French troops, marching on Mexico City, are subdued at Puebla**
1863	Juárez's government flees north as the French enter Mexico City and proclaim a monarchy; Napoleon III and exiled Mexican conservatives offer the throne to Ferdinand Maximilian, the Hapsburg archduke
1864	Maximilian and his wife, Carlota, a celebrated and dashing couple, arrive in Mexico; Maximilian alienates conservatives by endorsing reform policies
1865	The United States calls for the immediate withdrawal of French troops from Mexico
1867	The last French forces withdraw; Maximilian refuses to leave Mexico and takes command of a small army of loyalist Mexican troops, who are defeated; Maximilian and his generals, Miguel Miramon and Tomás Mejia are executed; Benito Juárez is confirmed as president
1871–1876	Juárez is re-elected president but dies before completing one year of his new term; Sebastián Lerdo de Tejada becomes president; the parliamentary government is changed to a two-chamber system
1873	The railway between Veracruz and Mexico City is completed by British engineers
1876	Porfirio Díaz, a man of modest origins and magnificent, self-aggrandizing dreams, assumes power; Lerdo de Tejada flees Mexico
1876–1911	**The Porfirian Era, lasting about 35 years, sees Mexico through a period of modernization and economic growth**
1880–1884	Manuel Gonzáles succeeds Díaz in deference to the law prohibiting immediate re-election
1884–1911	Díaz is elected once again and remains in power for 27 years
1910–1920	**Approximately one million Mexicans die in the Mexican Revolution**
1910–1915	Francisco Madero becomes president after Díaz resigns in 1911; Madero is overthrown by General Victoriano Huerta and executed in 1913; Huerta, governing as a dictator, is opposed by constitutionalist factions led by former ally Pancho Villa, as well as by the United States; Huerta flees Mexico
1916–1920	Venustiano Carranza becomes president
1917	A new constitution is put into effect; dissent toward Carranza grows, as the United States withdraws support from his government
1920	Carranza is assassinated; Alvaro Obregón becomes president of Mexico
1921–1933	**Revolutionary objectives are consolidated as the country is governed by revolutionary leaders, the *Claudillos***

1921–1924	The presidency of Alvaro Obregón sees significant growth in the areas of public education and the arts
1924–1928	The presidency of Plutarco Elías Calles amends the constitution to extend the presidential term to six years and to allow the president a second term if it does not directly follow the first; Obregón is subsequently re-elected but is assassinated shortly after he assumes office
1929–1933	Emilio Portes Gil, Pascual Ortiz Rubio, and Abelardo Rodriguez serve in three short presidencies; the National Revolutionary Party (PNR), uniting Mexico's major political factions, is founded. This party, renamed several times, dominates Mexican political life to the present day and is now known as the Partido Revolucionario Institucion-alisado (PRI)
1934–1940	**The presidency of Lázaro Cárdenas has a decidedly left-wing posture**
1940–1946	Mexico's gross domestic product doubles during the relatively untroubled presidency of Manuel Avila Camacho, whose policies encourage foreign investment in Mexico and promote private industry
1942	Mexico declares war on the Axis powers
1946–1952	The presidency of Miguel Aleman Valdés continues to improve Mexico's infrastructure, with development of better roads and systems of communication, and an eighty percent increase in Mexico's gross domestic product
1952–1964	During the presidencies of Adolfo Ruíz Cortines and Adolpho López Mateos, economic growth continues but there are problems with high inflation, government corruption, and illegal entry by agricultural workers into the United States
1964–1970	The presidency of Gustavo Díaz Ordaz is marred by the brutal repression of student demonstrations in Tlatelolco preceding the 1968 Olympic Games, held in Mexico City
1970–1976	President Luís Alvarez Echeverria aspires to play a dominant role in Third World politics; new tourist resort areas, including Cancún, are developed and become major sources of foreign revenue
1976–1982	The presidency of José López Portillo is marked by a temporary economic boom due to high oil prices; the peso gets devalued from 27 to 44 pesos per dollar; in 1982, in an unconstitutional act, the administration nationalizes the banks
1982–1988	The presidency of Miguel de la Madrid Hurtado takes the reins at a time of crisis; the peso continues to decline; inflation

rises; civil strife between the PRI and PAN, the opposing party, escalates

1988   The presidency of Carlos Salinas de Gortari begins with pressing problems to surmount; Mexico's economic crisis continues—with soaring inflation, the constant devaluation of the peso, high unemployment, crippling foreign debt, and some political unrest

VITAL INFORMATION

EMBASSIES AND CONSULATES

The following list of U.S., Canadian, British, and Australian embassies and consulates will be of help in case of any sort of emergency, including illness or death, accidents, theft, or legal problems. The embassies and consulates often have other interesting publications and brochures concerning Mexican business and cultural life, as well as information about retiring and studying in Mexico. The amount of help you can get depends largely upon the resources of the office. Obviously, the larger posts are better equipped to assist you. However, sometimes the smaller posts are able to take more personal interest in your situation.

U.S. Embassy and Consulates

MEXICO CITY
U.S. Embassy
Reforma 305
Tel. 5-211-0042

ACAPULCO
U.S. Consulate
Hotel Club del Sol
Costera M. Alemán, esquina (corner) Reyes Catolicos, Number 8
Tel. 748-5-72-07

CANCÚN
U.S. Consulate
Avenida Coba 30, esquina (corner) Nader
Tel. 988-4-24-11

CIUDAD JUÁREZ
U.S. Consulate
Avenida López Mateos 924N
Tel. 161-13-40-48

DURANGO
U.S. Consulate
Juárez Norte 204
Tel. 181-122-17

GUADALAJARA
U.S. Consulate
Avenida Libertad 1492
Tel. 36-25-27-00

HERMOSILLO
U.S. Consulate
Monterrey 141
Tel. 621-7-23-75

MATAMOROS
U.S. Consulate
Avenida Primavera 2002
Tel. 891-2-52-50

MAZATLÁN
U.S. Consulate
6 Circunvalación 120 at Venustiano Carranza
Tel. 678-5-22-05

MÉRIDA
U.S. Consulate
Paseo Montejo 453
Tel. 99-25-50-11

MONTERREY
U.S. Consulate
Avenida Constitución 411
Poniente 64000
Tel. 283-45-21-20

NUEVO LAREDO
U.S. Consulate
Avenida Allende 3330
Colonia Jardín
Tel. 871-4-06-96

OAXACA
U.S. Consulate
Calle Crespo 213
Tel. 951-6-06-54

PUERTO VALLARTA
U.S. Consulate
Parian del Puente, Number 12-A
Tel. 322-2-00-69

SAN LUIS POTOSÍ
U.S. Consulate
Venustiano Carranza 1430
Tel. 481-2-25-01

SAN MIGUEL DE ALLENDE
U.S. Consulate
Hernandez Macias 72
Tel. 465-2-23-57

TIJUANA
U.S. Consulate
Tapachula 96
Tel. 66-81-74-00

VERACRUZ
U.S. Consulate
Juárez 110
Tel. 29-31-01-42

Canadian Embassy and Consulates
MEXICO CITY
Canadian Embassy
Calle Schiller 529
Rincón del Bosque
Colonia Polanco
Tel. 5-254-32-88

ACAPULCO
Consulate of Canada
Hotel Club Del Sol, mezzanine floor
Costera Miguel Alemán
Tel. 748-5-66-21

GUADALAJARA
Consulate of Canada
Hotel Fiesta Americana, Local 30
Aurelio Aceves 225
Tel. 36-25-34-34, ext. 3005

MAZATLÁN
Consulate of Canada
Avenida Albatros 52 no. 705
Tel. 678-3-73-20

MÉRIDA
Consulate of Canada
Calle 62 no. 309 (near Avenida Colón)
Depto. 9
Tel. 99-25-62-99

TIJUANA
Consulate of Canada
G. Gedovius 5-201
Condominio del Parque
Desarrollo Urbano Rio Tijuana
Tel. 66-84-04-61

British Embassy and Consulates
MEXICO CITY
British Embassy
Lerma 71
Colonia Cuauhtémoc
Tel. 5-511-4880 or 5-207-2089

ACAPULCO
British Consulate
Las Brisas Hotel
Carretera Escénica
Tel. 748-4-66-05

CIUDAD JUÁREZ
British Consulate
Calle Fresno 185
Campestre Juárez
Tel. 161-7-57-91

GUADALAJARA
British Consulate
Calzada Gonzáles Gallo 1897
Tel. 36-35-82-95

MÉRIDA
British Consulate
Calle 58 no. 450
Tel. 99-21-67-99

MONTERREY
British Consulate
Privada de Tamazunchale 104
Garza García
Colonia Del Valle
Tel. 283-56-91-14

TAMPICO
British Consulate
2 de Enero no. 102
Tel. 121-2-97-84

Australian Embassy
MEXICO CITY
Australian Embassy
Plaza Polanco Torre
B-Piso 10
Jaime Balmes 11
Colonia Los Morales
Tel. 5-395-9988

Mexican Government Tourism Offices

The Mexican government's Secretaría de Turismo handles dissemination of information about travel in Mexico both within the country and abroad. The secretary of tourism is a cabinet post appointed by the president of Mexico and currently filled by Pedro Joaquin Coldwell.

The Secretaría de Turismo has its headquarters in Mexico City and maintains offices in the capital of each Mexican state and in other high-volume tourist destinations.

These offices should be able to provide you with pamphlets, brochures, and maps of their region, and give you information about current entertainment programs and special events. Here are their addresses:

MEXICO CITY
Secretaría de Turismo
Avenida Mazarik 172
Tel. 5-250-0123

ACAPULCO (Guerrero)
Costera Miguel Alemán 187
Tel. 748-5-11-78 or 5-13-03

CAMPECHE (Campeche)
Avenida República 159
Frente a la Alameda
Tel. 981-6-31-97 or 6-55-93

CANCÚN (Quintana Roo)
Avenida Tulúm 81
Edificio Fira
Tel. 988-4-32-38

CIUDAD VICTORIA (Tamaulipas)
2 and 3 Avenida Carrera Torres 1510
Tel. 131-2-37-87 or 131-2-38-41

COZUMEL (Quintana Roo)
Fideicaribe
Tel. 987-2-09-64

CUERNAVACA (Morelos)
Comonfort 12
Tel. 735-2-28-15 or 735-2-52-39

DURANGO (Durango)
Bruno Martínez 403 Sur 305
Tel. 181-2-76-44 or 181-1-56-81

GUADALAJARA (Jalisco)
Lázaro Cárdenas 3289, first floor
Tel. 36-22-41-30 or 36-22-41-52

LA PAZ (Baja California Sur)
Paseo Alvaro Obregón 2130
Tel. 682-2-11-90 or 682-2-79-75

MANZANILLO (Colima)
Juárez 244, fourth floor
Tel. 333-2-01-81 or 333-2-20-91

MAZATLÁN (Sinaloa)
Avenida del Mar 1000
Tel. 678-1-42-12 or 678-1-42-11

MÉRIDA (Yucatán)
Avenida de los Itzaes 501
Tel. 992-3-60-75 or 992-3-69-75

MONTERREY (Nuevo León)
Emilio Carranza 730 Sur P.B.
Tel. 183-44-01-72 or 183-44-50-11

MORELIA (Michoacán)
Santos Degollado 340, Altos 1
Tel. 151-2-05-22 or 151-2-01-23

OAXACA (Oaxaca)
Matamoros 105, corner of García Vigil
Tel. 951-6-01-44 or 951-6-00-45

PACHUCA (Hidalgo)
Plaza de la Independencia 110, third floor
Tel. 771-2-59-60 or 771-2-48-60

PUEBLA (Puebla)
Bulevar Hermanos Serdan and Bulevar Norte
Tel. 22-48-29-77 or 22-48-31-77

PUERTO VALLARTA (Jalisco)
Presidente Municipal P.B.
Tel. 322-2-25-54 or 322-2-25-55

SAN LUIS POTOSÍ (San Luis Potosí)
Jardín Guerrero 14
Tel. 481-4-09-06

TIJUANA (Baja California)
Linea Internacional
Puerta México, Planta Alta
Colonia Federal
Tel. 66-823-34-79 or 66-865-40-15

TOLUCA (State of Mexico)
Avenida Vicente Villada 123
Colonia Centro
Tel. 721-4-42-49 or 721-4-03-04

TUXTLA GUTIÉRREZ (Chiapas)
Avenida Central Poniente 1454
Colonia Moctezuma
Tel. 961-2-45-35

VERACRUZ (Veracruz)
Avenida Ignacio Zaragoza 20 Altos, Centro
Tel. 29-32-70-26 or 29-32-16-13

VILLAHERMOSA (Tabasco)
Lerdo 101, first floor
Corner of Malecón and Carlos A. Madrazo
Tel. 931-2-73-36 or 931-2-74-56

ZACATECAS (Zacatecas)
Bulevar López Mateos 923A
Tel. 492-2-67-50 or 492-2-67-51

ZIHUATANEJO (and **IXTAPA**, Guerrero)
Paseo de Zihuatanejo
Tel. 743-4-28-35

EMERGENCY PHONE NUMBERS

The following list of telephone numbers is for the Mexico City headquarters of various emergency units and agencies. If you are not in Mexico City at the time of a crisis, ask your hotel concierge or the nearest consulate for local emergency numbers.

Ambulance (Cruz Roja and Cruz Verde)   557-5758
Fire (Bomberos)   768-3700
Hospital (American-British-Cowdray)   515-8359
Missing Persons (Locatel)   658-1111
Police (Federal District and Transit)   588-5100
Police (Highway)   684-2142
Road Service (Green Angels)   250-4817
24-Hour Tourist Hotline   250-0589 or 250-0493

MANZANILLO

Minatitlán

Colirna

1

2

3

TEPEIXTLES

Laguna las Garzas

Laguna de San Pedrito

Laguna de Cuyutlán

PLAYA AZUL

Playa San Pedrito

E

SALAGUA

Playa Azul

CAMPOS

SANTIAGO

Bahia de Manzanillo

MANZANILLO

Armeria

Playa Las Hadas

see inset

Playas Olas Altas

Playa Ventanas

VILLA FLORIDA

D

Playa la Audiencia

Playa Campos

Laguna Peñitas

MIRAMAR

Bahia de Santiago

Pacific Ocean

C

International Airport

Playa Miramar

Laguna Cuyután

N

Bahia de Manzanillo

B

Muelle Fiscal

Bus Station

Niños Héroes

Chapultepec

Post Office

Aldama

Rail Station

Hidalgo

Constitución

Tourist Information

Market

Laguna de Cuyután

City Hall

Miguel

Alameda

Dávalos

Allende

Cuauhtémoc

V. Guerrero

circunvalación

Quintero

5 de Mayo

21 de Marzo

V. Zaragose

Núñez

Puerto

Mexico

Anaya

Zapata

A

N. Bravo

F. Villa

C. 2

A. Serdán

Calle 4

Calle 6

Calle 8

Camaron

Culiacán

A

B

C

El Toreo Bullring

Camaron Sabalo

PUEBLO NUEVO

Juan Carrasco

1

Rafael Buelna

DE MAYO

E. ZAPATA

Craftmanship Centre

Av. Revolucion

20 DE NOV.

Marine shells exhibition

Av. del Mar

Bahia del Puerto Viejo

Rail Station

Aquarium

Estero del Infiernillo

Bus Station

Av. Gabriel Leyva

2

Airport

Durango Tepic

Pacific

J. CARRASCO

A. Serdan

G. Najera

Planetarium

Estero

Fisherman's Monument

Ocean

Isla de Ocom

Urias

see inset

Av. del Puerto

Isla de Belvedere

Canal de Navegacion

Isla de la Piedra

3

Transferring Terminal

N

Cerro del Creston

Isla de los Chivos

MAZATLAN

Hidalgo

Genaro Estrada

Dr. Carbajal

Intubide

Arriba

Belisano Dominguez

Melchor Ocampo

Aquiles Serdan

Camanava

Carnava

5 de Mayo

G. Nelson

Juarez

Leandro Valle

Canizales

Roszles

Campana

H. Frias

Basilica

21 de

Marzo

J. Azuela

Plaza Hidalgo

City Hall

Post Office

Angel Flores

Escobedo

Constitucion

U. Guerrero

Progreso

A

MERIDA

N

B

C

Cankal

Izmal

PEDREGAL CHUBURNA

PENSIONES

Diametral

Calle 22

Paseo Montejo

Calle 28

Av. de los Capules

TANLUM

Av. Miguel Alemán

ALEMAN

Paseo Colon

Parque de las Americas

Bullring

LOPEZ MATEOS

GARCIA GINERS

Canton Palace

INDUSTRIAL

Calle 72

Calle 64

Calle 60

Calle 50

Av. de los Itzaes

Tourist Information

LAZARO CARDENAS

Calle 59

see inset

Zoological Park

Calle 65

ESPERANZA

Calle 69

Bus Station

VICENTE SOLIS

Calle 65

OBRERA

SN. JOSE

Campeche

Calle 76

Calle 74-A

Calle 72

Calle 70

Calle 64

Calle 62

Calle 51

Sta. Lucia Square

Calle 56

Calle 52

Calle 50

Calle 59

Calle 55

Rail Station

Calle 61

Telephones

Theatre

Calle 57

City Hall

Government Palace

Popular Art Museum

Parade Ground

Calle 65

Calle 68

Calle 66

Craftsmanship Market

Post Office

Calle 63

Calle 46

Calle 67

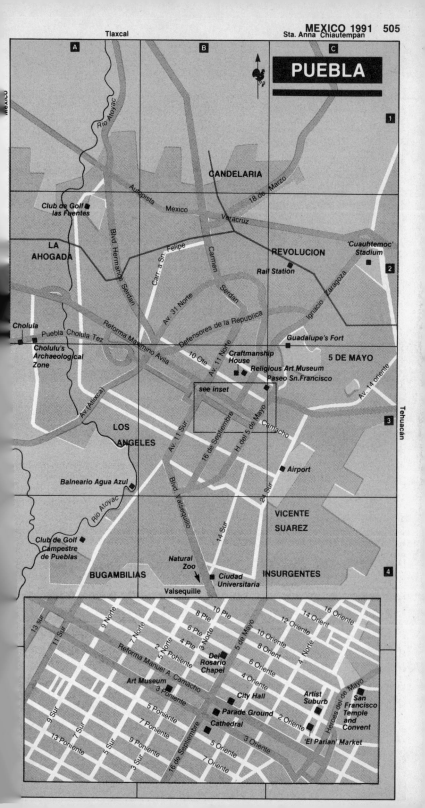

PUEBLA

Tlaxcal

A · **B** · **C**

1

CANDELARIA

Autopista Mexico

18 de Marzo

Veracruz

Club de Golf las Fuentes

LA AHOGADA

Blvd Hermanos Serdan

Carr. a Sn. Felipe

Carmen

Serdan

REVOLUCION

Rail Station

'Cuauhtemoc' Stadium

2

Ignacio Zaragoza

Cholula

Puebla Cholula Tez

Reforma Maximino Avila

Av. 31 Norte

Defensores de la Republica

Cholulu's Archaeological Zone

10 Ote

Av. 11 Norte

Craftmanship House

Religious Art Museum

Paseo Sn.Francisco

Guadalupe's Fort

5 DE MAYO

Av. 14 oriente

see inset

Av. (Atlixca)

LOS ANGELES

Av. 11 Sur

16 de Septiembre

H. del 5 de Mayo

Camacho

3

Tehuacan

Balneario Agua Azul

Rio Atoyac

Blvd Valsequillo

Airport

24 Sur

VICENTE SUAREZ

Club de Golf Campestre de Pueblas

14 Sur

Natural Zoo

Ciudad Universitaria

INSURGENTES

BUGAMBILIAS

Valsequille

Inset

13 sur

11 Sur

9 Norte

7 Norte

5 Norte

Reforma Manuel A. Camacho

3 Pohiente

10 Pte

8 Pte

6 Pte

4 Pte

2 Norte

4 Pohiente

5 de Mayo

10 Oriente

8 Orient

6 Oriente

4 Oriente

16 Oriente

14 Orient

12 Oriente

4 Norte

Del Rosario Chapel

Art Museum

3 Poniente

5 Poniente

City Hall

Parade Ground

Cathedral

2 Oriente

Artist Suburb

Heroes del 5 de Mayo

San Francisco Temple and Convent

9 Sur

7 Sur

5 Sur

3 Sur

7 Poniente

9 Poniente

16 de Septiembre

5 Oriente

3 Oriente

7 Oriente

'El Parian' Market

13 Poniente

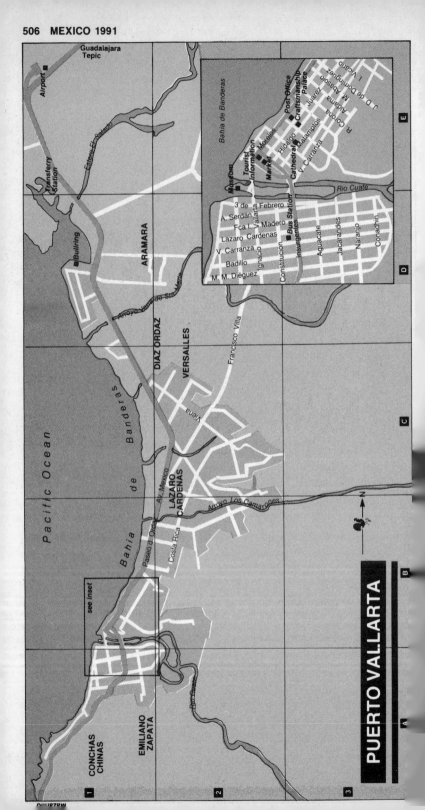

PUERTO VALLARTA

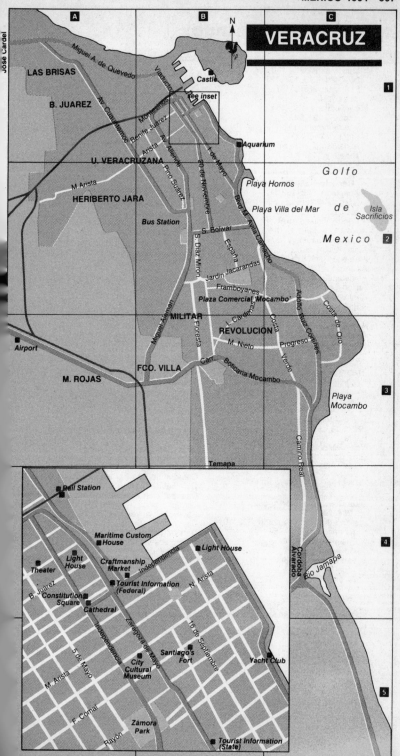

VERACRUZ

José Cardel

LAS BRISAS

Miguel A. de Quevedo

Viaducto

Castle

see inset

B. JUAREZ

Av Cuauhtémoc

Montesinos

Benito Juárez

Arista

A Allende

Pino Suárez

Aquarium

U. VERACRUZANA

M Arista

20 de Noviembre

Playa Hornos

Golfo

HERIBERTO JARA

Bus Station

S. Bolívar

Blvd M. Ávila Camacho

Playa Villa del Mar

de

Isla
Sacrificios

Mexico

S. Díaz Mirón

España

Jardín Jacarandas

Framboyanes

Plaza Comercial 'Mocambo'

Miguel Alemán

Floresta

MILITAR

L. Cárdenas

Costa

Adolfo Ruiz Cortines

Costa de Oro

REVOLUCION

Airport

M. Nieto

Progreso

Costa Verde

FCO. VILLA

Carr Boticaria Mocambo

M. ROJAS

Playa
Mocambo

Camino Real

Temapa

Rail Station

Maritime Custom
House

Light House

Theater

Light
House

Craftmanship
Market

Independencia

**Tourist Information
(Federal)**

N. Arista

Córdoba
Alvarado

Río Jamapa

B. Juárez

**Constitution
Square**

Cathedral

Zaragoza

5 de Mayo

Independencia

16 de Septiembre

Santiago's
Fort

Yacht Club

M. Arista

**City
Cultural
Museum**

F. Comal

Rayon

Zamora
Park

**Tourist Information
(State)**

Index